GRENADA DOCUMENTS:
AN OVERVIEW AND SELECTION

INTRODUCTION
BY MICHAEL LEDEEN AND HERBERT ROMERSTEIN

The military action by the United States and the members of the Organization of Eastern Caribbean States (OECS) in October 1983 brought to a close the four-year rule of the New Jewel Movement (NJM) on the island of Grenada. During their stay on Grenada, the combined forces found a considerable body of documents, constituting an extensive archive of the NJM regime. There were roughly 35,000 pounds of material, ranging from official government treaties, orders, minutes, and correspondence to personal diaries, telexes to and from many foreign countries, and bank documents concerning the finances of government and party leaders. Rarely has such a complete documentary picture of a Communist state been available to Western students. The entire lot is being made available to scholars and other interested parties through the National Archives in Washington.

Pending completion of the Grenada archive, we were asked to assemble a cross-section of documents to give a preliminary picture of Grenada during the rule of Maurice Bishop and the NJM, from April 1979 to October 1983. It was a daunting task, for the richness of the material made selection difficult. The collection presented here could easily have been replaced almost in its entirety by other, equally significant material. Nonetheless, we have striven to provide representative samples from areas likely to be of interest to students of communism and of international relations. We expect that in the future other scholars will produce more detailed studies using the substantial documentation in the archive. We judged the area we selected to be most important for a first look at the Grenada documents. To these we added some material dealing with life on the island during the NJM period, particularly documents illustrating human rights abuses by the Bishop regime. These include reports of treatment of prisoners and legal proceedings, as well as the attempts by the regime--with the help of its international allies--to deal with political opponents, particularly the churches.

Finally, while this work was authorized and paid for by the Government of the United States [Ledeen worked as a consultant to the Department of State; Romerstein is an official of the United States Information Agency], we are entirely responsible for the selection of the documents and for the introductory material. We did our work without any pressure from anyone, except insofar as we were urged to work as fast as was reasonably possible. We are grateful for freedom to make the selections we deemed most representative and for the patient support throughout the many months we worked on the documents. We are grateful above all to the two senior officials who authorized the project: the then Undersecretary of State for Political Affairs, Lawrence Eagleburger, and the Undersecretary of Defense for Policy, Fred Ikle.

We believe that the documents in this collection give an accurate albeit incomplete picture of Grenada under the NJM. In choosing a few hundred pages out of tens of thousands, the best that can be hoped for is that the selection was done fairly, with an eye to understanding. We believe that we have done this.

THE NEW JEWEL MOVEMENT

The revolution that overthrew the Gairy regime in Grenada in April 1979 was designed to create a Communist society and to bring Grenada into the Soviet orbit. While the leaders of the New Jewel Movement recognized that they needed to feign respect for political pluralism and a desire for good relations with all neighboring countries (above all the United States), the actual direction that Maurice Bishop and his NJM colleagues wished to take was clear from the outset. The close working relations the regime established with the Government of Cuba--both in Grenada and in Cuba itself--showed that Bishop intended to model his revolution on that of the Soviet Union and, more immediately, of Cuba. The attention shown to delegations from the Soviet bloc and from such radical regimes as Qadaffi's Libya and Kim-il Sung's North Korea, along with the lack of exchanges with traditional friends such as Great Britain, indicated the NJM's real intentions.

By September 1982, Bishop could give an extended "now it can be told" speech to the leaders of the Party and the Government, aptly entitled "Line of March for the Party" (Document 1). In that key presentation, Bishop flatly stated that the goal of the NJM was to "ensure the leading role of the working class through its Marxist/Leninist Party backed by some form of the dictatorship of the proletariat." Copies of the "Line of March" were closely held; each copy was marked confidential and consecutively numbered by hand. Many had been read, marked, and dog-eared, then returned. The minutes of the NJM Political Bureau reflect the use of the "Line of March" document in study classes attended by every member and candidate for membership.

The "Line of March" contains Bishop's reflections on the tactics he adopted shortly after seizing power. People from all social strata were included in the original ruling council and, according to Bishop, "this was done deliberately so that imperialism won't get too excited and would say 'well they have some nice fellas in that thing; everything allright.'" This little deception was abandoned by the time of Bishop's speech, when the NJM was in complete control, and Bishop was quite explicit about the way in which control was exercised:

> Consider how people get detained in this country. We don't go and call for no votes. You get detained when I sign an order after discussing it with the National Security Committee of the Party or with a higher Party body. Once I sign it--like it or don't like it--it's up the hill for them.

Candidates for "the hill" were identified through a clandestine system that monitored the population and foreign visitors (even the predominantly American student body at the medical school). The Special Branch (Secret Police) divided the island into regions for

surveillance; potential opponents of the regime were identified
(generally on a class or religious basis) and closely watched. In
addition, major institutions were targeted for surveillance: the
government, the trade union, the police, the medical school, and the
churches. That this represented a departure from previous practices
is indicated by a statement made by the head of the Special Branch,
Michael Roberts, in a May 1980 report to the Prime Minister and the
Minister of National Security (Document 9): "the old MI 5 (British
counterintelligence) methods of work, after experimentation, have
proven to be not effective enough."

THE CHURCHES

    Church leaders were subjected to particularly close
surveillance, and the Grenadans received considerable help from the
Cubans and Nicaraguans in countering religious activities. In a
document outlining the basic counterintelligence operations of the
Interior Ministry (Document 9), the scope of the NJM's concern with
the churches is evident from a list of duties of the Special Branch,
which included:
    --"Monitoring all sermons by the various parish priests and
       preachers in the society;
    --The controlling of all hirachy [sic] meeting of the
       church in particular the Catholic and Anglicans;
    --Controlling all elements of the society that pay visits
       to the hirachy [sic];
    --Tapping of the Hirachy [sic] of all the leading counter
       churches phones."
("Counter" was used as shorthand for "counterrevolutionary" by
virtually all Grenadans.)

    The NJM took these security measures against church leaders
because they believed that all major religious institutions on the
island were opposed to the revolution. In a top secret report
written in March 1983 (Document 4), Michael Roberts of the Special
Branch stated that the Roman Catholic, Anglican, Methodist, and
Seventh Day Adventist churches were all hostile to the NJM, and that
the Catholic Church was the most important because of its size and
internal discipline. Roberts was concerned about the Catholics' use
of the Jerusalem Bible because "this bible is written as a novel and
is very easy to understand not being written in old English...This
means that the Church in understanding the struggle...has
'revolutionized' is [sic] main ideological weapon--the bible."
Moreover, the Church distributed the Pope's New Year's message, and
Roberts considered it to be "the Church's foreign policy document
and no doubt will be used to criticize our foreign policy."
Similar concerns were expressed about the other churches, to the
point where, by July 1983, Interior Minister Keith Roberts could
write that "in the medium term, if serious measures are not taken,

we can find ourselves faced with a Poland situation....we see the Church in the immediate period as being the most dangerous sector for the development of internal counter revolution" (Document 5).

But perhaps most indicative of the great concern about the churches was the interest shown by the Cuban Communist Party (PCC). The Americas Department of the Cuban Communist Party prepared an extensive analysis of "the religious situation in the country, and the contacts for further cooperation between the PCC and the NJM regarding the question" (Document 2).

The Cubans concurred that the churches were "in harmony with the campaigns carried out by the reactionary governments in the Caribbean" and were distressed at the lack of effective action by the NJM. For example, the Cubans lamented that the Grenadans had not infiltrated the churches ("there are no signs of systematic progressive projections within the Grenadian clergy"), and, as of the time of the report (August 1982), the Grenadans had not even appointed a person to take charge of religious questions. This was remedied forthwith, as Selwyn Strachan was named to this position, and was supposed to spend nearly three weeks training in Cuba before starting work. The Cubans foresaw that Strachan's job would "basically include the information work at the beginning and regular contacts with collaborators from Christian organizations." In other words, he would place agents inside the churches, and then attempt to manipulate them from within.

The other main Cuban suggestion was to bring Grenadan religious leaders and laypersons into contact with Nicaraguan church figures "and other Latin American circles linked to the theology of liberation and, in general, to the idea of a church committed to the revolutionary positions."

THE SOVIET CONNECTION

From the beginning, Bishop and the other NJM leaders sought to bring Grenada into the Soviet orbit, and there are thousands of documents showing the intimate relationship that developed between the USSR and Grenada. Sometimes relations were embodied in formal treaties between Grenada and Soviet bloc countries, and such Soviet proxies as Cuba, Vietnam, and North Korea. On other occasions there were secret agreements, such as those for providing counter-intelligence or surveillance equipment, training for agents, and so forth. We have included several of the treaties and party-to-party agreements that gave Grenada a vast quantity of armaments as well as military and political training. Thousands of weapons, far more than could have been required for the security requirements of the tiny island, were shipped by the Soviet Union and Communist-bloc countries. Overall, the documents (samples of which can be found in this book) showed that the Soviet, Cuban, North Korean, and Czechoslovakian agreements included the following items, which were to have been delivered by 1986:

--Approximately 10,000 assault and other rifles;
--More than 4,500 submachine guns and machine guns;
--More than 11.5 million rounds of 7.62 mm ammunition;
--294 portable rocket launchers with more than 16,000 rockets;
--84 82 mm mortars with more than 4,800 mortar shells;
--12 75 mm cannon with 600 cannon shells;
--15,000 hand grenades, 7,000 land mines, 60 armored personnel carriers and patrol vehicles;
--More than 150 radio transmitters, 160 field telephone sets, approximately 23,000 uniforms, and tents for about 7,700 persons.

By U.S. Department of Defense estimates, equipment found on the island (not all of it had arrived) would have been sufficient to equip a fighting force of roughly 10,000 men. Furthermore, there evidently were some plans for special forces, since the Soviets promised to provide an airplane capable of transporting 39 paratroopers, as well as other special equipment.

All of this made Grenada a real military threat to its neighbors, most of whom had only local constabularies rather than standing armies. And there was little question that the airport was going to be used for military purposes, since General Hudson Austin's deputy, Liam James, reported in his notebook on March 22, 1980, "The Revo has been able to crush Counter-Revolution internationally, airport will be used for Cuban and Soviet military" (Document 23). This apparently reflected a decision of the NJM leadership.

The Soviets appreciated the geopolitical significance of acquiring another proxy in the Western Hemisphere, as can be seen from the picturesque account of a meeting between Major Einstein Louison, Chief of Staff of the Grenadan Army (who had gone to Moscow for military training), and his Soviet counterpart, Marshal N.V. Ogarkov. According to the Grenadan notes on the meeting (Document 24), Ogarkov told Louison, "over two decades ago, there was only Cuba in Latin America, today there are Nicaragua, Grenada and a serious battle is going on in El Salvador." The Grenadans saw themselves as Soviet proxies. Their Ambassador to Moscow, W. Richard Jacobs, reminded his comrades in Grenada that their importance to the Soviets would eventually depend on their success in exporting revolution: "To the extent that we can take credit for bringing any other country into the progressive fold, our prestige and influence would be greatly enhanced [sic]" (Document 26). Jacobs felt that the first such project should be Suriname.

There was no lack of Soviet support for Grenadan intelligence and counterintelligence operations. A draft letter dated February 17, 1982, from General Hudson Austin to Yuri Andropov, then the chief of the KGB, requested training courses for three Grenadans in counterintelligence and one in intelligence work. Austin thanked Andropov for the "tremendous assistance which our armed forces have received from your party and government in the past" (Document 27).

Perhaps the most intensive Soviet assistance to Grenada was in the field of indoctrination, for it was necessary to train a new, Communist generation on the island. The Soviets participated in some of the "ideological crash courses" that are referred to in the minutes of several meetings of the Politbureau and the Central Committee, and they also invited Grenada to send students to the highest level Soviet training school for foreign Communists, the Lenin School in Moscow. The Lenin School, in operation since the 1920s, has trained the leading Communists of almost every country of the world. The NJM students there reported on their training, including courses in "social psychology and propaganda" and "party organization--intelligence/security" (Document 28). The Cubans also assisted in courses in mass manipulation, offering training in journalism, crowd control, propaganda, billboard painting, newspaper and cartoon writing and drawing. A secret agreement between the Cuban Communist Party (PCC) and the NJM provided for training of Grenadans in Cuba and Grenada (Document 17). The document was signed for Cuba by Manuel Pineiro, the former head of Cuban intelligence (the DGI), and currently the head of the Americas Department of the Central Committee of the Communist Party of Cuba, the covert action arm of the Castro regime.

Twenty Grenadans were invited to Vietnam to study anti-chemical warfare, anti-radioactivity warfare, "reeducation of anti-social and counterrevolutionary elements," and "Yankee tactics and the weapons used in Vietnam" (Document 18). Others were invited to Czechoslovakia, Libya, East Germany, and North Korea. We do not know whether the invitations were accepted, but the proposals show how thoroughly Grenada was integrated into the Soviet world.

RELATIONS WITH THE UNITED STATES

The leaders of the Grenadan Government and the New Jewel Movement consistently regarded the United States with hostility. There were several contacts between the NJM and the Communist Party U.S.A., both to raise money for Grenada and to coordinate propaganda and public relations strategies in the United States. There was also guidance from the Cubans provided by Gail Reed Rizo, the U.S.-born wife of the Cuban Ambassador to Grenada, Julian Torres Rizo. Gail Reed had been active in American radical organizations, including the Venceremos Brigade, during the 1970s. Prior to the trip of Prime Minister Bishop to the United States in 1983, Mrs. Rizo gave him detailed suggestions on how he should conduct himself in his contacts with American officials, and recommendations on which Americans he should meet (Document 31). She also reminded him that Sanchez Parodi of the Cuban Interests Section in Washington would be available to him if needed.

Most helpful to an understanding of the NJM's attitude toward the United States are the handwritten notes, evidently written by a Grenadan participant in the conversation, describing Bishop's meeting with National Security Adviser William Clark (Document 32). The notes reveal the NJM perception of American concern about the ideological direction of the Bishop regime (Clark at one point purportedly stressed the U.S. desire that Grenada remain within a Western legal framework), and that the main obstacle to better relations between the two countries was not political, but geopolitical. According to the notes, Washington was worried about the large numbers of Cubans and Russians on Grenada. Clark, Deputy Secretary of State Kenneth Dam, and U.S. Ambassador to the Organization of American States William Middendorf stressed that the U.S. Government wanted actions, not mere declarations of good intentions from the Grenadans. The notes indicate that Bishop was "encouraged by [Judge Clark's] response."

In their efforts to persuade the United States to switch from perceived hostility to support, the Grenadans exerted considerable effort to create a lobby in Washington and to organize a propaganda network throughout the country. They carefully monitored the American media (with help from the Cubans, especially Ambassador Julian Torres Rizo and Gail Reed Rizo), and responded vigorously to criticisms, attempted to identify correspondents and television producers sympathetic to their point of view, and even discussed with the Communist Party U.S.A. the possibility of starting a new radio station in New York City. (These themes are found throughout the minutes of the Politbureau and the Central Committee. See, for example, minutes for Politbureau of 13 May 1982, for their preoccupation with a CBS broadcast they did not like.) A public relations firm in New York was hired to monitor less important publications.

Finally, Grenada coordinated its efforts with those of Soviet-bloc countries and international Soviet-front organizations in supporting and encouraging a worldwide "peace" movement, and in turning against U.S. policy. In April 1981, an NJM representative attended a World Peace Council Congress in Havana, and met with his counterparts from the USSR, Bulgaria, East Germany, Hungary, and the National Committee of Quebec. He reported that assistance would soon be forthcoming from the Soviets, the Hungarians, and the East Germans (Document 45).

THE SOCIALIST INTERNATIONAL

The Declaration of the Socialist International (SI) adopted in Oslo in June 1962, states that the Communist "one-party dictatorships represent in fact tyranny, denying those freedoms of speech, religion, criticism, voluntary organization and contacts with the outside world which are the essence of a democratic society." (See Declarations of the Socialist International, London, 1978, p. 13.) The SI was therefore a natural target for the Communists, and some of the Grenada documents show that "Active Measures"* were conducted against the SI by Grenadans and others acting under the direction of the Americas Department of the Central Committee of the Cuban Communist Party. To further the objective of subverting the SI, a "Secret Regional Caucus" was formed by the Nicaraguan Sandinistas, the Grenadan NJM, and some parties in the Latin American Committee of the SI (Document 39). The NJM had sent observers to SI meetings even before its successful revolution, and in late 1979 Bishop applied for membership in the Socialist International. The application was accepted in November 1980 at the SI Congress in Madrid.

The Grenadans, taking their cue from the Cubans and from the Soviets, viewed the Socialist International as a potential enemy, and one unsigned document (Document 38)--apparently from the 1980-81 period--defended the decision to join the SI, but made clear that it was not because of belief in the SI's principles. Membership was supported on two grounds:

---

*"Active Measures" is an expression used by the Soviets for their influence operations. Soviet Active Measures are coordinated by the International Department of the Communist Party of the Soviet Union (ID), which engages in both overt and semi-overt activities. The KGB conducts the covert Active Measures in coordination with the ID.

Covert Active Measures include forgeries, agents of influence, placement of false stories in the press, and so forth.

Some Soviet Active Measures are carried out through surrogates (usually the intelligence service of another Communist-bloc country). In the Western Hemisphere, the Cuban Communist Party's Americas Department conducts Active Measures on behalf of the Soviet Union. The Americas Department combines both overt and covert Active Measures by having officers of the Cuban Intelligence Service (the DGI) operate on behalf of the Department. For more details, see hearings of the U.S. House of Representatives, Permanent Select Committee on Intelligence, Soviet Covert Action, 1980 and Soviet Active Measures, 1982.

1.   It provided access to international movements which could be persuaded to support New Jewel Movement policies.

2.   The New Jewel Movement could use its membership in the SI to "express organized support for the progressive struggles in Southern Africa, the Western Sahara, Palestine, El Salvador, Nicaragua, and other parts of Latin America, etc."

There was evidently some concern within the government of Grenada that the NJM might be violating its own principles by being a member of a social democratic organization. The author of the document responded that the Socialist International was "sufficiently flexible to permit dissention [sic]" and therefore "membership in the SI should be retained. It has proved useful and if Grenada's foreign policy initiatives are strengthened it can prove even more useful in the future."

The most detailed documents concerning the Socialist International were apparently not written by Grenadans, but rather by Cubans. Two documents found stapled together appear to have been written by a Cuban and then translated into English. (The language is stilted and the author writes from a vantage point outside the SI. We believe they were written by the same person who wrote Document 37A, definitely a Cuban.) They contain sophisticated analyses of the SI from a Marxist/Leninist perspective. One of them--Document 35--is a report on the 15th Congress of the Socialist International held in Madrid in November 1980. The report refers to international documents that had been circulated confidentially among the members of the SI Bureau. These confidential documents showed that there were internal conflicts on a number of questions. The author of the report complained that the "rightist and conservative sectors of the International" (who, as we shall see, included persons who are now the heads of government in Italy, Spain, and Portugal) had succeeded in including in a draft resolution references to "the Afghan problem; events in Poland...[and] the USSR's alleged arms-race policy."

The nature of the conflict between communism and democratic socialism was spelled out in detail in the other document (Document 36): "in the main contradiction of our times between capitalism and socialism, led by U.S. imperialism and the USSR respectively, Social Democrats as a whole are on the imperialist side up to now." Thus the social democrats were enemies of the Communists, and efforts by the SI to exert influence on Latin America were to be resisted:

We see a dual nature in the projection of social democracy in Latin America and the Caribbean. On the one hand, it does represent a permanent enemy of the essential objectives of the communist and left movements in that this trend intends to prevent the triumph of socialist revolutions and the

materialization of the communist ideal. On the other hand,
it is obvious that certain political positions of the
social democracy can be used by the revolutionary and
progressive forces of the continent at given junctures of
the struggle against a repressive and fascist military
regime and of the confrontation with U.S. imperialism.
Hence, in our view, while ideological struggle is
necessary, we should implement ways and methods of
case-by-case treatment of the parties related to social
democracy whose positions coincide with certain tactical
objetives [sic] of the Latin American revolutionary
movement (Document 36, page 14).

DEMOCRATIC SOCIALISTS VERSUS THE MARXIST/LENINISTS

Unison Whiteman, minister of external relations of the
Bishop Government, attended a two-day emergency SI meeting on
Latin America and the Caribbean in Panama on February 28 and
March 1, 1981. Whiteman had a dispute over El Salvador with
former President Carlos Andres Perez of the Venezuelan
Democratic Action Party, who insisted that if the SI meeting
was going to condemn the United States for supplying arms to
the Salvadoran Government, the Cubans and the Soviets should
also be condemned for arming the guerrillas. Whiteman
responded that "the U.S. supply of arms to the Junta is a
notorious fact, that the U.S. officially and publicly stated
this; that SI should not speculate on where the freedom
fighters are getting arms from; that in any event we should not
equate arms for the oppressors with weapons to defend the
people in their just struggle." Whiteman worked for a
compromise resolution that named no names, and he implied that
the tone of the resolution was hostile only to the United
States (Document 41).

Whiteman's position was that of the Cubans. In this
regard, an illuminating document is a Spanish-language report
on an SI committee meeting held in Nicaragua on June 25, 1981
(Document 33). The report was signed by Manuel Pineiro Losada,
head of the Americas Department of the Cuban Communist Party.
In this document, Pineiro complained of efforts by the
democratic socialists to urge the Nicaraguan regime to move in
a more moderate direction. Pineiro was particularly upset with
the actions of Carlos Andres Perez and Felipe Gonzales, the
head of the Spanish Socialist Party (PSOE) and now the Prime
Minister of Spain. Attached to Pineiro's report were two
documents: an account in Spanish of the discussion between
Bayardo Arce (a member of the Sandinista National Directorate
in Nicaragua) and Felipe Gonzales and Carlos Andres Perez for
the SI; and an apparently intercepted telex from Hans Eberhard
of the German Social Democratic Party to Walter Hacker, the
International Secretary of the Austrian Social Democratic

Party. There was also a poor English translation (we have made a fresh translation, included here as Document 33A). Evidently, the Cubans' distrust of the Social Democrats was so intense that they carefully watched the behavior of their principal enemies within the SI.

Conflicts between the democrats and the Communists within the Socialist International emerged at virtually every meeting of which the Grenadans had a record. At a meeting in Bonn on April 1 and 2, 1982 (Document 37), for example, NJM representative Fennis Augustine found that while there was considerable support for Grenada within SI ranks, "some have reservations on what they see as a Marxist thrust of the NJM. I believe that close relationship with Cuba will continue. Nicaragua's position is a little more difficult, although there was a great degree of understanding and sympathy for them by the time the meeting was finished" (Document 37). Augustine noted that some of the social democratic parties were worried about the actions of the Sandinistas, and cited in particular Carlos Andres Perez' party's criticisms of the Nicaraguans. Augustine was also disturbed to encounter SI support for greater democracy in Nicaragua, including elections, a two-party system, human rights, freedom of religion, and freedom of speech and press.

The same meeting was the subject of another report, this one unsigned (Document 37a). Internal evidence (a reference to Cuba as "us") suggests that it was written by a Cuban, and it is quite similar to Documents 35 and 36. It would not be surprising to have a Cuban report of an SI meeting, since the Cubans were almost always present at the site of such meetings, even though they were not permitted to attend. But they gave instructions to the Grenadans (and perhaps also to the Nicaraguans), and were thus able to get detailed reports on what transpired. In any event, the author of the report, while disturbed that the democratic socialists were attempting to neutralize the "revolutionary" countries in the region so as to limit Cuban influence, boasted that the "right-wing" forces within the SI (identified as Felipe Gonzales of Spain, Mario Soares of Portugal, and Carlos Andres Perez of Venezuela, two of whom are now prime ministers and one a former president of their respective countries) were effectively neutralized.

But Cuban and Grenadan optimism turned out to be misplaced. At a meeting of the Socialist International European Bureau in Basle, Switzerland, on November 3 and 4, 1982, there was outspoken criticism of both the NJM and the Sandinista regime in Nicaragua. According to a report of the meeting submitted by Chris DeRiggs, a member of the NJM Central Committee and Minister of Health, there was strong opposition to a resolution expressing solidarity with Grenada and Nicaragua. Leading critics included Mario Soares, Bettino Craxi of the Italian Socialist Party, and Rita Freedman of Social Democrats USA. According to DeRiggs, "their major line of attack was that Grenada was a one-party state and, therefore, could not be considered a democracy" (Document 40, page 4).

Both DeRiggs and Paul Miller of the Peoples National Party (PNP) of Jamaica tried to justify the lack of an opposition party in Grenada, but apparently their rhetoric was not convincing, and so they pondered ways in which the Socialist International could be turned to their own purposes. DeRiggs suggested that the forces of the Latin American left within the SI could be used to lobby the European Socialists, and he observed that Guillermo Ungo of the Salvadoran National Revolutionary Movement (MNR)--affiliated with the Revolutionary Democratic Front (FDR), the political wing of the guerrilla movement--had achieved a certain degree of success along those lines. Thus, in DeRiggs's words, "it is felt that similar efforts from other SI members in the region can help to exploit contradictions existing even within the membership of SI parties like the Socialist Party of Portugal" (Document 40, page 8). In other words, it was necessary to work within the member parties to produce a shift in outlook. By January of 1983, these ideas had taken a more concrete form.

THE "SECRET REGIONAL CAUCUS"

January 6-7, 1983, a Secret Regional Caucus was held in Managua, consisting of five parties affiliated with the Socialist International, and the Communist Party of Cuba (See Document 39). The five SI parties were:
   --The FSLN of Nicaragua, represented by Antonio Jarquin (misspelled as Marguin and Harguin in the document), the chairman of the meeting;
   --The Salvadoran MNR, represented by Hector Oqueli (this party is one of the groups composing the guerrilla movement, and Oqueli is the Secretary of the Socialist International Committee for Latin America and the Caribbean, which has given a patina of respectability to the Salvadoran insurgents);
   --The Chilean Radical Party, represented by "Freda" (the leadership of the party later denied that it had sent a representative);
   --The Jamaican PNP, represented by Paul Miller;
   --The New Jewel Movement, represented by Chris DeRiggs.

The Socialist International was the main topic of the meeting. In DeRiggs's words, they considered "initiatives to neutralize forces within SI that are against us." And what were these forces? "Our principal enemies are to be found among the parties of Soares and Horgo [sic, Pietro Longo, the leader of the Italian Social Democratic Party] in Portugal and Italy respectively--the Social Democrats of the USA are also our sworn enemies." DeRiggs boasted that of the 14 members of the SI Committee for Latin America and the Caribbean, "there are seven parties that are generally progressive and some within a Marxist-Leninist trend." The Secret Regional Caucus report shows that a resolution on Latin America and the

Caribbean drafted by Hector Oqueli of the Salvadoran MNR, subsequently submitted to the SI, was actually based on guidelines laid down at the meeting. A decision was made to maintain the Secret Regional Caucus, and to "review membership in the future."

This document shows that the NJM was fundamentally opposed to the democratic ideals of the Socialist International, that the Grenadans, along with others in the region, worked in lockstep with the Cubans to undermine the SI's effectiveness, and that the Grenadans' greatest objection to the SI was its insistence on democratic institutions and democratic elections. In fact, on February 3, 1982, Benny Langaigne, the permanent secretary in Maurice Bishop's office, showed the Prime Minister a draft letter addressed to the official magazine of the SI, Socialist Affairs (Document 42). The letter protested a story in the magazine stating that Grenada would have elections in the near future. In fact, the NJM had no such intention.

CONCLUSION

The documents selected for this volume constitute, in our opinion, a representative sample of the total archive. We believe that those who take the time to study them will find a remarkable consistency, a single-minded dedication to the NJM's objective of creating, over time, a Communist society on the Soviet model.

Bishop and his colleagues not only wished to establish communism in Grenada; they wanted to be active members of the Soviet Empire. To this end, they sought ways to curry favor with the Soviets and other bloc countries, and loyally followed the instructions that came to them through Cubans. Thus, on both the domestic and international levels, the Grenadans emulated the USSR and tied their destiny to the Kremlin.

Nonetheless, and despite considerable assistance from the USSR and its proxies, the People's Revolutionary Government was a failure, and the failure led to intense internal conflict, and eventually to the overthrow and murder of Bishop.

The several documents that recount the internal crisis that led to the fall and murder of Maurice Bishop in the autumn of 1983 do not indicate any strong divergence of views between Bishop and those who replaced him; rather, the struggle appears to have been almost exclusively personal. The complaints against Bishop involved inefficiency, insufficient ideological coherence, and lack of strong leadership and guidance, not political deviation or betrayal of the goals of the revolution. We saw no evidence that Bishop was removed because the Cubans or the Soviets were dissatisfied with his political orientation; as far as we have been able to discover, there is no reason to think that his conversation with Judge Clark and other American officials earlier in the year led his colleagues to believe that he was "soft on imperialism."

An archive of the dimensions and richness of this one from Grenada will provide scholars with a wealth of information about Communist activities in the Caribbean, Soviet and Cuban foreign policy, and the problems encountered by Soviet-oriented Communists in their attempts to mold a new generation of Grenadans who had had little contact with Marxism/Leninism before the NJM took power. Of particular interest is the material related to international organizations, including negotiations with the International Monetary Fund and attempts to manipulate the Socialist International. We have given here only a brief overview of a few of the themes that most interested us. We will be pleased if this serves to whet the appetites of a wide audience for this collection of documents, and for the many documents that will be made accessible to the public with the opening of the Grenada archive.

Washington, D.C.
September 1984

CONTENTS

Note: Documents marked A-1 were Maurice Bishop's personal copies.
Notes on these documents seem to have been written by him.

SECTION ONE: LIFE UNDER THE NEW JEWEL MOVEMENT

SECTION TWO: INTERNATIONAL ACTIVITIES

SECTION THREE: MINUTES OF POLITICAL BUREAU and CENTRAL COMMITTEE

Political Bureau

Central Committee

NOTE: The material relating to the international crisis of the NJM and the People's Revolutionary Government, including the fall and death of Maurice Bishop, is found in Oct. 1982 to Sept. 1983 documents covering Central Committee meetings.

SECTION ONE:
LIFE UNDER THE NEW JEWEL MOVEMENT

CONFIDENTIAL

LINE OF MARCH FOR THE PARTY

PRESENTED BY

COMRADE MAURICE BISHOP

CHAIRMAN, CENTRAL COMMITTEE

TO

GENERAL MEETING

OF

PARTY

ON

MONDAY 13th SEPTEMBER 1982

Comrades of the Political Bureau and Central Committee of the Party, Comrades of the Party.

I will like to join with Comrade Strachan to say on behalf of the Central Committee that we are very happy to have all the comrades here this afternoon. As Comrade Selwyn has pointed out, essentially what we want to do today is to deal with the proposed line of march as examined by the C.C. of the Party in the last few weeks.

In our view the line of march needs to take into account four specific features:-

Firstly, the present character and stage of the Revolution. We regard that as fundamentally important. We must decide what exactly is a correct characterisation of the present stage of the Revolution.

Secondly, the line of march must address in a serious way the question of the main tasks facing the Party and Revolution at this time.

Thirdly, we must determine a correct prioritisation of those tasks; we must establish priorities bearing in mind particularly, the comments, criticisms, suggestions, proposals etc. which have been made by Party members and, of course, taking into account the totality of the objective and subjective situation.

The fourth and final factor is the need to emphasise the further development of the subjective factor, the need to place great emphasis and importance on the further development of the subjective factor, that is to say, the Party. In other words, we must look at the Party itself, review the history of the Party very briefly and deal with the question of criteria for membership into the Party and for remaining as members of the Party.

Comrades, in terms of the character of the Revolution, the first aspect to the line of march, we believe it is important for us to look at this question at this time for several reasons.

Firstly and obviously, because we must as a Party know where we are. As Party members, candidate members and applicants we have to face the broad masses out there; we have to answer questions about where we are, what we are trying to do and so on and therefore we must be able to answer those questions in precise terms. We believe further that there is some confusion on this question, that it has not been sufficiently dealt with in the past and therefore we want today to look at it that much more carefully. It is extremely important for us to get a better understanding of where we are, of what we are trying to build and of how we will be able to build it. That is why we feel that this whole question of what exactly is the present stage is so important.

Before looking at that, a few words on the question of where we have come from, in other words, the inheritance of the Revolution. All comrades know of course that we inherited a backward, undeveloped economy, with a very low level - one can say in fact, a primitive level, of technological and economic development in the country. There was a very low level, and there is still a low level of development of the productive forces, that is, of living human labour, objects of labour and instruments of labour. This low level of development of the productive forces in turn resulted in very underdeveloped class formations.

3.......

What we have in Grenada primarily of course, is a very
large pet.t bourgeoisie, particularly a large peasantry-
the rural petit bourgeoisie - small farmers who own
small means of production and who must therefore work
as they cannot live off their own plot of land alone.
Some of them employ labour; some do not. So a large
peasantry or bulk of our rural petit bourgeoisie.
Then there is the urban petit bourgeoisie in terms of
shopkeepers, garage owners, craftsmen, small restaurant
owners and such like. The whole range of the petit
bourgeoisie in our country. That of course is by far
the largest class formation in the country.

We also have a working class which is very small and
made up of agricultural workers based mainly in the
rural areas, transport   and communication workers on
the docks, in telephone, electricity, etc.,
manufacturing and industrial workers (the smallest
section of all) who produce garments, cokes, beer,
that sort of thing. Some sections of the working class
are employed by Government - garbagemen, the lowest
clerical workers, the daily paid workers and so on.
And of course we also have the commercial workers.
Some of these comrades of the working class are also
small owners of the means of production, but do not
rely on that to support themselves - at least not as
their main means of support.

In terms of the inheritance I also want to emphasise
the low cultural level of our population at large as
part of that inheritance and in particular the lack of
technical skills and technical expertise of the working
people. We must emphasise also the 19th century type
of capitalist that we have in the country, capitalists

4/ engaged.......

engaged primarily in comprador activity, in other words
largely in the importation and thereafter distribution
of goods. This is a particularly parasitic type of
capitalist in the full time service of international
capitalism on which they must depend for the manufactured
goods which give them their profits. They produce
nothing and the vast majority of them engage in no
form of manufacturing or industrial activity at all.

As part of the inheritance too, we must also note the
very low level of infrastructural development of our
country. Further, very backward agricultural development is also part of our inheritance and has relevance
to the present stage of the Revolution. This
inheritance of ours does have negative implications
for the road that we are travelling on, for our
objective to build Socialism in our country.

First of all, having a small working class is a very
very serious disadvantage because only the working
class can build Socialism. We know this is so because
the working class is the class that is always growing;
in fact, it has been historically, and it still is part
of capitalist development that the working class gets
larger and larger. Again, it is the working class that
is most prepared for organisation and discipline
because of having to work every day, having to arrive
on time, having to engage in collective organisation
and collective bargaining in their trade unions and so
on. The working class too owns no means of production,
in fact owns nothing except their labour and therefore
they are the ones who most of all have to fight to end
the oppression that comes about as a result of the
private ownership of the means of production which of

5/ course......

course enslaves them and ensures that their own development is stultified and, finally the working class does have the key role in building socialism because of their role in production.

This inheritance is a problem also because of the large r   bourgeoisie that it has left us. We of course have that number of petit bourgeoisie in our country precisely because of economic under-development, precisely because capitalist production was so undeveloped that they did not need much labour and therefore people were by large forced to try to make a living however they could and wherever they could. But because the petit bourgeoisie is a vaci   ting class it is more difficult to build Socialism when there is such a large amount of petit bourgeoisie in the country, precisely because they are in the middle and you have to fight hard to win them. Many of them of course have bourgeois aspirations, many more are deluded and   by bourgeois ideology and propaganda and therefore the struggle to win the petit bourgeoisie has historically been a very serious intense struggle in all countries that have embarked upon a path of Socialist transformation.

The question we must now pose comrades is whether a society such as ours with their primitiveness, with so little infrastructure, with so little development of productive forces, with such a small working class can really build socialism. This is a question that many other countries before us have posed and many other countries in the future will continue to pose. Of course, this question arises because socialism requires a good level of development of the productive forces, it requires infrastructural development, it

1 - 6

requires agricultural development, it requires
industrialisation, it requires a high level of cultural
development of the people, it requires an even higher
level of political development and political consciousness, it requires central planning of the economy and
society as a whole, it requires a serious Marxist
Leninist vanguard Party leading, guiding and directing
the whole process. All of these things are pre-
requisites for the building of Socialism, and, of course,
the vast majority of these either do not exist at all
or are at a very low level of development, at this
time. Nonetheless, the answer is yes, it is possible
for a country like ours to build Socialism. That of
course we all know. It is possible, but the question
is how and we think that this can be seen if we examine
some of the possibilities or models for economic development
in our country.

We believe that there are four main possibilities for
economic development of Grenada and countries like
Grenada. The first of these is a total private
sector free enterprise system of economic development,
your Seaga of Jamaica or your Puerto Rico model of
development, where free enterprise is given full rein,
where the private sector is able to rule uncontrolled.
The second model is a total state sector approach where
just about anything important is owned by the State,
where the State owns virtually everything that matters.
The third type is a mixed economy, but with a private
sector dominant, and of course, that is the model
that we have chosen in Grenada, the mixed economy -
state sector dominant type model. But even after
having said that, there are still questions of why

7/ we have.......

we have chosen that form and the question of precisely
how will that form assist us to build socialism are
two such questions that come to mind. Obviously, if
we are speaking of building Socialism and we are, then
it is clear that our objective as Marxist-Leninist
must in the first instance be to construct socialism
as rapidly, but scientifically as possible. That
being so, clearly we cannot choose the path of capitalism. We cannot choose the path of a total private
sector free enterprise model because that will be
inconsistant with what we believe in and what we
have been and are struggling for. We could not likewise choose that path of the mixed economy, with the
private sector dominant because that will have
tremendous dangers for the successful construction of
Socialism and will have us without the effective
possibility of guiding and regulating economic
development through the imposition of taxes, the
granting of credits and concessions and the use of all
arms of the State apparatus. This must necessarily
be so because it is, as we know, the objective material
basis of the economy that determines and directs the
political, social and cultural development of the
society as a whole.

Equally, we cannot opt for the total state sector model
as the state does not have the necessary material of
financial resources, management and skills resources,
access to markets, international contacts and so on.
All of this should be obvious, but for those who have
any doubts, please reflect on the tremendous
difficulties that we have in finding the dollars
necessary to pay the downpayment to the British
Company - Plessey's - that will be installing the

8/ radar......

radar, communications and navigational equipment for our new international airport, or reflect on how difficult it has been to find guaranteed markets for our primary products and our agro-industrial products, or how difficult it is to find engineers or architects or science teachers or managers - and note I did not even say good managers, I just said managers. No, it would be impossible at this time for the state on its own to build Grenada.

That, of course, means that an alliance is necessary, an alliance in the first place between the working class and the petty bourgeoisie, in particular the rural peasantry, and in the second place an alliance with those elements of the upper petty bourgeoisie and the national bourgeoisie who, for different reasons, are willing to be involved in building the economy and the country at this time.

$/.............

DEFINITION OF PRESENT STAGE OF GRENADA REVOLUTION

And this leads me at long last to the answer to the
question - what is a correct characterisation of the
present stage of development of the Grenada Revolution?
And the answer, course, as we all know, is that the
Grenada Revolution is a national-democratic, nti-
imperialist Revolution, involving the alliance of many
classes including sections of the small bourgeoisie
but under the leadership and with the dominant role
being played by the working people and particularly the
working class, through their vanguard Party the NJM.

This, Comrades is how we define the present stage of the
Grenada Revolution today. Obviously National Democratic,
anti-imperialist means what it says. I did not say a
socialist revolution as some comrades like to keep
pretending that we have. Obviously we do not have a
socialist revolution and it is not socialist precisely
because:-

  (1) The low level of development of the
       productive forces. You cannot have a
       socialist revolution with this low level
       development.

  (2) Our working class is too small and too
       politically underdeveloped.

For these primary reasons we cannot proceed straight
away to the building of socialism but must first pass
through a stage where we lay the basis, where we create
the conditions, including the socio-economic and political
conditions, for the building of socialism and the creation
of the socialist revolution, that is, for the full coming

to power of the working class. In other words, comrades,
what we are into now (this national democratic stage)
really means two things. What we are speaking about
now is not socialist construction, not the socialist
revolution, we are speaking about the national democratic
revolution, we are speaking about socialist orientation.
So the important   things to contradistinguish here
are socialist construction the second stage versus
socialist orientation the first stage, which is the
stage we are in at this time.

Comrades, these two things are completely different
and it is very important for us to grasp that
difference, because the experience of the C.C. and
study guides in the Party is that it is an area of
tremendous confusion and an area that has proven hard
to grasp. In some countries around the world it is of
course possible to go straight to socialism. That would
have been possible;.for example the French in 1789 at
the time of their bourgeois-democratic Revolution.
They could have gone straight to socialism because the
necessary objective material bases and conditions were
present. Or if tomorrow morning a revolution takes
place in the United States or one of the industrialised
countries of Western Europe they too can go straight
to socialism, because they have a large working class,
because the objective material basis in terms of
infrastructure, high economic development, high level
of development of the productive forces etc, etc are
present, so once there is a correct scientific political
leadership it is possible for them to proceed to socialism
straight away, but for us it is impossible. It really
is important for this first concept to be fully grasped.

11.......

On Saturday when we were doing the same presentation for
the Applicants, there was a particular example I gave which
I want to repeat for the Members and Candidate Members and
ask for the apologies of the promoted Applicants.

What we gave for ~ e...ple then was two different people
in Grenada who owned two separate plots of lands; let us
say one person owning land in Grand Anse and another in
Grenville, St. Andrew's. Both of them own plots of land,
both of them want to build a house on their respective
plots of lands. In the case of the man in Grand Anse, his
land is flat, his land already has the necessary attachments for telephone, water, electricity, he has a concrete
base, there is already some kind of access road to his
plot of land - therefore all he has to do is put up his
house.

In the case of the man in Grenville, what he has is a
rough piece of land, the land is hilly, the land has a
lot of bush, a lot of trees, a lot of stone. There are
no water pipes near to this man's plot of land; there are
no telephone poles near to this man's plot of land, no
electricity poles, no access road - he has to go through
a dirt track. This second man cannot just go and put up
his house. First of all he has to cut a piece of road to
the house to get the materials there; then he has to level
the land and he has to do all the necessary earth work;
and civil works; he has to put down his concrete base and
only then can he begin to talk about building his house.

The first man, the man in St. George's, he is ready for
socialist construction.
The second man, the one in Grenville with the rough
hilly land who has to do all the necessary preliminary
works is the kind of man like us here in Grenada who can't
go straight to socialism. He has to first lay the basis

and the foundations. We have to cut the land, cut the road, make sure the telephone poles are laid, the pipe borne water is available and so on before we can build the house.

That is the difference, comrades, between socialist orientation and socialist construction and that is the stage we are at, the first stage - the stage of socialist orientation.

Comrades, we speak of the national democratic anti-imperialist revolution and each of those words, of course, has a meaning. The national democratic anti-imperialist revolution is national because it arose from a national liberation struggle that was aimed to do away with the political, economic and ideological domination of an oppressive ruling elite that of Gairy, imperialism and their allies. It is national because it involved, and still involves, a vast majority of the people - that is why the national democratic Revolution is national.

It is democratic because it aims to give or restore rights and freedoms to the majority of the people. Under the Gairy dictatorship of course, many of the rights of the working people were taken away. The February 1978 Essential Services Act took away the right to strike from eleven of the most important categories of workers. The Public Order Act, 1974, prohibited political parties and even individuals from using loudspeakers, without police permission. The 1975 Newspaper Act made it impossible to publish a newspaper that was political and opposed to Gairy. These rights, as comrades know, have been restored. We have all created new rights because part of this national democratic path is the need to readily expand democracy and the democratic participation of the poor and working people in the country. That is why we have brought more democratic rights through the establishment of zonal councils, workers parish councils, farmers, women and youth councils - all of the organs of popular democracy.

The Revolution is also anti-imperialist because it is opposed to foreign domination and the exploitation of our country and its resources by the transnational co-operations. Of course, this looks only at the economic essence of imperialism for that is what I am trying to focus on at this time. The political, cultural and ideological aspects of imperialism are not what we are dealing with here, though they will also be struggles in this anti-imperialist stage.

We want to point out too, comrades, that the national democratic anti-imperialist stage can be led not just by the working class, not just by the petty bourgeoisie, but even by the bourgeoisie. It can be led by the bourgeoisie, petty bourgeoisie or the working class - any of these class forces can lead the Revolution. If it is led by the bourgeoisie, obviously, it could never go on to build socialism - that will be an impossibility; no bourgeois can build socialism. If it is led by the petty bourgeoisie, the only basis on which it can build socialism is if the petty bourgeoisie leadership in the course of the class struggle is transformed into a revolutionary Marxist-Leninist leadership and therefore develops a Marxist-Leninist Party that then guides and directs the process. Without that transformation, it would also be impossible.

Therefore, obviously it is only the working class that can build socialism. It is only under the leadership

1 - 14

of the working class, led by a Marxist-Leninist
vanguard Party that the process can be completed and
we can go on to socialist construction. That is the
only time it is possible.

That again, comrades, needs to be understood by us
because of its tremendous relevance to the nature of
the alliance we have and what we need to do from here
on.

This national democratic stage of the revolution has,
broadly speaking, two main components - a political
aspect and an economic aspect.

POLITICAL ESSENCE OF THE NATIONAL - DEMOCRATIC PARTY

In terms of the political aspect, the essence of that
political aspect is the dictatorship of the working
people, dictatorship of rule of the working people -
that is the essence. This essence implies a change in
the balance of forces that presently exists, a change
in the balance of forces that will usually be involved
in the anti-imperialist struggle of the national
liberation movements. In other words, in your Angolas,
Mozambiques, etc., what you would normally find
happening is that there is a class alliance involved
in the fight to end colonialism. And that class
alliance will involve the bourgeoisie, the petty-
bourgeoisie and the proletariat (the working class) -.
all three.

And in countries like ours, after independence, just
like in Grenada today, what you usually find happening
is that state power is wielded by an alliance of the
bourgeoisie, the petty-bourgeoisie and the working
class through a particular Party or combination of
Parties, and usually comrades, as you know, the
situation is that it is the bourgeoisie and the petty-   1 - 15

bourgeoisie that is pre-dominant, the combined bourgeoisie
and petty bourgeoisie that is pre-dominant, and the
working class is the minority influence. That is the
usual situation in countries like ours even after
independence. That is what is happening right now.
Right through the English-speaking Caribbean - in all
of them - you can see that the bourgeoisie and petty-
bourgeoisie are ruling and that working class representation is very small.

But when countries start to move to develop this essence
I was talking about - the dictatorship (or rule)of the
working people - is that in the course of class
struggle, the bourgeoisie begins to become subordinated and the influence of the petty-bourgeoisie
and working class together becomes pre-dominant. In
other words a drift begins to take place, at first
imperceptible, but gradually observable and at a certain
moment when quantity becomes quality, that shift becomes very clear and very noticeable. And at that
 time, the bourgeoisie becomes the minority force and
the petty bourgeoisie and proletariat begin to rule.
And when that happens, it becomes the first time at
which it is possible to shift the country away from
the path of capitalist development, because a
combination of bourgeoisie and petty bourgeoisie
pre-dominant necessarily means that the emphasis will
be on capitalist development. And equally, once the
shift takes place then the potential is there for the
first time to begin to move along the path of socialist
orientation and away from the path of capitalist development. That comrades, is our situation in Grenada, and
that was the situation when we took power on March
13th, 1979.

When we took power on March 13th 1979, as comrades know,
we did not take power as an alliance - we took power as

NJM. But within the first few hours of taking power,
we tried to build an alliance and we begun to build
that alliance for two main reasons:- Firstly to hold
on to power in the first few seconds, minutes, hours,
days and weeks. And the second reason was to defeat
imperialism. in the months and years thereafter,
because defeating imperialism is a complex process,
that requires a political orientation and an economic
transformation that involves crushing the rule of the
monopolies and of big business in your country, that
involves taking control of the commanding heights of
the economy and so on. And we cannot do what on our
own and that is why the alliance was and is needed.

But comrades, we have to be very clear that it was the
Party and the Party alone that took power. GNP didn't
help us; there was no UPP, there was no alliance with
any upper petty-bourgeoisie or any national bourgeoisie
in seizing power. In fact, most of these elements
might have run from the prospect of having to go down
to True Blue barr   to take power. NJM took power
on its own, but NJM then decided - correctly - that an
alliance was needed to hold power. We understood the
reasons for that because we knew we could not do it on
our own. The leadership of the Party and the Party
itself had a working class ideology and therefore an
understanding of what was required to ensure that the
working class will eventually take power. But we were
    way ahead and we still are way, way ahead
ideologically of the masses of our people in general
and also of our national bourgeoisie. We are much
more politically and ideologically developed than them,
we have a much deeper class consciousness then them.

So we have the objective to build socialism. We know
that objective could only be achieved if we built an

alliance but not all of our masses know that and in fact the vast majority still have no scientific understanding of this need for an alliance. So what we did, we did in their interest and acting in their name, even though they did not necessarily understand why we were doing what we were doing. And it is very significant Comrades that from the start, from the very first second of the Grenada Revolution (let us say 4.30 a.m. on March 13th 1979) from the very first second of the Grenada Revolution, what was established was a dictatorship of the entire working people. In its operationalisation; in its initial concretisation; it took the form of the anti-Gairy poor and working people, in other words, those people who were opposed to Gairy were the ones who appeared to be in the vanguard. And that is true, they were in the vanguard. But right from the start, the effective dictatorship was not only of the anti-Gairy working people. It was a dictatorship of the entire working people with the anti-Gairy working people initially being in the operational vanguard of that dictatorship. It is a very important concept for us to grasp and to agree on.

As the Revolu... deepened and strengthened and consolidated, as the Gairyite working people came to see that the Revolution was also in their interest, that we were not victimising them, that, in fact, we were bringing benefits to them, then they too joined the Revolution, and today, a majority of them support the Revolution. But right from the start the rule that was established by the NJM on behalf of the working class, was rule of the entire working people. It's a very important conceptual point.

From the start too, comrades, we had an alliance with
sections of the upper petty bourgeoisie and national
bourgeoisie right from the word GO. Within the first
few hours of the Revolution, we began to put that
alliance in place. I can remember all of us making
phone calls to different sections of the Petty-
bourgeoisie and the National bourgeoisie, inviting them
to come down to Radio Free Grenada and in some cases
beginning to feel them out as to whether or not they
were willing to serve on the ruling council of the
People's Revolutionary Government.

I can remember very well that the first set of names
we announced for the ruling council was fourteen (14),
not twenty-three (23). And these fourteen names were
made up mainly (outside of the immediate leadership),
of the petty-bourgeoisie, the upper petty-bourgeoisie
and the national bourgeoisie. You remember that?
Simon Charles and Sydney Ambrose - peasantry,
Bernard Gittens - professional middle strata, Lloyd
Noel - professional middle strata; Palm Buxo and
Norris Bain - middle capitalists; Lyden Ramdhanny -
big capitalist; that is who the People's Revolutionary
Government was. And this was done deliberately so
that imperialism won't get too excited and would say
"well they have some nice fellas in that thing; everything alright." And as a result wouldn't think about
sending in troops.

That was the mistake, for example, the comrades in
Gambia made a few months ago. Remember the Gambia
Coup E'tat a few months ago? What was the first thing
those comrades did? They say "we are Marxist-Leninists
and we have just had a Marxist-Leninist Revolution and
we go wipe out the bourgeoisie." The same day they

overthrow them - same day, they didn't even give them
three days. So fortunately, NJM had a little more
sense than that. And like I said comrades, the first
fourteen names were bourgeoisie, big capitalist, petty-
bourgeoisie, middle capitalist, peasantry and professional
middle strata - that is who made up the People's
Revolutionary Government. It is only after about a
week and a half (if I recall correctly), when we held
the Party General meeting in Radio Free Grenada's
studio (and some comrades here would have been present
at that meeting) that we finally got around to pulling
some more Party comrades. You all remember that
meeting down in Radio Free Grenada stud... It was
then we chose nine more comrades to make up the
twenty- three. But the first set of names were Lyden,
Pam Buxo, Norris Bain, Lloyd Noel and so on. That is
what I mean by saying th the alliance began from the
first few hours and the first few days. And that
alliance was and is extremely important.

From our point of view comrades, why do we need the
alliance?

We need the alliance firstly, as we pointed out already,
to hold power in the first few days and weeks.

We need the alliance, secondly, to consolidate and
build the revolution and to ensure the defeat of
imperialism.   this time we can't do this
effectively without the alliance.

We need the alliance, comrades, because we don
have enough managers, because we don't have enough
capital, because we don't have enough international
contacts, bec se we don't have enough markets. For
all of these reasons, we need the alliance.

If we were the State that owned the flour mill in Tempe
and not Geddes Grant, we won't be able to sell that
flour so easily to Jamaica and the others in Caricom.
If it were the State that owned the Gament Factory in
True Blue and not Hadeed, we won't be able to sell
garments to Barbados and Trinidad so easily. The
capitalist prefers to deal with the capitalist and
capitalist Governments allows other capitalists to come
in, even when their Government is a socialist oriented
Government like our Government in Grenada. It is very
important for us to see that.

And why does the bourgeoisie need the alliance?

They need the alliance first of all because they have
contradictions with imperialism. Imperialism especially
at this time because of the deep capitalist crisis,
has been putting the squeeze on the national bourgeoisie.
They can't always get letters of credit, every month
the banks make the terms for the letters of credit more
difficult instead of three month repayment, it becomes
one month. Sometimes they get not even one day. Also
they can't get the kinds of loans they want. And when
they do get loans, they have to pay high interest
rates. And overall, of course, the fact of the
recession - the capitalist crisis makes it more
difficult for them to develop in the way in which they
would like. This is so because the capitalist crisis
affects Grenada and helps to scueeze our economy because
their demand for our goods - cocoa, banana, nutmegs -
has fallen. And when we can't sell cocoa, banana,
nutmegs, then it means the standard of living falls
because there is less money floating around. So a lot
of the capitalists are vexed with imperialism. That
is the first point.

21......

The second p it is t   they have been watching the
Revolution and they are now convinced that the
Revolution gives them new possibilities for making
profits, new possibilities for expanding their businesses
and moving on. They have watched the growth of
infrastructure - the new International Airport, the
coming Sandino Plant, the Emulsion Plant, the Quarry
and Asphalt Plant, the new East Coast Road, the Feeder
Roads, the West Coast road to come, the new Telephone
system to come, the new Electricity system to come,
the new Storage ¯ank Farm to come, the 40% more water
in people's homes. They have watched all of that and
understand that it represents the necessary basis for
them to develop their business and to ake profits.
In other words they see the Revolution as providing
them with the possibility of developing and expanding.

And don't forget that we have been encouraging them
through holding many consultations with them. When we
have a National Conference on the Economy with the mass
organisations (as we did on 29th January), two weeks
later, we held a   itio al Conference with the Private
Sector, and we are sitting down with them just like we
did with the masses.

Now we are settling with their participation a Tourism
Code and an Investment Code. And Cde Coard, as the
Minister of Finance, has been meeting with them very
regularly and giving them incentives, giving them
concessions, helping them to develop the confidence
that the state is not going to crush them. And all
of this has now had a qualitiative effect on the
National Bourgeoisie.

A third factor, comrades, and   a factor we s ne-
times forget, is that the National Bourgeoisie has

22/ two sides.......

there is the un-patriotic capitalist and there is the patriotic one, and it is the patriotic ones who will form the alliance with us. The un-patriotic ones will sell out and go abroad or will try to engage in sabo...ge. So the reality of patriotism is something that must not be overlooked.

And fourthly and finally, it is important to remember that part of the reason we can form the alliance with them is because of their own low level of class consciousness. Therefore, they don't really fully understand what it is we are doing. It comes over in a million things they say from time to time. They are not really ...... d they are still hoping that what we are building is not sociali.... but no one of them puts it socialist capitalism or capitalist socialism - whatever that means.

So, there is that area of confusion. But comrades a few more words on the nature of the alliance that we have with these sections. First of all, it is important to understand that the alliance we have gives full, total complete control to the Party and the working people. The party and the working people have hegemony. A monopoly will mean total power, hegemony will mean total control, and that is the distinction we are drawing between hegemony and monopoly.

But there is absolutely no doubt that we have a hegemonic control on power and over all the capital ar.. of the State. We can see this in several different ways. If you consider the question Cabinet. The Cabinet of our country has ten (10) ministers and nine of these ten ministers are members of the Party; the only non-member of the Party is Norris Bain. If you look at the ruling

council of the People's Revolutionary Government, you
will see it no longer has twenty-three people because
Lloyd Noel is in detention, Pam Buxo is out of the
country, Lyle Bullen is no longer involved. There are
three people who are out, there are now twenty (20)
people who are in the P.R.G. And if you look at the
Party and   Cabinet and you analyse them carefully,
you will discover an over 90% direct control by the
Party of the ruling council of the P.R.G. and Cabinet.

Secondly, to see further this hegemony or control I am
talking about comrades, look at the composition of our
army and militia. We don't have any upper Petty-
bourgeoisie or bourgeoisie in our army or militia. When
you look at the officers in the army it is Working Class
comrades or petty-bourgeois revolutionary democrats or
communists who are the officers in the army - that's
the situation in our army.

Thirdly comrades, consider our Zonal Councils and our
Workers Councils and so on. The bourgeoisie is not
invited deliberately and consciously, so they don't
have the opportunity to come and try to confuse people
inside the councils. When we're having a Zonal Council
in this building or a Workers Parish Council, we send
out the invitations, we decide who we want to invite
and we live the bourgeoisie out deliberately and
consciously.

Consider the trade unions in our country, five of the
eight leading trade unions are under the direct leadership and control of full members, candidate members and
applicants of our Party. There is no doubt about it;
what we have is hegemony; we have full control.

24........

4

I want to think of another area. Just consider, comrades,
how laws are made in this country. Laws are made in
this country when Cabinet agrees and when I sign a
document on behalf of Cabinet. And then that is what
everybody in the country - like it or don't like it -
has to follow. Or consider how people get detained
in this country. We don't go and call for no votes.
You get detained when I sign an order after discussing it with the National Security Committee of the
Party or with a higher Party body. Once I sign it -
like it or don't like it - its up the hill for them.

It is also important to note comrades, that while we
are in an alliance with sections of the bourgeoisie
and upper petty-bourgeoisie, they are not part of our
dictatorship. They are not part of our rule and control -
they are not part of it. We bring them in for what we
want to bring them in for. They are not part of our
dictatorship because when they try to hold public
meetings and we don't want that, the masses shut down
the meeting. When we want to hold Zonal Councils and
we don't want them there, we keep them out. When they
want to put out newspaper and we don't want that, we
close it down. When they want freedom of expression
to attack the Government or to link up with the CIA
and we don't want that, we crush them and jail them.
They are not part of the dictatorship. In fact, if the
truth is told, they have been repressed by the
dictatorship. They have lost some of the rights they
used to have. Now it is the working people who have
these rights, not the bourgeoisie. When the working
people want to hold a public meeting, we don't stop
them. When the working people want to go and hold a
picket, we don't stop them. When they want to Picket
Bata, that is good, but if Bata want to picket workers
we jail Bata. The workers could Picket Bata, but Bata

25/ cannot.......

cannot picket no workers. When Torchlight workers
want to take over the company, we support them, not
publicly and through making noise because that would
not be in our interest. We pretend we don't know
what's happening and let the trade unionists do it.
But if the Torchlight owners try to crush the workers,
we jail the Torchlight owners.

The point is all rights are not for them, all freedoms
are not for them, but all rights and freedoms are now
for the majority who are no longer oppressed and repressed by a tiny minority. That is very important to
understand because that is what dictatorship or rule
means. And that is how every state operates. That is
why the state came about in the first case; so that
there would be a dictatorship and a minority, in the
case of the capitalist state, would crush and oppress
the majority. In the case of the Socialist State, the
majority will crush, oppress and repress the
recalcitrant minority. That is what it is, and that is
what the nature of the dictatorship is, so they are
not part of that. And that is very important for us
to understand.

Comrades, as we see it, this political essence - this
dictatorship of the working people - is what we have to
continue to develop and to build rapidly if we are to
make substantial progress in building the national
democratic anti-imperialist phase of the Revolution.
And I would say, there are six (6) things to watch and
to emphasise in terms of the political essence.

First, it means control by the Party and the working
people. So we have to be guided by that at all times.
The Party and the working people; the Party acting in
1 - 26   the name of the working people and particularly, of
course, the working class must control, guide and direct
the process - must rule.

Secondly, it means an alliance has to continue to be maintained, firstly, with the peasantry and other elements of the petty-bourgeoisie, and secondly with sections of the upper petty-bourgeoisie and the national bourgeoisie. That also means comrades, when we do work plans when we have particular actions we want to take or are about to take, we always have to be conscious of this alliance. In other words, comrades in St. Andrew's area for example, who historically have given extra ordinary trouble in their dealings with Norris Bain, Minister of Housing and member of the ruling FRG Council must be very careful Over and over again, there would be activities, where there is no no reason why the comrade can not be present, and they won't invite him. So we have him coming to us and complaining about all kinds of unnecessary problems because of stupidity. On the way in which some comrades choose to relate to, let's say a Lyden Ramdhanny or a Bernard Gittens. The fact is that we have an alliance and the alliance is important. And the same applies to the patriotic businessmen with whom we are developing joint ventures and whom we are encouraging to invest. We can't meet them and curse them or get on arrogantly with them for no good reason. Obviously, a trade union struggle is one kind of thing. But what I am saying is that for as long as the alliance is there, it calls for a certain kind of political maturity at the level of our behaviour in dealing with those with whom we are building an alliance. That is very important for us to watch.

The third thing, comrades, the question of our people; their education (political and academic); the development of further democratic mechanisms and organisations and means and methods of getting them to be involved and to participate and so on; The need for greater training in democracy for them, In other words, the

27/ preparation......

preparation for them to rule. That, of course, primarily
refers to the working class but it applies in general to
the working people and also to the broad masses in terms
of the development of democracy, in terms of the involvement in mass organisations, in terms of participation in
the organs of popular power.

The fourth point, the necessary emphasis we have to give
at all times to the working class (we are going to come
back to that so I don't want to say too much on it).
But for this political section, it has to be emphasised.

And the fifth point, the building of the Party, because
again it is the Party that has to be at the head of this
process, acting as representatives of the working people
and in particular the working class. That is the only
way it can be because the working class does not have
the ideological development or experience to build
socialism on its own. The Party has to be there to
ensure that the necessary steps and measures are taken.
And it is our primary responsibility to prepare and
train the working class for what their historic mission
will be later on down the road. That is why the Party
has to be built and built rapidly, through bringing in
the first sons and daughters of the working class.

And finally comrades, the need always for firmness and
inflexibility on political questions that affect the
building of socialism. On the economic front, you can
have a lot of flexibility; on the political front the
flexibility must be very little. We have to be firm
because we are walking a real tight rope. On the one
hand, you have to give encouragements and incentives
and build the confidence of the bourgeoisie. But on
the other hand, when they step out of line, we still
have to crush them. So it's that kind of tight-rope
that has to be walked.

28.,.......

ECONOMIC ESSENCE OF THE NATIONAL DEMOCRATIC PATH

I want to come corades, to the economic essence in the
non-capitalist path, or more precisely the path of
socialist orientation. That is what the economic
essence of this national democratic business is- the non-
capitalist path of economic development, the path of
socialist orientation. That involves in particular
building the state sector along particular lines which
I now want to describe quickly.

Firstly, the state sector must be built to be the dominant
sector. As comrades know, that's happening already.
Last year over 90% of all investments in this country
were by the public sector, by the state and at this time
the*controls about a quarter of the total economy.
Building the state sector to be the dominant sector means
a number of things:-

* state

(a) We must assume total control of all financial
    institutions over a period of time. I did not say
    total control tomorrow morning or next year, but
    equally over a period - that must happen:

(b) We must assume total control of all foreign trade
    and also of some aspects of internal trade. The
    MNIB, of course, is helping us in that area already.
    This year, the MNIB will have a turnover of $20m.
    Right now MNIB has $35m in stocks (quite a stagger-
    ing figure). Right now , MNIB is buying over 78
    agricultural items from the farmers in Grenada.
    Right now, one in every ten farmers is selling his
    produce to MNIB. Right now, the three main depots
    for the MNIB (Young Street, Hillsborough Carriacou,
    and Petit Martinique), in January, February, March
    of this year together, sold something like 300,000
    lbs of produce. And I'll give you something that's

29/ even ....

even more staggering than that which was told to me
by the Manager of the MNIB depot in Petit Martinique -
Linus Belmar. Belmar told us that the Petit Martinique
depot has a monthly turnover of $60,000 - a quite
staggering figure. The role of the MNIB, both in the
area of imports and exports, will have to be stepped
up in the coming period.

(c) We must assume total control of all Public Utilities -
electricity, telephone, water, National Transport
Service. And here again, as comrades know, we
already in fact control those four. The missing
one for us now is Cable and Wireless and the
Satelite Dish from the Soviet Union will be one
aspect of the timing in relation to Cable and
Wireless.

(d) We must continue the building of the infrasturcture -
air port, sea ports, roads etc. - all aspects of
infrasturcture.

(e) We must ensure the further development of tourism,
of the manufacturing and industrial sectors; of
the agricultural sector; of the agro-industrial
sector; of fisheries. In other words, all of the
main pillars of the economy - agriculture, agro-
industries, fisheries, tourism, manufacturing and light
industry.

(f) We must develop central planning mechanisms for
the economy and the society as a whole, But
first of all we must start with the economy. In
terms of the development of the economy comrades,
over the next 10 - 15 years; as we see it, the
next 5 years - emphasis will undoubtedly be
tourism. That is not to say that we like tourism,
That is because we have no choice. Tourism is

the sector that has the greatest potential for giving
us the profits to invest in the areas we really want
to invest in - agriculture, agro industries, fisheries,
and non-agro industrialisation generally. That's
really where we will like to go, but those cannot
produce the money at this time, while tourism can.
We estimate that we will spend about $350m in just
tourism alone over the next couple of years, including
the cost of the New International Air-port.

The question is how to control that tourist development? And the plan there as you know is the Tourism
Code, the Investment Code in general, and of course,
a very, very careful policy and the development of
careful guidelines at every stage to ensure that the
negative social effects of tourism are at all times
curbed. For example, take prostitution, if you catch
local prostitutes - lock them up and rehabilitate them.
If you catch foreign prostitutes coming in - deport
them. So we will have to develop a very careful set
of rules and guidelines to ensure that tourism doesn't
get our of hand. But at the same time, unfortunately
for us is the way I will put it, tourism has to be
the key for the immediate short term period.

For one thing, there is no way we can ever pay back
for that International Air-port in a short or medium
term if we don't have tourism developed. So that's
where it's at for the next five years or so. The
next five years after that - agriculture with a lot
more emphasis then too on Agro-Industries and Fisheries.
But of course, in this first five-year period we also
have to continue to do a lot of work on agriculture,
agro industries and fisheries, so don't misunderstand
what I am saying. I am talking about emphasis and
where the dollar bills will have to go because we

31/ don't have ....

don't have many dollars. But the fact of the matter is
that all of these phases I am describing we will have
to continue to work on all fronts. But we are not
going to be able to make the kind of returns we need
on Agro, Agriculture or Fisheries in the upcoming
period. Hence the importance of tourism.

And in terms of agriculture comrades, the Youth Employment Programme assumes predominant emphasis right now in
this first period.

In the third five year period (that is in ten years time),
light industry, especially non-agro based industry and
manufacturing will become more and more predominant,
more and more important.

It is important to observe comrades that all of this
lays the basis for the development of capitalism. And
that of course is a major problem because it means that
if we are not careful capitalism rather than socialism
will be the the end product, just like when Lenin had
formulated NEP right after the Great October Socialist
Revolution, the Bolsheviks too had that same problem
and concern.

Simultaneously we will be nurturing the shoots of
capitalism and the shoots of socialism and the question
is which one becomes predominant and how you control
and ensure that socialism is what comes out and not
capitalism. We have the same problem as the young
Soviet State faced but a million times more difficult,
because our state sector is much smaller and does
not have the potential in this immediate period for
providing the profits to build the economy and the
country. And of course, we have a much smaller and

32/ less.......

less ideologically developed working class. On top of
that we have this massive petty bourgeoisie; you have
this low level of development of class consciousness;
you have this total backwardness and primitiveness in
the economy. In other words comrades, we have a tight
rope that we have to monitor very carefully as we walk
it - <u>every single day</u>, understanding clearly that all
of this infrastructural development, and all of this
activity we are describing not only can build socialism
but also capitalism.

What this means is that our primary task must be to
sink the ideas of Marxism/Leninism amongst the working
people so that their own ideological level can advance
and they can begin to better understand what we are
trying to do and why their class consciousness can be
raised in this way. Secondly, of course we can control
the development of capitalism through the use of laws
and regulations; because one thing we do have is
political control (and we have that firmly) so we can
decide on how much taxes to charge, we can decide who
get credits, we can decide who gets concessions and
pioneer incentives, we can decide what of Laws to
pass and when, we can decide who to "manners" and when.
In other words, we can use the apparatus of the State
in order to effect those controls. But it is a tight
rope and we just need to be careful and understand what
we are involved in.

TASKS OF THE NATIONAL DEMOCRATIC STAGE

Comrades, the tasks of this national democratic stage
can perhaps be summarised in ten points; and I want to
just quickly list them.

(1) Ensure the leading role of the working class
     through its Marxist/Leninist Party backed by

1 - 33

33/some

some form of the dictatorship of the proletariat. But
please note that I said <u>some form</u> of the dictatorship
of the proletariat, because obviously at this stage we
cannot have the dictatorship of the proletariat or the
working class, but the form we would have at this first
stage is the dictatorship of the working people.

(2) Build the alliance between the working class and
mass of the working people; in other words, the
alliance between the working class and the urban
and rural bourgeoisie. At the same time, we must
also build an alliance with those patriotic sections
of the upper petty bourgeoisie and national
bourgeoisie who are willing to help develop the
country.

(3) Ensure over a period, public ownership of the means
of production. In other words, build the state
sector.

(4) Work towards the gradual transformation of
agriculture along socialist lines through development of voluntary co-operative farms and state
farms.

(5) Plan the development of the economy in order to
lay the basis for the building of socialism and to
raise living standards.

(6) Begin the implementation of the cultural revolution.
And this cultural revolution, as all of us know, is
one of the four revolutions we are building at the
same time - the political, economic, scientific and
technological and the cultural. And in the context
of the cultural revolution, I want to emphasise
three main points - the spreading of the socialist
ideology, the wiping out of illiteracy and the
building of a new patriotic and revolutionary-

1 - 34

34/democratic.......

democratic intelligentsia.

(7) Build the defence capacity of the country so as to
protect it and to protect the revolution from
internal and external enemies. Comrades, the
applicants on Saturday in one of the six workshops
came back reporting that they were very concerned
about the fact that there were so many non-party
comrades who were leading the militia; and that is
an area of concern that we share very strongly.
We have to get more party comrades into the leadership of the militia. Just in terms of the means
that we have here right now, we are short by over
one fifth of the comrades that we need to operate
them. Just in terms of what we have, I am not
talking about what is to come. So if comrades are
not prepared to come out and learn to use those
means, then it means that other comrades out there,
hopefully supporters and strong sympathisers would
be the ones using them, which means that at the
appropriate time we won't even have the guarantee
that the guns can't be turned back on us. So I
really hope comrades will take that comment from
the workshop seriously.

(8) Develop proletarian internationalism. As representatives of the working class in Grenada, we have to
ensure that our working class and the working people
always demonstrate maximum solidarity with all
international working class struggles. That is a
fundamental responsibility.

(9) Develop equal and friendly relations with all
governments in the world, except the fascist
military dictatorship and apartheid types. That
is why comrades, we have been making trips to
different countries in Latin America like Mexico,

35/ Venezuela....

Venezuela, Ecuador, Panama and so on. That is why in
a few days time we leave for France to another state
visit. We must develop relations with all different
kinds of countries - some of them revolutionary-
democratic, some of them social-democratic, some of
them, like in the case of many in CARICOM, straight
pro-capitalist and pro-imperialist in outlook.

(10) Build rapidly our links with the Socialist World,
especially the Soviet Union. And here I should
hardly need to say more; we have just come back
from an important visit to the land of Lenin, the
Soviets in the last two days have arrived, nine of
them including the Ambassador and their Embassy is
about to be opened and so on. So these links and
relations are building reasonably satisfactory.

FOR THE PRESENT PERIOD

Coming out of all of this comrades, what are the tasks
as seen by the Central Committee?

The first task is sinking the ideas of Marxism/Leninism
among the working class and the working people. The
main vehicle for this comrades is socialism classes. The
Central Committee feels very strongly that this is the
Number One task. And of course, there can be only one
Number One task, and this the Central Committee regards
as Number One - sinking the ideas of Marxism - Leninism
among the working class and the working people. The
fact of the matter is that a national democratic
revolution can be turned back easily. For example in
the case of Nasser's Egypt, not withstanding the years
of hard work put in by Nasser and his party into trying
to build the national democratic revolution in Egypt,
After his death it took only a few years to roll back

1 - 36

36/ all that......

all that had been accomplished. And there were several
reasons. One, the party was not in fact built along
Leninist vanguard lines and secondly, because the ideas
of Marxism/Leninism had not taken root, there was no
deep class consciousness in Egypt. We know that in many
of these national democratic revolutions -- in Iraq,
Somalia, Algeria and so on - the fact is that the ideas
of Marxism/Leninism were and are not being spread. And
therefore, with the ideological work being weak, at a
certain point it becomes easy for forces opposed to
revolutionary transformation to overturn what had been
accomplished.

2. The second task, comrades, the organisation of the
working class and the working people through their trade
unions, their organs for popular power, their mass
organisations and through sports and culture - the
Organisation of the working class and the working
people.

3. Thirdly, comrades, strengthening the Leninist character
of the party by bringing in the best elements of the
<u>working people and in particular the working class</u>, and
through building the internal organisation of the Party.

4. Fourthly comrades, building the economy along the path
of socialist orientation, thus providing more material
benefits for the masses and laying the basis for the
construction of socialism.

5. The fifth task, developing the defence capacity of the
country through building the militia both quantitatively
and qualitatively by strengthening the influence of the
Party in the militia.

We believe very firmly, comrades, that the tasks have been
put in the correct order of priority by the Central
Committee. Unless the party as a whole feels very strongly 1 - 37

37/ about.

about this, and we decide to change this   :ritisation,
these priorities in the order outlined will stand as
1.2.3.4. and 5. You can   e two number ones and you
can't ve three number twos. One is one and two is
 two. So we have to look at our workplans and committees
and look at the programmes that we are into and revise
them to make sure that they are in line with the line
of march set by the Central Committee. One is one,
Two is two, Three is three, Four is four and Five is
five. Because, comrades, as you know another historic
weakness of ours has been to set priorities one day
and then the very next day to break the priorities that
we have set; so we really need this time to take a very
strong and firm position on this question.

THE SUBJECTIVE FACTOR - THE PARTY

Comrades I want to close, but what I want to close by
saying will take another fifteen minutes or so. I want
to close by going into the question of the subjective
factor, in other words the party, a very brief history
of the party's development and the criteria for Party
membership at this time.

Over the past nine and a half years, our Party has
passed through many stages of development; all of us
know that. We have analysed recently that there have
been six major stages that the Party has gone through.
The first stage began on the 11th March, 1973, with
the merger, when came NJM out of JEWEL and MAP led by
:   intelligentsia and rural petty-bourgeoisie. The
Strategy adopted was one of mass mobilisation with
seizure of power coming through mass mobilisation,
general strike, street marches and thereafter
insurrection. Mistakes were made, a deep class
approach was not taken. no attempt was made to build

1 - 38

38/ a Leninist Party.......

a Leninist Party, there was an over-reliance on
spontaneity and the possibilities of crowd politics.
That period, comrades, March '73 to April '74 is the
period of mass mobilisation in action. Using the issue
of Gairy's incorrect approach to the question of independence
as a base   we went around the country agitating the
masses for popular insurrection. During that same
period in fact, within the first two months of the
Party being formed, we liberated 51 rifles from Gairy.
It is true we did not hold them for as long as we would
have liked; we had them for one year and then Belmar
took them back, but in fact we stole 51 rifles as part
of that preparation.

During this period of mass mobilisation, we held the People's
Convention on Independence and the massively attended
People's Congress where five historic, but nonetheless
ultra-leftist, decisions were taken. You remember the
decisions? Firstly, we tried Gairy, found him guilty
of 27 crimes and gave him two weeks to resign. We
suggested that a National Unity Council should be
elected and a National Unity Council was elected and
we said it would have the task of supervising the
orderly transition to power of the new regime. We also
decided that the people would take steps to remove the
Gairy dictatorship if he did not resign within 2 weeks.
So undoubtedly, this was ultra-leftism in action.
Nonetheless the major weakness of this period was the
subjective factor; the fact that a Leninist approach
to pary building and to strategy and tactics were not
adopted; and this is notwithstanding the notable
achievements of the period, including the publication of
our Manifesto.

After the defeat in January '74 the Party held its
first major evaluation in April 1974, we were then

exactly one year and one month old. We spent a few
days, a whole week-end, looking at the Party and
trying to decide where we went wrong and what corrective
action was needed. That is when we decided in theory
and in principle that we should build a Leninist Party.
That decision was taken in April '74 but in practice
that decision was not implemented for many years. In
fact, there was a constant struggle within the Party
to get Leninist principles, in practice and in a
concrete way going but it was always an uphill struggle,
particularly on the need for collective study. In
this second period, that is from April '74 to June '77,
the Party was very much going through its period of
early childhood, though our contesting of the 1976
General Elections and our policy on Alliances were
evidence of a developing political and ideological
maturity.

In the time period, July '77 to August '78, the party
did make a qualitative leap forward in terms of Leninist
standards and principles. That is the period when we
stepped up our work among the working class, the work
was not sufficiently deep, but at least it was starting.
We tried to organise the agricultural working class
but did not get very far because of Gairy's use of
repression in protecting his base among the agricultural
working class. But we did some work during that period
with the urban working class and with sections of the
rural petty bourgeoisie - the farmers and the fishermen.
That is the period too when the Organising Committee of
the Party was formed, thus taking some of the strain
off the Political Bureau and leaving matters of
discipline, party organisation and so on, for the
Organising Committee to handle - a critical step
forward.

40/ And then........

And then we came to the next period, the fourth period
from August '78 to March '79, when the Party really
moved into top gear. The timing was fortuitous for
us because at the exact moment that a revolutionary
situation was developing a number of key work committees
of the Party began to function. Inner party democracy
was also being strengthened; party study was going on,
and a mass scientific approach to organisation was
beginning to develop.

And from March '79 to this period, the fifth (5th) we
have had a lot of mass activity. It is the period
when we broadened and deepended our links with the
working people and the masses in general, through the
mass organisations - women, youth, pioneers-; through
the organs of popular power - workers, parish and
zonal councils-; through the socialism classes, very
critically and also through our greatly expanded work
in the trade unions. In this period, we have considerably deepened, broadened and expanded our links with
the working people and the broad masses in general.
This is the period too when the Party began to develop
a number of critical new structures and committees,
including the C.C. itself, PCB's and a Committee on the
economy for the first time. They have not all done
well as we would have liked but the fact is that
important new structures have been set up and have
begun to function.

During this period too, the Party has also been involved
in supervising many aspects of the State Apparatus and in
running the state generally. The party is involved in all
the key programmes of the Revolution, the Centre for
Popular Education Programme, the Land Reform Programme,
Youth Employment Programme, and recently in the

discussions around the Budget and the Economy. So this
is a period that has seen a number of new mechanisms,
new structures and new work committees and greatly
expanded work in dozens of different areas at the same
time.

But we believe very strongly, comrades, that as from
now, September '82 the Party is definitely entering a
new stage of the revolution and of our Party's development. We feel that because of the growing internal
and external complexity of this period, because of the
growing quantity of work required of the Party and in
order to cope with the new complexities that once again
we have to change gears and step up the pace. This
year we have a major role to play in the development
of the Economy because   this is the essential basis
for progressing on our path of socialist orientation.
Furthermore, the question of the Armed Forces,
especially the militia and of the Party assuming
leadership of the key positions there is something
that we have to be involved in a lot more this year.
The question of increasing the quantity and quality of
our socialism classes, as our priorities demand is
also,something that we must take much more seriously.
The C B Programme, in its second phase, must also get
a lot of attention this year. The Youth Employment
Programme and the Land Reform Programme are central to
agricultural and overall Economic development.

In other words, we are required to work on a dozen
critical fronts at the same time, and that is going
to require a lot more application of Leninist
standards of discipline, consistency and seriousness.
All of this, comrades, means that our ideological and
organisational level as a Party will have to rise
considerably. It is clear that if we had not insisted

1 - 42

higher standards we would not have reached where we have reached. But it is equally clear, comrades, that holding power is much more difficult than taking power. There is no doubt that the Party can be built more rapidly on the basis of lower standards but this will mean that the tasks we have set ourselves, including our historical task of building socialism, would not be accomplished. As Lenin told us a long time ago "better fewer but better". Immortal words that we must never forget.

During the Party's history, there are members who have dropped out; some for opportunist reasons; others because they were not willing to make the sacrifices required in the particular period; in other cases, as the Party's ideological outlook developed, they came to realise that they did not share the desire to develop socialism; some others just could not take the level of discipline, of organisation, of strain, of hard work, of sacrifice. But no one is a member for life in the serious Leninist Party and, at this point, the Central Committee would like to enumerate the criteria for party membership and to go into some details as to the qualities required for promotion in the Party.

REQUIREMENTS FOR MEMBERSHIP

The four basic requirements for party membership are:-

(1) Regular collective ideological study organised by the Party.

(2) Engage in consistent political work under the guidance of an organ of the Party.

(3) Consistent payment of party dues fixed at 5% of gross salary. And comrades, gross means gross, it doesn't mean net - after you pay tax, or after you take out money to give to some member of the family.

43/ So, if.....

So, if your salary is $800 per month and you are paying
$60 tax, that is not the Party's business; it is 5% of
the $800, so you have to pay $40. Unemployed comrades
and students must pay $1.00 a month. I don't know how
many unemployed comrades the Party has left, but we
certainly have students.

(4) Understanding, accepting and implementing the
    principles and programme of the Party. This last
    requirement includes a complete willingness to
    accept Party discipline in many, many areas of one's
    personal life, not just political life. To fully
    accept and really implement the principles and
    programme of the party requires you to let the
    Party decide <u>when</u> you can get vacation and sometimes
    even what kind of activities you can be involved in.
    In other words, even our personal life is under
    security to some extent.

POTENTIAL APPLICANTS

Comrades, we developed a new category called
Potential Applicants after the Revolution, so as to
ensure that opportunists, careerists, self-seekers and
other elements like that who want to come into the
Party because it seems easy, or because the new conditions
mean that they don't have to get "bull-pistle" if they
join the Party now or because the Party seems like a
badge and passport to fame and prestige, are not
allowed to enter the Party as applicants before they go
through a tight screening process. And what we have
been trying to do in choosing Potential Applicants is
essentially to look for people with four main qualities
and characteristics. Firstly, comrades with a
genuinely revolutionary democratic outlook; secondly,
comrades who engage in disciplined political work in
a particular area; thirdly, comrades who are basically
honest and not opportunist in character; and fourthly

1 - 44

44/ comrades whose

Comrades whose relations to private property do not involve them in the exploitation of labour.

POTENTIAL APPLICANTS TO APPLICANTS

From our experience, comrades, these are the people who are most likely to move to Marxism/Leninism. These comrades are then invited to join classes where they are tested to see whether they are hostile to, or accepting of the ideas of Marxism Leninism. If they are not anti-communist, and if they continue to work well and show an honest approach, they are admitted as Applicants. And as all comrades know the period of applicancy is one year. That gives both the Party and the applicant the time to judge whether the applicant really accepts the science of Marxism/Leninism and is willing to make the sacrifices necessary to become a Party member.

APPLICANTS TO CANDIDATE MEMBERS

When assessing an applicant for promotion to Candidate Member the following five points are looked at:-

(1) Whether the applicant accepts the principles of Marxism Leninism and shows willingness to continue to develop.

(2) Whether the applicant has been working consistently and effectively in his/her   of political work and developing in terms of organisational skills.

(3) Whether the applicant has in practice accepted party discipline, in practice.

(4) Whether the applicant has good relations with the masses, including party members and non-party members with whom he he works in his Union, Mass Organisation, Army, Workplace etc.

43/ Whether......

(5) Whether the Applicant continues to be of good
character so as to present an example to the masses
he/she comes in contact with; whether certain
petty bourgeois traits such as individualism,
hostility to criticism, arrogance, indiscipline
and so on are being eroded; and whether proletarian
qualities such as respect for the working class,
co-operativeness and co-operation, discipline,
modesty, self criticism are being built. If accepted
as a Candidate member, another year would now
elapse before the comrade is eligible for consideration for full membership.

CANDIDATE MEMBERS TO MEMBERS

At this stage, the stage of moving from Candidate Member
to Member, the Party looks for the fullest possible
development of six factors.

(1) Ideological development as seen in a development
of the ability to analyse and cope well with many
different situations and to correctly apply
strategy and tactics - the essence of correct
Marxism/Leninism Leadership.

(2) The development of correct leadership. A professional
approach to his/her political work, expressing
Leninist organisational standards in all aspects
of the work.

(3) The development of an ability to supervise and
guide the work of junior party comrades.

(4) The removal of petty bourgeois character faults
and the development of a character which
provides

46/ an.......

an outstanding example to other party comrades and the
masses alike.

(5) The development of very good relations with the
    masses and other party comrades.

(6) The development of the technical and professional
    skills needed by the comrade in his or her job.

Comrades, some comrades feel that it takes too long to
become a full member in our Party. Some comrades feel
it is rough enough to have applicants, then candidate
members and then members so that on top of that to
have Potential Applicants is really just pushing the
pace too much. And yet the truth is that some comrades
in the Party are right now proposing another new
category of not just Potential Applicants but of
Prospective Potential Applicant, to make it even more
difficult to gain entry. The fact is, comrades, that
we feel it is correct in our situation for us to have
this long process of what, at one level, can be seen
as probation before comrades can become full members.
We think it is important now because at the level of
party leadership we want to keep the number down; in
fact at the level of the Central Committee of the
Party, our anxiety and concern is to see the Party
lifted in terms of quantity and quality in the shortest
possible time. But we also know from experience that
this whole question of coming to accept full membership
in the party and really internationalism and
operationalising in a serious way party discipline and
party duties is something that does take time to really
sink home. Sometimes comrades might last two or three
years but then on a certain issue when the class struggle
is really heightened they break and then leave the Party.

The truth is that it is not really a case of the Party
Leadership laying down harsh conditions; it is real

1 - 47

life and the demand of the struggle that make it
necessary for us to have these difficult conditions and
for us to ensure that comrades who are full members,
and also candidate members, are truly the finest
representatives of the working class and the most
steeled in struggle, in discipline, in dedication, in
commitment and in total commitment for the working
class and their interests. That is not the C.C. laying
laws down, that is real life laying the laws down. And
that is why comrades, we feel very strongly that these
criteria are critical and necessary.

We believe it must become more and more difficult for
comrades to become full members and candidate members
and it must become more difficult for new comrades to
remain as members and candidate members;.and those who
are unwilling to live up to the demands of this
membership would have to be moved. We believe comrades
that this stage of our process requires this. Being a
Communist, comrades meansbecoming a different kind of
person. Our society is deeply petty bourgeois and
this means the majority of our people are deeply
individualistic, ill-disciplined, disorganised, un-
proletarian, hostile to criticism and so on. Many in
the middle strata and intelligentsia often find it
difficult to relate as equals with the working people
while at the same time many working people lack
confidence in dealing with certain types of people.
It takes time for a new proletarian person to be built.
It takes time for a Communist to be built. So in
reality, comrades, promotion is not decided on by the
Party but by the development of comrades themselves.

On behalf of the Central Committee of our Party, I
want to congratulate all the comrades who have been

48/ recently.......

recently promoted from applicants to candidate members
who are here with us today for the first time in that
capacity, and who as a result of that new status have
assumed new rights, duties and responsibilities. I
also want to congratulate in advance those comrades in
this room who will shortly be promoted from candidate.
members to full members. Comrades now know the basis
on which they have been promoted. Those comrades who
have not been promoted at this time will also, we hope,
understand and accept the reasons why they have not
been promoted.

We believe comrades, that this line of march will equipt
us to go into the field and to move rapidly to ensure
that this first stage of the path we are on - the
socialist orientation stage - is rapidly built. We
believe that we have correctly defined the new tasks
required to handle the new situation that has developed.
We believe that as Party, individually and collectively,
we must now develop ourselves into becoming more
professional, more disciplined, more Leninist so that
we would be able to meet the demands of this period.
We also believe firmly that the path we have chosen
is the ONLY correct one. We believe that this path
would certainly bring us to our second major historical
objective to seeing socialism, of seeing socialist
construction achieved in our country, thus ensuring that
the working class in Grenada would assume their rightful
role and become fully emancipated for the first time.

LONG LIVE THE NEW JEWEL MOVEMENT!

LONG LIVE THE MEMBERS, CANDIDATE MEMBERS AND
APPLICANTS OF OUR PARTY!

LONG LIVE THE REVOLUTIONARY HISTORY OF OUR PARTY!
LONG LIVE THE WORKING CLASS OF GRENADA!
LONG LIVE THE INTERNATIONAL WORKING CLASS!
LONG LIVE PROLETARIAN INTERNATIONALISM!
LONG LIVE THE GRENADA REVOLUTION!
FORWARD FROM SOCIALIST ORIENTATION TO SOCIALIST
CONSTRUCTION!

FORWARD EVER! BACKWARD NEVER!
**** _____ ****

REPORT OF THE DELEGATION SENT TO GRENADA BY THE AMERICA DEPARTMENT
WITH THE AIM OF STARTING THE GATHERING OF SOURCES FOR THE CHARAC-
TERIZATION OF THE RELIGIOUS SITUATION IN THE COUNTRY, AND THE CON-
TACTS FOR FURTHER COOPERATION BETWEEN THE PCC AND THE NJM REGARDING
THE QUESTION.

DELEGATION: Cde. Aurelio Alonso Tejada

DATE: August 13-24, 1982

This report was handed in on October 14, 1982,

"YEAR 24 OF THE REVOLUTION"

INTRODUCTORY NOTE

This report is the result of an initial ten days stay which, as it coincided with holidays, could not be used to the greatest advantage.

Two more difficulties must be taken into account: firstly, the total lack of informative or unofficial documentation by the NJM* comrades, which resulted in the need to find sources through our visit to the public library, the national museum, and religious bookstores; secondly, the absence of Judy Williams, the most important person among the Christian lay people that actively cooperate with the NJM who, in addition to her personal testimonies, should have arranged our contacts with other positive elements within the laity. This situation caused our interviews to be limited to representatives of the ecclesiastical institutions.

In spite of these difficulties, it can be considered that the work showed useful results so that the thought-out objectives were satisfactorily reached.

We received a decisive support by the revolutionary leadership through Cde. Selwyn Strachan, member of the Political Bureau of the NJM and Minister of National Mobilization, whom we met on three occasions. During the first interview, Cde. Strachan summarized the recent aggressive positions adopted by the Church against the revolutionary leadership and we, on our part, explained the concrete aims we had set for the visit. Cde. Strachan showed interest in receiving a written version. After working out a detailed project starting from the general plan we had thought out, we handed it in at a second meeting. On this occasion, arrangements were made for the interviews. At the same time, we had begun to work in the tracking down of written sources. We met Minister Strachan again at the end of our stay and gave him a brief account of the results of the contacts and tracking down of sources (some of which were supplied to him) and expressed our concerns about the educational

---

* New Jewel Movement

reform issue and about the mechanisms of response to the recent summons to the Church. We told Cde. Strachan that the report on the visit would be sent to him not before the second fortnight of September.

The constant, efficient, diligent support by Cde. Gastón Díaz, our Embassy's First Secretary who at the time was head of the Mission, played an important role in the positive results we might have achieved in this visit. We left him in charge of finding and sending two important informative sources: the Handbook of Caribbean Churches, 1982, to be bought in Barbados, and the book written by Raymund Devas in 1932, which in case of not being obtained from F. Martin Simmonds, efforts should be made to borrow it from the public library so as to photocopy it.

The documents that make up the report are ordered in the following way:

* CONCLUSIONS

* RECOMMENDATIONS

* REVIEW OF THE RELIGIOUS SITUATION IN GRENADA

  1. Characterization of the churches and religiosity in Grenada.

  2. Positions of the Church in the face of the revolutionary transformation.

* ANNEXES:

  I.- Outline for the study of religion in Grenada.

  II.- Summaries of interviews held and of observation carried out at the curches in St. George's.

III.- Articles from Caribbean Contact, August and September, 1982.

  IV.- Bibliography

The religious situation in Grenada shows a series of characteristics which can be summarised as follows:

1) Since the revolutionary triumph in 1979, the diocese showed signs of reservation and started to insist on the holding of elections. During the three years of revolutionary government, the Catholic hierarchy has added to its electoral claim a position of mediation in favor of the 1979 pro-Gairy prisoners and of advocate of the "freedom of the press" in the face of governmental measures to stop counterrevolutionary propaganda. The emphasis of the Church is in harmony with the campaigns carried out by the reactionary governments in the Caribbean against Grenada's PRG* and now has an institutional argument formalized in the pastoral of the Caribbean Catholic bishops in February this year. This pastoral marks a new reference, which goes backward in comparison with that of 1975, and starting from it, political sectors in the area have promoted the summons to the Church for a confrontation of forces with the PRG of Grenada.

2) For the Grenadian Church (particularly the Catholic one) the moment can be described as one of definitions. It cannot be said yet (in our opinion) that the hierarchy has decided on an open confrontation. Although the pressure from the reactionary forces in the region within and outside the Church is aimed at confrontation, the position of the diocese seems to lean towards a combination of the pastoral attacks with repeated reference to the disposition to dialogue and the insistence upon the fact that their position towards the PRG is not uncompromising.

3) There are reasons to think that there is a potential contradiction between the foreign clergy (mainly the British and the Irish) and the West Indian minority. That majority, whom the vicar of the cathedral himself think is alien and inadaptable to the local realities, is at

---

* People's Revolutionary Government of Grenada.

first sight the most active counterpart of the oppositionist dynamics brought about by the February pastoral and by the provocations of reactionary forces in the region.

4) There are no signs of systematic progressive projections within the Grenadian clergy. It seems that within the institution there is not a trend in the theological and social line sympathetic to the revolutionary project, and there are no indications of a community organization of this kind at the grass roots. However, some believers belonging to Catholic organizations, who gather around the Pope Paul Camp (with whom we could not get in touch during this visit) and who actively collaborate with the NJM, can constitute a ferment in this direction.

5) The strong point of the Grenadian churches (both the Catholic and traditional Protestant ones) regarding their social influence is the educational sector. The religious schools are, at a very high percent, in charge of elementary and secondary education because throughout the colonial period the State traditionally neglected this sector. The PRG does not have a public educational system. In our opinion, the teaching centers are the stronghold of the ecclesiastical institutions and the possibility of a reform that should bring about their exclusion is their main concern.

6) The incorporation of the Catholic churches of the Caribbean to the Conference of Caribbean Churches (CCC), which also includes over 20 Protestant churches since its creation in 1973, besides being an exceptional characteristic of ecumenism, establishes an associational link among the Christian institutions that admits a game of influences in their projection: the Grenada Catholic diocese is a member of the Conference of Churches of Grenada (CCG) and with its positions it can influence on the the Protestant churches, and the other way around; at the same time, the fact that the Catholic Church belongs to the CCC means a similar game of influences at the regional level. In this interaction, the most positive positions of the CCC act as a restraining factor to the behaviour of the Catholic Church at the local (and regional) level. However, the CCC is not a homogeneous body and the

possibility of a reversal of its positions should no be underestimated, which would be in harmony with the tone of the criticisms to
the PRG by the Grenadian churches (see diagram in page 4).

7) The estimated believing population is over 80 percent, made up
mainly by Catholics (59 percent), Protestant from the historical churches (Anglicans, Presbyterians and Methodists), and a number of sects
among which the Rastafarians seem to be widely disseminated. The level of participation observed in the Sunday service is high. There
does not seem to exist a significant difference in the degree of religiosity among Protestants and Catholics. The Charismatic Catholic
movement has expanded and it is thought to reach no less than a quarter of Catholics. The African roots and their possible syncretic expressions should be studied.

8) The Catholic Church is organized in a diocese with 20 parish churches. It has one Bishop and 22 priests, with a rate of one priest for
every 2,950 Catholics (baptized). Sixteen of the priests are religious and 6 are diocesan; 16 are English, Irish, and American; 4 are
from other West Indian countries and 2 from Grenada; 15 are white and
7 are mestizo or black. Thus, because of their origin and race this
is a clergy with characteritics that alienate them from the problems
of the Island.

9) The diocese is suffragan to the archdiocese of Castries (St. Lucia)
and belongs to the Episcopal Conference of the West Indies, whose main
seats are Jamaica and Trinidad-Tobago. Thus the ecclesiastical organization takes on a supranational character and the projection of the
Grenadian Church is linked to the strategy carried out by the West
Indian body. (Regarding the framework of institutional relationship of
dependence, see the following diagram.)

6

DIAGRAM OF REALITIES OF DEPENDENCE AND ASSOCIATION IN THE RELIGIOUS
INSTITUTIONS OF GRENADA

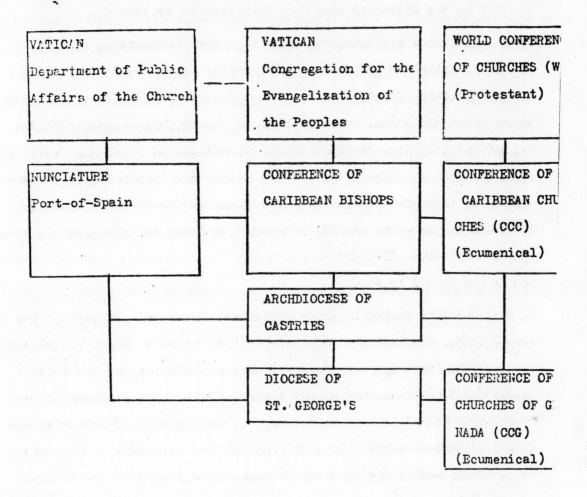

RECOMMENDATIONS

1. We underline the importance of the fact that a comrade responsible for the attention to the religious problems be appointed by the New Jewel Movement: This activity would basically include the information work at the beginning and regular contacts with collaborators from Christian organizations. If it is thought to be relevant, this can also include contacts with the clergy. We repeat the recommendation that the person to be appointed should spend 15-20 days in Cuba so as to be able to know our experiences, be trained in the tasks of systematic information on the subject, and exchange ideas on the most controversial aspects of the work. Comrade Strachan expressed his agreement on this proposal.

2. It would be advisable to study the possibility of formally creating a Register of Associations (or a similar mechanism) attached to the corresponding governmental body. Such a body could be legally established on the basis of the public need to make an inventory of the existing associations in the country and their activities (this would not only include the religious institutions, but the Chamber of Commerce, associations of professionals, clubs such as the Rotarians, the Lions, etc.). This would enable the counting of members, posts, premises, etc., the knowledge on special and regular activities, the means of financing of activities , etc. Both the terms of the resolution or law and the concrete contents of the register and modus operandi would be defined according to the specific conditions. This proposal is based on the need to regularize the access by the PRG to systematic factual information on the religious institutions and their activities. Our recommendation does not dismiss the fact that the resposibility regarding the register could be closely linked to the above-mentioned proposal.

3. To promote contacts among clergymen and members of the laity from Nicaragua and other Latin American circles linked to the theology of liberation and, in general, to the idea of a church committed to the

revolutionary positions, and the Christian sectors in Grenada through the Pope Paul Camp and maybe through talks with religious clergymen from a same order, particularly the Dominicans. These contacts should positively influence the Christian sectors of Grenada.

4. To consider the possibility of the Matanzas Evangelical Seminary inviting pastors from the Grenadian Protestant churches belonging to the Conference of Caribbean Churches (CCC), of which the Conference of Evangelical Churches of Cuba is a member, to short or annual courses. The language problem would be solved here.

5. To promote the invitation of Grenadian members of the laity and clergymen, through the appropriate channels, to visit Cuba. In my opinion, it would be useful to immediately invite F. Cyril Lamontagne, Vicar of the Cathedral of St. George's (second figure in the diocese), who in our interview expressed his willingness to visit Cuba and was interested in knowing how he could be invited. Afterwards, I think arrangements should be made for a visit of F. Martin Simmonds, superior of the Order of the Dominicans in the British West Indies, in case the trip he told us he was planning to make to Havana from Jamaica early next October would not take place. In case he would travel in October, we should be kept informed on his visit so as to organize activities that should help to positively influence his positions. F. Simmonds is the only clergyman who, in spite of his institutional responsibility, enjoys a positive reputation in the revolutionary circles of the Island. I think that after a new inquiry in Grenada we should assess the advisability of continuing this program of visits with other West Indian priests of the diocese.

6. The result of this visit ratifies an existing proposal in the sense of regularizing a reciprocal information link and an exchange of criteria on the strategy and tactics of the Church and the mechanisms of prevention and response. The action of the Church - particularly the Catholic one - has its origin in the policy of the Vatican towards

Central America and the Caribbean, and therefore, entails the existence of mechanisms of combined action within the institution. The exchange on our part should comprise two levels: a regular one with a NJM-PCC bilateral character, and another one with a trilateral character in which the FSLN of Nicaragua would also participate.

7. I think it is indispensable to make a second brief visit within a short time (if possible within the present year) with a view to widen and deepen the gathering of testimonial information and to carry out tasks of observation which were not possible to undertake during the first visit and that are essential both to complete the characterization of the phenomenon and to propose effective measures. I summarize below the main concrete aims which have been left for a second visit:

a) Interviews with Christian collaborators with the NJM (initially, Judy Williams, Annette Campbell and Susan Berkley) and visits to the Pope Paul Camp.

b) Interviews with Mons. Sidney Charles, Catholic Bishop; Rev. John Withington, Superintendent of the Methodist Church; and Rev. Hoskins Huggins, Archdeacon of the Anglican Church. According to the first contacts established, these interviews seem feasible and would result in direct assessments by the local hierarchies.

c) Visit to Catholic communities with F. Martin Simmonds, This was proposed by F. Simmonds during the interview with him, and it would give us a series of worthy elements.

d) Interview with officials of the PRG and leaders of the NJM who could contribute with criteria on the religious phenomenon in Grenada.

e) To keep active the contacts with F. Lamontagne and Deacon Lucky Bernard, for whose optimum preparation there are good possibilities.

NOTE:

We repeat what was stated in the outline presented to Cde. Strachan (Annex 1) regarding the provisional character both of the conclusions and recommendations of the present report.

ANALYSIS ON THE RELIGIOUS SITUATION IN GRENADA

1. Characterization of the churches and religions in Grenada.

1.1. Composition of the main churches and cults

Although the credibility of the numerical references within our reach is relative, by late 1979 out of a population of 110,000 inhabitants, a total of 65,000 was estimated to be Catholic, which makes 59% of the total[1]. The 1981 Pontifical Yearbook estimates 70,000, which makes 62%[2].

In any case, it is necessary to remember that the Catholic sources only take into account the amount of baptized people, that is why the actual number of believers is always inferior. The Anglican Church (official religion under the English Crown since 1795) follows Catholicism as to the amount of believers, and in smaller amounts, other traditional Protestant cults (Presbyterian and Methodist) and Apocalyptic sects (mainly Adventist and Pentecostal, followed by a score of smaller denominations). The Rastafarian sect, of Jamaican origin, seems to be widely disseminated, identified by the testimonies obtained in pre-criminal environments. Although in the first visit we did not achieve other statistical references than the ones mentioned regarding Catholicism, the criteria obtained shows that the believing population in the country is of no less than 80%. Though the number of Catholics is predominant, the proportion of Protestant cults is relatively high. As to the beliefs of African origin, there are references to the survival of elements of the Yoruba pantheon, particularly Shangó, which were supposed to enter the Island in the 19th century, with the trade of freedmen as salaried labor for the plantations after the abolition of slavery.[3]

Likewise we have heard about witchcraft practices under the rite of African origin called "Obeah". We still do not have references which

_____

(1) Figures from the Caribbean Catholic Directory, 1980, Kingston.

(2) 1981 Pontifical Yearbook, Vatican, 1982.

(3) Beverly A. Steele, "Grenada, an Island State. Its History and its People", Caribbean Quarterly, Vol. 20, No. 1, March, 1974.

analize Afro-Christian syncretisms, a question which should be taken into account. Neither we are in conditions to assess the specific weight of the Rastafarian sect in the framework of the most disseminated religions; for this reason, I have limited myself to indicate its existence.

In a summarized way, the study of Epica[4] recognizes that the institutionalized religions existing today in Grenada are the Catholic, Anglican, Presbyterian, and Methodist ones, the Salvation Army, the African Methodist Episcopal Church, the Church of God, three Baptist denominations, Berians, Pentecostals and Seventh Day Adventists, the Rastafarians, the Muslims, and the Bahaists. It does not mention, however, other religions also present, such as the Church of the Nazarene, and some Literalist sects whose temples I was able to see.

Regarding the Jehovah Witnesses, their presence was mentioned in some interviews, but it was described as insignificant. It should be noted that some sects are distributing pamphlets in Spanish in the streets, which seems to be purposely aimed at our internationalist workers.

1.2. Historical reference

In the British West Indies, Grenada seems to be the only one where the most disseminated religion is the Catholic one. In St. Vincent, Barbados, Antigua and the rest of the British West Indies the Anglican and Methodist Churches have greater influence, while in the French West Indies the Catholics are predominant.

This majority of Catholics in Grenada is explained starting from the colonization of the Island by the French Crown. The first Catholic missioners arrived in 1651 from France. Under the British domination, the Anglican Church was introduced, which became the official religion, and likewise other Protestant cults were introduced. The status of official religion gave the Anglican Church certain privileges over other religions. With the substitution of the French institutions by

---

(4) Grenada, the Peaceful Revolution, Epica Task Force, Washington, DC, 1982.

the British ones, the Catholic Church, which struggled for a successful survival, also became British: since 1795 on and throughout a
century Irish secular priests predominated in the Island, and since
the beginning of this century, the Dominicans from the English province have made up most of the Catholic clergy.

It is worth noting the historical weight which the order of the Dominicans has had in the ecclesiastical government in the Island and
the sub-region. The diocese of the West Indies was created in 1813
and since 1863 to 1930 (at least) it was led by Dominican bishops.
The Catholic historian E. Devas listed 202 Catholic priests in the
history of Grenada up to 1930, all of them foreigners, out of whom
52 have been Dominicans. Likewise the absence of Jesuists in this
list is significant.[5]

The year 1956 marked the creation of the diocese of St. George's,
in Grenada, suffragant to the archdiocese of Port-of-Spain up to
1974, when Castries (St. Lucia) acquired the rank of archdiocese,
with Grenada subordinated to it. The Benedictine Patrick Webster,
Bishop of Grenada sice 1970, was appointed Archbishop in Castries
in 1974, and then the diocesan priest Sidney A. Charles, from Trinidad, was appointed Bishop of the Grenada diocese, a post he still
holds.

The moving of Bishop Webster to Castries was considered in the Epica
study as a meneouver of the Vatican due to his position on the side
of the Conference of Churches of Grenada in the face of the repression by the Gairy regime after the 1973 Bloody Sunday. Webster de-
finitively retired last year and is living in Paris.

The coming into the Island of the Adventist, Pentecostal and other
sects is described as a phenomenon of the second post-war period and
as having a typically American influence. Even more recent is the
arrival of the Rastafarian sect, which took place in the second half

(5) Raymund Devas, Conceptio Island: The History of Catholic Church
    in Grenada, Sands & Co., London, 1932.

of the '60s and was linked to the "Black Power" boom in the United States, and which also had another aspect of political influence in the Island and in other West Indian countries.

1.3, The Catholic Church: Composition, structure and dependence relationship.

Grenada is a small diocese, made up by one Bishop and 22 priests (23 in 1979, 27 in 1972, according to various sources)[6], which represents a rate of one priest for every 2,950 believers, approximately.

Out of the 22 priests, 16 belong to religious orders and there are only 6 diocesan, the majority of them being Dominicans and the Irish Fathers of St. Patrick (Kiltegan). The Dominicans, who evidently play a predominant role in the Grenadian Church, also have four brothers who make up a small community of a dozen religious, who includes the regional Superior of the Order (F. Martin Simmonds) for the British West Indies. In relation to the nationality of the clergy, only two of them are Grenadians, four oothers come from other West Indian countries, and sixteen are missioners of European origin (13), and Americans (3).

Consequently, the clergy is mostly religious, foreign and white. The mmebers of the institution are completed with 24 nuns, 2 permanent deacons, 8 lay missioners and 4 seminarists (out of the country).

The two largest seminaries in the region, which depend on the West Indian Episcopal Conference, are: one in Trinidad, with about 20 seminarists, and another one in Jamaica with another 10 students. Both are diocesan and their teaching level is ratified by the University of the West Indies, with seat in Kingston.

---

(6) The present datum was facilitated by F. Lamontagne, Vicar of the Cathedral; that of 1979 is from the Caribbean Catholic Directory, 1980, and that of 1972 appears in the Handbook of Caribbean Churches of the CCC, 1973.

The Catholic institution has 20 parish churches and another 33 missionary facilities and chapels without resident priests.

In the framework of the social activity, the action of the Church focuses on education. They have 6 secondary education institutions, headed by 23 religious and with 52 lay teachers and around 1,400 students.[7] The source reports likewise 30 elementary schools with 11,141 students. In 1925 there was a total of 58 elementary schools in the Island, out of which 10 were public and 48 religious (27 Catholic and 21 Protestant). The work of the churches in education has historically prevailed in the country and even today it is advocated by the clergy as a contribution to the Grenadian society. F. Simmonds insisted upon this aspect, showing the intention of the Church to saveguard the continuity of the religious orientation through teaching.

The diocese in Grenada is subordinated to Mons. Kelvin Felix, Archbishop of Castries (St. Lucia), one of the four archdioceses integrating the Episcopal Conference of the West Indies. At present, the Conference is headed by Mons. Anthony Pantin, Archbishop of Port-of-Spain since 1979. This structure, which divides the region into four archdioceses with 13 suffragant dioceses, exists since 1975. With this organization, the country is a Catholic province which is articulated within a West Indian Episcopal body out of the national demarcation. This is one oof the most significant structural characteristics of the Grenadian Church. One cannot speak about autonomy regarding the national Episcopate, because the Episcopate has a regional character.

The second characteristic to be taken into consideration is that, unlike Cuba, the Dominican Republic, Haiti, Puerto Rico, and the rest of the continent, the so-called "Lesser Antilles" are considered territory of mission and answer to the supervision of the Congregation for the Evangelization and Propagation of the Faith, like the African

---

(7) 1979 data from the Caribbean Catholic Directory, 1980.

or Asiatic provinces. The explanation given by F. Lamontagne is that this dependence assures the West Indian churches the economic subsidy by the Vatican. It remains to be clarified the differences that could exist in their links with CELAM.

A third characteristic to be taken into consideration is that the Catholic Episcopal Conference is part of the Conference of Caribbean Churches (CCC), which has an ecumenical character. In no other part of the continent has the Catholic Church accepted to integrate the corresponding conferences of churches, which group the most representative part of the Protestant churches.

Finally, the relationship with the Holy See equally adopt supranational features. Between 1977 and 1979 Trinidad-Tobago, Barbados, Grenada, Jamaica and Bahamas initiated diplomatic relations with the Vatican, thus establishing the nunciature of the Caribbean with seat in Port-of-Spain and Archbishop Paul Tabet was appointed Internuncio.

1.4. Elements on religiosity

The rigurous characterization of religiosity requires data and tests which have not been carried out. However, at the risk of being neglectful, it is indispensable that we organize some assessments of these first contacts.

a) In the first place, the features of the present Christian religiosity have to be considered in the framework of cultural patterns of Anglo-Saxon origin; there seems to be little difference between Catholic and Protestant religiosity. It is the view of F. Lamontagne that there is no difference between the Protestant and the Catholic cults as to the proportion of participants in Sunday mass and in lay organizations within the total of the believers; he considers this proportion low, although he does not dare to estimate it in percentage.

b) In spite of Lamontagne's assessment, we counted around 200 attendants to Catholic mass and some 130 to Anglican mass, in both cases during the first session (between 7 and 9 in the morning). Throughout that Sunday we could observe a significant movement in around

a dozen halls and temples of diverse denominations. In sum, we got
the impression that the attendance to Sunday mass is high, if we
take into account that St. George's is a city of around 20,000 inhabitants. Attendance to mass maintains all the characteristics
not only of a religious but also of a social celebration, attention
being drawn to the care of Sunday clothes.

c) The Charismatic movement is considerably disseminated within the
Catholic Church. Having arrived in the country in the early '70s,
interviewed priests estimate that today no less than 25% of the Catholics belong to Charismatic groups. These are attended to by
priests. In November 1976, the Conference of Bishops of the West
Indies declared in an official document the legitimacy of the Catholic Charismatic renewal. This movement has gained followers mainly
in the humblest sectors.

d) In some of the information received the presence of elements of
African origin was mentioned, but we could neither observe nor ob-
tain concrete written or testimonial references to syncretism with
African elements, which require deeper research.

e) In conclusion, the first impression received is that of a Christian parish which constitutes a considerable percentage of the population and presents a degree of participation in the cult which can
be described as high.

2. The positions of the churches with regard to the revolutionary
transformations.

After the meeting held in Martinica, in november, 1975, the Episcopal
Conference of the West Indies then headed by the Archbishop of Kingston, Mons. Samuel Carter, S.J., issued a pastoral entitled "Justice
and Peace in a New Caribbean".[8]

---

(8) Justice and Peace in a New Caribbean, Martinica, 1975.

2.1. The 1975 Pastoral.

This document declared itself to be in harmony with the Report of the Opening Assembly of the Conference of Caribbean Churches (1973) in the praising of social justice, describing itself (the Church) as "being identified with the poor and the oppressed, making their struggle its own". It started from a strong self-criticism: "Our Church is also to be blamed on occasions for acts of racial discrimination and of perpetuation of social and class divisions". The Bishops go far enough to state here that "the Catholic Church does not indiscriminatedly condemn all forms of Socialism".[9]

The text differentiated Marxism as unacceptable for Christianism for being a Atheistic doctrine, and conditioned the Christian support to movements or parties carrying out Socialist programs to their links with materialist positions.

This pastoral, which indicates the adaptational shift of the Catholic Church when an epoch of definitions takes place in the Caribbean, is particularly important for measuring the orientation of the Caribbean Church after the germination and triumph of the people's revolution headed by the New Jewel Movement in Grenada. In it, after differentiating and conditioning the Christian positions around Socialism, the Bishops concentrate their attention on the rights of the individual, especially those referring to suffrage, the possibility of public dissent, and equal protection before the law. No mention is made here to the right to work, survival, education, and health. So the document presents a shift which begins by assuring an ethical cover which denotes a sense of guilt and by looking for an opportunity to make clear its rejection to atheism and to end by defending the constitutions in force to prevent the revolutionary transformation as elitist displacements. Likewise it formulates a reinforcement of the pastoral tactics towards family life and, what is much more interestin

––––––––––––––––––––––––––

(9) Although there is a Spanish version, in this case we use direct translation from the original in English.

politically, it openly criticizes racism.

Even with these ambiguities, one has to note that it is a highly tinged document, with statements which fragmentarily contain much more realistic references than most of the official ecclesiastic texts, which has caused it to be described as a document of a progressive cut in various analysis on the region.[10]

2.2. The 1982 Pastoral

Last February the West Indian Bishops issued a new Pastoral entitled "True Liberty and Development in the Caribbean". This new document presents explicit connections with the most recent encyclical of John Paul II, Laborem Exercens, which is quoted on 10 occasions. In the papacy line, it intends, since its first pages, to place itself over Capitalism and Socialism, adopting an equally critical attitude towards both regimes.

Here the Bishops reiterate the considerations around the possibility of a Socialism "without atheism" and without total abolition of private property (they admit the legitimacy of nationalization of key productive sectors).

But the main issue of this document is expressed in the next to last epigraph under the title "Political Coups". It begins with a reflection on the vulnerability of the West Indian governments, and leads to a decisive criticism of violence, noting that "frequently the political coups simply substitute one tyranny for another". It underscores that the coup does not legitimize the government and subordinates all such legitimization to the rights of the individual. The epigraph ends sanctioning that although in the Caribbean the "traditional pacific means of political change through elections" have been forced, "these are the only adequate ones even when they do not guarantee a good government".

This second pastoral contains, therefore, a tacit allusion to the people's revolution in Grenada, and the consequent warning as to what are the values that the Church is willing to defend and advocate. Surely this document was made public from the pulpit during the Sunday mass in the Grenadian churches, giving rise to the corresponding uneasiness among the Catholic parishioners.

Both pastorals show a high level of politization in their wordings. That of 1975 since its initial lines warns that "in reading this letter some will argue that the Church is once more meddling in politics". In the second letter there is no longer the need to prevent in spite of the fact that it has statements such as the following: "There are still strong efforts to submit our region to noxious foreign influences which threaten our peace"; followed by: "There are attempts to impose the ideology of atheistic Marxism on our peoples". After these affirmations, a brief critical mention to Capitalist exploitation, as a moderate counterweight, clearly shows what the Bishops are emphasizing as preeminent danger.

We have not heard – between February and the present time – about any document of the Conference of Caribbean Churches (CCC), which gathers both Catholics and Protestants, and whose positions are more open because they even admit complete progressive expressions.

2.3. The recent provocations

Under the enunciation on human rights, the Caribbean reaction has strengthened a campaign against the PRG of Grenada regarding a hundred of Gairy followers who are kept in jail since the arrests in 1979.

In this campaign the Church, which internally has functioned as mediator, can even become an open oposition factor, which is the aspiration of the reactionary forces in the subregion.

Last July the annual convention of the ruling party of Dominica served as framework for this campaign. In an allocution by the journalist of Grenadian origin, Alister Hughes, linked to political positions in the previous regime, the Church is reproached for its moderation and its action is demanded to move the public opinion against the PRG, taking advantage of its sensitivity to people's pressure.

The New Jewel Movement answered the provocation in two separate statements. The first one rejects the interference of the ruling party of Dominica in the Grenada internal affairs and characterizes the reactionary positions of that government. The second one places Hughes in his alignment with the Caribbean reaction and alerts the Grenadian people as to the call issued to the Church for them to join the positions of the Counterrevolution.[11]

The Church, which has interceded with the PRG regarding the question of the people kept in jail since 1979, has not pronounced itself on Hughes' summons. To a certain extent, it can consider that the response of the NJM tacitly frees it from that necessity.

In an interview with the Vicar of the Cathedral, F. Cyril Lamontagne, the question of the people imprisoned in 1979 was mentioned as a point of fundamental disagreement of the Church with the PRG. However, Lamontagne condemned Hughes' pronouncement in Dominica and expressed his disagreement in that the Church be taken as opposition instrument. He recognizes that the Church has to adapt itself to the new social situation existing in the country and says that its greatest difficulty is to move from being a Church that rules to one which is destined to serve.

In the interview F. Lamontagne underscores the differences between the positions of the Church and those of the foreign clergy, which cannot manage to understand the social situation. He raises objections to the PRG in that these positions be understood as those of the institution. He, however, admits that the inadaptation of a British or Irish clergy is an objective factor which has an unfavorable bearing on the understanding with the Government.

After our return, in its September 1982 edition the monthly publication of the CCC has published an article entitled "Church-State Relations in Grenada", which contains the points of view of Archdeacon

---

(11) Enclosed is a photocopy of the texts published in Caribbean Contact, August, 1982.

Hoskings Huggins, Chief of the Anglican Church and President of the Christian Conference of Grenada (CCG). Huggins expressly answered on behalf of the CCG, confirming the existing complete freedom of cult, the recognition of the achievements of the PRG, and the willingness of the churches to cooperate. At the same time, it lists the disagreements ("areas of concern") with the revolutionary government: 1) the differendum on the imprisonments in 1979; 2) the lack of elections; 3) the delay of working permission for clergymen; 4) restrictions to the local ecclesiastic publications; 5) an administrative contentious affair regarding the acquisition of a building; 6) difficulties to meet with the ministers of the Government.

The contributor includes afterwards answers given by the Prime Minister's office to all the points, as well as a rejoinder by Rev. Huggins limiting itself to the dispute around the building.[12]

In conclusion, I think it can be said that the position of the churches has become tense, but that it cannot be affirmed that it has reached a critical point because it is not expressed in the level of open confrontation. The tactics of the CCG seems more inclined to tone down the contentious problems with favourable statements, as the above article shows. There is a difference between the level of pressure against the PRG demanded by the West Indian reaction from the churches and that which the CCG is in a position to exert.

(12) Enclosed is a photocopy of the text from the Caribbean Contact, September, 1982.

ANNEX 2

SUMMARIES OF INTERVIEWS HELD AND OF OBSERVATION CARRIED OUT IN

THE CHURCHES OF ST. GEORGE'S

F. CYRIL LAMONTAGNE.

* Was born in St Lucia; 55 years old — diocesan with around 16 years in Grenada — General Vicar of the diocese.

* He explains that in St. Vincent, Barbados, and Antigua most of the believers belong to the Anglican and Methodist Churches, while in the French West Indies, as in the Spanish ones, the majority are Catholic. Grenada keeps the Catholic predominance of the colonial period under France, which has also culturally left other marks.

* He establishes a difference between the massive level of participation, which includes attendance to Sunday mass, and the intense participation, which is by a minority. His view is that in Grenada the levels of attendance to the historical Protestant churches are close to those of Catholicism: more intense during the festivities —Christmas, Holy Week, Lent.

* As to the liturgy, he says that there are several priests trying to assimilate the reforms of the Vatican II.

* On being asked about his opinion regarding the theology of liberation, and in general regarding this renewed line of thought, he answered that Grenada is not a country with a large concentration of wealth; that there are neither the very rich nor the extremely poor; that there is a predominance of a poverty characterized by a low standard of living, but not by misery (only in unusual cases); he adds that attendance to church is representative of this composition, and that he thinks this specific fact makes a theology of liberation that would adjust to other realities to be less adequate in the country. These observations follow his doubts about the strictly theological character of these theories.

* Composition of the clergy by countries: at present there are only 2 Grenadian priests and another four from the West Indies; there are 16 Irish, British, Canadians and Americans, which complete the present 22 priests.

2 - 24

* In the '70s three priests were brought from Nigeria with the aim of increasing the proportion of blacks, but he says this experience was a failure because they did not have a good adaptation and that 2 of them left, and the third one will soon go back to Nigeria. They chose Nigeria because of the experience and contacts of the Kiltegan friars there.

* On assessing negative reactions on the part of the clergy to social change in Grenada, he puts them down to the difficulties of the transition from a church that rules to a church that serves. He centers the problems on the European clergy whom he thinks should proportionally decrease in years ahead in favour of an indigenous clergy from the region.

* The Catholic Episcopal Conference (West Indies) has two major seminaries: one in Trinidad and another in Jamaica. Both seminaries are — diocesan and the former now has around 20 seminarists, while the latter has around 10. They are affiliated to the University of the West Indies (UWI) so that their level would fit to that which is tought — there and the degree confered would be correspondent.

* He explains the dependence of the West Indian dioceses on the Congregation for the Evangelization of the Peoples and the Propagation of the Faith instead of on the Congregation of Bishops, like in the rest of America, due to financial reasons. The Caribbean Church is not able to finance itself and subordination to the above Congregation assures its
/financing as the region is considered a territory of Mission.

* He points out that the relations Church-State under Gairy were not easy, but that the Church managed to keep its status because the government knew its social influence. He adds that the Church has to show — its capacity to carry out its mission beyond the ideologies being predominant in society.

* He said that at present the Church does not object the changes by the PRG, but that it has critical apprisals. He understands that there have been mistakes both by the PRG leadership and the Church. In the Church the foreign clergy is not as able as to understand the internal questions and reacts hastily, adopting wrong positions. The PRG has interpreted these positions as being those of the Church, but it has been made clear that those manifestations do not express the position of the Church.

* In spite of maintaining these criteria, he admitted that the statement by the journalist Alister Hughes in the Congress of the DFP of Dominica, summoning the Church to exert pressure on the public opinion around this question, was not an appropriate channel; and he says that this is not the Church's position. He recognizes that out of the 400 initial prisoners, over 75% have been set free, and that this shows that the PRG has not acted intransigently in this sense.

* He is interested in knowing whether Marxism necessarily assumes atheism, and whether we understand the building of Socialism as conditioned by atheistic positions. He has the opinion that in the Island (I think he means the political leadership without expressly affirming it) there is the view that religious faith and Socialism are not compatible and that they are willing to accept Socialism as long as one does not start from this criterion of incompatibility. He stresses that he is, above all and first of all, a man of the Church and that he will always react as such, but that he is willing to accept, within this framework, a Socialist transformation. That the Church would also have to facilitate the assimilation of these changes for the believers.

* He asks questions on Cuba, the Church, the training of the clergy (whether there is a major seminary, whether it is integrated to the higher education system, etc.). He says he is interested in visiting Cuba, but that he does not know in what way this visit could take place.

OPINION:

Lamontagne is, as he said, a man of the Church, representative of the positions of the institution. In my opinion, he cannot be evaluated as a progressive clergyman, but as one who could assimilate a Church within the framework of radical social transformations. I think that his willingness to visit Cuba and his interest in doing so should not be underestimated because his visit could contribute, on the one hand, to counteract the effects of propaganda schemes; on the other, it would help in differentiating his situation within the clergy of the diocese.

F. MARTIN SIMMONPS

* The Jamaican F. Martin, with around 30 years or more living in Grenada, is around 60 years old, and he is the SUPERIOR OF THE DOMINICANS for the BWI region within the English province of the order. He is known as the most sympathetic person towards the PRG within the clergy.

* He considers that Grenada is a country which presents a high degree of religiosity: that in the people's base the Christian faith is deeply rooted. The Catholic religiosity is the most generalized in the grass-roots. The religious practices and attendance to cult are significant, although they are not in correspondence, certainly, with the whole of the believers.

* He considers that the Grenadian Church is not traditionalist (but F. Martin himself wore white full-length soutane of the order when he visited me at the hotel), that on the contrary, there exists a spirit of renewal and of popular committment in the institution. He regrets my rapid departure and invites me to visit with him the communities he attends to, and to be present at some liturgical activities.

* He says he is familiarized with Gustavo Gutiérrez' texts and that he had likewise read Friar Betto's, but does not completely share these positions, that they are not really theologians; he recognizes that they are interesting and that there should be access to those readings in the ecclesiastic circles. He considers that the clergy residing in Grenada is interested in knowing these positions.

* He considers as a difficulty that a considerable part of the clergy in the country is of European origin, which does not facilitate the comprehension of the reality in the region. He does not formulate, however, any criticism regarding the behaviour of the clergy.

* With respect to the relations with the PRG, he recognizes that the comprehension from the churches is insufficient. Although he considers that there have been errors on the part of the government, he thinks

that "it is the first honest Government in the history of Grenada",
and in this way he states it within the Church whenever any disagree
ment is brought to the fore.

* He thinks that the Church plays a social role in Grenada, mainly dis
tinguished in the field of education. The religious schools are, in
his view, of capital importance within the general education. School
is paid for, although he stresses that the fee is very low and that
it has a wide range as to the possibilities of the population. The
State subsidizes the religious schools.

* The Charismatic movement within Catholicism goes back to the begining
of the '70s in Grenada. He himself attends to a Charismatic community. This movement covers at present, according to his estimates, -
over a quarter of the Catholic population.

* When asked about the Rastafarians, he expressed that in Grenada it
has been a way of covering a pre-criminal behaviour: vagrancy, easy
way of earning money, drug addiction (ganja), etc., are the features
of the Grenadian Rastafarians. He insists on differentiating the local situation from that in Jamaica, where -he says- such belief presents other features which deserve respect, and whose leaders refuse
to be identified with the Rastafarians in Grenada.

* F. Martin was recently removed from the parish in Grennville to the
Church of St. Paul in St. George's.

* He will visit Havana between the end of September and early October.
I consider we should program for him activities which will allow him
to know the achievements of the Revolution mainly in education.

OPINION:

F. Martin (as he is known by) has the reputation of being a priest —
closer to the revolutionary process than the rest of the clergy. His
expressions indicate a willingness to understanding, but not progressive
positions. His position should not be compared to that of the clergy-

men and theologians who promote the conception of the "people's church" in Central America. Martin is a leader of an order and expresses himself as a voice of the institution no less than Vicar Lamontagne, although with better knowledge and preparation than the latter.

LUCKY BERNARD

* Catholic lay deacon — Second Chief of the Police: he already had this post under Gairy, and the PRG has maintained the policy of not removing the police apparatus as long as it does not have a connection of repressive committment with the Gairy regime.

* He has a middle level education, deeply committed with the ecclesiastic structure.

* He thinks that before the triumph of the NJM the politicians maintained a position of respect to the CC because of its rootedness in the population of the Island, but that they did not completely trust it.

* He considers that around the '40s about 90% of the population in the Island was Catholic, that this percentage decreased due to conver——sions to other churches, mainly to Adventism and Baptism. He believes that the JW are very few and that they lack influence, and that the Pentecostals are not significant, although they are more in number.

* He thinks that the main Protestant churches, as to the number of believers and influence in the population, are the Anglican, the Methodist, and the Presbyterian.

* Regarding the social composition of the parishioners, he sees the merchant bourgeoisie in the Island agglutinated mainly in the Anglican Church, whereas the Catholic Church is made up by humbler sectors, which include the small farmers and the workers in general.

* He sees no difference between religiosity in the Protestant churches and the Catholic ones. He considers that although not all of the believers regularly attend mass, the participation is high, and similar in proportion to the participation within the Protestant churches.

* He refers to Charismatic Catholics as a very important part of the total number of Catholics. They indistinctly participate in the ordinary activities with the traditionalist Catholics (with no other difference than the diversity in meaning of the cult). At the same time,

they maintain the separation of the Charismatic celebrations, in many cases with sacerdotal orientation. He himself used to be a Charismatic during some years in the '70s. He thinks that the movement was brought from Europe in the early '70s.

* Regarding the presence of syncretic elements in religiosity, he says that there exist disperse superstitions inserted in the Catholic faith. He mentions three rituals of African origin:

1. SARAKA: He describes it as an African cult in the process of extinction.

2. OBEAH: Is characterized by fortune-telling through a glass of water; it is maintained as a practice inserted among Christians.

3. African dance: It seems to be a dancing ritual which, according to him, is revitalized with young people because it brings a recreational motivation.

* He states that the Catholic Church is made up by a foreign clergy, mainly Irish (he does not know the amount of people), that it does not understand the process, and that it would like everybody to develop according to its points of view. He considers that the Grenadian presence in the clergy should be reinforced.

* The PRG means an important step for the country; he thinks that in its action there are "errors", but that the intentions are good. The foreigners in the clergy do not understand. He assesses his personal contribution in making the foreign priests understand that they should be intransigent with the "errors" of the PRG, and that they should accept them in their exact dimension, realizing the possitive value of the action.

..10

OPINION:

A man of the Church who, at the same time, seeks to maintain his social
status before the PRG. He asks about the possibility of travelling to
Cuba to receive medical care for a chronic disease which has maintained
him away from work during the last two months. Attention and continui
ty should be given to him for combining the presence in the Church --
with a responsability in the Administration, but he gives no indication
of possibilities for progress in his positions.

NONSTRUCTURED OBSERVATION (SUMMARY)

Sunday mass in the Catholic, Anglican, and Presbyterian cathedrals, from 7:30 am to 9:30 am, Sunday, August 22. The observations in this regard are the following:

- In the Catholic cathedral there were 200 hundred persons of different ages; in the Anglican, between 120 and 150; and in the Presbyterian, around 20 persons.

- The composition observed among the believers: as to social position, the clothes they wore indicated a higher standard of living among Presbyterians and Anglicans than among Catholics, although all of them were dressed as for a festivity. From the racial point of view, in the Presbyterian Church the proportion of whites was higher than in the other two.

- Throughout that Sunday we observed that the flow of people attending religious services is high in the temples of different denominations, which are numerous in St. George's.

- There are neither credible statistics nor a register of associations which would allow an inventory of the religious institutions and of the numbers of believers they have, but undoubtedly the degree of denominationalism is very high and there is a considerable amount of participants.

- Informal talks with Anglican, Presbyterian, and Pentecostal believers show some elements to be taken into account:

1) The Anglican Church is considered in connection with the British colonial State, with emphasis in the fact that it belongs to the Commonwealth, as well as in the presence of other cultural signs of Anglo-Saxon character.

2) In the framework of Protestantism, the sectarian movement (Adventist and others) is more identified with an American influence, not only because of its origin, but also because of the way of thinking induced in the believers.

3) Catholicism, originating from the French colonial period, but with a historical change towards an English-speaking environment (Irish and British clergy) since the beginning of the 19th Century, has sought to maintain an image of independent creed, beyond the specific influences of either metropolises.

A series of publications are being put out by the Catholic Church. Most of those published so far are aimed at showing that Communism is atheistic and should be feared and that our party is Communist. The articles aim at creating fear in the minds of the religious.

So far five have been published in the series - the first three being the small leaflets of track size. NO. 4 was Civic Freedoms NO. 5 some notes on Marx - Leninism. The sixth publication in in the making but no definite date has <u>been given as to when it will be out.</u>

The typing of the 5th publication was done by an <u>Irish teacher at St. John's Christian Secondary School.</u>

Father Bernard Kadlec of Czechoslovakia is one of the writers. Father Austin is another. (I don't know which).

Publication is done by Mc Kie's Printery, and Torchlight Printery. (A track size publication Brown writing is <u>now being</u> printed in St. Lucia.)

Further information could not be had: the Priest was in a haste to leave for St. George's.

However, the Priest said that whenever he publishes any of these things he always send one to the Prime Minister.

He seems to have a hunch that the PRG will clamp down on these publications. I told him to to ensure me a copy of each of his publications when he replied yes with a statement to this effect.

Father Bernard was the writer of Civic Freedoms, but I have not found out who is the author of the 5th publication.

The Priest is also afraid of these leaving the hands of the PRA soldiers for fear they may lose their jobs.

And so fear to give it to soldiers.

TOP SECRET

15th.March 1983

TO: MAJOR KEITH ROBERTS

FROM: O/CDT.MICHAEL ROBERTS

ANALYSIS - THE CHURCH IN GRENADA

THIS report will seek to analyse the Main Churches against whom our work is directed and also a general view of the other Churches. The Main Churches are : (a) The Roman Catholic Church

  (b) The Anglican Church

  (C) The Methodist Church

  (d) The Seventh Day Adventist Church

) THE ROMAN CATHOLIC CHURCH

This Organisation continues to be hostile towards the Grenada Revolution and is now placing emphasis on two (2) main areas. They are 1. Control of all Catholic Youth Groups and 2. Education of priests through materials distorting the teachings of Marxism/Leninism and offering Christianity as the only way to solve societies problems.

At present there are eighteen (18) Roman Catholic priests in Grenada. They serve in forty (40) places of worship through out Grenada and Carriacou. There are two main Religious Orders in this Church in Grenada (a) KILTEGEANS and (b) DOMINICANS, other lesser Orders are Diocesean ~~Preient~~ priests and secular priests. These priest are in the main either conservative or out right reactionary with the most dangerous priests being FRS. TOM LUCY, OLIVER DAVY, PETER CLARKE, GILBERT COXHEAD, CYRIL LAMONTAGNE and BISHOP SYDNEY CHARLES.

Although all reactionary and conservative the Bishop does not have the control over the priests that he would like, this is because of the exclusiveness of the two aforementioned Orders, to which he does not belong, thus giving him limited control. These Orders are totally loyal to their Superiors firstly and secondly to the Bishop. The Kiltegeans are headed by FR.OLIVER DAVY and the Dominicans by FR.MARTIN SIMMONS. Thus the tendency is for the Bishop, who is very popular among the church goers, to ensure strict and direct control of the Diocesean priests and Organisations of Youth. Hence his thrust to control the Catholic Youth Organisations. Significantly also is the fact that the Advisory Body to the Bishop is made up of Lay People;

his Body is called the Diocesean Pastoral Council and is Chaired by Danny
ILLIAMS - a noted reactionary. This Body advises the Bishop on all matters
om Sex tp Politics. Also worthy of note is the little heard of Public
atements Committee which is headed by the Bishop and comprises such element
e Willie REDHEAD. Also the Finance Committee which is accountable ONLY to
Bishop.

therefore can be seen from the fore going that the Bishop understanding
at he is not popular with his priests (his colour is another reason for
lack of popularity) has moved to control key Church Organisations to
ntain his power. He understands that he is not ever invited to the meet-
s of the Orders and does not see their minutes. These meetings are used
only to review the work of the Orders but to come out with a common line
h they want the Bishop to adopt at the monthly general meeting of all the
sts. So by sheer weight of numbers at voting time the Bishop is easily
ipulated to take certain actions or to make certain statements on the
lf of the Church while the real authors remain hidden.

wever this Church remains considerably strong in Grenada and it will take
t of work to erode their influence. Particularly strong among the middle
and older people in the state.

e plan to reorganise the Catholic Youth Organisations which began since
ember 1982 has gone along very smoothly on paper. This plan is allegedly
"Combat the challenge faced by the Church in 1983". The Main decision
ing body will be the Diocesean Youth Commission which is headed for the
ent by the Bishop. But indications are that as soon as all the plans are
lized DOMNIC HAYNES will take the Chairmanship.This Commission, made up
reactionary elements will be the overall controlling body of all Catholic
th, a function previously held by the Catholic Youth Congress which the
hop sees as too Political, too pro-PRG. The CYC'S function will now be
ried out by the Catholic Diocesean Youth Council which will comprise two
resentatives from each Youth Organisation, thus by the numbers alone the
ce of the CYC will be silenced.
ow circulated for ALL priests to study is a document called "MARXISM, HUM-
ISM AND CHRISTIANITY ". Orginiating from Zambia Episcopal Conference and
ted August 1979. This document was in Grenada in 1981, but not circulated

among the priests to study as an "answer" to Scientific Socialism. This

ument is Anti-Scientific Socialism, anti- Communism and in general distorts

teaching of Marx and Lenin. The Bishop sees this document as important

erial to combat the "Challenge" to the Church. This "Challenge" obviously

he Bishops view will come from the Government. In fact on the 2nd.January

3 while addressing an indoor rally of the St,Vincent DePaul Society (a

holic Organisation which helps the poor) held at the Pierdmontemps R.C

ool the Bishop said "The Church is facing it's greatest Challenge, and, for

3 the Church will be looking on the youth to be more committed to the Church

a ever, there are people who want to dictate to the Church what to do and

1983 will even see attempts to CRUSH the Church". This veiled statement is

arly directed against the Revolution and the PRG.

ne Bishop left Grenada on the 20th.February 1983 to attend a meeting of the

hops of the Antilles which was held in Cayenne. He returned to Grenada on

ch 11th.1983. No doubt he used this forum to "report" on the Grenada situ-

on.

v in Grenada is a new priest, Fr.SHEAN, who is attached to Grand Roy R.C

rch. He is an Irishman and belongs to the Kiltegeans Order. He has worked

frica and England before coming to Grenada. This is in keeping with the

op's view to recruit priests who have worked in simular conditions as now

ist in Grenada. This is also to face the "Challenge".

so in keeping with the need to face the "challenge" the Church has brought

4,365 copies of the Jeresulem Bible; This bible is written as a novel and

very easy to understand not being written in old English. This bible is

d in Trinidad to train priests. Now on sale over the island at a cost of

ollars each. This means that the Church in understanding the struggle for

s has "revolutionized" is main ideological weapon -the bible.

Pope's new year message message is also now in the hands of the priests

study. This is the Church's foreign policy document and no doubt will be

d to criticize our foreign policy.

NCLUSIONS: From the foregoing it is abundantly clear that the Roman Catholi

rch is gearing up for confrontation with Government. Although not really

n the facts perviously outlined indicate the following - (a) Planning

Constant evaluation of it's power base and influence in the Society

nd (c) Counter measures against State in a most skillful way.

s Regards point (a) The explanation must be the new type of bibles, intro-
ction of new priests, control of the Catholic Youths,- this as a counter
tack against the NYO who has eroded a number of their Organisations-, new
ives to evangelism to attract more youths to the Church, circulation of the
pe's message, the paper on "Marxism, Humanism and Christianity" to prepare
iests to combat, from a Christian stand point, the ideas of Marxism Lenin-
m now being defused in the masses as part of the year of Political and
ademic Education.

int (b) The emphasis on Youth placed by the Bishop. Almost 50 per cent of
rch goers are Youth (Below 30Yrs) therefore to lose even a part of xtix
s percentage is to drastically erode the Church's power base and if unchec-
d can cause the Church to crumble. Something it will fight against at all
sts.

int (c) Exposing the so-called "Challenge" but not naming names the Church
 in fact laying the basis for it's Counter Revolutionary activities and
ipping up feelings of sympathy among it's followers. By hinting that the
urch will be persecuted in christ's name, any action taken against the
urch will be seen by the followers as "prophecy". We must remember that
l churches strive best in created conditions of persecution. Therefore
at we are up against is an experienced and skillful Counter Revolutionary
ganisation.

E ANGLICAN CHURCH

his Church is experiencing a number of internal problems foremost being t he
 of priests to carry out its work and to expand it's influence in the
iety. It is also in direct contradiction with the Roman Catholic Church
ause of that Church's historical control in Grenada. However the Anglican
urch now carries the common "Challenge" line although not in the same words
the Roman Catholic Church.

 December 24th.1982, Archdeacon Hoskins Huggins, the leader of the Anglican
urch in Grenada told a Congregation at the St.George's Church to "Guard
 e right to freedom of worship, and to do all in their power to ensure this
 t be always a part of the People". He also claimed that "for 1983 freedom
 worship may not exist and that this a grave challenge to us as a freedom
 ving people". This clearly is only a variation of the "challenge" line

4 - 4

ushed by the Bishop of the Roman Catholic Church. With the departure of
.Everton WEEKES (he left Grenada for good on 17th.December 1982) who was
sponsible for servicing the West Coast, the Church now has to rely on Lay
ople to preach sermons, and, has not been able to train more pepple to
o this work precisely because of this shortage of priests. Thus Archdeacon
s becoming more and more critical against the Revolution.

He is backed by a host of reactionary elements who dominate all the Church's
ganisations (men's league, Advisory Councils etc.). Prominent among them is
le Hosten who is Church Lawyer, Church Chancellor and Advisor to the Archdeacon.

:CLUSION: Not as influencial in the State as the Roman Catholic Church
it still a major threat to the Revolution. This is beaause the both churches
are a common outlook on the Grenada Revolution. No indications of concrete
anning just yet but it is my opinion this Church will go along with the
Church in ga it's general line if only from the position that the Anglican
urch is a member of the Conference of Churches of Grenada, an Organisation
which the RC Church dominates. I do not forsee immediately any independent
tion like what is being carried out by the RC Church.

E SEVENTH DAY ADVENTIST CHURCH

is Church is for the moment content to be the "Buisness Church" of Grenada
i at this period confines it's efforts mainly to it's "Ingathering" Prog-
amme. This is aprogramme which is designed to reach money goals set for xxx
ry church in the State. This Church is divided into six Districts. There
twenty Four (24) main churches in Grenada and fomm (4) smaller ones called
panies.

:CCLUSION: This Church is hostile towards the Revolution , but does nothing
nly. Now has itIs own Mission and Executive because of Currency restrict-
s; previously administered by the East Carribbean Conference of the Seventh
Adevntist Church. At present indicated internal contradictions among the
dership being investigated.

HE METHODIST CHURCH

is Church, Like the Anglican, is experiencing some difficulties with priest
dership. In fact Church services are being held over the island by Lay
ple. In st.John's by Fred Grant, in St.George's by Eileen Byer, Lennox

Phillip and Elliot Gittens (they Take turns). National membership is very small.

Of the above named group of people Eileen Byer is the most reactionary and clearly anti- PRG. In fact on the 30th.January 1983, she told a congregation in St.George's that the Church had applications sent to Government for two work permits for priests but up to now there has been no response. This statement taken in the light of the Ledson case is tantamount to telling the Congregation that Government is wilfully and deliberately blocking and hampering the work of the Methodist church. This is also a variation to the "Challenge" line by both Catholic and Anglican Churches.

CONCLUSION: This Church will not take independent actions not positions because of it's social base in the Society, historically a "town Church" and has no real broard social support. But will definitely go along with the position of the Conference of Churches of Grenada of which Eileen Byer is the Secretary.

OTHER CHURCHES

Generally the other Churches - Beraan, Jehovah's Witnesses, Baptists, Church of the Open Bible, Pentecostal, Garden of Prayer, Church of Christ - are very quiet. The Baptist and Church of the Open Bible are on the increase in numbers. These Churches also oppose the Revolution from the position that it is teaching "Atheism and turning away from God", but these Churches do not consistently attack the Revolution. Generally pre-occupied in the process of "winning souls" and attacking the Catholic Church in order to build their numbers. In my opinion the most reactionary of the lesser Churches are (1) The Jehovah's Witnesses (2) The Church of the Open Bible and (3) The Baptists.

SUBMITTED AS REQUESTED.

MICHAEL D.ROBERTS

TO:MAJOR KEITH ROBERTS

OM: O/CDT.MICHAEL ROBERTS

<u>ANALYSIS - THE CHURCH IN GRENADA</u>

IS report will seek to analyse the Main Churches against whom our work is

rected and also a general view of the other Churches. The Main Churches

e : (a) The Roman Catholic Church

     (b) The Anglican Church

     (CO The Methodist Church

     (d) The Seventh Day Adventist Church

) <u>THE ROMAN CATHOLIC CHURCH</u>

is Organisation continues to be hostile towards the Grenada Revolution

d is now placing emphasis on two (2) main areas. They are 1. Control of

l Catholic Youth Groups and 2. Education of priests through materials

storting the teachings of Marxism/Leninism and offering Christianity as

e only way to solve societies problems.

At present there are eighteen (18) Roman Catholic priests in Grenada. The;

rve in forty (40) places of worship through out Grenada and Carriacou.

ere are two main Religious Orders in this Church in Grenada (a) KILTEGEANS

d (b) DOMINICANS, other lesser Orders are Diocesean Priexi priests and

cular priests. These priest are in the main either conservative or out

ght reactionary with the most dangerous priests being FRS. TOM LUCY, OLIVER

AVY, PETER CLARKE, GILBERT COXHEAD, CYRIL LAMONTAGNE and BISHOP SYDNEY

ARLES.

though all reactionary and conservative the Bishop does not have the

ntrol over the priests that he would like, this is because of the exclusiv-

ess of the two aforementioned Orders, to which he does not belong, thus

ving him limited control. These Orders are totally loyal to their Superiors

rstly and secondly to the Bishop. The Kiltegeans are headed by FR.OLIVER

AVY and the Dominicans by FR.MARTIN SIMMONS. Thus the tendency is for the

shop, who is very popular among the church goers, to ensure strict and

rect control of the Diocesean priests and Organisations of Youth. Hence

is thrust to control the Catholic Youth Organisations. Significantly also

is the fact that the Advisory Body to the Bishop is made up of Lay People;

his Body is called the Diocesean Pastoral Council and is Chaired by Danny
WILLIAMS - a noted reactionary. This Body advises the Bishop on all matters
from Sex to Politics. Also worthy of note is the little heard of Public
Statements Committee which is headed by the Bishop and comprises such elements
like Willie REDHEAD. Also the Finance Committee which is accountable ONLY to
the Bishop.

It therefore can be seen from the fore going that the Bishop understanding
that he is not popular with his priests (his colour is another reason for
the lack of popularity) has moved to control key Church Organisations to
maintain his power. He understands that he is not ever invited to the meetings of the Orders and does not see their minutes. These meetings are used
not only to review the work of the Orders but to come out with a common line
which they want the Bishop to adopt at the monthly general meeting of all the
priests. So by sheer weight of numbers at voting time the Bishop is easily
manipulated to take certain actions or to make certain statements on the
behalf of the Church while the real authors remain hidden.

However this Church remains considerably strong in Grenada and it will take
a lot of work to erode their influence. Particularly strong among the middle
aged and older people in the state.

The plan to reorganise the Catholic Youth Organisations which began since
September 1982 has gone along very smoothly on paper. This plan is allegedly
to "Combat the challenge faced by the Church in 1983". The Main decision
making body will be the Diocesean Youth Commission which is headed for the
present by the Bishop. But indications are that as soon as all the plans are
finalized DOMINIC HAYNES will take the Chairmanship. This Commission, made up
of reactionary elements will be the overall controlling body of all Catholic
Youth, a function previously held by the Catholic Youth Congress which the
Bishop sees as too Political, too pro-PRG. The CYC'S function will now be
carried out by the Catholic Diocesean Youth Council which will comprise two
representatives from each Youth Organisation, thus by the numbers alone the
voice of the CYC will be silenced.

Now circulated for ALL priests to study is a document called "MARXISM, HUM-
ANISM AND CHRISTIANITY ". Orginiating from Zambia Episcopal Conference and
dated August 1979. This document was in Grenada in 1981, but not circulated

among the priests to study as an "answer" to Scientific Socialism. This
ument is Anti-Scientific Socialism, anti- Communism and in general distorts
teaching of Marx and Lenin. The Bishop sees this document as important
erial to combat the "Challenge" to the Church. This "Challenge" obviously
he Bishops view will come from the Government. In fact on the 2nd.January
3 while addressing an indoor rally of the St,Vincent DePaul Society (a
holic Organisation which helps the poor) held at the Pierdmontemps R.C
ool the Bishop said "The Church is facing it's greatest Challenge, and, for
3 the Church will be looking on the youth to be more committed to the Church
n ever, there are people who want to dictate to the Church what to do and
1983 will even see attempts to CRUSH the Church". This veiled statement is
arly directed against the Revolution and the PRG.

ne Bishop left Grenada on the 20th.February 1983 to attend a meeting of the
hops of the Antilles which was held in Cayenne. He returned to Grenada on
ch 11th.1983. No doubt he used this forum to "report" on the Grenada situ-
on.

v in Grenada is a new priest, Fr.SHEAN, who is attached to Grand Roy R.C
rch. He is an Irishman and belongs to the Kiltegeans Order. He has worked
frica and England before coming to Grenada. This is in keeping with the
iop's view to recruit priests who have worked in simular conditions as now
st in Grenada. This is also to face the "Challenge".

so in keeping with the need to face the "challenge" the Church has brought
4,365 copies of the Jeresulem Bible; This bible is written as a novel and
very easy to understand not being written in old English. This bible is
d in Trinidad to train priests. Now on sale over the island at a cost of
ollars each. This means that the Church in understanding the struggle for
s has "revolutionized" is main ideological weapon -the bible.

Pope's new year message is also now in the hands of the priests
study. This is the Church's foreign policy document and no doubt will be
d to criticize our foreign policy.

NCLUSIONS: From the foregoing it is abundantly clear that the Roman Catholi
rch is gearing up for confrontation with Government. Although not really
n the facts perviously outlined indicate the following - (a) Planning
Constant evaluation of it's power base and influence in the Society

nd (c) Counter measures against State in a most skillful way.

s Regards point (a) The explanation must be the new type of bibles, intro-
ction of new priests, control of the Catholic Youths,- this as a counter
tack against the NYO who has eroded a number of their Organisations-, new
ives to evangelism to attract more youths to the Church, circulation of the
pe's message, the paper on "Marxism, Humanism and Christianity" to prepare
iests to combat, from a Christian stand point, the ideas of Marxism Lenin-
m now being defused in the masses as part of the year of Political and
ademic Education.

int (b) The emphasis on Youth placed by the Bishop. Almost 50 per cent of
rch goers are Youth (Below 30Yrs) therefore to lose even a part of this
s percentage is to drastically erode the Church's power base and if unchec-
d can cause the Church to crumble. Something it will fight against at all
sts.

int (c) Exposing the so-called "Challenge" but not naming names the Church
in fact laying the basis for it's Counter Revolutionary activities and
ipping up feelings of sympathy among it's followers. By hinting that the
urch will be persecuted in christ's name, any action taken against the
urch will be seen by the followers as "prophecy". We must remember that
l churches strive best in created conditions of persecution. Therefore
at we are up against is an experienced and skillful Counter Revolutionary
ganisation.

E ANGLICAN CHURCH

his Church is experiencing a number of internal problems foremost being t h
of priests to carry out its work and to expand it's influence in the
iety. It is also in direct contradiction with the Roman Catholic Church
ause of that Church's historical control in Grenada. However the Anglican
rch now carries the common "Challenge" line although not in the same words
the Roman Catholic Church.

December 24th.1982, Archdeacon Hoskins Huggins, the leader of the Anglican
rch in Grenada told a Congregation at the St.George's Church to "Guard
e right to freedom of worship, and to do all in their power to ensure this
t be always a part of the People". He also claimed that "for 1983 freedom
worship may not exist and that this a grave challenge to us as a freedom
ving people". This clearly is only a variation of the "challenge" line

ushed by the Bishop of the Roman Catholic Church. With the departure of
.Everton WEEKES (he left Grenada for good on 17th.December 1982) who was
sponsible for servicing the West Coast, the Church now has to rely on Lay
ople to preach sermons, and, has not been able to train more pepple to
o this work precisely because of this shortage of priests. Thus Archdeacon
s becoming more and more critical against the Revolution.

He is backed by a host of reactionary elements who dominate all the Church's
ganisations (men's league, Advisory Councils etc.). Prominent among them is
le Hosten who is Church Lawyer, Church Chancellor and Advisor to the Arch-
eacon.

CLUSION: Not as influencial in the State as the Roman Catholic Church
t still a major threat to the Revolution. This is beaause the both churches
are a common outlook on the Grenada Revolution. No indications of concrete
anning just yet but it is my opinion this Church will go along with the
  Church in it's general line if only from the position that the Anglican
urch is a member of the Conference of Churches of Grenada, an Organisation
  which the RC Church dominates. I do not forsee immediately any independent
+ion like what is being carried out by the RC Church.

E SEVENTH DAY ADVENTIST CHURCH

is Church is for the moment content to be the "Buisness Church" of Grenada
d at this period confines it's efforts mainly to it's "Ingathering" Prog-
amme. This is aprogramme which is designed to reach money goals set for
ry church in the State. This Church is divided into six Districts. There
 twenty Four (24) main churches in Grenada and four (4) smaller ones called
panies.

CCLUSION: This Church is hostile towards the Revolution , but does nothing
nly. Now has itIs own Mission and Executive because of Currency restrict-
s; previously administered by the East Carribbean Conference of the Seventh
  Adevntist Church. At present indicated internal contradictions among the
dership being investigated.

HE METHODIST CHURCH

is Church, Like the Anglican, is experiencing some difficulties with priest
dership. In fact Church services are being held over the island by Lay
ple. In st.John's by Fred Grant, in St.George's by Eileen Byer, Lennox

Phillip and Elliot Gittens (they Take turns). National membership is very small.

Of the above named group of people Eileen Byer is the most reactionary and clearly anti- PRG. In fact on the 30th.January 1983, she told a congregation in St.George's that the Church had applications sent to Government for two work permits for priests but up to now there has been no response. This statement taken in the light of the Ledson case is tantamount to telling the Congregation that Government is wilfully and deliberately blocking and hampering the work of the Methodist church. This is also a variation to the "Challenge" line by both Catholic and Anglican Churches.

CONCLUSION: This Church will not take independent actions not positions because of it's social base in the Society, historically a "town Church" and has no real broard social support. But will definitely go along with the position of the Conference of Churches of Grenada of which Eileen Byer is the Secretary.

OTHER CHURCHES

Generally the other Churches - Beraan, Jehovah's Witnesses, Baptists, Church of the Open Bible, Pentecostal, Garden of Prayer, Church of Christ - are very quiet. The Baptist and Church of the Open Bible are on the increase in numbers. These Churches also oppose the Revolution from the position that it is teaching "Atheism and turning away from God", but these Churches do not consistently attack the Revolution. Generally pre-occupied in the process of "winning souls" and attacking the Catholic Church in order to build their numbers. In my opinion the most reactionary of the lesser Churches are (1) The Jehovah's Witnesses (2) The Church of the Open Bible and (3) The Baptists.

SUBMITTED AS REQUESTED.

MICHAEL D.ROBERTS

TOP SECRET

MINISTRY OF INTERIOR,
BUTLER HOUSE,
ST. GEORGE'S.

12TH JULY, 1983.

ANALYSIS OF THE CHURCH IN GRENADA

(1) A BRIEF HISTORICAL OVERVIEW:

The real history of the Church in Grenada can be said to have begun with the coming of Columbus to the island and the subsequent attempts by the different religious sects to "christianize" the inhabitants.

With the changing of the balance of power by the constant squabbles between the Colonial powers and the subsequent changing of ownership of the island of the religious institutions of those powers were extended to Grenada; first the English Anglican Church, then the Roman Catholic Church, Methodist and Presbyterian Churches.

All these Churches served the interests of the ruling classes and helped to strengthen the position of the Colonial Governments. While helping the ruling class, these Churches also played a key role in uniting different sections of our society. For example, the Anglican Church traditionally comprised the elite of Grenadian Society while the Roman Catholic Church drew it's members from the poor and oppressed classes. This serves, today, to explain why the Roman Catholic Church is the most powerful in Grenada with approximately 70,000 baptised members.

Poor living conditions, poverty and dispair during the era of Colonialism served to strengthen the position of the Church among the broad masses of our country because the Church is strongest where there exists poverty, illiteracy and an educational system designed to suit the interests of the Church, where religious knowledge was compulsory at schools controlled by the Church, served to entrench further a deep idealism among our people which today, is one of the main reasons for our people's deep and strong religious feelings.

To compound matters more a flood of new-fangled religious sects and denominations came to Grenada just after the Second World War. These are the Non-Traditional American types. This flood continues even to this day. Thus, the bases of the traditional religions have been somewhat eroded and the social composition of Grenadian society further subdivided into a multitude of various sects of different shades and creeds.

----/2

In conclusion, we can say that the Church, although at periods in it's history, sometimes played a progressive role if even in it's own interest is nothing but a fetter to our development.

2) THE CHURCH AS A THREAT TO THE REVOLUTION

March 13, 1979 forced all Churches in Grenada to take a new look at themselves and to analyse their role in a Revolutionary society. At first they played a wait and see game, but, when it became clear where the Revolution was going and what it stood for, they took up a clear position. It is safe, here, to say that there is no clear "left" religion in Grenada, but, since our Revolution enjoys popular support, then the broad mass of Church goers are to varing extents supporters of the Grenada Revolution. This cannot be said about the Leaders of the Churches in Grenada and I contend that we have no support among them, all are to different degrees hostile to the Revolution. This is true even though some are less vocal than others. The following analysis of events taken at different periods up to the present time will suffice to here identify the Church as the main potential source of major internal counterrevolution.

. 1980 - 1981 - The main line pushed for this period by the Traditional Churches was the question of the Detainees at Richmond Hill and the holding of elections. The Roman Catholic Church in particular used every forum to push this line. This Church organised retreats, seminars and conferences and at every one of these activities, hostile statements were hurled against the Grenada Revolution on so-called violation of Human rights. Every Sunday at one Church or another priests were heard to ask people to "pray for the detainees" whose rights have been denied.

While the Traditional religious were on the human rights/election line, the non-traditional religions were on a different line. They were preaching the so-called " last days doctrine" and saying that "man has turned away from god" a subtle attack on our ideological positions. This line was particularly strong among the Baptists and the Open Bible Churches.

1980-1981 period saw the Catholic Church making efforts to obtain priest versed in the knowledge of submitting our ideological position, and also saw the Roman Catholic Priests begin to print pamphlets on "civic and human Rights" and "notes on Marxism". In reality anti-Marxism/Leninism.

. 1982 - The first half of the year was relatively quiet as the Churches started to plan new strategy and tactics. In November 1982 the Roman Catholic Church emerged as the No. 1 antagonist of the Revolution.

The Bishop, Sydney Charles, began to push the line that the Church will face its biggest "challenge" in 1983. A new strategy was developed that of re-organization of all Catholic Youth under the direct control of the Bishop. Two new organizations were formed for this purpose (a) the Diocesean Youth Commission and (b) the Diocesean Youth Council. The latter organization whose chairman is appointed by the Bishop, replaces the Catholic Youth Congress (CYC) whom the Bishop saw as "too political".

On 10th December, 1982, 4,365 copies of the Jerusulem Bible arrived in Grenada for the Catholic Church. A very simple bible it is written in novel form so as to make it easier for the church masses to read. This indicates the Church's understanding of the ideological struggle. The call by A. Huges for the church to voice its opinion on matters of human rights, and the statement that it is the main hope at this time. The Bishop speaks of the "challenge" to the Church in 1983 in his Christmas Message.

The situation took on a new turn when Methodist Minister Ledson refused to officiate at the burial of Cde. Demo Grant and had to be kicked out of Grenada. All the traditional Churches saw this as "persecution" and hardened their position against the PRG and Revolution.

In December of the same year, in his Christmas sermon, Arch Deacon Huggins of the Anglican Church, spoke of the need to safeguard the right to worship, and acted in a way that would make anyone feel that this right was about to be taken away.

3. 1983 - Upsurge in open air crusades, house to house and tract giving
by the non-traditional religions. More house to house work done by Jehovah's Witnesses. There seem to be a frenzied drive by these churches to win new members. This process is continuing now. There has also been a number of visits to Grenada by pastors and preachers from abroad to "beef up" the work in "evengelization".

The Roman Catholic Clergy, for the first time, has instituted a prescheduled list of meetings led by the Bishop for the year. Nine (9) in all. Three (3) have been held so far, all at different venues. The fourth meeting will take place on 12th July, 1983 at the Grand Roy Presbytry. This activity indicates that the Clergy is becoming more and more organized under the leadership of the Bishop

The organization of the youths continue at an accelerated rate, with all ages included in this drive. The Bishop, at a meeting of all Catholic youths leaders in May, said that the enemy was organized and that it was

-----/4

necessary that the church organize also to combat the enemy. At an early
meeting in April, the Bishop again spoke of a subtle form of destabilization
against the church. The Anglican Church has started to re-organize its
Youth Groups after a lapse of three (3) years. This year was the first
time the Anglican and Catholic Churches had a joint Corpus Christi Pro-
cession.

Based on these developments and the knowledge of the large percentage
of Grenadians who have very deep trust in the church and also taking into
account the weakness in all our mass organizations and, therefore, our
influence over the masses, we see this development as a very dangerous one.
We think that in the medium term, if serious measures are not taken, we can
find ourselves faced with a Poland situation. In this light, we see the
church in the immediate period as being the most dangerous sector for the
development of internal counter revolution.

FUTURE TRENDS

1) We forsee the continuation of the organization of all Youths by the
   Catholic and Anglican Churches.
2) We forsee stronger unity among all G.C.C. churches.
3) We think that the unity among Catholic Clergy will grow steadily.
4) Infiltration of anti Marxist/Leninist from outside.
5) The Bishop becoming bolder in his attacks against the Revolution.
6) The Catholic Church overall hardening its position against the
   Revolution.
7) More and more foreign Pastors and Preachers of non-traditional
   religious will want to come to Grenada to work and hold crusades.

RECOMMENDATIONS

a) Ensuring that Michael Roberts continue a permanent and full time way
   to be in charge of church work.
b) Obtaining a second person to work in this area in order to control all
   churches, their leadership, membership and their activities.
   The establishment of a register of association including churches and
   all other organizations e.g. Jaycee, Unions, Association of Professional
   etc. which will make it necessary when registering to give some basic
   fact about the Associations or churches e.g. the knowledge on special
   and regular activities, counting of members, different posts within the
   organizations, means of financing activities, etc.
   Continuing to develop the co-operation in this area with the Cuban
   Comrades at the level of Party to Party.

-----#5

4. Ensuring that C.P.E. get a majority of working people involved in its classes.

5. Build the Mass Organizations - Pioneers, N.Y.O., N.W.O., P.F.U., Militia, to incorporate a majority of working people.

6. Organize the community work in the different areas more efficiently, start on time, and actively mobilize to bring out the masses to participate.

7. Removing from Primary Schools, all deeply religious head teachers by whatever means most suitable, replacing them with more progressive elements. This should be done no later that the end of this month.

8. Introduce Polical Education as that or Social studies in every classroom in the Primary and Secondary Schools from this September, use the most progressive teachers within the school system (chosen by teachers committee) to teach these classes. Use Merle Hodge and Didicus to write up the materials for the courses.

. Political Education for all teachers by this September.

. Strengthen Science Education - theory and practical - in every school and in the community through C.P.E. and Film shows.

. Cut back on all religious programmes on R.F.G. Substitute on Sunday morning voice cast of the masses on the progress of the projects.

. To promote contacts among Clergymen and members of Laity from Nicaragua and other Latin American countries linked to the theology of liberation and, in gereral, to the idea of a church committed to Revolutionary positions.

. To implement the visits of Pastors from the Grenada Protestant Churches belonging to the Caribbean Conference of Churches (CCC) of which the Evangilical Churches of Cuban in a number, to short annual course, in light that the comrades can solve the language question.

. More dialogue with West Indian Priests, Nuns and Brothers in the Church and schools by the Leadership.

. Opening up M-L Bookshop in different parishes of the country.

. Getting M-L literature into all schools by September.

. Explore possibility of getting Father Martin and La Montague to visit Cuba.

. Step up the systematic monitering of all Religious manifestation in the state, and position being taken as regard the work permit of way-side Preachers entering the country to preach, and immigration position on these way-side preachers.

7. Open Cinemas.
. Start progressive church (Talk with Neal.. + Cuban)

MAJOR KEITH ROBERTS.

I

LIST OF PERSONS IN DETENTION AS FROM ~~[struck through]~~ 1ST. JANUARY 1998

NO.	NAMES	ADDRESS	DATE
1.	NORMAN DESOUZA	LABORIE, ST. GEO.	13.3.79
2.	OLIVER RAEBURN	SAUTEURS, ST. PAT.	14.3.79
3.	OSBERT JAMES	MAMMA CANNES, ST. AND.	15.3.79
4.	RAYMOND DESOUZA	LABORIE, ST. GEO.	13.3.79
5.	CLINTY SAMUEL	ST. PATRICK'S	15.3.79
6.	KINGSTON BAPTISTE	GOUYAVE	14.3.79
7.	TANNIL CLARKE	ST. JOHN'S	14.3.79
8.	DENNIS RUSH	ST. ANDREW'S	17.3.79
9.	DONNALLY PATRICK	HAPPY HILL	23.3.79
10.	TERRANCE JONES	BYELANDS	23.3.79
11.	NOBLE PHILLIP	MT. RICH	25.3.79
12.	STEADMAN PATRICK	HERMITAGE	25.3.79
13.	DALTON POPE	SAUTEURS	25.3.79
14.	LESTER DESOUZA	LABORIE	30.7.79
15.	ANTONIO LANGDON	HAPPY HILL	15.8.79
16.	FRANCIS JONES	WESTERHALL	13.3.79
17.	TEDDY VICTOR	VINCENNES	15.10.79
18.	ANTHONEY MITCHELL	VINCENNES	15.10.79
19.	JAMES ANTOINE	WINDSOR FOREST	15/10.79
20.	WINSTON WHYTE	GRAND ANSE	15.10.79
21.	LESLIE PHILLIP	MT. RICH	15.10.79
22.	HAYES JAMES	CHANTIMELLE	15.10.79
23.	GOSLYN JONES	MIRLI, ST. PAT.	17.12.79
24.	JOHN THOMAS	GRAND ROY	17.12.79
25.	ERIC CHARLES	GRAND ROY	17.12.79
26.	JOSEOH PETERS	MT. GRANDBY	17.12.79
27.	CONROY PARAYAG	RIVER ROAD	18.12.79
28.	WAYNE LETT	GRAND ANSE	18.12.79
29.	JAMES MODESTE	GRAND ROY	18.12.79
30.	STEPHEN CUFFIE	GRAND ANSE	18.12.79
31.	MATTHEW ANTOINE	GRAND ANSE	18.12.79
32.	TWISTLETON PATTERSON	TEMPE, ST. GEO.	18.12.79
33.	WILTON DERAVENIERRE	POMME ROSE	18.12.79
34.	BENEDICT GEORGE	MT. CARMEL, ST. AND.	18.12.79
34.	JAMES BOWEN	WESTERHALL	18.12.79
35.	JEROMME ROMAIN	BELMONT	18.12.79
36.	ANTHONEY BUCKMIRE	RIVER ROAD	6. 3.80
37.	KENNEDY BUDHLAL	TIVOLI	29. 4.80
38.	DENNIS CHARLES	TIVOLI	29. 4.80
39.	VINCENT REUBEN	TEMPE	30. 4.80
40.	PETER LASHLEY	CARENAGE	5. 5.80

DETAINEES LIST CONTINUED

NO.	NAMES	ADDRESS	DATE
41.	EVAN BHOLA	RIVER ANTOINE	8.5.80
42.	MAURICE PATTERSON	LUCAS STREET	12.5.80
43.	RAPHAEL ROBERTS	ST. APULS	17.5.80
44.	NORRIS WALKER	TIVOLI	19.5.80
45.	ROLAND JOSEPH	TIVOLI	19.5.80
46.	BENEDICT HENRY	TIVOLI	19.5.80
47.	BRENDA J. PHILLIP(F)	TIVOLI	22.5.80
48.	RONNIE NYACK	LAFELLITTE	8.5.80
49.	JACQUELINE JOSEPH(F)	HERMITAGE	29.6.80
50.	THERESA PETERS (F)	LAPOTERIE	29.6.80
51.	CLARIBELLA WELLS(F)	TOP HILL ST. AND.	4.7.80
52.	MAUDLYN JOHN (F)	CHANTIMELLE	21.6.80
53.	ADRIAN ROBERTS	CONFERENCE	22.6.80
54.	DONVILLE NECKLES	PROSPECT, ST. PAT.	22.6.80
55.	JOSEPH JACOBS	PIEDMONTEMPS	22.6.80
56.	GLENN BEGGS	CONFERENCE	22.6.80
57.	MICHAEL MARK	MT. REUIL	22.6.80
58.	WINSTON SIMON	TIVOLI	22.6.80
59.	GODFREY WILLIAMS	LAPOTERIE	22.6.80
60.	LEON CALLISTE	LAPOTERIE	22.6.80
61.	FRANCIS ABERDEEN	BIRCHGROVE	22.6.80
62.	DAVID STANISCLAUS	MT. RICH	16.12.80
63.	JIMMY JULIEN	MT. RICH	16.12.80
64.	ALROY BELIXGY	MT. RICH	16.12.80
65.	RICHARD PASCAL	MT. RICH	16.12.80
66.	DENZIL RICHARDSON	MT. RICH	16.12.80
67.	ISAAC JAMES	MT. RICH	16.12.80
68.	ERROL GITTINS	MT. RICH	16.12.80
69.	TERRANCE BERNARD	MT. RICH	16.12.80
70.	ADRIAN ALEXIS	MT. RICH	16.12.80
71.	MATTHEW PASCAL	MT. RICH	16.12.80
72.	ETHELBERT JOHN	MT. RICH	16.12.80
73.	DAVE RICHARDSON	MT. RICH	16.12.80
74.	MAUDLYN RODERIQUE (F)	TIVOLI	16.12.80
75.	HELEN PASCAL (F)	MT. RICH	16.12.80
76.	CATHERINE PASCAL(F)	MT. RICH	16.12.80
77.	CATHERINE FLEMMING(F)	MT. ROSE	16.12.80
78.	ANNES PASCAL (F)	MT. RICH	16.12.80
79.	SELWYN FLEMMING	MT. REUIL	14.9.80
80.	KIPLIN FRANCIS	MT. REUIL	21.11.80

3

DETAINEES LIST CONTINUED

NO.	NAMES	ADDRESS	DATE
81.	KELLY RUDD	SNELL HALL	21.11.80
82.	ALSTON ROBERTS	MUNICH	23.12.80
83.	DENNIS AUGUSTINE	HERMITAGE	29. 6.80
84.	~~HUDSON NIMBLETTE~~	BEAULEAU	Corrected 6. 7.81 4.2.83
85.	LAWERENCE SIMON	TIVOLI	23. 2.81
86.	~~BERECK ROMAIN~~	WOODLANDS	Corrected 23. 2.81 /.82
87.	GODWIN CHARLES	FONTENOY	26. 2.81
88.	LYLE ST. BERNARD	ST. PAULS	26. 2.81
89.	HUGH ST. BERNARD	ST. PAULS	26.2. 81
90.	EMMANUEL CHARLES	SAUTEURS	26. 2.81
91.	JENSON OTTWAY	ST. PAULS	26. 2.81
92.	KENNY CHITAN	MOYAH	26. 2.81
93.	GROFTON CHITAN	MOYAH	26. 2.81
94.	RAYMOND ALEXIS	MUNICH	26. 2.81
95.	CHARLES FLEMMING	MT. REUIL	26. 2.81
96.	HERBERT JOHN	TIVOLI	26. 2.81
97.	BARRY JOSEPH	MT. GAY	26. 2.81
98.	DENNIS FARRIER	ST. GEORGE'S	9. 3.81
99.	COSMOS MCINTYRE	ST. GEORGE'S	9. 3.81
100.	STEPHEN SCOTT	MT. GAY	9. 3.81
101.	Raymond Steille	Morne Jaloux	9. 3.81
102.	Rondolf Charles	RIVER ROAD	9. 3.81
103.	DAVID AIRD	ST. GEORGE'S	9. 3.81
104.	CARLYLE PHILLIP	RIVER ROAD	9. 3.81
105.	SAMUEL BONAPARTE	ST. DAVID'S	11. 3.81
106.	FABIAN LEWIS	CARENAGE	11. 3.81
107.	IRIE CALLISTE	ST. DAVID'S	12. 3.81
108.	THOMAS GILBERT	ST. DAVID'S	24. 7.81
109.	WILFRED DERAVENIERRE	POMME ROSE	13. 7.81
110.	PAUL EDWARDS	LA TANTE	13. 7.81
111.	ALEXANDER NOEL	HERMITAGE	29. 6.81
112.	JARDIN REUBEN	POMME ROSE	11. 7.81
113.	LESLIE PIERRE	FORT JEUDY	11. 7. 81
114.	STANLEY ROBERTS	PIEDMONTEMPS	11. 7.81
115.	MARTIN FLETCHER	SAN SOUCI	25. 2.81
116.	WORREL LEWIS	BIRCHGROVE	3. 9.81
117.	RONALD MCSWEEN	ST. DAVIDS	13. 7.81
118.	BERNARD PATRICK	TIVOLI	11. 9.81
119.	DUNCAN CHARLES	LAPOTERIE	14. 8.81
120.	LLOYD NOEL	ST. JOHN'S	13. 7.81

DETAINEES LIST CONTINUED

NO.	NAMES	ADDRESS	DATE	OTHER
121.	TILLMAN THOMAS	ST. GEORGE'S	13. 7.81	
122.	WINSTON CROWE	ST. GEORGE'S	13. 7.81	
123.	EMMANUEL TOUSSAINT	TIVOLI	19. 3.80	
124.	RODNEY NELSON	TIVOLI	8. 5.80	
125.	VAUGHN NOEL	WALKER	15. 5.80	
126.	STEPHEN LEWIS	LAPOTERIE	22. 6.80	
127.	RONALD LEWIS	TIVOLI	22. 6.80	
128.	LOXLEY LOGIE	ST. PATRICK'S	26. 6.80	
129.	~~JEFFREY BRENDSHAW~~	~~ST. GEORGE'S~~	~~9. 3.81~~	CONVICTED 4.1.82
130.	MICHAEL ANDREW'S	ST. PAULS	13. 7.81	
131.	FABIAN TELESFORD	WINDSOR FOREST	20.12.81	
132.	DAVID GREENIDGE	WINDSOR FOREST	20.12.81	
133.	RAPHAEL BOYKE	GRANDANSE	23.12.81	
134.	CLARANCE BERNARD	ST. PATRICK'S	26. 6.81	
135.	DESMOND FREDERICK	HERMITAGE	27. 6.81	
136.	DOMINIC HAMLET	MADEYS, ST. PAT.	25. 6.81	
137.	DERICK GOODING	TIVOLI	27. 6.81	
138.	KENT BAIN	BELMONT	29. 4.80	
139.	LEROY CHARLES	TIVOLI	27. 6.80	
140.	ERROL CHARLES	BELMONT, ST. GEO.	6. 3.80	
141.	STEVE RICHARDSON	MT. RICH	25. 6.81	
142.	REGINALD PHILLIP	MT. PARNASSUS	6. 3.80	
143.	KENNETH WILLIAMS	HERMITAGE	26. 6.81	
144.	MARTIN BERROTTE	MT. GAY, ST. GEO.	9. 3.81	
145.	CLAUDE SIMON	ST. PATRICK'S	26. 6.81	
146.	CLIFTON AUGUSTINE	ST. DAVID'S	11. 3.81	
147.	HESLYN PHILLIP	MT. RICH	25. 6.81	
148.	MILTON ALEXANDER	BYELANDS	12. 7.81	
149.	LAWRENCE WILLIAMS	GRAND ROY	12. 7.81	
150.	EDMUND CHARLES	MOYAH	12. 7.81	
151.	EDWIN JALDOO	MOYAH	12. 7.81	
152.	KADE LAYNE	ST. GEORGE'S	6. 3.81	
153.	FRANCIS WILLIAMS	LAPOTERIE	22. 8.80	
154.	RODNEY GARRAWAY	ST. GEORGE'S	7. 3.80	
155.	HAROLD LEWIS	HERMITAGE	26. 6.81	
156.	SYDNEY BARTHOLOMEW	TIVOLI	19. 5.80	
157.	OUFTY HOUSTON	MOYAH	13. 7.81	
158.	CHESTER PAUL	HAPPY HILL	13. 7.81	
159.	BENEDICT CHARLES	TIVOLI	27. 6.81	
160.	VAUGHN THOMAS	LAFELLITTE	12. 7.81	

DETAINEES LIST CONTINUED

NO.	NAMES	ADDRESS	DATE
161.	COLVILLE PROSPER	PARADISE	12.7.81
162.	ROY ALBERT	PARADISE	12. 7. 81
163.	CLETUS ALEXANDER	MT. REUIL	12. 7. 81
164.	DAVID CLARKE	MIRABEAU	31. 7. 81
165.	GODWIN BAPTISTE	HERMITAGE	29. 7. 81
166.	KENNETH CLARKE	GRAND BRAS.	12. 7. 81
167.	RUPERT CHARLES	MIRABEAU	12. 7. 81
168.	TERRY HOUSTON	SOUBISE ST. AND.	31. 7. 81
169.	NICODIMUS TAYLOR	VICTORIA	26. 7. 81
170.	KEITH PAUL	VICTORIA	25. 7. 81
171.	GABRIEL JULIEN	VICTORIA	26. 7. 81
172.	FITZROY SIMON	PIEDMONTEMPS	15. 7. 81
173.	ISIAH HENRY	HARFORD'S VILLAGE	9. 7. 81
174.	WORREL NEDD	HERMITAGE	26. 2. 81
175.	MATTHEW FLEMMING	MT. RICH	26. 2. 81
176.	EDDIE RICHARDSON	TOP HILL, ST. AND.	26. 2. 81
177.	VAUGHN JOSEPH	SNELL HALL	26. 2. 81
178.	WINSTON JAMES	ST. PATRICK'S	27. 6. 81
179.	HARRY DALEY	ST. ANDREW'S	27. 6. 81
180.	CUTHBERT JOHN	ST. GEORGE'S	9. 3. 81
181.	SIMON ANTOINE	ST DAVIDS	13.12. 81
182.	DUNBAR SAMUEL	WESTERHALL BEAULIEU	13.12. 81
183.	DESMOND PTTS	TOPTON HALL FORESTS ST. MARKS	13.12. 81

NAMES	ADDRESS	DATE ADMITTED
10. Kiplin Francis (Abi)	Mt. Reuil, St. Pat.	21.11.80
11. Kellt Rudd (go cool)	Snell Hall, St.Pat.	21.11.80
12. Joseph Paul (Dabeau)	Montrose, St.Pat.	22.11.80
13. Alston Roberts (Imby)	Munich, St. And.	23.12.80
4. Dennis Augustine(Ants)	Hermitage, St. Pat.	29.6.80
5. Hudson Mimblette	Bealeau	6.1.81
6. Lawrance Simon	Tivoli	23.2.81
7. Derick Romain	Woodlands, Tivoli	23.2.81
8. Godwin Charles	Fontenoy	26.2.81
9. Lyle St.Bernard	St. George's	26.2.81
0. Dennis Alexander	Corinth, St.David's	26.2.81
1. Hugh O. Keith St.Bernard	St. Paul's	26.2.81
2. Emmanuel Charles	Sauteurs	26.2.81
3. Worrel Nedd	Hermitage	26.2.81
4. Matthew Flemming	Mt.Reuil	26.2.81
5. Jenson Otway	St. Paul's	26.2.81
6. Kenny Christian	Moyor,St.Andrews's	26.2.81
7. Crofton Christian	Moyor, St.Andrew's	26.2.81
3. Raymond Alexis	Munich	26.2.81
9. Eddy Richardson	TopHill St. Pat.	26.2.81
0. Charles Flemming	Mt.Reuil	26.2.81
1. Herbat John	Tavoli	26.2.81
52. Barry Joseph	Mt.Gay	26.2.81
5. Denis Ferrier	St. George's	9.3.81
4. Cosmus McIntyre		9.3.81
5. Martin Berrotte		
5. Stephen Scott		
7. Raymond Steele		
3. Sylvester Maitland		
9. Ronald Charles		
0. Phillip Donald		
. Jeffrey Marryshow		
2. David Aird		
3. Cuthbert John		
4. Carlyle Phillip		
5. Samuel Bonaparte		11.3.81
5. Fabian Lewis		11.3.81
7. Clifton Augustine		11.3.81
8. Irie Calliste		12.3.81
9. Clifton Marryshow		12.3.81
0. Winston Hinds		18.3.81
. James Modeste	Grand Roy	18.12.81

Total 147

7

NAMES	ADDRESS	DATE ADMITTED
75. Ronald Lewis	Tivoli	22.6.80
76. Vanrick Joseph	La Poterie/Snell Hall	22.6.80
77. Glenn Beggs	Conference, St.And.	22.6.80
78. Winston Simon	Tivoli	22.6.80
79. Michael Mark alias Battle Zone	Mt.Reuil, St. Pat.	22.6.80
80. Edward Nurse	Brich Grove	22.6.80
81. Godfrey Williams	La Poterie, St.And.	22.6.80
82. Leon Calliste	La Poterie, St.And.	22.6.80
83. Francis Aberdeen	Brich Grove, St.And.	22.6.80
~~84. Michael Charles~~	~~Sauteurs, St.Pat.~~	~~22.6.80~~
85. Stephen Lewis	La Poterie, St.Andrew's	22.6.80
~~86. Grace Augustine~~ (charge for murder)		
~~87. Pitilyn Joseph 9~~ (charged for murder)		
~~88. Raphael Phillip~~	~~Mt. Rich, St.Pat.~~	~~16.12.80~~
89. David Stanislaus	Mt.Rich	16.12.80
90. Jimmy Julien	Mt.Rich	16.12.80
91. Alroy Belingy	Mt.Rich	16.12.80
92. Richard Pascal	Mt.Rich	16.12.80
93. Densil Richardson	Mt.Rich	16.12.80
94. Isaac James	Mt. Rich	16.12.80
95. Emrol Gittens	Mt. Rich	16.12.80
96. Terrence Bernard	Mt.Rich	16.12.80
97. Adrian Alexis	Mt.Rich	16.12.80
98. Matthew Pascal	Mt.Rich	16.12.80
99. Matthew Jeremiah	Crouhu, St.And.	16.12.80
100. Ethelbert John	Mt. Rich	16.12.80
101. Dave Richardson	Mt. Rich	16.12.80
102. Maudlyn Roderique	Tivoli	16.12.80
103. Helen Pascal	Mt.Rich	16.12.80
104. Catherine Pascal	Mt.Rich	16.12.80
105. Catherine Fleming	Mt.Rose	16.12.80
106. Annas Pascal	Mt.Rich (Mt.Royal)	16.12.80
107. Francis Williams	La Poterie, St.And.	22.6.80
108. Selwyn Fleming	Mt.Reuil, St.Pat.	14.9.80
109. Philmore Williams alias Mucmin)	Conference, St.And.	18.11.80.

NAMES	ADDRESS	DATE ARRESTED
34. Godwin Charles	Sauteurs	17.12.79
35. Conroy Parayag	River Rd.	18.12.79
36. Wayne Lett	Grand Anse	18.12.79
37. Stephen Cuffie	Grand Anse	18.12.79
38. Matthew Antoine	Grand Anse	18.12.79
39. Twistleton Patterson	Tempe	18.12.79
40. Wilton DeRavineere	Pomme Rose	18.12.79
41. Bendict George	Mt.Carmel, St. And.	18.12.79
42. James Bowen	Westerhall	18.12.79
43. Jerome Romain	Belmont	18.12.79
44. Kade Layne	Belmont	6.3.80
45. Errol Charles	Belmont	6.3.80
46. Anthony Buckmire	River Rd.	6.3.80
47. Reginald Phillip	Mt. Parnassus	6.3.80
48. Rodney Garraway	Sptings	7.3.80
49. Kennedy Buhalall	Tivoli	29.4.80
50. Dennis Charles	Tivoli	29.4.80
51. Vincent Reuben	Tempe	30.4.80
52. Peter Lashley	Carenage	5.5.80
53. Kent Bain	Belmont	29.4.80
54. Evan Bhola	River Antoine	8.5.80
55. Rodney Nelson	Tivoli7	8.5.80
56. Maurice Patterson	Lucas St.	12.5.80
57. Vaughn Noel	Walker, St. Andrew's	15.5.80
58. Raphael Roberts	St. Paul's	17.5.80
59. Norris Walker	Tivoli	19.5.80
60. Emmanuel Toussaint	Tivoli	19.5.80
61. Roland Joseph	Tivoli	19.5.80
62. Sydney Bartholomew	Tivoli	19.5.80
63. Benedict Henry	Tivoli	19.5.80
64. Brenda J.E.Phillip	Tivoli	22.5.80
65. Ralph Thompson	Tempe	21.7.80
66. Ronnie Nyack	La Fillette (convicted)	8.5.80
67. Jacquline Joseph	Hermitage, St.Pat.	29.6.80
68. Teresa Peters	La Poterie, St. And.	26.6.80
69. Claribella Wells	TopHill, St. Pat.	4.7.80
70. Maudlyn John	Chantimelle, St.Pat.	21.6.80
71. John Forrester	Brich Grove	22.6.80
72. Adrian Roberts	Conference, St. And.	22.6.80
73. Donville Neckles	Prospect, St.And.	22.6.80
74. Joseph Jacobs	Perdmontemps, St.Geo.	22.6.80

Grenada Prison Service
Richmond Hill
St. George's.

25th March, 1981.

LIST OF DETAINEES:

NAMES	ADDRESS	DATE ADMITTED
Herbert Preudhomme	Abhibald Av. St.Geo.	13.3.79
Norman DeSouza	La Borie	13.3.79
Norton Noel	Westerhall, St.David's	5.4.79
Oliver Raeburn	Sauteurs, St. Pat.	14.3.79
Osbert James	Mamma Cannes, St. And.	15.3.79
Raymond DeSouza	LaBorie	13.3.79
Clinty Samuel	St. Patrick's	15.3.79
David Coomansingh	St. David's	13.3.79
Kingston Baptiste	Gouyave	14.3.79
Ashley Church	Grand Anse	13.3.79
Iannil Clarke	St. John's	14.3.79
Dennis Rush	Grenville	17.3.79
Dennally Patrick	Happy Hill	23.3.79
Terrence Jones	Byelands	23.3.79
Noble Phillip	Mt.Ritch,St.Pat.	25.3.79
Steadman Patrick	Hermitage	25.3.79
Dalton Pope	Sauteurs	25.3.79
Daphney Baptiste	St. George's	4.7.79
Lester DeSouza	Laborie	30.7.79
Antonio Langdon	Happy Hill	15.8.79
Francis Jones	Westerhall	13.3.79
Teddy Victor	Vincennes	15.10.79
Anthony Mitchell	Vincennes	15.10.79
James Antoine	Windsor Forest	15.10.79
Rasta Nang Nang	River Rd.	14.10.79
Winston Whyte	Grand Anse	15.10.79
Kenny Lalsingh	Sauteurs	15.10.79
Leslie Phillip	Mt.Ritch, St.Pat.	15.10.79
Hayes James	Chantimelle	15.10.79
Goslyn Jones	Marli, St.Pat.	17.12.79
John Thomas	Grand Roy	17.12.79
Eric Charles	Grand Roy	17.12.79
Joseph Peters	Mt. Gramby	17.12.79

INVESTIGATIONS DEPARTMENT
MINISTRY OF NATIONAL SECURITY
ST. GEORGE'S.

16th December 1980.

TO: THE COMMISSIONER OF PRISONS
     GRENADA PRISON SERVICE
     RICHMOND HILL
     ST. GEORGE'S.

SUBJECT: ADVICE OF RELEASES FROM PREVENTITIVE DETENTION.

Comrade Commissioner,

    You are hereby formally advised that the following named persons were taken
into Preventitive Detention and released on the dates indicated. Detention Orders
were accordingly issued and copies of such orders, are in your possession:

NAME	ADDRESS	DATE DETAINED	RELEASED	PLACE DETAINED
CALVIN JOHN ?	Montrose, St. And.	21-11-80	9th Dec.1980	Fort Rupert
NICODEMUS FORTEAU	River Sallee, St. Pat.	21-11-80	9th Dec.1980	Fort Rupert
BERNARD CHARLES	Rivoli, St.And.	23-11-80	9th Dec.1980	Fort Rupert
KLIARKIN FLANDERS	Moyah, St. And.	18-11-80	9th Dec.1980	Fort Rupert
AIRD VENTOUR	Conference, St.And.	21-11-80	9th Dec.1980	Fort Rupert
RAMLE HOUSTON	Seamoon, St. And	18-11-80	9th Dec. 1980	Fort Rupert
RODWAY JOSEPH	Windsor Forest,St.Dav.	14-9-80	9th Dec.1980	Fort Rupert
FRANKLIN LEWIS	Mt.Rich, St. Pat.	28-11-80	16th Dec.1980	Sauteurs
VERNON RODERIQUES	Mt. Rich, St.Pat.	28-11-80	16th Dec.1980	Sauteurs
ASHTON ALEXANDER	Snell Hall, St.Pat.	28-11-80	16th Dec.1980	Sauteurs
STEVE JOHN	Snell Hall, St.Pat.	2-12-80	16th Dec.1980	Sauteurs
JOHNNY FRANCIS	Mt. Rich, St.Pat.	28-11-80	16th Dec.1980	Sauteurs
DEBRA MURRAY	Mt. Rich, St.Pat.	28-11-80	16th Dec.1980	Sauteurs
JOAN FRANCIS	Mt. Rich, St.Pat.	28-11-80	16th Dec.1980	Sauteurs
FREDERICK RICHARDS	Mt. Rich, St. Pat.	28-11-80	16th Dec.1980	Sauteurs
CLARIE PAUL	Mt. Rich, St. Pat.	28-11-80	16th Dec.1980	Sauteurs
RICHARD BERNARD	Mt. Rich, St. Pat.	28-11-80	16th Dec.1980	Sauteurs
LOCKSTON PHILLIP	Mt. Rich, St. Pat.	28-11-80	16th Dec.1980	Sauteurs
WILBER SMITH	Mt. Rich, St.Pat.	28-11-80	16th Dec.1980	Sauteurs
BERTRAND PAUL	Mt. Rich, St.Pat.	28-11-80	16th Dec.1980	Sauteurs
DONNETTE RICHARDSON	Mt. Rich,St.Pat.	28-11-80	16th Dec.1980	Sauteurs
JOHN ST. CLAIR	Mt. Reuil, St.Pat	28-11-80	16th Dec.1980	Sauteurs
VENNIE PAUL	Mt. Rich, St.Pat.	28-11-80	16th Dec.1980	Sauteurs
YVONNE FRANCIS	Mt.Rich, St. Pat.	4-2-80	16th Dec.1980	Sauteurs
WILMA MARK	Mt. Rich,St. Pat.	28-11-80	16th Dec.1980	Sauteurs

    The above advice is forwarded for your information and guidance.

                                            Victor Husbands
                                            Special Investigator

MINISTRY OF THE INTERIOR,
GRENADA PRISON SERVICE,
ST. GEORGE'S,
GRENADA, W.I.

31st. January 1983.

Deputy Secretary
Ministry of the Interior
St. George's

I meet with the 23 Detainees at 10.00hrs. this morning and spoke to them on the following Subjects;-

(1) Restriction Order and what is entailed.
(2) The Progress of the Revolution.
(3) Released by goodwill of the P. R. G.
(4) Report at 10.00hrs. on the 15th. and end of month.
(5) Abstain from any activities.
(6) Heard complaints.

COMPLAINTS:-

   (1) Simon Charles, Grand Anse, working with a contractor day work but looses pay to-day.

   (2) Garvin Patrice, reason for not working is gas lines taken away and not returned and damaged to the Propeller.

   (3) Kade Layne, wants work and somewhere to stay.

   (4) Conroy Parayag, not working would like to get something to do. He request to get his passport to get it renewed.

   (5) Matthew Antoine, - Not working have four (4) children mother and father crippled.

   (6) Anthony Buckmire - Not working constantly, would like to get a constant job.

   (7) Reginald Phillip - Staying with his uncle , would like to get a job.

   (8) Ashley Griffith - Wants to continue his job trafficking between Grenada and Trinidad.

   (9) Raphael Boyke - Request to get some materials to fix his home. Empty boxes will do from the Airport site.

  (10) Rodney Garraway - Wants a Job at the Mental Hospital.

They all listened attentively but did not ask any question.
I must commend the CID. for keeping a Register of attendance, each signs his name, Address, and Restriction Order. Each Detainee has to sign in the presence of Lt. Bedeau.

P. MACLEISH, MAJOR,
COMMISSIONER OF PRISONS

SECRET

PADDOCK

ANALYSIS OF THE AREA:

Paddock is a small area and it is the nearest village to the town of St.Georges. There is many housewives in the area and also state workers.

Before the Revolution the area was a strong base for the N.J.M Party and was fully anti-gairy, moreso the youths. The residential lives of the people was a stable one, but moved to a petty bourgeosie character made up of the people from the middle strata. At that time the ones that support Gairy was much more vocal and active as for political work was concern. It was very easy during that period to rally around the youths, around the issues that were confronting them, because they were able to identify some of the problem.

But following the period after the Revolution things began to change some what. Some of the people who was living in the area then began to move out, being replaced by new comers, who really never settle down for any long time and this is the pattern up to this present time, leaving a small percentage of the people who actually grow up in the area. Presently they seem to moved with the tide, however things may go. They are very difficult to organised into groups and mass organisations, but the majority support the Revolution in what ever way.

PRESENT AND PAST COUNTER REVOLUTIONARY ACTIVITIES:

Nil

STRENGTH OF THE MILITIA:

15 - regular attendance
22 - highest at one time

ECONOMIC OBJECTIVES:

Ottway's Esso Servicenter Station (private)
France Resturant & Bar (private)
Grenada General Workshop (Allan Louis)
Ministry of Agriculture, Tourism etc
8 private shops

SOCIAL OBJECTIVES:

Regal Cinemea
Botanical Gardens

MILITARY OBJECTIVES:

None

POPULATION:

Paddock - Tanteen = 476

CHURCHES:

None

ENEMY FORCES:

Fred Taith and the woman he lives with in the house
     Dangerous - Worker.
David Ottway - Petty Bourg - Dangerous
Charlie Francis - Petty Bourg - Less Dangerous
Sonny Collins - Worker - Less Dangerous

OUR FORCES:

1 N.W.O - 9 - 11 persons
P.S.G - 9 persons

CONTACTS:

7 - 2

Patrick James
Lennox Adonis
Vincent Jackman
Harlym

SECRET

SPRINGS

ANALYSIS:

Before the Revolution, the Springs area was a strong Gairy area. When the G.U.L.P won its first election, the G.N.P had only 5- 10 supporters to Gairy 150 - 200 supporters. The Last election which was in 1976, Selwyn Stranchan won his seat in the area. This proved that the number of supporter just before the Revolution had increase for the N.J.M party.

After the Revolution the support for the Party and Govt. has increase. There is some benefits that reached the people in the area such as Milk feeding programme, and house repair programme. But most people in the area felt that the area is neglected by the present Government. This is felt so, because there is no group in the area to organise activities. Groups formation, most times, fail to be organised and to function.-

The majority of people in the area could be classified as Agricultral workers, farmers and some commercial workers.

ECONOMIC OBJECTIVES:

7 shops (private)

SOCIAL OBJECTIVES:

South St. George' Govt. School
Springs field
Springs Post Office
Grenada Baptiste Dental Clinic.

MILITARY OBJECTIVES:

None

POPULATION:

563 people

CHURCHES:

Grenada Baptiste Church - Pastor James -
St. George's Evangicial Church -
Open Bible Church - Pastor Hood -
Baptiste Church - Edmond Gilbert-

SECRET

ENEMY FORCES:

Roy Charles - Petty Bourg - Dangerous

Joseph Neckles - Petty Bourg - Very dangerous (Big Joe)

Dominique - Dangerous - Petty Bourg

Karan Pascal - Dangerous - Petty Bourg (Pastor)

Wilfred Thomas - Dangerous - Petty Bourg

Vendor at Charlie David Gas station - Very dangerous - Petty Bour

Mrs. Checkle - Dangerous - Bourg

George WORM - Very Dangerous - Worker

OUR FORCES:

Parish Council members of over 30 persons

STRENGTH OF THE MILITIA:

None

PAST AND PRESENT COUNTER REVOLUTIONARY ACTIVITIES:

None

CONTACTS:

Mr. Benioth

Maria Celestine

Mrs. Benioth

Saga

SECRET

ANALYSIS:

Belmont is one of the largest area in the south. Most families earn a living due to the father or the male in the house being a Dock worker. There is some commercial workers and agricultral workers.

Belmont before the Revolution was a Gariy strong area. Gariy had organise the Dock workers around him resulting in a strong base for his Government. The former government had a strong support base among the elderly people. Due to these facts there was still some conflict among the Dock workers and some of the elderly people that was supporting his Government, because there was constant clashes between the Mongoose Gang and the Belmont Dock workers during the reign of his Government. Although these clashes, some of the Dock Workers still remain loyal to the Gariy Government. During the latter years of Gariy ruling the middle class section of the people in the area was anti Gariy, but there is a few middle class elements who still loyal to Gariy.

After the Revolution the area have benefit from the programmes being put out by the P.R.G. In the beginning of the Revolution period many people came out in support of the overthrow, mainly the youths. The majority of these youths still give full support to the Revolution. The majority of mass activities organise by the P.R.G, there is always a large turn out to these activities.

ECONOMIC OBJECTIVES:

Butler House
Ministry of Agro Industries
Bryden and Minors(Lagoon Rd)
Grenada Yacth Service (Lagoon Rd)
Genreal Control (Lagoon Rd)
Gleans Garage (LagoonRd)
Grenada Tyre Service Lagoon Rd)
Mc Intyre Bros. (Lagoon Rd)
Patio Bar (Lagoon Rd)
Ross Combine Workshop (Lagoon Rd)
Univeral Supplies (Lagoon Rd)
The Ware House (Jean Anglias)
Maitland Garage
Papaty Garage
8 private shops
St. Ann Guest House
Skyline   "   "
Cresent Inn

C

SOCIAL OBJECTIVES:

International Mediation Society

Robertson Convalescent Home

Mrs. Black Pre- Primary School

Picker Patch Pasture (Lagoon Rd)

Reservoir (Jean Anglais)

Pandy Community Center

Belmont Soceity Hall

MILITARY OBJECTIVES:

Ministry of Interior Unit

POPULATION:

1,863 people

CHURCHES:

Grenada Baptiste Church - Paster James -

Catholic Church now under construction

ENEMY FORCES:

Vernon Edwards - Worker - Very Dangerous

Mr. Maitland (Lagoon Rd) - Petty Boug - Dangerous

Linclon Ross - (" ") - Petty Boug - Less Dangerous

Phinsley St. Louis - Petty Bourg - Dangerous

OUR FORCES:

Pioneer Group - 1

N.Y.O Group - 1

N.W.O Group - 1

Parish Council members - over 50 members

P.S.G

CONTACTS:

Ian Wilson

Isiah Trail

Kelvin Howell

Sharon Coutain

Brian Birzan

Nickolas St. John

Mrs. Beryl Coutain

James Eddie

7 - 6

PRESENT AND PAST COUNTER REVOLUTIONARY ACTIVITIES:

SECRET

GRAND ANSE

ANALYSIS:

Before the Revolution, the Grand Anse area was a Gariy strong hole. The people relied mostly on the Tourist Trade in the area, due to so many Tourist Vendors. The others wree made up of Hotels workers.

In that area Gariy had his Green Beast army, his personal business places, where most of his night life was spent. Gariy had organised the Community Buliders Movement, which had key persons in it , such as Dowson Calliste, Phillis Taith, the Mc Intyres excluding Jessey. Gariy had the largest percentage of unionise workers living in the area and there was a union office situated in the area. The Tourist vendors and hotel workers base in his union.

The army and police used to carry out regular checks and patrol in the area and made search in homes of the strongest supporters of the N.J.M party, one such example is Ambrose Phillip. Besides these roughnecks, Gariy also had many informers in the area. About 65% of the people support went to Gariy.

Grand Anse was one of the area that Gariy was determine to carry out Operation Boothstrap. He used to bring his supporters into the area to do the work. In the area of sports Gariy again organised the Grand Anse women, such as the Mc Intyres and many of the youths. A sporting complex built in the area also. The main people who control the sporting activities in the Grand Anse area are still the Mc Intyres A housing Scheme was also built in the area in which most of his supporters, his Green Beast men, Secret Policemen and policemen who obtain houses. In the area many of the Gariy supporters were armed, mainly in the Mt. Hartman area.

After the Revolution many of the Gariy supporters became inactive, due to the absent of the firm Gariy supporters, such as "Sparrow". The initial respond to the Revolution by the youths in the area was good, because at the beginning most of these youths picked up gun when their wree told to come out. The work done by the Revolutionaries among the Gariy supporters was able to moved them to the Revolution side (house repair, milk distribution programme, the drain project in the Mt. Hartman area and other programmes of the Revolution). The strength of the Revolution mobolisation manisfested itself in the clean up drive during the first Festival of the Revolution. Gariy had difficulty in mobolising the people.

The manners being put on the counters in the country prevented the most backward of the Gariy ites to keep calm. The Cubans presence in the area helped the Gariy supporters in organising maroons and helped out the peopel in general. The personal relationship some of the Cubans build the Gariy supporters also moved them to the Revolution side.

ECONOMIC OBJECTIVES:

Sheep and Pig Farm (Mt. Hartman)

ECONOMIC OBJECTIVES CON'T:

Carib Factory	Wave Crest
Guy Furniture	Sliver Sands
Cuban Airline Service	Riverea
Carin Travel Service	Spice Inn Hotel
Cocanut Grove	Cinimon Hill
The Sugar Mill Dico	Flying Dutchman
The Grand Anse Shopping Center	Flambouyant
Maffakihs Inn	Carifta Cottages
Palm Court	Apple Inn
South Winds	The Coffee Shop
Agro Industries Plant	Hibiscus Inn
Hubbards Warehouses	Blue Horizon
Southern Const. Ltd	Grenada Property Management Ltd (Golf Land)
Govt. Warehouse and Stored Room	P.R.A Garage
GRAND ANSE SERVICE ONTRE	

SOCIAL OBJECTIVES:

The Dome

The Day Nursery

School for the Mental Handicapped (limes)

Grand Anse Post Office

"   " R.C. School

Upper Grand Anse Pre- Primary School

Lower Grand Anse   "   "   "

Universal School of Med.

Grand Anse Community Center

The Grand Anse Sporting Complex

The Golf Course or Club

Grenada/Venezuela Corporation

MILITARY OBJECTIVES:

South St.George Police Station

Camp Boney

The Logistics Center(True Blue)

CHURCHES:

GRAND ANSE R C Church - Revrent Laventine -

Grand Anse Berean Bible Church - Pastor Briggs -

Jahovha Witness (not yet establish) -

Church of God (meet in the Community center)-

SECRET

ENEMY FORCES CON'T:

Knight – Petty Bourg – Dangerous (George)

Raymond Anson – Petty Bourg – Less Dangerous

Mrs.Ines – Working Class – Less Dangerous

Lela Mc Intyre – Working Class – Dangerous

Emison Mc Intyre – Working Class – Less Dangerous

Clovis Moore – Working Class

Mrs.Frank – (baby) – Working Class – Less dangerous

OUR FORCES:

2 – N.Y. O

2 – N.W.O

Parish Council members over 70

P.S.G.

COUNTER- REVOLUTIONARY ACTIVITIES:

None

PRESENT COUNTER- REVOLUTIONARY ACTIVITIES:

None

CONTACTS:

Elisha St Louis

Lennox Maximay

Brian Beggs

Ralph James

Martin Calliste

Vincent Nathan

population:

2,335

83- GOLF COURSE

208- FREQUENTE

STRENGTH OF THE MILITIA:

Average of 15 – 20

ANALYSIS OF THE AREA:

Before the Revolution the Marian area was a Gairy strong hole as the other villages in the south. The area is made up of many religious elements. The area is also a very backward area. Many of the older heads are farmers in which Sugar Cane is the main crop.

Since the Revolution, some benefits had reach the people in the Marian area. Due to those benefits the Revolution and the N.J.M Party have gain many support from the masses.

Although there is strong support from the masses in the area of Marian, there is some setbacks in the area when it comes community work in the area. Because of the large percentage of religious elements and persons that are going to church community projects in the area is very very low, an example of such project is the building of the Community Center which is a on going project for over two or more years. The people who come out to do the work, are always a few members of the P.S.G (Party Support Group).

ECONOMIC OBJECTIVES:

Evelyn Sugar Mill
3 private shops

SOCIAL OBJECTIVES:

Community Center
1 private school

MILITARY OBJECTIVES:

Nil

POPULATION:

526 people

CHURCHES:

Pentecostal Church -
Baptiste Church -

ENEMY FORCES:

Nil

SECRET

STRENGTH OF THE MILITIA:

    15 comrades

PAST AND PRESENT COUNTER REVOLUTIONARY ACTIVITIES:

    Nil

CONTACTS:

    Ivy Bain

    Ellioth Bishop

SECRET

CALIVIGNY

ANALYSIS OF THE AREA:

The Calivigny area is made up mainly of small farmers, some peasent and public workers. The area is also very religious as the Marian area. Before the Revolution, generally the area was a Gairy area. Gairy had the most support among the elderly people, to be more correct, the peasents and farmers, many of them still believed that Gairy will enter politics again in Grenada.

Youth before the Revolution was fully in support of the party in their struggle against the Dictatorship regime, and for a change just around the 1979 period and did support the Revolution when it came.

After the Revolution, because of the programmes of the Revolution such as milk feeding programme, house repair and other programme being put out, the majority of these youths are still supporting the Revolution.

The area is very quiet and some of the people are very selfish. But due to this fact, the people come out in large numbers to participate in what ever the P.R.G organise or the community organise.

ECONOMIC OBJECTIVES:

2 Garages

6 private shops

SOCIAL OBJECTIVES:

Nil

MILITARY OBJECTIVES:

Camp Fedon

POPULATION:

477 people

CHURCHES:

Calivigny Emmanuel Baptiste Church - Pastor Green -

Gospel Hall -

ENEMY FORCES:

7 - 12   Wilfred Ross - Less dangerous - Petty bourg

Banfield - Less dangerous - Bourg (Preacher)

SECRET

<u>PAST AND PRESENT COUNTER REVOLUTIONARY ACTIVITIES:</u>

Nil

<u>STRENGTH OF THE MILITIA:</u>

5 - 9 members

<u>CONTACTS:</u>

Ferron Lowe

Kenny James

Edwin Frank.

J B

SECRET

MORNE ROUGE Con't

PRESENT ENEMY ACTIVITIES:

Nil

OTHER SOCIAL OBJECTIVES IN THE SOUTH:

1 NTS from town to Calliste

1 NTS from town to Grand Anse and around Morne Rouge strecth

1 NTS from Morne Jaloux through Marian back to town

1 NTS from town through Springs to Woodlands and Woburn back to town.

SECRET

POINT SALINE Con't:

SOCIAL OBJECTIVES:

Point Saline Light House

MILITARY OBJECTIVES:

Cuban Mission

POPULATION:

39 people

MORNE ROUGE

ECONOMIC OBJECTIVES:

Carifta Cottages   Spice Inn Hotel
African Night Club   Blue Horizon
Flying Dutchman   Hibiscus Inn
B.B.C Night Club   Cinimon Hill
Flambouyant

SOCIAL OBJECTIVES:

Consulate Of The Netherlands
Radio Free Grenada
St. George's School Of Medcine
USSR Embassy

MILITARY OBJECTIVES:

Camp Boney
South Police Station

POPULATION:

270

PAST ENEMY ACTIVITIES:

SECRET

LANSE AUX EPINES

ECONOMIC OBJECTIVES:

    Lanse Aux Epines Cottages
    Steven's & Co Ltd
    Spice Island Charters (G/da)

SOCIAL OBJECTIVES:

    1 Playing Field

MILITARY OBJECTIVES:

    None

POPULATION:

    494

TRUE BLUE

ECONOMIC OBJECTIVES:

    Fishing School

SOCIAL OBJECTIVES:

    Selwyn Stranchan home
    St. George's University School Of Medicine

POPULATION:

    66 people

POINT SALINE

ECONOMIC OBJECTIVES:

CALLISTE

ECONOMIC OBJECTIVES:

Three (3) private shops
International Airport Site

SOCIAL OBJECTIVES:

Calliste Government School   Cuban Ambassador
Calliste Medical Center
Old Transmitting Station

MILITARY OBJECTIVES:

None

POPULATION:

495 people

CHURCHES:

Berean Bible Church - Mr. Miller -

ENEMY FORCES:

OUR FORCES:
1 N.Y.O
1 N.W.O
P.S.G

STRENGTH OF THE MILITIA:

ENEMY ACTIVITIES, PAST AND PRESENT:
None

CONTACTS:

SECRET

ANALYSIS OF THE AREA:

The political outlook and social outlook of the people and the area before the Revolution was a very backward one. The people was hostile towards the New Jewel Movement at the beginning. The area before the Revolution was a strong hole for government.

The lively hood of the people are made up mainly small cane farmers, some fishermen and small section involved in services with the majority engage in farming.

Just before the Revolution there was about 55% anti- gairy people in the area, but since the Revolution support for the Revolution and the Government has drop, due to the problem of political backwardness and some reactionary elements which makes it impossible for proper mobilization in the different activities organise by the P.R.G.

In the village there is no kind of facilities to carry out any social function, which as a result, maybe, the main reason for the high level of backwardness. However, inspite of the political outlook of the people there is no real signs of counter-revolutionary threath.

SECRET

WOODLANDS

ECONOMIC OBJECTIVES:

    The Grenada Sugar Factory
    Three (3) private shops

SOCIAL OBJECTIVES:

    Water Pump (behind the Sugar Factory)

MILITARY OBJECTIVES:

    None

POPULATION:

    611 People

CHURCHES:

    Berean Chapel - Wilmus Neptune - 30
    A.M.E Baptiste Church - Gladys Clarence -
    Woodlands Baptiste Church - Shirley Bowen -
    St. Philomena Church - Claris Peterkin -
    New Testiment - Phillip Bonaparte - 15

ENEMY FORCES:

    Cosmos Fitz Roy Williams - Petty Bourg - Very dangerous
    Lloyd Griffith - Worker - Dangerous

OUR FORCES:

    1 N.Y.O - 28 - 30 persons
    1 N.W.O - 8 - 10 persons

ENEMY ACTIVITIES, PAST AND PRESENT:

    None

STRENGTH OF THE MILITIA:

    10 - Persons

CONTACTS:

Confidentia

Subject: Movements of Visiting Nationalities

In January, February, March and April of 1980 a total of 519, 510, 450 and 300 visiting American Nationals, visited our country. The majority of whom came on vacation. This of course does not include Medical Students.

In the four above mentioned months a number of 200, 237, 175 and 230 British Nationals visited our shores, again the majority of whom came on vacation.

With respect to the Medical Students, studying at the St. George's University School of Medicine, a number of 420, students arrived in the month of January. As for February, March and April, some of the same students departed on private business for a short period. Also a small number of professors and students came for short periods to lecture and study. For the Regionals, there was a number of 420 Trinidadians arriving here for the month of April, while we had 100 Barbadian Nationals, the majority of whom came on vacation.

COMMENTS: For the month of April there was a considerable drop in the number of visiting American Nationals to our shores especially at the early stages of the month. However, there was a rise towards the ending of the month. Also there was a rise in the amount of visiting British Nationals for the month of April, as compared with the other months.

Laurie,

Submitted for your information:

Michael K. Roberts
7/5/80

John Jerome

PLAN OF C.I. OPERATIONS   *Ministry of Interior*

Setting up of command post comprising Major Keith Roberts.
Cpt. H. Romain, Lt. B. Pivotte.

Responsible for analysing all information that are coming in, in
order to pass on to members of the Central Committee.

- Also, one Comrade who we can send to verify situations and
  incidents that have been reported.
- Recorder of all the information coming into the Centre.

MONITORING REGIONALLY - ST. GEORGE'S

City - three (3) Officers

Dock, Carenage - one (1) Officer

St. Paul's - two (2) Officers

ST. JOHN'S

One (1) Officer plus Party Cadres - Valdon

ST. PATRICK'S

Reports from Jan

ST. ANDREW'S

Two (2) Officers plus Party Cadres - Re Gill
Regular hourly report from all officers and Party Cadres being
ed for this purpose.

Carenage

Monitoring of all Embassies a-nd Diplomats in this period

(ii)   To control the movements of all diplomats, with the purpose
         of revealing the links with possible counter elements.

(iii)   Stop any possibility of them actively using this period to
         create distrubances and confusion and a major counter-actions.

(iv)   Monitoring of all visitors who have been in Grenada ov = four
         weeks and more.

(v)   Study the incoming visitors of the various counters to see
         the composition of visitors.

(vi)   Checking and controlling the key middle class elements who
         have links with diplomats, and influence in some section of the
         society.

(vii)   Check the hotels to see if visitors are leaving before their
         scheduled time or the booking question.

MEDICAL SCHOOL

Monitor all students during this period.

Check the mood and movements of the school hirachy and professors
during this period.

CHURCH

Monitor all sermons by the various parish priests and preachers in
the society.

The controlling of all hirachy meeting of the church in particular
the Catholic and Anglicans.

Controlling all elements of the society that pay visits to the
hirachy.

Tapping of the Hirachy of all the leading counter churches phones.

ESSENTIAL SERVICES

Physical protection of the key installations against sabotage.

...... meeting of confidence people xx to ensure that any signs of

...... be identified.

Getting a general operative picture of the area in which the key installations are located.

Checking of mails of dangerous elements.

Tapping and disconnection of dangerous elements phones.

Check all Heads of Ministries to see if they have any important documents which needs to be secured.

Special control over technicians who are not very firm and cannot be replaced.

COAST GUARD

Establish communication with watch towers.

Boat patrols on a nightly basis.

Documentation of all telephone calls and security reports from various regions.

Special Branch Office,
St. George's,
May 21, 1980.

From: Head Special Branch

To :   Minister of National Security, Comrade Prime Minister.

Subject: Special Branch Areas of Work

    The old MI 5 methods of work, after experimentation,
have proven to be not effective enough. It consisted of speaking
to 'Confident Persons' and General 'Patrols'. The use of the agent
was not sufficently developed and utilized. Therefore upon the
completion of my instructions with Comrade JAMIL and BRUNO, I did
the following:

(a) Cut up the island into intelligence districts
and assigning officers to same.

(b) Lectured to officers on the use and control
of agents.

(c) Appoint a chief of Operations (which was not
in effect before my time).

(d) Organise areas of concentration.

(e) Hold regular meetings with my officers on
work, progress etc.

(f) Because of our limited transport resources
allowed officers in the out districts to
operate from their homes, instead, as was the
custom, coming to St. George's every day and
doing 'patrols'.

    Apart from these INtelligence Districts I have assigned officers
to deal with specific areas.

    Hereunder are the areas:

(a) Government Departments

/

578

(2)

(b) Trade Unions

(c) The Police

(d) School of Medicine

(e) The Churches

We are also requested by Cabinet, from time to time, to do Character Investigation on applicants who desire citizen-ship. The Immigration Department links directly with Special Branch into matter of issue of passports to certain persons and on matters of deportations, that we might have to carry out from time to time.

COMMENTS: Submitted for your information.

signature

HEAD SPECIAL BRANCH

c.c. P.H. File
    L. James

COMRADES TO COMPLETE FIVE (5) YEARS BY MARCH 13th '84

NO	RANK	NAMES	REMARKS
1.	Major	Einstien Louison	
2.	Major	Basil Gahagan	
3.	Major	Chris Stroude	
4.	Lt.	Cecil Prime	
5.	2Lt.	Chris Parke	
6.	Captain	Lester Redhead	
7.	2Lt.	George Cherebin	
8.	Lt.	Julien Andrews	
9.	2Lt.	Crispin Hypolite	
10.	2Lt.	Lennox Taylor	Studies USSR
11.	Captain	Carl Hyacinth	Studies USSR
12.	Lt. Col.	Ewart Layne	Studies USSR
13.	2Lt.	Allan Lowe	Studies USSR
14.	2Lt.	Adrian Dewsbury	
15.	O/CDT	David Francis	
16.	Sgt.	Daniel Franklyn	By April
17.	Sgt.	Alister John	
18.	Sgt.	Dorset Peters	
19.	Cpl	Norril Richards	
20.	Cpl	Aden Alexander	
21.	WO2	Richard Browne	
22.	2Lt.	Micheal Bridgeman	
23.	WO1	Vincent Richards	
24.	Sgt.	Wendell Redhead	
25.	WO2	Benedict Bubb	
26.	Pte	Winston Knight	
27.	L/Cpl	John Oliver	
28.	Cpl	Leroy Mc Sween	
29.	Cpl	Micheal Donald	
30.	Cde.	Bernadette Gittens	
31.	L/Cpl	Vernon Francis	
32.	Cpl	Keith Phillip	
33.	L/Cpl	Joshua Beggs	
34.	P.F.C.	Colley Bubb	By April
35.	Pte	Rodney Langdon	
36.	L/Cpl	Joseph Mc Donlad	
37.	WO1	Samuel Mignon	
38.	Sgt.	Joseph Philbert	

EC	RANK	NAMES	REMARKS
39.	L/Cpl	Lenard Thomas	
40.	P.F.C.	Yvonne Thomas	By April
41.	P.F.C.	Allen Williams	
42.	WO1	Morgan Gabriel	
43.	WO2	Kenneth Gilbert	By April
44.	2Lt.	Kenrick Fraser	
45.	L/Cpl	Thomas Alexander	
46.	P.F.C.	Jimmy Abraham	
47.	WO2	Stephen Kingston	
48.	O/CDT	Rudolph Charles	
49.	Pte	Stephen Cadore	
50.	2Lt.	Raeburn Nelson	
51.	Cpl	Ainsley Baptiste	
52.	Cpl	Anthony Whiteman	
53.	L/Cpl	Danley Thomas	
54.	P.F.C.	Danley Alexander	By April '84
55.	L/Cpl	Raymond Charles	By April '84
56.	WO2	Ian Jones	
57.	P.F.C.	Marrast Paul	
58.	WO2	Winston Francis	
59.	Cpl	Ian Joseph	By April
60.	Cpl	Eric Lambert	By April
61.	WO2	Vernon Gabriel	
62.	L/Cpl	Godwin Lashington	
63.	Sgt.	George Nowl	
64.	L/Cpl	Osbert Felix	
65.	L/Cpl	Christopher Andrews	By April
66.	P.F.C.	Charlie Surallie	
67.	WO2	Leslie Noel	Studies USSR
68.	WO1	Rudolph Philbert	
69.	L/Cpl	Alston Francis	
70.	Cpl	Nicholas John	
71.	Cpl	Vincent Joseph	
72.	WO1	Clyde Francis	
73.	Cpl	Joseph Pavy	
74.	L/Cpl	Charles Richards	
75.	Sgt.	Theophillus Walters	
76.	Sgt.	Byron Cameron	
77.	Wo2	Llewellyn Archibald	
78.	2Lt.	Junior Harris	
79.	Cpl	James Hazzard	
80.	L/Cpl	Cleveroy Lessey	
81.	Cpl	Layne La Mothe	
82.	Sgt.	Jude St.Bernard	

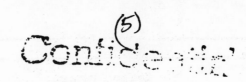

Head Special Branch (2)   SB St. George's,
                                              May 7, 1980.

                    Subject: Movements of Visiting Nationalities

        In January, February, March and April of 1980 a total
of 519, 510, 450 and 300 visiting American Nationals, visited
our country. The majority of whom came on vacation. This of
course does not include Medical Students.

        In the four above mentioned months a number of 208, 237,
175 and 230 British Nationals visited our shores, again the
majority of whom came on vacation.

        With respect to the Medical Students, studying at the St.
George'S University School of Medicine, a number of 520, students
arrived in the month of January. As for February, March and
April, some of the same students departed on private business for
a short period. Also a small number of professors and students
came for short periods to lecture and study. For the Regionals,
there is a number of 420 Trinidadians arriving here for the month
of April, while we had 100 Barbadian Nationals, the majority of
whom came on vacation.

COMMENTS: For the month of April there was a considerable drop
in the number of visiting American Nationals to our shores especially
at the early stages of the month. However, there was a rise towards
the ending of the month. Also there was a rise in the amount of
visiting British Nationals for the month of April, as compared with
the other months.

Maurice

Submitted for Your Information:

Michael K. Roberts
7/5/80

                                        John Jerome

GOVERNMENT OF GRENADA

FROM: LANGSTON SIBBLIES, DIRECTOR OF PUBLIC PROSECUTIONS .... FILE No ....

TO: CDE. MAURICE BISHOP, PRIME MINISTER .... DATE 26th January, 1982 ....

SUBJECT   DETAINEES

List of Detainees currently charged before the Courts:

	Name	Charge
A)	1. Teddy Victor	Possession of Explosive Substance (S.6 Terrorism (Prevention) Law)
B)	2. Wilton De Raviniere	"
	3. Kennedy Budhlall	Conspiracy to commit acts of terrorism (April 26th Plot) S.10 Terrorism Law
	4. Raphael Roberts	" "
	5. Joseph Jacobs	" "
	6. Keith St. Bernard	" "
	7. Lyle St. Bernard	" "
	8. Godwin Charles	" "
	9. Antonio Langdon	Attempting to escape lawful custody (S.3 Preventive Detention Regulations)
	10. Winston Crowe	" "
	11. Adrian Roberts	Failing to disclose information about terrorists (S.13 Terrorism Law)
E)	12. Glenn Beggs	" "
	13. Winston Simon	" "
	14. Ronald Lewis	" "
F)	15. Eddie Richardson	Conspiracy to commit acts of terrorism (June 19th) (S.10 terrorism Law) Also failing to disclose information S.13.
	16. Jimmy Julien	Causing death by explosive substance (S.3 terrorism law) (Nov. 17th)
	17. Richard Pascall	" "
	18. Denzil Richardson	Conspiracy to commit acts of terrorism (S.10)
J. (G)	19. Isaac James	" "
	20. Annas Pascall	" "
	21. Catherine Pascall	" "
	22. Matthew Pascall	" "
	23. Helen Pascall	Possession of Explosive Substance (S.6 Terrorism Law)
(H)	24. Terrence Bernard	" "
	25. Errol Gitters	" "
	26. Kent Bain	Assaulting Prison Officer (S.52 Prison Act)
(I)	27. Reginald Phillip	" "
	28. Rodney Garraway	" "
	29. Anthony Buckmire	" "

/ Detainees .....

(J) 30. Kent Bain

(K) 31.

B46

Detainees who have been referred to the Police for charges to be laid.

1. Raphael Boyke   Harbouring escapee (S.3 Preventive
                                    Detention Regulations)
2. Dutty Housten
3. Kade Layne
4. Rodney Garraway
5. Errol Charles
6. Martin Benoit

The following detainees have recently been convicted of Escaping
Lawful Custody and sentenced to one year imprisonment:

1. Emmanuel Charles
2. Derek Romain
3. Hudson Nimblette.

The following detainees have been committed to stand trial at the
Assizes:

1. Teddy Victor
2. Antonio Langdon
3. Winston Crowe

Langston Sibblies,
Director of Public Prosecutions.

LIST OF PERSONS IN DETENTION
AS OF 22ND JULY 1981

HOPE VALE

No.	NAME	ALIAS	ADDRESS	DATE DETAINED	PLACE DETAINED
1	NOEL ALEXANDER	Saga	Hermitage, St. Patrick's	29-6-81	Santeurs
2	HARRY DAILEY	Cultureman	Tivoli, St. Andrew's	27-6-81	Tivoli
3	DESMOND FREDERICK	Jah Idom	Hermitage, St. Patrick's	27-6-81	Hermitage
4	PERCY THOMAS		Montrose, St. Patrick's	27-6-81	Montrose
5	DOMINIC HAMLET	Rastafero	Madeys, St. Patrick's	25-6-81	Madeys
6	DERICK GOODING	Neptali	Tivoli, St. Andrew's	27-6-81	Tivoli
7	ALLAN MITCHELL	Bagga	Gouyave, St. John's	26-6-81	Gouyave
8	LEROY CHARLES	I Trad Rasta Geese	Tivoli, St. Andrew's	27-6-81	Tivoli
9	WILLIE JOSEPH		Belair, St. Andrew	26-6-81	Belair
10	STEVE RICHARDSON	Go Cool	Mt. Rich, St. Patrick's	25-6-81	Mt. Rich
11	LAWRENCE PHILLIP		Mt. Rich, St. Patrick's	25-6-81	Mt. Rich
12	KENNETH WILLIAMS	Ras Klacks	Hermitage, St. Patrick's	26-6-81	Hermitage
13	DEXTER BERNARD	Rasta Gay	Mt. Rich, St. Patrick's	26-6-81	Mt. Rich
14	WINSTON JAMES	Ras Ilie	Mt. Rich, St. Patrick's	25-6-81	Mt. Rich
15	CLARKE PAUL		Mt. Rich, St. Patrick's	25-6-81	Mt. Rich
16	MANLEY FRANCIS	Ras Cool	Mt. Rich, St. Patrick's	25-6-81	Mt. Rich
17	MERLYN PHILLIP	Ras Herb	Mt. Rich, St. Patrick's	25-6-81	Mt. Rich
18	CHRISTOPHER DELVES	Chris	Belmont, St. George's	4-7-81	St. George's
19	TREVOR HISSESSAR		Conference, St. Andrew's	12-7-81	Conference
20	HILTON ALEXANDER		Ryelands, St. Andrew's	12-7-81	Ryelands
21	LAWRENCE WILLIAMS		Grand Roy, St. John's	12-7-81	Grand Roy
22	EDMOND CHARLES		Mayah, St. Andrew's	12-7-81	Mayah
23	IRVIN CORNWALL		La Tasse, St. Patrick's	12-7-81	La Tasse
24	EDWIN JALDOO		Mayah, St. Andrew's	12-7-81	Mayah
25	PHILLIP CHARLES		Mamma Cannes, St. Andrew's	11.7.81	Mamma Cannes
26	WILFRED DE RAVENIERE	Calt	Pomme Rose, St. David's	11-7-81	Pomme Rose
27	ELVIN SPARKS	Fox	La Tante, St. David's	11-7-81	La Tante
28	GORDON REGHIN		Pomme Rose, St. David's	11-7-81	Pomme Rose
29	TERYL NOEL	Smalls	Piedmontemps, St. David's	11-7-81	Piedmontemps
30	GODWIN VICTOR	Sep	Vincennes, St. David's	11-7-81	Vincennes
31	JEROME MITCHELL	Gry Fox	Vincennes, St. David's	11-7-81	Vincennes
32	ANDERSON HAGLEY		Vincennes, St. David's	11-7-81	Vincennes
33	WAYNE HAGLEY		Vincennes, St. David's	11-7-81	Vincennes
34	PAUL EDWARDS		La Tante, St. David's9	11-7-81	La Tante
35	THOMAS GILBERT	"SGUARES"	Windsor Forest, St. David's	11-7-81	W/Forest
36	OUTTY HOUSTON	Ooty I	Mayah, St. Andrew's	13-7-81	Mayah
37	CHESTER PAUL	I Forward	Happy Hill, St. George's	13-7-81	St. George's
38	BENEDICT CHARLES	I Dreamer	Tivoli, St. Andrew's	27-6-81	Tivoli
39	FRANCIS CHARLES	I Man	Harford Village, St. And.	13-7-81	Harford Vill.
40	ISIAH HENRY	I Far I	Harford Village, St. And.	9-7-81	Harford Vill.

-2-

CENTRAL POLICE STATION

1.	GEORGE FERGUSON	Geek	Calliste, St. George's	11-7-81	St. George's
2	MICHAEL COARD	Sends	Baddeck, St. George's	11-7-81	St. George's
3	HAROLD KELLY	Funkie	River Road, St. George's	17-6-81	St. George's
4	GLENN BRUNO		Mardi Gras, St. Pauls	3-6-81	St. George's
5	ERROL MAITLAND		Belmont, St. George's	19-7-81	St. George's

FORT RUPERT

1	STANLEY ROBERTS		Piedmontemps, St. David's	11-7-81	Piedmontemps
2	VINCENT CLYNE		St. David's	14-7-81	St. David's
3	RONALD MC SWEEN	Ooo La La	Piedmontemps, St.David's	14-7-81	Piedmontemps
4	WINSTON CROME	Ras Mang Mang	River Road, St.George's	11-7-81	St. George's
5	TILLMAN THOMAS		Hermitage, St. Patricks	11-7-81	
6	LLOYD NOEL		Gouyave, St. Johns	11-7-81	Gouyave
7	LESLIE PIERRE		Fort Jeudy, St. David's	11-7-81	Fort Jeudy
8	MICHAEL JOSEPH	Mike	Green Street, St.George's	3-6-81	St. George's
9	TERRIE MCGINTY		Grand Mal, St. George's	3-6-81	St. George's
10	FITZROY SIMON	Sleepy I	Piedmontemps	12-7-81	Piedmontemps
11	KENNETH CLARK	I Jah Como	Grand Bras, St. Andrew's	12-7-81	Gran Bras
12	COLVILLE PROSPER	I More	Paradise, St. Andrew's	12-7-81	Paradise
13	TOGIE CHARLES	Jah I Live	Mirabeau, St. Andrew's	12-7-81	Mirabeau
14	VAN THOMAS	I Jah Ras	La Filette, St Andrew's	12-7-81	La Filette
15	ROY ALBERT	Roots I	Paradise, St. Andrew's	12-7-81	Paradise
16	CLETUS ALEXANDER	Eye Shine Bright	Mt. Reuil, St. Pat.	12-7-81	Mt. Reuil

Note: Of the above total of 61 Detainees, Thirty Three (33) have declared themselves avowed Rastafarians while there are about six (6) others sporting "Dread Locks" but disclaim any connections with Rastafarism.

Nine (9) persons wearing dread locks have elected to cut their hair since detention and have done so. Five (5) of this amount have been released while the other four (4) is still in detention. Signed voluntary requests were taken from each person.

RELEASES

PERSONS RELEASED FROM DETENTION BETWEEN 29TH JUNE and 21ST JULY 1981

NO.	NAME	ADDRESS	DATE DETAINED	DATE RELEASED
	FROM HOPE VALE			
1	EDWARD GEORGE	Hermitage, St. Patrick's	26-6-81	21st July 1981
2	FRANCIS FRANCOIS	Grand Anse, St. George's	26-6-81	14th July 1981
3	PETER LEWIS	Grand Anse, St. George's	26-6-81	14th July 1981
4	TERRANCE MURRAY	Mt. Rich, St. Patrick's	25-6-81	8th July 1981
5	RONNIE PHILLIP	Mt. Rich, St. Patrick's	25-6-81	8th July 1981
6	TERRY FLEMMING	Mt. Rich, St. Patrick's	25-6-81	8th July 1981
7	ANTHONY RICHARDS	Hermitage, St. Patrick's	26-6-81	21st July 1981
8	MICHAEL RAEBURN	Mt. Rich, St. Patrick's	25-6-81	8th July 1981
9	FRANK THOMAS	Hermitage, St. Patrick's	26-6-81	21st July 1981
10	LENOX LEWIS	Mt. Rewil, St Patrick's	26-6-81	8th July 1981
11	WILSON BAPTISTE	Tivoli, St.Andrew's	27-6-81	21st July 1981
12	LEROY GEORGE	Hermitage, St. Patrick's	26-6-81	21st July 1981
	CENTRAL POLICE STATION			
1	RUBY MURRAY	Mt. Rich, St. Patrick's	26-6-81	3rd July 1981
2	AUDITH ANDREW	Happy Hill, St. George's	12-7-81	20th July 1981
3	VERNON BUCKMIRE	La Mode, St. George's	11-7-81	20th July 1981

OFFICE OF SPECIAL INVESTIGATIONS
BUTLER HOUSE
BELMONT
ST. GEORGE'S-

29th September 1981.

TO: THE PRIME MINISTER AND MINISTER OF THE INTERIOR AND DEFENCE.

Comrade Prime Minister,

The Task Force appointed by the Prime Minister, Comrade Maurice Bishop, a few
months ago, with specific responsibility to deal with "Detainees Affairs" met
yesterday afternoon in the office of the Director of Public Prosecutions.

The Task Force is composed of Comrades Miles Fitzpatrick, Legal Consultant in
the Ministry of Legal Affairs, Langston Sibblies, Director of Public Prosecutions,
Pat Mc Leish, Commissioner of Prisons and Victor Husbands, Special Investigator.

In view of the following factors; (1) the over population of the Prisons which
now stand at 353 with detainees at Richmond Hill Prisons alone accounting for some
161 while at Hope Vale there are 46; (2) the attendant high costs of maintenance
and (3) the passing of an Amendment to the Preventive Detention Regulations (Peoples Law No.21 of 1979) providing for a Restriction Order which may be imposed upon
a released Detainee with severe penalties for infringement (vide Peoples Law No.29
of 1981), the Task Force has taken a unanimous decision to recommend the release
of a number of Detainees in the first instance, who it feels, are no longer threats
to the Security of the State, nor to Public Safety and Order.

Accordingly, I have been delegated to prepare the following report and to forward same to you for your consideration.

In the light of the provisions of the Restriction Order referred to above, a
copy of which is atached for your perusal, it is recommended that the following named
Detainees, regarded as common criminals whose specific crimes are burglary and
housebreaking and who were originally detained to preserve Public Safety during the
Festival of the Revolution on the recommendations of the Police, be released.

Since their detention was not accasioned by involvement in subversive and/or
counter revolutionary activities, their release is recommended under the imposition
of a Restriction Order compelling them to report to the Police Station in their
district or the nearest such Station, twice per month for a period of two (2) years:

1. KADE LAYNE (6-3-80) Belmont, St. George's.
2. ANTHONY HUCKMIRE (6-3-80) River Road, St. George's.
3. DENNIS FARRIER (9-3-81) St. George's
4. COSMOS MC INTYRE (9-3-81) St. George's
5. STEPHEN SCOTT (9-3-81) Mt. Gay, St. George's
6. DAVID AIRD (9-3-81) St. George's.
7. CUTHBERT JOHN (9-3-81) Tempe, St. George's.
8. FABIAN LEWIS (11-3-81) Carenage, St. George's.
9. IXXE CALLISTE (12-3-81) St. David's.
10. RONALD CHARLES (9-3-81) River Road, St. George's.
11. ERROL CHARLES (6-3-80) Belmont, St. George's.
12. REGINALD PHILLIP (6-3-80) Mt. Parnassus, St. George's
13. RODNEY GARRAWAY (7-3-80) Springs, St. George's
14. MARTIN BERROTTE (9-3-80) Mt. Gay, St. George's
15. RAYMOND STEELE (9-3-81) Morne Jaluax, St. George's
16. CARLYLE PHILLIP (9-3-81) RiverRoad, St. George's
17. SAMUEL BONAPARTE (11-3-81) St. David's.
18. CLIFTON AUGUSTINE (11-3-81) St. David's
19. KENT BAIN (29-4-80) Belmont, St George's.
    (Bracketed dates indicate date detained)

Detained since in the early stages of the Revolution, the following Detainees
are recommended for release based on the following factors; (1) That they are no
longer regarded as threats to the National Security; (2) Their good behaviour

....while in

516

while in detention, (3) Their decision to stay out of politics and most importantly (4) The difficulty in collecting sufficient evidence to bring charges successfully against them in the Courts. They are to be released under the imposition of a Restriction Order as indicated:

1. HERBERT PRUDHOMME (13-3-79)
   Archibald Avenue, St. Geo.

   His movements to be restricted to the Town and Parish of St. George's excluding Happy Hill, Brizan, Willys and New Hampshire, for a period of five (5) years.

2. OLIVER RAEBURN (14-3-79)
   Madeys, St. Patrick's

   His movements to be restricted to the Parish of St. Patrick's for a period of five years.

3. NORTON NOEL (5-4-79)
   Westerhall, St. David's

   His movements to be restricted to the Parish of St. David's for a period of three years and provided further, he signs the conveyance for the Property bought from the previous Govt.

4. ASHLEY CHURCH (13-3-79)
   Grand Anse, St. Geo.

   His movements to be restricted to the Parish of St. George's for a period of three years.

5. TERRANCE JONES (23-3-79)
   Byelands, St. Andrew's

   To report to the Police Station in his district twice monthly for a period of three years.

6. DALTON POPE (25-3-79)
   Sauteurs, St. Patrick's

   To report to the Police Station in his district twice monthly for a period of two years.

7. SYDNEY BARTHOLOMEW (19-5-80)
   Tivoli, St. Andrew's

   To report to the Police Station in his district twice monthly for a period of two years.

8. RALPH THOMPSON (19-6-80)
   Tempe, St. George's

   (Mainly on account of his failing health) To report to the Police Station his district for a period of two years.

9. DAVID COOMANSINGH (13-3-79)
   St. David's

   To report to the Police Station in his district twice monthly for a period of two years.

10. PETER LASHLEY (5-5-80)
    Carenage, St. George's

    To report to the Police Station in his district twice monthly for a period of two years.

11. DAPHNE BAPTISTE (4-7-79)
    St. George's

    To report to the Police Station in her district twice monthly for a period of three years.

12. MAURICE PATTERSON (12-5-80)
    St. George's.

    To report to the Police Station in his district twice monthly for a period of two years.

13. DENNIS ALEXANDER (13-6-80)
    Corinth, St. David's.

    To report to the Police Station in his district twice monthly for a period of two years. Also, must give a firm undertaking for repayment of the sum of $263.87 amassed through Overseas telephone calls while working as Prison Officer at the Richmond Hill Prisons.

14. TANHIL CLARKE (14-3-79)
    Concord, St. John's

    To report to the Police Station in his district twice monthly for a period of two years.

15. DONALLY PATRICK (23-3-79)
    Happy Hill, St. George's

    To report to the Police Station in his district twice montyly for a period of two years.

16. KINGSTON BAPTISTE (14-3-79)

    To report to the Police Station in his district twice monthly for a period of two years.

17. JOHN FORRESTER   (19-6-80)   To report to the Police Station in his dis-
    Birchgrove, St. Andrew's   trict twice monthly for a period of two years

18. FRANCIS ABERDEEN (19-6-80)   To report to the Police Station in his dis-
    Birchgrove, St. Andrew's   trict twice monthly for a period of two years

19. EDWARD NURSE   (19-6-80)   To report to the Police Station in his dis-
    Birchgrove, St. Andrew's   trict twice monthly for a period of two years

The following named Detainees whose release is also recommended, were detained in November 1979 for alleged involvement in the November 1979 plot. There is absolutely no evidence of an incriminating nature available and it is therefore difficult to lay charges against them. The accusations of their involvement cannot be firmly and factually established. Their release is recommended under the imposition of a Restriction Order as indicated:

1. JOHN THOMAS   (17-12-79)   To report to the Police Station in his dis-
   Grand Roy, St. Johns   trict twice monthly for a period of three years

2. CONROY PANYAG (18-12-79)   To report to the Police Station in his dis-
   River Road, St. George's   trict twice monthly for a period of three years

3. STEPHEN CUFFIE (18-12-79)   To report to the Police Station in his dis-
   Grand Anse, St. George's   trict twice monthly for a period of one year in the first instance. See Note below.

4. JAMES MODESTE (18-12-79)   To Report to the Police Station in his dis-
   Grand Roy, St. John's   trict twice monthly for a period of three years.

5. JOSEPH PETERS (17-12-79)   To report to the Police Station in his dis-
   Mt. Granby, St. John's   trict twice monthly for a period of three years.

6. GODWIN CHARLES (17-12-79)   To report to the Police Station in his dis-
   Sauteurs, St. Patrick's   trict twice monthly for a period of three years.

7. BENEDICT GEORGE (18-12-79)   To report to the Police station in his dis-
   Mt. Carmel, St. Andrew's   trict twice monthly for a period of three years.

8. MATTHEW JEREMIAH (16-12-80)   To report to the Police Station in his dis-
   Crochu, St. Andrew's   trict twice monthly for a period of two years.

9. KENNY LALSINGH (15-10-79)   To report to the Police Station in his dis-
   Sauteurs, St. Patrick's   trict twice monthly for a period of two years and also, his movements to be restri-
                                         cted to the Parish of St. Patrick's for a similar period.

10. JEROME ROMAIN (18-12-79)   His movements to be restricted to the Town
    Belmont, St. George's   and Parish of St. George's for a period of two years.

NOTE: Stephen Cuffie, an Ex Policeman, is a Vincentian by birth. His release had been sanctioned a few months ago on the basis of representations made by the St. Vincent Government and the Grenada Conference of Churches but due to the fact that he complained in a written statement, that he was subjected to torture and ill-treatment while held on Fort Rupert, it was decided to stay his release in the interests of unfavourable propaganda. His release was sanctioned at the time on the condition that he be deported to St. Vincent. It is suggested that he be released and allowed to remain in the country for at least one year after which time he may be deported. This might serve to counter any desire on his part to publicise the treatment he received on the Fort.

                                                     Victor Husbands   (183)
                                                                        184B

                                                                      12 - 3

SECTION TWO:
INTERNATIONAL ACTIVITIES

A G R E E M E N T

**between the Government of Grenada and the
Government of the Union of Soviet Socialist
Republics on deliveries from the Union of SSR
to Grenada of special and other equipment**

The Government of Grenada and the Government of the Union
of Soviet Socialist Republics,

guided by aspirations for developing and strengthening
friendly relations between both countries on the principles of
equality, mutual respect of sovereignty and non-interference into
internal affairs,

proceeding from the desire to promote strengthening the
independence of Grenada

and in connection with the request of the Government of
Grenada

Have agreed upon the following:

Article 1

The Government of the Union of Soviet Socialist Republics
shall ensure in 1980-1981 free of charge the delivery to the
Government of Grenada of special and other equipment in nomenc-
lature and quantity according to the Annex to the present Agreement to the amount of 4.400.000 Roubles.

Article 2

The delivery of the equipment listed in the Annex to the present Agreement shall be effected by the Soviet Party by sea, at the port of the Republic of Cuba.

The order of the further delivery of the above equipment from the Republic of Cuba shall be agreed upon between the Grenadian and Cuban Parties.

Article 3

The Government of the Union of SSR at the request of the Government of Grenada shall ensure rendering technical assistance in mastering of the equipment delivered under the present Agreement by receiving Grenadian servicemen for training in the USSR.

The Grenadian servicemen shall be deputed for training in the USSR without their families.

The expenses connected with the Grenadian servicemen's training, upkeep, meals, and equipment in the Soviet military educational establishments as well as with their travel fare from Grenada to the USSR and back shall be borne by the Soviet Party.

Article 4

The Government of the Union of SSR shall ensure free of charge the transfer to the Government of Grenada of necessary technical descriptions, instructions and manuals in standard composition on operation of the special equipment delivered under the present Agreement.

13 - 2

Article 5

The appropriate Grenadian and Soviet organizations shall conclude contracts in which there shall be stipulated the detailed terms and conditions of receiving for training Grenadian servicemen and other services connected with the implementation of the present Agreement.

Article 6

The Government of Grenada shall not without the consent of the Government of the Union of Soviet Socialist Republics sell or transfer, formally or actually, the special equipment, delivered under the present Agreement, the relevant documentation and information or give permission to use the equipment and documentation by a third party or any physical or legal persons but the officials and specialists of the citizenship of Grenada being in the service with the Government of Grenada.

The Government of Grenada and the Government of the Union of SSR shall take all the necessary measures to ensure keeping in secret the terms and conditions of the deliveries, all the correspondence and information connected with the implementation of the present Agreement.

Article 7

The present Agreement comes into force on the date it is signed on.

The Annex is an integral part of the present Agreement.

Done in Havana on October "27", 1980 in two originals, each in the English and Russian languages, both texts being equally valid.

FOR AND ON BEHALF
OF THE GOVERNMENT OF GRENADA

FOR AND ON BEHALF
OF THE GOVERNMENT OF THE UNION
OF SOVIET SOCIALIST REPUBLICS

ANNEX

to Agreement of October "27", 1980

L I S T

of special materiel to be delivered
to Grenada from the Soviet Union in
1980-1981 /free of charge/

Description	Unit of measure	Quantity	Years of delivery 1980	Years of delivery 1981
Artillery and small arms armament				
82-mm mortars, used reconditioned	piece	12	-	12
RPG-7V antitank hand grenade-launchers	piece	24	24	-
Group sets of spare parts /1:9/ to RPG-7V grenade-launchers	set	3	3	-
7,62-mm PKM machine-guns	piece	54	-	54
Group set of spare parts /1:50/ to PKM machine-guns	set	1	-	1
7,62-mm AK submachine-guns, used reconditioned	piece	1000	1000	-
7,62-mm carbines, model 1944, used reconditioned	piece	1500	500	-
Antiaircraft armament				
23-mm ZU-23 antiaircraft mounts	piece	18	6	12
Group sets of spare parts /1:6/ to ZU-23 mounts	set	3	1	2

Description	Unit of measure	Quantity	Years of delivery	
			1980	1981
Repair set of spare parts /1:18/ to ZU-23 mounts	set	1	-	1

Communication means

Radio stations:

Description	Unit of measure	Quantity	1980	1981
R-105M	set	12	12	-
R-108M	set	4	4	-
R-109M	set	4	4	-

Vehicles

Description	Unit of measure	Quantity	1980	1981
GAZ-66-05 vehicles	piece	28	6	22
UAZ-469B jeeps	piece	5	-	5

Ammunition

Description	Unit of measure	Quantity	1980	1981
82-mm mortar rounds with fragmentation shell	thous. pieces	4,5	-	4,5
PG-7V rounds to RPG-7V grenade-launchers	thous. pieces	2,4	2,4	-
23-mm rounds to ZU-23 antiaircraft mounts:				
with fragmentation, high explosive, incendiary projectile	thous. pieces	162,0	54,0	108,0
with armour-piercing, incendiary, tracer projectile	thous. pieces	54,0	18,0	36,0
7,62-mm rifle cartridges with steve-core bullet in clips	thous. pieces	675,0	675,0	-
7,62-mm rifle cartridges without clips:				
with steel-core bullet	thous. pieces	416,0	-	416,0
dummy	thous. pieces	75,0	-	75,0

Description	Unit of measure	Quantity	Years of delivery	
			1980	1981
with B-72 bullet with steel cartridge case	thous. pieces	27,0	-	27,0
with T-46 bullet	thous. pieces	97,2	-	97,2
7,62-mm cartridges, model 1943, without clips:				
with steel-core bullet	thous. pieces	600,0	200,0	400,0
with tracer bullet	thous. pieces	300,0	100,0	200,0
dummy	thous. pieces	75,0	-	75,0
Logistic equipment				
Soldiers'camp tents for 10 men	piece	20	-	20

Spare parts, auxiliary and
training equipment on specifications of the Soviet Party
to the amount of up to
400000 Roubles

СОГЛАШЕНИЕ

между Правительством Гренады и Правительством
Союза Советских Социалистических Республик о
поставках из Союза ССР в Гренаду специального
и другого имущества

Правительство Гренады и Правительство Союза Советских Социалистических Республик,

руководствуясь стремлением к развитию и укреплению дружественных отношений между обеими странами на основе полного равноправия, взаимного уважения суверенитета и невмешательства во внутренние дела,

исходя из желания содействовать укреплению независимости Гренады,

и в связи с обращением Правительства Гренады,

согласились о нижеследующем:

Статья 1

Правительство Союза Советских Социалистических Республик обеспечит в 1980-1981 годах безвозмездно поставку Правительству Гренады специального и другого имущества в номенклатуре и количестве согласно Приложению к настоящему Соглашению на сумму 4.400.000 рублей.

Статья 2

Поставка перечисленного в Приложении к настоящему Соглашению имущества будет произведена Советской Стороной морем в порт Республики Куба. Порядок дальнейшей доставки указанного имущества из Республики Куба к месту назначения в Гренаде будет согласован между Кубинской и Гренадской Сторонами.

Статья 3

Правительство Союза ССР по просьбе Правительства Гренады обеспечит оказание технического содействия в освоении эксплуатации поставляемого по настоящему Соглашению имущества путем приема на обучение в СССР гренадских военнослужащих.

Гренадские военнослужащие направляются для обучения в СССР без семей.

Расходы, связанные с обучением, содержанием, питанием и обмундированием гренадских военнослужащих в советских военных учебных заведениях, а также с их проездом из Гренады в СССР и обратно, Советская Сторона принимает на себя.

Статья 4

Правительство Союза ССР обеспечит безвозмездно передачу Правительству Гренады в установленной комплектации необходимых технических описаний, инструкций и наставлений по эксплуатации поставляемого по настоящему Соглашению специального имущества.

Статья 5

Соответствующие гренадские и советские организации заключат между собой контракты, в которых будут установлены подробные условия приема на обучение гренадских военнослужащих и других услуг, связанных с выполнением настоящего Соглашения.

Статья 6

Правительство Гренады не будет без согласия Правительства Союза Советских Социалистических Республик продавать или передавать, формально или фактически, поставляемое в связи с настоящим Соглашением специальное имущество, документацию и информацию по ним или разрешать пользоваться этим имуществом и документацией третьей стороне и каким бы то ни было физическим или юридическим лицам, кроме должностных лиц и специалистов из граждан Гренады, находящихся на службе у Правительства Гренады.

Правительство Гренады и Правительство Союза ССР примут все зависящие от них меры, которые обеспечат сохранение и тайне условия поставок, всей переписки и информации, связанных с выполнением настоящего Соглашения.

Статья 7

Настоящее Соглашение вступает в силу со дня его подписания. Приложение к Соглашению является его неотъемлемой частью.

Совершено в Гаване 27 октября 1980 года в двух подлинных экземплярах, каждый на английском и русском языках, причем оба текста имеют одинаковую силу.

ПО УПОЛНОМОЧИЮ
ПРАВИТЕЛЬСТВА ГРЕНАДЫ

ПО УПОЛНОМОЧИЮ
ПРАВИТЕЛЬСТВА СОЮЗА СОВЕТСКИХ
СОЦИАЛИСТИЧЕСКИХ РЕСПУБЛИК

13 - 9

ПРИЛОЖЕНИЕ

к Соглашению от "27" октября 1980 года

П Е Р Е Ч Е Н Ь

специального имущества, поставляемого Гренаде
из Советского Союза в 1980-1981 годах
/безвозмездно/

Наименование	Единица измерения	Количество	Годы поставки	
			1980	1981
Стрелково-артиллерийское вооружение				
62-мм минометы, бывшие в эксплуатации, отремонтированные	штука	12	–	12
Ручные противотанковые гранатометы РПГ-7В	штука	24	24	–
Групповые комплекты ЗИПа к гранатометам РПГ-7В /1:9/	комплект	3	3	–
7,62-мм пулеметы ПКМ	штука	54	–	54
Групповой комплект ЗИПа к пулеметам ПКМ /1:50/	комплект	1	–	1
7,62-мм автоматы АК, бывшие в эксплуатации, отремонтированные	штука	1000	1000	–
7,62-мм карабины образца 1944 г., бывшие в эксплуатации, отремонтированные	штука	1500	1500	–
Зенитное вооружение				
23-мм зенитные установки ЗУ-23	штука	18	6	12
Групповые комплекты ЗИПа к установкам ЗУ-23 /1:6/	комплект	3	1	2

Наименование	Единица измерения	Количество	Годы поставки	
			1980	1981
Ремонтный комплект ЗИПа к установкам ЗУ-23 /1:16/	комплект	1	-	1
Средства связи				
Радиостанции:				
Р-105М	комплект	12	12	-
Р-108М	комплект	4	4	-
Р-109М	комплект	4	4	-
Автомобильная техника				
Автомобили ГАЗ-66-05	штука	28	6	22
Автомобили УАЗ-469Б	штука	5	-	5
Боеприпасы				
82-мм минометные выстрелы с осколочной миной	тыс.штук	4,5	-	4,5
Выстрелы ПГ-7В к гранатометам РПГ-7В	тыс.штук	2,4	2,4	-
23-мм выстрелы к зенитным установкам ЗУ-23:				
с осколочно-фугасно-зажигательным снарядом	тыс.штук	162,0	54,0	108,0
с бронебойно-зажигательно-трассирующим снарядом	тыс.штук	54,0	18,0	36,0
7,62-мм винтовочные патроны с пулей со стальным сердечником в обоймах	тыс.штук	675,0	675,0	-
7,62-мм винтовочные патроны без обойм:				
с пулей со стальным сердечником	тыс.штук	416,0	-	416,0
для холостой стрельбы	тыс.штук	75,0	-	75,0

13 - 11

Наименование	Единица измерения	Количест-во	Годы поставки	
			1980	1981
с пулей Б-32 со стальной гильзой	тыс.штук	27,0	-	27,0
с пулей Т-46	тыс.штук	97,2	-	97,2
7,62-мм патроны образца 1943г. без обоям:				
с пулей со стальным сердечником	тыс.штук	600,0	200,0	400,0
с трассирующей пулей	тыс.штук	300,0	100,0	200,0
для холостой стрельбы	тыс.штук	75,0	-	75,0
Имущество тыла				
Палатки лагерные солдатские 10-местные	штука	20	-	20

Запасные части, учебное
и вспомогательное имуще-
ство по спецификациям
Советской Стороны
на сумму до 400000 рублей

A G R E E M E N T

between the Government of Grenada and the
Government of the Union of Soviet Socialist Republics on deliveries from
the Union of SSR to Grenada of special
and other equipment

The Government of Grenada and the Government of the Union
of Soviet Socialist Republics,

quided by aspirations for develcping and strengthening
friendly relations between both countries on the principles of
equality, mutual respect of sovereignty and non-interference into internal affairs,

proceeding from the desire to promcte strengthening the independence of Grenada

and in connection with the request of the Government of
Grenada

have agreed upon the following:

Article 1

The Government of the Union of Soviet Socialist Republics
shall ensure in 1982-1985 free of charge the delivery to the
Government of Grenada of special and civil equipment in nomen-
clature and quantity according to Annexes 1 and 2 to the present
Agreement to the amount of 10.000.000 Roubles.

Article 2

The delivery of the equipment listed in Annexes 1 and 2 to the present Agreement shall be effected by the Soviet Party by sea, at the port of the Republic of Cuba.

The order of the further delivery of the above equipment from the Republic of Cuba shall be agreed upon between the Grenadian and Cuban Parties.

Article 3

The Government of the Union of SSR at the request of the Government of Grenada shall ensure rendering technical assistance in mastering of the equipment under delivery by receiving in the USSR Grenadian servicemen for training in the operation, use and maintenance of the special equipment as well as by sending Soviet specialists to Grenada for these purposes.

The Grenadian servicemen shall be sent to the USSR for training without their families.

The expenses connected with the Grenadian servicemen's training, upkeep, meals in the Soviet military educational establishments as well as with their travel fare from Grenada to the USSR and back shall be borne by the Soviet Party.

The Government of Grenada shall provide at its own expense the Soviet specialists and interpreters with comfortable furnished living accommodation with all the municipal utilities, medical service and transport facilities for the execution of their duties and shall ensure their having meals at reasonable prices at the places of their residense.

The Soviet specialists and interpreters shall not be imposed by any taxes and duties on entering or leaving Grenada and during their stay there. All other expenses connected with deputation of the Soviet specialists to Grenada shall be borne by the Soviet Party.

Article 4

The Soviet Party in periods to be agreed upon between the Parties shall depute a group of Soviet specialists to Grenada to determine expediency, opportunity and scope of rendering technical assistance in the creation of the stationary shop for repair of the special equipment and transport, commanding staff trainer school, training facilities for Armed Forces as well as the deliveries of missing building materials for construction of the storehouses and road.

The deputation of a group of Soviet specialists shall be effected on the terms and conditions of Article 3 of the present Agreement.

Article 5

The Government of the Union of SSR shall ensure free of charge the transfer to the Government of Grenada of necessary technical descriptions, instructions and manuals in standard composition on operation of the special equipment delivered under the present Agreement.

Article 6

The appropriate Grenadian and Soviet organizations shall conclude contracts in which there shall be stipulated the detailed terms and conditions of deputing Soviet specialists, receiving for training Grenadian servicemen and other services connected with the implementation of the present Agreement.

Article 7

The Government of Grenada shall not without the consent of the Government of the Union of Soviet Socialist Republics sell or transfer, formally or actually, the special equipment, delivered under the present Agreement, the relevant documentation and information or give permission to use the equipment and documentation by a third party or any physical or legal persons but the officials and specialists of the citizenship of Grenada being in the service with the Government of Grenada.

The Government of the Union of SSR and the Government of
Grenada shall take all the necessary measures to ensure keeping
in secret the terms and conditions of the deliveries, all the
correspondence and information connected with the implementation
of the present Agreement.

Article 8

The present Agreement comes into force on the date it is
signed on.

Annexes 1 and 2 are an integral part of the present Agreement.

Done in Moscow on July "27", 1982 in two origi-
nals, each in the English and Russian languages, both texts being
equally valid.

FOR AND ON BEHALF

OF THE GOVERNMENT OF GRENADA

FOR AND ON BEHALF

OF THE GOVERNMENT OF THE UNION
OF SOVIET SOCIALIST REPUBLICS

A N N E X 1

to Agreement of July "27", 1982

L I S T

of special equipment to be delivered to the Army of Grenada' from the Soviet Union in 1983-1985

Description	Unit of measure	Quantity total	Years of delivery		
			1983	1984	1985
Armour materiel					
BTR-152V1 armoured personnel carriers, used, repaired	piece	50	–	30	20
7,62-mm rifle cartridges without clips:					
with steel core bullet	thous. pieces	100,5	–	60,3	40,2
with B-32 armour-piercing-incendiary bullet and steel case	thous. pieces	37,5	–	22,5	15,0
with T-46 tracer bullet	thous. pieces	49,5	–	29,7	19,8

6

Artillery armament and ammunition

Description	Unit of measure	Quantity total	Years of delivery	
			1983	1984
76-mm ZIS-3 guns, used, repaired	piece	30	18	12
76-mm rounds:				
with fragmentation and high-explosive-fragmentation grenade	thous. pieces	9,3	5,6	3,7
with armour-piercing-tracer shell	piece	540	330	210
with sub-calibre armour-piercing shell	piece	450	270	180
with hollow charge shell	piece	540	330	210
57-mm ZIS-2 anti-tank guns, used, repaired	piece	30	18	12
57-mm rounds:				
with fragmentation grenade	thous. pieces	5,4	3,2	2,2
with armour-piercing-tracer shell	thous. pieces	4,0	2,4	1,6
with sub-calibre armour-piercing shell	thous. pieces	1,3	0,8	0,5

Description	Unit of measure	Quantity total	Years of delivery 1983	1984	1985
"Grad-P" /9P132/ portable launchers	piece	50	20	30	-
Group sets of SPTA /1:4/ for "Grad-P" launchers	set	12	5	7	-
Repair sets of SPTA /1:8/ for "Grad-P" launchers	set	5	2	3	-
122-mm 9M22M fragmentation-high-explosive set projectiles in sets with packs of "Grad-P" launchers	thous. pieces	1,8	0,9	0,9	-
14,5-mm ZGU-1 AA mountain mounts	piece	30	-	30	-
Group sets of SPTA /1:10/ for ZGU-1 mounts	set	3	-	3	-
Repair sets of SPTA /1:50/ for ZGU-1 mounts	set	1	-	1	-
14,5-mm cartridges:					
with B-32 armour-piercing-incendiary bullet	thous. pieces	180,0	-	180,0	-
with BZT armour-piercing-incendiary-tracer bullet	thous. pieces	180,0	-	100,0	-
82-mm BM mortars, used, repaired	piece	60	30	30	-

Description	Unit of measure	Quantity total	1983	1984	1985
82-mm rounds for BM mortars:					
with fragmentation mine	thous. pieces	21,6	10,8	10,8	-
with inert charge mine	piece	200	100	100	-
Small arms					
RPG-7V light anti-tank grenade launchers	piece	50	-	20	30
Group sets of SPTA /1:9/ for RPG-7V grenade launchers	set	5	-	2	3
Repair sets of SPTA /1:01/ for RPG-7V grenade launchers	set	1	-	-	1
PG-7VM rounds for RPG-7V grenade launchers	thous. pieces	3,0	-	1,2	1,8
7,62-mm PKM machine guns	piece	60	20	20	20
Group set of SPTA /1:50/ for PKM machine guns	set	1	-	1	-
7,62-mm PKMS machine guns	piece	30	-	10	20
Group set of SPTA /1:50/ for PKMS machine guns	set	1	-	-	1

Description	Unit of measure	Quantity total	1903	1904	1905
			Years of delivery		
7,62-mm DP, DPM machine guns, used, repaired	piece	270	170	100	-
7,62-mm rifle cartridges without clips:					
with steel core bullet	thous. pieces	919,5	432,0	308,7	178,8
with B-32 armour-piercing-incendiary bullet with steel case	thous. pieces	45,4	21,9	14,0	9,5
with T-46 tracer bullet	thous. pieces	213,8	101,6	69,3	42,9
7,62-mm AK sub-machine guns, used, repaired	thous. pieces	2,0	1,0	1,0	-
7,62-mm cartridges of 1943 model without clips:					
with steel core bullet	mill.pieces	1,44	0,7	0,74	-
with T-45 tracer bullet	thous. pieces	324,0	162,0	162,0	-
for blank firing	thous. pieces	120,0	60,0	60,0	-
7,62-mm carbines of 1938/1944 model, used, repaired	thous. pieces	1,0	1,0	-	-
7,62-mm rifle cartridges with steel core bullet in clips	thous. pieces	60,0	60,0	-	-

Description	Unit of measure	Quantity-total	Years of delivery		
			1983	1984	.1985
7,62-mm SVDN-1 sniper's rifles	piece	10	-	10	-
Group set of SPTA /1:18/ for SVDN-1 sniper's rifles	set	1	-	1	-
7,62-mm sniper's rifles of 1891/1930 model, used, repaired	piece	270	207	-	-
7,62-mm sniper's cartridges without clips	thous. pieces	2,7	-	2,7	-
9-mm PM pistols	piece	150	-	150	-
Group set of SPTA /1:100/.for PM pistols	set	1	-	1	-
9-mm cartridges for PM pistols	thous. pieces	10,8	-	10,8	-
Hand grenades:					
F-1	thous. pieces	10,0	-	10,0	-
RGD-5	thous. pieces	3,0	-	3,0	-
Training grenades with fuzes:					
URG	piece	500	-	500	-
URG-N	piece	500	-	500	-

Description	Unit of measure	Quantity total	Years of delivery		
			1983	1984	1985
Mines:					
PMN	thous. pieces	5,0	5,0	-	-
TM-57	thous. pieces	2,0	2,0	-	-
Communication means					
Radio stations:					
R-104AM3	set	10	-	-	10
R-105	set	40	-	-	40
R-109M	set	20	-	10	10
TA-57 telephone sets	piece	60	30	30	-
P-193M switchboards	piece	10	5	5	-
P-274M two-wire field cable	kilometre	50	50	-	-
TK-2 reels	piece	100	100	-	-
Engineer materiel and workshops					
TZ-5 refuellers	piece	2	-	2	-

Description	Unit of measure	Quantity total	Years of delivery		
			1983	1984	1985
OP workshop	set	1	-	1	-
MRS-OR workshop	set	1	-	1	-
ESD-10VS/230 power plant	set	1	-	1	-
Other equipment					
10-place tents	piece	100	-	50	50
Aluminium soldier flasks	thous. pieces	1,5	0,5	0,5	0,5
Flask case	thous. pieces	1,5	0,5	0,5	0,5
Sets of soldier uniform	thous. pieces	1,4 x/	1,4	-	-
SSh-60 steel helmets	thous. pieces	1,5	0,5	0,5	0,5
BPTs5 8x30 field-glasses	piece	100	50	50	-

Spare parts, auxiliary and training equipment by the specifications of the Soviet Party
to the amount of 600000-00 Roubles

x/ Set composition: panama - 1, field shirt - 1, trousers - 1, sleeveless cest - 2,
shorts - 2, socks - 2 pairs, boots - 1 pair, waist-belt - 1.

ANNEX 2

to the Agreement of "27" July 1982

L I S T

of special materiel and civilian equipment to be
supplied for the Ministry of the Interior of Grenada from the Soviet Union in 1982-1985

Description	Unit of measure	Quantity	Years of delivery			
			1982	1983	1984	1985
Small arms						
Light antitank rocket launchers RPG-7V	piece	20	-	-	-	20
Group sets of SPTA /1:9/ to rocket launchers RPG-7V	set	2	-	-	-	2
Repair set of spares /1:81/ to rocket launchers RPG-7V	set	1	-	-	-	1
Rockets PG-7VM to rocket launchers RPG-7V	thous.pieces	1,2	-	-	-	1,2
7,62-mm machine guns PKM	piece	25	-	-	25	-

Description	Unit of measure	Quantity	Years of delivery			
			1902	1903	1904	1985
Group set of SPTA /1:50/ to machine guns PKM	set	1	-	-	1	-
7,62-mm rifle cartridges without clips:						
with steel core bullet	thous.pieces	115,5	-	-	115,5	-
with armour piercing-incendiary bullet B-32 with steel casing	thous.pieces	7,5	-	-	7,5	-
with tracer bullet T-46	thous.pieces	27,0	-	-	27,0	-
7,62-mm submachine guns AK	piece	50x/	-	50	-	-
7,62-mm cartridges, model 1943, without clips:						
with steel core bullet	thous.pieces	40,0	-	40,0	-	-
with tracer bullet T-45	thous.pieces	8,0	-	8,0	-	-
7,62-mm sniper's rifles SVD	piece	13	5x/	8	-	-
Group set of SPTA/1:18/ to SVD rifles	set	1	-	1	-	-
7,62-mm sniper's cartridges to SVD rifles	thous.pieces	6,8	4,4	2,4	-	-
9-mm pistols PM	piece	600	50x/	-	550	-
Group sets of SPTA/1,100/ to PM pistols	set	6	-	-	6	-

x/ Used, repaired.

Description	Unit of measure	Quantity	Years of delivery			
			1982	1983	1984	1905
Repair set of SPTA /1:500/ to PM pistols	set	1	-	-	1	-
9-mm cartridges to PM pistols	thous.pieces	44,7	5,1	-	39,6	-
Special Instrumentation						
Items:						
"Pobedit-M"	piece	20	20	-	-	-
B-2	piece	5	5	-	-	-
B-4	piece	5	5	-	-	-
"Moshka-M2"	set	30	5	15	10	-
"Moshka-MV"	set	20	5	10	5	-
"Bulavka"	set	5	5	-	5	-
"Nylon"	set	10	10	-	-	-
"Nylon-2U"	set	1	1	-	-	-
Photo cutter to "Nylon"	piece	1	1	-	-	-
Photo cuvette to "Nylon"	piece	1	1	-	-	-

Description	Unit of measure	Quantity	Years of delivery			
			1982	1983	1984	1985
Instrumentation:						
"Luza-2-Lakmus"	set	2	2	-	-	-
"Bridge"	set	2	2	-	-	-
Infrared viewers "Kustarnik"	set	5	5	-	-	-
Step-and-repeat machine ER-11K1	piece	1	-	1	-	-
Signalling systems "Rubin-3"	set	4	-	4	-	-
TV systems "PTU-47"	set	2	-	2	-	-
Equipment of general civilian use						
Videotape recorders "Electronika-video"	set	3	-	3	-	-
Tape recorders "Mayak"	piece	15	-	15	-	-
Photo cameras:						
"Zenit-TTL"	piece	10	-	10	-	-
"Zenit-E"	piece	10	10	-	-	-
Exposure meters "Leningrad-6"	piece	3	3	-	-	-

Description	Unit of measure	Quantity	Years of delivery			
			1982	1983	1984	1985
Photographic enlarger "Neva-3M"	set	2	2	-	-	-
Black-and-white film "FED"	cassette	100	100	-	-	-
Colour reversible film, 35-mm	meter	80	80	-	-	-
Various kinds of photographic paper and chemical agents /developer and fixer/	set	1 x/	1	-	-	-
Safes with key locks	piece	6	-	6	-	-
Metal cabinets	piece	50	-	50	-	-
Single-stand tables	piece	30	-	30	-	-
Clothing and equipment						
Cotton khaki tunics with trousers	set	600	-	600	-	-
Officers' equipment /belts and shoulder straps/	set	1500	-	1500	-	-
Kersey high boots	pair	1500	-	1500	-	-
Khaki kapi	piece	600	-	600	-	-
Officers' capes	piece	500	-	500	-	-

x/ To be supplied to specifications of Soviet Party.

Description	Unit of measure	Quantity	Years of delivery			
			1982	1983	1984	1985
Black cotton socks	pair	1500	-	1500	-	-
Kit-bags	piece	1500	-	1500	-	-
Vehicles						
GAZ-66	piece	4	4	-	-	-
UAZ-469B	piece	6	6	-	-	-
VAZ-2106	piece	3	3	-	-	-
Sets of spares for vehicles:						
GAZ-66	set	1 x/	1	-	-	-
UAZ-469D	set	1 x/	1	-	-	-
VAZ-2106	set	1 x/	1	-	-	-

Spare parts, auxiliary and training equipment to specifications of Soviet Party for a sum up to 100000 roubles

x/ To be supplied to specifications of Soviet Party.

СОГЛАШЕНИЕ

между Правительством Гренады и Правительством
Союза Советских Социалистических Республик о
поставках из Союза ССР в Гренаду специального
и другого имущества

Правительство Гренады и Правительство Союза Советских Социалистических Республик,

руководствуясь стремлением к развитию и укреплению дружественных отношений между обеими странами на основе полного равноправия, взаимного уважения суверенитета и невмешательства во внутренние дела,

исходя из желания содействовать укреплению независимости Гренады,

· и в связи с обращением Правительства Гренады,

согласились о нижеследующем:

Статья 1

Правительство Союза Советских Социалистических Республик обеспечит в 1982-1985 годах безвозмездно поставку Правительству Гренады специального имущества и имущества общегражданского назначения в номенклатуре и количестве согласно Приложениям 1 и 2 к настоящему Соглашению на сумму 10.000.000 рублей.

Статья 2

Поставка перечисленного в Приложениях 1 и 2 к настоящему Соглашению имущества будет произведена Советской Стороной морем в порт Республики Куба. Порядок дальнейшей доставки указанного имущества из Республики Куба к месту назначения в Гренаде будет согласован между Кубинской и Гренадской Сторонами.

Статья 3

Правительство Союза ССР по просьбе Правительства Гренады обеспечит оказание технического содействия в освоении поставляемого имущества путем приема в Советском Союзе гренадских военнослужащих для обучения эксплуатации, применению и ремонту специального имущества, а также командирование для этих целей советских специалистов в Гренаду.

Гренадские военнослужащие будут направляться на обучение в СССР без семей.

Расходы, связанные с обучением, содержанием, питанием и обмундированием гренадских военнослужащих в советских военных учебных заведениях, а также с их проездом из Гренады в СССР и обратно, Советская Сторона принимает на себя.

Правительство Гренады обеспечит за свой счет советских специалистов и переводчиков благоустроенными меблированными жилыми помещениями, обеспечивающими нормальные условия их проживания, медицинским обслуживанием и транспортными средствами для служебных целей, а также организует предоставление советским специалистам и переводчикам питания за умеренную плату в местах их расположения.

Советские специалисты и переводчики не будут оплачивать какие-либо налоги и сборы при въезде, выезде и во время их пребывания в Гренаде.

Все остальные расходы, связанные с командированием советских специалистов в Гренаду, Советская Сторона принимает на себя.

Статья 4

Советская Сторона в сроки по согласованию Сторон командирует в Гренаду группу советских специалистов для определения целесообразности, возможности и объемов оказания технического содействия в создании стационарной мастерской для ремонта специального имущества и транспортных средств, школы для подготовки командиров и специалистов, учебной базы для Вооруженных Сил, а также поставки недостающих строительных материалов для создания хранилищ и дороги.

Командирование указанной группы советских специалистов будет произведено на условиях статьи 3 настоящего Соглашения.

Статья 5

Правительство Союза ССР обеспечит безвозмездно передачу Правительству Гренады в установленной комплектации необходимых технических описаний, инструкций и наставлений по эксплуатации поставляемого по настоящему Соглашению специального имущества.

Статья 6

Соответствующие гренадские и советские организации заключат между собой контракты, в которых будут установлены подробные условия командирования советских специалистов, приема на обучение гренадских военнослужащих и оказания других услуг, связанных с выполнением настоящего Соглашения.

Статья 7

Правительство Гренады не будет без согласия Правительства Союза Советских Социалистических Республик продавать или передавать, формально или фактически, поставляемое в связи с настоящим Соглашением специальное имущество, документацию и информацию по ним или разрешать пользоваться этим имуществом и документацией третьей стороне и каким бы то ни было физическим или юридическим лицам, кроме должностных лиц и специалистов из граждан Гренады, находящихся на службе у Правительства Гренады.

Правительство Гренады и Правительство Союза ССР примут все зависящие от них меры, которые обеспечат сохранение в тайне условий поставок, всей переписки и информации, связанных с выполнением настоящего Соглашения.

Статья 8

Настоящее Соглашение вступает в силу со дня его подписания. Приложения I и 2 к Соглашению являются его неотъемлемой частью.

Совершено в Москве "27" июля 1982 года в двух подлинных экземплярах, каждый на английском и русском языках, причем оба текста имеют одинаковую силу.

ПО УПОЛНОМОЧИЮ
ПРАВИТЕЛЬСТВА ГРЕНАДЫ

ПО УПОЛНОМОЧИЮ
ПРАВИТЕЛЬСТВА СОЮЗА СОВЕТСКИХ
СОЦИАЛИСТИЧЕСКИХ РЕСПУБЛИК

ПРИЛОЖЕНИЕ I

к Соглашению от "27" июля . 1982 года

ПЕРЕЧЕНЬ

специального имущества, поставляемого для армии Гренады
из Советского Союза в 1983-1985 годах

Наименование	Единица измерения	Количество всего	В том числе по годам		
			1983	1984	1985
Бронетанковая техника					
Бронетранспортеры БТР-152N, бывшие в эксплуатации, отремонтированные	штука	50	-	30	20
7,62-мм винтовочные патроны без обоймы:					
с пулей со стальным сердечником	тыс.штук	100,5	-	60,3	40,2
с бронебойно-зажигательной пулей Б-32 со стальной гильзой	тыс.штук	37,5	-	22,5	15,0
с трассирующей пулей Т-46	тыс.штук	49,5	-	29 7	19,8

Наименование	Единица измерения	Количество всего	В том числе по годам		
			1983	1984	1985
Артиллерийское вооружение и боеприпасы					
76-мм пушки ЗИС-3, бывшие в эксплуатации, отремонтированные	штука	30	18	12	-
76-мм выстрелы:					
с осколочной и осколочно-фугасной гранатой	тыс.штук	9,3	5,6	3,7	-
с бронебойно-трассирующим снарядом	штука	540	330	210	-
с бронебойно-подкалиберным снарядом	штука	450	270	180	-
с кумулятивным снарядом	штука	540	330	210	-
57-мм противотанковые пушки ЗИС-2, бывшие в эксплуатации, отремонтированные	штука	30	18	12	-
57-мм выстрелы:					
с осколочной гранатой	тыс.штук	5,4	3,2	2,2	-
с бронебойно-трассирующим снарядом	тыс.штук	4,0	2,4	1,6	-
с бронебойно-подкалиберным снарядом	тыс.штук	1,3	0,8	0,5	-
Переносные реактивные установки "Град-П" /9П132/	штука	50	20	0	-
Групповые комплекты ЗИПа /1:4/ к установкам "Град-П"	комплект	12	5	7	-

Наименование	Единица измерения	Количество всего	В том числе по годам		
			1983	1984	1985
Ремонтные комплекты ЗИПа /1:8/ к установкам "Град-П"	комплект	5	2	3	-
122-мм реактивные осколочно-фугасные снаряды 9М22М в комплекте с вьюками к установкам "Град-П"	тыс.штук	1,8	0,9	0,9	-
14,5-мм зенитные горные установки ЗГУ-1	штука	30	-	30	-
Групповые комплекты ЗИПа /1:10/ к установкам ЗГУ-1	комплект	3	-	3	-
Ремонтный комплект ЗИПа /1:50/ к установкам ЗГУ-1	комплект	1	-	1	-
14,5-мм патроны:					
с бронебойно-зажигательной пулей Б-32	тыс.штук	180,0	-	180,0	-
с бронебойно-зажигательно-трассирующей пулей БЗТ	тыс.штук	180,0	-	180,0	-
82-мм минометы БМ, бывшие в эксплуатации, отремонтированные	штука	60	30	30	-
82-мм выстрелы к минометам БМ:					
с осколочной миной	тыс.штук	21,6	10,8	10,8	-
с осколочной миной в инертном снаряжении	штука	200	100	100	-

Наименование	Единица измерения	Количество - всего	В том числе по годам		
			1983	1984	1985
Стрелковое вооружение					
Ручные противотанковые гранатометы РПГ-7В	штука	50	-	20	30
Групповые комплекты ЗИПа /1:9/ к гранатометам РПГ-7В	комплект	5	-	2	3
Ремонтный комплект ЗИПа /1:81/ к гранатометам РПГ-7В	комплект	1	-	-	1
Выстрелы ПГ-7ВМ к гранатометам РПГ-7В	тыс. штук	3,0	-	1,2	1,8
7,62-мм пулеметы ПКМ	штука	60	20	20	20
Групповой комплект ЗИПа /1:50/ к пулеметам ПКМ	комплект	1	-	1	-
7,62-мм пулеметы ПКМС:	штука	30	-	10	20
Групповой комплект ЗИПа /1:50/ к пулеметам ПКМС	комплект	1	-	-	1
7,62-мм пулеметы ДП, ДПМ, бывшие в эксплуатации, отремонтированные	штука	270	170	100	-
7,62-мм винтовочные патроны без обойм:					
с пулей со стальным сердечником	тыс. штук	919,5	432,0	308,7	178,8
с бронебойно-зажигательной пулей Б-32 со стальной гильзой	тыс. штук	45,4	21,9	14,0	9,5
с трассирующей пулей Т-46	тыс. штук	213,8	101,6	6,3	42,9

Наименование	Единица измерения	Количество-всего	В том числе по годам		
			1983	1984	1985
7,62-мм автоматы АК, бывшие в эксплуатации, отремонтированные	тыс.штук	2,0	1,0	1,0	-
7,62-мм патроны образца 1943 года без обойм:					
с пулей со стальным сердечником	млн.штук	1,44	0,7	0,74	-
с трассирующей пулей Т-45	тыс.штук	324,0	162,0	162,0	-
для холостой стрельбы	тыс.штук	120,0	60,0	60,0	-
7,62-мм карабины образца 1938, 1944 годов, бывшие в эксплуатации, отремонтированные	тыс.штук	1,0	1,0	-	-
7,62-мм винтовочные патроны с пулей со стальным сердечником в обоймах	тыс.штук	60,0	60,0	-	-
7,62-мм снайперские винтовки СВД-1	штука	10	-	10	-
Групповой комплект ЗИПа /1:18/ к снайперским винтовкам СВД-1	комплект	1	-	1	-
7,62-мм снайперские винтовки образца 1891/30 годов, бывшие в эксплуатации, отремонтированные	штука	270	270	-	-
7,62-мм снайперские патроны без обойм	тыс.штук	2,7	-	2,7	-
9-мм пистолеты ПМ	штука	150	-	150	-

Наименование	Единица измерения	Количество всего	В том числе по годам		
			1983	1984	1985
Групповой комплект ЗИПа /1:100/ к пистолетам ПМ	комплект	1	-	1	-
9-мм патроны к пистолетам ПМ	тыс.штук	10,8	-	10,8	-
Ручные гранаты:					
Ф-1	тыс.штук	10,0	-	10,0	-
РГД-5	тыс.штук	3,0	-	3,0	-
Учебные гранаты в комплекте с запалами:					
УРГ	штука	500	-	500	-
УРГ-Н	штука	500	-	500	-
Мины:					
ПМН	тыс.штук	5,0	5,0	-	-
ТМ-57	тыс.штук	2,0	2,0	-	-
Средства связи					
Радиостанции:					
Р-104АМ3	комплект	10	-	-	10
Р-105	комплект	40	-	-	40
Р-109М	комплект	20	-	10	10
Телефонные аппараты ТА-57	штука	60	30	30	-?

Наименование	Единица измерения	Количество всего	В том числе по годам		
			1983	1984	1985
Телефонные коммутаторы П-193М	штука	10	5	5	-
Кабель полевой П-274М в двухжильном исчислении	километр	50	50	-	-
Катушки ТК-2	штука	100	100	-	-
Инженерное имущество и мастерские					
Топливозаправщики ТЗ-5	штука	2	-	2	-
Мастерская ОП	комплект	1	-	1	-
Мастерская МРС-ОР	комплект	1	-	1	-
Электростанция ЭСД-10ВС/230	комплект	1	-	1	-
Прочее имущество					
Палатки 10-местные	штука	100	-	50	50
Фляги алюминиевые солдатские	тыс.штук	1,5	0,5	0,5	0,5
Чехлы к флягам	тыс.штук	1,5	0,5	0,5	0,5
Комплекты солдатского обмундирования	тыс.комплектов	1,4 x/	1,4	-	-

Состав комплекта: панама - 1, гимнастёрка - 1, брюки - 1, майки - 2, трусы - 2, носки - 2 пары, ботинки - 1 пара, брючный ремень - 1.

Наименование	Единица измерения	Количество-всего	В том числе по годам		
			1983	1984	1985
Шлемы стальные СШ-60	тыс.штук	1,5	0,5	0,5	0,5
Бинокли БПЦ5 8х30	штука	100	50	50	-

Запасные части, учебное и вспомогательное
имущество по спецификациям Советской Стороны на сумму до 600000-00 рублей.

ПРИЛОЖЕНИЕ 2

к Соглашению от "27" июля 1982 года

ПЕРЕЧЕНЬ

специального имущества и имущества общегражданского
назначения, поставляемых для Министерства внутренних
дел Гренады из Советского Союза в 1982-1985 годах

Наименование	Единица измерения	Количество-всего	В том числе по годам			
			1982	1983	1984	1985
Стрелковое вооружение						
Ручные противотанковые гранатометы РПГ-7В	штука	20	-	-	-	20
Групповые комплекты ЗИПа /1:9/ к гранатометам РПГ-7В	комплект	2	-	-	-	2
Ремонтный комплект ЗИПа /1·81/ к гранатометам РПГ-7В	комплект	I	-	-	-	I
Выстрелы ПГ-7ВМ к гранатометам РПГ-7В	тыс.штук	I,2	-	-	-	I,2
7,62-мм пулеметы ПКМ	штука	25	-	-	25	-

Наименование	Единица измерения	Количество всего	В том числе по годам			
			1982	1983	1984	1985
Групповой комплект ЗИПа /1:50/ к пулеметам ПКМ	комплект	I	-	-	I	-
7,62-мм винтовочные патроны без обойм:						
с пулей со стальным сердечником	тыс.штук	115,5	-	-	115,5	-
с бронебойно-зажигательной пулей Б-32 со стальной гильзой	тыс.штук	7,5	-	-	7,5	-
с трассирующей пулей Т-46	тыс.штук	27,0	-	-	27,0	-
7,62-мм автоматы АК	штука	50[x/]	-	50	-	-
7,62-мм патроны образца 1943 года без обойм:						
с пулей со стальным сердечником	тыс.штук	40,0	-	40,0	-	-
с трассирующей пулей Т-45	тыс.штук	8,0	-	8,0	-	-
7,62-мм снайперские винтовки СВД	штука	13	5[x/]	8	-	-
Групповой комплект ЗИПа /1:18/ к винтовкам СВД	комплект	I	-	I	-	-
7,62-мм снайперские патроны к винтовкам СВД	тыс.штук	6,8	4,4	2,4	-	-
9-мм пистолеты ПМ	штука	600	50[x/]	-	550	-

[x/] Бывшие в эксплуатации, отремонтированные.

Наименование	Единица измерения	Количество всего	В том числе по годам			
			1982	1983	1984	1985
Групповые комплекты ЗИПа /1:100/ к пистолетам ПМ	комплект	6	-	-	6	-
Ремонтный комплект ЗИПа /1:500/ к пистолетам ПМ	комплект	I	-	-	I	-
9-мм патроны к пистолетам ПМ	тыс.штук	44,7	5,1	-	39,6	-
Специальная аппаратура						
Изделия:						
"Победит-М"	штука	20	20	-	-	-
В-2	штука	5	5	-	-	-
Б-4	штука	5	5	-	-	-
"Мойка-М3"	комплект	30	5	15	10	-
"Мойка-МВ"	комплект	20	5	10	5	-
"Булава"	комплект	5	5	-	-	-
"Нейлон"	комплект	10	10	-	-	-
"Нейлон-3У"	комплект	I	I	-	-	-
Фоторезак к изделию "Нейлон"	штука	I	I	-	-	-
Фотобачок к изделию "Нейлон"	штука	I	I	-	-	-

Наименование	Единица измерения	Количество-всего	В том числе по годам			
			1982	1983	1984	1985
Аппаратура:						
"Луза-2-Лакмус"	комплект	2	2	-	-	-
"Бриж"	комплект	2	2	-	-	-
Приборы ночного видения "Кустарник"	комплект	5	5	-	-	-
Копировально-множительная машина ЭР-ПКГ	штука	I	-	I	-	-
Системы сигнализации "Рубин-3"	комплект	4	-	4	-	-
Телевизионные системы "ПТУ-47"	комплект	2	-	2	-	-
Имущество общегражданского назначения						
Видеомагнитофоны "Электроника-видео"	комплект	3	-	3	-	-
Магнитофоны "Мелк"	штука	15	-	15	-	-
Фотоаппараты:						
"Зенит-ТТЛ"	штука	10	-	10	-	-
"Зенит-Е"	штука	10	10	-	-	-

Наименование	Единица измерения	Количество-всего	В том числе по годам			
			1982	1983	1984	1985
Фотоэкспонометры "Ленинград-6"	штука	3	3	-	-	-
Фотоувеличители "Нева-3М"	комплект	2	2	-	-	-
Фотопленка черно-белая "ФЭД"	кассета	100	100	-	-	-
Фотопленка обращаемая цветная 35-мм	метр	80	80	-	-	-
Фотобумага разная и химические реактивы /проявитель и закрепитель/	комплект	1 x/	1	-	-	-
Сейфы с замками под ключ	штука	6	-	6	-	-
Шкафы металлические	штука	50	-	50	-	-
Однотумбовые столы	штука	30	-	30	-	-
Обмундирование						
Костюмы с брюками, (комплект) защитного цвета	комплект	600	-	600	-	-
Снаряжение офицерское /ремни и портупея/	комплект	1500	-	1500	-	-

x/ Поставляется по спецификациям Советской Стороны.

14 - 35

Наименование	Единица измерения	Количество- всего	В том числе по годам			
			1982	1983	1984	1985
Сапоги кирзовые	пара	1500	-	1500	-	-
Кепи защитного цвета	штука	600	-	600	-	-
Плащ-накидки офицерские	штука	500	-	500	-	-
Носки хлопчатобумажные, черного цвета	пара	1500	-	1500	-	-
Вещевые мешки	штука	1500	-	1500	-	-
Автомобильная техника						
Автомобили:						
ГАЗ-66	штука	4	4	-	-	-
УАЗ-469Б	штука	6	6	-	-	-
ВАЗ-2106	штука	3	3	-	-	-
Комплекты запасных частей для автомобилей:						
ГАЗ-66	комплект	1x/	1	-	-	-

x/ Поставляется по спецификациям Советской Стороны.

Наименование	Единица измерения	Количество-всего	В том числе по годам			
			1982	1983	1984	1985
УАЗ-469Б	комплект	I x/	I	-	-	-
ВАЗ-2I06	комплект	I x/	I	-	-	-

Запасные части, учебное и вспомога-
тельное имущество по спецификациям
Советской Стороны на сумму до
I00000-00 рублей

x/ Поставляется по спецификациям Советской Стороны.

P R O T O C O L

to the Agreement between the Government of
Grenada and the Government of the USSR of
October 27, 1980 on deliveries from the USSR
to Grenada of special and other equipment

The Government of Grenada and the Government of the Union of
Soviet Socialist Republics

have agreed upon the following:

Article 1

The Government of the Union of Soviet Socialist Republics
shall ensure free of charge the delivery in 1981-1983 to the
Government of Grenada of special and other equipment in nomen-
clature and quantity according to the Annex to the present
Agreement to the amount of 5.000.000 Roubles.

Article 2

In all other respects the Parties will be guided by the
provisions of the Agreement between the Government of Grenada
and the Government of the USSR of October 27,1980 on deliveries
from the USSR to Grenada of special and other equipment.

Article 3

The present Protocol comes into force on the date of its signing.

The Annex is an integral part of the present Protocol.

Done in Havana on February " 9th ", 1981 in two originals, each in the English and Russian languages, both texts being equally valid.

FOR AND ON BEHALF
OF THE GOVERNMENT OF GRENADA

FOR AND ON BEHALF
OF THE GOVERNMENT OF THE UNION
OF SOVIET SOCIALIST REPUBLICS

Basil H. Grahagan.

ANNEX

to Protocol of " q " February, 1981

L I S T

of special equipment and vehicles to be
delivered to Grenada from the Union of
Soviet Socialist Republics in 1981-1983

/free of charge/

Description	Unit of measure	Total quantity	Years of delivery		
			1981	1982	1983
Armour					
BTR-60PB armoured personnel carriers	piece	8	8	-	-
BRDM-2 armoured reconnaissance and patrol vehicles	piece	2	2	-	-
14,5-mm cartridges:					
with B-32 bullet	thous. pieces	6,3	6,3	-	-
with BZT bullet	thous. pieces	6,3	6,3	-	-
7,62-mm rifle cartridges without clips:					
with steel core bullet	thous. pieces	30	30	-	-
with B-32 bullet and steel case	thous. pieces	5	5	-	-
with T-46 bullet	thous. pieces	15	15	-	-

- 2 -

Description	Unit of measure	Total quantity	Years of delivery		
			1981	1982	1983
GAZ-49B engines	piece	4	–	2	2
GAZ-41 engines	piece	2	–	2	–
Armament and munitions					
7,62-mm AK submachine guns, used, reconditioned	thous. pieces	1	1	–	–
7,62-mm cartridges of 1943 model without clips:					
with steel core bullet	thous. pieces	1000	1000	–	–
with T-45 tracer bullet	thous. pieces	300	300	–	–
9-mm PM pistols	piece	300	300	–	–
Group sets of spare parts /1:100/ to PM pistols	set	3	3	–	–
Repair set of spare parts /1:500/ to PM pistols	set	1	1	–	–
9-mm cartridges to PM pistols	thous. pieces	36	36	–	–
26-mm SPSh-2 signal pistols	piece	30	–	30	–
26-mm signal cartridges:					
red	thous. pieces	3	–	3	–
green	thous. pieces	3	–	3	–
yellow	thous. pieces	3	–	3	–
26-mm illuminating cartridges	thous. pieces	3	–	3	–
TZK-2 commander's periscopes	piece	5	2	3	–
B-8s/s binoculars	piece	100	100	–	–

- 3 -

Description	Unit of measure	Total quantity	Years of delivery		
			1981	1982	1983
Adrianov compasses	piece	300	300	-	-
F-1 grenades	thous. pieces	1	1	-	-
RGD-5 grenades	thous. pieces	1	1	-	-
Engineering equipment					
E-305V universal excavator	piece	1	-	1	-
KS-4561A crane	piece	1	1	-	-
DZ-109 bulldozer	piece	1	1	-	-
ESD-30-VS/230 diesel power supply stations	piece	10	5	5	-
AD-30-T/230M2 diesel power supply stations	piece	10	5	5	-
ESB-2-VO gasoline lighting power supply stations	piece	15	5	5	5
IMP induction mine detectors	piece	20	-	20	-
30-mm signal cartridges:					
red	thous. pieces	1	1	-	-
green	thous. pieces	1	1	-	-
30-mm illuminating cartridges	thous. pieces	2	2	-	-
PSO-M portable firing range equipment	set	2	2	-	-
RTK company tactical set	set	1	1	-	-
Communication means					
Radiostations:					
R-104 UM	set	5	5	-	-
R-105M	set	15	15	-	-

Description	Unit of measure	Total quantity	Years of delivery		
			1981	1982	1983
R-108M	set	15	15	-	-
R-109M	set	15	15	-	-
R-129, used, reconditionned	set	5	5	-	-
R-130M, used, reconditionned	set	5	5	-	-
TA-57 telephone sets	set	100	-	100	-
P-194M1 switch boards	set	5	-	5	-
M-3M2 mobile signal workshop	set	1	1	-	-
P-274M two-wire field cable	kilometer	150	-	150	-
GB-10-u-1,3 batteries	piece	150	-	150	-
TK-2 reels for military field cable	piece	100	-	100	-
Transport means, special vehicles and workshops					
GAZ-66 vehicles	piece	30	30	-	-
UAZ-469B jeeps	piece	5	5	-	-
UAZ-452-A ambulances	piece	5	5	-	-
TZ-5 refueling vehicles	piece	2	-	2	-
APM-90M automobile light-beacon stations for landing	set	6	3	3	-
MTO-AT technical maintenance workshop	set	1	1	-	-
SRZ-A storage-batteries repair and charging station	set	1	1	-	-
Logistic materiel					
PMKh mobile mechanized bakery plant	set	1	1	-	-
PKS-2M mobile kitchen-messes	set	2	2	-	-
KP-125M vehicle-towed field kitchens	piece	20	20	-	-

- 5 -

Description	Unit of measure	Total quantity	Years of delivery		
			1981	1982	1983
DDA-66 desinfection shower installations	set	5	-	-	5
SDP-2 sterilisation and distillation units on trailers	set	2	-	2	-
RDV-100 reservoires	piece	10	8	2	-
Vacuum flasks:					
of 12 litres	piece	400	194	206	-
of 36 litres	piece	400	200	200	-
B-1 sterilized bandage sets	set	50	-	50	-
Individual bandage packets	thous. pieces	5	-	5	-
USB-56 tents with fittings	piece	25	5	20	-
Camp tents for 10-persons	piece	100	25	75	-
MKT-T camouflage nets	piece	20	20	-	-

Uniform articles and clothing

Description	Unit of measure	Total quantity	Years of delivery		
Soldiers' field cotton olive-coloured shirts, without belts	thous. pieces	12,6	12,6	-	-
Soldiers' field cotton olive-coloured trousers	thous. pieces	12,6	12,6	-	-
Soldiers' cotton khaki-coloured shelter-halves	thous. pieces	6,3	6,3	-	-
Soldiers' cotton olive-coloured field caps	thous. pieces	12,6	12,6	-	-
White cotton shorts	thous. pieces	12,6	12,6	-	-

Description	Unit of measure	Total quantity	Years of delivery		
			1981	1982	1983
Knitted white undershirts	thous. pieces	12,6	12,6	-	-
Olive-coloured socks without rubbers	thous. paires	25,2	25,2	-	-
Soldiers' tarpaulin waist-belts with brown coating and plain zink-covered buckles	thous. pieces	6,3	6,3	-	-
Soldiers' khaki-coloured tarpaulin waist-belts with plain zink-covered buckles	thous. pieces	6,3	6,3	-	-
Tarpaulin shoulder-belts with brown coating	thous. pieces	6,3	6,3	-	-
Khaki-coloured cotton knapsacks	thous. pieces	6,3	6,3	-	-
Steel helmets	thous. pieces	6,3	6,3	-	-
High leather boots with rubber soles	thous. paires	6,3	6,3	-	-
Flanelette blankets	thous. pieces	6,3	6,3	-	-
Coarse calico bed sheets, 214x126 cm	thous. pieces	12,6	12,6	-	-
Coarse calico outer pillow-cases, 60x50 cm	thous. pieces	12,6	12,6	-	-
Inner cotton pillow-cases, 60x50 cm	thous. pieces	6,3	6,3	-	-

Description	Unit of measure	Total quantity	Years of delivery		
			1981	1982	1983
Cotton mattress-cases, 220x77 cm	thous. pieces	6,3	6,3	-	-
Foam plastic mattresses, 185x70x4 cm	thous. pieces	6,3	6,3	-	-
Foam plastic pillows, 80x50x4 cm	thous. pieces	6,3	6,3	-	-
Soldiers' aluminium water flasks	thous. pieces	6,3	3	3,3	-
Covers for soldiers' water flasks	thous. pieces	6,3	3	3,3	-
Soldiers' aluminium pots	thous. pieces	6,3	6,3	-	-
Officers' capes	piece	300	-	300	-
Summer cotton work-suits	thous. pieces	6,3	-	6,3	-
Officers' box-calf leather shoes woth leather soles	pair	300	300	-	-
Officers' field bags of artificial leather	piece	300	-	300	-

Spare parts, training equipment
and auxiliary equipment as per
specifications of the Soviet
Party to the amount of up to
0,9 mln.roubles

Совершенно секретно

ПРОТОКОЛ

к Соглашению между Правительством Гренады
и Правительством СССР от 27 октября
1980 года о поставках из СССР в Гренаду
специального и другого имущества

Правительство Гренады и Правительство Союза Советских Социалистических Республик

договорились о нижеследующем:

Статья 1

Правительство Союза Советских Социалистических Республик
обеспечит в 1981-1983 годах безвозмездно поставку Правительству
Гренады специального и другого имущества в номенклатуре и количестве согласно Приложению к настоящему Протоколу на сумму
5000000 рублей.

Статья 2

Во всем остальном Стороны будут руководствоваться положения-
ми Соглашения между Правительством Гренады и Правительством СССР
от 27 октября 1980 года о поставках из СССР в Гренаду специального
и другого имущества.

Статья 3

Настоящий Протокол вступает в силу со дня его подписания.
Приложение является неотъемлемой частью настоящего Протокола.
Совершено в Гаване, " 9 " февраля 1981 года в двух подлинных
экземплярах, каждый на русском и английском языках, причем оба
текста имеют одинаковую силу.

ПО УПОЛНОМОЧИЮ   ПО УПОЛНОМОЧИЮ
ПРАВИТЕЛЬСТВА   ПРАВИТЕЛЬСТВА СОЮЗА
ГРЕНАДЫ   СОВЕТСКИХ СОЦИАЛИСТИЧЕСКИХ
                                 РЕСПУБЛИК

Совершенно секретно

Приложение

к Протоколу от " " февраля 1981 года

П Е Р Е Ч Е Н Ь

специального имущества и автомобилей, поставляемых
Гренаде из Советского Союза в 1981-1983 годах

/безвозмездно/

Наименование	Единица измерения	Количество	Годы поставки		
			1981	1982	1983
Бронетанковая техника					
Бронетранспортеры БТР-60ПБ	штука	8	8	–	–
Бронированные разведывательно-дозорные машины БРДМ-2	штука	2	2	–	–
14,5-мм патроны:					
с пулей Б-32	тыс.штук	6,3	6,3	–	–
с пулей БЗТ	тыс.штук	6,3	6,3	–	–
7,62-мм винтовочные патроны без обойм:					
с пулей со стальным сердечником	тыс.штук	30	30	–	–
с пулей Б-32 со стальной гильзой	тыс.штук	5	5	–	–
с пулей Т-46	тыс.штук	15	15	–	–
Двигатели ГАЗ-49Б	штука	4	–	2	2
Двигатели ГАЗ-41	штука	2	–	2	–

- 2 -

Наименование	Единица измерения	Количе-ство	Годы поставки		
			1981	1982	1983
Вооружение и боеприпасы					
7,62-мм автоматы АК, бывшие в эксплуатации, отремонтированные	тыс.штук	1	1	-	-
7,62-мм патроны образца 1943 года без обойм:					
с пулей со стальным сердечником	тыс.штук	1000	1000	-	-
с трассирующей пулей Т-45	тыс.штук	300	300	-	-
9-мм пистолеты ПМ	штука	300	300	-	-
Групповые комплекты ЗИПа к пистолетам ПМ /1:100/	комплект	3	3	-	-
Ремонтный комплект ЗИПа к пистолетам ПМ /1:500/	комплект	1	1	-	-
9-мм патроны к пистолетам ПМ	тыс.штук	36	36	-	-
26-мм сигнальные пистолеты СПШ-2	штука	30	-	30	-
26-мм сигнальные патроны:					
красного огня	тыс.штук	3	-	3	-
зеленого огня	тыс.штук	3	-	3	-
желтого огня	тыс.штук	3	-	3	-
26-мм осветительные патроны	тыс.штук	3	-	3	-
Трубы зенитные командирские ТЗК-2	штука	5	2	3	-
Бинокли Б-8с/с	штука	100	100	-	-
Компасы Адрианова	штука	300	300	-	-
Гранаты Ф-1	тыс.штук	1	1	-	-
Гранаты РГД-5	тыс.штук	1	1	-	-

- 3 -

Наименование	Единица измерения	Количе- ство	Годы поставки		
			1981	1982	1983

Инженерное вооружение

Экскаватор универсальный Э-305В	штука	1	–	1	–
Кран КС-4561А	штука	1	1	–	–
Бульдозер ДЗ-109	штука	1	1	–	–
Электростанции силовые дизельные ЭСД-30-ВС/230	штука	10	5	5	
Агрегаты питания дизельные АД-30-Т/230М2	штука	10	5	5	–
Электростанции бензиновые осветительные ЭСБ-2-ВО	штука	15	5	5	5
Индукционные миноискатели ИМП	штука	'20	–	20	–
30-мм сигнальные патроны:					
красного огня	тыс.штук	1	1	–	–
зеленого огня	тыс.штук	1	1	–	–
30-мм осветительные патроны	тыс.штук	2	2	–	–
Переносное стрельбищное оборудование ПСО-М	комплект	2	2	–	–
Ротный тактический комплект РТК	комплект	1	1	–	–

Средства связи

Радиостанции:

Р-104УМ	комплект	5	5		
Р-105М	комплект	15	15	–	–
Р-108М	комплект	15	15	–	–
Р-109М	комплект	15	15	–	–
Р-129, бывшие в эксплуатации, отремонтированные	комплект	5	5	–	–
Р-130М, бывшие в эксплуатации, отремонтированные	комплект	5	5		

- 4 -

Наименование	Единица измерения	Количество	Годы поставки		
			1981	1982	1983
Телефонные аппараты ТА-57	комплект	100	-	100	-
Коммутаторы П-194М1	комплект	5	-	5	-
Подвижная мастерская связи М-3М2	комплект	1	1	-	-
Кабель полевой П-274М в двухжильном исчислении	километр	150	-	150	-
Батареи ГБ-10-у-1,3	штука	150	-	150	-
Катушки ТК-2 для военно-полевого кабеля	штука	100	-	100	-
Транспортные средства, специальные автомобили и мастерские					
Автомобили ГАЗ-66	штука	30	30	-	-
Автомобили УАЗ-4695	штука	5	5	-	-
Санитарные автомобили УАЗ-452-А	штука	5	5	-	-
Топливозаправщики ТЗ-5	штука	2	-	2	-
Автомобильные посадочные светомаячные станции АПМ-90М	комплект	6	3	3	-
Мастерская технического обслуживания МТО-АТ	комплект	1	1	-	-
Станция ремонтно-зарядная аккумуляторная СРЗ-А	комплект	1	1	-	-
Имущество тыла					
Полевой механизированный хлебозавод ПМХ	комплект	1	1	-	-
Полевые кухни-столовые ПКС-2М	комплект	2	2	-	-
Кухни походные автоприцепные КП-125М	штука	20	20	-	-
Дезинфекционно-душевые установки ДДА-66	комплект	5	-	-	5

- 5 -

Наименование	Единица измерения	Количество	Годы поставки		
			1981	1982	1983
Стерилизационно-дистилляционные установки СДП-2 на автоприцепах	комплект	2	-	2	-
Резервуары РДВ-100	штука	10	8	2	-
Термосы:					
12-литровые	штука	400	194	206	-
36-литровые	штука	400	200	200	-
Комплекты Б-1 /перевязочные стерильные/	комплект	50	-	50	-
Пакеты индивидуальные перевязочные	тыс.штук	5	-	5	-
Палатки УСБ-56 с такелажем	штука	25	5	20	-
Палатки лагерные 10-местные	штука	100	25	75	-
Маскировочные сети МКТ-Т	штука	20	20		-
Обмундирование и вещевое имущество					
Рубашки верхние солдатские полевые без пояса оливкового цвета из хлопчатобумажной ткани	тыс.штук	12,6	12,6	-	-
Брюки навыпуск солдатские полевые оливкового цвета из хлопчатобумажной ткани	тыс.штук	12,6	12,6	-	-
Плащ-палатки солдатские защитного цвета из хлопчатобумажной ткани	тыс.штук	6,3	6,3	-	-
Фуражки солдатские полевые оливкового цвета из хлопчатобумажной ткани	тыс.штук	12,6	12,6	-	-
Трусы белого цвета из хлопчатобумажной ткани	тыс.штук	12,6	12,6	-	-

Наименование	Единица измерения	Количество	Годы поставки		
			1981	1982	1983
Майки трикотажные белого цвета	тыс.штук	12,6	12,6	-	-
Носки без резинок оливкового цвета	тыс.пар	25,2	25,2	-	-
Ремни поясные солдатские тесьмяные с покрытием коричневого цвета с пряжками оцинкованными, гладкими	тыс.штук	6,3	6,3	-	-
Ремни поясные солдатские тесьмяные защитного цвета с пряжками оцинкованными, гладкими	тыс.штук	6,3	6,3	-	-
Лямки плечевые тесьмяные с покрытием коричневого цвета	тыс.штук	6,3	6,3	-	-
Мешки вещевые из хлопчатобумажной ткани защитного цвета	тыс.штук	6,3	6,3	-	-
Шлемы стальные	тыс.штук	6,3	6,3	-	-
Ботинки с высокими берцами юфтевые на резиновой подошве	тыс.пар	6,3	6,3	-	-
Одеяла байковые	тыс.штук	6,3	6,3	-	-
Простыни размером 214х126 см из бязи	тыс.штук	12,6	12,6	-	-
Наволочки подушечные верхние размером 60х50 см из бязи	тыс.штук	12,6	12,6	-	-
Наволочки подушечные нижние размером 60х50 см из хлопчатобумажной ткани	тыс.штук	6,3	6,3	-	-
Наволочки тюфячные размером 220х77 см из хлопчатобумажной ткани	тыс.штук	6,3	6,3	-	-
Матрацы поролоновые 185х70х4 см	тыс.штук	6,3	6,3	-	-

- 7 -

Наименование	Единица измерения	Количество	Годы поставки		
			1981	1982	1983
Подушки поролоновые размером 60х50х4 см	тыс.штук	6,3	6,3	-	-
Фляги алюминиевые солдатские	тыс.штук	6,3	3	3,3	-
Чехлы к солдатским флягам	тыс.штук	6,3	3	3,3	-
Котелки алюминиевые солдатские	тыс.штук	6,3	6,3	-	-
Плащ-накидки офицерские	штука	300	-	300	-
Комбинезоны рабочие летние из хлопчатобумажной ткани	тыс.штук	6,3	-	6,3	-
Полуботинки хромовые офицерские на кожаной подошве	пара	300	300	-	-
Сумки полевые офицерские из искусственной кожи	штука	300	-	300	-

Запасные части, учебное и
вспомогательное имущество
по спецификациям Советской
Стороны на сумму до 0,9 млн.
рублей

PROTOCOL

OF THE MILITARY COLLABORATION BETWEEN THE GOVERNMENT OF THE
REPUBLIC OF CUBA AND THE PEOPLE'S REVOLUTIONARY GOVERNMENT
OF GRENADA

The Government of the Republic of Cuba and People's Revolutio
nary Government of Grenada, in full exercise of their sovereign
right as free and independent State, based on the fraternal
relations existing between both countries with the aim of making a constribution to the strengthening of the defensive capacity of Grenada, have agreed upon the following:

ARTICLE I

The Government of the Republic of Cuba in agreement with the -
request formulated by the People's Revolutionary Government of
Grenada, will maintain Cuban Military specialists in that coun
try in quantities and specialists established in Annex No. 1 -
of this document. (Protocol).

ARTICLE II

The Military specialists from Cuba in behalf of strengthening
the military capacity of the Armed Forces will assist grenadian military men on the questions of Organization of the Or-
ganic Structure, Organization of the Instruction and combative
and campaign training of the troops and staffs in the preparation of cadres and minor specialists, and in the elaboration
of the operative and mobilization plans for the defense of the
country.

ARTICLE III

The Government of the Republic of Cuba will grant scholarships
to military personnel of Grenada in the Military Training Cen
tres of the Revolutionary Armed Forces with the quantities -
and specialist with the requirements that will be established
in Annex No. 3 which will be elaborated afterwards.

ARTICLE IV

The Government of the Republic of Cuba has the pleasure of recie
ving during 1982 four delegations of the Armed Forces of up to
three members each, of the following specialities:

- Engineering, (the fourth-three months period)
- Communication, (the first three-months period)
- Logistics, (the first three-month period)
- Exploration, (the fourth three-month period)

The dates in which these delegations should travel to Cuba will
be communicated to the grenadian side, by the cuban side twenty
days in advance.

ARTICLE V

In order to lead the activities of the Cuban Military Specialists, the post of chief of the Cuban Military Specialists is
established who will develop functions in the Ministry of Defense.

ARTICLE VI

The Cuban side according to the plans approved by its governments will carry out the systematic change of Cuban Military-
specialists in the quantities foreseen in the present Protocol.

ARTICLE VII

The People's Revolutionary Government of Grenada will give facilities to the chief of the Cuban Military specialists in the
work places and for using the communication means existing in
the country in order to assure the direction of his activities
of Technical Military assistance to the Armed Forces.

ARTICLE VIII

The Cuban and grenadian Military specialists who in virtue of
the present Protocol are in the Republic of Cuba or in Grenada
will respect the sovereignty and costums and will observe the
laws.

ARTICLE IX

The People's Revolutionary Government will give facilities to the Ministry of the Revolutionary Armed Forces of the Republic of Cuba to check the work of the Cuban Military Specialists.

ARTICLE X

The medical, technical and material assurance and the expenses as a result of the permanency of the Cuban Military Specialists on the Granadian territory will be implemented according to the time period established in Annex No. 2 of this Protocol.

ARTICLE XI

The People's Revolutionary Government will pay the expenses of the Custom-House and fees of the means sent to the Cuban Military specialists, by sea and by air.

ARTICLE XII

The Government of the Republic of Cuba and the People's Revolutionary Government of Grenada, will take all measures depending on them in order to assure the secrecy of the permanency of the military personnel in both states and the character of the activities, as well as the mail and information related to the present Protocol.

ARTICLE XIII

Any kind of situation that comes out in respect to the present Protocol or its accomplishment, it will be solved by friendly conversations between representatives of both sides in Havana City or in the City St. George's.

Any charges or additions to the Present Protocol will only be effective in case they are elaborated in a written way and signed by authorized personnel of both sides.

ARTICLE XIV

Annex No. 3 of the Protocol of Military Collaboration on scholar

ships to the People's Revolutionary Government of Grenada will
be included in the present Protocol, by means of a written request through the chief of the Group of Military Specialists -
after having finished the studies that will be carried out.

ARTICLE XV

The Present Protocol will be put into effect from the date of
signature and it will be effective until Dicember 31st, 1984.

The Annexes No. 1, 2 and 3 are part of this Protocol.

Written up in two copies, original, in spanich and english, --
both texts are valid and signed in the City of _____
on the _____ days of _____ of 19____

By the Government of the   By the People's Revolutio
Republic of Cuba   nary Government of Grenada

ANNEX No. 1

PROTOCOL OF THE MILITARY COLLABORATION ABOUT THE LEVELS OF WORK OF THE CUBAN MILITARY SPECIALISTS IN THE PERMANENT ARMED FORCES.

The Government of the Republic of Cuba will maintain military specialists in Grenada whose composition will be as follows:

1.- Permanent Specialists

    a) In the General Staff of the Armed Forces.

       - Chief of the Military Specialists ————————— 1

       - Specialists ———————————————————————— 8

    b) In the Military Region.

       - Specialists ———————————————————————— 3

    c) In the Permanent Company.

       - Specialist ————————————————————————— 1

    d) Internal Assurance Groups of the Military Specialists.

       - Officers, Sergeants and soldiers ————————— 16

                                TOTAL 27

2.- Specialists for short periods and for 2-4 month periods

    a) In the General Staff.

       - Specialists ———————————————————————— 6

    b) In the assurance units.

       - Techinicians ———————————————————————— 3

    c) Transport Repairing Brigades ————————————— 3-4

                                TOTAL 12-13

ANNEX No. 2

PROTOCOL OF THE MILITARY COLLABORATION ABOUT THE MATERIAL MEANS, SERVICE AND ASSURING PERSONNEL.

The Government of the Republic of Cuba and the People's Revo lutionary Government of Grenada agree to guarantee the mate- rial, technical and medical assurance of the Cuban Military Specialists according to the time period mentioned below:

CLAUSE No. 1

The People's Revolutionary Government of Grenada will guarantee the material means, equipments and the following services:

a) Maintainance of furniture and properties sent and construc- ted by Cuba and those given by the country to the Cuban mi- litary personnel.

b) Equipment and office material for the usage of the Cuban mi litary specialists.

c) Fresh food-stuff for the feeding of the Cuban Military per- sonnel.

d) The necessary transport means for the develpment of their - functions inside the Armed Forces, guaranteeing the fuel and lubricants, its maintainance and repair.

e) Armament and ammunition for the Cuban Military specialists.

f) Qualifield medical assistance in the Hospital of the country as well as the necessary medicines for desease prevention and the maintainance of health of the Cuban Military Specia- lists.

g) Means of personnel hygiene of every kind.

h) National transportation required for the accomplishment of the service activities.

i) Public Services (water, electricity, telephones and others)

j) A small stipendium for the personal expenses of every members equivalent to (30) U.S. Dollars.

k) Entrance visa and Identification Documents which accredit them for the civilian and military authorities of the — country.

1) Personnel that guarantee the driving and usage of the trans port Technique, the elaboration of food, washing ang ironing of the clothes, the cleaning of furniture and properties and the security of the house.

11) Other means and services non-specified which are required - for the development of the work of the Cuban Military perso nell.

CLAUSE No. 2

The Government of the Republic of Cuba will guarantee the means equipment and services we mention as follows:

a) The sending of technical personnel, material means and nece- ssary furnitures for the construction of the necessary ins- tallation for the living conditions and work of the Cuban - Military Personnel.

b) Dried foodstuff of every kind for the feeding of the Cuban- Military Personnel.

c) The trip clothes of the Cuban Military Specialists.

d) The necessary consultive material for the execution of the functions of the Cuban Military Specialists.

e) The salary in Cuba of the Military Personnel.

PARTIDO COMUNISTA DE CUBA / COMITE CENTRAL

<u>SECRET</u>

<u>COOPERATION AND EXCHANGE PLAN BETWEEN THE COMMUNIST PARTY OF CUBA AND THE NEW JEWEL MOVEMENT OF GRENADA, FOR THE 1983 PERIOD.</u>

<u>INTRODUCTION</u>

The Communist Party of Cuba and the New Jewel Movement, brotherly united by the same ideals of struggle in their respective countries, as well as of active solidarity in favor of the peoples that struggle for national liberation, and likewise, sharing the same convictions against imperialism, colonialism, neo-colonialism, Zionism, and racism, become aware of the need to unite efforts and coordinate actions of cooperation in the different activities within their scope.

Both Parties, on agreeing that the many-sided relations of cooperation be governed by the widest and justest spirit of cooperation, solidarity, and internationalism, reach agreement on the following:

<u>CHAPTER I</u>

a) The CPC and the NJM will exchange delegations for the mutual study of the experiences in the different fields of Party work, according to agreements and needs that will be established between the parties. To this end, they will carry out regular meetings and exchange of experiences between the different departments and secretaries of both Parties, whose agreements and commitments will be annexed to this protocol.

PARTIDO COMUNISTA·DE CUBA / COMITE CENTRAL

2.

b) The CPC expresses its willingness to send, according to the requests formulated by the NJM in this sense, technical advisers for the organization of public meetings and propaganda of the Party in Grenada.

c) Regarding the political upgrading and professional assistance, the NJM and the CPC express their willingness to receive, at the "Ñico López" School, the NJM cadres that will be decided on mutual agreement.

d) The CPC and the NJM of Grenada will exchange information of mutual interest, both on the field of the development of the two revolutions and their experiences, as well as on the international situation and, fundamentally, that of the Caribbean in its struggle against imperialism, neo-colonialism, racism and Zionism. Likewise, they will exchange information on the liberation movements as well as coordinate actions and positions of mutual interest to be adopted at events, conferences, and other Party activities of an international character, with special emphasis on the problems in the Caribbean.

e) Both organizations, vanguard of the peoples of Cuba and Grenada, express their mutual solidarity in the struggle against imperialism, and they are committed to struggle and make sure that they develop to the utmost the mutual solidarity and understanding of the International Revolutionary Movement regarding both revolutions.

f) Both Parties will exchange information and join efforts in strengthening their relationship with the socialist and

PARTIDO COMUNISTA DE CUBA / COMITE CENTRAL

3.

progressive countries, and in favor of the peoples that
struggle for their liberation, particularly within the
Movement of Non-Aligned Countries.

CHAPTER II

On political and mass organizations:

Both Parties agree on developing to the utmost the cooperation
and assistance in the development and strengthening of the mass
organizations of Cuba and Grenada.

In this sense, the CPC and the NJM will promote, according to
the needs of the NJM and its mass organizations, a work plan
of the Workers' Central Union of Cuba, the Cuban Women's Federation, the Association of Small Farmers and the Young Communist
Organization, with their counterparts in Grenada, both for the
exchange of delegations, advice, and collaboration in their different fields, and for receiving cadres from those Grenadian organizations in the schools and courses of the Cuban organizations which are arranged and agreed to these purposes.

These agreements on cooperation will include exchange of information, publications, and expertise built up by them.

Likewise, they will coordinate their positions at international
events and conferences, by mutually advising each other on the
common interests of both Parties.

CHAPTER III

On the exchange and cooperation between both Parties:

The CPC and the NJM of Grenada will approve, control, and en-

SECRET

4.

sure the fulfillment of the understandings and agreements of
cooperation and exchange to be established at state level,
for which they will create the mechanisms and controls that
they consider relevant.

Similarly, both Parties will periodically oversee the development of the cooperation and exchange between both governments,
formulating the readjustments that become necessary for practical purposes.

The CPC and the NJM will coordinate the positions of the governments of Cuba and Grenada at international events, conferences,
and agencies where they participate, in attention to the political, economic and social interests of both Parties.

Besides, both Parties, through their state apparatus, will pro-
pitiate the exchange of information, publications, research,
and scientific and propaganda works related to their political
interests.

CHAPTER IV

On their fulfillment:

The CPC and the NJM commit themselves to inform the counterpart,
in due time, the implementation of the agreed exchange plans.
Also, both Parties will aprove the agreements to be established
among the above mentioned political and mass organizations,
making sure that they are fulfilled.

The agreements adopted in the different fields of Party life,
as well as those to be concluded among the Cuban and Grenadian
political and mass organizations, will be incorporated as annexes to this protocol in force until December 31, 1983.

5

SECRET

5.

1983 PLAN

The New Jewel Movement of Grenada and the Communist Party of Cuba, ratified the general lines established in the Coopera- tion and Exchange Plan between both Parties, and pursuant to the spirit of such Agreement, they establish the following plan for 1983:

I. The Cuban Party will recieve in 1983:

a) Five comrades with secondary educational level to study at the "Ñico López" School, for one year.

b) Two technicians in drawing for specialization in mak- ing billboards and posters.

c) Two comrades for specialization in sound equipment for public meetings.

d) A press photographer for training in Cuba.

e) Training of a technician in microfilm for the press.

f) A newspaper librarian, for training in Cuba.

g) Training of a press cartoonist.

h) Training of a technician in general graphic arts.

i) Two comrades linked to the work on religion for exchang ing experiences and coordinating regional and interna- tional work.

j) Two comrades linked to the work on the Socialist Inter- national for exchanging experiences and criteria on this aspect.

17 - 5

6

6.

k) A delegation made up of three comrades of the Ministry of
Mobilization who have to do with the work of Foreign Affairs, fundamentally with the Caribbean, for exchanging
experiences, criteria, and coordination in the region.

l) A delegation made up of a Memeber of the Political Bureau
and two other persons for exchanging experience on the
work of organization, internal education and propaganda
of the Party.

m) Two Members of the Political Bureau and two other persons,
each one for one week of rest in Cuba.

n) Two Members of the Central Committee for one week of rest
in Cuba.

II. The Grenadian party will recieve in 1983:

a) Two technicians in sound equipment for public meetings,
to train and increase the level of their counterparts in
Grenada.

b) Two technicians in billboards and posters for exchanging
experience and increasing the technical level of the Grenadian comrades.

c) A delegation of two comrades from the Department of Organization for exchanging experience on the organization work
of the Party.

SECRET

7.

d) A specialist in the work with the religious people for exchanging experiences in the work of the Party on this sector.

e) A specialist in internal education plans of the Party.

The Communist Party of Cuba and the New Jewel Movement of Grenada, satisfied by the discussed and agreed aspects, which fully correspond with the fraternal relations between both Parties, underwrite this document in the City of Havana, Cuba, June 29th, 1983.

The Communist Party of Cuba   The New Jewel Movement

8

17 - 8

EMBAJADA DE GRANADA EN CUBA

STA. AVENIDA No. 8409 Esq. 84
MIRAMAR. C. HABANA
CUBA

TELEFONOS:
29-5429
29-3913

In accordance with the requests put forward at the 2nd Congress of the Communist Party of Cuba by the Prime Minister, the Vietnamese Ambassador has reported the following:

1. The Ministry of Defence and Interior is ready to receive from Grenada starting in April 1982 twenty appropriately qualified people to train in the following:
   (a) anti-chemical warfare
   (b) anti-radioactivity warfare
   (c) re-education of anti-social and counter-revolutionary elements
   (d) Yankee tactics and the weapons used in Vietnam

2. The Government of Vietnam is not in a position to send people to Grenada nor are they in a position to train pilots.

3. I enquired as to who will pay the passages for these people. The Ambassador promised to check on this question but pointed out that it was unlikely that Vietnam would be able to pay. He suggested that we approach a friendly country which has airline facilities.

signature
18/2/82

Headache,

We need to decide who and how many.

You can keep this copy.

initials

EMBAJADA DE GRANADA EN CUBA

5TA. AVENIDA No. 8409 Esq. 84
MIRAMAR CIUDAD HABANA
CUBA

RSO 295/83

TELEFONOS:
29-5429
29-3913

"YEAR OF POLITICAL AND ACADEMIC EDUCATION"

SUMMATION OF THE WORK and DECISIONS OF GENERAL MEETING - NJM
(CUBA)

1. The General Meeting of the New JEWEL Movement (NJM) branch
   in Cuba was held on Saturday 7th May 1983 at 9.30 am in
   Santa Clara according to the decision of the previous GM.

2. In attendance were 28 comrades. The meeting heard excuse
   for the abscence of Cde. James Clarkson but could not account
   for Cde. Augustine Vesprey's absence. Comrades Cletus St.
   Paul and John Houston (Lion) were welcomed by the GM.

3. The meeting re elected Cde. Springle as recording secretary
   and adopted the following agenda:
   a) Report on decisions and tasks of last GM.
   b) Report and discussion on Party work in the institutions
   c) Proposal on Cultural activity.
   d) Discussion on collective assessment of comrades.
   e) A O B

4. The GM reviewed all the decisions that were taken at its
   last session. In all cases (14 cases) a responsible attitude
   was taken to implement the decisions. The results are as
   follows:

DOCUMENT 19
19 - 1

EMBAJADA DE GRANADA EN CUBA

5TA. AVENIDA No. 8409 ESQ. 84
MIRAMAR. CIUDAD HABANA
CUBA

TELEFONOS:
29-5429
29-3913

cont'd....

a. Travel arrangement for 97 students return from Cuba for
August vacation including all the economic students who
have been requested by the Ministry of Finance has been
arranged with Aero Caribbean as follows:

Departure	Return
i. June 15th or July 9th for Econ. students	August 25th
ii. July 11th	August 27th
iii. July 13th	August 29th
iv. July 24th	August 31st

All monies for buying tickets to be sent in bulk to the
Embassy via Ministry of Education. The Ministry already
informed of this.

b. Emulation plan for national emulation for period September 1983 to March 1984 already prepared and discussed with
students. It was noted that students are looking forward
for this.

c. Discussion on pregnancy and birth control in progress –
to date no report on pregnancy among Grenadian students.

d. Celebration of 10th Anniversary of NJM & 4th Anniversary
of Revolution held in provinces and were successful.

EMBAJADA DE GRANADA EN CUBA

9TA. AVENIDA No. 8409 Esc. 84
MIRAMAR CIUDAD HABANA
CUBA

TELEFONOS:
29-5429
29-3913

cont'd. /.3/

e. Discussion on transfer of students in progress although
   several lmodifications are being made based on the desire
   of the students and the availability of their speciality
   in the particular province.

f. Discussion on holiday plan for students remaining in Cuba
   held. The main difficulty with this has to be resolved
   by the FEU.

g. Efforts have been made to resolve the academic problem of
   Laurie Frederick. He still experiences difficulties but
   the school is prepared to give him another chance.

h. The problem of Allan Benjamin was frankly taken up with
   him. Over the last 3 moths there has been marked improvement.

   A study of OPPP completed by all except the Havana applicants

   More attention is being given to the middle level students
   by the respective party group.

   members now have study material (report on 1982 eco-
   performance), although this was only done recently.
   study material is being prepared for september.

EMBAJADA DE GRANADA EN CUBA

AVENIDA No. 8409 Esc. 84
MIRAMAR CIUDAD HABANA
CUBA

TELEFONOS:
29-5429
29-3913

cont'.....4/

1. collective assessment was held in all party groups.

5. During the report on decisions of last GM matters arose on which decisions were taken, namely,

   a. that the embassy must have a direct hand in the placement of students in the future,

   b. that it be suggested to Grenada that career weeks be held with students about to leave school so they can better appreciate what they want to study and/or what they should study in relation to national development.

   c. need for a common approach to members, candidates and applicants study in different provinces and how this can be achieved.

6. The General Meeting heard reports on the work of the party groups in Havana, Santiago de Cuba and Camagüey as well as Cde. Allan Roberts work in Santa Clara. It was noted that the work in Santiago de Cuba had significantly improved since last GM. The applicants completed study and the NYO group organised quite a number of political, cultural and social activities as well as attended several political activities of other student bodies. It was however, stressed that the situation was not yet consolidated and several students still sho political indifference thus the need to focus more attention there. In Camagüey the work is still good with the applicants and M & CM completing their study. The NYO
set and they ...

EMBAJADA DE GRANADA EN CUBA

5TA. AVENIDA No. 8409 Esg. 84
MIRAMAR CIUDAD HABANA
CUBA

TELEFONOS:
29-5429
29-3913

cont'd...5/

group held several political, cultural (for the first time)
and social activities which were successful. However, a
slight drop in attendance and punctuality was beginning to
develop. In Havana the work is satisfactory. The applicants
are completing their study, the M & CM are now on chapter
4 of Political Economy. With the NYO several activities were
realised - political, cultural and social that were all very
successful. It was however, noted that the failure to provide
study material to NYO affects all the groups. The NWO which
was recently started held several successful activities and is
proving to be a step forward for all the sisters. In Santa
Clara the NYO is operating and held some successful activities.
The group however has some disciplinary problems which must
be resolved urgently. The group takes part in all activities
that other students bodies hold.

7. A general problem of all the groups which was identified was
that of information from Grenada. It was noted that a more
consistent centralised and responsible approach must be taken
by Grenada on this problem.

8. The General Meeting heard a proposal from the Havana party
group and approved it. The proposal is for the students returning home on holidays to hold 3 cultural shows in Grenada
the proceeds of which would be all given to the defense of
the homeland. Various tasks were distributed to three provinces and they would immediately begin preparations. It was

19 - 5

EMBAJADA DE GRANADA EN CUBA

5ta. AVENIDA No. 8409 Esq. 84
MIRAMAR CIUDAD HABANA
CUBA

TELEFONOS:
29-5429
29-3913

cont'd...6/

decided that the OC be contacted on this to get the organisational help of the party.

9. The results of the collective assessment were given. It was noted that there was some timidity in the assessment, however, the GM agreed that this exercise is very fundamental and as such must be continued but greater attention must be paid to frank, open and objective assessments with comradely criticism and advice given.

10. The GM looked at other matters such as the problem of the French students which has been referred numerous times to the Ministry of Education (Gda); the problem being created by the boastful attitude of the economic students in relation to their trip to Grenada; the problem of the monthly newsletter as a result of no one to type it; the need for Grenadian students to more actively participate in voluntary productive work in Cuba.

The GM ended at 5 pm after deciding on the date and place of its next meeting - 5th November in Camagüey. The Meeting was carried out in a disciplined and businesslike manner.

General Meeting - NJM branch (Cuba)
May 7th 1983

A G R E E M E N T

between the People's Revolutionary Government of
Grenada and the Government of the Democratic
People's Republic of Korea on the free offer of
military assistance to the People's Revolutionary
Government of Grenada by the Democratic People's
Republic of Korea.

For the purposes of further cementing and developing the

friendship and solidarity between the peoples and armies of

the two countries established in the common struggle to oppose

against imperialism, consolidate the national sovereignty and

safeguard independence, and strengthening the national defence

power of Grenada, the People's Revolutionary Government of

Grenada and the Government of the Democratic People's

Republic of Korea have agreed as follows ;

Article   1

The Government of the Democratic People's Republic of

Korea shall give, in 1983-1984, the free military assistance

subject to weapons and ammunitions covering US $ 12,000,000
indicated in Annex to this Agreement.

Article 2

The Grenadan side shall be responsible for the transport of weapons and ammunitions to be rendered to the People's Revolutionary Government of Grenada by the Democratic People's Republic of Korea.

Article 3

Both sides shall strictly keep the secrecy of the military assistance to be executed according to this Agreement and have an obligation not to hand over any matters of this Agreement to the third country.

Article 4

This Agreement shall come into force on the day of its signing.

This Agreement has been prepared in duplicate in the Korean

and English languages and signed in Pyongyang on April /4

1983, two original equally authentic.

By the authority of the   By the authority of the

People's Revolutionary   Government of   the

Government of Grenada.   Democratic   People's

                                        Republic of   Korea.

A N N E X

of Agreement on the free offer of military assistance
to the People's Revolutionary Government of Grenada
by the Democratic People's Republic of Korea.

Hand flares	200	pcs
Ammunition for hand flares	4,000	rds
7.62mm automatic rifle	1,000	pcs
7.62mm light machine gun	50	pcs
Ammunition for 7.62mm auto. rifle	360,000	rds
7.62mm blanks	300,000	rds
7.62mm heavy machine gun	30	pcs
Ammunition for heavy machine gun	60,000	rds
RPG-7 launcher	50	pcs
RPG-7	500	rds
Hand grenade	200	rds
Instruction hand grenade	20	rds
Binoculars (8 x)	30	pcs
Anti-gas masks	1,000	pcs

Sirens	50	pcs
Tactical drawing instruments	15	sets
Coast guard	2	boats
Uniforms	6,000	suits
Knapsacks	6,000	pcs
Camouflage nets	50	pcs
Ultrashort waves wireless set (□ -3)	3	pcs
Ultrashort waves wireless set (□ -4)	3	pcs

조선민주주의인민공화국이 그 녀 네이더인인혁명정부에
무상으로 군사원조를 줄데 대한 그 녀 네이더인인혁
명 정부와 조선민주주의인민공화국 정부 사이의

협   정

그 녀 네아더인인혁명정부와 조선민주주의인민공화국 정부는 제국주의
룰 반대하고 나라의 독립을 공고히 하며 자주성을 옹호하기 위한
공동투쟁에서 맺어진 두 나라 인민들과 군대들 사이의 친선과 단
결을 더욱 강화발전시키며 그 녀 네이더의 국방력을 강화할 목적으로
다음과 같이 합의한다.

제   1   조

조선민주주의인민공화국 정부는 그 녀 네이더인민혁명 정부에 이 협
정을입료에 지적된 1200만 미달라에 해당한 무기와 탄약들을
1983-1984년도에 무상으로 군사원조를 준다.

6 . . . . .

제 2 조

조선민주주의인민공화국이 그레네이더인민혁명정부에 무상으로 군사

원조하는 무기와 탄약들에 대한 수송은 그레네이더측이 책임진다.

제 3 조

쌍방은 이 협정에 의하여 진행되는 군사적협조에 관한 비밀을 엄격히

지키며 그 어떤문제도 제3국에 넘겨주지 않을데 대한 의무를 지닌다.

제 4 조

이 협정은 수표한날로부터 호력을 가진다.

이 협정은 1983년 4월 14일 평양에서 서명되었으며 조선

어와 영어로 각각 2부씩 작성된 두 원문은 같은 호력을 가진다

Maurice Bishop.

그레네이더인만혁명 정부의   조선민주주의인민공화국 정부의

위임에 의하여   위임에 의하여

조선민주주의인민공화국이 그 례네이귀인민혁명정부에

무상으로 군사원조를 줄데 대한 협정눌입료

소형신호권총	2 0 0 정
소형신호권총탄	4.0 0 0 발
7.6 2 미리자동보총	1.0 0 0 정
7.6 2 미리경기관총	5 0 정
7.6 2 미리자동보총탄	3 6 0,0 0 0 발
7.6 2 미리총탄	3 0 0.0 0 0 발
7.6 2 미리중기관총	3 0 정
7.6 2 미리중기관총탄	6 0,0 0 0 발
7 호발사관	5 0 정
7 호발사관탄	5 0 0 발
수 류 탄	2 0 0 발
고유탄수류탄	2 0 발

쌍 안 경 (8배)	3 0개
방 독 면	1,0 0 0개
사 이 렌	5 0개
지 도 작 업 용 도 구	1 5조
경 비 정	2척
군 화	6,0 0 0별
배 낭	6,0 0 0개
세 장 망	5 0개
초 단 파 무 선 기 우-3	3대
초 단 파 무 선 기 우-4	3대

The Ambassador reported that on his last trip to Venezuela, he met with the Ambassadors from the Socialist Community and raised with them the fact that, since his eight month stay in Trinidad, none of them had visited.

He explained that he had spoken with the General Secretary of the Venezuelan Communist Party and among other things, had raised the question of the level of counter-revolutionary activities in Venezuela. The General Secretary explained that there was, he thought, contact between the Venezuelan Government and the counter-revolutionaries and thought, but wasn't sure, that the President knew of it. The Ambassador asked him to work on it and send more precise information.

The Prime Minister thanked him and pointed out that the General Secretary had never been to Grenada kept contact with the Grenada Embassy in Caracas.

The Ambassador added that the International Relations Secretary of the Venezuelan Communist Party said he is coming to Grenada.

The Ambassador gave to the Prime Minister, copies of articles on Grenada published in the Soviet press.

The Ambassador reported that special equipment, 2 Coast Guard patrol boats and foodstuff were being sent direct to Grenada. This included 3,000 military uniforms in 1984 and 2,000 spades in 1985.

ITEM	1983	1984	1985	TOTAL
Flour	440	660	770	1870
Grains	88	132	154	374
Canned Meat	82	124	144	350
Canned Fish	73	110	128	311
Sugar	48	72	83	203
Salt	23	31	38	91
Vegetable Oil	14	21	25	60

ITEM	1983	1984	1985	TOTAL
Gasolene	240	300	370	910
Lubricants	600	400	200	1,200
Army Type Pick Up VAZ 21	18	6	–	24
Military Jeeps UAZ	25	15	–	40
Trucks SAZ	15	35	–	50
Fire Engines	5	–	–	5

(handwritten: } 114)

(handwritten: How many years Spare parts)

The Ambassador indicated that the supply of the vehicles and the fire-engines was based on the intergovernmental protocol of 11th July, 1980. The conditions were:

(1) 15% within 1 year of date of delivery;
(2) 85% over 10 years from date of delivery in equal half-yearly payments with the first to be made 3 years after date of delivery,
(3) 4% interest rate.

This, the Ambassador said are the most favourable conditions given to any body by the Foreign Trade Division of the U.S.S.R.

Talks and agreements can be conducted and signed in Moscow.

Prime Minister promised reply before the Ambassador leaves on 1st June, 1983 for vacation in Moscow.

Ambassador informed that General Chief of Staff, Ogarkov, will like appointment with Cde. Hudson Austin. He reported that 12,000 roubles supply of 14.5mm shells for BTR Armoured carriers delivered to Cuba in January 1983. Another 80,000 will be supplied this year through Havana. 35,000 roubles in spare parts can be delivered in the 3rd quarter of 1983 after letter of credit comes from Grenada. Soviet trade representative now in Grenada, can discuss this. The P... promised to have someone contact him.

Ambassador said agreement reached to exchange 2,000 pairs of boots for larger sizes (40-45); Grenada to follow up with the Cubans who have already been contacted and agreed to principle.

● 10 copies of Soviet Military Review coming in May 1983.

Cde. Layne had made requests on those two things and P... is to check him to follow up.

C.C. of C.P.S.U. has agreed to receive 5 members of Leadership for rest and treatment; Cde. Strachan had given name of Cde. Board, wife and three kids.

On P.M.'s request, Ambassador will clarify whether this will account for the five places. However, Ambassador explained that in event of necessity, a request can still be made.

Aircraft to be supplied to Grenada will be delivered to Cuba. Can seat 39 paratroopers and hold 6 tons of cargo. Has 4,000 flight hours capacity and 4,000 landings. If used actively can last four years without repair. Can be assembled in 90 days and will be done in Cuba. Has been designed with Sofa and car space and can accomodate 10-12 under those conditions.

P... explained that plane can be used for a dual purpose with the other being a Grenada/Cuba weekly run. He explained that the car will not be used as it can have negative political repercussion. He also pointed out that the kind of plane, a military make, can pose problems landing in the more reactionary countries in the region as civilian make craft will not have those problems.

Fifteen specialist will travel from Moscow to Havana to work on the aircrafts. An additional engine and spare parts enough for five planes will be attached. All spare parts will be left in Cuba under supervision of Specialists from the U.S.S.R. who will do all warranty services.

The Ambassador said that they will prefer Cubans Pilot to use it. Electrical equipment for starting the engine will be supplied to Grenada. Grenada must indicate what colours, emblems, service number are to be put on the plane.

The Ambassador pointed out that technicians can be sent to help develop the socio-economic plan for 1983-85. Two Specialists and and one interpreter can arrive September/October for three months.

He reported that equipment had been sent to G.I.S. from TASS Agency.

The Ambassador provided the P.M. with an overview of Venezuela's Foreign Minister, Zambrano's, visit to Moscow 25-30.4.83 and gave him a document on it.

The Ambassador informed that some projects for assistance to Grenada had been drafted but were done without taking into consideration the specific conditions on Grenada, therefore, he needs to know Grenada's position on these. They included:

(a) Technical and economic feasibility for sea-port project;
(b) Fifteen teachers coming to Grenada.

The P.M. pointed out he was glad the Ambassador raised this as he was going to raise a number of things:

(1) more sales of nutmeg and cocoa,
(2) gratuitous supply of 20,000 tons of fertiliser over 5 years (4,000 per year); (Ambassador explained that fertiliser is only product never granted - will still explore the possibility);
(3) Cement Plant;
(4) Satellite Station;
(5) East Coast Harbour;
(6) I.F.E.
(7) Steel.

The P.M. suggested the Ambassador meet with Cde. Strachan or Cde. Louisson before departing.

The Ambassador pointed that they have received no names from the Ministry of Education for scholarships granted - 20 per year.

The P.M. reminded the Ambassador about a request made to the Cde. Lronyks for EC$15M for International Airport; Ambassador promised to raise again.

The P.M. then gave the Ambassador, on request, an overview on the situation of the imperialist threat to Grenada.

The Ambassador thus pointed out that the state section was strengthening; he was concerned about the newspaper not being published for three weeks and about the level of propaganda and ideological activity by the mass media.

He offered to consider assistance to the media and requested an outline of what the problems were and what assistance was required.

The P.M. told him about the imminent closing down of R.F.G.
and explained that the problem was the Transmitter which could no
longer be repaired and a new one could not be bought. He ~~arranged~~
promised to arrange to have the media get the outline of the problems
and assistance need to the Ambassador before leaving.

The Ambassador indicated that Specialist can come to look at the
problems of the R.F.I.

The P.M. asked the Ambassador to express his greetings to
Cdes. Andropov, Pichonov, Pronyks and the C.C. of the C.P.S.U. and to
indicate his satisfaction on the progress in the development of the
relation and anticipation for even more deepened relations.

FOR FOLLOW UP

(1) Supply of special equipment, foodstuff, vehicles, cartridges.
    Talks and agreement possible from the Soviet side this year in
    Moscow. Promised reply to Ambassador before he leaves - 1.6.83.

(2) Delegate someone to meet with Soviet Trade representative now
    in Grenada re spare parts for 35,000 roubles to be delivered
    third quarter in 1983.

(3) Check Cde. Ewart Layne re (i) exchange of A, 56 pair of boots for
    larger sizes through Cuba, and (ii) 10 copies of Soviet Military
    Review coming for May 1. I.

(4) Inform Cde. Strachan to clear with Ambassador question of whether
    Cde. Board's five (wife and kids and himself) takes care of
    five agreed to for rest and treatment or just one place.

(5) Decide what colours, emblem and service number should be placed
    on plane.

(6) Read document on Lambran's visit to Moscow in light of Contadora
    group position on Central America as part of your preparation for U.
    S.S. trip.

(7) Ensure Grenada's position on projects for collaboration from USSR
    is prepared in time for disc. by Soviet bodies in March.

(8) Speak to Minister of Education re scholarships to USSR - 20 per
    year but no names have been given.

(9) Arrange for Cde. Strachan or Louison to meet with the Ambassador
    before he leave and give answer on questions.

(10) Arrange for comrades in the Media to prepare outline of their
     department's problems and assistance necessary and provide same
     to Ambassador before he leaves.

FEDERAL MINISTRY OF FOREIGN TRADE
T.D.PRAHA

Consignee

ORDER OF AMBAJADA DE GRANADA 5 AVENIDA
No.8409 MIRAMAR,LA HABANA — C U B A

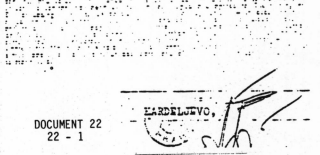

CZECHOSLOVAK OCEAN SHIPPING
INTERNATIONAL JOINT-STOCK Co.

POŠTOVNÍ SCHR. 140

110 91 PRAHA 10

CABLES PRACCS PRAHA

"Ocean" vessel	Port of loading			
"SITNO"	KARDELJEVO			
Port of discharge	Final destination (if on-carriage)	Freight as stated at		Number of original Bs/L
HAVANA		FREIGHT PREPAID		THREE/3/

2110054/D	1.250	CASEES EXPLOSIVE AMMUNITION	32.500	72,292
1.250/1-1.250		(WARHEADS,ROCKET)		
		ČECHOFRACHT PRAHA		
		Ref: 144/80664		
		FEDERAL MINISTRY OF FOREIGN		
		TRADE T.D.PRAHA		
		Ref:121/0839		

ABOVE PARTICULARS DECLARED BY SHIPPER

FREIGHT PREPAID

KARDELJEVO,

DOCUMENT 22
22 - 1

FEDERAL MINISTRY OF FOREIGN TRADE
T.D. PRAHA

Consignee

ORDER OF AMBAJEDA DE GRANADA 5 AVENIDA
No. 8409 MIRAMAR LA HABANA C U B A

B/L No: 6.-

ORIGINAL

CZECHOSLOVAK OCEAN SHIPPING
INTERNATIONAL JOINT-STOCK Co.

POCERNICKA 168

103 99 PRAHA 10

CABLES PLAVBA PRAHA

(Ocean) vessel	Port of loading	Final destination (if on-carriage)	Freight payable at	Number of original B/L
"SITNO"	KARDELJEVO		FREIGHT PREPAID	THREE /3/
Port of discharge HAVANA				

Marks & Nos.	Number and kind of packages, description of goods		Gross weight	Measurement
2110054/D ——— 1.250/1-1.250	1.250 CASES	EXPLOSIVE AMMUNITION (WARHEADS, ROCKET)	32.500	72,292

CECHOFRACHT PRAHA
Ref: 144/80664

FEDERAL MINISTRY OF FOREIGN
  TRADE T.D. PRAHA
Ref: 121/0859

ABOVE PARTICULARS DECLARED BY SHIPPER.

Freight and charges

KARDELJEVO,

168

Ofe Meeting - 25/3/80

Present: B, Kaman, ther, Bonner, SfB, Heesveld, Kent, Sebory, Bego, Challie, Clavette, Bello, Coldwell, ana ard Mr. / Malcolm Ardoin

Ghana

① Present Bilateral Aid Packages
② How are we going to build the Roads.

- left lots of Complicated - threat to the Revolution
- Several asking Ap of Congita

- Meeting of Caribbean Spokesman
  guns + ammo threat to independence

- Pattern of Rotor in the Army
- entirely the Hands of Gen Staff
- Clearance Program org to form turkmen war

- Prospective of Radio Scarborough

- Maximize Albanian conflicts between

- the Rivo has been Old & Great Counter-Revolution internationals, Expat hold to aid for Cubans and Soviets Militias.

- Init / Saritano / Rzick - Statement

- Proctor Laney - Norman main Speaker Sola Conkero au positive Traore Elekia Robberry Patrik

- Destabilized
  Popularity of the Revolution is a main element being held the elements.

- Fairman member of Bodyguard - Soprano to Gees guardian in Lookout Current lon Scorpion.

(3)

- Patrik Nomai - Actively engaged in organizing Guajika for Traore election

- Gorie & base aware of slack lookin in stellar in last couple of weeks

EMBASSY OF GRENADA IN THE USSR

Dobryninskaya Ulitsa 7
Apartment 221
Moscow
USSR

Telephone:
237-25-41
237-99-05

MEETING BETWEEN CHIEFS OF GENERAL STAFF OF SOVIET ARMED FORCES AND PEOPLE'S REVOLUTIONARY ARMED FORCES OF GRENADA

DATE: Thursday 10 March 1983 (4.00pm)

Representing the Soviet side were:

1.Marshal of the Soviet Union Ogarkov N.V.	-Chief of Staff
2.Colonel General N.A. Zutov	-10th Department
3.LT.-General G.A. Borisov	-Foreign relations Department
4.Colonel Soloviev	-10th Department
5.Captain M. Globenko	-Foreign Relations Department.

Present on the Grenada side were:

1.Major Einstein Louison	-Chief of Staff
2.Bernard Bourne	-Minister-Counsellor

The meeting commenced promptly by Marshal Ogarkov who extended a warm welcome to Major Louison. In doing so, Marshal Ogarkov enquired whether Major Louison was having any problems with his studies and living conditions.

Major Louison expressed thanks for the words of welcome and explained that he had no difficulty with studies and thought that he was making progress because there was no report to the contrary from the professors at the school.

Speaking about the Grenada Revolution Major Louison pointed out that the economy had grown by 5.5%(percent) in 1982 and living standards by 3 percent. He explained that the United States continues with its plans to destabilize the revolution, undermine tourism, linking our international airport with military potential and training of mercenaries in Venezuela. in addition

EMBASSY OF GRENADA IN THE USSR

Dobryninskaya Ulitsa 7
Apartment 221
Moscow
USSR

-2-

Telephone:
237-25-41
237-99-05

to the United States itself. Major Louison then emphasised that
the Grenada Revolution got around these problems and still
continued to make advances. He also informed Marshal Ogarkov
that at the Seventh Non-Aligned Summit Grenada was again
elected to the coordinating Bureau of the Movement.

At that moment Marshal Ogarkov said that he was glad for the
information on Grenada. About the situation in the world
Marshal Ogarkov pointed out that the United States would try
now and in the future to make things difficult for progressive
changes in all regions and continents. The Marshal said that
over two decades ago, there was only Cuba in LAtin America,
today there are Nicaragua, Grenada and a serious battle is
going on in EL Salvador. The Marshal of the Soviet Union then
stressed that United States imperialism would try to prevent
progress but that there were no prospects for imperialism to
turn back history.

Moreover, Marshal Ogarkov emphasised that in an aggressive
climate the military people have tasks to do. He explained that
since Grenada was located close to US imperialism and was not
developed militarily the Grenada Revolution would have to be
specifically vigilant at all times. Furthermore, the Marshal
declared that once the masses have a burning desire for progress
the leadership should move ahead decisively and firmly. On
that point Marshal Ogarkov assured Major Louison that the plans
outlined by Prime Minister Maurice Bishop during his visit to
the Soviet Union in 1982 were good and had the support of the
Grenadian people.

Further still, the Marshal of the Soviet Union reminded Major
Louison that the Soviet Union would contribute to raising the
combat readiness and preparedness of the Armed Forces of Grenada.

24 - 2

EMBASSY OF GRENADA IN THE USSR

Dobryninskaya Ulitsa 7
Apartment 221
Moscow   **-3-**
USSR

Telephone:
237-25-41
237-99-05

He informed the Grenada Chief of Staff that according to the
agreement signed in July 1982, one-third of the means for 1983
were already supplied and the rest would be delivered during
this year.

In response Major Louison expressed his gratitude for the
supplies sent to Grenada and mentioned that he was confident
that more deliveries would be sent to Grenada in the future.

However, Major Louison explained that he wished to introduce
another matter for discussion which was not included in the
protocol. The Chief of Staff of Grenada explained that he was
refferring to the text of a letter from Prime Minister Bishop
addressed to Prime Minister Tikhonov dated 28th July 1982.
Major Louison said that in the letter, Grenada was requesting
additional assistance in: food, fuel, spare parts, transportation,
engineering kits, uniforms and others. He disclosed that the
greatest part of the budget was used for food and fuel and that
spare parts were also of serieus concern because many vehicles
were grounded since the basic spare parts were unavailable.

Marshal Ogarkov replied rather jokingly that students should be
concerned with studies, but that Major Lousion who would grad-
uate on 10th May was also concerned about the problems of his
soldiers. Nevertheless, the Marshal indicated that he was aware
of such requests, but hastened to assure Major Louison that all
items contained in the protocol would be delivered. Marshal
Ogarkov further assured Major Louison that the requests contained
in the letter to P.M. Tikhonov were presently under consideration and that even though they were handled by GKS and Ministry
of Foreign Trade, the Ministry of Defence would exercise some
control on the solution. He said, with confidence, that his
Ministry would participate in the settlement of these requests.

EMBASSY OF GRENADA IN THE USSR

Dobryninskaya Ulitsa 7
Apartment 221
Moscow   -4-
USSR

Telephone:
237-25-41
237-99-05

Further still, the Marshal disclosed that there was a possibility that some of the main questions would be solved and as soon as a decision was taken, the Ministry of Defence through Col-General Zutov would inform the Embassy.

Additionally, referring to the question of deputation of Soviet specialists to Grenada to conduct studies related to the construction of military projects the Marshal informed the Grenadian side that the team of specialists would be sent in one month's time and that they await an indication from Grenada confirming readiness to accommodate the specialists.

Finally, towards the end of the meeting the Marshal of the Soviet Union and Chief of Staff of the Soviet Armed Forces proposed a toast 'from the bottom of our hearts'- in his words- to Major Louison on the eve of the 10th Anniversary of the New JEWEL Movement and the fourth Anniversary of the Grenada Revolution.

In his turn, Major Louison expressed thanks and appreciation to the Marshal for the kind words about the Grenada Revolution; Major Louison also expressed thanks for the assitance to the Armed Forces of Grenada and then raised a toast towards the strengthening of relations between the two countries, parties, people's, and their armed forces.

Marshal Ogarkov was thankful for the warm meeting and reinforced both toasts by raising a final toast for the growth and futher strengthening of the relations between the Soviet Armed Forces and the People's Revolutionary Armed Forces of Grenada.

In conclusion, it should be pointed out that the entire meeting
24 - 4   was conducted in an atmosphere of warmth, friendliness, simplicity and unpretentiousness.

EMBASSY OF GRENADA IN THE USSR

Dobryninskaya Ulitsa 7
Apartment 221   -5-
Moscow
USSR

Telephone:
237-25-41
237-99-05

The meeting ended with warm embraces.

Bernard Bourne

Bernard Bourne

Minister-Counsellor.

СВИДЕТЕЛЬСТВО
CERTIFICATE

МИНИСТЕРСТВО ОБОРОНЫ СССР	**THE MINISTRY OF DEFENCE, USSR**
# СВИДЕТЕЛЬСТВО	# CERTIFICATE
АН № 46207	AH № 46207

Настоящее свидетельство выдано ....
...... *майору*
...... *Луисону Эктейну*
в том, что он .... в *декабре* 19 *82* г. поступил ....
и в *мае* 19 *83* г. окончил .... *Вкшие*
офицерские курсы
„ *Выстрел* "
по специальности ....
командная тактическая
мотопехотных войск

Настоящее свидетельство дает право на
самостоятельное выполнение работ, связанных с полученной специальностью.

Регистрационная № *2123*

This is to certify that ....
...... *major*
...... *EINSTEIN T. LOUISON*
entered in *December* 19 *82* and graduated
from ....
VYSTREL ACADEMY
.... in *May* 19 *83*
majoring in ....
motorized infantry
tactical commander

The bearer of the Present Certificate enjoys
the right for independent activity associated
with Major subject.

Commanding Officer, VYSTREL ACADEMY
Major-General of the armour
D. DRAGUNSKY
" *10* " *May* 19 *83*
Registration No. *2123*

25 - 2

EMBASSY OF GRENADA IN THE USSR

Dobryninskaya Ulitsa 7
Apartment 221
Moscow
USSR

Telepho
237-25-
237-99-

Typed personally by W.Richard Jacobs.
Distribution as follows: Minister Unison Whiteman
                          PM
                          Deputy PM Coard
                          PB Member Ewert Layne who is in the USSR

11th. July 1983

EMBASSY OF GRENADA IN THE USSR

Dobryninskaya Ulitsa 7
Apartment 221
Moscow
USSR

CONFIDENTIAL

Telephone:
237-25-41
237 99-05

Grenada's relations with the USSR

Our relations with the USSR are influenced by a number of inter- connecting factors. Among the more important are:
1. Perceived ideological direction of the NJM Party and the PRG.
2. The management of state affairs.
3. The development of state to state relations.
4. Grenada's role in the world (region).
5. Our relationship with other members of the socialist community.
6. Relationship between the NJM and CPSU.
7. Our activity in international organizations.

Perceived ideological direction - xxx PRG

Grenada is regarded as being on the path of socialist orientation. There is a general acceptance among Soviet authorities that we are at the national democratic, anti-imperialist stage of socialist orientation. The USSR assigns a special place to these types of countries in its foreign policy. This is, of course, also the case with other socialist countries. In terms of their priorities, the countries of socialist orientation come right after the socialist community. Therefore, whatever, the internal debate, it is important that we continue to maintain our public assessment of our stage of development as the national democratic, anti-imperialist stage of socialist orientation. After all the PM himself made that assessment when he was here in Moscow as well as during his visit to Berlin. This has recently been reinforced by the Foreign Minister during his visit to Vietnam, Kampuchia and Laos. So it seems to me absolutely necessary that we maintain this line. This is made all the more important by the very high priority that is placed on consistency of analysis here.

- NJM

The Comrades responsible for Grenada in the International Section, have told me that they operate on the basis that the NJM is a "communist party". Given the relatively low level of these comrades (Nicholi etc.) one is not too sure about the authoritativeness of this statement though, I doubt that they would make a statement like that without the necessary authority. In any event, my clear impression is that we are being treated as a fraternal party — ie a M-L Party. My impression too, is that the CPSU delegation that visited in March formed a positive impression of the work of the NJM and have communicated that impression. The CPSU is x in a position to know almost everything about the NJM - its size, programme, objectives, orientation etc. and they cannot fail to recognize and accept the authenticity of our credentials. The problem of protocol — the proper level at which our leaders should be met etc. remains. This could perhaps be explained on two levels: 1. They sometimes adopt an over-protective attitude towards us and argue that if we meet at too high a level the USA would use this as an excuse to further squeeze Grenada.(This is one of the explanations floated as to why the PM did not meet with Andropov in April)2. Although we are regarded as a fraternal party we are not in the "inner group" ie members of the socialist community — their highest party officials are reserved for these kinds of encounters. Their answer as to why Nicaragua is treated differently — and at a higher level — would presumably be that Nicaragua is already under direct US attack and it is necessary for them to openly show solidarity. They would like Grenada to avoid that direct attack. The core of the matter however, is that they regard Grenada as a small distant country and they are only prepared to make commitments to the extent of their capacity to fulfill,and if necessary, defend their commitment. (I recall on one occasion explaining the situation in St. Vincent to the Party comrades. Their response was that this is all very interesting but St. Vincent is so far away!!)

Recommendations

1. The Soviets have a correct perception of our ideological line both at the Government and Party levels. We should continue along these lines.
2. The problem of "protocol" has to be solved but it must be handled gently. At the diplomatic level, we could keep on insisting that counterparts meet. To the extent that this is not achieved, the principals would mention it in passing - not a substantive point, just in passing. We must not fail to mention the matter to their Ambassador at social activities. Gestures are also important - cutting conversations short with junior people etc. Receprosity is also important. BP Members should not be easily available to low-ranking Soviet officials on visits. As a rule, the PM in particular, and I would also say the Deputy PM should only entertain courtesy calls not exceeding 15 to 30 minutes.

The management of state affairs

The Soviets have been burnt quite often in the past by giving support to Governments which have either squandered that support, or turned around and become agents of imperialism , or lost power. One is reminded of Egypt, Samolia, Ghana and Peru. They are therefore very careful, and for us sometimes maddingly slow, in making making up their minds about who to support. They have decided to support us for two main reasons. 1. Cuba has strongly championed our cause.
2. They are genuinely impressed with our management of the economy and state affairs in general. They are impressed with our commitment to planning, the absence of corruption, the ethic of hard work among the leadership, the ability of the leadership to spread this ethic among the population, the willingness to sacrifice. They are also impressed with the policy on the communication media, the close links with the masses, the practice of popular democracy and the implementation of the policy of democratic centralism as a guiding principle and not a dogma. Also of importance is the stability of our leadership.

Recommendation

The Soviets are very impressed with our management of state power. We should continue along this line with a continuing emphasis on the "step by step" approach.

Development of State to State Relations

The principal item here is the implementation of the Agreements signed in July 1982. In the area of Trade and Collaboration — this is generally being implemented in accordance with the agreements. Some collaboration agreements however, have been delayed as a result of procrastination on our part. In particular, the sattelite dish agreement has not yet been signed by our side. As far as the Soviets are concerned, this is the centerpiece of our July agreements, the only negotiable items in it are how we house and transport the technicians, and how we pay them in local currency. The other items are fixed. The credit for this project cannot be utilized for any other project. We really need to get on with this matter. The same holds true for the Fifteen Teachers project. In any event, the reasons for not signing these agreements promptly, sould be routinely communicated to the Embassy. We are not infrequently faced with the question as to what is the state of affairs on this or that project and we are plac in the very embarassing possition of not being able to answer. Meanwhile, our Soviet colleagues who ask these questions often know the answer because their Embassy in Grenada has informed them. But even with these shortcomings, I would say that we are OK in this area of trade and collaboration.

State to state relations are also fundamentally influenced by the development of relations in other field as well. We have a good record of collaboration at the military and trade union levels. These are positive factors in the development of our state to state relations. A lot more could be done at the NWO and Peace levels. It is important always to remember that plans for visits and interchanges should be made at least one year in advance. The NYO level is developing satisfactorily satisfactorily.

One of the most difficult areas is at the University and Technical education levels. As in all the above, the Soviets assess the level of state to state relatio by, among other things, the extent to which we are willing to share our experiences with them, and learn from their experiences. When trade unionists, youth, women and pioneers come to study in the USSR, we are in effect signaling to them that we recognize that we can learn from their experiences and thereby sending the correct ideological message as well. The same holds true for our University and technical students. The presence of ten of our top planners has made a very favourable impact on the development of our state to state relations. But the same is not true in the area of the University and Technical education. To date we have been offered 80 (eigthy) University or Technical scholarships - 20 in 1981, 20 in 1982 and 40 in 1983. We have accepted eighteen (18) of which two of our students have given up the course. Of the remaining sixteen (16) at least eight (8) do not have the minimum requirements for entry to the level of education they expected to receive upon leaving Grenada. This, it seems to me, is requesting more than we know that we can absorb. It is much better to ask for five scholarships and fill four than to ask for 40 and send only four people. This gives the impression, false as it may be, that our students prefer not to study in the USSR. It introduces a certain question mark and works in a negative way on state to state relations. Of course, it need hardly be mentioned that the behaviour of our students can also have an effect on state to state relations, and we must therefore be carefull to select highly motivated students.

The establishment of the Grenada-Soviet Friendship society has a positive effect on our relations. It is now critical that this organization function.

State to state relations are very seriously affected by the use that is made of the aid and assistance rendered to Grenada at the material and technical levels. In the case of technicians, it is important that proper provisions be made for their stay in Grenada and they be full fully utilized for the entire time of their stay in Grenada. In general we have received very good feed-back on this aspect and the technicians are full of praise for the enthusiasm and commitment of their Grenadian hosts.

In the case of the use of some materials, the feedback has also been generally good. But there have evidently been some lapses, and and we must always take care to ensure that we order the correct item with full information and specifications for everything associated with its use. The case of the first set of tractors which arrived without the necessary attachments simply because the Soviets did not know what "attachments" we were talking about; the case of waterpumps going unused because of no hose; and the case of military vehicles without spare-parts in part because of poor specifications on our part - all contribute to a negative impression. There seems to have been some slip-up also in relation to the AN-2. The information needed for certification should certainly have been requested before the completion of the assembly of the plane. The Soviets have serious concerns about the operation and maintenance of the AN-26. We have assured them that we have a suitable stand-by agreement with the Cubans on this one, but it is urgent that we select and despatch as soon as possible ten(10) people - at least - to be trained for the operation and maintenance of this aircraft.

An important aspect of the development of state to state relations is the operation and functioning of the Embassy. All countries use the quality and quantity of personnel assigned as diplomatic staff to particular Embassies as an indication of the nature of a country's priorities in domestic and international affairs. The Soviet Union is no exeption in this regard. Their own Embassy in Grenada is not only an indication of their resource base, but equally a reflection of the fact that they have considerable interest in the development of relations with Grenada.

I have on a previous occasion pointed out that for any Embassy to operate efficiently, the following officers are absolutely essential - Ambassador, Deputy (at the level of 1st. Secretary or above) Secretary to the Ambassador, Accountant. This is emphasized even more in the case of the Embassy in Moscow by the fact that the Ambassador is accredited to nine other countries - GDR, Bulgaria, Checoslovakia, Hungary, Korea, Rumania, Mongolia, Poland, Yougoslavia and Afghanistan - ten in fact - and at least the first five plus the USSR are countries with which we have some serious relations. This means that the job requires a lot of travel. Both inside and outside of the USSR, I would say that about 60% of the Ambassador's work is representational. This responsibility requires two essential elements 1. Information from Grenada 2. Sophisticated analyses of the information available from each country. The first one is lacking but I am confident that a political decision can correct this situation. The second requires a person of high cultural level with some formal training and/or experience in international relations. Equally, we need someone with the appropriate training to undertake the task associated with the maintenance and development of our trading relations with the socialist community. Because of the structure of the diplomatic corps in the USSR both of these people need to be at the level of 1st. Secretary or above. We have a mountain of experience in the proper selection of these people. The fact is that a trained person can absorb and apply the experience to which he exposed in a creative way. An untrained person can be little more than a messenger, and length of service becomes a repetative experience. It is important too, to recognize that particularly in the socialist community, training is highly valued and contributes to the development of the kind of prestige necessar to achieve our objectives.

All members of our leadership with whom I have raised this matter of staffin agree that we need additional staff at the Embassy in Moscow. This matter should be given the most urgent attention. Inadequate staff prevents this Embassy from developing state to state relations to the level necessary to preserve and advanc our interests.

I mentioned earlier about the representational role of the Ambassador and th need for information for this task to be properly performed. I wish to draw on th example of the PM's recent mission to the USA. I was in the GDR at the time of th mission and I happened to hear on VOA a report of the PM's mission just before a meeting with the Foreign ~~Minis~~ Ministry. The PM's mission turned out to be the main item on the agenda. I was able to handle the issue because as part of the information package on the March mobilization, the PS (Foreign Affairs) had sent an up-to-date package on ~~the~~ our relations with the USA. When I returned to Moscow, the issue was raised by Kazimirov – Director of the First Latin American Department – who handles Grenada's affairs in the Foreign Ministry. Basically, he wanted to know what was the nature of the meeting with Clark. I told him that thus far the results are confidential. He said to me in the usual light vein of t types of conversations that if he were friends with the American Ambassador he could get the information from him!! The basic point that he successfully got ove to me is that in the circumstances of our relations with the USSR and their and our relations with the USA, it would have been courteous to inform them of the intention to visit. I agree with that. The contents of the discussion with Clark is another matter since, among other things, I am certain that the USA could ~~declxre~~ break our code if they wanted to. Kazimirov told me that he first read of the visit in the newspapers and that he first heard that the PM had a meeting with Clark when the Canadian Ambassador, who was on a visit to his office, mentioned it to him. I feel sure that either his Ambassador in Grenada or USA would have informed him of this but the basic point that he is making is that he would have expected the information to come from me.

The other piece of information which is really crucial for our state to stat relations deals with the IMF loan that I understand that we are negotiating or ha signed. Now, when the PM raised the possibility of a US$6 million with Gromyko in April he made the point that we could get the money nowhere else. I have been monitoring the response here and the latest thing that they told me is that we may get a reply by mid July. I assume that the IMF loan has nothing to do with th airport project and therefore we are still going ahead with the US$6 million request which is strictly for the airport. But this is only an educated guess on my part, I have no hard information, and it would have been appropriate to let the Soviets know through our Embassy here that we were about to apply for thi loan. Of course, as I understand it, they have no problem with us going to the IMF. But the communication of this kind of information adds to a stable, reliable friendly state to state relations atmosphere. And equally important, it developes an expectation of ~~repre~~ resoprosity – they will give us information in the future

Recommendations

1. We should make every effort to implement ~~xxx~~ all collaboration and personnel-exchange agreements. In the case of personnel exchange, when it is not possible for the Grenada party to fulfill the agreement, the Embassy must be promptly informed. No individual should arrive in the USSR without previously informing the Embassy.

2. Both the Embassy and an appropriate Unit in the Ministry of Trade should monitor the implementation of trade agreements on a monthly basis and exchange this information. The Embassy and the Misnistry of Planning should do the same thi

with other collaboration agreements.(I have in the past received such a monitoring report from the Macro-Planning Unit. But only on one occasion.)

3. We should as a matter of principle never request materials and opportunities that we are not in a position to utilize within a defined period.

4. A political decision should be immediately communicated to the International Department of the Party or the FS(Foreign Affairs) to keep the Embassy informed on all important issues.

5. Urgent steps be taken to recruit three new members of the diplomatic staff for the USSR Embassy with the appropriate qualifications.

Grenada's role in the world (region)

By itself, Grenada's distance from the USSR, and its small size, would mean that we would figure in a very minute way in the USSR's global relationships. Our revolution has to be viewed as a world-wide process with its original routs in the Great October Revolution.For Grenada to assume a position of increasingly greater importance, we have to be seen as influencing at least regional events. We have to establish ourselves as the authority on events in at least the English-speaking Caribbean, and be the sponsor of revolutionary activity and progressive developments in this region at least. At the same time, we have to develop and maintain normal state to state relations with our neighbours and concretely operationalize our good-neighbourlyness policy. The twice per year meetings with the progressive and revolutionary parties in the region is therefore critical to the development of closer relations with the USSR. Inorder to keep both the Embassy and the Soviets informed of the outcome of such meetings, perhaps a good model would be for a member of the CC to pay a visit to the UBSR after each such meeting. The mission of such a person could without difficulty be mixed with other activities. We must ensure though that we become the principal point of access to the USSR for all these groups even to the point of having our Embassy serve as their representative while in the USSR.

Equally important is our relationship with those neighbours who the Soviets regard as our potential adversaries. We have not been making a big deal of the Regional Defence Force but the Soviets never fail to mention that to their mind this is one of the most serious future dangers that we face. It is perhaps possible to use the GG on some kind of good-will mission to the other islands as a prelimilary to the signing of some type of treaty of Friendship and Co-operation with them.It seems to me too, that we need to maintain a high diplomatic profile in these islands.

Of all the regional possibilities, the most likely candidate for special attention is Surinam. If we can be an overwhelming influence on Surinam's international behaviour, then our importance in the Soviet scheme of things will be greatly enhanced. To the extent that we can take credit for bringing any other country into the progressive fold, our prestige and influence would be great enhanced. Another candidate is Belize.I think that we need to do some more work in that country.

Recommendations

1. Establish a system of informing the Soviets of the outcome of the meetings between NJM and the progressive parties in the region.

2. Maintain these party to party meetings.

3. Examine the possibility of concluding formal treaties of Friendship and co-peration with our neighbours.

4. Explore ways and means of influencing the international behaviour (voting at UN etc) of Surinam and Belize.

Our relationship with other members of the socialist community

It is well to remember that there is a constant and very detailed consultatio process that takes place between members of the socialist community. For example, on my recent mission to the GDR (June 1983) they made it very clear to me that they had been briefed on the PM's discussions with Gromyko, and this is to be expected.As a result, our performance in verious aspects of our relations with members of the socialist community directly affects our relations with the USSR - not to mention the fact that it directly determines the relationship between Grena and the country involved.

There have been some positive points that has promoted our image throughout t socialist community. Among the most recent are: 1. The excellent to very good performance of our students who went to the CPSU Party school –this has become generally known. 2. The excellent contribution made by comrade DeRiggs and the generally good impression made by the Grenada delegation at the Berlin Conference on Karl Marx – this is a constant cause of congratulations in various countries. (Incidentally, as a further indication of the communication problem, it is worth noting that I have not yet received a copy of this presentation which I am sure will serve as a good guide of policy.) 3. The fact that I have been presenting credentials and participating in the important occasions of the states involved. But there have also been negative factors. I think chief among them is the very slow process of implementing the agreements signed between Grenada and Bulgaria and GDR. This is very bad for our relations with the countries involved as well as for the USSR because they not only look at the process of implementation of our bi-lateral agreements with them, but also with the rest of the community. In particular, the GDR has floated the view with me that we appear to want to rewrite a solemn agreement agreed to by their President and our PM. (This refers principally to the method of paying for the bananas.) This, to them, is entirely inconceivable. My own view is that once the agreement is signed at that level, there is no going back and even if it is disadvantageous to us we just have to implement it. It is indecent to be seen as wanting to revise an agreement arrived at by the two Heads of Government. I have no evidence that this view ~~has been communicated~~ regarding our apparent desire to revise a solemn agreement has been communicated to other members of the community, but I would be very surprised if it has not. In any event, I ~~s~~ have not formed the impression that there is any such generalized view within the community and it is of course in our interest to ensure that we retain the reputation as honest brokers who keep their word regardless. It is worth noting also that any effort to revise an agreement signed by the two Heads of Government below the level of Heads of Government will be next to impossible and could only serve to undermine the prestige and authority of the office of the Prime Minister.

~~brother·negative·work·six·years~~

As far as the relations with the other socialist countries are concerned, it is useful to have our people visit there as frequently as possbile as well as to have state officials visit us as frequently as possible. I think that officials who travel to Eastern Europe should as a matter of policy include on their itinerary, at least one other socialist country in a planned and rotational way so that we get to touch as many bases as possible. If we are informed of such visits atleast ten days in advance, we can get the host country, I am sure, to stand most of the costs. The benefits to us will be very great. As a rule, our officials have made a very ~~positive~~ positive impression on their hosts.

Recommendations

1. Continue high profile, well prepared participation in important events of the socialist community eg Karl Marx Conference and World Peace Council
2. Implement agreements between Grenada and other members of the socialist community promptly and faithfully.
3. Encourage officials to visit at least two countries in Eastern Europe during official missions to this part of the world.

Party to Party Relations

In the socialist community, it has emerged that there is a very close inter-relationship between party to party and state to state relations. Many of the things that the Party was able to arrange in Cuba (eg airline tickets and special considerations of several kinds) are passed on to the state here. Further, as we discovered during the PM's mission and after, there is such an intimate linkage between the party and state at all levels, and notably at the highest levels that the distinctions that we have been inclined to make are not applicable in the socialist community.

One of the direct consequences of this is that the perception of party to party relations is fundamentally influenced by the nature of state to state relations and it is important to constantly keep this in mind.

Of course the implementation of the party to party agreements is paramount. By and large, we have implemented these agreements faithfully. Our first batch of party school students, although they were some two years late, have made a very good impression. Our implementation of the rest and recreation agreements have been good for our relations. But there are a number of negative points. I think the most telling is the fact that Comrade Strachan undertook during his mission here in December to send a team of party mobilizers to the USSR for a couple of weeks, to experience the Soviet experience. As is known, these people were not sent. This did some damage which could have been minimized if we had received some instructions to explain to the CPSU comrades that this undertaking was not possible at the moment. As it is, they cancelled it when the time ran out. Another example, has to do with the Public address system. We said that we needed it urgentl for March 13th. 1983. They rushed it down by air to Cuba at the end of January, as promised, and the P.A. system stayed in Cuba for a very long time. I am not even sure if it has arrived as yet. They have brought this matter to our attention on a number of occasions, we have sent messages to Cuba and Grenada to try and co-ordinate our excuses by we have received no response.

We have to insist too that they stick to their agreements. For example, they agreed with Comrade Strachan to send down to Grenada "a high level delegation" - in March 1983 - you know of course, the very low level that was sent. They also agreed to send two people for rest and recreation in 1983, and we must make sure, that they stick by their agreement. They have also fallen down in relation to their undertakings to supply books, magazines, newspapers, films and projection equipment for the political education programme. We have to stick them to their word. I can raise it here at the diplomatic level but it will be twice as effective when it is repeated at the party political level.

The problem of what might be called counterpart protocol remains. That is, we have never been able to meet with our strict counterparts at the party level when we have our leaders here. On 27th. June, I had a very frank and friendly discussion with Boyko Demitrov - the former Bulgarian Ambassador to Grenada who is now Director of International Relations in the Party. He told me that even Bulgaria sometimes face this problem and that Grenada has to face the reality that it is a question of size, distance and priorities. I think that he is correct. But we then have to deal with these realities. Inorder to elevate our priority in the socialist scheme of things, the recommendations contained in the section dealing with our role in the world (region) becomes all the more relevent. In addition, we have to raise and discuss with the highest authorities, <u>global and regional</u> issues rather than parochial or national issues. In other words, our legitimate begging operations have to be cast in the larger world context. We have in fact done this in the past quite successfully, linking our national requests to a global analysis. What we need to do now, it seems to me, is to become the spokesman for a broader constituency - perhaps the countries of socialist orientation. It is in this context that I have prepared the attached paper dealing with a bank of last resort sponsored by the socialist community for countries for socialist orientation. This will give us an opportunity to discuss the highest issues of policy both with the countries of socialist orientation and with the socialist community, lift our profile, and heighten our priority. Here we can clearly see the close link between party to party and state to state relations.

All that is said about the CPSU holds true for the other parties as well. We have a very sympathetic hearing in Bulgaria with Boyko Demitrov and we should perhaps draw ever closer to the Bulgarian Party.

In the GDR, we also have made a good impression and there is great sympathy there for the NJM. Four comrades will be coming for rest and recreation in 1983.

I doubt that we will encounter the protocol problems that we have found in the CPSU. But we must at all cost continue to regard relations with the CPSU as the highest priority.

Recommendations

1. Strictly implement all agreements and insist on implementation on the other sides as well.
2. Send prompt explanations when it is not possible to implement an agreement.
3. Seek to become spokesman for the countries of socialist orientation.
4. Develop even stronger relations with the Bulgarian and GDR parties by sending delegations etc.

International activity

From the point of view of our relations with the USSR, our international activity is important from the following persepctives:
1. The consistency of our political line.
2. The influence of Grenada in the international community
3. The degree of support offered to the positions taken by the USSR.

Our performance is assessed at the folling levels:
1. The United Nations and its agencies - UNESCO, UNCTAD etc.
2. Organization of American States
3. Non-aligned Movement
4. Missions in various countries (Embassies).

It is very difficult for me to assess their view of our performance in the UN, its agencies and the OAS because, we receive only the minimum of information on our voting and performance etc. But during the period of the threats etc. in March 1983, they advised us to play a more active role in the UN ecpecially at the Security Council and spoke approvingly of Nicarigua's performance at the Security Council. But I suspect that we need a bigger staff at the UN to do the kind of job that would impress internationally. The same probably holds true for the OAS. They have however, praised our role in the Zone of Peace resolution and activity.

At the non-aligned movement, they have a high vlauation of our role. You will recall that before the New Delhi Conference they gave me a detailed briefing on their positions and when Comrade Whiteman visited afterwards they expressed admiration for our performance. I think however, that we must insist that we form the inner circle of the advisers to Mrs. Gandhi in line with our leading role in New Delhi especially in regard to the New International Economic Order and the Small States Conference. We have an excellent case - especially since Guyana did not participate when they were invited to in May 1983 in New Delhi. The Guyana Amba sador here tells me that the Foreign Minister decided that the Heads of Mission meeting then taking place in Guyana was more important.

As far as our Embassies are concerned, the most important thing is that they carry the same line on all matters - economic and political, internal and external. To do this successfully, we need to have a common fund of information. Obviously, each mission would have its area of specialty and would have more information on that area than any other Embassy. But a regular series of directives, instructions and information from the Party or the Foreign Ministry would ensure that a common line is maintained throughout.

As far as the role of the mission in the USSR is concerned, the reality of size came to me very early in the game. It therefore became necessary to establish ones influence in the corps by making strategic associations and alliances. Latin America - our natural constituency - lacks cohesiveness and leadership. The Dean of the Latin American group - Venezuela is lazy and uninterested in leadership. The Cuban Ambassador is not very out-going. So I have had to maintain individual relationships especially with Cuba, Nicarigua and Mexico. Ecuador is also a good man. The African group is much more cohesive and influential in Moscow. They have also been very welcoming. My informal inclusion in the group has raised Grenada's profile and influence in the corps as a whole.

The socialist countries to which I am accredited are a natural area of interest Of these, Bulgaria is the Dean and has little time for socio-political interaction. Checoslovakia, GDR and Rumania have been particularly warm. We have it as a high priority to establish and maintain the closest personal and official relations with these countries. And although the Korean Ambassador for example, is regarded as a recluse, I have had him over to dinner and he has reciprocated, as is the case with many of the others.

On the whole, I have formed the view that the USSR is satisfied with the degree of support that they receive from Grenada. Indeed, I would say that they have every reason to be satisfied especially if our vote on Afganistan for example, is recognized as one of two Latin American votes (the other being Cuba) in their favour. Considering the risks that we have taken on this and other matters, it might be fair to say that their support for us is actually below our support for them. We must therfore work to establish a balance of interests. This might best be done by gentle reminders at critical stages by members of our leadership. We might also seek to develop our links with what has ebeen called the "middle" countries like Yougoslavia and Greece for example and strengthen our links with "off centre" countries like Korea, and Rumania, and Hungary. But these calculations have to be done very carefully and in a very sophisticated way. We have to think them out very carefully.

Recommandations

1. Continue our international support for the Soviet line.
2. Strengthen our political efforts in the UN and OAS and their agencies.
3. Seek a more critical role in the non-aligned movement.
4. Examine the desirability, ways and means of developing closer relations with the "middle" and "off centre" countries.
5. Provide all missions with a regular common fund of knowledge so that there can be a guarantee that a common line is being pursued on all matters.

MINISTRY OF INTERIOR

~~PRIME MINISTER'S~~
~~BELMONT~~
~~GRENADA~~

BUTLER HOUSE
ST. GEORGE'S
GRENADA
WEST INDIES

TEL: 3383   3020

17th Feb. 19 82

TO: Commander Andropov
         Chairman of the Committee of State Security
         Member of Politburo

FROM: General of the Army Hudson Austin

Dear Comrade,

Warmest revolutionary greetings to you, the Communist
Party of Soviet Union and all Soviet people, from the
Political Bureau of the New Jewel Movement, Government, Armed
Forces and all the Grenadian people.

Let me first of all extend our deepest sympathies to your
Party and people on the passing away of comrade Suslov, a true
Bolshevik and hero of revolutionary people worldwide.
                I WRITE AT THIS TIME TO
~~Secondly, I write this letter in the form of a~~ request ~~for~~
assistance in the strengthening of our Ministry of Interior. •
                                       HELD BETWEEN
This request stems from discussions ~~held with~~ Cde. Vladmir
Klimentov, then attached to the Soviet Embassy in Jamaica,
~~During the course of these discussions held with~~ ʰComrade
                        ʰ
Maurice Bishop, Chairman of the Central Committee of our Party
the New Jewel Movement, Prime Minister and Minister of Defence
and Interior of the People's Revolutionary Government, ~~comrade~~
~~and~~ Comrade Liam James, Member of the Central Committee of our
Party and Head of the Ministry of Interior ~~and~~ *myself.*

*[handwritten: Peoples Revo. Govt. ... may formally
request the following: ... of our ...]*

~~Request~~ Training courses for four (4) comrades:—

a) Basic course in Counter Intelligence for the
   period of one (1) year - three (3) comrades.

b) Basic course in Intelligence for a period of one
   (1) year - one (1) comrade.

We thank you once again for the tremendous assistance
which our Armed Forces have received from your Party and
Government in the past. We recognise the tremendous
internationalist obligation of your people, yet we sincerely
hope that these courses will be made available to our
comrades in 1982, given the pressing needs in our Ministry
and the continuing threat being posed to the Grenada
Revolution by United States Imperialism.

I close by once again extending our greatest warmth
and embrace to you and your Party - Sons and Daughters
of the heroic Lenin. I look forward to hearing from you
soon.

Yours Fraternally,

....
General Hudson Austin
Member of the Political Bureau of NJM
Secretary of Defence and Interior.

The course was divided into two aspects, theoretical and practical. The Theory included the following subjects:-

1) Social Psychology and propaganda.
2) Philosophy.
3) Theory and tactics of the International Working Class Movement.
4) Political Economy.
5) The Historical Experience of the CPSU.
6) Party Organisation - Intelligence / Security.
7) General Lectures which covered a wide range of topics.

The practical aspect involved being assigned

(1) To a texile factory - The October Factory; from which we gained real work experience in two days of Subbotnik - ie. Voluntary work days; one on Dec 18th, 1982 in honour of the 60th Aniversary of the formation of the USSR; and the other on April 16th, 1983, in honour of Lenins 113th Birthday. We created 66 Roubles in the first Subbotnik and received a Certificate for that service. For the second day we were not informed about the Roubles created. At the factory we were given an explanation on how cost accounting is implemented in the factory.

(2) Visiting places of historic importance eg. museums and monuments, exhibitions etc. This was done mostly on afternoons and Sundays.

(3) Visit to three places outside of Moscow - Leningrad in the Russian Federation; Kiev in the Ukraine and Volgograd in the Russian Federation. In each place one week was spent. The whole Collective visited Leningrad and Kiev but only two were invited to Volgograd. Anslem De Bourg and Fabian Otram were chosen by our Collective to go to Volgograd.

The course also involved Symposiums and Theoretical Conferences.

Our Collective took part in the Latin American Symposium at which we were given a special chance to present seven papers in five days. Others Collectives had a maximum of five (5) papers, however, none of the countries presented their five papers. The following persons presented our papers:-

. Rita, Spooner, Glen, Fabian, Samuel, Superville and Derrick.

We were also invited by the chair of theory and tactics to speak on behalf of Latin America at the African Symposium. Ian Lambert presented that paper.

- For the Theoretical Conference which was to mark the 165th Birthday of Karl Marx, Ian Lambert presented a paper on the Social psychology and propaganda section, and Anslem De Bourg on the Theory and tactics section.
- All the presentations made are available for reference.

During the course students were given a chance to meet and have discussions with important persons from parties of foreign countries including General Secretaries of Communist & Workers parties.

The various parties present at the Institute also celebrated their party's day with an exhibition of what's happening in their various countries. That was very informative and we learnt a great deal from them. Few Collectives also held celebration meetings which we attended.

There were also other extra curricula activities which included cultural activities and sports. Our Collective took part in them and did well. The activities included carnival, festival of political songs etc. A: ? sports like athletics and football. The sports report will give the details.

28 - 2

On our own we celebrated and commemorated our historic days.

(1) March 11th & 13th.

(2) Bloody Sunday Nov 18th.

(3) Independence Day Feb 7th.

(4) Harold Strachan 27th Dec.

(5) Jeremiah Richardson April 1st.

(6) Lenins Birthday 22nd April.

(7) A round table solidarity conference of Latin American countries at the time of the threat of invasion of Grenada.

Items (1), (2) and (7) were public events where as the others were internal, either with our own Collective only or with the party branch in Moscow.

For March 11th & 13th the 10th Anniversary of the NJM and the 4th anniversary of the Revolution, this was organised by our March 13th Cttee. headed by Cde. R. Spooner. The celebration involved three aspects:-

(1) Political aspect / Formal Meeting.

(2) Exhibition / propaganda.

(3) Reception.

The formal meeting was chaired by Rennie Spooner. The Deputy Rector gave a speech on behalf of the Institute. Cde. Ambassador Richard Jacobs was the main speaker. The El Salvador Collective gave a solidarity message on behalf of the students of the Institute and Rita Joseph closing, made the speech of the Session on behalf of the Grenada Collective. It was well received by all present - Students, Staff and Officials.

The exhibition which turned out to be very impressive was prepared by all members of the Collective. In fact the Studies department requested the materials for resource as well as to use as an example for other collectives doing exhibitions.

The reception was also very well organised and well attended. It gave us and our Cde. Ambassador a chance to tell more about the process in Grenada as well as learn about other countries. Our Senior Professor remarked to us that it was the best they had in ten years.

- Because of the threat of invasion of our homeland Grenada, our Co Collective undertook the task of alerting the staff and students of our situation and therefore organised with the jelp of the Social psychology & propaganda department, a round table solidarity conference with Latin America. Taking part were Grenada, Nicaragua. El Salvador, Guatemala, Honduras, giving our countries position at that time and representatives from Canada and Argentina expressed solidarity. That took place as a T.V. programme, which was viewed by students of the Institute.

Bloody Sunday was commemorated at which we invited representatives of all collectives present at our section of the Institute and the Rector of the branch.

- Our relatic ship with other collectives developed throughout the course. We held formal bilaterals with Nicaragua, El Salvador and Guatemala, Tanzania and other informal sessions with Greece, Zambia, Portugal. Other social sessions were also held with Tanzania, Zambia, Nicaragua etc. Our collective held send off get togethers for Tanzania, Zambia, Chile and Nicaragua.b An informal send off was also held for our department by Guyana, Jamaica, Canada, South Africa among others.

Bilateral were requested by West Berlin and Ethopia which we did not fulfil because of our impromptu notice to leave Moscow.

The Collective internal structure was developed as the necessity arose.

First the Leadership of four as appointed by the OC. - Rita Joseph, Anslea De Pourg, Gordon Raeburn and Ronnie Spooner, and later :-

- Tae Secretary — Derrick James
- Education / Study cttee — Chaired by Ian Lambert
- Propaganda cttee. — Fabian Otram
- Cultural cttee. — Ian Lambert
- Emulation cttee. — Ronnie Spooner
- Sports personnel — Derrick James
- District — Patrick Supperville
- Financial Secretary. — Samuel B--thwaite
- March 13th cttee — Ronnie Spooner
- A different Cttee for each important day that was celebrated.

Meetings were held regularly on Sundays from 8-10 p.m. The agenda was tiped and always included criticism & self criticism and the singing of the International. The various cttees reported on a regular basis.

The discipline of the Collective grew as the course went on. Our Social psychology course was particularly helpful to us in learning how to deal with the problems which turned up. However, there were few exceptions. As reported earlier, Patrick Supperville found problems in adjusting to the demands of being a member of such a Collective. He reported that he lost confidence in the Leadership and throughout the whole course the Leadership and the collective had to struggle with him in an effort to help him to adjust and to understand what is required of him. Incidents kept repeating themselves until the matter was referred to the party branch leadership in Moscow.

After constant struggle with the Comrade by the branch leadership he admitted that he acted incorrectly, that he had repeated his mistake and that he pledged to comply with the norms of party life. He promised to do a report to be presented to Cde. Bourne concerning his behaviour.

All other disciplinary matters were dealt with by the collective with satisfactory results. It should be noted however, that the collective had to struggle with Cde. William St. Louis and Roy Cooper, but they responded better to criticism. However it must be noted that when the collective experienced some unexpected difficulties in Cuba on our way home. Cde. William St. Louis displayed shockingly ill disciplined behaviour. After serious criticism by the entire collective present, he accepted his criticisms and pledged never to behave that way again. Cde. Roy Cooper also displayed unaccepted behaviour. He too was criticised. He however insisted that he would not change his position that "the living conditions were worst than in prison" but that he would tolerate it until he left Cuba.

Criticism and Self criticism was a norm in the development of the collective and every member of the collective was criticised at some point or another. This exercise certainly helped our collective to emerge successfully.

The collective was faced with problems which included:-

((1) Late arrival for the course which partly caused us to have to do a six months course instead of 10 mths. The 10 months course offers International relations normally and Economic Management if requested also other topics and were indepth study of the regular subjects.

Late arrival also caused our collective to be deprived of the photography and driving courses.

(2) The low cultural level of four of our Comrades. To a greater extent Mr. Fred Burris, William St. Louis and Roy Cooper and a lesser extent Gordon Raeburn. This of course caused them some frustration and low level of achievements

(3) (3) Inadequate means of communication re:- propaganda - newspapers etc. Despite repeated efforts of our propaganda cttee.

(4) Cde. Purris was sick throughout the course and had to be hospitalised on two occasions. Also Cde. Andre Mc. Queen was hospitalised for almost three months March 5th to May 25th. These two Comrades did not do the final exams. They were still both ill at the time.

Other Comrades William St. Louis, Rita Joseph and Anslem De Bourg were also hospitalised but it did not affect their study greatly.

Overall one can say that the strength of the Collective lie in its high level of co-operation and collective spirit coupled with its level of organisation and serious sense of purpose of the collective. Despite limitations of some members all comrades took the course seriously. For example Cde. Roy Cooper stuck at his books tenaciously.

The various committees were very helpful in bringing up the collective; in particular the study and emulation committees.

However the collective experienced some weaknesses. The leadership sometimes "dragged its feet in dealing with certain issues", eg. ill discipline; doing bilaterals with each member of the collective to discover personal problems. This was requested by the Collective.

The NJM Party branch to which our collective belonged was very helpful also in helping to deal with the disciplinary problem of Patrick Superville. At the branch we engaged in party study and general discussion on the present situation at home in Grenada.

At a dinner hosted by Cde. Ambassador Richard Jacobs and his wife June Jacobs, the Deputy Rector and all our professors and two members of the International Department of the party were present. Speeches were made by all of them and they all expressed their satisfaction with the collective of Grenada and its leader.

The Deputy Rector also commended our Cde. Richard for consistantly showing interest in the progress of the students. This he said was done by very few other Ambassadors who had students there.

- Each Committee will be presenting a report on its work as we think it necessary for other collectives to learn from our experience.

- Each member will also be doing a personal evaluation of the course.

Recommendations:

(1) That the new group be sent up on time for beginning of September.

(2) That our CC decide whether they will study for 6 or 10 mths. and communicate their decision to the CC-OFSC.

(3) That all comrades chosen for the course be of a similar cultural level and high level. The course is meant for developed comrades in the party.

(4) The new group should carry documents of the NJM party and gifts a and tokens for visits to party cttees etc.

(5) They should also travel with songs. - political songs of Grenada.

(6) That William St. Louis and Roy Cooper and Patrick Superville be e seen by the D.C. of the party.

Rita B. Joseph,
Leader of Collective.

EMBASSY OF GRENADA IN THE USSR

(SAINT GEORGE on 20.7.82 in MOSCOW) 706

Dobryninskaya Ulitsa 7
Apartment 221
Moscow
USSR

Telephone:
237-25-11
237-99-05

TO: COMRADE MAURICE BISHOP, CHAIRMAN OF THE CENTRAL COMMITTEE OF THE NEW
     JEWEL MOVEMENT.
FROM: COMRADE BERNARD BOURNE

I wish to express my warmest, militant regards to the Central Committee of our Party, the NEW JEWEL MOVEMENT and to you personally.

Allow me comrade, to use this opportunity to raise a matter which, in my opinion, is a necessary and urgent one. This matter concerns my area of work while operating as Minister Counsellor in the Embassy of Grenada in the Soviet Union. The fact that I have been appointed by the Political Bureau of the Central Committee of the New Jewel Movement to be the Minister Counsellor in itself is clear to me, even though I have not received a letter of appointment nor have the guidelines, terms and conditions of work been brought to my attention six months later.

Nevertheless, what concerns me and I wish to add, what bothers me from time to time, is the fact that while in Grenada I considered myself to be a senior member of the Party as I was a member of one of the leading arms of the Party – the Organising Committee and yet, neither the Political Bureau, the Central Committee nor the Secretariat has ever informed me as to whether as part of my diplomatic work I am supposed to be additionally responsible for the co-ordination of the work of the Embassy with the CPSU, KOMSOMOL, TU. etc, etc.

In my view, the diplomatic work is two-fold: STATE TO STATE and PARTY TO PARTY and MASS ORGANISATIONS. I will appreciate it and be gratified if the exact situation is made clear to me as soon as possible and in writing preferably. Additionally, and until such time that a Military Attache is appointed, it is my suggestion that security and military matters should be handled by me.

Furthermore, all that this entails concretely when it comes to the question of reports to Grenada is two reports: one to the Ministry of Foreign Affairs; the other to the Party.

Please comrade, could you or the Party clarify these points for the benefit of the diplomatic staff of the Embassy and for better organisation of our work at the soonest possible time.

In the meantime however, I wish to report on the Party Political work of the Embassy during the last two to three months. In this report, the following points will be discussed:
1. Meetings with North American and English- Speaking Caribbean
   Department of the CPSU;
2. Upcoming State and Party Visit;
3. Party Work of Party Members;

1. MEETINGS WITH CPSU

During the last two months comrade Ambassador and myself held three
meetings with representatives of the CPSU responsible for our area. The meetings
were held on April 22, May 7 and June 9. In the meetings we discussed a wide
range of issues, some of which are included in this report. These points are as
follows:

    i Nature of our Party;
    ii 6Cth Anniversary of the formation of the USSR;
    iii Rest and familiarisation;
    iv Party School;
    v Party Headquaters.

i. During our first meeting the nature of our Party was raised by the Soviet
side. They said that in their view NJM is a Communist Party, but what they do not
understand clearly is our membership in the Socialist International. We had to
point out that NJM's membership in the SI is a tactic which depends on the
peculiar conditions faced by Grenada under the Gairy dictatorship and the nature
of the governments in the region.

Our assessment is that our Party is not fully known; the Soviet comrades are
gathering information about NJM and the peculiar conditions of the region and
that is why they are dealing with us cautiously and sometimes skeptically.

However, we think that this matter would be settled during the upcoming STATE
and PARTY VISIT.

ii. This year is the 60th anniversary of the formation of the USSR and this
occasion will be celebrated in December. The Soviet comrades informed us that NJM
would be invited to participate in this big activity. Other parties from the
Eastern Caribbean, like UPM, have asked for invitations. The final decision on
these invitations will be taken by the CPSU after consultations with NJM via the
Embassy.

iii. With reference to an existing agreement between the CPSU and NJM, the comrades have asked us for details from Grenada of Central Committee comrades who
will come for rest and familiarisation this year, 1982. It is possible for us
under the agreement to send leading members of our MASS ORGANISATIONS for rest
and familiarisation.

Additionally, we recommended that the CPSU should create the possibilities for
comrades of the Left Parties in the region to enjoy similar facilities. To this
the Soviet comrades think that it is necessary and will like to take the final
decisions only after getting all necessary information from NJM.

In our assessment, our Embassy will also serve as a bridge between the CPSU and
the LEFT PARTIES in the English-Speaking Caribbean. We will be decisive in their
work by being able to give details of the situation in each of these countries.
In that way, we are certain to develop good working relations and become a trust-
worthy ally of the CPSU. It goes without saying, therefore, that we will have to
be supplied with details of analyses and assessments by the CC NJM and information
on developments at home and in the region.

29 - 2

iv. On the question of attending the CPSU Party School, we were informed that ten (10) of our cadres can attend the school; they are waiting on us. The system is such that if students begin classes in September, the course will be for 9 months. Also, there are three and six months courses which begin in January and it depends on us to decide how we are to utilise the scholarships.

The comrades are pressing us to take up the scholarships. At our last meeting I promised the comrades that as of this September we will take up the offers.

(NOTE: It is my opinion and also that of other comrades that in order for the CPSU to have greater confidence, trust and reassurance in our Party and our process it is absolutely necessary that we should take up these offers and attend the Party School courses. It is important for the image of our Party, the NEW JEWEL MOVEMENT.)

v. This question of Party Headquarters was discussed during our first and second meetings. The comrades were bewildered to learn that no work had began on the construction of our Party Headquarters. Even more so, they were shocked to hear that the Cuban comrades, including PB members, did not know about the agreement to construct NJM Party Headquarters.

The Soviet Ambassadors in Havana and Kingston were to convey the decision to NJM which was done. The present problem lies in the fact that the decision was not conveyed - so it seems - to the Cubans. This is the main problem: the PCC claimed that it was not informed on any decision to provide all materials to Grenada (NJM) which will be compensated for by the CPSU.

Furthermore, the comrades of the CPSU told us that they were ready to send the materials but they hadn't any details from our side. Comrade Jacobs informed them that the details were presented to the Soviet Embassy in Cuba.

On this matter, however, there are two outstanding points to be clarified:
    a. That the PCC be contacted on decision;
    b. That we follow up details of materials needed to the CPSU.

Finally, in our first meeting with the CPSU, we presented to the comrades a letter from Comrade Chalkie, on behalf of the CC NJM, thanking them for the Literature which they have been sending us. We also gave them the list of materials received then and copies of 'IS FREEDOM WE MAKING', REPORT ON THE 1981 ECONOMY ...' and 'GRENADA IS NOT ALONE.' They were grateful for the little gift.

2. UPCOMING STATE AND PARTY VISIT

- On this subject the document on the proposed agenda for meeting with the CPSU during the visit was handed over to the Chief of the Department for North-America and the English- Speaking Caribbean, comrade Nikolai. With reference to Party to Party collaboration we would have to prepare beforehand written documents and hand over to the CPSU.

Additionally, we conveyed your desire to meet with the General Secretary, Comrade Brezhnev and asked for confirmation on all three occasions. Up to now there is no final word on that score. However, we were told that comrade Boris Ponomaryov will be present during the Party to Party discussions.

3. PARTY WORK OF PARTY MEMBERS

At present, the Grenadian staff of the Embassy are all within the Party. The comrades are Richard Jacobs, Marlene Bourne and Bernard Bourne.

Today only two of us are working in the Embassy. And in order to organise the work of the Embassy efficiently, we held Party Meetings- only three such meetings were held.

The other area of Party work is STUDY. Other Party cadres who are in Moscow can attend Study sessions which take place on Sundays from 9 to 12 noon. So far five (5) sessions were held, and all during the month of May. The material which we have been studying is the 'REPORT ON THE 1981 ECONOMY AND PROSPECTS FOR 1982.' We chose this material because we did not get a chance to participate in the discussions at home and we believe that it is necessary for us to be familiar with our Economy - 2nd PILLAR OF THE REVOLUTION. Further, we have decided to write up a report, which has some recommendations coming out of our studies. This report is an appendix to this note.

Finally, I wish to reiterate my desire to have greater clarity on my area of responsibility while in Moscow in the nearest future. Maybe, with such clarity, future Party reports will be sent to the relevant structure - the International Department of the Party.

With A FIRM EMBRACE,
Comrade Bernard Bourne
30th June, 1982.

Bernard Bourne

EMBASSY OF GRENADA IN THE USSR

Dobryninskaya Ulitsa 7
Apartment 221
Moscow
USSR

Telephone:
237-25-41
237-99-05

MEETING WITH THE MINISTRY OF DEFENCE

DATE:24th November 1982

Present at the meeting were:

Colonel Petrov-Chief for preparing Students for Military

    High School;

Colonel Germark-Resposible for Grenadian Military Students;

Bernard Bourne-Minister-Counsellor.

For the purpose of information, Colonel Astremsky is overall

Head of Department of all Foreign Students; he was *absent*.

There were two (2) points on the Agenda:

1.Grenadian Students in/expected in the Soviet Union;
2.Military Projects.

Grenadian Students

At present there are fifteen (15) students pursuing courses in
three cities of the Soviet Union:

a.Ten students are at the High School for Infantry in Odessa;

b.Two students are in Simferopoll; and

c.Three students are in Volsk.

These 15 students will complete their training on 1 February,1983.

Additionally, ten (10) more students, including officers, are
expected to come to the Soviet Union within the next seven months.

i. On December 1-two officers are expected to arrive to study in

        the city of Solnechnogorsky at the Vystrel

        institute;

ii.On January 1- three more officers are expected to pursue

        studies at the same institute;

iii.On March 1 — three comrades will arrive , one will study

        in the Political Academy and two will be trained

        as communication experts in Ulyanovsk;

iv. June 1   Two officers will arrive for studies.

All courses will be of five (5) months duration and it is expected
that the names of these students would be communicated to the
Ministry one full month in advance. This last point is necessary
to observe in order to avoid problems at the airport.

Recognising that 2 officers are due to arrive by Wednesday, 1
December, I promised to try to get the names and flight details
of the men within two days. *

Further, on this point, Colonel Petrov mentioned that if we are
thinking of increasing the number of students to pursue Military
courses in the Soviet Union in 1983 then the Commander-in-Chief
should send a letter to the Ministry of Defence on this matter
not later than January 1, 1983 ~~~~ letter went. Asking
for 10 men for coups

Under this item, I asked the Colonels about the possibility of
visiting our Military students. The comrades responded that that
was possible and necessary in order to ensure that the students periods
are properly taken care of. However, the Colonels explained that
if it is decided that we visit the students, the Ministry of
Defence should be informed 5 to 10 days in advance in order that
it can render necessary assistance. Such letters should mention
the flight or train details. This information is necessary so
that the Ministry of Defence can inform the school, arrange to
meet the visitor on the airport, arrange meetings and to carry the
visitor to the hotel.

It is *also* possible to visit the students as a tourist but the tourist
would have to make all the arrangements personally.

MILITARY PROJECTS

Two departments are involved in Military Projects:
Main Technical Department (GTU) and Main Engineering Department,
both attached to the State Committee for Foreign Economic Relations.

It was agreed that a meeting should be organised with GTU which is
the Department connected with Military Projects. Colonel Petrov
suggested that we contact comrade Bogomolov of GTU to arrange such
a meeting
The meeting was later arranged for Friday 26 November.

* A telex was sent to Cde Bishop the same day, but no response was
received by Sat. 27 November.

Bernard Bourne

Bernard Bourne
Minister-Counsellor

30 - 2

CC EWART LAYNE

EMBASSY OF GRENADA IN THE USSR

Dobruninskava Ulitsa 7
Apartment 221
Moscow
USSR

Telephone:
237-25-41
237-99-05

YEAR OF POLITICAL AND ACADEMIC EDUCATION

MEETING WITH STATE COMMITTEE FOR FOREIGN ECONOMIC

RELATIONS (GKS)

DATE: FRIDAY 29 TH APRIL 1983 (9.15 A.M.)

Representing the GKS were :

1. Colonel General M.A. Sergeichik — First Deputy Chairman of the
USSR State Committee for For-
eign Economic Relations (GKS)

2. Rear Admiral V.A. Vlassov — Deputy Chief of the General
Engineering Department of GKS

3. Colonel V.P. Evteev — Chief of Section of the General
Engineering Department

4. A.Yu. Allianov — Expert of the Section and
interpreter

Present on the Grenada side was ;
Comrade Bernard Bourne — Minister-Counsellor.

At the commencement of the meeting comrade Bourne expressed his
appreciation for the speed in which the meeting was arranged(less
than twenty-four hours) and that he was thankful to be received
by Colonel General Sergeichik at short notice.

Moreover, comrade Bourne explained that the fraternal relations
existing between the Soviet Union and Grenada were developing
impressively, that the Grenada Government was happy about the
development of the bilateral relations and was grateful for all
assistance rendered, including the means delivered already in 1983.

Furthermore, Bourne pointed out that at present the United States
imperialists were posing a serious threat to the Grenada Revolution
and that the Party, Government and people were fully prepared to
respond to any United States inspired invasion of Grenada. Comrade
Bourne explained that although the people of Grenada were ready to
rebuff any intervention, the People's Revolutionary Armed Forces

EMBASSY OF GRENADA IN THE USSR

Dobryninskaya Ulitsa 7
Apartment 221   -2-   *Telephone:*
Moscow   237-25-41
USSR   237-99-05

were having serious difficulties at home,namely, that some 27
trucks were out of action because of lack of basic spare parts
and tyres and that fuel and food for the Armed Forces were providing a strain on the national budget.

Bourne pointed out that at present the People's Revolutionary
Government was focusing on the need to build up the defence
potential of the Revolution by putting everything in order. At
that moment cde Bourne explained that the PRG had instructed him
to meet with the relevant Soviet officials in order to get an
urgent response to the various requests for spare parts and tyres;
fuel; food; transport; engineering means etc. which were made in
letters in 1982. The opportunity was used to present copies of two
letters recently sent to the Ministry of Defence (one from General
Austin; the other requesting air rifles or 0.22 rifles).

After comrade Bourne's presentation Colonel General Sergeichik comm
ented by saying that the General Engineering Department (GTU) of
the GKS was responsible for questions of armaments,but that the
Ministry of Foerign Trade was responsible for the questions of
transport, food, fuel, spare parts. Additionally, Col. General
pointed out that some proposals on spare parts were handed over to
the Government of Grenada through the Soviet Trade Representative
in Havana and was not certain if the proposals were signed. The
Colonel General also said that some quantities of spare parts were
delivered to Grenada from the Soviet Ministry of Defence and that
the copies of the latest letters would be carefully studied and the
results conveyed in the future.

As for the Inter-Governmental Agreement signed in July 1982,Col.
General Sergeichik explained that everything contained in the
agreement would be delivered and the greater part for 1983 had already been delivered. He pointed out futher that another shipment
of means was being prepared; this shipment would include all submachine guns, carbines, sniper rifles, mortars, anti-tank guns,
mines, ammunition; small arms and vehicles for the Ministry of
Interior.

Dobryninskaya Ulitsa 7
Apartment 221
Moscow
USSR

-3-

Telephone:
237-25-41
237-99-05

Moreover, Deputy Chairman of GKS, Col. General Sergeichik informed the Grenada side that the Soviet Government had positively consider-ed the additional requests from Grenada Government and the results were conveyed to Ambassador Sazhenev who was charged to visit Prime Minister Maurice Bishop to inform him of the decisions. However, in general terms, Colonel General pointed out that on April 22 the decision was taken to deliver to Grenada: automobiles; foodstuff; fuel and lubricants; two patrol boats; 3000 units of uniform; sol-diers' spades etc.

On all these matters, Col. General Sergeichik explained that the Soviet Government would like to know the response of the People's Revolutionary Government of Grenada to the proposals for supplying the abovementioned things. This was necessary before a contract could be signed, he pointed out. Colonel General also mentioned that the Soviet Government had proposed to the PRG that talks on these questions be held in Moscow and that the contract be signed too in Moscow.

Finally, comrade Bourne asked that the GTU kindly arrange a meeting with the Ministry of Foreign Trade in the nearest future to discuss the relevant questions. The Soviet side agreed and promised to inform the Embassy on the date of the meeting.

The meeting ended by exchanging kind words of appreciation on the success of the meeting.

CDE.   Bernard Bourne

Bernard Bourne

Minister- Counsellor.

EMBASSY OF GRENADA IN THE USSR

Dobryninskaya Ulitsa 7
Apartment 221
Moscow
USSR

Telephone
237-25-41
237-99-05

Course name: WCM - World Communist Movement
SPP - Social Psychology and Propaganda
- Historic Experience of the CPSU

<u>Names of Students</u>

School name	Real name
Pear Achebe	Derrick James
David Gill	Sam Braithwaite
Justin Lorainey	Fabian Outram
Bill Jordan	Anselm DeBourg
Francis Che	Glen Noel
Bernadine Peters	Rita Joseph
David Allen	Ian Lambert
Dave Gordon	Andre Mc. Queen
John Franklyn	Ronnie Spooner
-	William St. Louis
-	Gordon Raeburn
-	Roy Cooper
-	Patrick Superville
-	Fred Burris

[handwritten notes at top]

EMBASSY OF GRENADA IN THE USSR

Dobruninskaya Ulitsa 7
Apartment 221
Moscow
USSR

Telephone:
237-25-41
237-99-05

Report of meeting with Acting Rector of the CPSU party school Caidun Oleg P
23rd. May 1983

This meeting between the Acting Rector and the Ambassador was arranged at the request of the Ambassador to receive a confidential assessment of the performance of our students during the six-month course just completed.

The Acting Rector informed the Ambassador that normally, it is necessary to apply to the International Department of the CPSU inorder to receive an official report of the performance of the students. However, in this case, since this was the first batch of Grenadians students he would be prepared to make available to the Party (NJM) the confidential assessments of their teachers as well as to communicate to the Ambassador in a confidential manner, the general opinion of the teachers regarding the overall performance of our students. The Ambassador thanked the Acting Director for his cooperation in this matter and pointed out that he will also request an official report from the CPSU.

The Acting Director reported that since this was the first group of Grenadians to attend the school, it was the policy of the administrators and teachers to pay very close and careful attention to the performance and behaviour of the students. After a collective assessment of the students, he could inform the Ambassador that he was expressing the unanimous opinion of the teachers and administrators of the school.

The students fully covered the syllabus of the six month course. It was the view of the school however, that the students would have benefited more from a one year course.

As a whole the students were well disciplined and oriented towards collective work. Minor evidences of indiscipline were never repeated once they had been identified and explained.

The internal relations of the group were generally good. Friction was kept to a minimum, problems were resolved in time, and due to the excellent leadership of Rita Joseph, the collective maintained a very marked cohesion throughout the course. It is worthy of note that Comrade Joseph was greatly helped in the exercise of her responsibility and authority by the following Comrades: Gorden Raeburn, Ronnie Spooner, Ian Lambert and Fabian Outram.

Comradely relations between members of the group steadily improved over the period of six months.

Attendance at classes was excellent, but punctuality was occasionally weak. All comrades displayed a conscientious attitude towards their work.

With the sole exception of Fred Burris, our students actively participated in classroom discussions. They always adopted a very serious attitude towards the work, asked relevant questions and all except Burris have been assessed as having achieved good to excellent knowledge. Burris was satisfactory.

All the students made consistent efforts to link up the theoretical points with the tasks to which they have been assigned by the NJM. This was particularly true of Ian Lambert, Rita Joseph and Roy Cooper.

There was a marked difference in cultural levels of the students as well as in levels of health. Both Fred Burris and Andre Mc Queen (David Gordon) were ill for long periods. A Report on Mc Queen's illness is enclosed.

The group took several good initiatives, and undertook the responsibilities associated with these initiatives. Three examples: Celebration of the 10th. Anniversary of the NJM, 4th. Anniversary of the Revolution, Round table solidarity Conference of the Americas.

As part of their practical work, the group had a permanent link with the CPSU Party committee of the October factory. They went to the factory on several occasions, participated in voluntary work on two occasions and had a lecture on the cost accounting procedures of the factory. The management of the factory was pleased with the students' performance and the students were satisfied with their

EMBASSY OF GRENADA IN THE USSR

Dobryninskaya Ulitsa 7
Apartment 221
Moscow
USSR

Telephone:
237-25-41
237-99-05

experience.

The two most outstanding students were: Rita Joseph and Ian Lambert. The weakest student was Fred Burris. The teachers considered that Burris would be well placed in an area of work requiring inter-personal relations with non-intellectual workers. He can carry out instructions and is very tenacious in his determination to implement agreed procedure, but he is neither an ~~intertentual~~ intellectual nor initiator.

The Acting Rector said that the performance of our students demonstrate a real thirst for knowledge and he recommended that the NJM think very seriously about the establishment of a Party School as a top priority. He pointed out that there were very positive achievements as a result of the establishment of the Party School in Yemen, Afganistan, Angola, Mozambique and very soon Ethiopia. In this context he suggested that the NJM might think of sending students who could qualify as teachers in the future Party School.

In closing the Acting Director said that he would like to emphasize that the teachers and Administrators had come to develop great respect for the abilities of Rita Joseph as a leader. In the beginning they were a bit apprehensive about her ability to manage thirteen men and she was a bit shakey in the beginning, but as time went on, it emerged that it was a wise decision.

V.Richard Jacobs

Dear Maurice—

I've given some thought to what you raised over the phone, and come up with a couple of ideas, although without ~~even~~ the general picture of what the trip looks like and perspectives you have on it -- a big limitation. But, for what it's worth:

1) I think being pressured into coming up with a "major announcement", declaration, etc. or even a gimmick along these lines is a bit of a trap. ~~certain ~~~~ ~~~~~~ ~~~~ ~~~~~~~~ ~~~~~~~~~~ With all due respect to the power of the U.S. media, once you've got their attention, the agenda must be yours, not theirs. Although I haven't been in the States recently, certain things don't change: the U.S. media go after violence, and when there's no war, controversy will due just as well -- especially in an election year. I would say they're most interested in the visit as it fits in to their idea of a "faceoff" with Reagan and his administration, in the midst of the election campaign. But, of course, Grenada's interests are far different. And it seems to me the best idea is to stick with those interests and objectives, and use the media as far as possible to advance them, ~~to~~ without getting "cornered".

2) Why the visit? (Of course, you've given the answer to this one more thought than I.) But for the media, how does this sound: "Grenada and the United States have a long history of relations -- many ~~trade~~ thousands of Grenadians live in the United States, their work contributing to the development of that country; many thousands of U.S. citizens travel to Grenada to enjoy its hospitality and natural beauty; cultural similarities unite Grenada with cultural currents in the U.S.; other economic links, etc., etc. The purpose of the visit is to reaffirm and develop these ties at as many <u>levels</u> as possible, and by so doing to help lessen the tensions that have cropped up at <u>one</u> of these levels: the current White House administration. (~~Of a meeting with the administration~~ ~~~~ ~~~~ ~~~~)." Thus, the importance of accepting the Black Caucus (another <u>governmental</u> level) and Transafrica invitations -- as <u>important in themselves</u> -- leaving open the possibility of meeting with the Reagan administration if it were to come off.

I think any suggestion that accepting these invitations is really a "cover" for another (larger) purpose (such as a meeting with Reagan) needs to be denied flatly and strongly. After all, what is contained in the suggestion, besides the implication that

31 - 2

the PRG is opportunist, is the racist and anti-popular emplication — "why would he come here just because a bunch of Black folks ~~were~~ invited him?"

The strong answer is that of course it is legitimate ~~—~~ in its own right — to speak directly to the people, to other levels of their government, etc. That is what the PRG is all about.

3) I still think it might be a good idea to launch the organizing of the "US- Grenada Friendship Flight" ~~————~~ (or some such better name), the inaugural flight direct to Grenada's new international airport for March 13th. Beyond a tourism boost, I think it would go a long way to promote the "open-ness" of Grenada and its airport to U.S. citizens, as well as the idea that the airport is a normal one, a good thing for U.S. travellers, too. Over time, the flight itself could be a focus for publicity -- of the important figures that will be on board, the Grenadians going home. (Wouldn't the medical school like to donate cash for a few seats so "prize trips" could be awarded, let's say, to a ~~couple~~ Grenadian ~~by~~ couple from New York, a trade unionist from Detroit? — Anyway, that's just a thought for the future.)

[left margin notes:]
ARRANGE MEETING W/ R MODICA GR...

Belafonte, Black Caucus member, Television, Charles Modica, tourists who've been regulars to Grenada

31 - 3

4) On the specific meetings, I think I'm too out of touch to be helpful. ~~Commission~~ Parodi from the Cuban Interests Section will be the single most clear person on this whole question. (Only comment: I think the contact with Gil Noble is important.)

Reading this over, it's pretty rambling, but I hope of some use.

By the way — the ABC interview was beautiful!

Take care of yourself.

Warm regards,

Gail

We must protest the meeting not occurri
as we were led to believe.
- long delay
- Mittendorf the chief host.

Clarke, Dann, Mittendorf, Bosch, Browne.

My - Glad for mting, been requesting
it for some time.
→ Need to ~~start~~ on the long lister
of good people to people relation
↳ Bottom line : dialogue & normal
relations.
- Commission : ⓐ discuss, differe
ⓑ discuss coopera

Clarke - No problems with dialogue,
more interested in conduct
→ concerned with Soviet influe
among our neighbours
→ Soviet influence in region is
not acceptable.
→ Can communicate to you our resp
to your proposals
→ Agreed to off the record meeting,
a secret meeting) in a way open.
↳ Not only to refer to this meet
expect change in criticisms in
future.

(A2) - Have common strands / history - legal 2
practice. Hope this can lead to great
progress.

    - M - Encouraged by live response, that
    they are willing to accept talks on the
    normalisation of relations.
      - But Our language (careful) should
      noted
      - Toning down of attacks - must be mutual

Clarke - Their preference is to sit around the
    table re Discussions rather public
    attacks.
      → Referred to morning / location of the
      School - not for this conference.
      → Hope that we return to the basic form
      of govt. rather than model of E. Euro

    [Judge's Departure]
- M - Time perspective re reply to our propos
Dam - Key thing is Sov. / Cuban influen
      → Need to see some change in conduct
    before this agreement; ≠

    M - - will have to look at - Econ Destabt.
                ↳ CDB, IMF
           - Terrorism re Reg
               attacks

      - We can explore any range of subjec
    and give fullest assurance that we
    constitute no threat to the US

Dam — Interested in assurances

"Thank you for coming to ~~see~~ meet me
w Judge Clarke."

— Re shift in venue
— Length of time Judy stayed
— Points he made
— Tone / atmosphere
— State Dept. component (Dam)
— meaning of the press / press state

A continuación le traslado algunas informaciones y apreciaciones sobre la reunión del Comité de la Internacional Socialista para la Defensa de la Revolución en Nicaragua, efectuada el 25 del presente mes de junio en Managua.

Esta reunión es la segunda que celebra el Comité. La primera se efectuó en Washington el 6 de diciembre de 1980.

El Comité fue creado oficialmente por iniciativa de Willy Brandt, en el XV Congreso de la Internacional Socialista celebrado en Madrid en noviembre pasado; quedó integrado por los siguientes miembros: Willy Brandt, Bernt Carlsson, Bettino Craxi, Michael Foot, Felipe González, Michael Harrington, Anker Joergensen, Bruno Kreisky, Michael Manley, Francois Mitterrand, Olof Palme, José Francisco Peña Gómez, Carlos Andrés Pérez, Michel Rocard, Pierre Schori, Mario Soares, Kalevi Sorsa, Joop den Uyl y Hans-Juergen Wischnewski.

Esta reunión es la segunda que efectúa el Comité; la primera se celebró en Washington el 6 de diciembre de 1980.

Entre las personalidades que asistieron a esta reunión en Managua, se encontraban Bernt Carlsson, Secretario General de la I.S.; Felipe González, presidente del Comité; Carlos Andrés Pérez de A. Democrática, -

Pierre Schori, del Partido Socialdemócrata Sueco y Michael Harrington del DSOC de EE.UU., todos miembros del Comité.

Resultó muy significativa la ausencia de los germanoccidentales en la reunión, hecho que sin dudas revela la intención del SPD de moderar su actuación frente a la situación centroamericana e imprimirle a su gestión latinoamericana dentro la I.S. un perfil bajo y de menor compromiso con los procesos que en esa zona se desarrollan. Se adjunta carta enviada por el Secretario Internacional del SPD al Secretario Internacional de Partido Socialdemócrata Austríaco presente en el evento, - en ocasión de esta reunión.

Las presiones norteamericanas y la difícil situación interna por la que atraviesa el SPD, explican en buena medida la cautela germanoccidental frente a la Revolución Nicaragüense.

A partir de los contactos bilaterales que se desarrollaron con los participantes, el documento que se aprobó y el propio desarrollo de la reunión, consideramos:

1) Se observaron en general, dos tendencias entre los participantes. - Una, encabezada por Felipe González y Carlos Andrés, con abiertos -- objetivos neutralizadores, asumiendo posiciones de relativa presión interesados en dejar claramente expresado los límites de la "solidaridad de la I.S." con Nicaragua, y subrayando que el apoyo de la I.S. es al "proyecto político democrático y pluralista". Este sector reflejó temores por el curso que a su juicio estaba tomando el proceso, y en especial por el asunto de lo que llamaron el suminis-

tro de armas de Cuba y la URRS; en síntesis, preocupados por la --
"cubanización" y "sovietización" del proceso.

Esta tendencia, en términos cuantitativos era minoritaria, pero --
cualitativamente es la de mayor peso.

El otro sector, no hizo de estas consideraciones el centro de su -
atención, y en general mostraron comprensión e interés por conocer
objetivamente las dificultades del proceso, coincidiendo en censu-
rar a EE.UU. como el máximo responsable de la situación por la que
atraviesa Nicaragua y denunciado los peligros que acechan el pro--
ceso.

En esta línea se ubicaba Pierre Schori, Jim Fulton, del Nuevo Partido Democrático de Canadá, Antoine Blanca, del Partido Socialista
Francés, entre otros.

2) Desde el punto de vista de los objetivos que el FSLN se propuso con
la reunión, a nuestro juicio se obtuvieron; se reconoció en la De--
claración aprobada por el Comité, los peligros y amenazas sobre el-
proceso y se ratificó el apoyo de la I.S. al proyecto "políticos --
democrático y pluralista que tiene lugar en Nicaragua". Por otra -
parte, las declaraciones públicas formuladas por la mayoría de los-
participantes, fueron en general positivas en la actual coyuntura-
para el proceso, pero muestran en alguna medida, las aprehensiones-
de algunos sectores con el actual rumbo del proceso.

3) Se evidenciaron las contradicciones y tendencias en el seno de la -
I.S. en cuanto a cómo encarar la política frente a Nicaragua y en -

general la actitud a asumir frente a la problemática latinoamericana. Las presiones de los EE.UU. sobre la I.S. y los partidos que la integran, la difícil y compleja situación internacional y el curso que van tomando los procesos en la región, determinan que los sectores más derechistas en el seno de la I.S., adopten una posición de cierto repliegue y moderación, y se propongan evitar que la I.S. continúe comprometiéndose como hasta el momento, sin que ello signifique renunciar a los objetivos estratégicos de incidir en el rumbo de los procesos centroamericanos y en particular Nicaragua, con claros propósitos neutralizadores.

4). Con esta reunión, la I.S., ha dejado expreso los límites de la "solidaridad" con Nicaragua, y de hecho sus sectores de derecha se propusieron ejercen presión e incidir directamente en el curso de la Revolución. No se trata de que la I.S. varíe estrategicamente su política frente a Nicaragua, pero si mostrará en lo adelante mayor cautela y discreción, y estará muy atenta a los próximos pasos de la Revolución.

Finalmente, le adjuntamos una versión de la entrevista que sostuvo Bayardo Arce con Felipe González y Carlos Andrés, antes de iniciarse la reunión, y que refleja nítidamente la óptica de las posiciones de derecha en la I.S.

Con saludos revolucionarios,

Manuel Piñeiro Losada

33 - 4

tanques.

Pidieron a Bayardo que ellos quisieran tener una reunión con toda la -
Dirección Nacional, para abordar todos estos temas y otros que no se -
pueden tratar en el marco de la reunión de la I.S.

Bayardo resumió las dificultades y problemas que confrontaban, subra--
yando que ellos (los sandinistas) no eran los que cerraban las puertas,
y que si todos los caminos se les cerraban a la Revolución, ellos tenían
que acudir donde se les brindara la ayuda; que la revolución tiene que-
garantizar su derecho a subsistir y defenderse.

Respecto a los tanques y el armamento, Bayardo revirtió el problema, --
cuestionando por qué se hacía tanto ruido con ese problema, y nadie ha-
blaba de los tanques ingleses que estan entrando en Honduras. En sín--
tesis no negó categoricamente el asunto, pero tampoco lo afirmó.

Refiriéndose a la aludida presencia cubana, Bayardo se preguntó de qué-
presencia cubana se trataba, agregando que acababa de venir de La Habana
donde fue a convencer a Fidel para que se reponga en un plazo breve el-
contingente de maestros que saldrá próximamente, porque 60,000 niños se
quedarían sin maestros, y ellos necesitab 2,000, y hasta ahora nadie,--
ningún país se había ofrecido a enviárselos excepto Cuba. En esta lí--
nea, Bayardo argumentó todo el plan de colaboración de Cuba con Nicara--
gua.

Dijo además, que los sandinistas entendían perfectamente la situación -
que confrontaba la socialdemocracia y que incluso comprenderían que en-
un momento determinado, los socialdemócratas dejaran de apoyar la revo-

...../3

lución; pero también pedía se asimilara cuales eran las alternativas que
el proceso tenía ante sí.

En cuanto a la reunión que solicitaron con la Dirección Nacional en ple-
no, Bayardo evadió el asunto, argumentando razones de carga de trabajo,-
aunque, en una de las sesiones de la reunión, los participantes tuvieron
la posibilidad de sostener un intercambio directo con los miembros de la -
Comisión Política (Bayardo, Humberto Ortega y Wheelock).

CARTA ENVIADA POR HANS EBERHARD, SECRETARIO INTERNACIONAL DEL PAR-
TIDO SOCIALDEMOCRATA ALEMAN A SU HOMOLOGO WALTER HACKER, DEL PARTI-
DO SOCIALDEMOCRATA DE AUSTRIA Y REPRESENTANTE DE BRUNO KREISKY EN
LA REUNION DEL COMITE.

Bonn, 19 de junio de 1981

Profesor Walter Hacker
Secretario Internacional del
Partido Socialdemócrata Aus-
tríaco.

Estimado Walter :

Con respecto a Nicaragua tengo que informarle que ni Willy Brandt ni
Hans Juergen Wischnewski podrán asistir a la reunión del comité de
la IS para la defensa de la revolución de Nicaragua que se celebrará
en Managua el 25 de junio. Desafortunadamente tampoco podremos asistir Klaus Lindenberg y yo. Explicaremos esto directamente a los
amigos nicaragüenses. De todos modos, hemos pedido a nuestro colega
Lutterbach que actúe como observador en las discusiones y reuniones.

Willy Brandt le escribió a Felipe González y le expresó sus opinio-
nes y las nuestras con respecto a ciertos acontecimientos que han
tenido lugar en Nicaragua. Usted también debía leer esta carta.

Espero que usted esté de acuerdo conmigo en que nuestra solidaridad
con la revolución no puede ser interpretada por algunos colegas sandinistas como un tipo de carta blanca para cualquier acción que lle-
ven a cabo. Por muchas razones nuestra asistencia tanto en lo político como en lo moral no puede ser interpretada como si fuera en una
sola dirección.

Supongo que conoce de la última lucha interna en el movimiento sandinista, con los hermanos Ortega enfrascados en una batalla desespe-
rada contra los que practican la política de "mano dura" que muchos
consideran que respaldados por Arce, Wheelock y Borge.

Con más interés que el de costumbre, deseo leer su informe, deseo sa-
ber si no debo ir a Estocolmo o debo encontrarme con usted a mitad
del camino después de su regreso de Managua.

...../2

Con relación al viaje de nuestro amigo Marten Van Traa y otros a --
Uruguay y Argentina considero que todo marcha bien.

Le escribí a Marten y le pedí que fuera precavido y prudente porque
la situación real de Argentina está llena de complejidades; algunos
círculos del gobierno seguramente agradecerían que se llevara a cabo cierto diálogo con nuestras fuerzas políticas en Europa siempre-
que no turbemos su orgullo nacional.

Con respecto a la reunión del Comité de la IS sobre América Latina-
y el Caribe que se celebrará el 25 de julio en Granada dudamos, por
razones obvias, la razón y decisión de celebrar esta reunión en esa
isla, podría ser interpretada por algunos como una provocación. Espero que nuestros amigos salvadoreños no serán los que más sufrirán
por esto.

Saludos,

Hans Eberhard.

~4195 st zent a

~std bonn 19/6 1110 hr.=

<3>
 professor walter hacker
internationaler sekretaer der spoe
wien

lieber walter-
nachstehend uebermittle ich dir,was ich an pierre shori und
marten van traa zu nikaragua,argentinien und ye grenada
geschrieben habe. elena flores hat auch kenntnis davon:

''1. with regard to nicaragua i have to inform you that neither
willy brandt nor hans-juergen wischnewski will be able to
attend the meeting of the si committee for the defence of the
revolution in nicaragua at managua on june 25th. unfortunately
klaus lindenberg as well as myself are unable to come either.
we shall explain this directly to the nicaraguan friends. anyhow
we have asked our colleague lutterbach to act as an observer
to the discussions und gatherings.
willy brandt has written to felipe gonzales and expressed some of
his or our feelings concerning certain developments in nicaragua.
you should read that letter too.
i hope y you will agree with me that our solidarity with the
revolution cannot be interpreted by some of the sandinista

... ... many reas... ... ...ance politically ...
...rc... ...n.t be under... ... a one-way road.

...n... ...t you know of the ...n..n infighting in the sandinista
...vement,with the ortega brother... being in a desperate battle
against the "hardliners" who ...y think to be backed by arce,
...eelock) and borge.

...th more than the usual interest i am looking forward to read
your report, i am wondering if i should not come over to stockholm
..r meet you halfway after your return fro.......... from managua.

.. as regards the trip of our friend marten van traa and
..thers to uruguay and argentine i do hope that everything goes
..ell.

. have written to marten and asked him to use his caution and
..rudence the actual situation in argentine is full of x
..omlexities, some circles within the government would certainly
..ppreciate a certain dialogue with our political froces in
..urope provided we donnot stumble over their national pride.

.. with regard tó the meeting of the si committee on latin
..merica and the carribean on july 25th at grenada we doubt,
.or obvious reasons,"the reason and the wisdom of that decision
.c have kee the meeting on that island. some might regard it
.s a provocation. i do hope that our salvadorian friends will
..ot be those who will suffer most from that."

.lles gute und viel glueck fuer die reise
.erzlichst
.ein
.ans--eberhard

.nde+
'4198 spzent a

I TRANSFER TO YOU BELOW SOME INFORMATION AND APPRECIATIONS ABOUT THE MEETING OF THE SOCIALIST INTERNATIONAL COMMITTEE FOR THE DEFENSE OF THE ~~NICARAGUA~~ REVOLUTION IN NICARAGUA, HELD ON JUNE 25 IN MANAGUA.

THIS IS THE SECOND MEETING THE COMMITTEE CELEBRATE. THE FIRST ONE TOOK PLACE IN WASHINGTON ON DECEMBER 6, 1980.

THE COMMITTEE WAS OFFICIALLY CREATED BY INITIATIVE OF WILLY BRANDT, IN THE XV CONGRESS OF THE SOCIALIST INTERNATIONAL HELD IN MADRID LAST NOVEMBER; IT WAS INTEGRATED BY THE FOLLOWING MEMBERS: WILLY BRANDT, BERNT CARLSSON, BETTINO CRAXI, MICHAEL FOOT, FELIPE GONZÁLEZ, MICHAEL HARRINGTON, ANKER JOERGENSEN, BRUNO KREISKY, MICHAEL MANLEY, FRANCOIS MITTERRAND, OLOF PALME, JOSÉ FRANCISCO PEÑA GÓMEZ, CARLOS ANDRÉS PÉREZ, MICHEL ROCARD, PIERRE SCHORI, MARIO SOARES, KALEVI SORSA, JOOP DEN UYL AND HANS-JOERGEN WISCHNEWSKI.

THIS MEETING IS THE SECOND ONE ~~HELD~~ HELD BY THE COMMITTEE, THE FIRST ONE TOOK PLACE IN WASHINGTON ON DECEMBER 6, 1980.

AMONG THE PERSONALITIES WHO ATTENDED HIS MEETING IN MANAGUA WERE BERNT CARLSSON, SECRETARY-GENERAL OF THE S.I.; FELIPE GONZÁLEZ, PRESIDENT OF THE COMMITTEE; CARLOS ANDRÉS PÉREZ FROM DEMOCRATIC GERMANY, PIERRE SCHORI, OF THE SWEDISH SOCIAL-DEMOCRAT PARTY AND MICHAEL HARRINGTON FROM THE DSOC OF THE U.S, ALL MEMBERS OF THE COMMITTEE.

IT WAS VERY SIGNIFICANT THE ABSENCE OF WESTERN GERMAN REPRESENTATIVES TO THE MEETING, THAT UNDOUBTEDLY REVEALS THE INTENTION OF THE SPD TO MODERATE ITS ACTIVITIES BEFORE THE CENTRAL AMERICAN SITUATION AND GIVE ITS LATIN AME

...rican negociation within the S.I. A low outline less commited to the processes takin
place in that zone. We enclose letter sent by
international secretary of the SPD to the
international secretary of the Austrian Social-
Democrat Party present in the event, on the
occasion of this meeting.

The North American pressures and the difi-
culte internal situation the SPD goes through,
xplains to a good extent the Western German
caution towards the Nicaraguan Revolution

Starting from the ~~multiple~~ bilateral contacts
developed among participators, the document
pproved and the development of the meeting
tself, we consider.

1) It was noticed, in general, two tendencies
among the participators.- One headed by
Felipe González and Carlos Andrés, with
open neutralizing objectives, assuming
positions of relative pressure interested
in expressing clearly the limits of the
"S.I. solidarity" with Nicaragua, and underlining that the support of the S.I. is for
"democratic and pluralist political project".
This sector seemed to be afraid of the
course that, to their opinion, the process
was taking, and specially of the matter
they called the supply of weapons of Cuba
and the USSR; summarizing, they were
worried about the "Cubanization" and
"Sovietization" of the process.
This tendency, was inferior in terms of
quantity but qualitatively it has more weight.
The other sector, did not became these
considerations, the centre of its attention,

AND IN GENERAL DEMONSTRATED COMPREHENSION
AND INTEREST TO KNOW, OBJECTIVELY, THE DIFFI-
CULTIES OF THE PROCESS, COINCIDING IN CENSU-
RING THE US AS MAXIMUM RESPONSIBLE FOR
THE SITUATION NICARAGUA GOES THROUGH
AND DENOUNCING THE DANGER THAT THREATEN
THE PROCESS.

IN THIS LINE WERE UBICATED PIERRE SCHORI,
JIM FULTON, FROM THE NEW DEMOCRATIC PARTY
OF CANADA ANTOINE BLANCA OF THE FRENCH
SOCIALIST PARTY, AMONG OTHERS.

2) FROM THE POINT OF VIEW OF THE ~~SEE~~ OBJEC-
TIVES PROPOSED BY THE FSLN, WE CONSIDER
THEY WERE ATTAINED, IT WAS RECOGNIZED
IN THE DECLARATION APPROVED BY THE COMMI-
TTEE, THE DANGERS AND THREATS ON THE PRO-
CESS AND IT WAS RATIFIED THE SUPPORT OF
THE S.I. TO "POLITICAL, DEMOCRATIC AND
PLURALIST PROJECT OF NICARAGUA". ON THE
OTHER HAND, THE PUBLIC DECLARATIONS FORMULA-
TED BY THE MAJORITY OF THE PARTICIPATORS,
WERE, IN GENERAL, POSSITIVE FOR THE PRO-
CESS IN THE PRESENT SITUATION, BUT SHOW
TO A GIVEN EXTENT, THE APPREHENSIONS OF
SOME SECTORS IN RESPECT TO THE PRESENT
COURSE OF THE PROCESS.

3) IT WAS EVIDENCED THE CONTRADICTIONS AND
TENDENCIES WITHIN THE S.I. IN CONNECTION
WITH HOW TO FACE POLITICS TOWARDS NICARA-
GUA AND IN GENERAL, THE ATTITUDE TO BE
ASSUMED BEFORE THE LATIN AMERICAN
PROBLEM. THE PRESSURES OF THE U.S ON THE
S.I. AND THE PARTIES THAT COMPOSE IT, THE
DIFFICULT AND COMPLEX INTERNATIONAL SITUATION
AND THE COURSE PROCESSES IN THE REGION

ARE TAKING, DETERMINE THAT THE MOST RIGHTIST SECTORS WITHIN THE ~~S~~ S.I., ADOPT A POSITION OF CERTAIN CONVOLUTION AND MODERATION, AND PROPOSE THEMSELVES TO AVOID THAT THE S.I. CONTINUE TO COMMIT ITSELF AS IT HAS DONE SO FAR, WITHOUT IMPLYING THE RENOUNCIATION TO THE STRATEGIC OBJECTIVES OF IMPINGING ON THE DIRECTION OF THE CENTRAL AMERICAN PROCESSES, AND IN PARTICULAR ON NICARAGUA, WITH CLEAR NEUTRALIZING OBJECTIVES.

4) WITH THIS MEETING, THE S.I. EXPRESSED THE LIMITS OF THE "SOLIDARITY" WITH NICARAGUA, AND IN FACT ITS RIGHTIST SECTORS HAVE SET FORWARD TO EXHERT PRESSURE AND IMPINGE DIRECTLY ON THE COURSE OF THE REVOLUTION. IT IS NOT THAT THE S.I. STRATEGICALLY CHANGES ITS POLICY TOWARD NICARAGUA, BUT IT WILL DEMONSTRATE FROM NOW ON MORE CAUTION AND DISCRESSION, AND WILL BE MORE ATTENTIVE TO THE NEXT STEPS OF THE REVOLUTION.

FINALLY WE ENCLOSE A VERSION OF THE INTERVIEW MAINTAINED BY BAYARDO ARCE WITH FELIPE GONZALEZ AND CARLOS ANDRÉS, BEFORE STARTING THE MEETING AND THAT CLEARLY REFLECTS VIEW OF THE POSITION OF RIGHT ~~C~~ IN THE S.I.

WITH REVOLUTIONARY GREETINGS

MANUEL PIÑEIRE LOSADA

33 - 14

BAYARDO ARCE TALKS WITH CARLOS ANDRES AND FELIPE GONZÁLEZ.

CARLOS ANDRE'S AND FELIPE, INDICATED THAT THEY WERE ABSOLUTELY CONVINCED OF THE DANGERS, THREATS AND PRESSURE BEING EXHERTED ON NICARAGUA, MAINLY BY THE U.S, AND THE DIFFICULT SITUATION THE PROCESS UNDEGOES. THAT PRECISELY WHAT THE U.S WANT IS TO HARASS NICARAGUA, PUSH IT TO A RADICALIZATION OF THE PROCESS, AS TO HAVE PRETEXT AND EVIDENCES TO IMPLEMENT THE MILITARY AGGRESSION.

BOTH SHOWED THEIR CONCERN THAT THE SANDINIST DIRECTION MIGHT FALL INTO A SNARE AND SUIT THE U.S., AND ~~THAT~~ TO THEIR OPINION, THEY WERE FALLING IN THE SNARE, THEREFORE IT IS NECESSARY THAT SANDINISTS TAKE THAT REALITY INTO ACCOUNT AND NOT ALLOW THEMSELVES TO BE PROVOCATED. SO IT IS QUITE INDISPENSABLE THAT THE REVOLUTIONARY PROJECT IS MAINTAINED WITHIN THE ~~FRAMEWORK~~ DEMOCRATIC AND PLURALIST FRAMEWORK AND THAT THIS WAS A CONDITION TO MAINTAIN THE SUPPORT OF THE S.I. THEY POINTED OUT THAT THEY (THE SOCIAL DEMOCRATS) WERE IN A VERY DIFFICULT SITUATION, RECEIVING STRONG AND CONTINUOUS ATTACKS AND PRESSURES FROM THE U.S. THEY ADDED THAT THE ABSENCE OF THE GERMAN TO THE MEETING WAS A CLEAR EXAMPLE OF THAT DIFFICULT SITUATION.

THEY EMPHASIZED THAT IT WAS AN URGENT NEED TO DELIMIT A MINIMUM PLATFORM THAT SAFEGUARDS RELATIONS OF THE SOCIAL DEMOCRACY WITH THE NICARAGUAN PROCESS AND TO ACHIVE AN UNDERSTANDING THAT IN CASE ~~WE~~ THEY CONTINUE ~~THE~~ THE TENDENCING OF APPROXIMATION TO THE SOVIET BLOCK, IT WOULD BE VERY DIFFICULT FOR THEM TO BEAR THE

PRESENT POSITION OF SOLIDARITY.

In REFERENCE TO SOME MEASURES THAT COULD BE TAKEN BY THE SANDINISTS, CARLOS ANDRES SUGGESTED TO DIMINISH THE CUBAN PRESENCE. BOTH MENTIONED THEIR CONCERN ABOUT THE SOVIET PRESENCE PARTICULARLY THE TANKS.

THEY ASKED BAYARDO THAT THEY WOULD LIKE TO HAVE A MEETING WITH THE ENTIRE NATIONAL DIRECTION, TO APPROACH ALL THIS TOPICS AND OTHERS WE CANNOT DEAL WITH IN THE MEETING OF THE S.I.

BAYARDO SUMARIZED THE DIFFICULTIES AND PROBLEMS BEING FACED, UNDERLINED THAT THEY (THE SANDINIST) ARE NOT THE ONES WHO CLOSE THE DOORS, AND THAT IF ALL THE PATHS ARE CLOSED TO THE REVOLUTION, THEY WOULD HAVE TO GO TO WHERE AID IS GIVEN. THAT THE REVOLUTION HAS TO GUARANTEE ITS RIGHT TO SURVIVE AND DEFEND ITSELF.

IN RESPECT TO THE TANKS AND ARMAMENT, BAYARDO REVERTED THE PROBLEM, QUESTIONING WHY SO MUCH NOISE WAS MADE AROUND THIS PROBLEM, AND NOBODY SPEAKS OF THE ENGLISH TANKS THAT ARE ENTERING HONDURAS. IN SYNTHESIS, HE DID NOT DENY THE MATTER CATEGORICALLY, BUT HE DID NOT AFFIRM IT NEITHER.

IN CONNECTION WITH THE ALLUDED CUBAN PRESENCE, BAYARDO ASKED HIMSELF WHAT CUBAN PRESENCE WAS THAT, ADDING THAT HE HAD JUST COME FROM HAVANA WHERE HE TRIED TO CONVINCE FIDEL ABOUT REPLACING AS SOON AS POSSIBLE THE CONTINGENT OF TEACHERS THAT WILL DEPART IN SHORT, BECAUS 60,000 CHILDREN WOULD BE LEFT WITHOUT TEACHERS, AND THEY NEEDED 2,000 AND SO FAR NOBODY, NO COUNTRY HAD OFFER THEM BUT CUBA

In this point, Bayardo argued all the collaboration plan Cuba - Nicaragua.

In addition he said, that the Sandinists understand pecfectly well the situation social democracy faces and they would even understand that in a determined moment, social democrats ~~would~~ will stop supporting the revolution, but he also asked to assimilate were the alternative ~~the~~ the process had before itself.

In respect to the meeting they requested with the whole national direction, Bayardo evaded the point, arguing reasons of excessive work, although, in a session of the meeting, participators had the possibility of having a direct exchange with the members of the political commission (Bayardo, Humberto Ortega and Wee lock)

SECOND CONGRESS OF THE COMMUNIST PARTY OF CUBA

<u>LETTER SENT BY HANS EBERHARD, INTERNATIONAL SECRETARY OF THE GERMAN SOCIAL DEMOCRAT PARTY TO HIS COLLEAGUE WALTER HACKER, OF THE AUSTRIAN SOCIAL DEMOCRAT PARTY AND REPRESENTATIVE OF BRUNO KREISKY IN THE MEETING OF THE COMMITTEE</u>

Bonn, June 19, 1981

PROFESSOR WALTER HACKER
INTERNATIONAL SECRETARY OF THE
~~COMM~~ AUSTRIAN SOCIAL DEMOCRAT
PARTY.

ESTEEMED WALTER:

In connection with NICARAGUA I HAVE TO INFORM YOU THAT NEITHER WILLY BRANDT NOR HANS JUERGEN WISCHNEWSKI WILL BE ABLE TO ATTEND THE MEETING OF THE S.I. COMMITTEE FOR THE DEFENSE OF THE NICARAGUAN REVOLUTION TO BE HELD IN MANAGUA ON JUNE 25. UNFORTUNATELY NEITHER KLAUS LINDENGERS NOR ME CAN ATTEND. WE'LL EXPLAIN THIS DIRECTLY TO OUR NICARAGUAN FRIENDS. ANYWAY, WE HAVE ASKED OUR COLLEAGUE LOTTERBACH TO ACT AS OBSERVER IN THE DISCUSSIONS AND MEETINGS.

WILLY BRANDT WROTE TO FELIPE GONZÁLEZ AND EXPRESSED HIS OPINIONS AND OURS IN RESPECT TO CERTAIN EVENTS THAT HAVE TAKEN PLACE IN NICARAGUA. YOU SHOULD ALSO READ THAT LETTER.

I HOPE YOU AGREE WITH ME IN THAT OUR SOLIDARITY WITH THE REVOLUTION CAN NOT BE INTERPRETED BY SOME SANDINIST COLLEAGUES AS A KIND OF WHITE CARD FOR ANY ACTION THEY CARRY OUT. DUE TO MANY REASONS OUR ASSISTANCE BOTH IN POLITICS AND

MORALITY CAN NOT BE INTERPRETED AS IF IT WERE
IN ONLY ONE DIRECTION.

I SUPOSE THAT THE LAST INTERNAL STRUGGLE — *→YOU KNOW ABOUT*
IN THE SANDINIST MOVEMENT, WITH THE BROTHERS
ORTEGA DEVOTED TO A DESPERATE STRUGGLE AGAINST
THOSE WHO PRACTICE THE POLICY OF "HARD HAND"
THAT MANY CONSIDER IS INDORSED BY ARCE, WHEELOCK
AND BORGE.

WITH MORE INTEREST THAN USUALLY, I WANT TO
READ YOUR REPORT, I WANT TO KNOW IF I SHOULD
NOT GO TO STOCKHOLM OR I MUST MEET YOU
IN THE MIDDLE OF THE WAY IN YOUR RETURN FROM
MANAGUA.

IN RELATION TO THE TRIP OF OUR FRIEND MARTEN
VAN TRAA AND OTHERS TO URUGUA AND ARGENTINE,
I CONSIDER EVERY THING IS GOING O.K.

I WROTE MARTEN AND ASKED HIM TO BE CAREFUL
AND PRUDENT BECAUSE THE REAL SITUATION OF AR-
GENTINE IS FULL OF COMPLEXITIES, SOME RULING
CIRCLES ~~THAT~~ WOULD SURELY THANK TO HAVE A
DIALOGUE WITH OUR POLITICAL FORCES IN EUROPE
PROVIDED WE DON'T AFFECT THEIR NATIONAL PROUD

IN RESPECT TO THE MEETING OF THE COMMITTEE
THE SI ON LATIN AMERICA AND THE CARIBBEAN
TO BE HELD IN JULY AS IN GRENADA, WE DOUBT,
DUE TO OBVIOUS REASONS, THE REASON AND DECISION TO
HELD THIS MEETING IN THAT ISLE, COULD BE INTER-
PRETED BY SOMEONE AS A PROVOCATION. I HOPE OUR
SALVADORIAN FRIENDS ARE NOT THE ONES WHO SUFFER
THE MOST AS A RESULT.

GREETINGS,

HANS EBERHARD

20

SORRY NOT TO HAVE
BEEN ABLE TO TYPE
IT. TIME PRESSURED
ME.

The following is a transcription of some notes on the meeting of the Socialist International Committee for the Defense of the Revolution in Nicaragua, held the 25th of this month of June in Managua. This meeting is the second held by the Committee. The first took place on December 6, 1980 in Washington.

The Committee was officially created on the initiative of Willy Brandt, at the XV Congress of the Socialist International held in Madrid last November; it consisted of the following members: Willy Brandt, Bernt Carlsson, Bottino Craxi, Michael Foot, Felipe Gonzalez, Michael Barrington, Anker Joergensen, Bruno Kreisky, Michael Manley, Francois Mitterrand, Olof Palme, Jose Francisco, Pena Gomez, Carlos Andres Perez, Michel Rocard, Pierre Schori, Mario Soares, Malevi Sorsa, Joop den Uyll, and Hans-Juergen Wischnewski.

Attendees at this meeting in Managua included Bernt Carlsson, Secretary General of the Socialist International: Felipe Gonzalez, chairman of the Committee; Carlos Andres Perez of Accion Democratics; Pierre Schori of the Swedish Social Democratic Party; and Michael Harrington of the DSCC of the United States, all members of the Committee. The absence of one of the West Germans proved to be very significant, since it undoubtedly reveals the intention of the SPD to moderate its actions vis a vis the Central American situation and to give its Latin American administration within S.I. a low and less conspicuous profile with developments in that region. Attached is a letter sent by the International Secretary of the SPD to International Secretary of the Austrian Social Democratic Party on the occasion of this meeting.

U.S. pressures and the difficult domestic situation experienced by the SPD explains in good part the West German caution toward the Nicaraguan Revolution. From the bilateral contacts developed with the participants, the document which was approved, and the development itself of the meeting, we considered:

1) In general, two tendencies were observed among the participants. One, led by Felipe Gonzalez and Carlos Andres, with open, neutralizing objectives, assuming positions of relative pressure interested in clearly expressing the limits of "S.I.'s solidarity" with Nicaragua, and stressing that the support of S.I. is to the democratic and pluralist political project. This faction reflected fears of the course which, in their judgment, the process was taking, and especially of what they called the supply of Cuban and Soviet arms; in short, concern over the "Cubanization" and "Sovietization" of the process. This tendency, quantitatively, was in the minority, but, qualitatively, carries the most weight. The other faction did not give much attention to these considerations

and in general showed understanding and interest in getting to know objectively the difficulties of the process, joining in censuring the U.S. as the most responsible for the situation in Nicaragua and denouncing the lurking dangers in the process. On this side could be found Pierre Schori, Jim Fulton, of the New Democratic Party of Canada, Antonie Blanca, of the French Socialist Party, among others.

2) From the point of view of the objectives that the FSDN proposed for the meeting, in our opinion, they were accomplished. The dangers and risks of the process were recognized in the Declaration approved by the Committee and S.I. support was voted for the "Nicaraguan democratic and pluralist policy" project. On the other hand, the public declarations formulated by the majority of the participants were generally positive, but showed to some degree the apprehensions of some factions with the current direction of the process.

3) The contradictions and tendencies within S.I. were highlighted insofar as how to deal with the policy toward Nicaragua and, in general, the attitude to assume toward the Latin American situation. U.S. pressures on the S.I. and its parties, the difficult and complex international situation and the course being followed by the processes in the region, determine that the most right-wing factions in the heart of the S.I. adopt a position of conciliation and moderation, and propose to avoid that the S.I. continue to behave as it has been up until now, without renouncing the strategic objectives of influencing the direction of the Central American and, in particular, the Nicaraguan processes with clear neutralizing proposals.

4) With this meeting the S.I. has made clear the limits of its "solidarity" with Nicaragua, and in fact its right-wing factions proposed to exert pressure and direct influence on the course of the Revolution. This is not a case of the S.I. strategically varying from its policy toward Nicaragua, but rather demonstrates, to the highest degree possible, caution and discretion, and it will watch very closely the next steps in the Revolution. Finally, we attach a copy of the interview that Bayardo Arce had with Felipe Gonzalez and Carlos Andres, before the meeting started, which clearly reflects the veiwpoint of the right-wing positions in the S.I.

With revolutionary best wishes
[signed]
Manuel Pineiro Losada

Conversation Between Bayardo and Carlos Andres and Felipe Gonzalez

   Carlos Andres and Felipe indicated that they were absolutely
convinced of the dangers, threats, and pressures which were being
exerted on Nicaragua, principally by the U.S., and the difficult
situation which the process is experiencing. That precisely what
the U.S. wants to do is harass Nicaragua, pushing it into a
radicalization of the process, and thus giving itself a pretext and
evidence for implementing military aggression.

   Both were worried that the Sandinista junta would fall into this
trap and play into the hands of the U.S. and that, in their
judgment, it was already doing so; therefore, the Sandinistas must
take into account that reality and not let themselves be provoked.
So it becomes absolutely indispensable that the revolutionary
project be kept within the democratic and pluralistic guidelines,
and that this was the condition for maintaining the support of S.I.
They indicated that they (the social democrats) were in a very
difficult situation, undergoing strong and continuous attacks and
pressures from the U.S.; they added that the absence of the Germans
at the meeting was a clear example of that difficult situation.

   They stressed that it was urgent that a minimal platform be
drawn up which protects the relationship of social democracy with
the Nicaraguan process and that they come to some understanding.
That to continue the trend toward closeness with the Soviet bloc, it
would be very difficult to sustain the present position of
solidarity.

   Referring to steps which could be taken by the Sandinistas,
Carlos Andres suggested a decrease in the Cuban presence. Both
mentioned the concern over the Soviet presence and in particular the
tanks. They requested that Bayardo set up a meeting for them with
the whole National Junta to bring up all of these questions and as
well as others outside the framework of the meeting of the S.I.

   Bayardo summarized the difficulties and problems which they
faced, emphasizing that they (the Sandinistas) were not the ones who
had closed doors, and that if all the roads were closed to the
Revolution, they would have to go where they could get help; that
the revolution has to guarantee its right to continue to exist and
defend itself.

   Regarding the tanks and weapons, Bayardo went over the problem,
questioning why so much was being made of that problem when nobody
was saying anything about the English tanks which were entering
Honduras. In sum, he did not categorically deny the matter, but
neither did he confirm it.

Referring to the previously alluded to Cuban presence, Bayardo wondered what Cuban presence was being talked about, adding that he had just returned from Havana where he went to convince Fidel to quickly replace the contingent of teachers which will soon leave since 60,000 children will be left teacherless, and 2,000 are needed, although up until now no one, no country has offered to send any except Cuba. Bayardo argues the plan of Cuban operation with Nicaragua along these same lines.

He also said that the Sandinistas understood perfectly the situation faced by social democracy and even understood that at a given point in time the social democrats would cease to support the revolution; but he also asked that the alternatives be considered.

Insofar as the meeting that was requested with the full National Junta, Bayardo evaded the issue, citing reasons of workload, although, in one of the meeting's sessions, participants had the opportunity to engage in a direct interchange with the members of the Policy/Political (?) Commission (Bayardo, Humberto Ortega, and Wheelock).

Letter Sent By Hans Eberhard, International Secretary of the German Social Democrat Party, to his Counterpart Walter Hacker, of the Austrian Social Democrat Party and Representatives of Bruno Kreisky in the Committee Meeting

Bonn, June 19, 1981
Professor Walter Hacker
International Secretary of the Austrian Social Democrat Party

Dear Walter:

Regarding Nicaragua, I have to inform you that neither Willy Brandt nor Hans-Juergen Wischnewski will be able to attend the meeting of the S.I. committee for the defense of the Nicaraguan revolution to be held in Managua on June 25. Neither, unfortunately, will Klaus Lindenberg nor I. We will explain this directly to our Nicaraguan friends. At any rate, we have asked our colleague Butterbach to act as an observer in the discussions and meetings.

Willy Brandt wrote Felipe Gonzalez and gave him his and our opinions on certain things which have taken place in Nicaragua. You should also read this letter.

I hope that you agree with me that our solidarity with the revolution cannot be interpreted by some Sandinista colleagues as carte blanche for whatever they do. For many reasons our assistance not only politically but also morally cannot be interpreted as if it were in only one direction.

I suppose you know of the last internal struggle in the Sandinista movement, with the Ortega brothers enmeshed in a desperate battle against those who advocate the hard-line policy considered by many to be supported by Arce, Wheelock and Borge.

With more than normal interest, I would like to read your report and to know if I should go to Stockholm or meet you halfway on your return from Managua.

With respect to the trip of our friend Marten Van Traa and others to Uruguay and Argentina, I expect that everything is going well. I wrote to Marten and asked him to be careful and prudent because the real Argentinian situation is full of complications; some government circles will certainly be thankful that a dialogue has been started with our political forces in Europe as long as we do not upset their national pride.

Regarding the meeting of the S.I. Committee on Latin America and the Caribbean to be held July 25 in Grenada, we question, for obvious reasons, the rationale and decision to hold this meeting on that island; it could be interpreted by some as a provocation. I hope that our Salvadoran friends are not the ones to suffer most because of this.

Best Wishes
Hans Eberhard

K

3

REPORT ON THE GENERAL CONGRESS OF THE WORLD CENTER FOR THE
RESISTANCE OF IMPERIALISM, ZIONISM, RACISM AND REACTION.

FROM: The N.J.M. Delegate
TO: The Central Committee of the N.J.M.
DATE: June 26th, 1982.

Comrades, I left Grenada on June 11th to attend what I was informed to be a Conference in Solidarity with El Salvador. It was only on my arrival in Cuba, together with delegates from other Caribbean Revolutionary and Democratic Parties and Organisations that I learnt the true Character of t Conference in Libya.

On Saturday June 12th the Caribbean Delegates met with Cde Phinera, a member of the Central Committee of the P.C.C. in charge of American Affair: He explained to us the nature of the Conference and put forward key guide-lines for our approach to the major issues of the meeting.
ie(1) That we should avoid giving support for the idea of Libya being the center of the World anti-imperialist struggle and its military implications of a rapid Deployment force against imperialism.

(2) That we should only give solidarity expressions for the proposed World Center.

(3) That the Secretariat of the World Center should include Latin American and Caribbean Revolutionary Forces, he also said that Cuba will be partici-pating as Ospal in the Congress and that they would be leaving that very ni(for Libya.

After the meeting with Cde Phinera the Caribbean Delegates continued to meet to analyse the new information and to take some common positions. The full implications of Cuba's participation in the Congress as Ospal and not as the PCC suddenly dawned on us and was a source of great concern but this did not prevent us from taking common decisions ie:
(1) That the English speaking Caribbean take a multi-lateral approach to:" Material assistance from the Libyans for the different Organisations and Parties, as compared to the Bi-lateral approach which can give range for organisations requesting arms, and its possible repercussions in terms of imperialist reaction.

(2) The tentative decision that N.J.M. should speak on behalf of the Cari-bbean, because there were other Caribbean Delegates who took another route to Libya, because they also received invitations from the Libyan Embassy in Guyana, and therefore would have to be consulted with, on the decisions.

N.J.M. agreed to speak on behalf of the Caribbean but pointed out its concern over the level of Cuba's participation in the conference, The fact that they were not attending as the PCC indicates the low profile being taken by the Cubans and that it is of concern to us since Cuba is the leader of the Revolutionary Movement in this part of the world. We should therefore expres our concern about this to Cde Otto Marrero.

DOCUMENT 34
34 - 1

W.P.J. response was that it seems that N.J.M. is implying, taking a low profile if Cuba is doing the same and since they are the two parties with State Power, therefore in that case the other Organisations should not speak and infact we should go underground.

The Libyans met with us on Monday June 14th and apologised for not getting in contact with us earlier. We left Cuba that day and arrived in Libya on Tuesday 15th June. We were driven to the Congress from the Airport. There were Delegates from over 80 States and 240 Organisations at the Congress.

The opening session of the General Congress included a welcoming address by the Congress Chairman, The feature address by the Libyan Leader and Solidarity statements. The Leader's address was adopted as a Working Paper of the Congress Papers.

The second day of the General Congress included a Morning session of Solidarity Statements. During the latter part of the morning session, The second item of the Congress was introduced. The draft Charter of the World Center or the World Sanctuary was presented verbally to the Congress, None of the Delegates had a written Copy of the draft, But sometime later Copies of the draft Charter was brought to the Congress Center while it was still being read.

After all delegates received copies of the draft, it was suggested that since the document was not studied before, the Congress should break for lunch so that delegates could study it. On resumption the draft was discussed and amendments were called for in the documents. A redrafting Committee was set up, and delegations submitted their admendments in writing to the Committee The third Day of the General Congress was Characterised by Solidarity Statements.

The closing session of the General Congress focused on three Major items i.e. (1) The ratification of the Charter. (2) The ratification of the Tripoli Declaration. (3) The setting up of the organs of the Sanctuary Comprising The General Secretariat of the Congress and the selection of the Secretary General.

The New Draft was ratified after much comments and criticism about it. At one time it appeared as if the Congress would break up in confusion and disarry. Criticism flew across the hall at the Latin American Delegates from Arab and African Delegates generally. The Latin Americans called for amendments to the Charter and a break in the Meeting so that they can meet among themselves first, and with the Libyans and the redrafting Committee after. The Chairman called for all amendments to be in writing. It was clear that the Arab Belegations and African Delegations like, Benin, Ghana, Senegal and Uganda comprised the Core of the forces which wanted the Charter ratified as presented by the redrafting Committee.

There were expressions from several delegations of the fact that they were invited to Libya to attend a Conference in Solidarity with El Salvador and now being confronted with the real nature of the Conference, they cannot concretely commit themselves to the center because they have no mandate from their organisations to do so. They suggested bringing back the documents home so that their organisations can study them.

The question of the membership of the Soviet Union in the Center was raised. It was pointed out that the Center is for the small Countries of the world, The Third World Countries, not for the big Countries. One or Two delegations also pointed out that the Latin Americans were trying to prevent the ratification of the Charter because the Soviet Union was excluded from membership. This charge was denied by the Latins saying, that all they wanted were some amendments to the New draft Charter.

The Congress adjourned for 30 minutes at the request of the Latins. On Resumption the Latins put forward their proposed amendments i.e. :
(1) That all reference to the United Nations be removed from the draft.

(2) That the Word 'United' be removed from objective Two of the Charter.

(3) That the word 'Weapon' be deleted from the Charter.
The Congress accepted the amendments and the Charter was ratified.

The second item the Tripoli Declaration was discussed. Suggestions were made on adding some details to the declaration and it was also ratified. The Chairman of the Congress presented the third item of the closing session. The item included the setting up of the General Secretariat and the Secretary General. The Congress agreed that the Secretariat be composed of the representatives of 18 Countries and Organisations. There were proposals for membership of the Secretariat of a number of Countries.

PROPOSALS FOR MEMBERSHIP

1. Iran 2. P.L.O. 3. Lebanon 4. Libya 5. Ghana 6. SWAPO
7. Senegal 8. Cyprus 9. Greece 10. El Salvador 11. Nicaragua
12. Cuba 13. Syria 14. Egypt 15. Polisario 16. Benin 17. Seychelles
18. Chile 19. Grenada.

Grenada was proposed for membership by W.P.J. Zimbabwe and Vietnam were also proposed for membership. El Salvador and Nicaragua withdrew from proposed membership in the Secretariat and suggested Guatemala.

Grenada was proposed for membership again by Seychelles. Other Countries proposed themselves for membership.
Bolivia took the floor and told the congress Chairman that Grenada has been proposed again and again and that he was not responding to the proposal, there fore she would like to propose Grenada for membership again.

- 4 -

The entire Congress showed its approval by exploding into loud applause. The Chairman said that we had agreed on 18 members which we now have, but it seems that you want it to be 19, - more loud applause, Grenada was accepted as a member of the Secretariat. The Secretary General of the General Secretariat was bestowed on Libya.

The Secretariat met at 12 noon on Saturday June 19th. Cuba was not informed in time of the meeting, so that the Leader of the P.C.C. delegation Cde. Fundora and other top members had already left Libya. Only Cde. Luis was in Libya and he represented Cuba at the meeting only as an observer.

I and the rest of the Caribbean delegation left the Hotel at 11 a.m. to attend a meeting at the International Green Book Center, up to that time I was not informed of the Secretariat Meeting, but I met with the Cuban Delegate Cde Luis who brought me up to date on the meeting.
He said that the meeting of the Secretariat was a complicated one. Some Countries did not understand changes in the names of members of the Secretariat. Nicarguai El Salvador membership was a major issue. The Arabs suggested translations problems as reason for the issue. The Libyans want a meeting with Nicargua and El Salvador to find out why they do not want to be members of Secretariat.

Some members of the Secretariat were concerned about the Latin Americans behaviour. The Libyans suggested outside pressure from the Soviet Union through Cuba on the other Latin Countries.

The question of Grenada membership was not challenged.

Cuba was proposed a member of the Executive Committee in the meeting along with Benin, Iran, Syria, and Libya.

Secretariat to meet in six (6) months again.

Based on this report and the attached documents, and detailed analysis of the global situation, our party will have to decide whether Grenada should participate in the World Center for resistance to Imperialism, Zionism, Racism and Reaction.

Godwin Horsford

THE CARIBBEAN DELEGATION

The Caribbean Delegation Comprised the following Representatives.

ANTIGUA - TIM HECTOR -A.C.L.M.

BAHAMAS - LIONEL CAREY - VANGUARD

BARBADOS - FRANCIS BELLE - MONALI

DOMINICA - BILL RIVIERE - D.L.M.

          - PIERRE CHARLES - D.L.M.

GRENADA - GODWIN HORSFORD - N.J.M.

GUYANA   - MICHAEL CHAN   - P.P.P.

        - ROHIT WILLIAMS - P.P.P.

JAMAICA - ELEAN THOMAS   - W.P.J.

        - MAXINE HENRY   - P.N.P.

ST. LUCIA - GEORGE ODLUM   - P.L.P.

       - MIKE PILGRIM   - P.L.P.

       -EARL BOSQUET   - W.R.M.

ST. VINCENT SIMEON GREENE   - U.P.M.

TRINIDAD/TOBAGO MICHAEL ABERDEEN- P.P.M.

There were sharp differences in views among delegates from the Caribbean on issues regarding a Common approach to material assistance from the Libyans and also who should speak on behalf of the Caribbean. N.J.M., W.P.J., W.R.M. and P.P.P. generally carried a common position on these two issues and generally had a common outlook on most issues.

There was a line that Cuba was using Grenada to influence the other Caribbean parties and organisations. The reason I believed that this line developed was the fact that Cuba was always keeping in touch with Grenada. Cuba always contacted Grenada to invite the Caribbean to the Latin American and Caribbean meeting, and generally made Grenada aware of the behind the scenes issues involved in the Congress and what is their position and general guidelines for us to follow.

CONTENTS

A) GENERAL CONSIDERATIONS

B) LIST OF ANNEXES

C) TEXT OF THE REPORT

GENERAL CONSIDERATIONS:

1. The 15th Congress of the S.I. held in Madrid and conceived as the programmatic grounds for the projection of the so-called democratic socialism in the 80's, could not implement the political basis for the offensive initially conceived by that international organization.

2. Various concurring factors in the field of international relations, the election of Ronald Reagan, the world's economy and East-West relations contained in the text of this report affected this.

3. The Congress could rather be defined as the expression of a policy of expectation and of partial tactical retreat of the S.I.

4. Despite the aforementioned, it should be stressed that the S.I. maintained, in essence, its basic global positions set forth at the Geneva and Vancouver Congresses which opened a new stage in the international organization's political life.

5. It can be stated that the policy toward Latin America became the central issue and the probatory touchstone of the S.I.'s opening to the Third World and of its will to confront the new Republican Administration.

Undoubtedly, the contradictory nature of the actions of international Social Democracy lies in its very roots. In its Latin American projection, obviously without loosing its feature of being a permanent adversary of the left and of the revolutionary forces it becomes a tactical ally of the latter; an important ally in the peoples' democratic and anti-imperialist struggle.

The effective use of the tactical space offered by the forces of
social reformism in this juncture, will depend greatly on the left's
ability and capability to project it to serve its own objectives
in the struggle; a clear proof of which has precisely been the scenario
of the Congress.

On the other hand, it should be borne in mind that the Social Democrat's
reformist project —in the face of the harsh socioeconomic reality of
our continent, characterized by a deepening of the system's structural
crisis and a growing polarization of the class struggle —has, objectively,
no cristalization prospects whatsoever in most of our countries.

6. In spite of these restrictive circumstances, the Congress fully ratified
Western Europe's will to practice an independent policy with respect
to the United States in all vital matters of international life.

This is evidenced in the:

- Petition of the ratification of SALT-II

- Adherence to the convening of the Pan European Conference on Disarmament.

- Support to the proposed moratorium or to the non-stationing of new
intermediate range missiles in the area.

7. In the Congress, judgements were passed on the problems of Afghanistan,
Cambodia and Poland, as well as on the arms race with expressions
which, although of anti-Soviet content, differed in emphasis.

8. In the item or chapter devoted to African problems, an underlying
political reference is made of our country concerning that region,
althoug in a general context it implies other nations.

9. The existence of multiple trends and nuances within the attending Social Democratic parties and personalities became manifest in the Congress, which reiterates our criteria on the heterogeneity of the reformist movement in our times.

10. The S.I.'s social reformist theoretical basis became manifest in issues such as the economic crisis, North-South Dialogue, problems of employment, etc., although the progressive nature of some of its central approaches on these matters should be acknowledged.

11. In our view, the Congress as a whole ratified the convenience of maintaining a line of access to the S.I.'s political information sources and of frequent relations with its activities, specially under the circumstances of the Republican Party's rise to power in the presidency of the United States..

REPORT ON THE 15TH CONGRESS OF THE SOCIALIST INTERNATIONAL - MADRID,
NOVEMBER 13-16, 1980.

The purpose of this report is to make a global political
assessment of the results of the S.I.'s Congress and of the agreements
contained in its General Resolution, the only document adopted at
the meeting. References on the most significant activities that took
place within the framework of the Congress that permitted, through
different channels, the knowledge of important political situations
in the Social Democracy's leadership and in many of its component
factors are also included. This report excludes the minutes of the
working sessions, the analysis of the delegations' speeches, press
conferences and other activities which, due to their lengthy nature,
would require a different treatment.

The preparatory work for this Congress and the direction given
to it at various previous meetings of the Bureau of the International,
as well as the documents and reference available to us, clearly
indicate that the objective of the S.I. leadership was to turn the
Madrid Congress into a new important offensive in the worldwide
political strategy of Social Democracy, stressing that this Congress
was to substantiate and make a breakdown of the so-called "projection
of the S.I. in the 80's".

In other words, the attempt was to strengthen S.I.'s activities
and to arrive at political statements that would mean an important
step forward in the implementation of the three main objectives
set forth at the 1976 Geneva Congress and ratified at Vancouver in 1978.
As is known, they are: to expand East-West cooperation; a plan of
measures for the solution of the North-South conflict and to promote

human rights. Coinciding with said goals, the Third World phase
or phase of rupture with Eurocentrism that continued developing in
subsequent years, was opened. As foreseen, the new political objectives
of the International were to be contained in a new programmatic
platform whose drafting project was entrusted to a working group
presided over by Felipe González and made up by Vice Presidents Reiulf
Steen and Karel van Miert of Norway and the Flemish Socialist Party
(Belgium) respectively. The idea was to elaborate a set of doctrines
of the S.I. or declaration of principles, structurally similar to
the one adopted at Frankfurt in 1951 but that would basically
underline the political tasks that constitute the S.I.'s present profile
and to express its main present political goals in a more invigorated
way.

As is known, the preparatory work of S.I.'s Congress covers a
lengthy period to plan their activities, in which the Bureau of the
international body establishes various tasks related to the preparation
of the reports and proposals that will be debated within the
framework of the Congress. In order to have more information available
concerning the preparatory stages of the Madrid Congress and of the
aims we have referred to, at the end of this report there is a list
of the main documents to be consulted as references.

Unquestionably, the international junctures which occurred during
the last months of the preparatory stage of the Congress, critically
affected the plans of the International to turn the Congress into a
new basis for the projection of its worldwide political activity. In
our view, among the most relevant facts in this regard, the
following can be mentioned: Ronald Reagan's election as President of
the United States; the suspension of the Conference on European
Cooperation and Security in Madrid; the events in Poland; the Iraq-Iran

war and its repercussions in the region; the sharpening of the
international economic crisis and particularly its effects on the
industrialized countries of the West.

We believe that the impact of these situations can be clearly
observed, with respect to the Congress, by examining two of its
documents:

1. Opening speech of the Congress, delivered by the President
    of the S.I., Willy Brandt.

2. The introductory speech on the Declaration of Principles by
    Felipe González, where reference is made to the inconvenience
    of presenting at the Madrid Congress a new programmatic
    basis, postponing its elaboration for the next Congress, using
    various pretexts.

If to all the aforementioned elements we add the information about
the strong pressures exerted on the S.I.'s leadership and on Brandt
himself by the US State Department of which we learned through Latin
American delegations' sources, one understands even more clearly
the political context within which the S.I. leadership had to work
in its Congress. The main US pressures that we learned of were:

1. A personal letter of Secretary of State Edmund Muskie
    addressed to Willy Brandt, about which he reported
    of the Bureau to stress the pressures being exerted on him.

2. Various documents of the State Department itself where
    concrete demands are made on the treatment of the situation
    in El Salvador and Central America. (see annexed list).

Due to the aforementioned, one can understand that the frustation
of the S.I.'s initial plans and the difficult political circumstances
in which the Congress was held, made Brandt himself ask publicly
the following in his opening speech. "I don't know what will be the
fate of minkind in the 80's: How would I know will be that of the
S.I.?"

The verification of the aforementioned political circumstances
led us to state, in different messages sent during the initial days
of the Congress, that attitudes of retreat were being observed in the
S.I. in the face of the new situations. We believe that the final
results introduced some alternative elements, specially concerning
Latin America which we shall later on discuss, that would indicate
that the strategy adopted before the existing difficulties by the
leadership of the S.I. could be defined more accurately as a "waiting
stage" or as a policy of expectation and restrain awaiting for the
development of international events.

We shall now break down the main formulations of the text of the
Final Resolution adopted, using as reference the draft prepared by
the already mentioned working group (Circular 89/80) and the different
versions containing the modifications resulting from the political
debate during the Congress. In our comments, we shall refer to the
confidential information and political circumstances that allow us
to make assessments of some of the problems put forth.

The aforementioned draft presented as a basis for discussion and forwarded to the members of the Bureau on September 17, 1980 was elaborated by the Resolutions Committee that met in Bad Neuenahr, FRG, on September 14. The Committee was presided over by Hans-Jürgen Wischnewski, Vice Chairman of the SPD and the following affiliated parties:

- British Labour Party

- New Democratic Party of Canada

- Radical Party of Chile

- French Socialist Party

- Social Democratic Party of Germany

- Labour Party of Israel

- Social Democratic Party of Italy

- Social Party of Japan

- Socialist Party of Senegal

- Workers' Socialist Party of Spain (WSPS)

- Social Democratic Party of Sweden

- UISY

In our opinion, the text is deliberately moderate and extremely cautious in its political statements. It could be said that, by omission, it was poor and weak. The reasons for this were, undoubtedly, the heterogeneity of the Drafting Committee on the one hand, and the purpose for the document to serve exclusively as basis for the debate in the Congress on the other.

It should be pointed out that Latin America was dealt with in an obscure and indiscriminate fashion, and that the global approach on Latin America proved hollow, politically weak and negligent.

Nevertheless, it should be noted that the draft contained two issues of major importance to measure the S.I.'S political position:

- Support to the French-Polish idea favoring a European Conference on Disarmament, which undoubtedly was a bridge with the socialist countries.

- Petition of the immediate ratification of SALT-II, which naturally clashed with the election of the Republican candidate in the United States.

Since the first working day of the Congress (November 13), the efforts of the rightist and conservative sectors of the International aimed at depriving the text of the previously mentioned positive features and at introducing wordings denoting anti-Sovietism and enhancing the ideological values of Social Democratic reformism became manifest. Through various friendly sources worth mentioning -- some Latin-American delegations, Pierre Schori and members of the WSPS participating in the organizational work -- we learned of the passionate debate on this issue in the Bureau meeting.

On the 14th, a second draft General Resolution -- which we obtained through the same sources -- also circulated confidentially among the members of the Bureau. As can be seen in this text, the debate within the Bureau resulted in the inclusion of various issues: the Afghan problem;

events in Poland; charge on the USSR's alleged arms-race policy; and to restrain the formulation of economic problems only to monetary and comercial matters. As to Latin American matters, the text reflected, however, some of the main problems of the region, although still in a weak and insufficient manner.

Saturday evening (November 14 to 15) a very lengthy session of the Bureau was held -- also reported to us by the same sources -- which resulted in the formulation of a third draft General Resolution. In general, this was the text finally adopted by the plenary on Sunday 16th with the addition of three topics proposed by the delegations of the countries concerned: Cyprus, Malta and Grenada, aimed at higlighting, of course, the political objectives of their respective S.I. member parties (EDEK, consultative party; Labor Party of Malta, full member; and New Jewel, admitted as full member during this Congress).

In its introduction, the document describes the present international situation by the aggravation of the economic crisis, the speeding up of the arms race, the deepening of the North-South gap, and the increasing violation of human rights. As can be noted, all these assertions oppose the S.I. programmatic objectives. It goes on affirming that "peace is threatened more seriously than at any other moment in the past ten years and relations among the great powers have worsened considerably". We believe that the S.I. deliberately starts with such a statement to conceal the sharp differences in the political atmosphere of the Madrid Congress and the previous Geneva and Vancouver Congresses, where the atmosphere was of relative success.

Additionally, -- and this can be considered undoubtedly as a victory of the progressive positions and of the will to oppose the future Republican Administration -- the International calls for the ratification of SALT-II.

-11-

although in a subtle manner backs the beginning of the SALT-III negotiations soon. In this chapter of the text, a formulation remained -- which, in our opinion, is the most important concession of the Congress to US interests -- stating that should negotiations on the limitation of strategic weapons be suspended, this "could lead to the USSR's greater accumulation of new missiles" It should be understood that in spite of the negative content of this formulation, it does not fail to reveal also a pressing intention on the United States.

Another element contained in the introduction is the Iran-Iraq conflict. After refering to its dangerous nature, the document cautiously speaks of the actions Olof Palme had just initiated, by making his success lie on "the commitment of non-interference by the great powers and the nations of the region". According to our knowledge, it seems that Palme's actions were preceded by a commitment expressed in the form of a declaration of intentions by the factors potentially involved in the conflict favoring the actions and refraining from any material implications in the confrontation between the two countries.

Following the introduction, the Polish issue is dealt with also in cautious terms although reiterating the reformist S.I.'s traditional stand on the organized labor movement to be found also in Brandt's opening speech.

Another significant element is the insistence on the need to saveguard the continuation of the Madrid Conference on European Security and cooperation. It should be stressed that this formulation becomes particularly important if we take into consideration that the atmosphere in Madrid and the general political assessments concerning the Conference seemed to indicate then a general blocking of its possibilities to go beyond the formal opening on November 11. Without doubt, the strong support given by the S.I. to the Conference was aimed at highlighting a constructive position as opposed to the situation prevailing then.

It is also particularly important that, although limitedly, the introduction contains support to the holding of a European Conference on Disarmament. We believe it reveals the interest of the International to please the positions of the French, the SDP and of a group of major European social democratic parties, and also constitutes a political gesture towards the socialist countries, particularly the USSR.

Immediately, the Resolution approaches a chapter on the economic crisis, stressing its aggravation and stating that it is "the proof of the existing economic order's inability to achieve a more just distribution of wealth". Analyzing this paragraph within S.I.'s characteristic approach, we believe that it presents more advanced theoretical formulations than those agreed upon in the Geneva and Vancouver Congresses, since, although the International naturally stresses its false distribution solution as a remedy for economic exploitation and insists on the formula of productivity and purchasing power increases as miraculous panaceas, it is also true that the need for reform in the international economic order is clearly established and opposition to the thesis on the solutions through free market economies is formulated, which undoubtedly constitutes a direct attack against the US Republican Party's policy.

Then comes an extremely brief chapter on Europe that reflects caution and care in its formulation. It contains, however, two very significant aspects:

a) Reiteration of S.I. support to all measures contributing to the withdrawal or non-stationing of new intermediate-range missiles in Central Europe, which is an endorsement of the idea of a moratorium promoted by the FRG.

-13-

b) Reiteration of the need for Western Europe to express and publicize
its own interests and responsibilities concerning the problems of
world peace, even by opposing them to the United States.

Both issues without doubt reveal two basic aspects of S.I.'s political
objectives in Europe and, in its broader sense, in East-West relations, and
clearly emphasize the will of not yielding before the new US Administration.
In a conversation with Francois Mitterand at a reception given at the
Ayuntamiento de Madrid, he said that the inclusion of these two issues in the
Resolution meant a face-to-face confrontation with the United States and
embodied the will of the S.I. to persevere in its objectives.

Concerning the Middle East, the most relevant element was the decisive and
full support given to the efforts of the Labor Party of Israel to return to
the government of that country. It is noteworthy to stress that the
leadership of the S.I. undoubtedly took two bold measures that reveal its
degree of commitment in this connection. On the one hand, Brandt, Kreisky
and Felipe González, among others, signed a joint document together with the
Egyptian Foreign minister Boutros Ghali and Shimon Peres himself -- which was
afterwards mentioned in the Resolution only in terms of "noting", thus
revealing the degree of internal debate aroused. In this connection, we
were able to learn that in the Bureau meeting where this topic was dealt with,
a sharp confrontation aroused in which the position that intended to make the
Congress adopt a more direct support to the content of the Declaration in
its Resolution was defeated by 14 votes against 5.

Moreover, the Congress decided to acknowledge consultative status to the
MAPAM Party of Israel, inviting it to make up a joint representation with
the existing member party.

The position adopted on the Middle East became one of the most vulnerable
points and a critical factor for Brandt himself, who was blamed on several

-14-

ocassions during the press conference held at the closing of the meeting,
as can be seen in the Memoires published.

UU16

360

Moreover, as can be seen in the Resolution, the formulation on the Palestinian problem actually does not go beyond the Camp David Agreements established by the governments of Israel and the United States.

We believe that a relevant element in the chapter devoted to the Middle East is the recognition of Malta's new policy of neutrality; this position of the S.I. should lead us to a closer examination of the present actions of the government of Malta -- which has recently adopted firm stands on issues as important as Italian-Maltese and Libyan-Maltese relations -- and Malta's position at the Belgrade Conference on the European Security and Cooperation Conference, which was further stressed in the present round of negotiations in Madrid. This topic is interesting when determining the degree of Yugoslav influence in Malta's policy.

In the chapter devoted to Asia two central elements should be pointed out:

1. The position on China

2. The treatment of the Cambodia and Afghanistan problems.

As for China, the strategy adopted by the S.I. clearly favors the position of the US, enhancing the new Chinese policy of broader "international dialogue". It is significant that the Resolution also denotes interest in the development of events in China.

It should be pointed out that in spite of our inquiries in this respect, we could not learn of the presence on any Chinese officials in the Congress with any capacity.

Concerning the Cambodian and Afghan problems, the Resolution calls for a "reconciliation of the Cambodian people to guarantee its neutrality".

And although no reference is made on Vietnam or on any specific claims --
which are expressed in connection with the situation in Eastern Timor
and the presence of Indonesian troops there -- undoubtedly, the nature
of the demand is negative.

In the case of Afghanistan, it should be pointed out that the
S.I. adopted an overtly aggressive style in stating "that it is terrified
and deceived" because the USSR has not yet withdrawn its troops from
Afghanistan, and concludes saying that it "supports the resistence of
the Afghan people to the occupation of the country". In a conversation
held with many journalists attending the Congress and in the speeches
delivered by most speakers at the Congress, an extraordinary insistence on
the Afghan problem as an element of denunciation of the USSR became
manifest. These circumstances should be taken into consideration when
evaluating this part of the text.

Lastly, in connection with Asia, India's position as a decisive
force in the Non-Aligned Movement is stressed, but no further mention
of the Movement itself or its policies is made.

As for the chapter devoted to Africa it is also extremely brief, and
is dealt with very conventionally, as usual in S.I.'s congresses and
conferences. Its main considerations refer to the denunciation of the
South African regime and the struggle against apartheid. The S.I. seems
to consider that the phenomena of class exploitation, neocolonialism
and military dictatorships in the region do not exist.

We wish to stress that this Congress Resolution contained an entirely
new formulation which constitutes an implicit attack against ~~~~~~~~ out
demanding   the withdrawal of foreign troops from the African Horn
conflict "and others".

The only positive element to be stressed in this chapter is the
actual recognition of the POLISARIO Front within the context of the
reaffirmation of the right of the Saharan people to self-determination.

The analytical section of the Resolution that refers to Latin America
and the Caribbean is specially significant both for its content and for
its length, when compared with the rest of the Resolution. An assessment
of the document reveals a sharp contrast between the chapter devoted to
Latin American problems and the treatment of other topics such as détente,
disarmament, the Middle East, Africa, and others. The chapter devoted to
Latin America is undoubtedly the most positive and advanced in the document.

The most important issues in the analysis of the Latin American
situation were:

- Central America, particularly El Salvador

- Latin America policy of the new US Republican Administration

- Nicaragua

It is enlightening to note the positions contained in the Resolution
that show the positive trend we have already referred to:

a) "The Socialist International challenges the US government to put
   an end to its political and military support to the present
   Salvadorian Junta and to admit its inability to prevent more bloodshed.
   We reject the thesis of the Salvadorian problem is that of a Junta
   fighting against an extreme right or an extreme left. It is rather
   that of a despotic regime whose actions have led to a state of civil
   war".

b) "We believe that the victory and achievements of the Nicaraguan revolution reflect the expectations for social change in the entire region. We reiterate our support for the Sandinista National Liberation Front".

c) "The Socialist International voices its solidarity with the people of Grenada and our new affiliated party, the New JEWEL Movement. The International will never admit foreign interference in the economic or military affairs of Grenada".

d) "The Socialist International seriously warns against any attempt from foreign powers at interfering in the internal affairs of Latin American and Caribbean countries".

e) "We are concerned about some remark of the then Republican candide to the presidency of the United States on Latin America, particularl his expressions of support to the dictatorial regimes of El Salvador and Guatemala, and his attacks against Grenada and Nicaragua,. We hope that our fears be groundless. We will await for the political statements of the new Administration before passing judgement. But we see the attitude of the new Administrati towards Latin America and the Caribbean as a sample of its stand towards the whole world".

To sum up, the position of the S.I in the Final Resolution on El Salvador represented a defeat for the United States and Latin American center right sectors, who could not impose their thesis.

From the point of view of the progressive and left forces, the analytical chapter on Latin America is in essence -- given the present international juncture-- undoubtedly positive and to a great extent meets the objectives pursued in this context.

Suffice it to reiterate that the first draft Resolution represented a set back not only when compared with the results of the Santo Domingo Conference but also with what was stated at the previous Vancouver Congress; it was simply hollow, full of rethorics, and avoided any definition on the most burning and relevant problems of the continent.

In this positive evolution of the Resolution concerning Latin American issues, the action of the delegates from MNR and FDR of El Salvador and the Nicaraguan delegation headed by Commander Bayardo Arce was most influential.

The behavior of the three key elements in the analysis of the Latin American situation -- the Europeans, the Latin American group and the actions of the US State Department -- gives an approximate picture of the contradictions and trends dealing with the treatment of the Latin American issue in the Congress.

a) <u>The Europeans</u>

In general, the position of European parties on the Latin America reality was good; this was reflected both in public addresses in the plenary and in the Bureau meetings and bilateral conversations and contacts. The Spanish, Swedes, English Laborites, Dutch, Finns, Belgians, French, Canadians, among others, were part of this trend.

To give an example: the drafting of the paragraph where the S.I. challenges the United States to put an end to its political and military support to the present Junta in El Salvador, was proposed by Jenny Little from the British Labour Party, when Willy Brandt was presiding over one of the Bureau sessions. It was also she, who, together with the PNP delegation from Jamaica, defeated a motion presented by Fanny Simon from the US Social Democratic Party against Cuba, which received only one vote in favor, from said party.

The German Social Democratic Party which was divided into two main trends on the Latin American problem deserves special mention: one trend was led by SPD Vice Chairman, Hans Jürgen Wischnewski with more conservative positions and more susceptible to US influences, and the other led Willy Brandt with a realistic and receptive attitude towards the positions of the most progressive and radical sectors of the Latin American group.

It must be taken into account that Wischnewski has been leading the conversations of the SPD with the State Department on S.I.'s positions on Latin America.

In his opening and closing speeches, Brandt ratified S.I.'s line of solidarity with the Nicaraguan Revolution and of support for the struggle

in El Salvador, which means to reject U.S. strong pressures to change the
situation. It was precisely at the second Bureau meeting where the
wording of the Latin American chapter was discussed, that Brandt
sarcastically revealed that he had received a letter from Secretary of
State, Muskie, stating that the positions of the S.I. Congress on El
Salvador should be strictly moderate.

b) The Latin American group

In the Latin American group, differences were more clearly defined:

- The center right sector, led by Carlos Andrés Pérez, Daniel Oduber
and the Panamanian representation led by Blandón. The main objective of
this sector was to make the S.I. change positions on Central American
realities, particularly on El Salvador, attempting to receive support
for an alleged immediate political or negotiated solution of the
Salvadorian conflict and for this to be included in the Congress
Resolution on those terms. They cited the military weakness of the
revolutionary forces in El Salvador and their incapability to defeat the
army, stating that negotiations were the sole solution — which would in
essence entail the capitulation of the revolutionary forces and the
implementation of a formula acceptable by the United States. Basically,
this position agrees with the alternatives the State Department is
planning for El Salvador.

- The center left sector, made up by Peña Gómez, Anselmo Sule and
Jorge Arturo Reyna, did not speak in favor of the positions of the center
right sector but maintained an eclectic attitude and showed little
activity, reflected ups and downs and attempted to conciliate the formulations
of the most progressive and left sectors.

- The sector of progressive and revolutionary   forces, made up by
the Salvadorian representatives (DRU, FDR and MNR), Commander Bayardo
Arce of the FSLN, Jamaica's PNP, the New JEWEL of Grenada, and others.
The positive role played by Manuel Ungo and Hector Oqueli of the MNR
should be stressed, as well as the work done by Commander Bayardo Arce.
The main objective of these forces was to thwart the maneuvers of the
center right, strongly stimulated by the Panamanians, and avoid a set back
of S.I. positions on Latin America and the Caribbean.

To this end, a plan of action was scheduled to held meetings and
contacts with the main European and Latin American leaders, the results of
which were positive.

c) Actions of the US State Department

After the Santo Domingo Conference, the State Department intensified
its efforts and activities to change the policy the S.I. was following
toward Latin America and the Caribbean which, as is known, shows important
signs of friction with the Latin American projection of Carter's
Administration.

Contacts and meeting took place before the holding of the Congress
among State Department officials and Social Democracy leaders. The main
interest for the US government remained unchanged: to avoid the S.I.'s
condemnation of the Junta in El Salvador and actually to promote its
support, and to prevent criticisms on the policy of the United States
toward Latin America and the Caribbean.

As stated before in this report, during the Congress we learned of
four documents that had been distributed by the State Department and
the US Embassy in Madrid, in which the basic issue demanded was for the
"Socialist International to condemn the use of violence whatever its

UU 24
368

origin, making an appeal to all those involved in the conflict of El Salvador to stop the violence and accept the mediating offers of the bishops".

It was also learned, on the other hand, that the State Department sent a large group of officials for lobbying, including Roy Prosterman, who is well known for his participation in setting up the "strategic villages" in Vietnam and for his being at present an adviser in the implementation of the agrarian reform intended for El Salvador. Also present, and on the same job, was Rey Prendes, the Major of San Salvador, who was sent by the Americans.

The continued presence of the US Ambassador to Madrid, Terence Todman in the Congress halls was also common.

In making a comparative analysis of this Congress' section on Latin America and the Caribbean with the previous Congress, one clearly observs important progress. The formulations adopted relate to the most important issues of the region's political life at present and to a large extent meet the objectives that the progressive and revolutionary forces aspired to have reflected in the document, although when compared with the Santo Domingo Conference, there are important elements that are not contained in the Resolution of the Congress:

- Support to the struggle of the people of Puerto Rico for their independence, an itchy issue for the United States, that brought about strong reactions on the part of the State Department.

- The recognition of the "legitimacy of the use of violence when other paths to attain the peoples' objectives of liberty and social justice are closed".

In this regard, it is significant that no reference was made about the Santo Domingo Declaration, while only satisfaction was expressed on the September 13, 1980 Declaration of the Latin American Parties meeting in Caracas. This was, undoubtedly, a concession to the United States.

On the other hand, one should not forget that due to this forum's hierarchy, the weight and significance of the statements on Latin America contained in the Resolution of the Congress relevantly go beyond the scope of the Declaration of Santo Domingo, which was a regional meeting.

In our view, the reasons that explain the positive projection of the position on Latin America adopted by the 15th Congress of the S.I. are the following:

1. Since the early part of this decade, the S.I. started to make a turn in its relations with the so-called Third World and specially with our region. This change takes place within a period of deepening of the structural crisis of State monopoly capitalism, which imposes new demands on the main European countries. The collapse of the system of colonial domination, the blows dealt to the traditional structure of neo-colonial domination beginning with the change in the international correlation of forces and the economic attraction the countries of the region offer, are basic elements behind the actions of the Socialist International.

2. Undoubtedly, Latin America is a touchstone of the political opening of the S.I. to the so-called Third World. There are factors of greater socio-economic development and of the region's socio-classist structure among others, that offer Social Democrats better possibilities of influence when compared to other areas of the underdeveloped world.

UU 26

$ 370

3. On the other hand, we cannot lose sight of the existance of interimperialist contradictions, mainly between the FRG and the United States. West Germans are aware of the changes occurring in the continent and of the transformations that will undoubtedly take place in the future; they also know that this reality is affecting and will affect US hegemony to a great extent. Their aspiration, in the face of this displacement, is to guarantee space and influence that, to be efficient, must count on the credibility and acceptance of the democratic, progressive and even left forces of the area.

4. The way the Congress dealt with Nicaragua is truly illustrative. The Nicaraguan Revolution is, without doubt, a trial test for the S.I. policy toward Latin America. The establishment of an International Committee for the Defense of the Nicaraguan Revolution and the support of the S.I. to the Sandinista Front, is an unmistakable proof of its interest to continue making efforts to influence this process, which is decisive for their influence work in the area and specially in Central America.

5. In the Congress, therefore, a set back in the positive formulations the S.I. had maintained on Latin America and the Caribbean until then, would have meant the failure and collapse of a policy that represents the main achievement Social Democracy can show in its Third World projection; and an open defeat of its efforts to neutralize revolutionary processes in the continent.

6. The prospect for the new Republican Administration's Latin American policy has aroused fear and almost the conviction of important sectors of the European Social Democracy that Reagan will militarily attack Latin America. In our view, that assumption favored the

receptive attitude of most European Social Democratic Parties in the Congress before the positions adopted on the area. From their point of view, it is a matter of warning the new Administration to act persuasively in the future policy to be implemented by the US Government.

The last part of the General Resolution contains, in various sections, the main problems for the 80's from the S.I. point of view. Undoubtedly, what was most significant was the statement contained in the second paragraph of this chapter in the sense that "The political pendulum has moved to the right in certain parts of the world".

The treatment given to the remaining items, through having once again a bearing on the Social Democrats' theoretical ground, shows some formulations that are more positive than others in past Congresses and Conferences. This is particularly significant concerning the:

- Treatment of the role of transnationals, while underlining the need of their subordination to the "peoples' interests".

- Deep reforms, not only in the international monetary system, but also in its institutions.

- Formulation of a thesis on the overcoming of the economic crisis in the developed world that rejects the unilateral interpretation of its inflationary origin and proposes a world-wide social solution in the search for employment sources.

- Adoption of the postulates of the Report of the Brandt Commission, which basically implies the ratification of its most positive considerations.

Presentation: Social Democracy in Latin America and the Caribbean (until 197

In this presentation we intend to examine how Social Democracy has become
ever more active in Latin America and the Caribbean in the past few
years, which are the objectives and characteristics that make up its
projection in the area, which are the elements that have conditioned it
and the true possibilities Social Democrats count on to develop their
strategy in the continent.

In the past five years, the international Social Democracy has intensified
its activities in the so-called Third World, specially in Latin America
and the Caribbean, showing particular interest in expanding its political
space and influence in this region.

It is timely to recall, --in order to evaluate the true dimensions of this
offensive -- that Social Democracy as a political trend had, until then,
expressed itself basically as a European phenomenon. This does not mean,
nevertheless, that our sub-continent was marginated within the framework of th
strategic interests of certain European Social Democratic parties such as
the German Social Democratic Party that -- as an expression of West German
monopoly interests and through the "renowned" Friedrich Ebert Foundation
-- created the basis for its work of systematic and long-term penetration
in the area. The establishment of the Latin American Institute for
Social Research (ILDIS) in Chile (1966) and of the Center for Democratic
Studies on Latin America (CEDAL) (1968) proves this.

Although it is true that since the 70's the SI maintained relations with
some Latin American parties such as the Socialist Party of Uruguay, the
MNR of Bolivia, APRA in Peru, amongst others, these relations were very
weak and lacked true prospects.

On the other hand, Latin America's political history does not record
the existence of a significant movement which could be defined as Social

Democrat -- in view of its goals, programs and structures, if we use as point of reference the European Social Democratic pattern, -- except in the English-Speaking region of the Caribbean, where they emerged under the protection and incentive of the colonial bonds with the British Labour Party.

In our Opinion, many elements condition and explain to a great extent the deployment of the SD's efforts to plant itself in the so-called Third World countries, particularly in Latin America and the Caribbean.

1.- One of the basic reasons are the new demands and pressures on the main European countries originated by the deep structural crisis of State monopoly capital -- in the form it had in the 40's and the 50's. The collapse of the system of colonial domination, the blows dealt against the traditional structure of neo-colonial domination that started with the changes that occurred in the world's correlation of forces, greatly affecting the so-called Third World, demand actions from State monopoly capital to overcome the crisis.

2.- For European Social Democracy --especially for parties in power -- the economic attraction of the so-called Third World countries becomes greatly important: market possibilities for their products; the transfer of processing industries; cheaper labor and, above all, the revaluation of raw materials as a relevant element in the productive process.

The following data concerning the FRG-Latin American relations are illustrative in this respect.

According to official 1978 reports, Latin America is the most important recipient country of the FRG's goods and capital when compared with Asia and Africa. The FRG is the main commercial partner of Latin America of the capitalist European countries.

-3-

In the field of capital investments, an accelerated increase of West German presence is observed; in the past 10 years, investments have multiplied by five. In 1978, West German investments in Latin America represented 63.3% of their total investments in the so-called Third World and 13.5 % of the total direct investments of the FRG abroad.

3.- On the other hand, the estimates of the Social Democracy concerning Latin America take into account the existence of historical and cultural bonds and similarities of the latter with the Old Continent and the most favorable conditions offered by the area's dependent capitalist development (when compared with Africa and Asia)in terms of class structure and of more appropriate socio-economic conditions when compared with the rest of the underdeveloped world to implement the Social Democratic project .

Seen from a different prospect, this SD offensive is launched in a period of development of military dictatorships and of the establishment of fascist regimes in the continent as a result of the deep crisis in the representative democratic-bourgeoise system and of the development of the revolutionary and democratic forces; in this manner, Social Democracy presents itself as an "alternative to save the system" by offering an alleged path that would exclude both fascism and socialist revolutions.

The following statements by some of the most outstanding European Social Democratic leaders, contained in an exchange of letters between Willy Brandt, Olaf Palme and Bruno Kreich from 1972 to 1975 are truly eloquent.

In one of these letters, Olaf Palme states: "The talks I have had during the past few years with representatives from Third World countries have indicated that those countries are searching for their own path in a world like today's, subject to a clear polarization of forces...Most Third World countries reject both Soviet communism and US capitalism and do not accept any of those systems as valid development models. The strength and value of Social Democracy lies in the fact that it does not constitute a political threat for these countries at all".

Palme goes on saying: "What we do want is to have close and open contacts with these countries and discuss with them the problems that the world's progressive forces are faced with. Our International cannot become an exclusively European organization. We must find responsible and non-bureaucratic formulas to make of the International a forum open for debates and the cooperation of representatives from all over the world. To do this, the basic thing is not that we all fully agree on all ideological matters".

On his part, Willy Brandt stated: "We should not end this exchange of views without clarifying our criteria on which is the best way to improve cooperation among Social Democrats and other forces of similar ideology throughout the world. In order to efficiently carry out this task, our International is quite limited. We must attain a flexible and non-schematic cooperation with political forces from other parts of the world that somehow coincide with our parties although with different starting points ."

Brandt goes on saying: "Let us take Central America as an example. There are various parties there that come very close to what we understand as democratic socialism, but these parties do not fit within a framework as rigid and conditioned by traditions as the Socialist International. Therefore, some form of exchange of views among our parties and theirs would have to be found...We should speak of fundamental theoretical matters, but also of basically practical topics. We should be flexible enough to establish contacts with these forces and find common fields of action in spite of possible differences. This is an important goal for all European Social Democrats".

The 13th Congress of the SI, held in Geneva in 1976, considered the new changes that were taking place in the projection and relations of Social Democracy with the so-called Third World, specially Latin America and the Caribbean; it planned the SI's interest to overcome its Eurocentrism and expand its political space; a special resolution on Latin America was adopted for the first time, denouncing the military dictatorships and existing repression in various countries of the continent; the Dominican Revolutionary Party and Costa Rica's PLN were added to the list of SI's member parties and Accion Democratica and Movimiento Electoral del Pueblo, both from Venezuela, and Paraguay's Partido Revolucionario Febrerista were given consultative status, thus making up a total of 5 new full member parties and 3 with consultative status. Daniel Oduber of the PLN of Costa Rica and Anselmo Sule of the Partido Radical de Chile were elected vice-chairmen of the organization, which is significant if we take into account that Latin Americans had access to those positions for the first time.

It should be stressed that the documents adopted did not contain the traditional formulations of obstinate anti-communism of the times of the "cold war" that had characterized SI's stand, which, naturally, does not mean it has abandoned the anti-communist objectives that inspire the organization, nor the negative references to socialist countries.

Besides,,the so-called "democratic socialism", expression of the doctrines of contemporary bourgeoise reformism, was not stressed as an "alternative project" between capitalism and communism; a certain flexibility of the stubborn stand concerning relations with other communist parties and progressive forces took place.

Since the 13th Congress of the SI was held up to now, the activities and actions of the SI concerning Latin America have multiplied: holding of international meetings, visits of delegations of the organization and of

its main leaders to various countries of the continent have taken place,
such as those of Willy Brandt, Mario Soarez, Al Herand and Felipe Gonzalez;
added to this is the fact that at all ordinary meetings of the SI Bureau,
the Latin American issue has been relevant.

These actions of the SI have included denunciations, of the military and fascist
dictatorships of the area in such terms, the ceasing of repression, the
need to make democratic changes and the promotion of the so-called "democratic
socialism" as a feasible alternative for the countries of the continent
in the face of decaying capitalism and "totalitarian socialism".

To this one must add the meetings and reunions that have been held on various
ocassions and that had not been officially convened by the SI, that is, not
organically committed to it and that counted with a large participation of
Latin American parties, including some of the left. This type of informal
meetings are part of the SI's policy of dialogue and rapprochement with the
progressive and left forces of the area, outside of its organizational framewor
using for this purpose somewhat powerful parties such as Mexico's PRI,
Venezuela's AN and Portugal's PS, amongst others.

In general, the agreements and resolutions of this type of meeting have had
a marked progressive content, even to the point of denouncing the US for
its policy on the area.

The international Social Democratic organization showed particular activity
concerning the struggle of the Nicaraguan people against Somoza, waging
an international solidarity campaign with their struggle and speaking in
favor of the armed line as an exception in the case of Nicaragua, as stated
by Willy Brandt at the 15th Vancouver Congress held in November last year.

Representatives of over twenty parties and political organizations of
Latin America attended this meeting and two resolutions signed by
them were adopted, a general one on Latin America and another one
supporting the independence of Puerto Rico, which were basically more
progressive than the one officially passed by the Congress on the area.
Besides, four Latin Americans were elected as Vice-chairmen of the SI,
two other parties of the area joined the organization and the establishment
of a Committee of the SI on Latin America was proposed.

Let us now briefly examine, stricly from the Latin American perspective,
the real forces Social Democracy counts with in the region.

At present, there are 10 Latin American parties organizationally linked to
the SI. As full members we have: Partido Socialista de Argentina, Barbados
Labour Party, Partido Radical de Chile, Partido Liberacion Nacional de
Costa Rica, Partido Revolucionario Dominicano , El Salvador's Movimiento
Nacional Revolucionario, Jamaica's Peoples National Party and with
consultative status: Partido Revolucionario Febrerista de Paraguay,
Acción Democrática and Movimiento Electoral del Pueblo, both of Venezuela.

Undoubtedly, in spite of its heterogeneity in classist terms, these ten
parties are a political expression of the interests of sectors of the
bourgeoisie in their respective countries; this general classist framework
does not, of course, exclude the difference in the class compositions of the
parties, a circumstance that, among others, gives each party a more or less
liberal or progressive, or more or less conservative orientation.

On the other hand, we should add that some of these parties, like the
Partido Revolucionario Dominicano, Jamaica's PNP and Costa Rica's PLN to
a lesser degree, represent important forces of the small and middle
bourgeoisie and, above all, the former one, whose influence reaches somewhat
large sectors of the people, counting with leaders of the charisma of
Francisco Peña Gómez, Secretary General of the PRD.

Besides, it should be stated that out of these parties, there are four with a specifically important influence in the political life of their respective countries:

- in Santo Domingo, the PRD won the past elections and is, without doubt, the main political force of the nation,
- the PNP of Jamaica was elected to government by a majority support.
- Venezuela's AD and Costa Rica's PLN continue being, in spite of having lost the majority in the past elections, the most important political forces in their respective countries.

There is another group of organizations and parties in the sub-continent which, although presently lacking organizational bonds with the SI, have relations and contacts of relative importance with said organization, or move within the sphere of influence of the "Social Democratic trend", or if anything, flirt with it.

Among the main forces of this category, we have the following organizations:

- Partido Revolucionario Hondureño
- Frente Unido de la Revolución de Guatemala (FUR)
- Partido Socialista Democrático de Guatemala
- Partido Revolucionario Institucional de México (PRI)
- Partido Liberal de Colombia
- Movimiento Nacionalista Revolucionario de Izquierda de Bolivia (MNR-I)
- Izquierda Democrática de Ecuador
- Unión Cívica Radical de Argentina
- Partido Revolucionario Democrático de Panamá
- Partido Intransigente de Argentina
- Partido Socialista Unificado de Argentina
- APRA de Peru
- Partido Traballista Brasileño

- Partido Democrático de Curazao
- Partido Independentista de Puerto Rico

These organizations have attended the activities, seminars and meetings sponsored by the S.I. or the West German SDP, and most of them have declared their ideological adherence to the Social Democratic trend.

The differences in the programmatic formulations, national projections, composition and actual political force in their respective countries among the parties listed above are unquestionable. However all these parties establish their political projects and actions within the framework of the capitalist system and in line with representative democracy.

There is another group of parties and movements, a minority indeed, which has maintained irregular and peripheral contacts with the S.I. or some major European social democratic parties. We are referring to the Montoneros, the Partido Socialista Uruguayo, the Partido Socialista Revolucionario del Peru, sectors within the Partido Socialista of Chile and the PSLN, among others.

These revolutionary and left forces affirm that they have nothing to do with social democracy ideologically -- in some cases we have no doubts --, and that they simply use these contacts circumstancially to promote their objectives in the struggle, in terms of requesting solidarity for their causes, denouncing fascist regimes, and so on.

The parties organically linked to the S.I. -- which we have mentioned -- declare with varied approaches, their basic programmatic goal to be the so -- called democratic socialism based on the theoretical and ideological bequest of Bernstein's revisionism of the Second International which Lenin brilliantly defined and rejected in his struggle against this trend.

VV 10

38ι

To this we must add that these parties vindicate, to a greater or lesser degree, the alleged solutions offered by European Social Democracy to the serious problems the countries of the area face. In the socio-economic field they favor a just redistribution of income, the creation of stable sources of employment for all, demand fair treatment in international economic relations, more advantageous prices on raw materials, and so on; in the political sphere they demand a democratic opening, the elimination of military and fascist regimes, respect for individual freedom, and others.

In analizing the past six years of European Social Democracy's activity it is imperative to record an objective fact: in 1973 European Social Democrats had more or less stable links with 8 or 10 related organizations in the area, while at present more than 24 parties are linked with Social Democracy.

Let us now review how do other mechanisms of the European Social Democracy — specifically West German as predominant force in the S.I.— operate in the continent, to do its penetration work in the area in order to promote its strategic objectives.

We are refering to the Friedrich Ebert Foundation, a tool of the German Social Democratic Party and, to be exact, of West German monopoly capital.

The essential objectives of this institution in the area can be briefly described as follows:

- to create favorable conditions for West German capital penetration and the promotion of its economic interests in the region,

VV 11

382

- to curb and/or neutralize the revolutionary movement by encouraging the development of the political forces related to Social Democracy,

- to subtly nurture anti-communism and hostile activities against the socialist camp.

These aims, of course, are not manifest nor evident in the activities carried out by the foundation. An outstanting feature of its work its subtle and refined methods and practices.

For this purpose, its relies on training and research institutions covering almost all countries of the area, such as the Costa Rica-based Center for Democratic Studies on Latin America, and the Latin America Institute for Social Research with branches in Caracas and Quito. It also has experts and advisors on different matters in charge of representation offices in various countries of the continent.

Through all these means it organizes numerous international seminars and training courses for trade union, peasant, business, youth, political party leaders and others.

Moreover, it provides material and financial support to political parties and movements that favor the Social Democratic trend.

CEDAL alone organizes some 65 to 70 varied annual seminars in which approximately 2000 persons participate every year. It is estimated that CEDAL operates on a 2-2.5 million dollar annual budget.

It is appropriate to recall, as an example, the holding of an International Seminar in Solidarity with Nicaragua convened last April

VV 12

383

by CEDAL to assess the situation in Nicaragua and agree upon concrete solidarity actions with the FSLN, the Patriotic Front and the Group of Twelve, as was publicly announced.

Apart from the representatives of the main Nicaraguan groupings that fought against Somoza, this meeting was attended by 19 parties and organizations from 13 countries linked with the Social Democracy.

The following significant formulations in the resolutions of this event are worth mentioning:

- the denunciation of US policy of intervention in Latin America and the Caribbean, specially Carter Administration's abetment of Somoza's regime. Imperialism was condemned and denounced by name;

- recognition of the need for unity of the left in every country and in Central America; therefore, a proposal was advanced for launching a campaign to resolutely struggle against anti-communist and anti-socialist mentality;

- the Central American projection of the struggle that was then being waged against Somoza was stressed, and it was literally stated that: "Nicaragua's liberation trascends to the freedom of other Latin American peoples such as Guatemala and El Salvador, and that the will to support Nicaragua's liberation, will mean the pormotion of freedom for the Guatemalan and Salvadorian peoples."

An overall assessment of the results of the event we have refered to should inevitably include the following:

VV 13

384

- First, it was an international meeting of Social Democracy-related parties but not binding on the S.I. organically since it was held outside of its structure.

- Second, the positive formulations and decisions made passed the filter of coined phrases — also included in the document — such as "changes only in democracy and freedom", "social justice in freedom" and others obviously intended to differentiate them from the achievements of real socialism.

- Third, in the case of Nicaragua, European Social Democracy knew well that the struggle waged against Somoza was irreversible. On the one hand, they tried to prevent that process from becoming a true revolution of socialist nature while searching for a possibility to obtain political and economic benefits in a Somoza-free Nicaragua. In this respect, FRG's intention to compete with the US is evidenced in its clear purposes of appearing as "alternative partner", taking advantage of the anti-US sentiments and positions of a majority of the Nicaraguan opposition forces.

- Lastly, we must not lose sight of the positive role played in the Seminar by Jamaica's PNP, Guatemala's FUR and PSD, El Salvador's MNR and by most representatives of the Group of Twelve, the Patriotic Front and the FSLN.

To sum up we would like to conclude with the following considerations on the abovementioned items:

VV 14

385

1. We see a dual nature in the projection of Social Democracy in Latin American and the Caribbean. On the one hand, it does represent a permanent enemy of the essential objectives of the communist and left movements in that this trend intends to prevent the triumph of socialist revolutions and the materialization of the communist ideal. On the other, it is obvious that certain political positions of the Social Democracy can be used by the revolutionary and progressive forces of the continent at given junctures of the struggle against the repressive and fascist military regimes and of the confrontation with US imperialism.

2. Hence, in our view, while ideological struggle against this trend is necessary, we should implement ways and methods of case-by-case treatment of the parties related to Social Democracy whose positions coincide with certain tactical objetives of the Latin American revolutionary movement.

3. On the oder hand, we must bear in mind that, although in the main contradiction of our times between capitalism and socialism, led by US imperialism and the USSR respectively, Social Democrats as a whole are on the imperialist side up to now, is not always from a position of more satelites, since inter-imperialist contradictions also affect social democracy. This is the case of West German Social Democracy— representative, in essence, of German financial capital — which is at present one of the leading contenders of US imperialism, although remaining as its patner in the struggle against socialism, the USSR and the socialist camp with compromising and often contradictory policies.

4. In this sense, the demagogic policy of " human rights " and of encouragement of "democratic openings in the countries ruled by

repressive military regimes, insistently promoted by Carter's Administration in its early years in power, favored the deployment of Social Democratic policies in the region. To this we must add that it is extremely difficult to conceive of the development of this overall Social Democratic offensive without the consent and encouragement, or at least the implicit tolerance of Us imperialism, including a certain degree of political agreement on basic aspects.

Nevertheless, recently, and beginning with the reactivation of Christian Democracy in the area with the victory of COPEI in Venezuela and the defeat of the PLN in Costa Rica by a coalition in which Christian Democracy holds a prominent place, there are signs that the US is favoring the projects of Christian Democracy more than those of Social Democracy, considering, among other things, that the first is a more moderate force and less dangerous to its interest than Social Democracy.

5. As for the strategy of the international Social Democracy on Latin America and the Caribbean, in our opinion, it points to the following directions:

- to oppose the "model of democratic socialism" to scientific socialism in an attempt to recover the essential values of the bourgeois representative democracy system

- to deviate and neutralize the revolutionary and progressive movement, that is to prevent the victory of new socialist revolutions

- to undermine the influence and progress of the socialist camp, particularly of Cuba and the URSS.

VV16

387

To this end:

- it tries to secure its presence in countries ruled by military dictatorships or fascist regimes in case of an eventual "opening". This has been the case in Santo Domingo, Bolivia, Ecuador, Nicaragua and lately in El Salvador.

- it strengthens its bonds with those countries related member parties and implements a recruitment policy -- including revolutionary movements -- with those organizations capable of becoming suitable counterparts for its policy in the area.

6. Finally, we would like to stress that, -- irrespective of the repercussion and propagandizing impact of the activation of Social Democracy in the area in recent years -- the real effects of this policy so far show that, in spite of the circumstantial or eventual sucesses Social Democracy may have achieved in given countries by contributing to implement oportunistic openings its medium - and long-term historic prospects are doomed to failure.

The continent's harsh socio-economic reality and the degree of polarization of the class struggle make the "solutions" being fostered by Social Democracy actually precarious.

To: Cde. Unison Whiteman, Foreign Minister

From: Cde. Fennis Augustine, High Commissioner

Report on Meeting of the Praesidium of Socialist International held in Bonn,
West Germany on 1-2 April 1982

I arrived at the Tulpenfeld Hotel, Bonn where most of the delegates were staying
at about 4.00 p.m. Unfortunately, I was unable to obtain accommodation at that
hotel. Arrangements were subsequently made for me at Astoria Hotel, a reasonable
distance away from Tulpenfeld.

After settling in, I returned to Tulpenfeld. There was a meeting with the Cuban
delegation, the Nicaraguan delegation, the British delegation which was headed by
Michael Foot, leader of the Labour Party, the Guatamalan delegation, the
Venezuelan delegation headed by Carlos Cuidros Perez, a member of the Swedish
delegation and Guillermo Lingo of the El Salvador delegation.

Before these meetings I spoke to representatives and later on Bernt Carlsson
Secretary General of the Socialist International seeking observer status for
Grenada at the meeting. The decision was firm that only members of the
Praesidium and specially invited guest could attend. (The composition of the
Praesidium is; President, General Secretary, six Honorary Presidents, and
twenty-one Vice Presidents).

ISSUES:

The special meeting of the Praesidium was called because of the confusion
existing in S.I. over a number of issues, one delegate said to me that if
nothing is done about the present situation S.I. would lose credibility.

(a)   The most immediate was the cancellation of the Bureau meeting which
      was to take place in Venezuela, when the party Democratic Action bowed
      to American pressure and refused to invite Nicaragua. It was cancelled
      on the personal intervention of Bernt Carlsson and Willy Brandt.

(b)   The declaration by Nicaragua of a state of emergency, seen in the context
      of the debate taking place within S.I. as to the principles involved in
      Social Democracy i.e. elections, two party system, human rights questions,
      freedom of religion, freedom of speech (free press).

(c)   Disarmament - The recent visit of the S.I. disarmament committee to
      the Soviet Union within the context of world disarmament.

(d)   The East - West conflict as it is seen being aggravated by Poland,
      Afghanistan and the debate about the relationship with Cuba.

The meeting started at 09.45 on the 1st April, although a number of delegations
had not yet arrived. Some of the late arrivals were, French delegation,
Israeli delegation, Austrian delegation, Jamaican delegation (only Michael
Manley attended Cde. Paul Miller did not attend), Danish delegation and the
Netherland delegation and the Chilean delegation Radical Party (Cde. Anselmo
Sulle was the only delegate attending)

Central America and the Caribbean was down for discussion in the afternoon
session (see agenda attached) it generated the most interest.

My information is that the discussion on Central America and the Caribbean went very well, this is substantiated by the fact that:-

(a)   There appear to be some dissatisfaction with Felipe Gonzales's report on Nicaragua - one delegate referred to the report as somewhat vague.

(b)   A committee was appointed to draft resolution on the area (resolution attached) the composition of the committee was Ed Broadbent, Canada; Carlos Perez, Venezuelan; Michael Manley, Jamaica; and later on Gunselmo Sule was coopted.

(c)   A decision was taken that Willy Brandt should appoint a committee to visit the area and report back (I asked Brent Carlsson that Grenada be included in the itinerary of the committee).

(d)   It was decided that the S.I. Secretariat will continue to invite Nicaragua to attend its meeting, implication being disapproval with Democratic Action of Venezuela over its decision to exclude Nicaragua from the Bureau meeting in November.

I had a short discussion with Michael Manley - his stay was extremely short - he advised that, based on the letter he received from Maurice, Grenada's case was put firmly by him. My understanding is that this was so, although there appear to be some confusion on the invitation. In a follow up discussion, Brent Carlsson informed me that N.J.M. will have to send our individual invitations to Sister Parties.

On the East/West question - it appears that the meeting supported West Germany's position on Ostpolitick and to press for constructive dialogue on disarmament.

Comments

Most sister parties seemed well disposed towards Grenada, although some have reservations on what they see as the Marxist thrust of the N.J.M. I believe that close relationship with Cuba will continue. Nicaragua's position is a little more difficult, although there was a great degree of understanding and sympathy for them by the time the meeting was finished.

N.B. Carlos Perez informed me that he may be visiting Grenada in May next year.

Had meetings with Chile Radical Party, Anselmo Sule and the delegation from Panama who was lobbying for admittance to S.I.

Fennis Augustine

1)   To fully and objectively evaluate the results of the Bonn meeting, the following background must be kept in mind:

-Calling off the meeting in Caracas was undoubtedly the first significant setback for the SI on the Latin American scene. It revealed more clearly than ever the existing internal contradictions in the organization, the pressures being exerted in this regard and the aims of the conservative sector to negatively modify SI's Latin American policy and to recall its support for the Nicaraguan Revolution.

-The decision by Brandt and by the vast majority of the social-democratic parties of Europe, to refuse to bow to the demands of the right-wing forces, reaffirmed the interests of the most pragmatic and realistic circles of the SI, oriented towards continuing their neutralization strategy based on penetration of and influence on the political processes in the area. In this situation the rivaly between Western Europe and the US also comes to the fore, as well as the aim of European monopoly capitalist circles to dispute actively but without confrontation terrain which falls in the area of the US. Brandt's decision to cancel the Caracas meeting reveals his conviction and that of the interests he represents to refuse to sacrifice strategic objectives for momentary situations which may present themselves.

-The consultations carried out by Felipe González in the region last December, which ended in January with the meeting he held with Haig in Washington, had negative results for the SI, in that, as seen by various European and Latin American parties, mainly the SPD of West Germany, Felipe didn't handle adequately the various situations he found himself in; he tried to monopolize the handling of the SI's policy towards Central America; and he contributed to stirring up the crisis he confronted in the SI by stimulating anti-Sandinista attitudes and positions and helping to spread opinions and confusion about the direction of the Nicaraguan process.

-Brandt's designation of Jospín to accompany Felipe on the consultations in the region after the Caracas cancellation showed his aim of compensating for the waivering and negative positions of Felipe with a more realistic point of view, such as that of PSF. Felipe is playing his own game, aspiring to the presidency of Spain, for which he needs the nod from the US and from the Spanish right-wing policy-makers and military.

-Carlos Andrés Pérez--for various reasons, from the internal pressures in his own party, to pressures brought to bear by the US, and to the inconsistencies in his own demagogic positions--became the main spokesman for the anti-Sandinista attitudes.

-With the virtual failure of the overtures made by Felipe González and the cancellation of the Caracas meeting, the SI lost ground in the region, which was largely gained by the Mexican initiative, strongly reenforced by López Portillo's visit to Managua, his proposals for a solution in Central America and the efforts being made to implement them. The COPPAL meeting held in Managua February 19-20 was an important step forward for PRI in terms of its intent to play a primary role in regional developments.

2)   Regarding both its organizational structure and its content, the Bonn meeting was prepared by its hosts so that its results would confirm the continuity of the positions which the SI has been adopting towards Latin America and the Caribbean, foreseeing and controlling all those elements or factors that were potentially risky, and which could have blocked this objective. The

291

right-wing positions were isolated or neutralized. No one questioned the SI's continued support for the Nicaraguan Revolution,
and what's more, no one objected to Brandt's proposal that the
FSLN be invited to the Bureau's next meeting in Helsinki. The
subject of Nicaragua--the most conflictive problem debated--
and the situation in El Salvador, were treated positively.

3)   As far as the SI's stand on Latin American issues is concerned, the results of the meeting were generally positive.
In addition to the resolution on Central America and the Caribbean, a commission was approved including Wischewsky (vice-
president of the SPD), Ed Broadbent (vice-president of the SI
and president of the NPD of Canada) and Carlos Andrés Pérez
(from Acción Democrática) which would travel to the region,
including to Cuba and the United States, with the mandate to
hold conversations to promote a political solution to the tensions in Central America and the Caribbean. This commission
will present a report on the results of its work to the SI
Bureau meeting next May in Helsinki.

4)   The tone of the document approved on Central America is
moderate, cautious, without adjectives, but expresses clear
positions on basic problems of the area:

-Notes that the so-called elections in El Salvador are no solution at all, and opts for a global negotiated settlement that
would include all political sectors, specifying the inclusion
of the FDR-FMLN.

-Says that the Sandinista government of Nicaragua should receive
support for its commitment to pluralism, social justice, democracy and non-alignment; and condemns all attempts at destabilization and interference against its sovereignty.

-Emphasizes the importance of a total regional negotiation process that would include the countries of the region, and in
particular the United States and Cuba. This is an essential
aspect, in that it constitutes pressure on the US for negotiations.

-Adopts the proposals formulated by López Portillo and other
regional leaders as the basis for achieving a solution for
regional security, peace and cooperation.

5)   Nevertheless, proceeding from the social-democratic view-
point of not provoking the United States and of facilitating
a channel of communication to the Administration, the resolution makes no reference to the US responsibility for the situation the region finds itself in, nor to the dangers of its
interventionist actions. The resolution limits itself to underlining the importance of the suspension of any intervention by
one state in the affairs of another.

6)   Negative aspects of the document are: its unilateral and
self-seeking mention of the subject of elections in Grenada;
and on the other hand, the formulation on Guatemala, that while
general and vague, contributed to creating favorable expectations of the military coup recently carried off there.

7)   In summary, the net results of the meeting were positive;
it represented a blow against the policies of the present
US Administration towards the region and a setback for its aims
of changing the Latin American policy of the SI. The US Government's reaction against the results of the meeting was immediate,
reflected in a State Department communiqué dated April 6, which
strongly attacks the SI for its positions regarding Nicaragua and
El Salvador.

8)   Internally, the SI managed to control and neutralize the actions of the conservative and right-wing sectors. Felipe González was excluded from the commission to be sent to the region; Carlos Andrés Pérez outdid himself to demonstrate that his position had not changed, and that he continued to support Nicaragua; Mario Soares did not participate in the debate, and publicly stated that he fully subscribed to the resolution adopted; the PLN sent no representative to the meeting, so as not to commit itself, aware beforehand of the correlation of forces.

9)   Together with the objective factors that shaped the results of the meeting, the actions and speeches of Michael Manley, Ed Broadbent, Olaf Palme, Anselmo Sule and Riulf Steen played a very important role.

10) It can be stated that the positive positions of the SI towards the area, which correspond to its strategic interests, were strengthened. In the context of the present world situation, faced with the aggressive policies of US imperialism and the polarization of political forces especially within the region, socialdemocracy sees its possibilities strengthened to act as an intermediate alternative and to increase its role as a neutralizer against the radicalization of, the revolutionary processes in the region. And they also include Cuba in this perspective, thinking to compromise in a negotiation process with the US our incidence in regional developments, or as they see it, "tying our hands and limiting our influence."

11) On the other hand, it can't be forgotten that posed against the US, the influence and terrain gained by social democracy in Latin America are resources and possibilities it has for negotiating global problems with the United States, with which, apart from strategic questions uniting the two, the SI maintains tactical differences of importance in the present situation.

BACKGROUND

1. Many claim for the Socialist International a history dating back to more than a century. It would appear that initially the name was the First International.

2. This International was born out of the rise of Socialist thought in Europe, the workers struggle in that continent and the internationalization of Capital and social and economic problems which many socialists felt demanded an internationally organised response.

3. Born in Europe at the historical epoch when vast areas of Asia, Africa and Latin America were yet colonised by Europe the Socialist International was a European organisation. However, since the second world war and the subsequent decolonisation process which saw the emergence of numerous nation-states, and since the heightened class struggle and formation of progressive nationalist and socialist parties in the newly independent nations, the horizon of Socialist International has widened considerably, stretching beyond Europe.

4. Thus, today only 20 of the 48 full member parties of the Socialist International are European. From Latin America and the Caribbean there are eleven (11) parties enjoying full membership.

5. Because of this widening of the Socialist International (SI) the concerns of the organization have advanced beyond mere European ones and today reflect to a certain extent, truly international concerns which progressive, democratic forces must confront.

PRINCIPLES AND IDEOLOGICAL ORIENTATION

6. The SI has sought to commit itself to the principles of "Peace, Freedom and Solidarity". This is its broad banner.

7. More specific principles are reportedly contained in two documents: The Frankfurt and Oslo declarations of principles. The Frankfurt declaration was forged in 1951 and the Oslo declaration in 1962.

QQ2

8. It is said that the Frankfurt 1951 document presented 326
    the Socialist doctrine mainly
            " as a permanent human liberation movement,
        aiming at a fully democratic organisation of
        society, spreading from the political to the
        Economic, social, Cultural and International
        Fields."

9. Democracy was seen "as the Synthesis of Freedom and
            equality whereby economic and social exploitation as
        well as political and Cultural enslavement of men
        by men and people by people is rendered impossible."

10. Recently the SI set up a <u>Working Group on a New Declaration</u>
    <u>of Principles</u>. To the Norwegian Labour Party was assigned
    the task of analysing the current situation from the point
    of view of Democratic Socialism exposed by the SI.

11. One of the findings of the Norwegian Labour Party was that:

            "Democratic Socialists disagree, on the one hand
        with the point of view that Social evolution should
        ideally be coordinated by an <u>invisible</u> hand as is
        justified by the liberal theory of the market; on the
        other hand, we do not agree that power should be
        concentrated in <u>one hand</u> as justified in leninist
        theories of absolutism. One solution divests the people
        of power; the other establishes power over the people."

12. The Norwegian conclusion continues:

            "According to one theory, power is decentralised and
        left at the doors of the market; according to the
        other it is completely concentrated in the Central
        Committee. In one the perfect society is identified
        with the perfect market; in the other, with the
        perfect leaders. In the one, the freely competitive
        market, no one holds power; in the other the
        dictatorship of the proletariat degenerat into a
        dictatorship over the proletariat. In   people
        are made impotent by the economy; in the   , by
        the police. Democratic Socialists rejec   ."

Q Q 3

327

13. Advocating these principles and coming from such a
philosophical orientation, the SI can be viewed as
wanting to form a sort of third bloc or third force
between the two main opposing poles of politics:
Capitalism and Socialism. Thus, in Foreign Policy
SI would repudiate both the U.S.A. and the U.S.S.R.
and would blame both for international tensions and
the cold war. For soem of the Europeans the principles
and ideological orientation of the SI is a means of
escaping US hagemony over Europe while not attaching
Europe to the U.S.S.R. Thus, Europe would, in this way,
be back on the road to global supremacy.

14. However, the establishment of a New declaration of principles
can prove a very torturous undertaking particularly as the
SI is no longer monopolised by Europe but is now a fairly
heterogenous body. And as President Welly Brandt put it
    "the European Concept of democracy cannot be
    exported to other regions on the earth."

15. Thus, as the "other regions" assert their sovereignty
and their definitions of democracy and socialism the SI
can become even more diverse. This has been recognised
by Felipe Gonzalez of the Socialist Workers Party of
Spain which hosted the last SI Congress. Gonzalez pointed
out that "the risk of a new declaration of principles
    which is a letter of introduction of our identity,
    in which present and future members of the SI
    must be able to recognise themselves, is great".

16. Developing the point Gonzalez continued:

    "We could fall into the temptation of preserving
    the principles of identity of European Socialism,
    excluding the others, thereby not giving an
    answer to the new problems..... Alternatively, we
    could be guilty of the fault of making a declaration
    so vague that, while including everybody, would
    satisfy no-one, even minimally, and which in
    consequence would not differentiate us from liberal
    or Christian democrats,......"

Q Q4

328

17. This then in the dilemma confronting the SI as it attempts to forge a new declaration of principles. A possible way out as one perceives it will be to agree on certain basic and broad ideological foundations and to create a body of ideas which condenses the SI position on Fundamental World problems and issues.

18. In this manner some real harmony can be established between the parties; between a party like the Izquierda Democratica (Democratic Left) of Ecuador which rejects the concept of the dictatorship of the proletariat because, it says, the concept produces a new elite which usurps the power of the proletariat, a party which rejects a single class party and wants a mass party; and between movements like the FSLN of Nicaragua, the National Revolutionary Movement of El Salvador and the N.J.M. of Grenada which believe that the party in one which only the most serious and conscious elements can join. This divergence in views shows up the underlying fundamental contradiction between revolutionary socialists and democratic socialists.

19. However, in the SI a working relationship can be established between the democratic socialists who assume a middle ground position between socialism and capitalism and the revolutionary socialists who are committed to the application of marxists-Leninist principles in the construction of scientific socialism. One thinks the strategy is to agree on very broad principles and take a SI position on world issues on which there exists a consensus.

POSITION ON MAJOR ISSUES

20. The SI on most of the major problems and issues today assumes/liberal progressive position, on others it takes /a a position equidistant from both the USA and the USSR.

21. Evidence of the SI, position of equidistance is its categorisation of the USA and the USSR as superpowers both seeking global dominance.

22. On the questions of the arms race, disarmament and international tension the SI attributes blame to both the USA and the USSR. Thus on disarmament the SI makes representation to both nations on an identical basis.

QQS

In May 1979 the SI sent its Study Group on Disarmament 32⁹
to discuss with Carter, Mond ale and U.S. Government
experts. In November 1979 the same Group went to the
Soviet Union and talked with Brezhnev, the Soviet
Government, the CPSU and other institutions.

23. The SI blames both the USA and the USSR for international
    tension and the set back to detente. SI cities: (i) the
    Cuban brigade crisis of late August 1979; (ii) U.S.
    reluctance to ratify SALT II; (iii) NATO decision on
    eurostrategic missiles as the main causes and is convinced
    that the situation was exacerbated by (i) the Soviet decision
    to deploy the SS-20; (ii) the Soviet occupation of
    Afghanistan.

24. In Poland the SI Congress Resolution coming out of the last
    Congress held in Spain on November 13-16, 1980 states:

    "As the democratic socialists committed to the
    right of workers to organise free and independent trade
    unions, we welcome the recognition of these rights
    in Poland. We regard this as an importance advance
    for economic and civil rights . We salute the courage
    shown by the leadership of solidarity. We welcome the
    pragmatic and realistic approach taken by the Government
    so far.

    Our solidarity with the struggle for trade unions
    rights is clear. We recognise these advances as
    achievements of the Polish Workers and believe that
    any further progress will be made only by them."

25. SI takes no side in the Iran/Iraq war but views it as
    "a serious blow to stability in the Middle East and to
    Security internationally." SI appeal to both to cease
    hostilities and to take part in mediation efforts.

26. On the Kampuchean question SI Congress Resolution takes
    a broad position. It says: "We express our great concern
       and deep sorrow at the tragedy of the people of
       Cambodia. The SI reminds all Government's of their
       responsibility to help heal the effects of this
       terrible genocide.

       The unity and integrity of Colombia must be
    respected. We support any initiatives towards
    a solution which will secure a reconciliation of
    the Cambodian people and its neutrality status."

Q Q 6

33°

27. The SI position on Southern Africa is firm. It states
in part: "We condemn the continued aggression by South
Africa against independent Angola."

28. It also undertakes the commitment to continue working
"with all elements of the South African
resistance, especially the ANC and SWAPO."
and demanded the release of Nelson Mandela and
Herman Toiva Ja Toivo.

29. On the Palestinian question the SI is somewhat split.
Some parties are supportive of the Camp while others
see the PLO as the sole legitimate representative of
the Palestinian people and think that the PLO must
be included in the negotiation of any solution.

30. The SI is soft on Morocco, though not supportive of it,
on the Western Sahara issue. The SI; however, recognise
the Polisario Front and thinks that the Polisario Front
and thinks that the Polisaris Front/Mauritania peace
accord can be a model by which the problem of the Western
Sahara can be resolved.

POSITION ON LATIN AMERICA AND THE CARIBBEAN

31. The SI has been following developments in Latin America,
particularly in the Central America and the Caribbean
sub-region, very keenly. The progressive struggles unfolding in this troubled region, long dominated by
European colonialism and, later, U.S. imperialism, have
earned the support of the SI.

32. Thus, in the Congress Resolution the SI extended support
for the Panama Canal treaties, for the valiant struggle
by Michael Manley and the PNP in the face of numerous
adverse odds. for the Nicaraguan resolution and the
FSLN, for the Grenadian revolution and the NEW JEWEL
Movement and for the exemplary struggle of the people
of El Salvador led by the Frente Democratics Revolucionario
(FDR). The SI rejected the imperialist line that the
Junta is a "moderate" one "fighting the extreme right
or left." The SI declares:

Q Q 7

331

"It is rather a despotic regime whose activities have led to a state of Civil War."

33. The SI supports independence for Belize "secure within its present borders."

34. The SI has repudiated the so-called "referendum" conducted by Pinochet in Chile and also the so-called "new constitution and "Join(s) with the people of Chile in their ongoing resistance to the military Junta.

35. A similar stand is taken on Bolivia which is ruled "by a vicious military dictatorship."

    Full support from the SI goes to the people and the National Unity Government led by Hernam Siles Zuazo and Jaime Paz Zamora.

36. The <u>Fronte Democratics Contra ta Represion (Democratic Front Against Repression)</u> (FDCR), the body which united all the progressive and democratic Forces in <u>Guatemala</u> opposing the bloody dictatorship led by Romeo Lucas Garcia, enjoy the full solidarity of the SI.

37. The SI has frequently resolutely condemned the dictatorships in Argentina, uruguay and Paraguay.

38. In sum then the SI policy in Latin America indicates firm support for the struggles unfolding in that region.

<u>N.J.M. AND THE SI</u>.

39. The NEW JEWEL Movement became a full member party of the SI at the last Congress of the SI in Madrid, Spain. Previously, for a brief period, the N.J.M. had observer status.

40. The question of whether the N.J.M. - Grenada ought to be a member of SI has arisen. It is opportune that it has a at a time when the Ministry of External Affairs   cided to assess Grenada's membership in all internati   bodies.

41. Now it has een established beyond dispute that the Grenada Revolution of March 13th. faces grave threats from imperialism, mercenaries and external reaction.

QQ8

332

Given this, one of the ongoing objectives of Grenada's Foreign Policy has to be: to <u>harness moral political, economic and other support from the international community so as to stave off and combat external aggression and subversion.</u>

42. One of the means of achieving this objective is through forging broad alliances internationally; through becoming a part of the international organisations which condemn firmly, militantly, imperialism and its aggressive manoeuvers and henchmen. The SI is such an organisation; thus, Grenada N.J.M., is correctly a member.

43. As Grenada seeks this international support, and as one fundamental aspect of the NJM's ideological orientation is internationalism, another objective of the foreign policy is: to support the struggles of oppressed people.

44. Through membership in the SI Grenada can express organised support for the progressive struggles; in Southern Africa, the Western Sahara, Palestine, El Salvador, Nicaragua and other parts of Latin America etc. Thus, the objective is realised; thus, N.J.M. is correctly a member of SI.

45. Some would argue yes, these are your objectives, yes, they are realised through membership in SI. But what about principles? The ideology of the SI is Democratic Socialism. The Grenadian revolution aspires to advance beyond democratic socialism. Thus, there are differences between the N.J.M. (Grenada) and the SI.

46. Of course there are differences. There exist fundamental contradictions between revolutionary socialists and democratic socialists. But this does not mean that the two cannot strike a working relationship under certain conditions when the objectives are sufficiently broad.

47. There is a world of differ_ce between the mildly reformist Social Democratic Partie: Europe, the Accion Democratica (AD) of Venezuela and t_ _dos Labour Party, on the one hand, and the N.J.M. of _ _a on the ot_er. However, on certain broad issues a p_ _sive conser_us can be effected. Thus, N.J.M. i_ _he SI is not a contradiction of its states objectives a__ philosophical orientation.

Q Q 9
333

48. In paragraphs 20-30 of this paper the SI Position on Major Issues was outlined 'A Comparison with Grenada's position reveal that there exist a tangible coincidence of views on many issues. The SI fully supports the struggle in Southern Africa, condemns strongly apartheid and racism, is in firm solidarity with the FDR IN El Salvador, the FDCR in Guatemala, the FSLN in Nicaragua and generally takes a very progressive position on Latin American issues. Those views and positions are identical to Grenada's. Thus, a working relationship, membership, is quite in order.

49. On issues where there exist a difference of views - Afghanistan, the two Superpowers, two imperialisms thesis, Kampuchea, the structure of the SI is sufficiently flexible to permit dissension. Thus, Grenada's sovereignty and principles are not compromised by being in the SI.

50. One can also point out to critics that if states like vietnam, Oman, Zambia, Saudi Arabia, Cuba, Libya, Iran, whose economic, political and social philosophy is so enormously divergent, if these states can cooperate and agree in the Non Aligned Movement on very sensitive issues, then there is no reason why Grenada cannot effect some relationship with the Democratic Socialism of the SI. The fact is that the international situation demands that bodies with divergent views cooperate, discuss and agree on some broad and sensitive issues.

51. The U.S.A. and the U.S.S.R. represent two fundamentally opposing poles of world politics, let they sit together, take joint decisions, agree on a number of issues at the United Nations, its Security Council and other bodies. Grenada and the Social Democratic parties can do the same in the SI.

52. In sum then Grenada's membership in the SI is quite consistent with its principles and objectives. Differences exist but they do not compromise the revolution, its goals and tenets. As a matter of fact give Grenada's near isolution in the Caribbean sub-region   est defence might be a broad stretch of Foreign re   ons. The SI can be a useful element in that stretc .

QQ10
334

RECOMMENDATIONS

53.   Already Grenada has achieved statements of support
       from the SI. This must be consolidated.

54.   The SI has mobilised economic support for Nicaragua.
       Grenada can approach the SI with a request for obtaining
       economic assistance. Grenada should point out to the SI
       (i) Grenada's particular economic constraints as a small
           island; (ii) the attitude of the British and the
           Americans over the question of aid through WINBAN
           for banana rehabilitation must be revealed to the
           SI with a view to showing the urgent need for assistance
           and to obtain an SI condemnation of this economic
           aggression on the part of Britain and the U.S.A.

55.   Now that the Social Democratic Party (SPD) of West
       Germany is in office, Grenada should initiate some
       dialogue with West Germany with a view to obtaining
       economic assistance. The possibility of trade should
       also be raised particularly as our traditional markets
       are in the hostile U.S.A. and Great Britain. In the
       event of an economic blockade by these two the West
       German Market might be an alternative. The SPD is a
       leading member of SI with Willy Brandt being the President.
       Its Government in Bonn might be more cordial to Grenada
       than the conservative Christian Democrats. Also, now that
       West Germany has an Ambassador accredited to Grenada it will
       be easier to communicate with Bonn.

56.   Finally, membership in the SI should be retained. It has
       proved useful and if Grenada's foreign policy initiatives are
       strengthened it can prove even more useful in the future.

REPORT ON MEETING OF SECRET REGIONAL CAUCUS OF
HELD IN MANAGUA FROM 6TH-7TH JANUARY, 1983

The following Organizations were represented:-

F.S.L.N.	- Nicaragua	- Antonio Marguin
M.N.R.	- El Salvador	- Hector Oqueli
R.P.	- Chile	- Freda
P.N.P.	- Jamaica	- Paul Miller
P.C.C.	- Cuba	- Silva
N.J.M.	- Grenada	- Chris DeRiggs

The following items constituted the agenda:

(I) An analysis of the balance of forces within the Socialist
International -
- the Regional situation.
- the International situation.

(2) Initiatives to be taken to strengthen the position of
progressive forces of Latin America and the Caribbean
within the organization.

(3) Initiatives to neutralize forces within S.I. that are
against us.

(4) Upcoming activities of S.I. - Regionally and
Internationally.

(5) Activities of Copaal - combining S.I. work with
Copaal work.

(6) Conference on non-intervention and peace in Central
America.

(7) Political character of projected growth of S.I.
- Conference of African S.I.

(8) Structure of S.I.

- Chairmanship of Regional Committees.
- Proposed Regional Executive Secretary.

(9) Proposed Institute of Economic and Political studies.

(IO) ALDHO.- Latin American Human Rights Organization.

(II) Work of Social Democracy in the Region.

The meeting was organized for the purpose of deepening the process of co-ordination among the most progressive S.I. forces of Latin America and the Caribbean with a view towards expanding the influence of the Region as a whole in the Organization and outlining a number of concrete initiatives related to the upcoming Congress of S.I. in Sydney, Australia.

The meeting was chaired by Antonio Harguin of the International Relations department of the F.S.L.N.

I.   ANALYSIS

   i) Regional Situation - the progressive forces are in control.

      a) There are fourteen members of the S.I. Committee
          for Latin America and the Caribbean.
      Of these fourteen, there are seven parties that are
      generally progressive and some within a Marxist-
      Leninist trend.

      There are three (3) new parties that have recently
      gained consultative observer status in S.I. They are:

(i) Puerto Rico.
(ii) W.P.A. - Guyana
(iii) P.L.P. - St. Lucia

The presence of these parties will help to strengthen the influence of the progressive forces within the Regional Committee. These parties can, in effect, function like full members of the organization. We must always consult with them and keep them informed.

2.   EUROPE IN RELATION TO LATIN AMERICA

a)   There are sharp divisions among the European parties
       in their outlook on Latin America.

b   Our friends in this area are prepared to accept the Latin American Revolutionary process as being palatable if restricted to the Latin American context.

c)   There is a great amount of misunderstanding about Latin America both among our friends and our enemies - some amount of fear and uncertainty.

d)   Many of the European S.I. parties expect us to understand the concept of "the Soviet Menace".

e)   Some European parties are concerned that, by the Latin American presence in S.I., they have let in a

f)   Many European Parties are willing to hold discussions with us at levels which indicate the contradictions among themselves -
- the difference between Kryski of Austria and Braudl of Germany on the P.L.O. question.

g)   Our strongest allies in Europe are the Nordic S.I. parties and that of Holland. There is also good potential with the U.D.P. of Canada.

h)   Our principal enemies are to be found among the parties of Soares and Horgo in Portugal and Italy respectively - the Social Democrats of the U.S.A. are also our sworn enemies.

i)   The reason why the European parties did not allow W.P.A. and P.L.P. to get beyond the consultative membership status is because of their fear of the growth of membership with parties that they do not control.

j)   A Mission to Europe comprising of our most trusted forces in Latin America and the Caribbean can be strategically valuable before the Sydney Congress. It can help to assure our friends and confuse our enemies.

DECISIONS

1)   The next meeting of the Broad Latin America Region S.I. Committee will be in any one of the following places:-

> Las Paz - Bolivia
> Mexico
> Caracas
> Canada

Michael Manley of P.N.P. and Auselmo Sule of P.R. will co-ordinate with B. Carlson of the S.I. Secretariat on this matter. Member parties will be informed according.y.

2. A broad resolution on the Latin American and Caribbean situation will be passed at the meeting of the Regional Committee.

   Agenda for this meeting will include:

   a) Analysis of current political situation.
   b) Attitudes to S.I. in Latin America.
   c) Issues for Sydney:
      i) New situation
      ii) Expansion of S.I.
   d) S.I. Latin America Committee:
      i) Structure
      ii) Staff
      iii) Officers
   e) Christian Democracy in Latin America.
   f) Actions to strengthen ALDHU.
   g) Sydney Resolutions.

3. Hector Oquel of M.N.R. of El Salvador will draft a Resolution on Latin America and the Caribbean by 31st January, 1983. This Resolution will be specifically for the Sydney Congress and will address only the most major issues.

   The following guidelines will be the basis for the Resolution:-

   (a) The Basle Resolution - including such themes like Peace and Non-Intervention, Anti-Militarisation in the Region, Anti-dictatorship, the settlement of disputes, etc.
   (b) Solidarity with Nicaragua, Grenada and the F.D.R., F.M.L.N. and M.N.R. of El Salvador.
   (c) A limited number of other key issues in the Region.

(d) The creation of a platform and frame of reference in S.I. for the approach on the Latin America and Caribbean Region until the next Congress in Belgium (in the subsequent 2 years).

4. Subject to the approval of N.J.M., the next meeting of the Secret Regional Caucus of progressive S.I. parties will be in Grenada around the 13th and 14th March. This meeting will have strategic value in that it will provide the opportunity to:

   i) Assess the results of the tour of Europe by the selected parties, and

   ii) Conduct a final assessment on issues related to the Sydney Congress - questions of tactics and levels of co-ordiantion can also be discussed.

6. Grenada should consider inviting a few key S.I. personalities to March 13th celebrations.

7. Bilaterals will be held with new Regional S.I. forces before Congress - Grenada will speak with W.P.A. and P.L.P.

8. In the meeting in Grenada, we are going to consider what initiatives can be taken to support Surinam. If the Surinam Government wishes, an unofficial familiarization visit can be organized subsequent to proposed Grenada meeting. This, it is felt, may have value in preparing members of the Regional Caucus to be able to speak with authority if the question of Surinam is raised in Sydney. If a decision is made to go ahead with this, the team can comprise:

   Radical Party of Chile
   F.S.L.N.
   P.N.P.
   N.D.P.

N.J.M. will establish contact with Surinam and guide the Regional Secret Caucus accordingly.

At the meeting of the S.I. Resolution Committee and Finance Committee in Madrid and Italy respectively during the middle of February, Regional parties should try to have the   possible presence.

Subsequent to the Madrid and Italy meetings, a tour
of Europe should be organized to hold Bilaterials with all
European parties who belong to S.I.

The participants of this mission should include:
    Ungo of M.N.R.
    Oquel of M.N.R.
    Sule of P.R.
    Manley of P.N.P.
    Miller of P.N.P.
    A senior representative of N.J.M.

This mission will seek to counter the forces of Portugal,
Italy and the U.S..

Seek to spreak discussion within hostile European parties.

Work of the expulsion of the (C.I.A.) U.S.A. Social
Democratic Party.

9. Progressive S.I. forces in the Region should seek to
    attend COPAAL meeting scheduled for Brazil in March and
    secure reinforcement of Sydney S.I.L.A. Resolution.

10. To push ahead and implement the proposal for the
    establishment of a Regional Institute for Political and
    Economic Research.

    - Paul Miller of Jamaica as Director
    - Open bank account in the Bahamas with signatures of
      Miller and Hector Oquel.

    Maintain the Secret Regional Caucus with periodic and
    special meetings.

    Review membership in the future.

Submitted by.
CDE. CHRIS DE RIGGS.

(1)

REPORT ON SOCIALIST INTERNATIONAL BUREAU MEETING
3-4TH NOVEMBER, 1982
IN BASLE, SWITZERLAND

A.   Agenda, list of Participants and important resolutions
     are submitted as Appendix I, II and III respectively.

B.   The N.J.M. Delegation consisted solely of myself.
     I arrived in Basle on the evening of Wednesday 3rd
     November. I missed the first day of the Conference.
     This was largely due to late Booking and difficult
     flight connections.

     On arrival at the meeting I immediately established
contact with the delegation of P.N.P. of Jamaica which
consisted of Michael Manley and Paul Miller. The following
morning I held a Bilateral with Paul Miller (Michael
Manley had left after the first day) who gave me a summary
of the first day's Agenda.

     He indicated that Manley had presented to the S.I.
Bureau Meeting a report on the Caribbean and Latin America.
Paul Miller indicated that Michael Manley had, in his
report, outlined the case for Grenada along the following
lines:-

   i)   that the Country, under the P.R.G., had made
        important strides forward in the development of
        its Economy;

  ii)   that a number of forums of peoples' participation
        had been developed;

 iii)   that the basis was being laid for the formation
        of a New Constitution and the organization of
        elections in the future;

  iv)   that there were certain objective difficulties
        which affects the rate at which the Country can
        proceed in developing the objectives stated in
        No. ii.

                                    ..../2

On the 2nd day of the Meeting, attention was focused on:-

(I) Resolutions to be sent to the Congress of S.I. scheduled for Sydney, Australia in April 1983,

(2) Invitations to the S.I. Congress, and

(3) other matters related to the up-coming Congress.

RESOLUTIONS I

As a consequence of discussions held between representatives of Socialist Parties of Latin America and the Caribbean, a joint resolution was submitted to the Bureau Meeting. This resolution was presented by Amselmo Sule of the Partido Radical of Chile who is presently living in exile.

The resolution did the following:-

i) It called for unconditional support for the National Revolutionary Movement of El Salvador (MNR),

ii) it condemned plans for military aggression against Nicaragua,

iii) it welcomed the decision of the Frente Patriotico de la Revolucion de Nicaragua to request to the Junta Government the elaboration of an electoral law, a law for political parties, a law for foreign Investment's, of a law regulating the means of communication and the reform of the law of the state of emergency that will allow political parties to function,

......./3

40 - 2

iv) it called on the S.I. to accept the invitation forwarded by Nicaragua to send a fact-finding Mission into Nicaragua. The following members of S.I. have been designated:

Ed Broadbent, Carlos Andres Ferez, Michael Manley, David Oduber, Mario Soares, Auselmo Sule.

Other representatives, including General Secretary Bernt Carlsson,

v) S.I. was asked (in this resolution) to condemn and denounce the policy of genocide by the Military Regime of Guatemala against the Indian population,

vi) the resolution proposed a Conference aimed at Non-intervention, stability and peace in Central America,

vii) the resolution also expressed support for the process of strengthening democracy in Colombia and Brazil - at the same time, it pointed out the need to expose the discovery of clandestine cemetries in Argentina, the misery and hunger in Chile which result from the failure of the Economic Model in that country and also expressed support for the people of Paraguay in their struggle against dictatorship.

ON THE CARIBBEAN

(I) The Resolution called on the Socialist International to deplore and condemn the attempts to isolate and destabilize Grenada and to publicise its satisfaction for the process of democratization on the island.

(2) S.I. was asked to denounce the increase of crimes by the Regime of Haiti and to express its solidarity with the opposition forces in that country.

3   40 - 3

(3)   S.I. was requested to support the Partido Idependista
       de Fuerto Rico in its fight for Independence.

       Finally, the resolution called on S.I. to publicise
       its support for the Latin American Association of
       Human Rights (ALDHU) and to request governments,
       parties and friendly organizations to collaborate
       with the Association.

       A number of minor amendments were made to the
Resolution, but there was substantial opposition to the
section which expressed solidarity with Grenada and Nicaragua.
Mario Soares of the Socialist Party of Portugal led off
the opposition followed by Brettino Craxi of the Italian
Socialist Party, Eita Freedman of the Social Democrats of
the U.S.A. also spoke against solidarity with Grenada.
Their major line of attack was that Grenada was a one-
party state and, therefore, could not be considered a
democracy.
       Both myself and Paul Miller of P.N.P. responded on
the behalf of Grenada. My response took the following
form:

       (a) A brief analysis of the History of Grenada
           through Slavery and Colonialism and Neo-
           Colonialism.

       (b) An explanation of the historical basis for
           the existence of one party in Grenada.

       (c) The major Economic and Social gains of the
           Revolution.

       (d) Special emphasis was given to the process of
           building and strengthening the forums of Peoples'
           participation which is the basis for a new
           constitution and an approach to the question
           of Elections.

       (e) I made reference to our Adherence to the
           principles of accountability, peoples participation,
           responsibility and the rule of law.

--------/5

40 - 4

7

(f) I ended by expressing amazement that ignorance
of the existing reality within Grenada had been
expressed from certain quarters of the meeting
and reminded them that Grenada has always been
willing to receive fact-finding Missions because
our record simply cannot be challenged.

The ammended Resolution went through.

RESOLUTION 2

The other resolution of major importance was the
resolution on the Beirut Massacre - a draft resolution
was presented to the meeting denouncing the Massacre,
calling on S.I. to mount its own investigation and calling
for S.I. to formally recognize the P.L.O.

There was widespread division on this resolution with
considerable hedging on the part of the more conservative
parties within S.I. Eventually, the dissention was so
great that there was no agreement on the draft.

INVITATIONS TO CONGRESS

A number of parties and individuals were identified
for invitation to the Sydney Congress. They include;

1)   Afghanistan - Social Democratic Party (Resistence
                                             Movement).

2)   Angola - M.P.L.A.

3)   Bolswana - Democratic Party

4)   Czechoslovakia - Charter 77 - (dissident groups)

5)   Eritrea

6)   Ethiopia

7)   Ghana

8)   Greece

------/6

8) Guatemala - National Revolutionary Movement

9) Guyana - W.P.A. - Now having consultative member status

10) St. Lucia - P.L.P. - now having consultative member
     status

11) Iran - National Council of Resistence

12) Korea - unification group

13) Mozambique - Frelimo

14) Nicaragua

15) Panama

16) Peru

17) Somalia - Revolutionary Socialist Party

18) Tanzania

19) Tunisia

20) Uruguay

21) U.S.A.

22) Yugoslavia - Y.C.L.

23) Zimbabwe - Z.A.N.U.

24) Suriname - (to be verified)

     Individuals include:

     i) Lech Walesa
     ii) Nelson and Winnie Mandela
     iii) Prince Sianhonk of Cambodia
     iv) Rudolph Botleck (in prison in Czechoslovakia)

                                        ------/7

40 - 6

6

A definite decision was made not to invite the
P.L.O. This decision was primarily to the benefit of the
Israel Labour Party and the Australian Labour Party -
In the case of the Australian Labour Party, the argument was
that it would embarrass the Government of Malcolm Fraser.

SOME OBSERVATIONS

(i) The heated debate on issues like Grenada, Nicaragua
and the P.L.O. could be an indication of sharpening
contradictions between left and right forces in
W.I.
This question was discussed in caucus with Hector
Aqueli, Paul Miller and others. They generally
agree that the right wing forces in S.I. are becoming
more aggressive.

(ii) Latin America and the Caribbean need to formalize
and maintain the Regional caucus. It is clear that
the right forces are going to attack again in the
Sydney Congress. The proposal, therefore, is that
a number of Regional Countries be organised
between the present period and the Sydney Congress.
One such caucus can be held if enough parties are
present at the inauguration of Miguel de la Madrid
in Mexico. In this context, co-ordiantion with
P.N.P. is important.

(iii) There is the suspicion that contradictions between
right forces of S.I. are growing - for example:
(a) between the French and the Germans for Leadership,
(b) between the Nordic and German Socialists.

(iv) I have picked up that there is a move spearheaded by Willy Brandt to isolate and remove
Bernt Carlson - This, it is alledged, is part of
the struggle by the German Socialists to tighten
their control of the organisation.

.... /8

(v)   It was also reported at caucus level that there
is a growing momentum for the secretariat to be
moved from London to a European Capital - Vienna
has been one name mentioned.

(vi)   It is felt that Regional Parties of S.I. need to
put a lot more diplomatic footwork into the
organization - the example is quoted of Ungo
of El Salador who has spent a lot of time lobbying
the European Socialists. It is felt that similar
efforts from other S.I. Members in the Region can
help to exploit contradictions existing even within
the Membership of S.I. Parties like the Socialist
Party of Portugal.

RECOMMENDATION

I recommended that a full consultation be held
between N.J.M., P.N.P., W.P.A. and P.L.P. on the current
situation in S.I. with a view towards working out a co-
ordinated approach for the wider Regional caucus leading up
to the Sydney Congress.

In closing, I wish to indicate that a decision
was made based on a recommendation by the Finance and
Administration Committee, that N.J.M. subscription to S.I.
be upped to £160 per year.

A copy of the new publication "Making the Peoples'
Budget" was given to each delegation present.

Submitted by,

Cde. Chris DeRiggs,
International Relation Sec.

Monday 8th November, 1982.

TO: N.J.M. Leadership   SUBJECT: Emergency S.I. Meeting in Panama

FROM: Comrade Whiteman   DATE: March 3, 1981

The emergency S.I. meeting of Latin America and the Caribbean took place in Panama on Saturday, 28th February and Sunday, 1st March. Basically, it was a one item agenda; the situation in El Salvador.

There were representatives of the following countries:

    Argentina, Barbados, Bolivia, Chile, Costa Rica, El Salvador, Ecuador, Guatemala, Grenada, Honduras, Panama itself, Peru, Puerto Rico, Dominican Republic, Venezuela, Uraguay and Nicaragua. P.N.P. was absent. From Europe came Spain, West Germany, France, Portugal and Sweden arrived. Brent Carlsson, Secretary General attended. Media coverage was wide.

The Conference was designed to counter these two carefully worked out tactics by the United States:

(1) To project the struggle of the people of El Salvador as a direct East West ("Communist - Capitalist") confrontation as a means of completely wiping out from the consciousness of the world the domestic causes, the oligarchy, the semi-feudel system, the incredible poverty of the masses.

(2) To show that the freedom fighters ("Marxist hardliners") do not want a negotiated settlement, that they prefer the bloodshed.

Because of airline difficulties, I missed the first day of the Conference. Although S.I. has a clear concensus on El Salvador, somehow Carlos Andre Perez insisted on adding the names of Cuba and the Soviet Union to the resolution demanding an end to the supply of arm to El Salvador!
(He claims that he is not anti-Cuba or anti-Communist but that S.I. must appear to be objective and even handed. He also claims that he whole heartedly supports the El Salvador liberation struggle. This is strange because there was a quiet meeting where the military commanders in the field explained their need for support in this ~~critical~~ critical situation and Carlos agreed with them).

For hours he persisted. Sweden and Grenada spoke out forcefully on the issue. Grenada pointed out that the U.S. supply of arms to the junta is a notorious fact, that the U.S. officially and publicly stated this; that S.I. should not speculate on where the freedom fighters are getting arms from; that, in any event, we should not equate arms for the oppressors with weapons to defend the people in their just struggle.

Finally, the El Salvador Comrades said they were prepared to accept a compromise formula that names no country but makes it clear that it is the U.S. that is being condemned. The house accepted this approach.

It should be noted that Vernon Walters, the ex-deputy C.I.A. Director
insisted on presenting to the meeting (he is on a tour of the region to dr⌐
up support for a U.S. invasion of El Salvador and/in Panama by 'coincidence')
he happened to be
proof of Cuban and Soviet arms supplies. This offer was not accepted.

As a means of defeating the second U.S. tactics ("hardliners, not wanting
to negotiate"), the Conference offered the services of S.I. Chairman, Will
Brandt as mediator in the conflict.

This initiative ensures that the U.S. cannot propose someone favourable to
their own interest. Brandt is sympathetic for the freedom fighters but th⌐
U.S. will have difficulty rejecting him for he is a Nobel Peace Prize Winne⌐
with stature world wide.

This counter tactic would therefore give the comrades time to carry on the
military and the political struggle together.

Another resolution expressed support for the Nicaraguan and Grenada revolutionary processes and solidarity with the Government and people of Panama
who were undergoing pressures from the U.S. There was also support for
Michael Manley and for the independence of Puerto Rico.

A Working Group for Latin America and the Caribbean was chosen. The members
are Jose Pena Gomez, Carlos Andres Perez, Hector Oqueli, Bernt Carlsson,
N.J.M. and P.Ñ.P. This group will propose to S.I. structures and a work
programme for the region.

For a number of reasons, I proposed a regional conference in Grenada in May.
The conference enthusiastically accepted. Delegates from all over have
expressed interest in coming to Grenada to the meeting and this will be
ex⌐⌐⌐⌐⌐y useful to us also. If the N.J.M. Bureau ratifies this, plans
for the conference will have to begin soon after the Festival.

The General Secretary, Bernt Carlsson, will be visiting us for a few days on
April 18, and Pierre Schori sometime in May. These are also two important
visits for us since they are stalwart supporters of the revolution in S.I.
and internationally.

Anselmo Sule will xxxxx speak with Carvajal about arranging the meeting in
Mexico? (Neutral ground if the Tom Adams matter is on) towards the end
of this month with Pena Gomez and Maurice to work out a concrete programme
of S.I. activity on behalf of Grenada. This is a follow-up to Maurice's
proposal in Havana. If we wish this same committee to mediate on the Tom
Adams affair, then Tom can be invited for a part of the proceedings. We
will have to keep in touch with Sule.

Many of the leading comrades will be at the Aruba meeting. They look forward to seeing Comrade Maurice.

The next two major S.I. (International) events are the Party Leaders' Conference - Amsterdam - April 29, and the Bureau meeting - Tel Aviv on June 11, and 12. I strongly recomend that Comrade Maurice attend one of these.

P.S. On may way back from the Conference I noted the following from press reports:

(1) That the mission of Vernon Walters to the region has been considered a failure. Of course, he claims that his objective was not to gain support for a U.S. invasion of El Salvador but merely to explain and give evidence of Cuban and Soviet military involvement.

(2) That the big four Latin American powers: Argentina, Brazil, Venezuela and Mexico have issued a statement in Buenos Aires rejecting any U.S. intervention in El Salvador.

(3) That Duarte has agreed to participate in the mediation talks as proposed by Socialist International.

(4) That Bernt Carlsson is on his way to Washington to discuss the mediation offer with the State Department.

(5) That the U.S. has ~~first~~ just announced a massive step up of military aid to El Salvador. (Many U.S. Senators, even Senator John Glenn who once supported such a policy are now opposed to this).

(6) It seems that both sides are applying the tactic of talk more, appear the one more willing to talk, but fight harder.

ROUTING SLIP   42

TO: Cde. Prime Minister.

FOR ACTION		
FOR APPROVAL		
FOR SIGNATURE		
PREPARE DRAFT		
FOR COMMENTS	X	
MAY WE DISCUSS?		
YOUR ATTENTION		
AS DISCUSSED		
AS REQUESTED		
NOTE AND FILE		
NOTE AND RETURN		
FOR INFORMATION		

Draft letter to Socialist Affairs on article carried
claiming that you promised in October elections in
1982.

Date:	FROM:
February 3, 1982	Permanent Secretary, P.M.O.

February 2, 1982.

Socialist Affairs,
8 Flowers News,
Archway close,
London N19 3TB
United Kingdom.

Dear Cde. Carlsson,

I address myself to you in your capacity as editor of the magazine
Socialist Affairs, the mouthpiece of our organisation, the Socialist
International.

In issue No. 6/81 of the magazine an article on Grenada appeared
on page 239 of the English edition. In that article entitled "Bishop
pledge to hold elections" it was reported that Prime Minister
Maurice Bishop, leader of the People's Revolutionary Government and
the New Jewel Movement, "pledged in early October that general elections
would be held in the island some time in 1982, after Public approval
of a new constitution currently being formulated."

Please be advised that the above statement, quoted from the article
referred to above, is fundamentally incorrect. Prime Minister Maurice Bishop
has at no time placed any particular time frame on the holding of elections
and certainly on no occasion has he uttered any pledge to hold elections in
1982.

The People's Revolutionary Government led by Prime Minister Maurice Bishop
is committed to the formulation of a new constitution. Currently the
necessary legal experts to do the drafting and models of other constitutions
are being sought. When those are obtained the concrete formulation will
commence with the draft concluded being submitted to the entire populace –
mass organisations, workers, women, youth, farmers.

The comments, criticisms and ideas arising out of that process of
discussion and debate will be submitted to the experts for study and
incorporation and then they will present a second draft which will again
be studied and adopted with amendments by the entire populace.

/..2

Only out of this process will elections emerge and since there are several phases involved it is impossible and even foolhardy to put any definitive time frame on the holding of elections. This has been the consistent policy and pronounciation of the PRG and its leader Prime Minister Maurice Bishop.

I therefore, request that in your next issue you publish the text of this letter so that the position of the People's Revolutionary Government on the question of elections can be clarified and made known to your readership.

Yours Fraternally,

Benny Langaigne
Ag. Permanent Secretary
Prime Minister's Office.

Bishop pledge to hold elections

The prime minister of Grenada's two-and-a-half-year-old revolutionary government, Maurice Bishop, pledged in early October that general elections would be held in the island some time in 1982, after public approval of a new constitution currently being formulated. Bishop's New Jewel Movement (which is a member party of the International) seized power in March 1979 and has since been engaged in the long process of social and economic reconstruction in difficult circumstances.

Earlier in the year a major cabinet reshuffle was announced by Bishop on 29 July intended to put the small Caribbean island on a 'war footing' to face the 'tremendous challenge' posed by US hostility to the New Jewel regime. The changes included the creation of a new ministry of national mobilisation and the appointment of the first woman member of the revolutionary government, the full composition of which became as follows: Maurice Bishop (prime minister, information, health, defence and interior); Bernard Coard (deputy prime minister, finance, trade, industry and planning); Kenrick Radix (attorney-general, legal affairs, agro-industries); Unison Whiteman (foreign affairs and tourism); Hudson Austin (communications, works and labour); George Louison (agriculture, lands and fisheries, cooperatives and rural development); Jacqueline Creft (education, youth and social affairs); Selwyn Strachan (national mobilisation) and Norris Bain (housing)

In carrying out the reshuffle Bishop stressed the need to increase efficiency and output 'in the face of economic aggression and propaganda destabilisation by US imperialism'.

The following month the Grenada prime minister issued a statement detailing US moves against his regime, claiming in particular that recent American military exercises off Puerto Rico were a rehearsal for a planned invasion of Grenada. Bishop added that the government's conclusion concerning the real purpose of these exercises 'is shared by many in the region and elsewhere who are fully aware of the Reagan administration's hawklike attitude towards our resolution and the steps it has already taken to destabilise our development process', and listed the following as examples of the US approach:
● attempts to block funding for the construction of an international airport on Grenada;
● attempts to gain the supp of other governments in region for the blocking Caribbean Development B credits;
● allowing mercenaries train openly in Miami future invasions of Nicar: Cuba or Grenada;
● drawing up plans for a r blockage of Grenada;
● pre-election threats by k Reagan and George Bush: teach Grenada a lesson';
● daily illegal spy flights : Grenada in violation of airspace.

The Grenada prime mini concluded: 'We firmly bel that the Caribbean will r be able to achieve true so justice and equality for people in an atmosphere tension and insecurity. It surely the right of the peo of Grenada, as it is the righ all peoples, to develop tl own processes in their c way free from all forms external dictation, intimidat and pressure.'

Award of Kreisky and Czernetz prizes

This year's Bruno Kreisky Foundation prizes for services to human rights have been awarded to ten individuals and two organisations, ranging from the imprisoned South African nationalist leader, Nelson Mandela, to the Israeli Histadrut trade-union federation. Worth between 100,000 and 400,000 Austrian schillings, the prizes were awarded by a jury chaired by Karl Blecha (deputy chairman of the Austrian Socialist Party) and including SI President Willy Brandt and Chancellor Kreisky himself.

Among the individuals awarded prizes were Simcha Flapan, for his contribution to Arab-Jewish dialogue, and Raimonda Tawil, for her work in the field of Arab women's emancipation. The Histadrut was honoured for its efforts to integrate Arab workers in Israel, while Nelson Mandela, currently serving a life sentence in South Africa, was commended for his commitment to the struggle for black equality.

Also awarded prizes were two South Korean opposition activists, Kim Dae Jung and the poet Kim Chi Ha; Domitilia Barrios de Chungara, a Bolivian miner's wife who has championed the rights of workers and women in her country; the late Enrique Alvarez Cordoba of El Salvador, who was murdered in November 1980 after playing a leading role in the opposition to the military junta; the Colombian sociologist Orlando Fals Borda, for his relentless opposition to fascist forces; Rosa Jochmann and Felix Ermacora, both of Austria, f their tireless efforts in vario human-rights campaigns; a the Foundation for the Suppo of European Intellectuals. f its work in assisting E European scientists a intellectuals.

The Kreisky Foundati was founded on the occasi of Chancellor Kreisky's 65 birthday. Banks, insuran companies and other bodi have contributed 9 milli schillings to finance the priz which are awarded every tv years to individuals and orga isations for outstanding servic in the cause of human rights.

Earlier in the year, the 198 Karl Czernetz prize (whic honours the memory of tl former international secreta of the Austrian Socialist Part was awarded in four sections t local party organisation (including two young sociali groups) for outstanding achiev ments in the educationa cultural and information field

Domitilia Barrios de Chungara

Enrique Alvarez Cordoba

① 43

SUMMARY REPORT ON THE REGULAR MEETING OF SOCIALIST INTERNATIONAL COMMITTEE FOR LATIN AMERICA AND THE CARIBBEAN

SANTO DOMINGO, D.R. February 24-25th 1983

SUBMITTED BY: DESSIMA WILLIAMS, NJM'S REPRESENTATIVE AT THE MEETING

This report does not claim to be exhaustive or comprehensive. Further follow up with cde. Victor Oqueli will be necessary. Please also see the short papers prepared for the press on the Conference. (Press Communique)
Basically, the _public_ Conference report reiterated previous previous positions. taken by some Latin American Governments on the region. This report attempts to report on some internal issues.

OUTCOME OF THE AGENDA ITEMS :

Item 1: Political situation in Latin America. Oqueli proposed a paper which was quite satisfactory as a start. (appendix 2). Off the record Andres Perez said it was too "anti-American" and introduced a completely new draft. (appendix 3) Several ammendments were submitted. Grenada's written ammendment is contained in appendix 4. Although a committee of four was set up, no conclusion was reached and all draft ammendments etc. are being sent to the drafting committee for the SI Congress which will be in _Lisbon, Portugal_, April 1983. (although there is still talk from Bernt Carlson about Sydney, Austrilia)

Item 11: Other Matters/ Special Developments.

1. The SI _Congress_ will be in _Lisbon Portugal_. Bernt Carlson is not happy with that but this seems more or less final.

2. _Andres Perez_ (as per usual) was extremely aggressive, almost hegemonistic on (a) the content of the assessment on Latin America, which he wanted to be very soft, almost no reference whatsoever to the US.
(b) On the first day, apparently he advanced a thesis on what should be the character of SI. He apparently wants it to be significantly identifiable from the christians and the communists. Ungo repeated this..o them

.......¬/2

(c) He wanted clear and firm statements against Suriname.
(d) He lost a definitive, but not-made-public bid for the Presidency
   to replace Pena Gomez. It appeared he was not popularly favoured
   by forces such as Oqueli.

3. The Guatemalan Carlos Gallardo of the Social Democrats informed
   the meeting that some elements of the party had been engaged in
   diversive action. They called a special and contestable 'Congress'.
   Also some progressive forces feared these same elements are co-operating
   with the Rios Lott government. The other side presented their C
   case. In summary, it appears that: (a) there is an ideological
   and/or tactical difference between those who want to build relations
   with the freedom fighters (Gallard's position, more or less) and those
   who want to concentrate now on rushing to take advantage of Rios Lott
   March 23rd "Political Abierta" (opening). And (b) there appears to
   be a struggle for leadership by a younger wing of the party. The SI
   Presidium advised them to settle the matter internally and they later
   announced the establishment of an internal Commission which will
   report on progress/or lack of it at the Lisbon Congress.

4. The Nicaraguans who are only observers, attended very few sessions
   and delivered less than a one-minute greeting. They were very
   active bilaterally and in the other structured activities. e.g. tours.

Item 111. What should be the SI Strategy in Latin America?

Several proposals were put forward.

(i) Andres Perez proposed a committee to look into the situation in
    Suriname (the Dutch Labour Party Representative gave a very poor
    report on the human rights situation there)
(ii) A proposal for a fact-finding mission to the Eastern Caribbean

(iii) an SI meeting should be held soon in Brazil to get a better
     understanding of the situation and work with all socialist
     parties there, similar discussions around Argentina as well.

Item iv. Internal organisation of the committee: First Pena Gomez
    was emphatically urged to remain as President, by Reuben
    Berrios, (PIP) Carlos Morales (PRC Chile) from the floor.
    Pena Gomez said the serious domestic crisis in the D.R. had
    more or less eased and he was now once again in a position
    to accept the presidency as offered to him.

    Secondly, a paper on "Terms of Reference" was adopted and
    it is attached as appendix 5. (it does not include all the
    ammendments)

......./3

43 - 2

Item 5. On Christian Democracy in Latin America was not discussed.

This is more or less in summary what occured. I arrived at the meeting one day late, and in any case the meeting was not very disciplined so items became merged.

MY OVERALL ASSESSMENT

First on the meeting itself. There are a number of storms inside SI at this time. Among them are: Elections for President and Secretary General; left-right splits over issues such as Nicaragua. It is rumoured that Suarez of Portugal wants the Congress in Lisbon. So he can invite and parade Eden Pastora (Commandente Zero) and thus embarras the Sandinistas. The Central American situation continues to be an issue of major controversy, to the extent that even Latin Americans are, or seem divided on SI strategy for the region. e.g. Andres Perez vs Hector Oqueli) There is also the charge that the Isrealis have and continue to manuver via certain Scandinavian parties to get an indication for Isreal's position. Thus the Lisbon Congress could be very important in deciding whether Socialist International takes a more anti-imperialist, anti-zionist position, or whether the right will be victorious.

Second, what is the political situation as seen by Latin American social democrats.. Unfortunately, I was not able to get a clear reading on this. I sensed that there is a certain amount of turmoil and most people are waiting to sort things out at the Congress. This appears to be Oqueli's position.

Third, was NJM's presence useful? Jamaica's Paul Miller did not come, neither was Barbados present. So even though we arrived at the end of the second day, an English-speaking party's presence was very useful. Furthermore NJM is well respected and its leaders well-known and equally respected. It was therefore very useful to continue to be working and to be seen among such regio parties and figures. Pena Gomez, Sule (Chile), Oqueli, Reuben Berrios (PR)., even Andres Perez took time out to listen and to come out and greet me, but particularly to send greetings to cde. Laurice Bishop. Our input in the meeting may not have been all that critical (with the exception of appendix 4) But as the 1981 hosts, as a member, as English-speaking Caribbean, and as a party well-loved, the answer is yes, the presence was very useful.

The delegate was given about one week's notice and quite unfortunately, no brief whatsoever. This was due to communications/transportation problems encountered by the International Relations Committee.

..... /4

Added to this, the meeting was moved up one day earlier and the delega
missed a full two-thirds of the first day.

On the morning of the second day, Grenada was given the floor without
soliciting it. I made a very short statement, the text of which is
attached as appendix.G
The third and final interview was towards the closing of the meeting
to thank and congratulate the host/president Mr. Pena Gomez, attached
as an appendix.H

<u>BILATERALS</u>   (these were mostly very brief meetings and with no real
agenda. I really want to report comprehensively on the meeting)

(a) Carlos Gallard (SDP_ Guatemala) He briefed me on the internal
conflicts in his party. Regarding the March 23rd Political opening
offered by Gen. Rios Mott, he was of the opinion that it could be used
but with great caution and without compromise. He thought it would be
difficult because the dictatorship has moved large sections of the
people into virtually concentration camps, and this makes it even more
difficult to do political work, given the repression etc. I told him
that our Party/cde. Bishop would welcome him to Grenada anytime.
He sends cde. Bishop very warm greetings.

(b) Hector Oqueli (for El Salvador) We did not really speak on the
El Salvador situation but on SI , it's work and problems. He advised
me that there was a personality struggle between Willy Brandt and
Bernt Carlson. The popular feeling inside SI is that Carlson should
resign. (He has already been offered a post as ambassador-at-large
Swedish foreign ministry). Oqueli reminded NJM and cde. Kojo about
the proposed meeting for Grenada, on/around March 13th 1933. I urge
someone to contact him. Oqueli's name has been proposed for Secretary
General of SI. He was generally cool and helpful.

(c) Zaarndem from Aruba's LEF and Carlos Marquez were very friendly
and advised me that Betico was at this moment in Holland on the independence talks. He said that Holland continues to be adamantly oppos
to Aruba's independence outside of the bloc of six islands.

(d)Rodrigo Borja (Democratic Left -Ecuador) discussed the very poor
economic situation in Ecuador. He said public opinion polls inside
Ecuador showed that his party, the democratic left will win the next
elections in January 198 . Some at this meeting (e.g Sule) told me
this man Borja will be the next president of Ecuador.

(e) Guillermo Ungo (FDR _ El Salvador) sends greetings to cde. Bisho
He seems in very high spirits. His circles were Andres Perez and Ans
Sule.

...../5

(f) Oscar Britez (RFP- Paraguay) remembers visiting Grenada as part of a Latin American Socialist Youth Conference.

(g) Andres Perez (AD-Venezuela) He sends greetings to cde. Bishop I asked him when he is coming to Grenada and he said "Sometime hopefully this year" then he moved quickly again.

(h) Reuben Berrios (PIP _ Puerto Rico) We travelled to PR together and he selected a hotel for me to stay. He showed me old San Juan, next morning, his party paid for my hotel room and political Affairs chief Hiram Melendez took me to the Party Office before going to the airport. The PP also gave NJM a small tape Recorder. Bro. Reuben told me that some of the US troops used in the recent provocative military exercises in Honduras to intimidate Nicaragua came from the US troop supplies in Puerto Rico. I also learnt that Cyrus/ or someone fitting his discription has addressed a CLAT trade union meeting some two months ago, in which he denounced the PRG. (ref. Hiram Melandez)

ON P.D.R. AND THE DOMINICAN REPUBLIC

Pena Gomez seems to be in control, politically speaking. Someone also observed that the military was well under control as well. I did not meet with him though he was very warm, but understandbly busy. The party machinery seemed to function well for the meeting (the Party) also paid for room and meals for all 2-3 days.
The trade union, youth and women's movement, all are attached as appendices.
The delegations were taken on a tour of the city and shown the main political economic centre piece of the Blanco Administration. Housing projects. Some 512 house units are being constructed to satisfy a housing crisis (10,000 units must be built in 4 yrs: a political promise) Meanwhile one party member told me re unemployment was about 50%

RECOMMENDATIONS

1. an immediate consultation with Hector Oqueli: The proposal meeting of select regional parties (arch 1983) would be excellent followup especially since no one from St. George 's attended this meeting. This is of highest importance.

2. We must begin to prepare immediately for the Lisbon Congress, April 7-10 or 4-7 1983. Two of the important issues NJM must raise (which are also likely to win broad support from latin America) are: 'the Caribbean as a zone of Peace, independence and Development and the need for special consideration of small island states in the context, of the severe financial and economic crisis.

.......6

Given the ,any struggles inside SI at this time, we must start early to catch people's attention before they are carried away by internal politicking.

3. NJM could assist the committee with its fact-finding mission to the eastern caribbean. Oqueli could best suggest how.

4. NJM must strengthen its relations with Pena Gomez.

6. Respond to the invitation for the Socialist Youth Conference March 23-3 Cappendix 10

Expenses

1. Airline ticket	$832.00	
2. Tel. Calls and meals	95.55	
3. Lodging paid by PDR	0 0	
4. Overnight in B/Dos	58.60	
Total	986.15	

Please ~~regard~~ refund soonest to Washington Mission.

List of appendices.

2. Resolution on Latin America and the Caribbean - Hector Oqueli draft

3. "   "   "   "   - Andres Perez   "

Grenada's proposals to the text
Terms of reference for the latin American /caribbean committee
list of participants, agenda and daily schedule.

16

REPORT ON S.I. COMMITTEE FOR LATIN AMERICA AND
THE CARIBBEAN

This S.I. Committee for Latin America and the Caribbean
was held between 19th and 21st of August, 1983. However
because of late organisation of our part I was only ablee
to attend the second half of the second day and the final
day. The agenda for that period and the entire conference
is enclosed. Enclosed also are a list of participants,
the (only) Portuguese version of the Rio declaration and
all other documents I received from the Conference.

First of all let me raise what seemed to me, the "unexplain-
able" presence of a number of European Parties. My
understanding was that the meeting was a Latin American
caucus and as such some fourteen Latin American countries
were to be present. This concern of the presence of the
European parties stemmed from the fact that most of the
representatives of these parties held backward and in
some cases reactionary positions during the day and a half.

Two examples in particular could be cited.

One: The position of the Holland delegate on the Social
and Economic Crisis was that the crux of the problem with
the Third World was and is the question of the internal
distribution of wealth. The debt problem and all other
external economic and social problems affecting the third
world stem from the internal distribution system in
operation. True enough. but the position went further
to say that the Third World's problems have nothing to do
with their external economic relations. In other words
we are laying blame on the developed capitalist economics
for their problems. This position, however, was successfully defeated by the Brazilian delegation.

Two: In the case of Portugal their position on a
solution to the problem was for Portugal and its former
colonies (ie. Brazil , Angola, Mozambique etc.) should
bond themselves together in a sort of union to work
collectively by themselves to solve the Third World problem.

Those, among others, were prominent points coming from
those parties. The European parties came from Holland,
Italy, Spain, France, Portugal and even Isreal.

On the issue of the Social and Economic porblems within
the context of a world in crisis most presentations were
purely descriptive and less analytical. The Brazilians
dominated the floor. As such nothing beyond the general
call for a restructuring of the international financial
and trading system was called for. There were some feeling (I think it wa s from the Venezuelans) that Third World
countries should unilaterally refuse to pay their debts.
There was all tacit support for the creation of a Third
World currency. In the context of that entire discussion,
I made the call for an inclusion in the final declaration,
the meeting support for the struggle for the N.I.E.O. The
call was made in my presentation which lasted for about
twelve to fifteen minutes. Details follow.

Having arrived late and learning that a number of parties
have made contribution on the situation in their respective
countries I decided to ask for the floor on the final day.
The presentation made can be divided into five parts viz.

1. Attacks made on the Grenada Revolution,
   centering on   a. The International Airport
   (carrying a similar line as was carried by the
   Comrade Leader, Hunter College Address)   and
   b. the allegation of human rights abuse in
   Grenada, constitutionality and elections.
   Again the Hunter College line was given.

2. The threat of imperialism to the Revolution
   focussing on   a. negative propaganda around our
   Carnival festivities; the aim of which was to
   scare our people and detract tourism.   b. the
   presence of Gairy in Barbados at a time of U.S.
   Military Monouveres in the Region. Gairy
   himself, confortable in Barbados and using the
   media there.   c. attempts made to isolate Grenada
   again at the Caricom Heads of Government
   Conference in Port-of-Spain and the   struggle

that had to be waged by our delegation.

3. The performance of our economy and the negative
   implications of the world capitalist crisis.

4. The present political situation in Central America
   and expressing firm support for the Contadora
   Initiative; also, expressing condemnation of all
   acts of military (and otherwise) aggression against
   the Nicaraguan Revolution. Support for the peoples
   of El Salvador and Guatamala was also expressed as
   well as support for a negotiated political settlement to the problems in Central America.

5. The final part called on the meeting to express in
   its final decleration concern and support for the
   following:

   a. The preservation of World Peace
   b. The struggle for a N.I.E.O.
   c. That the Caribbean be declared a zone
      of peace, Independence and Development
      and implemented in practice.
   d. The Contadora Initiative

In terms of criticism of the presentation two specific ones
could be made. In the first instance the correctness of
naming Barbados as the country from which Gairy was operating is questionable. In the context of the type of gathering it seemed later to me that implying Barbados without
naming it could have been more appropriate. Secondly, the
final part of the presentation did not call on the meeting
to express concern and condemnation of U.S. interference in
the internal affairs of Grenada. However, implicit in the
presentation was the cry for such, but specific reference
to it would have gone a longer way. A mild concern for the
Grenada situation was in the final declaration.

By way of general criticism of the entire planning and arrangements for Grenada to attend the meeting let me make a few remarks. In the first instance late preparation (or even no preparations) were made. As a result I was able to attend only half of the meeting. Besides that the lateness meant the following:

1. Lost of time and money. I had to fly north and then south and vici verse on my return. It was possible to fly south only.

2. Absolutely no briefing with respect to the content of the meeting (before leaving) and what we as a party wanted from the meeting.

3. No contacts on information as to the venue of the meeting. I only knew it was in Rio. I was therefore stranded in Rio for over five hours.

4. There was also a security problem related to point three in that I had to unavoidably release information of myself and my mission in Rio before I could have established contact with St. George's. This is in the context of Bernt Carlsson, a V.P. of S.I. been arrested at the airport and detained for couple hours and a murder at the airport only fifteen minutes after I left it. Anything could have happened.

Finally, I want to make a few recommendations on our approach to future missions.

1. The I.R.C. have someone specialised in S.I. matters (and other organs of equal or greater importance). My experience was that continuity and personal contact, relations and familiarity are necessary at these fora.

2. All travel requirements should be found out at least three days before someone goes on a mission. (Visa, routing etc.). This will save time, money and minimise security risks.

3. Thorough briefing of comrades going to these sessions with particular emphasis on objectives.

4. At least two party comrades should be singled out for full time work in I;R.C. with specific responsibility of carrying our line to these sessions.

Wayne Sandifed.

EMBASSY OF GRENADA IN THE USSR

Dobrynınskaya Ulitsa 7
Apartment 221
Moscow
USSR

Telephone
237-25-41
237-99-05

TO: THE GRENADA PEACE COUNCIL
SUBJECT: REPORT ON PEACE MEETINGS IN LISBON

DATE: 6TH NOVEMBER 1982

There were two meetings held:

1. Presiduim of the World Peace Council from October 30 to 2nd November
2. International Preparatory Committee of World Assembly for Peace and Life, Against Nuclear War on 3rd November.

OBJECTIVES

The main objectives of the meeting were:

a. To review the work of the World Peace Council since the last Presidential Committee met in Havana in April 1981;

b. To work out the 1983 programme of the World Peace Council;

c. To begin preparations for the most important meeting of the World Peace Council in 1983, that is, the World Assembly for Peace and Life, Against Nuclear War to be held in Prague from June 14 to 19.

PARTICIPANTS

Participants for both meetings, respresenting millions of people, came from all parts of the world. A list of some of the names of the participants is included with the report. It is instructive to note that onl two Caribbean countries were represented, Jamaica and Grenada.

OBSERVATIONS

From the Caribbean, both St.Vincent and Guyana (2 Peace Councils in Guyana) are vice-presidents of the WPC and all were absent from the meeting. This cannot be the only indication, but it seems that the Caribbean Peace Movement is underdeveloped and immobilised.

A very important development - in my view - in the World Peace Counci and Movement at the present international situation is the great urge to build the strength and unity of the world's peace forces, regardles of political, ideological or religious persuasions, on the question of the need to avert a thermo-nuclear catastrophe. The Leadership of the WPC puts it this way,"the only condition/qualification for joining the Peace

EMBASSY OF GRENADA IN THE USSR

Dobryninskaya Ulitsa 7
Apartment 221
Moscow
USSR

Telephone
237-25-41
237-99-05

Movement is the support of the struggle to prevent a nuclear war".

Furthermore, a very significant focus of the World Peace movement and its leadership is the inextricable link between the struggle for World Peace and the struggle for national liberation, independence, democracy and social progress. This link is profoundly proclaimed at every opportu nity.

For this last reason, it is my genuine recommendation for us to develop our Grenada Peace Council to a very high and prominent level. Since Grenada leads the struggle in the Eastern Caribbean for national liberation, social progress and economic independence, it behoves of us that we have a dear role to mobilise and put in action the Caribbean peace forces. The WPC expects that of the Grenada Revolution and the GPC Members of the WPC Secretariat informed that Trinidad and Tobago has a good Peace Council which is a good starting point for our regional activities; so too is Jamaica and Guyana. St.Vincent's peace movement is not vibrant.

RESULTS

The assessment of the WPC is that the results of the meetings were good. This is based on the concensus reached by all the participants on the documents* and resolutions adopted. A copy of these documents - witho the final amendments - forms part of this overall report. The list of th final documents will be sent to the GPC at a later date.
Of interest to Latin America and the Caribbean; the result is as follows
1.The Latin American Commission at the meeting agreed to coordinate these activities in 1983: a.The bicentenary of Simon Bolivar;b.The 10th anniversary of the fascist coup in Chile and c.support for Nicaragua in United Nations Security Council.
2. A resolution was unanimously adopted which gives support to progress: ve forces in the region, including the Grenada Revolution.
3. A press conference was held by all representatives of the region, th focus being the situation around Nicaragua, fully expounded by the Nica gua delegation. A renounciation of the aggressive activities against Nicaragua was signed by participants of peace movements from Latin Ameri and the Caribbean.

4. The WPC decided to make the first week in December 1982 "a week in

45 - 2

* One of the document- the most important one- is the Lisbon Appeal

Solidarity with Nicaragua" in view of the dangerous schemes planned
by the Reagan Administration in collusion with the reactionary
Hoduran Government in Central America for, the beginning of
December.

INITIATIVES BY GRENADA

1. I spoke with the WPC President Romesh Chandra and extended an
invitation to come to Grenada for the 4th Anniversary of the
Grenada Revolution on March 13, 1983, on behalf of Prime Minister,
Maurice Bishop. He was thankful for the invitation and accepted it
orally; he expressed his eagerness to come to Grenada. On his
suggestion, I publicly announced the invitation from the Prime
Minister to President Romesh Chandra, in my intervention at the
meeting.
Prime Minister, Maurice Bishop would, therefore have to send this
letter of invitation to Moscow by December in order for us to
present it to Romesh Chandra, President of the WPC soon afterwards.
2. A meeting was held with WPC Vice- President and several dicussions
with officials and workers at the WPC headquaters.
They all turned out to be very useful.
I presented three proposals for WPC activities in Grenada in 1983.
i. That a meeting of the Caribbean peace movements should be held
in Grenada in April as a build up to the Prague Assembly in June so
that the region's peace movements could present a united position;
ii. That the WPC should convene a conference in Grenada in November,
the Theme being: The Caribbean as a zone of Peace, Independence
and Development.
iii. Solidarity posters with Grenada for March 1983. These proposals
were presented in the form of a letter to the Latin Amercian Department of the WPC and the last two were also give to the President of
the WPC.
It was later reported to me that in principle the suggestions were
accepted but that they would be further discussed in Helsinki,
headquaters of the WPC, before a final decision is taken.
Additionally, three other suggestions were put forward:
a. That the WPC should circulate information of the World Peace
Movement to the Peace committees in the Caribbean;
b. That the WPC should invite representatives of the regions' peace
committees to participate in WPC meetings, seminars, conferences etc;

c. That the WPC should send films of the Peace Movement to the GPC.

On this suggestion I was advised that the WPC does not make films, and that we should approach the GDR Peace Movement because they have good films of the Peace Movements. I spoke with a German on the subject and asked that he raise it for the GPC with the GDR Peace Committee.

On this matter the GPC should follow up directly and immediately.

During a meeting with WPC Regional Secretary comrade Hill Arboleda of Panama, a member of the WPC Secretariat, he mentioned that the WPC highly assess the Grenada Revolution and the work of the GPC. However, he pointed out that the flow of information from the GPC to the Secretariat of the WPC is not very good. In fact, this is more or less the same situation with the Peace movements in the Caribbean. The WPC knows little about the activities of the region's Peace movements except Cuba and Guyana.

On this score I firmly recommend, with a degree of urgency and consistency, that the Grenada Peace Council should immediately undertake to circulate regular information to the WPC Secretatiat on its activities and events of the Revolution. The information could be in the form of ;reports on its work, news, articles, upcoming activities, letters etc. This is urgent and absolutely necessary. We should bombard the WPC with information on the Revolution and work of the GPC. This is important if we are going to raise our standing and prestige in the WPC.

The WPC has several magazines and news-sheets, but has never written an article on the Grenada Revolution for the simple reason that the WPC has little or no information on Grenada.

Additionally, the WPC is leaning and depending on the Grenada Peace Council in order that the WPC could develop wider and deeper relations with the Peace movements in Guyana, the Eastern Caribbean French Caribbean, Cayenne, Barbados and Trinidad and Tobago. This was mentioned to me by Comrade Hill Arboleda.

45 - 4 Further still, Cde. Arboleda of the WPC suggested that the WPC would like the GPC to send addresses of the Peace Movements of the Caribbean to it. Also mentioned was that the GPC could organise visits to the various peace movements in the Caribbean.

Since the new Presidental Committee of the WPC would be elected
during the Prague Assembly in June 1983, we spoke about the possibility of Grenada putting up a candidate for vice-president. This
was strongly supported. The GPC should groom someone and present
a written recommendation to the WPC before the Assembly, ie. by
April 1983 or earlier. Also, the GPC should recommend to the WPC
its desire to work in one of its commissions.

Finally, on the question of participation in WPC activities,the
one drawback of the WPC is finance to buy tickets. I was told
that the Soviet Peace Fund, through AERFLOT, Soviet Airlines and
Cubana make some contributions; plus the various Peace committees
around the world. For example, at previous meetings the Latin
American Peace Committees assisted the WPC by paying 80 000 US
dollars for tickets.

Concretely, as far as the GPC is concerned, it would be invited
to participate in WPC activities, but would be called upon to
pay for its participants for <u>part</u> of the flight, namely, from
Grenada to Havana where the future delegates would collect
Aeroflot and get a free ticket. If the GPC could raise sufficient
funds and pay up to Havana, it could send up to six (6) delegates
to the Prague Assembly from June 14 to 19, 1983.

My last recommendation to the GPC is that it should send all
information to the World Peace Council via the Embassy of Grenada
in the USSR.

Magazines, booklets, newspapers posters are attached to this
report.

Bernard Bourne
Minister- Counsellor

45 - 5

SECTION THREE:
MINUTES OF POLITICAL BUREAU
AND
CENTRAL COMMITTEE

POLITICAL BUREAU

MINUTES OF THE POLITICAL BUREAU MEETING
WEDNESDAY, 8TH December, 1980

46

Comrades present:-

Maurice Bishop
Selwyn Strachan
George Louison
Hudson Austin
Ewart Layne

Comrades absent:-

Unison Whiteman)
Liam James   ) away

Agenda:-

1. Minutes
2. Correspondence
3. Items for Decisions
4. PB Consultation on Item 5
5. "Areas of Work" - Workers Work

1. MINUTES
   1.1 Corrections
      i)   Re comrades absent - Cdes. Whiteman and James were out of the country.
      ii)   Re TFG, Cde. Austin to meet the staff on behalf of the Chief, re disciplinary matters.
      iii) Reported sub points of the Comrade Leader (re main feature of the present political situation) were points made/arising out of the discussion on the topic.
      iv)   1983 slogan reported as "Year of ~~Agriculture~~ +ACADEMIC Political Education" was not decided on as reported; it was the suggestion of Cde. Bishop reported from discussions held with Cde. Coard.
      v)   Re visiting countries in 1983, Cde. Whiteman to visit the Latin American and Caricom countries and the Comrade Leader to visit the others. Ghana and Mozambique were also raised as possibilities.
      vi)   Draft of the Comrade Leader's New Year Speech to be circulated to the mass organisations leaders and Party members for their suggestion/imput

   1.2 Tasks
      i)
      ii)
      iii)   Not done.
      iv)   Done. (Excluded was that Cde. St.Bernard to go to Carriacou.)
      v)   Done
      vi)   Done
      vii)   Done; new ammendment will be circulated to CC for discussion
      viii) Implemented; now a OC member
      iX)   Was not done
      x)   Capt. Belfon to be installed on Monday 13 December.
      xi)   Done
      xii)   Only the economic aspect was done.

                                        3/...

xiii) Outstanding
xiv) Implemented.
xv) Ongoing
xvi) Duplication of Task No. x
xvii) To be done next week.
xviii) Suggestion to make IRC responsible from the Party point of view on the foreign/regional tasks; Cde. Whiteman should be made responsible for the IRC, with Cde. DeRiggs reporting to him. Cde. Coard together with IRC will prepare the workplan and budget for this.
xix) Done
xx) Started, ongoing.

1.3 Outstanding Tasks:
i) Discussions have taken place
ii) Being done
iii) Still outstanding; not completed
iv) Still outstanding; not completed

1.4 Other
i) Cde. Austin reported on the tasks he was assigned to speak to the TFG staff on matters of discipline, he pointed out the following:-

* met first with Patrick Smikle, Peter David and Cheryl Fletcher the the general staff
* told them of their high level of ill discipline, their feeling of being indispensible, that they would be dismissed if notimprovement; that regulations for the use of the vehicle will be implemented with the coming of a new Manager; spoke of the budget and the 28 staff members overall compared to the work been done presently; the violation of no use of drugs; the issue of workscheldules and tasks assignment; technicians to prepare report on the equipment; staff relations raised; spoke on the role of the TV on building a new society; physical condition of the place is very bad

2. CORRESPONDENCE
2.1 Letter from Joe Charter: sent to the Comrade Leader raising the financial problems related to salary and operating costs; requested another diplomatic officer be sent to the mission - suggested Thaddeus McEween. PB suggested James Clarkson to be the other diplomatic officer. Decision - Matter to be raised with Foreign Affairs - financial question re the acutal agreement made with the Lybians re the operations of the Mission there.
2.2 Telex was received re the issue of a vessel been shot at while in Egbert Harbour and after been given permission to be there. This took place on 24th November, at 11.00 p.m. Tele to be sent in reply stating that the matter is being investigated and a response will be received by them.

3. ITEMS FOR DECISIONS:
3.1 Grand Bacolet Issue: A report on the issue was submitted to the PB by the

2/...

46 - 2

AGWU Comrades. There was an industrial dispute at the estate,
the comrades were given instructions by the PB (through Cdes.
Louison and Bishop) as to h w to handle the situation, but
they acted contrary to the instructions given for the solution
of the problem.

The overseer was given six hours to move out ofrom the farm;
the keys were handed over to the workers for it to be run by
them.

The OC has looked at the matter and sent the relevant comrades
to face the Disciplinary Committee.

3.2 Internaional Relations Department: UWI: A proposal from Henry Gill
for 20 - 25 UWI students to do an educational visit of Grenada
January 31st - February 5. They will hold one hour presentations
on mornings with 30 - 45 minutes discussion following the presentations. Topics to be presented on are:-

i)	Role of the Party....	:Cde. Strachan
ii)	Foriegn Policy.....	:Cde. Whiteman
iii)	Economic Development....	:Cde. Coard
iv)	The Private Sector in the Revolution	:Richard Menez
v)	Agricultural Development....	:Cde. Louison
vi)	Education, Training, Culture	:Cde. Creft
vii)	Women in the Revolution	:Cde. P. Coard
viii)	Law in the Revolution	:Cde. Radix
ix)	Presentation by the Comrade Leader	

They have requested assistance in ground transportation; they will pay
all other expenses. We are also committed to hosting a reception for
them. The visits to the projects will take place in the afternoons.

The proposal was agreed to by the Political Bureau.

3.3 Paul Miller: Cde. Strachan reported that Cde. Miller had been here
over the last few days for the prupose of discussing a proposal from
the Socialist International for the setting up of a Institute for
Political Studies.

Agred too by P.B.

3.4 IICA Industrial Dispute: Mario Franka, the Head of the IICA office here
has recently fired a few sisters employed with the Institute and since
then has refused to meet with the Union.

3.5 Atlanta Conference: This conference on the CBI to be held in Atlanta
from December 11 (date not absolutely clear) is organised by the
liberal left and they are requesting that somebody from the leadership be there, apart from the Ambassador (Dessima). Decision to
get more details and then take decision.

4/...

5. <u>WORKERS WORK</u>; Two documents re the report on the workers work were already submitted to the Bureau. The report looke at the structures of the WC and an anlysis of each WC member:

o   suggested that Cde. Anslem should not be on the Board of Directors of the ~~Luing Association~~
o   that Cde. Winston Ledlow should be made a member of the WC
o   all WC members should be made to submit a workscheldule
o   Judlyn's presence on the WC should be looked at; maybe she should be put to deal with emulation at the workplaces
o   also suggested for dealing with emulation was Jenny Donald and that she be put full time in the TAWU work
o   a check should be kept on the classes every day on a union by union basis; the aim should be to have classes going on 90% of the work-places
o   have to find comrades for all areas of work ranging from political/ideological work to sports and culture
o   the following areas should be given priority:-
    i)   socialism classes
    ii) CPE
    iii) emulation/production committees
    iv) work on the international airport site
    v)   propaganda: WV, billboards and charts at the workplace; declaration of different categories of workers days;

o   it was decided that one PB comrade to be assigned to each of the five areas outlined above.
o   Cde. Ventour to head the political/ideological/pfopaganda work

<u>DECISIONS/TASKS</u>:
1. Matters raised by Cde. Charter to be discussed with Foreign Affairs.
2. Reponse to telex re been shot at in ███████ Harbour to be sent stating that the matter is being investigated and will send repponse.
3. Relevant AGWU comrades to face the Disciplinary Committee re the Grand Lacolet issue.

MINUTES OF THE POLITICAL BUREAU MEETING
APRIL 22ND, 1981

Comrades present:-   Absent:-
    Maurice Bishop   Unison Whiteman - out of the country
    Bernard Coard
    Selwyn Strachan
    Vincent Noel
    Hudson Austin
    Kenrick Radix
    George Louison

Agenda:-

(1) Airport Committee meeting at 11.00 a.m.
(2) Left Parties Conference
(3) Amsterdam trip
(4) Comrade Radix's report

The meeting did not follow the patter of the planned agenda. Instead, many different topics were discussed, which were not on
the agenda. They included:-

(1) SITUATION ON THE DOCKS - Comrade Strachan reported that Eric
Pierre had telephoned him saying that there was a conflict on the
docks, as Sawney wanted to use the BGWU workers to off load the c
cement that is here. Pierre was insisting that the other workers
from the SWWU be allowed oto do it. Sawney was called to the meeting and explained that what he was trying to do was to get a compromise of 60% of the workers from SWWU and 40% from BGWU. But
Pierre was not willing to accept that, When he was leaving he said,
they (Pierre and others) were trying to forcibly enter the ship .
Decision-As one solution, BGWU should sign a contract with the MNIB
to be their shipping agent. Comrade Noel then left to complete
that by the end of the day. This will make it easier for BGWU workers to be allowed to off load the goods coming for the MNIB. In the
meantime, the arrangement Sawney suggested should continue to be
as he suggested, i.e. 60% of the workes from SWWU and 40% from BGWU.
Also, Sawney should not be playing a visibly leading role in all
this. The BGWU should get somebody else to play that role.
Comrades Bishop and Strachan are to meet with the Executive of the
SWWU on May 7th, at 11.00 a.m. at the P.M.O. Comrade Strachn to
meet with Eric Pierre before than. He is also to contact him for a
proposed agenda for that meeting.

(2)GRENADA RESORTS CORPORATION-Four names have been suggested for
Managers - Paul Redhead, ? Minors (Manager of Rum Runner), Winston
Bullen and Evelyn Ross. It was noted that the G.R.C. hotels are in
dire need of repairs.

Comrade Radix reported that Pinar Gomez of the Dominican Republic
wants to come to Grenada and is also interested in forming a Gre-
nada/Dominican Republic Friendship Association. He wants to know
when it is best to come. Decision - He should come ton or around
May 22nd - the time of the Socialist International Conference here.

Comrade Coard reported that the Board of Directors of both the I.M.F.
and the World Bank wanted him to come to Washington. Decision - He
replied that he is unable to do so. Instead, they should send somebody to see him instead.

This item formally on the agenda was discussed:-

NATIONAL AIRPORT COMMITTEE MEETING 11.00 A.M. - It will be chaired
by Kurt Strachan, Comrade Strachan to give a short address on the
schedue of work at the site and apologise for the later invitations. Bernard will give a detailed report on the Co-financing conference and Maurice will speak on the formation of the Committee

/...and on the ....

-2-

and on the idea of the formation of Airport Committees in every work place, school and village. A National Committee to draft a programme for the Airport Committees is also to be formed with representatives from the youth, women, business, workers, farmers, middle strata, civil organisations.

CARRIACOU WORK - Comrade Louison who visited Carriacou over the last weekend reported that George Prime still has not been appointed Deputy Secretary for Carriacou Affairs as yet. Decision - Comrade Radix to work on this. Comrade Louison met with Comrades Prime and Bullen. The latter is thinking of resigning and also responded to allegations made against him, which he said were unfounded and false. Bentley Thomas is now doing his own thing and Comrade Louison said he is to be called here to work for a few weeks.

Comrade Radix reported on a hydro-power report done by some French which reveals areas that we can receive power from. Comrade Coard said that this is being worked on.

Comrade Radix also reported that Minor Spices is in a financial crisis. That is to be discussed on Friday, 24th at Economic Bureau.

The Sugar Factory he said also, ishas a large quantity of sugar lying there and a cash flow problem. Comrade Coard said that this is being worked on also.
                                    but
This was not on the agenda/was discussed:-
The new D.P.P., Comrade Sibbles from Jamaica is to be paid $2,000.00 monthly and given a monthly housing allowance of $500.00 with 50% duty free on the purchase of a car. His contract is to last one year. Comrade Coard is to discuss the matter with him.

                              Hazel-Ann
                              RECORDING SECRETARY

MINUTES OF THE POLITICAL AND ECONOMIC BUREAU
MEETING ON SATURDAY 25TH
APRIL, 1981.

Comrades present:-   Comrades absent:-
Maurice Bishop   Kenrick Radix - outof the country
Bernard Coard
Selwyn Strachan
Hudson Austin
George Louison
Unisn Whiteman
Vincent Noel

AGENDA:

(1) Prioritisation of the Capital Budget
(2) Housing
(3) Bestlait
(4) MNIB
(5) PWU
(6) A sterdam
(7) Mexico
(8) Suriname
(9) GRC

(1) PRIORITISATION OF THE CAPITAL BUDGET - The plan here is to cut out some $25M from the budget because of not getting some promised $12M from the I.M.F. Some programmes were cut, but it did not amount to the required sum. There has been a drop in the revenue - going lower that expected. But the possible reasons for that are being looked at presently.

----Comrade Strachan reported that hemet with four representatives of the S.W.W.T.U. Their greviance was that the presence of the BGWU workers was denying them their job. Also, they have decided to boycott the May Day Celebration. Comrade Strachan replied to the first issue, that the PRG had no desire to see thwm without jobs and that is not what was bein" done. The second, May Day Celebrations - is being organised by the T.U.C. and their boycott will be against the T.U.C. and not the P.R.G. They also want to discuss the question of the Cuban boats and will send a agenda for the meeting with the Comrade Leader on may 7th.

(2) PUBLIC WOKRERS UNION - At the last meeting, they w re willing to accept PRG's offer if the letters will :then be withdrawn. That was not the agreement - they will be withdrawn when the whole agreement is signed. The PWU has put out a call to its members to come out on May Day and show their solidarity with their members now on suspension. Decision - Lauriston Wilson is to tell them, that if they do as planned, regarding the present stage of the negotiations, PRG will be free to do anything they see necessary.

------Comrade Noelppointed out that AGWU must apply to TUC formembership now, in order that the latter remains in our control.

------The CIWU, BGWU, AND PFU must ensure to be at the May Day Celebrations.

————

(3) G.R.C. - Comrade Whiteman reported on the GRC situation with specific regard to Cruickshank and allegations of corruptions against him. He reported however that the State hotels had improved, largely due to Alva James's enthusiasm and attention and that the allegations against him (Alva) mustbbe investigated.
The Comrade Leader pointed out that Alva's approach has been one of by passing the GRC Board and dealing with Unie on a none to one basis. He was refusing to attend board meetings. Comrade Whiteman confirmed that he had told Alva that there shoukd be no board meeting in his (Unie's) absence.

At this point, I had to leave.

Hazel-Ann
RECORDING SECRETARY

REPORT TO THE POLITICAL BUREAU:

ON WORLD PEACE CONFERENCE

HAVANNA, CUBA. 19th - 21st APRIL, 1981.

The Conference was attended by seventy-nine countries, and nine international organisations. Delegates came from working class parties, in and out of political power, religious organisations and national peace movements. Delegates from the caribbean came from Grenada, St. Vincent, Barbados, Jamaica and Guyana.

The Conference got on with a positive start with a fiery anti-imperialist speech from Cuban Comrade Jesus Montane Cropesa alt. member of the politburo of P.C.C, and was then followed by ROMESH CHANDRA, President of World Peace Council (W.P.C).

This session of the presidential committee of W.P.C was held in solidarity with the peoples of Cuba, Grenada, Nicaragua and El Salvador.

At the opening session Cde. Whiteman delivered a short speech to the conference on Imperialism manoeuvers in and around Grenada. Condemning their attempts of economic sabotage and their provocation of violating our air space and territorial waters.

Speeches were made by members of Communist parties and Presidents of National Peace Movements. All of which called for mass participation of the peoples in dealing with bringing the arms race to a halt and creating an atmosphere of PEACE. This session was very businesslike. There wasn't any mood of militancy on the part of the speakers nor delegates.

The following day April 20th were the sitting of the various Commissions, and discussion of two items on the agenda viz "THE

STRUGGLE OF LATIN AMERICA AND CARIBBEAN PEOPLES FOR GENUINE ECONOMIC AND POLITICAL INDEPENDENCE FOR PEACE AND AGAINST THE ARMS BUILD UP." AND "WORLDWIDE FOR DISARMAMENT AND DETENTE." These discussion were held in frankness. All findings of the commissions were document and brought forward as resolutions.

On the final day, reports on organisational matter i.e(finance, regional bodies and campaign) were discussed. The work of National Peace Committee were discussed, and suggestions were given as to ways in which the movement can get stronger.

Resolution rom commission, Grenada and other countries were read and adopted.

The sessions ended with an address from Cde Fidel Castro, President of Cuba.

Besides this general report on th. conference, I also took time
to meet with leaders and President of various Peace Committees,
representative of El Salvador, Cayman, Soviet Peace Committee,
U.J.C. and other personel. They are as follows.

RAPHAEL GOU.AIGE: Representative of organisation of solidarity
with the peoples of Africa, Asia and Latin America (OSPAAAL).

A delegation from (OSPAAAL) wants to pay a visit to Grenada on
May 8th. Ambassador Jacob in Cuba will be co-ordinating the
visit. OSPAAAL has proposed doing more solidarity work with G/da.
He also want to carry out an interview with the leadership of
N.J.M. for Tri-Continental Magazines.
As Co-ordinators of W.P.C for Latin America and Caribbean they
want to take on joint initiative with G/da, and hold a conference
sometime next year, on the experience of the Caribbean peoples.

There were also a proposal of English speaking National Peace
Movements in G/da, so that organisational matters in co-ording
the work of the Next Committee, Africa, Asia and Latin America
can be dealth with.

ALBERTO RAMOS: (Int Relations Department and members of FMLN
of El Salvador;
At present seven (7) zones which in El Salvador is under military
and political control of the FMLN. These area is about one-tenth
(1/10) of El Salvador territory..

The Junta troops have never been able to defeat them in that
region, which is mainly in the Northern part of El Salvador.

At present there have been a lull in the fighting, due to the
heavy lost and demoralise state of the Junta troops. Troops are
also being trained by U.S personnel and this will take six (6)
months.

In the city the (FMLN) are facing many problems in moving their
troops. Their fight take the form of blowing up transmission and
power lines, in an effort to halt production. This would affect
foreign exchange and the gov't won't be able to meet the people's
need. One third(1/3) of the country has been put out of production
by these methods. The country lost $3 billion in 2 years. Im-
perialism is giving financial and military assistance to the Junta.
Due to these measures the FMLN is planning a second offensive.
However, their problem is that there are more people, than
weapons.

Diplomatic offensives are also taking place. In Europe against
the Italian Christian Democratic Party which supports the Junta.
they face ab election next year. Venezuela Democratic Party also
supports the Junta. Presure is being brought upon them to cease
their support.

The FMLN doesn't support the move by Socialist
in seeking a political situation.

The reason is the Junta is unpopular and have no support among the masses. A proposal was that the country may be divided in two i.e North and South. The Cde. want G/da to mobilise campaign for their struggle.

They are also requesting that on May 1st, solidarity is shown with the people of El Salvador and firm support for their struggle. They also ask that we call for direct non-intervention of America in El Salvador.

FEROTE MOHAMMED$ (PPP GUYANA) The present issue in Guyana is one concerning the border dispute between Guyana and Venezuela. The Cde. think that Burnham shouldn't have opened up talks again in 1970 with protocol. The point is that the British and the Venezuelan did agree with the border lines in 1962.

It is the feeling that Burnham will use this opportunity to whip up political support, by appealing to the patriotism of the masses. They aslo see it as an attempt by imperialism to leave the question of the border open, so that, it can always be made use of in the future, e.g. if Burnham had to be removed from power and the progressive forces take over.

There is also moves between the Guyanese and Brazilian Gov't to conclude an agreement in the disputed regions.

To sum up, the Cdes, see it as an attempt by Burnham to save the imagine, provocation by Imperialism to push Venezuela to open the issue again, and an overall act to get the progressive orces out of the way.
A BOOK BY Dr. CHEDDIE JAGAN " BORDER CONSPIRACY EXPOSED" deals more with the issue.

The government of Guyana Representative Agnes Kirton, informed me of an invitation sent to the party on a Conference to be held in Guyana from April 30th - May 3rd. The Theme being " TOWARDS THE LIBERATION OF SOUTHERN AFRICA"

The Y.S.M of Guyana also extended an invitation to the N.Y.C inviting them to their congress in May-June. Two members are asked to attend.

HUMBERTO HERNANDES: (Head of U.J.C).

Concretely; The party is offering five(5) scholarships to the N.Y.O to attend their National School in August 1981. Offers have been given for 5 Cdes to attend the International Pioneers Camp to be held from July-August, 1981. One of those places going to a guide.

Two (2) members of the U.J.C will be ComingWhere after the Y.S.M conference held in Guyana. They will exchange organisational experience with the N.Y.C.

An update of youth work was given to Cde . We expressed continuation of correspondence and growing and strengthing relation between both organisations.

..../ Meeting

Meeting of a very brief nature were held with representative of
the following peace committee. Soviet Peace Committee, Bulgaria,
German Democratic Republic, Hungary and the National Committee of
Quebec. All of these express wanting to know G/da and to establish
relations with our peace committee.. The Soviets, Hungaria and
German Peace Committee will be sending materials films and other
sorts of assistance to the G/da peace committee. These relations can
go a very far way.

Dr. Carlton Goodlett and Publisher U.S Peace Council, and a
Canadian representative in a effort to raise funds for the W.P.C
has expressed their desire of organising cultural exchanges with
G/da for this venture. A letter was written expressing this
desire. Cde Whiteman took the opportunity , to establish some sort
of correspondence with the Canadian representative, to get tourist
from Canada to come to G/da.

Other exchanges and update on political situations in countires
such as Afghanistan, Ethiopia, Zimbabwe, Namibia and other region
in Latin America, could have been held but this wasn't possible,
due to the time I had and the fact that we had only one representative present at the conference.

I think that the conference itself was very successful, as far
as representatives and the businesslike and serious discussions
which were held. This was also by the Nat resolution adopted and
the strength and growth of the Nat Committee.

I have benefited and gain some more experience in dealing with
such type of conference. There should have been a bigger dele-
ations which to the conference, so that much more could be achieved.
We were most fully prepared for this world peace conference.

It is important that when G/da is invited on attending any
xonference that all information concerning such conference be
known. We are looked upon by our caribbean, and Latin American
Cde to play a leading role in solidarity support and presenting
papers and positions of economic and political issues.

This was also evident in the number of Cdes who checked me out to
discuss for e.g the latest political situation in G/da etc.. and
also of giving our support on contraversal issues of Guyana.

This was also the case with Cdes from the Socialist world which
checked me out, and want to establish some sort of contact with
us.

We must move quick to get the GRENADA PEACE AND SOLIDARITY
COMMITTEE ESTABLISHED. The sooner the better.

Yours Truly

Swinton Lambert.

Rep. of N.J.M at World Peace
                            c...

Comrades Present:-	Comrades absent:-	
Bernard Coard	Maurice Bishop	) out of the
Selwyn Strachan	Unison Whiteman	) country
Vincent Noel	Kenrick Radix	)
Hudson Austin		
George Louison		

Agenda:-

(1) Beausejour compensation - Report
(2) Maitland issue
(3) Ministry of Education
(4) May Day Programme - a. Content b. TUC Guest
(5) Rizo discussion/ Cuban Technical Assistance
(6) Johnson Chase vehicle
(7) Letter from Ralph Thompson's wife
(8) Robby Robinson/Labour Department

(1) BEAUSEJOUR COMPENSATION - At the request of the Economic Bureau
meeting of April 24th, a report was received from Orgias Campbell
on the Beausejour situation regarding compensation for persons
who have been affected by the placing of RFG's transmitter there.
The report revealed that a total of $10,000 was owing to different
persons. However, the profit made from the sugar cane   is
$2,000. Therefore, the net cost is $8,000.
DECISION - All debts owing to be paid today, with proper receipts
issued.

(2) Maitland has dismissed two workers because they are unionised.
But he has gave Comrade Strachn other reasons for their dismissal.
After discussion with the Minister, he agreed to take them back,
but when they returned, he again dismissed them. Two suggestions
were made, as ways of handling the situation - (1) matter should
be taken to court, (2) strike. However, the DECISION - Comrade
Strachnn to give Maitland 24 hours to take back the workers.

On the general question of workers, it was noted that Woodroffe
of Y. DeLima should be dealt with for firing a worker because
she was pregnant. Also noted, was the case of a beer factory
worker who met in two on-the-job accidents and has apparently
been changed since then, but received no form of compesation -
case being worked on by Comrade Noel. He also reported that
the Beer Factory is planning to lay off some workers because,
they have said that sales have dropped.

(3) MINISTRY OF EDUCATION - Sister Jaqueline Creft, who has been
recently appointed Secretary for Education, has not been giving
that area any attention, has said she is not capable of doing
the job and is not even trying. This has resulted in the Ministry collapsing. This report was given by Comrade Louison, who
himself has been directed to concentrate on the farmers' work
and spend less time in the Ministry. Somebody is urgently needed. DECISION - Comrades to think about it over the next 48 hours
and make suggestions.

(4) MAY DAY PROGRAMME - CONTENT: The programme will be chaired by
Comrade Noel. Solidarity messages will come from the following
unions:-

T.A.W.U.		Jim Wardally
C.I.W.U.	–	Chalkie Ventour
P.G.W.U.	–	Nelson Louison
P.W.U.	–	Simon Charles

Comrade Strachan will speak on the PRG programmes that benefit
workers in particular, on the recent maternity leave violation
case won in court and the Maitland issue (without calling names)
for about 20 minutes. Comrade Coard will speak on the state of
the economy including foreign assistance from the IMF and World
Bank, expand on the points made at the Jeremiah Richardson Day,
the race riots in Britain and the blacks being killed in Chicago.

/...his presentation

His presentatoon should last about 30 minutes.

A T.U.C. Guest here, Blair is to stay at Horse Shoe Bay at the expense of the Ministry of Labour.

Comrade Noel reported that the mobilisation for the May Day is going good - over 600 jerseys sold and there are demands for more..Comrades in charg of the different cells in the P.W.U. and those in C.I.W.U. B.G.W.U. and T.A.W.U. to bring out their membership. The S.W.W.T.U. and the Taxi-Drivers are expected to boycott the event. The President General and Secretary of the T.U.C. are to meet with the latter to try to convince them to attend.

B.G.W.U. to use Rivera grounds for their May Day Party.

Comrade Noel reported that Raymond Redhead attended a seminar for Bank workers in Barbados. He returned reporting that all the bank employees at the seminar have expressed the desire to come to Grenada and are in support of our Revolution. Comrade Noel sighted the need to establish contact with the trade unions in the region.

The labour budget is to be reviewed.

Nigel James will be helping with the accounts of Chester's bar, AGWU, CIWU AND BGWU.

(5) RIZO DISCUSSION/CUBAN TECHNICAL ASSISTANCE - Comrade Strachan reported that Ambassador Rizo has been pressing him for a discussion
on the state of ouf Party and has been "ducking" him until a P.B. decision was taken on the question.
DECISION - Such discussions should take place on a Party-to-Party basis at the appropriate levels of the two parties. This discussion should not take place now, since we are in the process of reorganisation andmmust wait until Sister Isabelle has done an a assessment with us. Comrade Strachan is to convey to Ambassador Rizo, the decision i.e. it is to take place at the appropriate level.
A sister is coming in the middle of May to do ideological development with the Party. She needs accomodation - Comrade Strachan to find out the length of her stay.

(6) JOHNSON CHASE VEHICLE - Johnson Chase has received a land rover from England and is requesting the duty off. Reasons-he has a lot of land and will be using the vehicle to do plenty PFU work.
DECISION - agreed. The request to be sent to the Ministry of Finance and then to cabinet. It must be stated aliso, that the vehicle will be used for militia purposes also and Comrade De Riggs to also sign the letter.

(7)A letter from Ralph Thmpson's wife which was written to Comrade Bishop was read to the meeting. In it she state that Ralph who is now in hospital is extremely ill, should be forgiven for whatever he did and be released. On this , Comrade Coard pointed out that Maureen St. Bernard had also been to see him on the issue. It is speculated that Ralph is suffering from an advanced stage of Syphyllis, which can eventually lead to death.
DECISION - A medical report to be submitted to the P.B. - Comrade's Austin's task to get such a report from the Prison's doctor and the letter should come from Ralph himself.

(8) ROBBY ROBINSON/LABOUR LEPARTMENT - Comrade Strachan wanted to know whether he should pull Robby Robinson into the work now or after the FWU issue is settled. He is anxious to get him back in the work because of the Labour Ministers meeting in Antigua and the ILO conference in Geneva, both coming up soon
DECISION - Robinson to be brought back and sent to Antigua and Philbert to Geneva It was also decided that Robinson should be a S.A.S. AND Philbert a A.S. Comrade Strachan also reported that t o labour inspectors have resigned and two party cadres are n needed to fill the spaces   a
DECISION - SECRETARIAT to compile/ list of allPPotential Applicants and Applicants who are unemployed and their qualification.,
Two comrades are also needed for the Budget Department of Finance, Malcolm is to be placed in the Mi istry of Trade to work with Clement Kirton and Nazim Burke.

                                        Hazel-Ann
                                        RECORDING SECRETARY

50 a

AGENDA

1. Electricity Company
2. Housing
3. Letter to Richard Jacobs
4. G.U.T
5. Secretariat Budget
6. Party Headquarters
7. Union Headquarters
8. C.P.C Conference
9. Carriacou report - Petite Martinique
10. NJAC
11. SL Report - Mario
12. Court of Appeal Judge
13. Proposal form Caldwell
14. John Stockwell
15. Antorio Langdon
16. Roads.

ITEMS ACCOMPLISHED

1. C.P.C Conference
2. Party Headquarters
3. Court of Appeal Judge
4. John Stockwell
5. Secretariat Budget
6. Union Headquarters
7. G.U.T
8. Roads
9. Proposals from Caldwell

C.P.C CONFERENCE

It was reported by Cde. George Louison that the Caribbean Peace Council will be hosting a Conference in the Dome, Grand Anse on May 10th to 14th 1981. Comrade Louison gave the P.B an insight as how the Conference will look like, he mentioned that sixty (60) overseas guests will be attending such a conference. Comrades will come from USSR, Bulgaria, G.D.R, Cardinal Jamaica and other progressive countries. Comrade Mauric asked for an overall theme of the Conference from Cde. Louison.

DECISIONS:- It was decided that Cdes Maurice and George speak at the Conference.

* That a Press Conference be held on Friday 15th - Prime Minister Office - the Conference Room.

* Cde. Ruggles Ferguson to assist in the mobilization network and interview the comrades individually.

TASKS:-

The Secretariat to contact all Applicants, C.M's and M's to be at the Dome on May 10th at 5.30 p.m.

PARTY HEADQUARTERS:-

After broad discussions in relation to a new Party Headquarter the P.B came up to the needs of such a headquarters and its location Some of the needs that were suggested are as follows.-

(1) Twelve individual offices

2. Two offices that con hold 6 people and six desks
3. An auditorium which can accommodate 500 people and 4 class rooms.
4. A receptionist office
5. Library and documentation centre.
6. Production area in regards to hold printing press, dark room.
7. Four bedrooms in the headquarters.
8. Living quarters for any personnel - i.e senior visitors
9. A reading room
10. A kitchen, cafetaria, a small
11. A radio transmitter room
12. Two secrete rooms
13. A room for Central Committee members where 50 could sit.
14. Room for Political Bureau
15. A bunker
16. Recreation -, table tennis, gymasium, weight lifting etc.
17. Six committee rooms.

The suggested location for the headquarters as brought forwa by the P.B - Mt. Royal. It was agreed that the area is a fantast spot, and should be of tight security.

JOHN STOCKWELL

It was brought to the attention of P.B by a written letter fr Cde. Stockwell to reside in Grenada. The matter was taken up and it was decided for the Cde. to come for at least 6 months wit his family. Cde. Maurice said that Sister Dessima will handle the tickets up in Washington. It was stated that a detailed Code should be sent to N.Y and then N.Y send it to Sister Dessima for preparing the necessary documents.

SECRETARIAT BUDGET

A budget made up by the Secretariat was presented to the P.B, it was given full thought by the comrades and agreed to expand it by another$50,000. A number of concrete areas were looked at re its expansion.

UNION HEADQUARTERS

Cde. Vincent Noel brought to the attention of the P.B of the small space in the Union Office. Cde. Coard and other members of the P.B gave the comrade concrete ideas in getting another building. Comrade Maurice said that Cde Vince should get in contact with Mr. Dean Whiteman re the building above the telephone Company as he had agreed to purchase it.

G.U.T.

Comrade George Louison reported on a seminar which was scheduled for for May 7th at Bucage St. John's. He said that 60 comrades are expected to attend, he said that it is for mainly the left elements in the Union.

ROADS

Comrade Selwyn reported that the roads throughout the country are in bad condition. He said that Lanse Aux Epines area is terrible and this will cause us to loose plenty of tourists. The comrade stated thathe has received 400 drums of bitumen and that 250 drums will be used for the Munich and Byelands area, and theother 150 will be used on the St. George's road. It was suggested by the P.B that deep drainage be done and a total road plan for the country should be set up to know exactly what is

50-2

needed to upgrade the system.   Comrades suggested that a team of engineers should be got to look into the roads and a supervision team to over look the project.

CALDWELL TAYLOR PROPOSAL

A letter came from Cde. Caldwell Taylor re Stone Brook University for students who are interested in doing a field Study Work Campaign. The I.E had a close look at the proposal and came up to some vital points:-

(1)   Find out from the Cde the cost

(2)   Get the full nature of the field work

(3)   Cirriculum Vitae

The meeting adjurned at 12.30 p.m.

Hazel-Ann & Justin
RECORDING SECRETARIES

Comrades present:-   Absent:-

   Maurice Bishop   Kenrick Radix - out of the country
   Bernard Coard
   Selwyn Strachan   50 b
   George Louison
   Vincent Noel
   Hudson Austin
   Unison Whiteman

Agenda:-

(1) Telephone Company
(2) Electricity Company
(3) Comrade Coard s visit to Lybia and Iraq after Gabon
(4) CFTC Oil Exploration Report
(5) Housing
(6) Letter to Richard Jacob
(7) FWU - a. Elections, b. negotiations
(8) Meeting with the S.W.W.T.U.
(9) G.U.T.
(10) Mongolian Party Congress
(11) Martinique and Gaudeloupe activities
(12) Secretariat's Budget
(13) Union Headquarters
(14) Party Headquarters
(15) CPC Conference
(16) Carriacou report - Petite Martinique
(17) NJAC
(18) Venezuela meeting - a. Group of 77 b. Movement for Socialism
(19) SI Report
(20) Proposal from Cladwell
(21) Court of Appeal Judge
(22) John Stockwell
(23) Antonio Langdon
(24) Roads

Before the officail start of the meeting, Comrade Coard gave Comrades a
brief report on the situation with the IMF regarding the request for a
loan from them. The programme has been redrafted and the money can be
received, with a repayment period of 3 - 5 years. Decision - the period
for repayment is too short and should be 9 - 10 years instead. The IMF
has to been informed.

(1) TELEPHONE COMPANY -These following persons are to attend Cabinet
   meeting this afternoon to discuss the offer from the GDR for our
   telephone system; Terry Moore, James Lashley, ? Lashley, ?
   O'Brien and Clement Kirton.

(2) VISITS TO LYBIA AND IRAQ - Requests are to go by two telexes,
   through our appropriate embassies to Lybia and Iraq, requesting
   that discussions be held between our two countries to discuss
   "matters of great concern to Grenada". These talks should take place
   place at the highest possible level. The visit to Lybia will be
   from 24th - 26th May with a request to them for $75M (US). Iraq
   should be visited if the request to Lybia has not been met,
   from 27th - 29th May.

(3) VENEZUELA MEETING - The Group of 77 is sponsoring a conference on
   Economic Co-operation Between Developing Countries. Officials
   are to attend from 13th - 16th May and a Minister from 17th -
   19th May. Merle Collins and Mathew Williams will attend as officials and Cladwell will attend as the Ministerial representative.
   b. The Movement for Socialsim has sent an invitation to the
   ComradeLeader to   speak on the topic "The New Paty To Socialism In The Caribbean". Decision - It will be tactically incorrect to do so right now given our present relations with
   the Venezuelan Government and the potential for receiving other

benefits from them.

(4) CFTC OIL EXPLORATION REPORT - Comrade Coard reported that the company that has done the oil exploration here have disclosed that there might be some oil somewhere between Grenada and Venezuela. Hence the importance of wooing the Venezuelan Government and building a popular base with them.

(5) MONGOLIAN PARTY CONGRESS - This is to be the 25th - 28th May. Comrade Austin will attend the Congress. He will carry Comrade Fraser with him to help seek military and other assistance in the countries including the U.S.S.R. and Vietnam. Both comrades Austin and Fraser are to speak to Gloria Payne, Clement Kirton and or Nazim Burke to get a full briefing on the projects before leaving. Among the projects to be discussed on the trip are the International Airport and the Party's headquarters. Comrade Austin should set up meetings with the foreign and military ministries in the different countries and should carry with him (a) Comrade Bishop's address at the SI Conference and (b) Comrade Noel's address while in the GDR last year.

(6) MARTINIQUE AND GUADELOUPE ACTIVITIES - The Communist Parties of these countries are holding some activities in the middle of May. Comrades Noel and Burke to attend and to particularly "tie up" the economic aspect of things in case of a economic blockade against us. Comrade Noel is to get the specific dates and more information on the activities and report to Economic Bureau meeting of Friday, 8th May.

(7) P.W.U. - A. Elections - This could be anytime now ant therefore the OC has formed a PWU Sub-Committee: President - Nazim Burke, Vice President - Ian Jacobs. The work should start immediately with worker education courses. The question of elections should not be raised with them until the night before the elections. If the elections clash with the visit to Guadeloupe and Martinique, then Comrade Burke should not go. Ian Jacobs should be brought on to the Party's Workers Committee. B. Negotiations - they should not be left to Larry Wilson alone. A letter should be sent to the Union explaining that our offer still stands and that letters will be withdrawn after the entire agreement is signed.

(8) A HUNGARIAN PROFESSOR - is presently here - the programme for him has been inadequate. Comrade Coard reported that he wants to do a demonstration farm using 25 acres including a dam. The Hungarian Professor also said that they can send two experts here for a period of 3 - 6 months, but everything must be ready for them. The La Sagesse Farm House is to be used to accomodate them and two rooms need to be air-conditioned. When the experts can come will depend on when the equiptment from the Airport site will be available. Comrade Whiteman is to check this out.

Comrade Coard reported that the Hungarian revealed that 2.2 lbs. of hybrid tomato seeds is worth $1,000 (US) on the world market. He also stated his concern about farmers using the wrong fertilizers on our soil. It means that the farmers need to be educated on the proper fertilisers to be used.

(9) S.W.W.T.U. MEETING - Comrades Bishop and Strachan are to meet with the S.W.W.T.U. tommorrow (May 7th) The Agenda is as follows:-

    1. Off-loading of Soviet and Cuban ships
    2. PRG's attitude to the Union
    3. Allegations against certain executive members
    4. Unions attitude to the PRG

IS The first three items were suggested by the Union.

The meeting was then adjourned to continue at 8.00 p.m.

MINUTES OF POLITICAL BUREAU MEETING ON
WEDNESDAY, 13TH MAY, 1981
_____

Comrades present:-   Comrades absent:-

Maurice Bishop   Bernard Coard - away
Selwyn Strachan   Unison Whiteman - sick
Vincent Noël
Hudson Austin   51
Kenrick Radix
George Louison

AGENDA:-

1. New York propaganda   5. Dock Workers
2. Walter Rodney   6. Invitations from the .U.S.S.RR.
3. Isabelle   7. Regina Taylor
4. Airport Committee   8. Drivers

(1) NEW YORK PROPAGANDA - Cde. Owusu who came to the meeting specifi-
     cally on this question reported that Dave Maresh of CBS televi-
     sion in the United States and was here for the Airport Rally,
has now returned to the U.S. and has been on a wicked, massive propaganda campaign against Grenada. Before coming, Maresh had said
that he was impressed with the social and economic developments of
Grenada.
     While he was here he was picked up by the Police, but only
spent two, three hours in custody.. Now he has returned home and has
a thrice-weekly TV programme called "Prisoner In A Police State".
This programme comes on at the peak television viewing hours; 6.00
p.m. and 11.00 p.m.
                    . The programme according to Cde. Owusu has been
on the defensive and has been advertised in the entire media for the
past three weeks. He has also made allegations of torture of police
prisoner and about while in custody. He also raised the issue of
Grenada being a one-party state and that of the Torchlight. In general, the CBS programme has been on the defensive and apart from the
television, the attacks have been coming from both the radio and the
press. A half/one hour programme increases according on Saturday and
they   also plan to feature Grenadians hiding their faces to say
what's happening here.

DECISION-Cde. Radix to leave for New York tommorrow (May 14th) to
combat the propaganda. Among other things, Comrades felt that a 5,
10, or 15 minute video tape using appropriate clips from the Airport
rally with Dave Maresh and the other US press men be compiled for
Cde. Radix to leave with. He was also given some political lines to
take on the issue, one of them being that he should respond to their
local affairs, e.g. the killing of balcks in Atlanta. Cde. Radix
is to carry information regarding detainees, pointing out that of
all the people picked up during the first six weeks of the Revolution, only 14 are left in custody. Apart from Cde. Radix's visit,
a demonstration is being paanned for New York on Saturday, 16th
and Cde. Radix will be given TV time on CBS to respond to the propaganda. While he is in the U.S., he is also to take the opportunity to meet with the state department, since he is still accredited as our Ambassador to the U.S.

(2) WALTER RODNEY - Cde. Bishop reported that in a telephone con-
     versation with Ricky Singh, the latter pointed out that June
13th will mark the first anniversary of Walter Rodney's assa-
sination. He wanted to know if the Party was doing anything in
this regard. DECISION - The Secretariat to contact Swinton
Lambert and ask him to let the Peace Council put out a statement on that day.

(3) ISABELLE - Cde. Bishop reported that Cde. Coard had spoken to
     Isabelle from the Cuban Federation of Women, who has been here
for a while assisting the NWO. He had hinted to her that we
want her to stay longer to assist the NYO and suggested that

                    /2...both cdes. Bishop

both Comrades Bishop and Strachan speak to her on this also.
Cde. Bishop disclosed that Cde. Fidel had told Isabelle she
should stay here as long as Cde. Bishop requested her to do
so. However, she has been hinting that what she think will
happen is that Cde. Castro will call her back and send a
youth representative to assist NYO. Cde. Bishop will meet
with Isabelle this afternoon.

(3) AIRPORT COMMITTEE - Cde. Bishop stated that the drafting
committee of the airport committee has submitted a report to
him. This report stated that the committee can sell the project, but will need some details and recommended the following:-

4.1 drawings of he project to be placed in show windows
islandwide
4.2 national lottery
4.3 tax-free bonds
4.4 charts and figures of expenditure and work done
4.5 telefund system - people calling in on radio to pledge
money
4.6 compensation for calliste residents who have been re-
housed
4.7 night lighting
4.8 name of the contractors and where they are from
4.9 information of the infrastructure
4.10 stand by generator plant(s)
4.11 expansion and diversification of tourism
4.12 visits abroad to sell the project
4.13 all progress to be known by the committee
4.14 PRG to ask the Canadian Government to help build the
terminal
4.15 getting all the requirements needed for landing here
e.g. licence, fees, etc.
4.16 representation from the taximen union on the committee
4.17 public kept up to date - information committee to get
radio time
4.18 competition to name the Airport
4.19 NYO to help form ADC's islandwide
4.20 committee wants a guided tour of the Airport

Comrades agreed on the above suggestions, xexcept Nos. 2, 11,
and 17. In the case of No. 2 - that of the national lottery -
it was decided that the committee should prepare a more detailed plan, consider a bingo instead and this to be submitted by them to Cabinet for approval. On no. 11 - the expansion and diversification of tourism - same as No. 2. And
No. 17 - the public being kept tp to date - the committee
should meet with Cde. McBarnette of RFG to discuss the idea
and then report to Cabinet.

The agenda for the Airport Committee meeting at 3.00 p.m.
is set as follows:-

1. Recommendations
2. Structure of the committee
3. Regularity of meetings
4. Assignment of tasks
5. Next meeting

(5) DOCK WORKERS - The contract which was to be drafted by Cde.
Noel some two weeks ago, still has not been completed. This
proposed contract is to let BGWU be the gagent for MNIB. Cde.
Coard had already spoken to Cde. Rizo about contacting the
Cuban ships and Cde. Noel is to follow up on this by contact-
ing Cde. Rizo.

(6) INVITATIONS FROM THE U.S.S.R. - They have sent to sets of invitations to the Central Committee. The first invites five

3/...CC members to visit

51 - 2

CC members to visit the Soviet Union for a period of rest
and recreation lasting one month and another five to come
for a period of 18 days for a working visit and also to
familiarize themse,ves with that country. These two sets
of invitations will be discussed at the CC meeting for
this p.m.

(7) REGINA TAYLOR - Cde. Louison reported that in a conversation
with Regina Taylor she stated that there is a great potential
for her to get funds for the youth, CPE and other programmes.
In fact, she has already gotten some. But in order to be able
to do so at the fullest, she must not be working with Government because these agnecies are Non-Governmental Organisations
that do not give money to Governments. DECISION - Sister
Taylor should be put in an "independent" office with a Secre-
tary/Typist, but be accountable to Cde. Coard.

Cde. Louison
is to contact Cde. Miles on the formation of ART (Agency for
Rural Transformation) or THRUST (Through U Service and Transformation). This will be the department Sister Regina will
be employed with.

(8) DRIVERS - Cde. Bishop disclosed that 50 persons are needed
as soon as possible to be trained to be car, truck and
jeep drivers.

OTHER BUSINESS:-

- Aerial survey; Cde. Austin to check Joe Campbell on what
  facilities he has do do the aerial survey of country.
- Carnival plans are on the way
- Certain mistakes were made in the organisation of hthe
  CPC conference:-
                    (1) leaving Judy in charge and
                    (2) neglecting to invite the CCC
                    (3) weak or no mibilisation at all
                        for Sunday's opening.
- Cdes. Bishop and Louison are to meet with the executive
  members of the Christian Peace Council.

                                    Hazel-Ann
                                    RECORDING SECRETARY

                                                        51 - 3

MINUTES OF POLITICAL BUREAU MEETING ON

~~MINUTES OF POLITICAL BUREAU MEETING ON~~

WEDNESDAY, 20TH MAY, 1981

Comrades present:-

Maurice Bishop - Chariman
Selwyn Strachan
Unison Whiteman
George Louison
Vincent Noel

Comrades absent:-
Bernard Coard)
Kenrick Radix) all out
Hudson Austin) of the
country

Agenda:-

1. The Chruch
2. Dr. Gonsalles
3. Cato of St. Vincent
4. Barbados report
5. P.W.U.

6. Electricity
7. Carriacou report
8. S.W.W.U. situation
9. African Liberation Day
10. Ian Cheret

(1) THE CHURCH - Cde. Louison led off the discussion here
stating that four church events have taken place in the
past week here:- (1) The CPC Conference, (2) Catholic
Teachers Annual Convention, (3) CYC Annual Convention,
(4) CADEC Conference. He reported that Bishop Charles
raised the issue of two Prime Ministers with him on Friday last, saying that he hopes nobody is peeved about
him having made that statement. Cde. Louison responded
by saying that as far as we know, there is only one
Prime Minister here and that if there is claim about
another one, we will have to look for his power base.

He also stated that at the Catholic Teachers Convention,
last Friday, he (Cde. Louison) spoke of the two inter-
pretations   Christian Education can have; that being
part of the theme.

At Sunday's CYC Convention - the Nicaraguan Priest who
was here for the CPC Conference gave a very good speech
that went down very well. Bishop Charles was obviously
extremely angered and responded by himself asking the
priest questions, which is very unusual for that forum.
He even went so far as to ask the crowd questions such
as, "Do you want to see your priests in the Militia?"
Cde. Louison stated that Bishop Charles was "put under
manners" by the thunderous applause the Nicaraguan
priest received. The CYC people who spoke also, were
very good.

CADEC CONFERENCE - Cde. Louison reported here too. He
disclosed that Bishop Charles was very low-keyed and
defensive in his presentation. David Mitchell, he said
also gave a good speech and the general mood there was
very good and warm. Cde. Louison's speech also went
down good. He touched on a number of points including; (a) CADEC in development in the past ten years and
that the conditions that existed then still exist now,
(b) the achievements of the Revolution are similar to
the work they are trying to do in terms of the social
and economic programmes, (c) the regional and interna-

2/...tional economic and

tional economic and peace situation, (d) that they
as church people, recognising the struggle to form
CADEC must not be side-tracked in their efforts.

It was suggested that Peggy Nesfiedl should work with
the CADEC people presently here to show them around.

David Mitchell also made a presentation ant the CADEC
Conference. In it he spoke of the importance of the
balck power struggle in the early 70's, the present
day World situation, that CADEC must look at the social
context in which developments are taking place, detente, and developing strategies.

Cde. Bishop then reported on a meeting he had with
Rev. Lett of the CCC from Antigua on Sunday morning
last. The latter wants;to know what is happening in
Grenada and of our relations with the Chruch. Cde.
Biship told him that there is no other Bishop or
hedd of Church in Grenada that could have made such
a statment as Bishop Charles made. He also told him
that what Charles was implying when he made the
statement about there being two Prime Minister -
one forthe Chruch and one for the State - and in
another chruch other than Catholic, and with other
denominations present, is that his church is the ·
real chruch and all others should join it.

Rev. Lett disclosed to Cde. Bishop that the progressive chruch in the region is under serious pressure
in that there is a great chance of the reactionaries
taking power in the upcoming elections for the CCC.
As. a result, he expressed the view that Grenada
can not and would not just sit down and not respond
any counter-revolutionary activity from the Church.
He pointed out to Rev. Lett that they would have to
carry the struggle themselves and expose Bishop
Charles if necessary. What he suggested is that Rev.
Lett should talk to Bishop Charles himself.

Rev. Lett disclosed that it is hard to dispell all
the theology picked up during one's school days regarding the concept of "pie in the sky". He also
made a distinction between what he called "atheistic
communism and just plain communism.

The General observation was made that the Church has
decided to make a major thrust against the Revolution
again and that hthey are in close contact with the
backward Church teachers.

The following points were noted:-
(a) Sydney Charles' clandestine meeting with the
    Venezuelan OAS Ambassador, Cardozo.
(b) Chalres'speech at the CPC Ecumenical Service
    (at which he made the statements about PRA
    and PRAY, two P.M.'s, etc.)
(c) meeting with Regina Taylor, calling the

3/...priests at the

priests at the CPC Conference leftists and querying
the decision to hold the Conference here and not in
Ecuador as was suggested.
(d) meeting with Phil Wheaton of EPICA
(e) meetings with the CPC crowd (some of them)
(f) his interview (the only one) on the recent CBS
    TV Station, which viciously attacks the Revolu-
    tion.
(g) his three encounters with Cde. Louison at dif-
    ferent occasions during the last week.

Cde. Strachan flet that the time had comw when Bishop
Charles should be called in andgiven a strong warning.

Cde. Whiteman expressed the view and Comrades agreed
that the present problems being experience with the
Chruch are a result of the Party's negligence in c
forming a committee for that specific purpose. In
this regard, Comrades are to start looking for such
possible people.

Here, Cde. Louison reported that he met with the Cuban comrade who is in charge of regilious affairs in
the PCC -he was here for the CPC Conference. He spoke
of the development of the Party's work in the Chruch
and said that a CC member is in charge of that area
of work.

Comrade Bishop also disclosee that because of Cde.
Louison's presentations, he has been the target for
criticisms from both Fathers Bernard and Petcr.

In light of all the above, the following decisions
were taken:-

A. The following taped speeches should be transcribed,
   to be edited by Cde.Louison:-

   i.   Cde. Bishop's speech at the Opening of
        the CPC Conference   - 10th May
   ii. Costa Rican priest at the opening of
        the CPC Conference   - 10th May
   iii. The Soviet priest at the opening
        of the CPC Conference   - 10th May
   iv. Cde. Louison at the CPC Conference   - 12th May
   v.   Bishop Charles at the CPC Ecumeni-
        cal Service   - 14th May
   vi. Cde. Louison at the Catholic Teachers
        Annual Convention   - 15th May -
   vii. Cde. Louison at the CYC Annual Con-
        vention   - 17th May
   viii. Nicaraguan priest at the CYC Annual
        Convention   - 17th May
   ix. Cde. Louison at the CADEC Conference-   19th May

B. The following package was also agreed upon:-
   i.   Cde. Bishop to speak to Fr. Martin(he being
        the most progressive of the priests).
   ii. Cde. Whiteman to speak to Lucky Bernard
        (Those two discussions will center around
        the present situation with the Chruch's re-
        lation with the PRG - a "Lett-type discus-
        sion".)
   iii. A letter to the F.W.I. (decided upon after
        much discussion)
   iv. identify the people in the Roman Catholic

                    4/...Chrurch Executive Council

... ...ve Council and get them to raise
... ...ce, Cde. Louison is to check Sis. Judy
on th... ... report by Friday, 22nd.
    v. Cde. Vince to check the Presbyterian pirest(?)
  vi. Go above Bishop Charles and let somebody speak
      to the person above him who will them probably
      speak to Bishop Charles himself.

There was a very long. intense discussion on the question
of religion generally, especially among Cdes. Bishop,
Strachan and Louison. This consumed a great portion of
the time. The view was expressed that it should be a
PB and CC agenda item.

Also taking up much discussion was the question as to
where the middle class was now in terms of support for
the Revolution. Some comrades felt that presently the
middle class was showing firm support for the Revolution, while others felt that this was not the case -
that in fact, that strata was moving away from the Revolution. Comrades also questioned the position regarding national unity at this time.

Comrade Louison is to talk to Mrs. Byer. She was requesting that either a group of chruch people go to
Cuba to look at the question of the Chruch there, or
that a group from Cuba comes here. It was decided
that the latter would be the better model and Cde.
Louison is to try to get her to agree to it.

(2) The Dr. Gonsalles issue was discussed.

(3) P.W.U. - Cde. Noel reported he held a meeting
with the PWU Cell. He said that it seems that elections will be next week and that the cell can
bring out about 80 people as opposed to 230/250
by the Union. He was suggesting that if an announcement could be made regarding the increased
salaries, the turnout would be more. He wondered
whether a clear announcement in this regard could
not be made about this between now and Monday.

Cde. Bishop explained that this would be difficult,
because of certain problems and that the issue was
due to be discussed this afternoon at Cabinet meeting.

(4) ELECTRICITY - Cde. Strachan disclosed that Salfarie
of the G.E.S. called him yesterday morning, stating
that there is a crisis in the company. The crisis
is that they chly have two days supply of fuel in
storage and that the boat is ue to pass here during
that time. However, ESSO has threatend to let them
by-pass Grenada unless they are paid the $478,000
owing them. He also said that the Company has not
been able to collect their money because no bills
have been issue, which is a result of the NCR
machine not functioning.

    G.E.S. was told that they should ask for a 60-day

5/...instead of a

instead of a 30-day line of credit. This they
have done, but ESSO has refused to agree.

Cde. Strachan stated that he told Salfari that
Taylor should berung up and told explicityly that
he must pau off his debts.

Cde. Bishop suggested that Cde. Strachan call
him in and speak to him about the money from
Taylor.

OTHER THINGS:-

- The Hermitage/Tivoli area is "on the biil" again a
  and Cde. Bishop said that he had received reports
  saying that there was a "jump-Up" in the streets
  there last night.
- there will be the launching of a Party in June,
  "come hell or high water".
- Stanley Roberts has been saying since April, that
  when June comes, "they go see".
- The Lybian Chagee D'ffairs says that he has received information saying that America plans to
  move decisively on us in the next three months -
  to get us out of poer in that time.
- all this must be linked and co-ordinated.

                    Hazel-Ann
                    RECORDING SECRETARY

MINUTES OF POLITICAL BUREAU MEETING HELD ON
WEDNESDAY, 27TH MAY,
1981

Comrades present:-   Comrades absent:-

Maurice Bishop   Bernard Coard
Selwyn Strachan   Hudson Austin
Unison Whiteman
Vincent Noel - late   5 3
Kenrick Radix
George Louison

AGENDA:-

(1) GRENLEC
(2) Agricultural Sub-Division Law
(3) GCNA Account
(4) Comrade Radix's report
(5) Barbados Report/Trinidad trip
(6) African Liberation Day delegates

Before starting the agenda, the decisions of the last PB
meeting were "looked through" to see whether they were implemented and the Secretariat was told to keep check RFG
to ensure that the tapes get done. On decision Bi., Cde.
Bishop did not speak with Fr. Martin, Bii., Cde. Whiteman
did not speak to Lucky Bernard as the latter is out of the
country, Biii., the letter to FWI was done, Biv., Cde.
Louison leaves for Trinidad this afternoon.
                                        Cde. Louison
spoke to Sister Judy, but she was not sure as to the
members on the R.C. church council and she is to try to
get the information and contact Cde. Louison. However,
she did confirm that the Bishop personally chosses the
people who are to be Council members.
                                        Cde. Radix said that
in spealing to his mother, she had the same to say about
the R.C.Chirch Council - she said that democracy is dying
in there.

(1) GRENLEC - Barclays Bank will send a letter, saying
that they will grant GES a loan of $400,000 if Cde. Bishop
signs the letter, thus taking on the personal undertaking
to see that the loan is repaid. Cde. Bishop asked Mr.
Commission to add "or the Minister he designates" to the
letter. This was agreed upon and Cde. Strachan signed
the letter, thus making the money available to GES. It
is to be repaid by September, 31st, 1981.

It was noted that somebody from Cuba will be arriving here
on Friday to look at the machinery and make recommendations,
that Trevor Farrel should do a economic survey of the company and that we should look for alternative sources of
fuel - GES has 8,000 customers.

Cde. Bullen, thenew Manager of GRENLEC gave the Political
Bureau a idea as to what is being done. He said that the
Board of Directors of the company met yesterday (May 26th)
and made some decisions:-

        a. to pay ESSO thebalance and work out with
           Tony Joseph an arrangement for the future,
        b. they have sdt up a committee to look at

                2/...the cash flow situation.

the cash flow situation.

    c. they are requesting a loan of $960,000 from the CDB
       to do a complete overhaul of the machines and to buy
       new ones. In this regard, he suggested that Cde.
       Bishop speak to Willam Demas
    d. considering employing 10 persons temporarily to
       write out the outstanding bills
    e. Pursoo to give a report on the generating plant and
       the present supply of spare parts
    f. the accountant (Salfarli) to give a report on the
       company's fixed assests, cash projection for the
       next 6 months and expenditure.

It was disclosed that GES collects about $700,000 -
$800,000 monthly.

Cde. Bullen also said that the main problem now is the cash
flow which has been affected by the NCR machines which have
been non-functional for some time. Consequently, bills are
6 weeks old. In this regard, Cuba might be willing to lend,
give or sell us such a machine. Cde. Bullen is to get the
specifics of the present NCR machine, inform Ashley Taylor
who will then contact Richard Jacobs to give Sister Coard,
presently in Cuba to see if it is available there. However, thefollowing people all versed in computers, will
be checked to see what other possibilities are open;
Boson Radix, Errol Coard and Byran Campbell. There is
also a computer at the Ministry of Planning, which was
given to us as a gift from David Wellington, that is to
be checked for possible use.

Mario Bullen and Fennis Augustine to be telephoned on obtaining spare parts.

The new Manager disclosed that under Rodney Beorge's contract, he received $36,000 yearly, a house, car and $1,000
entertainment allowance. Rodney George is also liable to
get paid for three months after the termination of his
services. The end of May will be the end of the three
months.

Comrades felt that the "surplus" from Rodney George's contract should be adjusted appropriately.

Comrade Bullen also disclosed that CDC is paid a Management fee and a Commission fee which runs into thousands
of dollars. This money comes from GES.

Twoletters are to be sent by Angus Smith, as Acting Per-
mament Secretary in the Ministry of Finance to CDC and
GRENLEC, outlining Government's position.

Comrades suggested that some propaganda be done to persuade customers to pay their bills and that a pamphlet be
done which can be used for house to house, outlining the
present situation in GRENLEC. Cde. Whiteman suggested
that Cde. St. Bernard write the pamphlet and said that he
would inform him at CC meeting later that day.
It was also agreed that the 1960 Law on GES be repealed.

(2) AGRICULTURAL SUB-DIVISION LAW - A law has been drafted
to generally bring the land "under manners". It is called

            3/...the LAND DEVELOPMENT

the LAND DEVELOPMENT AND UTILISATION LAW. It is based
on examples from countries like Jamaica and St. Kitts.
It allows for the Land Commission to declare certain
lands, agricultural and iddle and requires for a development plan for that land. It also makes it legal for
the transfer of the land title to Government and compensation later.

Cde. Radix has been given the draft
which was done by Miles Fitzpatrick to be studied and
for him to report to Economic Bureau on Friday 29th
May. Cde. Raidx is also to check Miles Fitzpatrick on
the purchsed of a house in St. Paul's going for
$200,000.

(3) GCNA ACCOUNTS - Cde. Whiteman reported that there are
reported irregularities in the GCNA account and that some
½ million lbs. of nutmeg is allegedly missing from the
Grenville Nutmeg Pool. He felt that this should be discussed at CC level, but it was decided that it will be discussed at Economic Bureau meeting on Friday 29th May.

(4) COMRADE RADIX'S REPORT - Cde. Radix reported on his tr
trip to the U.S. which was mainly to beat back the adverse
propaganda that was being spread up there, through the
television programme on CBS, done by Dave Maresh.

He said
that a programme on WIIB Radio Station, organised to beat
back the propaganda that was supposed to be ½ hour, ended
up being 1½ hrs. During the radio programme, there was
only one caller who supported Dave Maresh.

Comrade Radix
said that about 5 meetings were held to mobilise people
for the demonstration against the CBS programme. The demonstration did come off and was very good with about
150 persons participating. Most of this number were
middle aged people, including some whites. He did not
take part.

He said no equal time was allowed on CBS and
that lawyers are looking in the programme for possible
chrges of libel.

When he went oto Washington, he held a
"get together" at Sister Williams' house where people from
the Black United Front and Friends of Grenada were present.

Cde. Raidx said that in New York, he held a Press Conference with some 35 pressmen, including some from the
Caribbean and CBC. He and Sister Williams attended the
Conference of Black Journalists. Cde. Raidx brought
greetings from Tony Monteo.

Cde. Radix reported that he
met with Robert Mann, Director of The Caribbean Section
of the State Department. They have admitted that they
interferred in the Airport/IMF issue. They also slipped
out the fact they they want to finance an independent
newspaper here and wanted to know if we have given Cuba
permission to use the Airport as a military base. Re-
gardingto their acceptance of our US Ambassador, they
said that the matter is still iunder consideration and
that we will hear from them, but they could not say
what the decision will be. Cde. Radix also raised with
them the fact that President Reagan has not replied to

4/...P.M. Bishop's

P.M. Bishop's letter. They replied that a verbal reply
was given by their representative in Barbados. Cde. Radix told them that he did not have any knowledge of
this. The State Department expressed disappointment that
we had given publicity to the letter, without waiting
for a reply. Cde. Radix protested their interference in
the Airport/IMF issue and they said they saw it as legitimate. They also said that they are still formulating
their policy towards Grenada. They also raised the
questions of election and the press.

Cde. Radix reported
that the BUF is gaining in prestige and that the Black
Political Party is having their conference in August and
they want somebody from the Party to attend it. He said
that they were able to mobilise 45,000 people for the anti-
war march that took place in Washington. He said also that
the 7th Pan African Congress organisers want to hold the
Congress here and that they are setting up a Steering Comi-
ttee with people responsible for different areas. He also
stated that there is a conference coming up soon to be
held in Paris, to press for Namibia's independence.

Cde.
Radix also said that he met Baseo who claims to know a
former CIA man. Baseo says that he discovered that a decision was made to bring down the PRG. He also felt that
we should try to form some support in the churches and
that he will soon be seeing Archbishop Pantin who he
described as being simplified.

Baseo wants permission
to write on Grenada, would also like to seek Kennedy
Budhlall and wants to know if anybody will be able to
see him if he comes here.

Here, Cde. Bishop analysed that
Baseo is trying to get back into the West Indian community
and is seeking to use Grenada for that purpose. He also
made the following points:-

- Bill Schaap and Ellen Ray send their greetings.
- Cde. Burke said he send down a telex to Cde. Louison
  about some students and 28 teachers who want to come he
  here to help for a while,
- Cde. Taylor should move from Manhattan to Brooklyn in
  order to do more community work
- Cde. Burke is also not doing enough community work
  and somebody is needed to do that
- Samorie is to send down his proposed programme
- The Grenada Friendship Society is to be re-launched
  on June 19th
- the NY mission has put together a March 13th Programme
- the Rally that was held in NY had about 250 persons

Cde. Radix ended his report by suggesting that for future
anniversaries of the Revolution, different comrades should
go to different places to hold celebrations, e.g. North
America, London, Europe and the Caribbean.

Cde. Louison said that Ricky Parris of Barbados wants us
to print their minimum programme. Decision - it can be
done once FWI has the facilities.

Hazel-Ann
RECORDING SECRETARY

MINUTES OF POLITICAL BUREAU MEETING HELD ON
WEDNESDAY, 3RD JUNE, 1981

Comrades present:-

Maurice Bishop
Selwyn Strachan
Kenrick Radix
George Louison
Unison Whiteman
Vincent Noel

Comrades absent:

Bernard Coard)
Hudson Austin) away

5-1

AGENDA:-

(1) Detention Tribunal
(2) OECS
(3) E M A Welsh
(4) June 19th
(5) Grace James
(6) Spare parts from South Korea
(7) PWU/ILO Conference
(8) Sonny Mark's phone call
(9) Foreign Ministers' Conference
(10) Lybia/USSR Ambassador
(11) Letter from Richard Jacobs
(12) Security
(13) Lybian delegation
(14) Ashley Wills/Russel
(15) Venezuela fuel
(16) Response to CPS
(17) CC assessment weekend

(1) DETENTION TRIBUNAL - Cde. Radix has been assigned the task of getting three new names to replace those presently on the Tribunal.

(2) ORGANISATION OF EASTERN CARIBBEAN STATES - Cde. Bishop said that the signing of the Treaty is to take place next week, but that there are some articles in it that he is not pleased with, eg. Article 8. The decision - the topic will be discussed at Cabinet meeting that afternoon.

(3) WELSH - Cde. Radix stated that E M A Welsh had resigned, but had later withdrawn his resignation. Decision - Welsh is to be transferred to the National Secretariat under Kurt Strachan to do organising and protocol work.

(4) GRACE JAMES - Cde. Radix told the P.B. of Grace James' connection with the rastas. A decision was already taken on this issue - i.e. that she should be fired from her present job. Cde. McBarnette was told to check on it and ensure that it is done.

(5) JUNE 19TH - That day is now called HECKES DAY instead of BUTLER/STRACHAN DAY. A Propaganda Plan and a draft pamphlet were sumbitted by Cde. McBarnette. The Propaganda Plan dealt with ways of encouraging the masses to come out to the Rally - getting rid of the fear left from the bomb blast last year. Both the Plan and the pamphlet were accepted by the Bureau with minor changes.

2/...The pamphlet will

The pamphlet will be published by Friday, 5th June. They were submitted to the P.B. on the O.C.'s suggestion. A draft letter to the T.U.C. was also accepted.

(6) SPARE PARTS FROM SOUTH KOREA - Cde. Whiteman disclosed that spare parts are needed for some tractors and that they are only available from South Korea. DECISION - Cde. Whiteman is to organised the purchase of the parts.

(7) PRG MEETINGS - It was noted that there has been a long lapse since the last PRG meeting and that some people are feeling isolated and are drifting. Cde. Bishop felt that if all Ministers are unable to attend the meetings, then a conscious effort should be made to ensure that about 2-4 ministers be present at any one meeting. DECISION - PRG meetings to be held fortnightly on a Tuesday, starting next Tuesday, June 9th at 2.00 p.m.

A Secretary to the PRG is to be appointed in the person of Rachel Bain, who is presently the Recording Secretary to the Cabinet. The Cabinet Secretary, Marcella David, has been told to draft a letter informing the relative PRG members of the recommencement of PRG meetings and these meetings are to proceed on a pre-set agenda. Rachel Bain is also responsible for reminding members of the meeting.

(8) PWU/ILO CONFERENCE - Under PWU, it was reported by Cde. Bishop that the negotiations had taken a drastic turn. The Unions are claiming that they know what their members want and that that the teachers and nurses should not get the increases that had already been agreed upon. Cde. Bishop felt that two errors were made (a) agreeing to the communique and (b) giving Chris Ram the negotiating power. DECISION - We are now back to "Square One".

ILO CONFERENCE - Robby Robinson is to be recalled from the Conference being held in Geneva. Cde. Fennis Augustine is to replace him to be accompanied by Cde. Strachan who leaves here on Sunday. Cde. Strachan will telex Robby Robinson to return home and will brief Cde. Fennis Augustine on the situation re. PWU negotiations.

(9)SONNY MARK'S PHONE CALL - Cde. Bishop revealed that Sonny Mark had telephoned him about the recent CBS programme. The latter said that he is concerned of the damage done by the programme and that Grenadian nationals in New York are demoralised. He said that he has asked the Mission to send a copy of the Grenada Human Rights Council's report to every national. Apart from that, he is also suggesting that an "independent" person goes to New York to address a rally that will be organised by him.

Comrades felt that the suggestion is worth a try and names as Bristol, Chasley David and Danny Williams were suggested for the "independent"

54 - 2

3/...type. However, the

type. However, the tentative feeling of the Bureau is
that Dr. John Watts should be that person. However, the
topic is to be placed on the agenda for next week's
P.B. meeting. In the meantime, Cde. Whiteman is to
check Dr. Watts when he (Dr. Watts) returns.

(10) FOREIGN MINISTERS CONFERENCE - Cde. Bishop gave
the Bureau an idea as to which countries/islands will
be attending the Conference;

Guyana	-	No official reply
Trinidad	-	no reply
Barbados	-	said
St. Kitts	ᴀ	
Monsterrat	-)	
Belize	-)	no reply
Bahamas	-)	
St. Vincent	-)	
St. Lucia	-)	will attend
Dominica	-)	
Grenada	-)	

It was decided that the following Comrades call these
different countries, trying to persuade them to attend
the Conference:-

Guyana	-	Cde. Bishop
Trinidad	-	Cde. Radix/Louison
Jamaica	-	Cde. Coard (and also to contact the INI and WFU to press JA)
St. Vincent	-	Cde. Bishop will telephone Cato (Also speak to Monica Joseph about the situation there)
Dominica	-	The P.S. in the Ministry of External Affairs there said an official will come
Monsterrat	-	Cde. Louison
Belize	-	Cde. Bishop

Cde. Bishop explained that to get a quorum, there must
be five independent countries and one MDC. He is also
due to meet with Mr. Cato on Mustique Island which is
privately onwned but has Vincentian Police and Immigration authorities.

(11) The Lybian/USSR Ambassdor - It was noted that both
ambassadors are urgently needed in these two countries
and whoever it is needs to leave here this month. Cde.
Bishop siad that the only person in mind now is Cde.
Gellineau James, but no firm decisions were taken on
this issue. It was also noted that Cde. Coard has
said that the Lybian Ambassador is more key than the
one for Iraq.

(12) LETTER FROM RICHARD JACOBS - Cde. Bishop read parts
of a letter he received from Ambassador Jacobs. In it
he raised many issues relating to Grenada's relations
with different socialist countries. One of the things
he said that they are most upset about is that many

4/...offers (particularly scholar-

offers (particularly scholarships) are being made to us
and they have not been getting any reply. They felt that
if we do not want to accept the offers, we should say
so and they will give them to other countries.

Cde.
Jacobs raised the issue of the Cde. Leader's visit
to the U.S.S.R. in his letter. He said that the visit
is not sure and that the best way to "get to" the
Soviet Union is through Bulgaria and or the G.D.R.
He suggested that Cde. Bishop first pay a visit to
these countries. He pointed out that Cde. Ortega has
been to Moscow on four ocassions, but has not seen
Cde. Brehnev on any of these visits.

Cde. Jacobs also
stated that there are plans to have one Ambassador
to Grenada representing all the socialist countries.
He also conveyed an invitation to Cde. Noel to visit
Yugloslavia for two weeks in December to look at workers' participation there.

We have also received offers
from Bulgaria to send 24 Comrades to their Party
School - 12 in June and another 12 in December. They
also want 2 children between 6 - 14 years who are
good in singing, drama etc. to visit there from
12th - 26th August. The C.C. is to look at that. Ten
university scholarships are being offered by the GDR
- Cde. Louison will check it out.

Still in Cde. Jacobs'
letter, the question of the construction of our Party's
Headquarters was raised. Ambassador Jacobs said that
the S.U. is willing to give us cement and other construction materials worth $150,000(US). They want to
get the information on the quantity of our needs, the
address it should be sent to and the route the materials should be sent through to reach here.

Two engineers
from the GDR will be arriving here on June 12th in connection with a Printing machine that they will be giving
FWI - the Secretariat to inform Don Rojas, to organise
transport, accomodation and other arrangements for them.

Finally, Cde. Jacobs said that the Hungarians will be
sending down some crates of food, clothes and medicine to
us. It will arrive here on June 6th.

(13) SECURITY - This item was not really discussed, but
Cde. Noel pointed out the Cde. Owusu that he noticed
some detainees, particularly "Buck" Buhdlall on the prisons' truck yesterday(June 2nd) on Young Street with
very little security. He also told him that they ("Buck"
etc.) were in the Court House likewise, to the extent
that a priest was able to pass a note to "Buck". Cde.
Owusus was asked to check it out.

It was also noted that
the Security for the detainees in the hospital is "dread"
and that Langdon (who is one of them) is reported to
be in possession of two knives there. Cdes. felt that
any day, he (langdon) can escape.

54 - 4

(14) LYBIAN DELEGATION - two Lybians will be arriving
here this week.

5/...(15) ASHLEY WILLS/RUSSEL

(15) ASHLEY WILLS/RUSSEL - This item was not discussed.

(16) VENEZUELA FUEL - This item. was not discussed.

(17) RESPONSE TO CBS - Cde. Radix has a "package" response, according to Cde. Bishop. But the former had to leave earlier to attend a meeting with the Cuban Collaboration team. So this item was not discussed.

(18) CC ASSESSMENT WEEKEND - The agenda for this has been changed. Instead of AGWU, TEACHERS, MILITIA, NATIONAL SECURITY etc., it will now be Analysis, Evaluation, Criticism, Self-Criticism and a Line of March. The Secretariat is to inform the relevant comrades.

These items not formally on the agenda were discussed and the following decisions taken:

* Cde. Bullen at GRENLEC should be given close daily supervision. (Nobody was assigned specifically to the task).
* The S.U. wants the CC Comrades scheduled to visit there to come in the two groups of five - they are to go in groups of two and three.
* Cde. Owusu told the P.B. of reports he received stating that Carl Drakes has been putting the money from the Fisheries industry into his personal account. He takes the fish directly from the boats unto the truck and sells to Food Fair, Buy Rite, Holiday Inn, etc. Nobody seems to know how much fish is being sold and how much it is being sold for. Apart from that, he has been "bad-talking" the PRG to the small fish vendors saying that the PRG is planning to take over their business. He has also been heard saying that he cannot work for Government unless he is making something for himself. He also seems to have a line to Angus Smith, with the latter believing anything he tells him. A decision was already taken that Carl Drakes should not be allowed to handle finances of that industry. However, Cde. Owusu is to speak to Cde. Radix on the issue.

* It was reported that there is a conflict between the constrctors, St. John and James Phillip. St. John was given the job of construction of the Sauteurs Health Clinic initially, but later the Ministry gave it to James Phillip without recalling St. John, so that both are constructing the clinic. Cdes. also described Arthur George of the Health Ministry as incompetent and guilty of sabotage. It was the general feeling that that Ministry is very disorganised and that there is a group there that are consciously trying to throw out the progressives eg. Candia Alleyne etc. The P.B. will discuss getting a Secretary for Health at the next meeting.

* The delegation to the Conference in Mexico from 17th - 22nd June will be headed by Cde. George Louison.

6/...* Grenada should

* Grenada should take the initiative at the UN
on the zone of peace. Kenny Langaine is to do the
research by checking the documents he has and
checking Cde. Caldwell Taylor.
* Cde. Nazim Burke is to attend Economic Bureau meeting on Friday, 5th June, to give the Bureau an
idea on the state of relations with the socialist
world - i.e. our requests to them and their responses.
* Cde. Louison should get a taped list of all the
scholarships that have been offered to us. Comrades felt that there is need to take a more serious approach to that question.
* Cde. Bishop stated that he desperately needs a
Personal Assistant. He said that the person has to be
to be a CC member - Ian/Kojo type. The topic is
to be discussed at next P.B. meeting.
* The minutes of Political/Economic Bureau meetings
must include; (a) items left back to be discussed
(b) decisions requiring follow-up action. The Recording Secretary is to ensure that the left over
items be put on the agenda of the following PB/EB
meeting.
* External Affairs has bust their budget for the
year in the first five months of this year.

DECISIONS REQUIRING FOLLOWUP ACTION:-

* Did Cde. Radix get the three names for the Detention Tribunal?
* Was the OECS issue discussed at Cabinet meeting?
* Was EMA Welsh transferred to the National Secreta-
riat?
* Has Cde. Whiteman organised the purchase of the
spare parts for the tractors from South Korea?
* Has the letters gone off to the relevant comrades about the recommencement of the PRG meetings and is Rachel Bain now the PRG's Secretary?
* Is a pre-set agenda been organised for the meetings?
* Has Robby Robinson being recalled from the ILO
Conference - did Cde. Strachan telex him?
* Has Cde. Whiteman contacted John Watts about addressing the rally in New York?
* Did the following comrades get in touch with
the following countries to persuade them to
attend the Foreign Ministers Conference here:-

Bishop   - Guyana, St. Vincent, Belize
Radix/
Louison   - Trinidad
Coard   - Jamaica and FNI, WPJ
Louison   - Monsterrat

* Did Cde. Bishop also speak to Monica Joseph on the
situation in St. Vincent?
* Did the O.C. look at the question of the 24 scholarships to the Party School in the GDR and the 2
children to go there for two weeks?

54 - 6

* Has Comrade Louison:-

> - checked out the ten university scholar-
> ships to the GDR?
> - prepared the lists of scholarships
> offered to us?

* Did the Secretariat:-

> - contact Cpt. Belfon re. the drawings
> for the Party's HQ?
> - inform Don Rojas about the engineers
> arriving here on June 12th?
> - call the relevant CC comrades re.
> the change in agenda for the week-
> end assessment?
> - contact Nazim to come to EB meeting on
> Friday, 5th June?

* Has Cde. Owusu checked out:-

> - the security for "Buck"?
> - the security for the detainees at
> the hospital?
> - the two knives Langdon is alledged
> to have in his possession?
> - speak to Cde. Radix re. Carl Drakes

* Who is to supervise Cde. Bullen's GRENLEC work?
* Was Benny told to do the research on the zone of
peace initiative to be taken at the UN and is he
doing it?
* Was Grace James fired?
* What is the position with the decision that the
socialist world send a team to look at the possibility of setting up a maufacturing industry here?

THESE ITEMS WERE NOT DISCUSSED:-

1. Ashely Mills/Russel
2. Venezuela fuel
3. Response to CBS

THESE NEW ITEMS ARE TO BE DISCUSSED:-
1. Sonny Mark's proposal (re.Watts addressing rally in
                            New York)
2. P.M.'s personal assistant
3. Secretary for health

Hazel-Ann
RECORDING SECRETARY

MINUTES OF POLITICAL BUREAU MEETING
ON WEDNESDAY 10TH JUNE
1981

Comrades present:-

Maurice Bishop
Selwyn Strachan
Vincent Noel
Kenrick Radix
George Louison

Comrades absent:-

Bernard Coard)
Hudson Austin) away
Unison Whiteman)

AGENDA:-

(1) Minutes - Decisions requiring follow-up action
(2) TWU
(3) NISTEP
(4) RODNEY'S DAY
(5) NCBL Conference
(6) BUF Conference
(7) A.H. Hall
(8) Soweto Day
(9) June 19th
(10) Detainees
(11) Carl Drakes/NCB
(12) Socialism Classes

(1) MINUTES - From the look at the minutes of the last
P.B. meeting, the following is to be done;

a. Cde. Bishop to speak to Kurt Strachan about the
transfer of EMA Welsh
b. The CC to look at the offer of 24 scholarships to
the Party School in the GDR and 2 children to go
there
c. Cde. Radix to get the names for the Detention Tribunal by Friday, June 12th
d. Cde. Louison to complete the type-written list of
scholarships by Friday, 12th June
e. -The C.C. to decide if Nigel James is to be put in
Fisheries as suggested by Cde. Radix within 72 hours
of today
f. Cde. Radix will have the agricultural law package
ready by Friday, June 12th.

(2) NISTEP - Cde. Louison reported on this programme -
that it is going very bad, basically because of the
weak leadership in the person of Judith Bullen. He has
not been meeting with the Comrades in that programme
for a while. The programme, he said had taken a drastic turn in the last 6 weeks and Sis. Creft has only
started doing some work with them in the last 2 weeks.
Cde. Louison reported that some time ago, "Radio"
called a meeting of the students in the programme,
trying to close down the programme. However, he was
beaten back. There was also indications that the
programme was going to see a period of massive ab-
senteeism. Some 79 persons have missed classes 5 or
more times already.
            Cde. Louison disclosed that what
the students are really objecting to is the quality
of the lectures, the syllabus is not up-to-date, the
lack of co-ordination and planning. He felt that, po-

2/...litical problems

litical problems could arise there.

He once again said
that the fundamental problem is the leadership and
that the option of moving Judith Bullen from there
has to be seriously considered or the programme will
fall. She had initially wanted to give up the programme, but Cde. Louiosn questioned whether she
would be as inclined now.

Chris Searle, who has a MA
degree in Teacher Education, can head the programme,
Cde. Louison suggested. DECISION - Cde. Louison is to
speak to Judith Bullen and according to her response,
he should go ahead and let Chris Searle head the programme or discuss it with the Bureau again. Cde.
Bishop is also to speal Wiht Winston Bullen on the
issue.

(3) PWU - Cde. Bishop told the Bureau that the PWU
have been recommending more cuts in the salary increases put forward by the PRG. DECISION - Chris Ram
is to "stand firm" on the figures recommended. He
had called to get directives as negotiations were
to recommence today.

(4) RODNEY'S DAY - June 13th, this Saturday, will
mark the first anniversary of the assassination of
Walter Rodney. The Grenada Peace Council had sent
a draft statement to be published on the day, for
the Bureau to look at. It was read and comrades
felt that the statement is a bit too "rough" and
showed that some guidance is needed. It was decided that it should be done over and Cde. Bishop
is to speak to Cde. Lambert about it. The general
feeling was that the statement should express concern about nobody being arrested for the crime yet,
it should also carry a anti-imperialist line, say
something about Rodney's life and urge the authorities to expedite the matter.

(5) NCBL CONFERENCE - Cde. Bishop has received an invitation from the National Conference of Black Lawyers (NCBL) in the U.S.A. to attend and address their
conference, taking place in Atlanta, Georgia next
month. The theme of the conference is "Committment,
Organisation and Struggle - Moving a Peoples Agenda
in the '80's". DECISION - Caldwell Taylor will attend the conference. Cde. Strachan to reply to the
NCBL, informing them of the decision, stating that
the Comrade Leader is unable to attend.

(6) BUF CONFERENCE - The Black United Front is having
their annual conference on 3rd - 5th July. They are requesting that Cde. Coard or a PRG member attend. DECI-
SION - Cde. James will attend it.

(7) A.H. HALL - Cde. Radix said Hall gave up his gun
sometime ago. Now, he can hardly walk and thieves
have stolen his household items. He is therefore requesting his gun be given back to him. DECISION - Cde.
Radix is to explain to Hall that he spoke to the Security Minister who has tol` him:-

3/.... a) there are many

a) there are many cases as his, but if he is given
   back his weapon, it will set a precedence - Cde.
   Bishop does not want to make exceptions
b) that a review is being done and he will be informed appropriately.

(8) SOWETO DAY - Next Tuesday, June 16th will be
"SOWETO DAY". DECISION - The Secretatiat to inform the St. George's FCB that they are to organise a indoor rap/rally for that day.

(9) JUNE 19TH - Cde. Bishop read parts of a note
that Jaqueline Creft left before her departure. She
said that the Principal of the B.B.S.S., Harris,
wanted to know if the school was going to be involved
in the June 19th activities. It was suggested that a
chidren's rally be held in that school during the
morning of the day. Cde. Louison is to speak to the
Principal of the school on something concrete - maybe
a student saying a roem at the rally.
                                   As part of the
mobilisation for the rally, the following Bureau members are to speak at these indoor raps;

PLACE	DATE	COMRADE	TIME
Grand Mall Com. Centre	~~Mon. 15th~~ Thur. 11th	Bishop	7.00 p.m.
Butler House	Mon. 15th	Coard	7.30 p.m.
Beaulieu	Mon. 15th	Whiteman	7.30 p.m.
St. Paul's	Wed. 17th	Radix	7.00 p.m.
Hinsey School	Wed. 17th	Noel	7.00 p.m.

Cde. Bishop told the Bureau that the applicants in his
study group had suggested the following to help the
mobilisation for the June 19th rally:

o talks in all schools, using the fact that 2 of the
  3 murdered on June 19th, 1980 were students - Carol
  Davis is working on that
o work place visits by MB - being organised by Cde.
  Noel
o block raps
o PA advertisement around town on the morning of 19th
x o children voices for a promo
o invitations to groups, trade unions, mass organisations to send a representative to sit at the platform
o the church could probably say something the day before
  being Corpus Christi - very unlikely
 o get the teachers to tell the students about the
   day/matrys (next week is Teachers week)
o radio interview explaining that security is tighter
  than last year - should not be done
It was noted that this year, there are four graves to visit
instead of one. Therefore, Bureau members will have to
split up to cover all four. Mobilisation should not concentrate on the wreath-laying ceremonies, but on the
rally itself.

(10) DETAINEES - There is need to review the detainees
and come up with a package for the release of some.
Cde. Noel expressed concern over Ralph Thompson's
health. He said he had received reports saying that

4/...Ralph's health is

Ralph's health is very bad. Cde. Bishop said he received a report on Ralph's health from the Cuban doctors and is due to get another one soon.

(11) CARL DRAKES - Cde. Noel reported that Carl Drakes has deposited $11,000 in the NCB recently - $10,000 incash. He said that the Bank workers are suspecting something and that the word has started going around in the banking world or corruption in the state sector and that the FRG is now becoming the "laughing stock".

Cde. Raidx responded that Carl Drakes has been asked to hand over all the vouchers, and bills that he has and that the accounts are being audited. However, Cde. Radix stated that the Ministry of Fisheries is in dire need of an accountant who is a "party-type". Carl Drakes suggested somebody to him, but other bureau comrades advised against getting him. Cde. Radix was insisting on Nigel James being the person. DECISION - The O.C. is to take a decision and inform Cde. Radix within 72 hours of today.

(12) SOCIALISM CLASSES- Cde. Noel reported that he had spoken to workers who have been attending the classes. They claim that the classes are not related to our situation and uninteresting. He felt that the wrong material is being used also.

A lenghtly discussion followed as to whether colonialism is a part/tactic of imperialism. And it was felt that since some comrades have different views, the topic should be one for study.

(handwritten margin note: CAPITALISM produced Colonialism before IMPERIALISM was formally institutionalised.)

Comrades also had different opinions on why the numbers at the Socialism classes are falling. Some suggested that it is because of organisational problems, while others felt that it is because of the topic being taught and that too many terminologies been used.

As to the content of the claaes themselves, some comrades felt that the first thing that should have been done is the History Of Grenada, highlighting the different phases. The way it is been done now, is that the topic Development of Society is taught with reference to our history. Although there is not much documented material on our history, comrades felt there was enough to make a start (could start from Fedon period) and that that the syllabus being used presently is wrong. Cde. Bishop thought that a "Why are we poor?" approach might be a good start.

However, it was clearly expressed that the syllabus should be looked at carefully to determine its suitability.

These items not formally on the agenda were discussed:-

- Cde. Raymond Layne's work at the Agro-Industrial Plant is being seriously affected by his regular absence from that job. This is because he is also Chairman of the St. George's PCB - the two

jobs are clashing. DECISION - The O.C. is to look
at the matter.

- Cde. Radix suggested that all the bodies of our
matrys be brought together in one central place
- have a memorial. It's a good idea, but might
meet families' disapproval.

- Fr. Bernard has written Cde. Bishop a letter. In
it he says that he went to visit Langdon at the
hospital, who knowing that Fr. Bernard was leaving on vacation, gave him the phone numbers to
contact his family who he has not been in contact with for a while. However, the guard, having seen
seen Langdon pass the paper to him, took it from
Fr. Bernard. Fr. Bernard is alledged to have fired a
cuff at the guard in response and is now claiming
that the guard took his notebook also. DECISON -
Cde. Owusu should do an investigation into the matter and submit a formal report to the Bureau in
about 2 weeks.

- Cde. Bishop has received a letter from the Conference of Churches here stating;

   a) complaining that they are asked to do the
   March 13th Church Service at the last minute
   - they should receive   the invitation 3
   weeks in advance
   b) The service should begin at 7.00 p.m.
   c) it should start the activities for the
   Festival

- Need to make a formal reply to the CBS programme.

DECISIONS REQUIRING FOLLOW-UP ACTION:-

* Have the tasks under Item (1) from a to f being
completed?
* Did Cde. Louison speak to Judith Bullen re. NISTEP?
* Did Cde. Bishop speak to Winston Bullen?
* Has Cde. Bishop spoken to Swinton Lambert re.
GFC statement on Rodney's assassination anniver-
sary?
* Did Cde. Strachan reply to the NCBL re. their con-
ference?
* Has Cde. Owusu been informed that he is to attend
the BUF Conference in July?
* Did Cde. Radix speak to A.H. Hall re. his weapon?
* Did the Secretariat contact the St. Geroge's PCB
re. Soweto Day?
* Has Cde. Louison spoken to Harris of E.B.S.S.
re. June 19th?
* What is the result of the look into bills and
vouchers from Carl Drakes?
* Has the O.C. looked at;-

   o Nigel James being attached to Agro-
   Industries/Fisheries?
   o Raymond Layne - PCB/Agro Plant
   conflict?

* What is the position with the decision that the
socialist world send a team to look at the possibility of setting up a manufacturing industry here?

Hazel-Ann
RECORDING SECRETARY

MINUTES OF POLITICAL BUREAU MEETING HELD ON
WEDNESDAY, 17TH JUNE, 1981.

Comrades present: Comrades absent:-

Maurice Bishop   56   Selwyn Strachan
Bernard Coard   Hudson Austin
Vincent Noel   George Louison
Unison Whiteman
Kenrick Radix

AGENDA:-

1. Party Headquarters
2. Mexico trip
3. Lybian delegation
4. PWU
5. Two ambassadors
6. OECS Treaty
7. Heroes Day

(1) PARTY HEADQUARTERS - A third cable from the Soviet Union
has been received re. materials we need for the construction
of the Party headquarters. DECISION - Rec Secty. to contact
Cde. Burke who is to send off a response by cable saying that
the architectual drawings for the building are in the process
of completion. Cde. Radix and Noel are now in charge of the
drawings.

(2) MEXICO TRIP - Cde. Louison who is to head the delegation
to the conference in Mexico next week was absent from the
meeting, but Cde. Coard reported that he had contacted
Gloria Payne to co-ordinate the plans for the trip. He also
said that Terry and Paul are critical to the trip. It was
also suggested that the team should get a briefing from the
comrades in Cuba - Cde. Bishop will work on this. He is also
to send a letter to President Portillo.

(3) LYBIAN DELEGATION - Nobody seems to be able to say where
the Lybian delegation that was supposed to be visiting here
is at present - not even the Lybian Embassy in Guyana knows.

(4) PWU - None of the Bureau members have received a report
on the negotiations with the PWU which was schelduled to
take place last Saturday, June 13th. Cde. Coard felt that
teachers and nurses should get a bigger increase.

(5) TWO AMBASSADORS - Grenada has to designate an ambassador
to the USSR and one to Lybia. Cdes. Coard suggested Sister
Dessima Williams for the first, saying that he felt she
will do a good job, plus, gain more experience. He also
pointed out that she will be a disaster if she is based
here.
        To fill her place in Washington, Ashley Taylor, Mathew
Williams and Merle Collins were suggested.
                                        As our Ambassa-
dor to Lybia, Comrades, Leon Cornwall. Fitzie Bain, "Headache" and Ge'lo James were suggested. The Bureau is to
look at the possibility of sending Cde. James again.
                                        It
was reported that the Guyanese community here is spreading
adverse propaganda about Carrol Davis.

(6) OECS TREATY - Cde. Bishop was due to leave on Thursday

morning for St. Kitts to sign that treaty. He raised
the topic of the arctilces on Security and Defense.
Cde. Coard riased that of Foreign Policy. Cde. Bishop
read the relevant part of the document. However, it
was decided that   the issue was to be discussed later
that day.

(7) HEROES DAY AGENDA- Cdes. felt that the three comrades to speak at the rally on that day should be
the Comrade Leader, Fitzie Bain and Coard.

THESE OTHER ISSUES WERE RAISED:

o Cde. Coard expressed worry about the need to make some
  key critical decisions on the economy in the light of
  the present situation.

o Cde. Ventour called from Havana. Cde. Bartholomew and
  himself are still stranded there, waiting to go to
  Moscow. Cde. Ventour told Cde. Bishop that the Soviets
  are still insisting on all 5 invitees going at the
  same time. It was pointed out that this will be impossible and that if they cannot accept the 2-3 model,
  then the comrades might have to return home.

o Cde. Strachan also called. He is attending the ILO
  Conference in Geneva, which he thinks he underestimated, where there are about 2000 delegates. He
  spoke to the Comrade Leader and told him that he
  goes to London on Friday and will be addressing a
  rally there on Sunday. He should be home early next
  week.
        The Rec. Secty. is to ensure that when the pam-
  phlet on "The Grenadian Voice" is out, that it is
  sent to the London Mission and the other missions, on
  Friday morning. This information Comrade Strachan will
  need to have in time to address the rally. The Rec.
  Secty. is also to ensure that he is sent a telex,
  summarising the rally.
                        Cde. Strachan also reported that
Lloyd Noel who is abroad has held two meetings. It was
  disclosed that he also has acsess to the Gouyave Militia and that he has received ammunition from them already.

DECISIONS REQUIRING FOLLOW-UP ACTION:-

o Did the letter go off to President Portillo?
o Were the telexes sent off to Cde. Strachan?
o Did Cde. Burke send off the telex re. the Party
  headquarters to the S.U.?

                                    Hazel-Ann
                                    RECORDING SECRETARY

MINUTES OF POLITICAL BUREAU MEETING ON
WEDNESDAY, 24th JUNE, 1981.

Comrades present:-

Maurice Bishop
Bernard Coard
Kenrick Radix
Unison Whiteman
George Louison
Vincent Noel

Non-P.B. Members:-

Liam James
Ewart Layne
Einstein Louison

Comrades absent:-

Selwyn Strachan
Hudson Austin

AGENDA :- No firm agenda was set.

(1) Comrades James, Louison and Layne came to discuss the present threat being posed by the rasta elements - particularly since
it was learnt that they are planning to attack one of the FRA camps
on Friday - and possible measures to deal with that situation.

Major Louison stated that all camps were on alert last night and
that a place is being constructed to house the 300 rastas that
will be "picked up". Cde. Bishop stated that he was totally against
taking up 300 of them and cutting their hair as was proposed.

Cde. James stated that he had spoken to Cde. Rizo about the issue.
The latter showed concern about the issue and felt that we would
be isolated regionally and internationally. Cde. James questioned
what would be the attitude/mood after the operation, the implications for the youth work, how will the rastas be influenced to
work, the reaction of the population. He suggested that in order
to 'legitimise' our grabbing any rastas, we should allow them to
carry out their attack as planned and then take them. The Comrade
leader felt that is too dangerous - it could very well end up in
people being killed on both sides.

A very detailed discussion followed on the different ways of handling the situation. Cde. Coard reminded the meeting that the Party,
for the last 2½ years has always been reluctant to take firm decisions on key issues e.g. Torchlight, Nang Nang, Stanley Cyrus, etc.

Major Layne expressed very deep concern on what would be the effect
on the Army, Militia and NYO.

At the end of the lengthly discussion, it was decided:-

a. Major Louison continues his camp model
b. Cde. James to focus on identifying major national rasta
   leaders and sub-leaders
c. infiltration of the rasta camps (at least one - Belmont)
d. ammend the powers of the magistrates
E. propose nat. service later

(2) PNC INVITATION - The PNC of Guyana has sent an invitation for
our Party to attend their Fourth Biennial Congress from August
22nd - 29th. The invitation was accepted and the Rec. Secty. is to

.2/...send a reply.

send a reply. However, the Bureau did not decide on any names
as yet.

BUF CONFERENCE - Cde. James was due to attend this conference
from July 3rd - 5th. However this decision has been reversed in
light of the present situation. Instead, Cde. Taylor will go
- Cde. James is to inform him.

(4) ADDITIONAL FLIGHT - Cde. Bishop reported that if we are to
get an additonal flight from Cuba, it will mean that the plane
will have to stop off at Aruba or Curacao. But somebody needs to
go there to discuss the proposal - Cde. whiteman is in charge
of this,

(5) TRAINING - Cde. Bishop reported that Ambassador Rizo has
told him that we need to train more specialists for the airport
equiptment - Cde. Strachan is to be informed of this on his
return.

(6) S.I. CONFERENCE - George Price should be invited to the conference. However, Grenada is only hosting the conference and is
not in a position to issue invitations.

(7) EAST GERMAN - A CC comrade who is in charge of his Party's
finances is here. Cde. Louison has spoken to him, but other
comrades should check him.

(8) RASTA - Desmond Trottter is to be sent back to Dominica
before the rasta leaders are picked up. They should be picked
up as they are seen.

                              Hazel-Ann
                              RECORDING SECRETARY

MINUTES OF POLITICAL BUREAU MEETINGS ON DSATURDAY, 27TH JUNE, AND WEDNESDAY 1ST. JULY, 1981

SATURDAY - Cdes. present:-   Cdes. absent:-

    Maurice Bishop   Bernard Coard
    Selwyn Strachan   Vincent Noel
    Unison Whiteman
    Hudson Austin
    George Louison
    Kenrick Radix
    Non-PB Member: Liam James

AGENDA:- No firm agenda was set

Only the following two (2) decisions were taken;

1. Hope Vale to be used as the centre for housing the
   rastas picked up
2. Cde. James to contact Winston Bullen re. switching on
   the lights in the Hope Vale building

WEDNESDAY - Cdes. present:-

    all above plus Cdes. Noel and Coard

AGENDA:- No firm agenda was set. Cde. Louison presented a
budget of $2.1M for work among the farmers. It was approved
and decided that Cde. Louison should get Cde. Burke to send
off telexes to all the countries including the socialist ones
to get information re. the cost of fertilisers; this programme
should have a separate accounting.

o Winston Bullen rang re. the Medical School. They had owed
GRENLEC $159,000.00. However, they paid the amount with a
cheque but it has bounced. DECISION - they should be cut off
and charged 12½% daily interest on the amount owing.

o Ambrose Phillip has returned to Grenada. He should be
placed in the Ministry of Agriculture.

                                  Hazel-Ann
                                  RECORDING SECRETARY

Comrades present :- ①

Maurice Bishop
Selwyn Strachan
Unison Whiteman
Kenrick Radix
George Louison
Vincent Noel
Hudson Austin

Comrade absent :-

Bernard Coard   -   sick

5/

AGENDA :-

1. Ministdrial reshuffle
2. ESSO/CDC
3. Counters
4. Guyana
5. Socialist International

6. Work places visits
7. Liat Shareholders meeting
8. Errol Maitland
9. Ken Milne
10. Samori Marksman

1. MINISTERIAL RESHUFFLE (30 mins.) - Cde. Bishop reported that he met with Cde. Bain yesterday re. separating the Ministry of Health and Housing. According to the former, Cde. Bain is "okay with the proposal" and wanyed to know when it would be implemented. Cde. Bishop told him to think about which of the two buildings he woyld prefer to house his ministry and his staff overnight for an emergency cabinet meeting this morning. Cde. Bishop also reported that he discussed the question of the hospital administration with the McLeishes. However, this he will discuss with Cde. N. Bain.

> o Cde. Bishop and "Fayo" Nyack are to discuss the proposal that the latter be made an Ombudsman.
> o Cde. Strachan to speak with Leroy Neckles about the latter being Comptroller pf Income Tax

Regarding Bernard Gittens, it was suggested that he be put in charge of a health plan for schools, a special advisor to the PM, or a resident ambassador.

2. ESSO/CDC (5 mins.) - This item was not discussed

3. COUNTERS (15 mins.) - This item was discussed and certain decisions taken. The discussion went beyond the time allocated, but this was agreed to by the meeting.

4. GUYANA (5 mins.) - Cde. Louison disclosed that he was leaving for Guyana that afternoon and wanted to know if there is "anybody to check". Comrades felt that there is nothing wrong if he does so. Cde. Whiteman said that Guyana Airways has aksed for lading rights here and we have agreed.

5. SOCIALIST INTERNATIONAL (15 mins.) - Cde. Bishop reported that the S.I. Conference coming up soon were sent and that the conference will cost the PRG $75,000. St. Kitts and Guyana will be left and out and Belize (who is very important) has not received an invita-

2/...tion, we should

tion, we should focus on Austria, France, Sweden and the Netherlands.

- o Cde. Bishop to telephone Cdes. Jimmy Emmanuel, Mario Bullen and Fennis Augustine
- o Kurt Strachan to send regional telexes

A questionaire concerning our Party was also received and it was noted that NJM has not paid its dues to SI as yet.

- o Our dues of £150 - £200 shpuld be paid
- o Cde. Strachan, as OC representative, to fill out the question-aire.

6. WORK PLACE VISITS (2 mins.) - The workers committee is to draw up a new programme for a series of visits to work places by the Com-rade Leader.

7. LIAT SHAREHOLDERS MEETING (5 mins.) - Cde. Strachan disclosed that this meeting is coming up soon. He said that Lyden Ramdhany will be attending it and that an item on the agenda will be "Worker Participatipn". The Managing Director, Ian Archer has re-signed. We are to be pushing for a director from each island in-stead of a rotation system.

8. ERROL MAITLAND - (5 mins.) This item was not discussed

9. KEN MILNE (5 mins.) - Cde. Whiteman said that Ken Milne has com-plained of not getting his rent fee from the Medical School for his hotel on the beach which they are using. He wants to use it for an economic venture, but first wants to consult with the PRG. It was reported that this issue was raised already and that Ian Jacob was to have replied to him.

- o Cde. Radix to check Ian Jacobs on whether a reply was sent

0. SAMORI MARKSMAN (5 mins.) - This item was not discussed

* SELA IS ASKING FOR OBBERVER STATUS AT CARICOM COUNCIL OF MINISTERS MEETING. CDE. BISHOP SEES NO REASON WHY THIS CANNOT BE AGREED TO BY GRENADA.

* IRAQUI CONVENTION - THE IRAQUI SOCIALIST PARTY WILL BE CELEBRATING THE ANNIVERSARY OF THEIR REVOLUTION ON JULY 7TH. THEY WANT US TO SEND SOMEBODY TO BE PART.

- o The Rec. Secty. to contact External Affairs and let them inform Mario Bullen that he is to attend it.

DECISIONS REQUIRING FOLLOW-UP ACTION:-
==

o Did Cde. Bishop and "Fayo" Nyack discuss the latter being an Om-budsman?
o Did Cde. Strachan speak to Leroy Nerkles about him being made Comptroller of Income Tax?
o Did Cde. Bishop phone Jimmy Emmanuel, Mario Bullen and Fennis Augustine - SI Conference?
o Has K. Strachan sent the regional telexes?
o Is our dues to SI being paid?
o Has the relevant questionaire sheet been filled out?by Cde. Strachan?
o Is the programme of the PL's visits to work places been done by the Workers Committee?
o Did Cde. Radix check Ian Jacobs re. the reply to Ken Milne?

3/...o Did the Rec.

③

o Did the Rec. Secty. get in touch with External Affairs for a telex
  to be sent to Mario Bullen requesting that he goes to the Iraqui
  Revolution Anniversary celebrations on July 17th?

ITEMS TO BE DISCUSSED:-

1. 2060/CDC
2. ERROL MAITLAND
3. SAMORI MARKSMAN
4. CHURCHES:-

        a. Date of meeting
        b. Neehall's letter

                              Hazel-Ann
                              RECORDING SECRETARY

MINUTES OF POLITICAL BUREAU MEETING HELD ON
WEDNESDAY, 29TH JULY, 1981

Cdes. Present:-

Maurice Bishop   Kenrick Radix
Selwyn Strachan   George Louison
Unison Whiteman   Hudson Austin

Cde. absent:-

Bernard Coard

60

AGENDA :-

1. Ministerial Reshuffle
2. US Cable re. Danga
3. GDR Proposal
4. Report on the New York Situation
5. Request from Patrick Bubb
6. Request from Bernadette
7. New York Public Relations Firm

1. MINISTERIAL RESHUFFLE - Cde. Bishop said that the Bureau needed
   to look at the physical location of some of the Ministries in
   light of the reshuffle. Comrades suggested a total of thirteen
   buildings for their location:-

   i. McIntyre Brothers'   - Young Street
   ii. Former Veronicas'   - The Carenage
   iii. Kirpalani's   - River Road
   iv. Ken Milne's building   -
   v. Albany Inn ✓   -- Upper Lucas Street
   vi. Jackie's house ∕   - Upper Lucas Street
   vii. Grand Hotel
   viii. DeAllie's
   ix. Green Gables   - Lucas Street
   x. Derek Steele's House ✓
   xi. Noble Smith's House
   xii. 2nd Floor HRC ✓   - Lucas Street
   xiii. Winston Bullen's House-

It was decided that Cdes. Radix and Strachan will check the owners
of Albany Inn and HRC respectively to house the two Ministries of
Agriculture and National Mobilisation.

(2) US CABLE RE. DANGA - Cde. Radix read a cable sent to the Prime
    Minister's Office by the US Embassy in Barbados. They alledged
    that their staff member Danga, was unduly searched and harrassed
    on the compound of Butler House. They wanted a response from us.
    It was decided that our immediate response should be that we are
    investigating the charges.

ITEMS 3,4,5,6, and 7 were not discussed.

DECISIONS REQUIRING FOLLOW-UP ACTION:-

o Did Cdes. Radix and Strachan check the respective buildings -
  Albany Inn and HRC?

o Was the response sent off to the US Embassy re. Danga's
  charges?

ITEMS TO BE DISCUSSED:-

See above Nos. 3 - 7.

Hazel-Ann
RECORDING SECRETARY DOCUMENT 60
                     60 - 1

MINUTES OF THE POLITICAL BUREAU MEETING ON WEDnesday,
AUGUST 5TH, 1981.

Comrades present :-   61   Comrades absent :-
Maurice Bishop   Bernard Coard
Hudson Austin   Unison Whiteman
Selwun Strachan
George Louison
Kenrick Radix

AGENDA :-

1. Minutes   8. Tom Adams' Statement
2. In-Service Training Unit   9. Nutmeg Association
3. Party Headquarrers   10. Park House
4. Maureen St. Bernard   11. Reagan's letter
5. Chester Humphrey   12. Workers work report
6. RFG Antenna   13. Fionerr Camps
7. Mike Forshaw

1. <u>MINUTES</u> - Resulting from the last PB meeting, Cde Louison was
assigned to check the possibility of obtaining Albany Inn to be
used as the Ministry of Agriculture. He reported that he had done
so and found out that Mr. Squires had already paid down some money to the owners with the intention of buying it to make a
"down town apartment building and hotel". However, the latter
stated his willingness to negotiate with the PRG in order
that we get it. It was the general feeling of the Bureau that
is going to be a good form of investment and thus should be
left as is.

A correction was made to the Minutes of the Friday's EB meeting, which said that the letter to President Reagan was soon to
be completed. In fact, it was already completed.

3. <u>IN-SERVICE TRAINING UNIT</u> - Cde. Bishop reciived some documents
on that programme. He said that Marilyn Harris is requesting
a monthly salary of $3,000 (US). (However, she will be paid by
an external agency.) She is also supposedly to have South Africa
connections, which raises the question of whether we want her to
work here. It was decided that Cde. Bishop is to look further
into the aspect of Canadian assistance and that Cde. Creft will
speak to Marilyn Harris on the South African issue. Comrades of
the Bureau expressed their concern and worry over the fact that
there is no Party imput into the I.T.U., although Swinton Lambert is now working at the National Secretariat.

3. <u>PARTY HEADQUARTERS</u> - Cde. Strachan suggested that Lennox Archibald be given the task of doing the drawings for the Party Headquarters. The former said that he wanted to take on the responsibility to get this "off the ground , as it has been dragging
for a while now. Both Cdes. Strachan and Austin will see that
the drawings are done.

This topic is to be made a recurring item on each Bureau agenda.

4. <u>MAUREEN ST. BERNARD</u> - Members of the Political Bureau read a
copy of a letter from Maureen St. Bernard, sent to the Comrade
Leader. The letter was also sent to the Organising Committee.

2/...It was disclosed

It was disclosed by Cde. Strachan that a Sub-Committee of the O.C. will be looking at the issue. It was noted that Sis. St. Bernard was not doing any work at the present time.

5. **CHESTER HUMPHREY** - Cde. Strachan made a request for Cde. Humphrey to be transferred to a job that will enable him to be full time in urban workers work, and that will make him eligible for elections to the executive of TAWU. Cde. Strachan felt that Cde. Humphrey can be replaced at G.F.C. by Ambrose Phillip. The proposal was agreed upon and Cde.

Humphrey is to be placed in the Ministry of Communications, Works and Labour.

6. **RFG ANTENNA** - Cde. Strachan revealed that an antenna has to be put up near to RFG which will require 5 acres of land. The decision is that a microwave should be the first option - it will not require much space. If that is not possible, then the space at the back of RFG can be used. Cdes. Strachan and Austin are both responsible for this.

7. **MIKE FORSHAW** - Cde. Radix told the Bureau that Mike Forshaw has resigned from his job at Spice Island Charters and wants to know if the Government can employ him. He had been offered a job at the Port Authority, but was only going to receive $1200. Cde. Radix suggested that he can be placed in a job with the fishing fleet. Cde. Radix is to check both Cdes. James and Coard, before this is done.

8. **TOM ADAMS' STATEMENT** - Comrades of the Bureau felt that a reply should be made to a statement made by Tom Adams that there is no human rights in Grenada and that we should hold elections. A statement was been drafted by Cde. McBarnette and will be looked at later.

9. **NUTMEG ASSOCIATION** - Cde. Louison reported that there is an urgent need 'move on' Renwick and Gittens in that association. He suggested Evelyn Ross and Ambrose Phillip. However, the latter is already being placed in G.F.C. Comrades felt that Evelyn Ross will not be able to "work for anybody". In spite of this however, he can still be checked to do the job. It was also noted that both the Nutmeg and Banana boards need an Assistant Manager.

10. **PARK HOUSE** - Cde. Radix reported that concrete dog kennels are being built beside Park house, which is a suitable Protocol house and that was not good. The Comrade Leader is to speak to Cde. Owusu on the issue, since he is the person responsible for putting up the kennels.

It was also decided that Park house should be added to the list of Protocol houses.

11. **REAGAN'S LETTER** - Only one copy of the draft letter to President Reagan was received. The Recording Secretary is to contact Ashley Taylor to send copies of the letter to the other members of the Bureau in time for it to be discussed at Friday's bureau meeting.

12. **WORKERS WORK** - Cde. Strachan gave the Bureau a verbal report on the work of the Workers Committee. He said that for the last 2 weeks, the committee has been re-organising. The unions are now compiling a list of about 150 of all their strong Party activists. There is also a plan to set up political committees in each work place. Priority, he said, is been given to the Socialism classes - they will be started soon and the Chris Holness material will be used. Telco and Grenlec are starting this week. The one at the Airport site has already started.

3/... The plan is

61 - 2

The plan is to meet with the 150 activiststto outline the plan for the work, starting with those workers at PMO and CWL. Cde. Strachan stated that the main question is one of structures and implementation. He suggested that Cde. Wardally should be made a Socialism Classes tutor and that a crash ideological course for the 150 comrades should be organised and they should be trained in leadership.

13. FIONEER CAMPS - A letter was received from the organisers of the Pioneer camps. They are requesting a Bureau member to officially open and close each of their six camps, from August 6th - September 4th. The following was agreed upon :-

      6th Aug. - 10th Aug. ----------Cde. Bishop
     12th Aug. - 16th Aug. ----------Cde. Strachan
     19th Aug. - 23rd Aug. ----------Cde. Radix
     25th Aug. - 29th Aug. ----------Cde. Austin
     25th Aug. (Carriacou) ----------Cde. Louison (Open)
     29th Aug. ("   ) ----------Cde. George Frime (close)
     31st Aug. - 4th Sret. ----------Cde. Coard

All the camps, except that of Carriacou, will be held at the GBSS Auditorium and on the 6th September, there will be a National General Meeting of the Pioneers to which the whole Bureau is invited.

Each comrade who opens a camp, will also close it.

OTHER THINGS RAISED:-

o Hutchinson's is selling out
o The house near Telco can be used for a ministry
o The houses at Grand Etang can be used for Agro-Industries, Forestry and Tourism

DECISIONS REQUIRING FOLLOW-UP ACTION:-

o Did Cde. Creft speak to Marilyn Harris?
o Has Cde. Bishop looked forther into the Canadian issue?
o Have Cdes. Austin and Strachan started to work on the drawings for the Party Headquarters?
o Did the Sub-Committee of the O.C. look at the issue of Maureen St. Bernard
o Has Chester Humphrey being transferred to the Ministry of Communications Works and Labour?
o Did Ambrose Fhillip replace Chester Humphrey at GFC?
o Did Cde. Radix look into the question of Mike Forshaw been employed by the PRG?
o Has Evelyn Ross being checked to be on the Nutemg Association?
o Has the Comrade Leader checked Cde. Owusu about the dogs at Park House?
o Was Ashley Taylor told to send copies of the letter to Reagan?

ITEM TO BE DISCUSSED:- Party Headquarters

                                        Hazel-Ann
                                        RECORDING SECRETARY

Comrades present :-

Maurice Bishop   Kenrick Radixx
Bernard Coard - late with excuse   Hudson Austin
Selwyn Strachan   Unison Whiteman
George Louison

AGENDA :-

    1. Carnival/Security Arrangements ...5 mins.
    2. Letter to President Reagan.......10 mins.
    3. Land Utilisation Law............20 mins.
    4. Nutmeg Board.....................5 mins.
    5. Militia Mobilisation.............5 mins.
    6. New York Report.................5 mins.
    7. Paul Miller's proposal..........5 mins.
    8. Pioneers........................ -
    9. Party Paper Report.............15 mins.
    10. Party Headquarters..............5 mins.
    11. FWI Building....................5 mins.
    12. Socialism Classes Report........ -
    13. Grenlec Propaganda.............. -

(1) CARNIVAL/SECURITY ARRANGEMENTS - It was clarified that only
    Carnival Monday is a public hol-
    half holiday. As regards the Security
    Festival, Cde. Bishop stated that the S and D Committee are
    the ones to look at that aspect.

(2) LETTER TO PRESIDENT REAGAN - Cde. Bishop read the changes
    made to the original draft of the letter to President Reagan.
    Cde. Coard suggested that a copy of the letter be sent to
    every head of Government, Kurt Waldheim and every US Con-
    gress member at the end of the time period for the President
    to reply. (End of September)

(3) LAND UTILISATION LAW - Cde. Louison reported that together
    with the Comrade Leader, and Miles Fitzpatrick and himself,
    they discussed the law. A long discussion follwoed about
    different technicalities of the law, but it was finally
    decided that the law would be gazatted and it was given to
    Miles Fitzpatrick.
                          It was decided that Michael Kirton will be
    the Chairman of the Land Commission.

(4) NUTMEG BOARD - Cde. Louison told the Bureau that he met with
    the Nutmeg Board and it seems that a woman named Bishop will
    have to be given back her job, after being fired, He disclosed
    that, not only must Renwick and Gittens be removed from the
    Board, but the whole Nutmeg Board must be changed. It was de-
    cided that Cde. Louison is to submit names for the Board at
    Friday's Bureau meeting and he is also to make suggestions
    as to what board Sylvia Belmar must be placed on. He is also
    to get some detailed information on Renwick's contract.

(5) MILITIA MOBILISATION - Cde. Strachan gave the Political Bu-
    reau an update of the state of mobilisation. He said that
    the route marches today will end at different centres. It
    was decided that the following Bureau members wukk be at
                          2... the these centres:

at these centres:

```
          Bishop & Austin............Market Square
          Radix  & Austin............Ferdmontemps
          Whiteman & Louison.........Sauteurs Court Yard
          Coard & Louison...........Gouyave
          Strachan..................Tivoli
```
Another route march was also decided upon for Sunday, 23rd August
before the Militia Parade on Wednesday, 26th August.

(6) <u>NEW YORK REPORT</u> - This item was not discussed.

(7) <u>PAUL MILLER'S PROPOSAL</u> - Cde. Coard reported that Paul Miller
said he had arranged meetings for somebody from the Party to
speak with two of three of the leading members of the NDF of
Canada. This is to take place on August 13th and 15th. Therefore somebody (Cde. Whiteman) needs to leave here today, in
order to attend the meeting.

                          However, the decision was made,
that in light of the possibility that the arrangements for
the meeting were hot finalised, Cde. Whiteman should telephone Paul Miller or Jimmy Emmanuel to clarify this question.

(8) <u>PIONEERS</u> - Cde. Bishop told Cde. Strachan that one of the Pioneers Camp is being opened this afternoon, which means that
he will have to leave Cabinet in order to open the camp and
then return in time for PRG meeting. Also, the camp is
schelduled to close on Sunday morning at 10.00 a.m. - it means
therefore, that Cde. Strachan will have to leave Study to
close the camp and then return.

(9) <u>PARTY PAPER REPORT</u> - A report on the Party paper which was
distributed to CC members the week before was discussed by
the Political Bureau. The report came from Cde. Strachan's
Study Group which made recommendations about the way the
paper must be written and suggested that the Editorial Committee be comprised of ideologivally clear comrades.

The Bureau moted that the Party has five organs presently
being published, but not one one of them has a full-time
Party comrade assigned to it, as opposed to the FWI, which
has a fairly-large reporting staff.

Cde. Whiteman, Chairman of the Party's Editorial Committee,
said there is no representation on that Committee from the
Workers and Women committees and that someboy was needed to
be a full-time Party propagandist and reporter. Thus, it was
decided that Cde. Ken Lewis be such a person.

Comrades also suggested that there be a body to co-ordinate
the publication of the five Party organs and that 'Publication'
Committee be changed to 'Propaganda Committee. It was felt too,
that non-Bureau members of the CC be requested to write articles for the paper.

Cde. Whiteman is to speak with Don Rojas re. Ken Lewis' new
area of work and try to find a replacement for him.

(10) <u>PARTY HEADQUARTERS</u> - Cde. Austin gave a report on the progress of the plans for the Party's Headquarters. He did
meet with Galston and the former promised to bring the draw-

                    3...ings of the
```
```

ings of the building on Friday so that the Bureau can look
at them.

(11) FWI BUILDING - Cde. Bishop said that he had asked the Police
to vacate some rooms in the building and that Cde. Whiteman
should take a look at the space available with a view to
assigning some to the Editorial Committee and Cde. Lewis.

(12) SOCIALISM CLASSES REPORT - This item was not discussed.

(13) GRENLEC PROPAGANDA - Cde. Strachan read out a plan sent in
by Cde. McBarnette, as to how the change and restructuring
of the electricity rates (as opposed to 'increases') will be
announced to the public. A few slight changes were made to
the original plan.

Cde. Coard noted that the chnages in the rates include an
increase for the high users; a decrease for small users;
no chance for industrial users,; increase for commercial
users.

The Bureau agrred that the phrase 'change and restructuring
of electricity rates' should be used instead of 'increase
in electricity rates'. They also noted that the way the propaganda is worded on this issue will be very important.

OTHER ISSUES DISCUSSED:-

- Kamau's Kolumn in the FWI should be re........
- The British Labour Party Conference is coming up soon.
- Study classes on Monday 16th (Carnival Monday) will not be
coming off, but those on Tuesday morning remain as schelduled.
- Vietnam and Non-Aligned Day is Tuesday 1st September - Cde.
Strachan to get a Vietnamese and or Non-Aligned official to
come here for the occassion. The O.C. will plan details of
the event for that day.

DECISIONS REQUIRING FOLLOW-UP ACTION:-

o Has Cde. Louison submitted the names for the Nutmeg Board,
suggested a Board for Sylvia Belmar and gotten the details
re. Renwick's contract?
o Did Cde. Whiteman call Paul Miller or Jimmy Emmanuel re. the
proposed meetings with the NDF members?
o Did Cde. Whiteman speak to Don Rojas re. Ken Lewis' new area
of work? Has he found a replacement for Cde. Lewis?
o Did Cde. Austin bring the drawings of the Party Headquarters
to show the Bureau?
Has Cde. Whiteman looked at the space available for the Editorial Committee to use?
o Did Cde. Strachan get a Vietnames and or Non-algined official
to come here for September 1st and jas the OC looked at the
topic to plan details?

ITEMS TO BE DISCUSSED:-

1. New York Report
2. Socialism Classes Report

Hazel-Ann
RECORDING SECRETARY

MINUTES OF POLITICAL BUREAU MEETING HELD ON WEDNESDAY, 19TH AUGUST, 1981.

Comrades present:-

63

Maurice Bishop
Bernard Coard
George Louison
Selwyn Strachan
Unison Whiteman
Hudson Austin
Kenrick Radix

Liam James - Non-Bureau member

AGENDA:- An agenda was not set

Cde. James reported to the Bureau that he is organising a programme for Phillip Agee, former CIA Agent, who is presently here. Among other things, he is to attend the following:- the St. David's NWO Parish GM, the St. Johns and St. Patrick's NWO Parish GM's and the St. George's Workers Parish Council.

The following decisions were taken:-

a. Public rally on Friday night (August 21st) at the Market Square for Marcus Garvey, which will also be used to bring the people up to date on the present threat of invasion. Agee will also speak.

b. A National rally on September 13th, for the following; 1)formal opening of the Agro-Industries Plant at True Blue, 2) commemorating the overthrow of Allende and 3) the recent threat of invasion.

c. Cdes. Whiteman and (maybe) Bourne to attend the INC Congress starting this Saturday, 22nd August. Cde. Whiteman will attend only the opening and will speak to Forbes Burnham and then return to Grenada. Cde. Bourne will stay on for the rest of the conference.

d. Eugenia Charles' statement re. her reasons for not attending the Foreign Ministers conference here, should be replied to.

e. Telex on the United States' manouvres in the region will be sent to all heads of Governments. However, it has to be re-written because comrades felt it was too unconvincing. The telex will come from the P. M.

f. The following countries and/or fraternal parties in those countries will be contacted re. the present situation:- Puerto Rico, St. Vincent, St. Lucia, Dominica, Barbados, Antigua, Nicaragua, Venezuela, Jamaica, Belize, St. Kitts, Mexico, Canada, Trinidad and Tobago, Aruba, Suriname, El Salvador, Cuba, Martinique, Guadeloupe and Guatemala. It was decided that the countries will be prioritised.

g. Cde. Bourne should be pulled into foreign affairs.

DECISIONS REQUIRING FOLLOW-UP ACTION:- Sec A to F above.

FS - Cde. Bishop proposed a package of getting statements on Grenada, solidarity rally, protesting to the USA and informing Party cadres.

MINUTES OF POLITICAL BUREAU MEETING HELD ON
WEDNESDAY, 26TH AUGUST, 1981

Comrades present:-   C4

Maurice Bishop   Unison Whiteman   Hudson Austin
Bernard Coard   Kenrick Radix
Selwyn Strachan   George Louison

AGENDA :-

1. Visitors Committee Report
2. Solidarity Conference Committee Report
3. Third Festival of the Revolution
4. Health documents
5. Cde. Whiteman's Report
6. NCB
7. Miles Fitzpatrick's contract
8. Cde. Gibbson
9. RFG and Beausejour Transmitter
10. Militia Parade and Manouvre
11. Party Headquarters

1. VISITORS COMMITTEE REPORT - This item was not discussed
2. SOLIDARITY CONFERENCE COMMITTEE REPORT - Cde. Bishop reported he
met with Kurt Strachan of the National Secretariat on the issue.
The conference is carded to start on November 18th to 22nd. The
programme includes:-

   18th November ----------------Field trip
                                 Formal public opening (Butler House)
                                 Speeches and Culture

   19th November ----------------Addresses by FRG ministers
                                 Culture, etc.

   20th November ----------------Rap to each other

   21st November ----------------Field Trip

   22nd November ----------------Field Trip
                                 "Bloody Sunday" Rally

The following proposals regarding the conference were made:-

     i. All Governments, fraternal parties, organisations
        and individuals should be invited to the Conference.
    ii. The conference committee should be chaired by Cde.
        Strachan.
   iii. The Ministers' presentations should be prepared in
        advance and circulated to the delegates.

3. THRID FESTIVAL OF THE REVOLUTION - Cde. Bishop again reported on
   his meeting with Kurt Strachan. This time in regards to the upcoming 3rd anniversary of the Revolution. These proposals were
   made:-

     i. Mass organisations, Pioneers, Trade Union representatives
        should be on the committee.
    ii. Waldheim, Ramphal and Samora Machel or Mugabe should be
        invited to the Festival.
   iii. Harry Bellaforte and the Mighty Sparrow should also be
        invited.

        2/...iv. There should be

DOCUMENT 64
64 - 1

iv. There should be a competition for the design of a Monument of the Revolution.

v. Streets, parks and places should be re-named.

vi. The True Blue barracks of March 13, 1979 should be re-created.

vii. The socialist countries should be invited from <u>now</u> and asked to send high level representation.

viii. There will only be two official days of celebration and 6 weeks of village activities.

ix. This Festival must be the biggest in light of the imperialist propaganda.

4. <u>HEALTH DOCUMENTS</u> - This item was not discussed - it will be done at Cabinet meeting.

5. <u>CDE. WHITEMAN'S REPORT</u> - Cde. Whiteman submitted a written report to the Bureau on his visit to Suriname and Guyana. He also reported that a CARICOM Foreign Ministers Meeting is being planned for early September. Comrades felt that the meeting could be aimed at taking away Grenada's chairmanship of the Council and that this is a bad time for such a meeting, given the present balance of forces in the region. It was the feeling that it will be politically disadvantageous for Grenada.

It was decided that the CARICOM Secretariat should be checked to obtain information on the status of the meeting. After this is received, a decision can be taken regarding the issue.

6. <u>NCB</u> - Cde. Strean stated that 3 employees of the St. George's branch of the National Commercial Bank were dismissed and that there are presently about 6 vacancies there. He therefore wants to ensure that firm Party supporters are employed to fill the places. It was his feeling that the Cabinet Directive regarding employment in the state sector was not firm and clear enough. It was therefore decided that this will be checked with the Cabinet Secretary, Marcella Dacid and the Bureau agreed that firm Party supporters should be the ones to be employed at the NCB.

7. <u>MILES FITZPATRICK'S CONTRACT</u> - Cde. Radix said that Miles Fitzpatrick's one-year contract includes:-

```
salary---------------2,600
housing-------------  550
travel--------------1,000
small car (to be bought)
holiday (6 weeks)
travel to Guyana for 2 (one way)
gratuity (10%)
```

8. <u>CDE. GIBSON</u> - Cde. Radix stated that Cde. Earl Gibson in the Ministry of Agro-Industries and Fisheries is asking for a car, as was agreed in his contract. Cde. Coard responded by saying that this is alright and that the Ministry of Agro-Industries and Fisheries can buy a car from the money allocated to it in the budget.

9. <u>REG AND BEAUSEJOUR TRANSMITTER</u> - Cde. Austin reported that he met with Galston and the engineers. They said that the transmitter is ready for testing on September 1st and they are requesting that

3/...the engineers and

the engineers and technicians who went to Cuba for training, be
with them now. Official broadcast they said, will start in October at 75 KW of power in the day and 50 KW at night.

Cde. Austin also stated that there is a Geneva-based organisation dealing with monitoring radio frequencies used by different stations. He thinks that we should join it. There is also
a conference being planned for Canada next year to deal with
allocation of frequencies.

Some comrades suggested that RFG should be transmitting from
Beausejour.

It was suggested that Ray Smith be spoken to regarding the technicalities mentioned above.

10. **MILITIA PARADE AND MANOUVRE** - It was decided that the Militia Parade scheduled for this afternoon should be put off in order to
place complete emphasis on mobilisation and organisation for the
up-coming manouvre. It was also felt that there have been many
activities in the last two weeks, that might have caused people
to feel a bit tired.

A meeting to discuss the manouvres was scheduled.

11. **PARTY HEADQUARTERS** - This item was not discussed.

OTHER ITEMS DISCUSSED:-

o A regional Lions Conference will be held here soon
o We should get our regional and UWI sympathisers eg. Trevour Farrel
  to write articles in the regional newspapers.
.o The NJM should respond to Eugenia Charles' recent statement, pointing out the following:-
  i. we arned not to interfere in our internal affairs - we will
     respond
  ii. We are taking up the challeng of the Freedom Party
  iii. we are now preparing a documentation of all violations of human
      rights violations in Dominica
  iv. From now on, we will be speaking out on all the incidents of
      violation of humnan rights in Dominica.
  v. The region has gotten more aid in the last 2 years that the pre-
     vious 5 years.

TASKS:-

1, Cde. Whiteman to get Ashley Taylor or somebody else to get the information regarding the question of aid to the region.
2. A department in the Secretariat to be set up to deal with the region, with a progressive from each country on the committee - Cde.
   Strachan's responsibility to get the name to head the committee.
3. The OC to look at the scholarships for the Party School in Bulgaria.

o The Comrade Leader will attend Belize's independence on Spetember
  21st.
o The African Peoples Socialist Party is holding their First Party
  Congress from 5th - 7th September. They are inviting us to send a

representative. Cde. Miguel Mitchell at the New York Mission will represent the Party.

o Cde. Radix is due to leave for Rome for the EFAD negotiations and will also be in Cuba. In Cuba he will therefore become the emissary to Cde. Fidel and the ambassadors of the socialist countries.

o We should ask Guyana if they want Grenada to put out a statement on the refusal of the loan to them.

o The two Korean fishing boats that were caught in our waters last week were expected in Suriname and should be released, as they were not fishing.

o A Federation of Senior Workers under Curtis Stuart was registered some time ago. They are trying to reactivate themselves - the Federation should be struck off the books.

o "Crottey" Antoine of the GFC has been overruling the decision of the Board - he should be replaced.

o The International Airport is to be discussed at Economic Bureau meeting on Friday 28th August, 1981.

TASKS REQUIRING FOLLOW-UP ACTION:-

1. Does Cde. Strachan have a report for the Bureau regarding the committee for the 3rd Festival of the Revolution?
2. Were the health documents discussed at Cabinet meeting?
3. Was the CARICOM Secretariat contacted to find out the status of the proposed Foreign Ministers meeting in Jamaica?
4. Was the Cabinet Directive regarding an employment policy for the state sector looked at, to see whether it was firm and clear enough?
5. Was the car bought for Cde. Gibbson?
6. Were the technicalities about the GFC and Beausejour transmitter discussed with Ray Smith?
7. Did Cde. Whiteman get Ashley Taylor or somebody else to get the information regarding the aid to the region in the last 2 years compared to the previous 5 years? And was the statement from the NJM put out in response to Eugenia Charles'?
8. Has Cde. Strachan identified somebody to head the regional department in the Party's National Secretariat?
9. Has the OC looked at the Party Scholarships to Bulgaria?

ITEMS TO BE DISCUSSED:-

1. VISITORS COMMITTEE REPORT
2. HEALTH DOCUMENTS
3. PARTY HEADQUARTERS

Hazel-Ann
RECORDING SECRETARY

MINUTES OF POLITICAL BUREAU MEETING HELD ON
WEDNESDAY' 2nd September, 1981.

Comrades present   Comrades absent

    Maurice Bishop   Kenrick Radix - away
    Bernard Coard
    Selwyn Strachan
    Unison Whiteman
    George Louison
    Hudson Austin

AGENDA

1. School book. and uniforms programme
2. WPJ Five
3. Investment and Tourism Codes
4. Report on 3rd Festival oupcoming
5. RFG Antenna
6. Cocoa Law
7. Medical School
8. Party Headquarters
9. Rizo's report
10. Delegation for Australia
11. St. Lucia situation
12. Mexico

1. SCHOOL BOOKS AND UNIFORMS PROGRAMME - Cde. Coard reported that the NWO
is asking for an additional $60,000 for this programme because of the
great influx of request for hlep in this regard. The additional money was
agreed on - this would make the total sum allocated for this programme -
$1M.

Somewhat connected to this was Cde. Louison's report that Lorrianne Of the
Pionners had spoken to him recebtly. She said that the total money allocated for the Pioneers Camps was not utilised. It was her suggestion
therefore, that the balance be used for assisting with school books and
uniforms for the pioneers. However, comrades felt that giving them those
could be co-ordinated with the programme spearheaded by the NWO and that
the excess money should not be used for that purpose. Cde. Coard
pointed out that the money sis desperately needed.

2. WPJ FIVE - This item was discussed and the proposal agreed upon.

3. INVESTMENT AND TOURISM CODES -- This item was not discussed and was
put on the agenda for Economic Bureau meeting on Friday, 4th September.

4. REPORT ON 3RD FESTIVAL UPCOMING - Cde. Strachan reported on the first
meeting of the Planning Committee for the 3rd Festival of the Revolution. He said there were four aspect co-ordinators present. Candia
Alleyne has been removed as head of the Education Committee, at her request. Replacing her is Valarie Cornwall or Didacus Jules. Chris Del.
Riggs will no longer head the of the Cultural Committee. In his place
will be Captain Cecil Belfon. Cde. Strachan reported that the committee has agreed to meet weekly - on Mondays - from now on. The following suggestions were made -

- The March 13 rally to start at 1.00 p.m. instead of
10.00 a.m.

2... - All regional and

- All regional and international fraternal parties should be contacted as early as now.

- Tours should be organised for the event.

- The March into Queen's Park to be done sectionally ie. women, workers, farmers, youth, students, etc.

- Different work places to organised banners for the big day.

- A competition for the best design for the monument of the Revolution.

The planning committee is scheluled to meet next, on Monday, 7th September.

5. RFG ANTENNA - Cde. Austin reported on this issue and said that the technicians want a decision on the proposal to test the new transmitter.

Cde. Coard suggested that we should really have two radio stations. The other one, he said will play non-stop music with breaks only to "hook up" with RFG for the newscasys.

6. COCCA LAW - This item was not discussed.

7. MEDICAL SCHOOL - Cde. Bishop reported to the Bureau that the Medical School wants a review of the agreement and he mentioned a few specific areas. However, a committee has been formed comprised of Larry Wilson, ? Borson, Dorcos Braveboy, Langston Sibbles and "Punjab" who will meet with the school officials.

8. PARTY HEADQUARTERS - This item was not discussed.

9. RIZO'S REPORT - The Comrade Leader reported on a conversation he had with Ambassador Rizo and he got responses from the rest of the Bureau on specific issues raised which involved them.

10. DELEGATION TO AUSTRALIA - This item was not discussed.

11. ST. LUCIA SITUATION - Cde. Coard raised this issue, made some suggestions, some of which wre more or less agreed to by the Bureau.

12. MEXICO - This item was not discussed.

ITEMS TO BE DISCUSSED:-

1. Investment and Tourism Codes
2. Cocoa Law
3. Party Headquarters
4. Delegation to Australia
5. Mexico

Hazel-Ann
RECORDING SECRETARY

MINUTES OF **POLITI**CAL BUREAU MEETING HELD ON
WEDNESDAY, 9TH SEPTEMBER
1981

_____

Present

Maurice Bishop   66
Selwyn Strachan
Hudson Austin
George Louison

Absent

Bernard Coard
Kenrick Radix
Unison Whiteman

AGENDA

1. CPTU MEETING
2. DENNIS HENRY
3. JIM WARDALLY DOCUMENT
4. HAM COMRADES
5. NATIONAL BUS SERVICE
6. BULGARIA ICE PLAN
7. ROAD CONSULTANT - WEST COAST
8. INTERNATIONAL SOLIDARITY CONFERENCE
9. PORT AUTHORITY

10. APPROPIRATION LAWS
11. PRG RESOLUTION ON CONSUMPTION DUTIES
12. RFG ANTENNA
13. PARTY HEADQUARTERS
14. CHILE DAY RALLIES
15. SOCIALISM CLASSES IN THE BUREAUCRACY
16. OC DECISION

(1) CPTU MEETING - The council of Progressive Trade Unions (Trinidad) has organised a public meeting on Grenada for tonight and want somebody to come to speak on the Revolution. DECISION - Cde. DeRiggs will represent the Party and Revolution. He was called to the Bureau meeting; told of the decision and was given a briefing.

(2) DENNIS HENRY - Cde. Bishop reported that Dennis Henry leaves for England tomorrow (10th). The former's house will be bought by the PRG. He will be allowed to leave here with 50,000 punds (notes) nand the rest
- of his three quarter million dollars will be drawn out in three differett batches.

Mr. Henry has expressed his willingness to work for the PRG while in London and wants to talk with Cde. Fennis Augustine about it.

Cde. Austin will be checked by Carrol Bristol (Dennis Henry's lawyer) about the furniture in his house. The former is to find an old man type to occupy the house 24 hours daily.

(3) JIM WARDALLY'S DOCUMENT - Cde. Wardally submitted a document to the PB on the question of payment for some 1,344 unestablished workers. DECISION - These workers are to be paid - Larry Wilson informed accordingly.

(4) HAM COMRADES - Some will be arriving on the weekend.

(5) NATIONAL BUS SYSTEM - Cde. Strachan disclosed that the 26 buses will be ordered from the Mitsubishi Company, through Glean's garage instead of the other brand through Huggins. The order has been placed and they should be here by November or December.

(6) BULGARIA ICE PLANT - Cde. Louison reported that regarding the purchase of an ice plant. Our offer is a letter of credit, two and one half to three percent interest and repayment over 15 years. Their offer is 20% advance payment and 80% by letter of credit.

He said that Cde. Nazim was recommending we ask them for the $80 letter of credit and take the other things apart from the Ice Plant. However,

2...the feeling was

the feeling was ;that we should take just the ice plant at this time.

(7) ROAD CONSULTANT - WEST COAST - Cde. Terry Moore to telephone Vin Lawrence of Jentech to ask him to reduce their bid further. Second ly, the PB's preference is that Jentech and not the other company gets the contract. And thridly, PRG will pay addtional sum (above the $100,000 being provided by the CDB) out of its resources.

(8) INTERNATIONALSOLIDARITY -CONFERECNE - Cde. Bishop reported on this. Barbara Lee is here and according to the documents she brought, the porposed conference will start on November 20th instead of the 18th as thought of by us. Cde. Strachan will check her to co-ordinate the proposals. The draft agreement of friendship is to be looked at by Miles Fitzpatrick.

(9) PORT AUTHORITY APPOINTMENTS - The Board has suggested EBA Welsh and Renwick to be General Manager and Port Manager respectively of the Port Authority. Both names were rejected and other names are to be suggested and looked at on Friday's EB, when Cde. Radix should have been through.

(10) APPROPIRATION LAWS - Cde. Bishop signed the relevant document. How-ever, the figures are to be double checked.

(11) PRG RESOLUTION ON CONSUMPTION DUTIES - PRG or Cabinet to pass resolu-tion this afternoon (9th).

(12) RFG ANTENNA - Cde. Austin's report on this, is that wherever the an-tenna is, the transmitter has to be near by. In the case of RFG, it must be placed, not further than the area of Carifta Cottages. It was suggested that the area near Groomes House could be used - Cde. Austin to speak with Bob Evans on the effett it will have on the International Airport.

(13) PARTY HEADQUARTERS - Cde. Austin gave the report. These are to be done - a. structural designs, b. elevation designs and c. soil tests.

(14) CHILE DAY RALLIES - This is on Friday, 11th with them in St. David's and St. Andrew's. Cdes. Louison and Austin will attend them res-pectively.

(15) SOCIALISM CLASSES IN THE BUREAUCRACY -- Cde. Strachan said that according to reports given by the tutors taking those classes there has been some resistance from some students. He is therefore propos-ing that a letter from his Ministry be sent to all Permanent Secreta-ries, stating that the classes are complusory and must be attended to by all workers.

However, it was decided that the classes should be linked to the ITU programme, still making it complusory, but in a different formulation.

(16) OC DECISION - Cde. Strachan told the Bureau of the OC decison/ propo-sal that Francis Gill should head the St. Andrew's PCB and wanted to know how it will affect the Army. DECISION - Cde. Austin to discuss it at a meeting Thursday morning, to see if a replacement for Gill can be found.

66 - 2

Hazel-Ann
RECORDING SECRETARY

MINUTES OF THE POLITICAL BUREAU MEETING HELD ON
WEDNESDAY, 23RD SEPT. 1981.

Present :-

Bernard Coard
Selwyn Strachan
Hudson Austin
Kenrick Radix

Absent :-

Maurice Bishop)
George Louison) all out of
Unison Whiteman) the country

AGENDA :- 1. Land Utilisation Law
2. State of political work in the army
3. National Bus Service
4. Party Headquarters
5. Mass Activities upcoming
6. Trade Union Conference
7. Dredging contract

(1) LAND UTILISATION LAW - Cde. Radix explained that the final draft
of the Law will be ready on Friday morning (25th) and CC comrades
are scheduled to meet at 9,00 a.m. that same morning to discuss
the law.

(2) STATE OF POLITICAL WORK IN THE ARMY - Cde. Strachan told the
Bureau that a present and for a long time now, there has not
been any political education going on in the Armed Forces. He
said that a meeting was held with some Party comrades (A?s,
CM's and M's) in the army to discuss the situation. One of
the major decisions form that meeting was to set up a Department of Politics within the Army. Another decision was to start
Socialism classes there. A proposal is also to go to the CC,
that the person in charge of political education in the Army
be a member of the OC. If agreed, the relevant comrade will be
brought on to that body.

The Bureau decided to make these temporary changes for a period
of six months; Cdes. Layne, Louison, Belfon, Gill, Redhead and
Stroude were called to the meeting and told of the changes.
These changes are:-

1. Major Louison - Deputy of Defense, Chief of Planning
2. Major Layne - Chief of Staff, Head of Region 1
3. Captain Belfon- Acting Chief of Operations, Chief of Mobilisation and Organisation
4. Captain Stroude-Chief of Politics and Academics
5. Captain Redhead- Deputy Chief of Staff (For discipline)
6. Captain Gill - Out if the Army: Head of St. Andrew's PCB

Cde. Coard called this a compromise, since it is his strong feeling that the leadership of the Army should be changed.

(3) NATIONAL BUS SERVICE - Cde. Strachan said that Egbert Francis was
recommended by Cleveland Dolland for the job of Manager of the
NBS and that the latter has displayed the interest in that job.
The Bureau decided:-

1. Employment of Egbert Francis as Manager - NBS
2. His tasks between now and when the buses arrive in January
1981 are:-

a. identify a place to house/service the 26 buses
b. advertise for drivers to be interviewed by Cdes.

Cleveland Dolland, Egbert Francis and Hudson Austin or Selwyn Strachan.

   c. Study the best routes, hours, weekend scheldule, scheldule to facilitate school children, fares etc.

   d. Identify a good accountant.

3. Interview to include questions about the applicants' age, record of accidents, background, etc.

4. The buses are not to travel on the Grand Etag roda.

5. The NBS will be registered as a private company owned by the Government.

6. The NBS Board of Directors comprises:-

   a. Permanent Secretary - Ministry of Communicationsm Labour
   b. Trade Union representative
   c. NYO representative
   d. NWO representative
   e. Cleveland Dolland

7. The Manager (Egbert Francis) will be Secretary to the Board of Directors, but not a member of the Board.

8. Ticket system to be used by NBS

(4) PARTY HEADQUARTERS - Cde. Austinnreported that the structural designs are being done and that by next week, everything will be ready.

(5) MASS ACTIVITIES - The list of mass activities taking place and the FB comrades assigned are as follows:-

Thursday, 24th:-

o Rural Workers Farish Council, St. David's
  RC School, 5.00 p.m.   : Cde. Radix
o Zoanl Council Meeting, Victoria   : Cde. Coard
o St. George's S.E. Zonal Council Meeting
  St. Paul's Model School, 7.00 p.m. : Cde. Austin
o Panel discussion, Woburn, 7.30 p.m. : Cde. Strachan

Friday, 25th:-

o NYO Extra-Ordinary General Meetings:
o St. Mark's, Waltham Junior Secondary School,
  7.00 p.m.   : Cde. Strachan
o St. David's, RC School, 7.00 p.m.   : Cde. Austin
o St. Andrew's, Junior Secondary School,
  7.00 p.m.   : Cde. Radix

Saturday, 26th:-

o Opening of MNIB, Petite Martinique Branch,
  4.00 p.m.   : Cde. Coard
o

Sunday, 27th:-
o NWC Membership rally,
  Elizabeth Park, Victoria, 2.00 p.m. : Cdes. Strachan and Radix

Monday, 28th:-
o Rural Workers Farish Council, West Coast
  Anglican School, 6.00 p.m.   : Cdd. Coard
o Urban Workers Farish Council, St. George's

3/... Butler House, 7.30 p.m.

Butler House, 7.30 p.m.   : Cde. Radix
o St. Patrick's, S.E. Zonal Council
  Meeting, River Sallee Government
  School, 7.00 p.m.   : Cde. Strachan

Sunday, 4th October:-

o AGWU National Get-together, La
  Sagesse,, from 10.00 a,m. until...   : Everybody
o Opening of the 2nd Ecumenical Human
  Rights Encounter, The Dome, 5.00 p.m.: Everybody

Sunday, 18th October:-

o NWO Parish Rally/Opening of Primary
  Health Care Programme, St. David's,
  Belle Vue Park, 2.00 p.m.   : Everybody

Saturday, 31st October:-
o FFU Annual General Meeting, 10.00 a.m.: Everybody

Sunday, 1st November:-
o PFU Mass Rally, Seamoon, 2.00 p.m.   : Everybody

Wednesday, 18th November:-
o Opening, Caribbean Trade Union Con-
  ference, The Dome, 1.30 p.m.   : Everybody

Sunday, 22nd November;-
o Bloody Sunday Rally, Seamoon   : Everybody

Monday, 23rd November:-
o Opening, 1st International Solidarity
  Conference, The Dome, 10.00 a.m.   : Everybody

Sunday, 6th December:-
o NWO National Rally,

12th and 13th December:-
o NYO Congress, The Dome

                                          Hazel-Ann
                                          RECORDING SECRETARY

MINUTES OF THE POLITICAL BUREAU MEETING HELD ON
WEDNESDAY, 30th September, 1981

Present :-   Absent :-

Bernard Coard   Maurice Bishop
Slewyn Strachan   68   George Louison
Hudson Austin   Unison Whiteman
Kenrick Radix

Agenda :-

1. Cadet Mobilisation   8. Callist Playing field
2. Party Headquarters   9. Upcoming activities
3. Festival Committee   10. Angola Independence Day
4. Solidarity Conference Report   11. Analysis of recent council
5. Letter from WPJ   meetings and parish NYO GM's
6. Letter from GCFS   12. Decision of Llyode Noel's
7. Cde. Bourne's ambassadorship   letter
                                  13. Recommendations for detainees
                                      release

(1) CADET MOBILISATION - Cde. Strachan explained that he held a meet-
    ing with the comrades responsible for this area. They felt that this
    must be given more attention and that Cde. Cherebin (Forgie) should
    have this as his full time job. However, comrades pointed out that
    this decision was already taken since last year, so it was thus
    irrelevant now and that the important thing is to get the work
    done.

(2) PARTY HEADQUARTERS - Cde. Austin showed the Bureau the drawungs of
    the Party Headquarters. The estimate of the qunatities of materials
    needed is to be done - they should be ready by next week.

(3) FESTIVAL COMMITTEE - Cde. Strachan wanted to look at one aspect of
    this re, the site for the monument. Places as the Botanical Gar-
    dens, the site of DeAllie's burnt house in St. Paul's, the area
    between Apple Inn and Carifta Cottages, etc. There was a very
    strong feeling that the monument be on "Freedom Hill". A number
    of ideas as to what the monument should be were expressed includ-
    ing, a sculpture that incorporates the years of NJM struggle, the
    heroes of the Revolution, the adhievements and symbolises the
    future. Cde. Strachan is to follow up on this.

(4) SOLIDARITY CONFERENCE REPORT - The report here, according to Cde.
    Strachan, is that "things are moving", but the invitations are out-
    standing. However, he explained that somebody will be leaving on
    Friday for North America for the purpose and that the aim is to get
    100 delegations.

(5) LETTER FROM WPJ - The WPJ has invited NJM to send 2 comrades to
    their 2nd Party Congress on 17th - 20th December.

    It was decided that NJM will attend, but no names were decided on.
    The topic is to be on the PB's agenda on Novdmber 11th. A reply is
    to be sent confirming our attendance.

(6) LETTER FROM THE G.C.F.S. - A request was received from the Grenada
    Cuba Friendship Society for Cde. Radix and the PB to attend their
    upcoming activity on October 8th. The former's attendance was con-
    firmed.

(7.) <u>CDE. BORNE'S AMBASSADORSHIP</u> - Cde. Bourne's appointment as Ambassador to Lybia was confirmed. He and "Bengie" are to leave for Cuba in the next two weeks and should get to Lybia by the end of November. Cde. Radix is to inform Winston Davis so that the Lybians will have the information.

(8) <u>CALLISTE PLAYING FIELD</u> - Cde. Strachan told the Bureau of a present conflict with one Pilgrime, owner of that Playing field who wants back the land that Gairy had acquired from him. But the youths are protesting this. Cde. Strachan is to handle the matter.

(9) <u>UPCOMING ACTIVITIES</u> - The following is a list of zonal council meetings scheduled for St. Andrew's during the month of October:-

    a. South West - B/Grove Community Centre - Thurs. 8th
    b. South East - G/ville Anglican School? - Thurs. 15th
    c. North East - Pearls Community Centre - Thurs. 22nd
    d. North West - Byelands Old School - Thurs. 29th

             They all start at 7.00 p.m.
The PB member to attend each of these meetings will be selected during the week.

(10) <u>ANGOLA INDEPENDENCE DAY</u> - This is on November 11th. We are to invite Angola's representatives at the U.N. and in Cuba to speak at two indoor parish rallies to be organised. The propaganda committee is to do a 'build up'.

(11) <u>ANALYSIS OF RECENT COUNCIL MEETINGS</u> - Comrades reported on the different council meetings and NYO parish GM's they had attended. All went well, except the St. Andrew's NYO GM, which was poorly attended.

(12) <u>DECISION ON LLOYD NOEL'S LETTER</u> - Lloyd Noel has written a letter, seeking permission to have his wife sell his car - this was agreed to by the Bureau.

(13) <u>RECOMMENDATIONS FOR DETAINEES RELEASE</u> - The list was read out and some names were agreed to by the Bureau. However, it is to be discussed with the relevant ICB's also.

                                 Hazel-Ann
                                 RECORDING SECRETARY

MINUTES OF POLITICAL BUREAU MEETING HELD ON WEDNESDAY, 14th OCTOBER, 1981

Present :-

Maurice Bishop
Hudson Austin
Kenrick Radix
Bernard Coard
Selwyn Strachan

Absent :-

George Louison
Unison Whiteman

AGENDA :-

1. Cde. Coards bilaterals with Dominicans, St. Lucians and Puerto Ricans
2. Bulgarian Ambassador's visit
3. OC Decision
4. Discussion with Cde. Gahagan
5. Carriacou's Mass Activities
6. Secondary School Emulation Night
7. Lyle Bullen's Lobster Trade
8. Draft speech for reopening of NISTEP
9. Beryl Rattan
10. Meeting with Korean Ambassador
11. Ray Smith
12. Resettlement of Calliste Residents
13. Eastern Main Road
14. Western Main Road
15. Tourists routes
16. Medical School
17. Sonny Mark's letter
18. Regina Taylor
19. Street
20. OCCBA'S letter
21. Neehall's letter
22. Date for next CC meeting
23. Education Committee Report
24. Spanish Socialist Workers Party, 29th Congress
25. Report on Commonwealth trip
26. GDR Communications Equipment
27. Cde. Bihsop's visit to the GDR, etc.
28. Antigua's Independence
29. Holiday Inn Sewage Plan
30. Langston - detainee
31. Cde. Coard's visit to Ralph Thompson
32. Meeting with Judy Williams and Ricky Charles
33. Meeting with representatives/members of the Chamber of Commerce

(1) COE. COARD'S BILATERALS - Cde. Coard reported that he held meetings with comrades from Dominica, St. Lucia and Puerto Rico, all separately.

(2) BULGARIAN AMBASSADOR'S VISIT - The Bulgarian Ambassador to Cuba due to visit here onfrom Friday, 15th, as part of the 1300th anniversary of the Bulgarian State. Some of the activities he will attend include :-

i) NWO/PRIMARY HEALTH CARE RALLY - Sunday, 18th, St. David's
ii) NYO National Council Meeting - Saturady, 17th
iii) South Zonal Council, Calliste Government School - Monday 19th
iv) Reception in his honour (tentative) - Tuesday, 20th
v) Press Conference

(3) OC DECISION - Cde. Coard told the BB that the Oc had suggested/decided that our Trade and Student Attaches in Havana should be Ken Roberts and one Mitchell respectively. Cde. Keith Roberts is to try to convince Ken Roberts to do trade instead of piloting as he wanted to do. A Military Attache is yet to be identified.

(4) DISCUSSION WITH GAHAGAN - Cde. Coard reported tha he held a discussion with Cde. Akie Gahagan regarding what the latter's job should be. He was given three alternatives. He decided to remain here and be attached to Cde. Strachan's Ministry. He will be part of the delegation to the 29th Congress of the Spanish Socialst Workers Party.

(5) CARRIACOU'S MASS ACTIVITIES - Carriacou's Parish Council to be held on Thursday, 15th and their Women's Parish Council on Friday 16th. Cdes. Coard and Radix to attend them respectively.

(6) SECONDARY SCHOOL EMULATION NIGHT - This was discussed, based on the report sent by Sis. Creft. A few changes were made.

(7) LYLE BULLEN'S LOBSTER TRADE - Cde. Coard received a report/complaint from Cdes. Creft and Jules that the Bullen brothers in Carriacou have been sending out lobsters by the planeloads out of Carriacou, apparently without any customs regulations or restrictions.

(8) SPEECH FOR MISTEP RE-OPENING - The draft speech was accepted, with only a few changes made to it.

(9) BERYL RATTAN - Cde. Radix told the Bureau that this woman was making requests for the pardoning of her son who was involved in some corruption. It was the feeling that the son involved should travel out of Grenada.

(10) MEETING WITH KOREAN AMBASSADOR - Cde. Radix reported on a meeting he had with the Korean Ambassador. The latter said that his country is willing to give technical, scientific and military assistance to Grenada. They also want the Comrade Leader and a delegation from the Mass Organisations to visit Korea next year.

(11) RAY SMITH - Here again, Cde. Radix explained that a site was being looked at for the re-locating of the radio transmitter. He said that he is "on top the situation".

(12) CALLISTE RESIDENTS - Cade. Austin disclosed that the Calliste residents have been slow in re-locating themselves. He also said that the specifications for the re-building of some residents' houses have not been followed and that he will handle the issue personally.

(13) EASTERN MAIN ROAD - Some problems are being experienced here - a few engineers are needed.

(14) WESTERN MAIN ROAD - A vehicle is needed for this project. The one

3/...being used by

being used by "Highead" will be used for this purpose.

(15) TOURIST ROUTES - Some tourist routes are to be repaired.

(16) MEDICAL SCHOOL - They want to add one floor to Ken Milne's building on Grand Anse beach, and are also complaining that they cannot get the use of the Dome, although they pay $1,000 (US) monthly rent. No decisions were taken on this.

(17) SONNY MARK'S LETTER - This letter was received by Cde. Bishop who said that Sonny Mark is complaining about the NY mission. It was suggested that Cladwell Taylor be given a copy of the letter and asked to reply to each complaint.

(18) REGINA TAYLOR)
(19) STREET   )   These items were not discussed.

(20) OCCBA'S LETTER - A letter was received from the Organisation of Caribbean and Commonwealth Bar Associations, signed by Elliot Mottley. They want to know the reasons why Lloyd Noel and Tillman Thomas are in detention. The Bureau decided that a reply will be sent to them.

(21) NEEHALL'S LETTER - Re. Roy Neehall of the CCC sent a letter to Comrade Bishop expressing concern over information he received that Lloyd Noel and Kennedy Budhlall have been tortured. He also stated that a CCC team will be coming to Grenada to meet with the church.

ITEMS 22 to 26 were not discussed.

(27) CDE. BISHOP'S VISIT TO GDR, ETC. - This is planned for 10 - 23 December and also includes Bulgaria.

(28) ANTIGUA'S INDEPENDENCE - This in November 1st and the Comrade Leader is due to attend the ceremony.

(29) HOLIDAY INN SEWAGE PLAN - Complaints had been received by Cde. Bishop that the Sewage Plan at the Holiday Inn is bad. They were given a deadline in which to correct the sityatuion. If it was not meet, the Ministry of Health will do the job and bill it to them.

Complaints were also received about the security at that hotel - Cde. Keith Roberts was duly informed.

ITEMS 30 and 31 were not discussed.

Hazel-Ann
RECORDING SECRETARY

MINUTES OF THE POLITICAL BUREAU MEETING OF
WEDNESDAY, 21ST OCTOBER
1981

Present:-

    Maurice Bishop   70
    Bernard Coard
    Selwyn Strachan
    George Louison
    Hudson Austin
    Kenrick Radix
    Unison Whiteman

Agenda:-

1. Budgetary situation
2. Nutmeg bonus
3. Low income housing
4. Letter from Cde. Croft - Cuban schols
5. Mexico Report
6. Ralph Thompson
7. Date for CC meeting
8. Bulgaria
9. Teachers for Nicaragua
10. Solidarity Conference
11. Trade Union Conference
12. Third Festival of the Revolution
13. Washington Mission Administrator
14. Causual workers pay
15. Idle equipment in Queen's Park
16. P.S. for Cde. Austin's ministry
17. Party Headquarters

(1) BUDGETARY SITUATION - The budget is on the way to a $9M shortfall in the revenue for this year. In order tfor the fall to be reduced, most ministries' budgets will habe to be cut. This item was due to be discussed at the Cabinet meeting schelduled for this afternoon.

* FWI needs a Business Manager immediately - Cde. Rohas cannot do the job.
* Ministries' budget for 1982 should be submitted soon.

(2) NUTMEG BONUS - Cde. Louison said that the GCNA has decided tp pay out $3.1M in bonus this year, compared to the $4M paid last year and the year before.

He also stated that the nutmeg sales in 1982 could just be the same as this year unless the sales improve.

Comrades agreed on the $3.1M.

(3) LOW INCOME HOUSING - The Ministry of Housing send a list of persons interviewed who have made application for the houses. The Secretariat is to make copies of the list and give it to the St. Andrew's and St. George's RCP leaders and PB members. The

latter is to discuss the item on Friday, 23rd.

(4) SCHOLS FROM CUBA - Cde. Creft has requested that the FB gives her an idea as to what areas scholarships are needed in for the 1982 - 1983 period. Alist of the areas given in 1979 - 1981 was sent. The document to be copied and distributed to FB comrades. The item will be discussed on Friday 23rd at EV.

(5) MEXICO REPORT - Cde. Louison reported on the COPPPAL meeting he attended in Mexico. He said that the regional SI group met. A Grenada Solidarity Committee was formed. It's president is France and Secretary - the Dutch. It includes Norway, Britain and the FNP. Some others have given their verbal support and say they will sign.

The next COPPPAL meeting: Panama, end of November

Cde. Louison met with Mexico's Vice Minister of Finance. They are willing to give us some money - a team will be visiting here from 26th October - 6th November.

The CLADE meeting is scheduled for 5th and 6th November.

* The Party needs to decide on an International Secretary very soon - comrades to think of names and the item to be discussed at Friday's EB meeting.

(6) RALPH THOMPSON - Cde. Bishop visited him, he wants to go home. Cde. Bishop thinks that he should be sent home also. It was decided upon and his name is to be taken off the list of detainees.

(7) DATE FOR CC MEETING - The date for the next CC meeting is October 28th (every last Wednesday in the month). That is, November 25th and December 30th. Time 8.00 a.m. to 4.00 p.m.

(8) BULGARIA - There will be an exhibition at Marryshow House on Thursday, 22nd in honour of the 1300th anniversary of the Bulgarian state. It is to become part of a reception in honour of Ambassador Dimitrov.

(9) TEACHERS FOR NICARAGUA - About 12 Grenadian teachers are to be identified to go to Nicaragua. Cde. Jules is presently working on this - it was suggested that NYO unemployed members be used.

ITEMS 10 to 12 and 14 to 17 were not discussed.

(13) ADMINISTRATOR FOR WASHINGTON MISSION - That mission needs an Administrator - no decisions were taken.

ITEMS TO BE DISCUSSED: - 10,11,12, 14, 15, 16, 17

ITEMS TO BE DISCUSSED AT E.B. MEETING: -

1, Low income housing
2, Schols from Cuba

Hazel-Ann
RECORDING SECRETARY

REPORT TO POLITICAL BUREAU, NJM

WORLD CONFERENCE OF WOMEN & WIDE CONGRESS, PRAGUE AND VISIT TO BULGARIA
BY SISTERS P. COARD' R. JOSEPH AND E. CALLISTE, OCTOBER 3-30th, 1981

World Conference of Women 8-13th - attended by 1000 delegates from more than
200 organizations.

We travelled via Cuba and had a brief discussion with the head of the International Affairs Department of the F.M.C., P. Coard had also had a discussion
over lunch with the International Secretary, Esther Veliz in September. These
centred around what Cuba sees as a difference in emphasis between the
European organizations and those of the underdeveloped world in the question
of the conference theme "Equality, Nationality Independence, Peace." The
F.M.C. felt that the European organizations emphasize peace at the expense
of the importance of the National Liberation struggles. They felt that this
was the result of those countries being so far removed from the underdeveloped
world. We were given the impression that this would be the major contradiction
of the conference. However, in the event, the Socialist organizations of
Europe led with a principled and, we thought, correct position and no such
struggle developed. In fact, it was clear that the struggle for peace was
closely linked with the struggle for National Independence, both facing the
same enemy, US Imperialism - this turned out to be the major theme of the
conference. The conference was highly successful in drawing the Socialist
World closer to the progressive organizations of the Third World, both
because of the firm and factual position taken by the CP organizations, and
also because of the excellent treatment given by the Czech Women's Union.

MAIN BENEFITS OF CONFERENCE FOR GRENADA

1) We discovered that Grenada was practically unknown to most of the
   Women's Organizations. However, by the end of the conference everyone
   knew about us because of our wide distribution of literature, our
   presentations in the two (2) major committees, the fact that Grenada
   was elected to speak for the English speaking Caribbean within the
   Latin American group, and our extensive contacts made with other
   organizations. We received fraternal greetings and solidarity every
   where by the end of the conference, and established relations with

   -2- many........

many organizations.

2)   Our two representations were well received and several Socialist countries
      asked for copies and commented on the high standard and the "firm position".

3)   We established very friendly relations with USSR, Hungary, GDR, Czechoslo-
      vakia and Bulgaria, whose delegations were led by outstanding women.
      The GDR will be sending a representative for our December 6th rally. The
      others regretted that their budgets for 1981 were exhausted because they
      had paid for many countries to go to the conference. However, they all
      promised to visit us next year and USSR, Czechoslovakia and GDR invited
      us to visit them, probably in May-June. This would need to be at the
      highest level - it would be a decisive step in drawing us closer to them.
      We need to improve the consistency of our written communications with the
      Socialist world.

WIDF CONGRESS 14-15th - 96 ORGANIZATIONS

Here we were accepted as members. The CWP - JA was also accepted. The WRSM
(Guyana) was not accepted - their application was delayed for further consideration. It was our impression that the Socialist organizations of Europe supported the WPO in its plea to have them rejected. All the English-speaking territories, as well as Cuba, maintained a neutral position. The INP-WM stated
that their Party Congress, being held at that time, was deciding the issue
of their relations with the PNC. We explained our position to the WPO in
terms of our desire not to do anything that would increase the rupture in
CAribbean unity, they accepted this. However, the WRSM adopted a quietly
hostile attitude to all the other English-speaking territories: on two (2)
occasions when we tried to join them at lunch they told us they were expecting
another delegation. Their tatics were to give a brilliant and progressive
presentation in the major committee(by contrast, the WPO's was very weak) and
to buy the favours of the Progressive African group by telling them of their
party's support for the African Liberation Movements. ($100,000 p.a.). However,
this didn't work, perhaps because of Zimbabwe's relationship with Rodney,
perhaps because of the closeness of relationships between the Socialist
bloc and the African organizations.

71 - 2

3/ Re.the WIDF.....

Re: the WIDF Bureau Elections, there was a slight possibility that we could have been elected. In practice, the old Bureau "proposes" the new one after consultations with the different geographic blocs; but candidates should declare their candidature in advance. Because of being unable to obtain up to now a copy of the WIDF constitution despite requests made in the past as well as at the conference, we were unsure as to how things worked; and an indirect hint to the FMC in September (re the WPO proposing us) produced no positive response from them; we had therefore concluded that the organization may not wish a brand new member to stand. However, because of the WPO's bad behaviour during the past year and some unprincipled positions taken, it timed out that the Bureau did not wish to retain the WPO on the Bureau. The day before the Congress, an FMC delegate suggested to us that we could be an alternative. We agreed but did not campaign. It then turned out that because of other Latin American organizations pressure within the Bureau it was decided to drop WPO and substitute several months ahead. However, this was a tatical error, as the WPO (which would have been forced to accept Grenada as a substitute) immediately mobilized the rest of the English-and French-speaking Caribbean to protest against their replacement on the Bureau by a 6th Spanish speaking territory of this hemisphere when there were already 5. The final decision was to delay the decision and let the Bureau decide at the next meeting in 6 months time.

However, the WPO also revealed itself as unprincipled by telling a lie against Cuba (that the FMC had proposed their replacement by Nicaragua-actually it was Argentina who did so) and both the CWP and ourselves spoke to Nalini about how incorrect and unwise we felt their attitude to the FMC and Cuba was using many examples. It's clear that it has affected the attitude of the Socialist countries to the WPO.

We are not particularly impressed by the efficiency of the WIDF (as opposed to their ideological stance) - their programme for the next 5 years was very vague, no real work-plan; and they never seem to be able to answer letters although they send thousands of press releases.

We ordered 200 copies of each issue of the WIDF journal, which is very good one for each group.

                              4/ Visit to

VISIT TO BULGARIA (17th-25th OCTOBER)

This was highly successful. We spent 3 days in Sophia, and 5 in Rousse, a manufacturing town with an ancient history of resistence to both the Turks and Nazis. We were able to learn a great deal about the history, and present level of economic development and social organization. of Bulgaria. Our hosts treated us extremely well and spoke very frankly to us about their own social problems and also the problems of Poland (they brought this up).

We formed a very warm relationship with the Women's Committee in Rousse; also with the President of the National Women's Committee, who is an outstanding woman, she was a guerrilla partisan from age 14; is now a CC member.

Prague 25th-26th We were warmly received, put at the CC hotel (Hotel Praga) and had very good discussions with the Women's Union International Secretary.

A note re the Organization of Women and Youth in the Socialist Countries.

Women: The USSR, Bulgaria and Hungary have Women's Committees which organize women on the basis of work-places (85%-90% of women in those countries work). There is usually a woman elected to represent the Committee in the Trade Union branch in each workplace. There is also usually a branch of the Committee in every community, which seeks to mobilize women for social goals, but this is like an executive. Thus, the committees are not mass organizations.

The GDR, Czechoslovakia and Cuba have mass women's organizations like ours, based in the communities. Czechoslovakia had a committee until 1968 - following the Dubzcheck crisis the party decided to transform it into a mass organization in order to deepen its links in the communities.

YOUTH: Apparently only the USSR and Cuba have vanguard youth Organizations. In Bulgaria, Czechoslovakia and the GDR the Youth have mass organizations, and very strong ones.

MINUTES OF POLITICAL BUREU MEETING ON
WEDNESDAY 4th NOVEMBER
1981
_____

Comrades present;-   72   Comrades absent :-

    Maurice Bishop   Unison Whiteman - sick
    Bernard Coard
    Selwyn Strachan
    George Louison
    Kenrick Radix
    Hudson Austin

Agenda :-

1. West German delegation
2. Plan
3. RFG's transmitter
4. Venezuela Boat
5. Bloody Sunday
6. Solidarity Conference
7. Soviet Union Embassy
8. Lybia, Iraq Embassies
9. Deputy Ministers from Cuba
10. Discussion with Denzil Wilks
11. WFA'S Union
12. Military Alert
13. Party Headquarters
14. NACDA'S Board

(1) WEST GERMAN DELEGATION) These items were not discussed
(2) PLANE   )
(3) RFG'S TRANSMITTER - Changed from 1010 om the meduim wave to
    690. Ray Smith will be attending the international communications
    conference, as the CECS and Grenada's representative. However,
    it was the Bureau's decision that Ashley Taylor should accompany
    Ray Smith, as the latter is too naive and may not make the cor-
    rect political decisions in this area.
(4) VENEZUELA BOAT - Cde. Radix reported on the negotiations taking
    place with Venezuela's representatives in regard to the boat
    that was found in our waters. Cde. Radix is to follow up on
    this.
(5) BLOODY SUNDAY - Cde. Strachan stated that   this Rally will
    have to be highly successful and must be the biggest. The mas-
    ses will be mobilised sectionally and by parish. A meeting of
    the PCB heads and leaders of the mass organisations is schel-
    duled for the next 48 hours to work out the plan of mobilisa-
    tion leading up to the 22nd. The aim is to have at least 1500
    persons at the rally. Transportation, he said, would be the
    main problem.

(6) SOLIDARITY CONFERENCE - Cde. Strachan:-
6.1 Invitations - between 225 to 250 invitations sent out to Asia,
    Africa, Europe, North America and the Caribbean. To date, only
    13 responses (12 of which are positive), have been received.
    The organisers in the U.S. (Barbara Lee and Carlatta, etc.)

..../2

DOCUMENT 72
72 - 1

have promised they will bring 10, 15 or even 20 delegations. Today, 150 telegrams will go out as a reminder. Dessima and Cladwell kept the US invitations 2 weeks before delivering them. Overall aim is to bring 100 delegates.

Cde. Coard: Use our seven ambassadors to make telephone call reminders.

6.2 Accomodation:- Lou Bone is in charge and has been doing a good job. 111 rooms (hotels and homes) have been confirmed. Attempting to get 50% discount from the hotels. The key to cutting done on accomodation costs is to get delegates to stay at some private homes.

6.3 Programme/Content:-

Cde. Leader's address is the major speech. Solidarity messages should be 2 minutes each. Presentations on Agriculture and Agro-Industries and Fisheries to be followed by workshops and reports. The presentations to be ready by 18th November. Time to be allocated for delegates to make pledges to avoid duplicating.

Cde. Bishop's speech should bemade into a booklet and given to the delegates before they leave.

PB: key right now is to "pull out all the stops", to make sure that the conference is a success.

(7) SOVIET UNION EMBASSY

(8) LYBIA & IRAQ EMBASSIES - Cdes. Berune and Benjamin have returned from Cuba and will leave for their respective missions shortly. The countries are to be informed.

(9) DEPUTY MINISTERS FROM CUBA - The deputy Ministers of Trade, Economic Collaboration and Foreign Affairs of Cuba will be arriving on Friday, 6th. Cdes. Lyden Ramdhany and Radix are to meet them at the Airport. In the latter's case, this will be done if Cde. Whiteman is still unwell.

(10) DISCUSSION WITH DENZIL WILKS - Cde. Bishop reported that Cde. Wilks had met with him and raised the issue of Clemont Kirton's salary. Cde. Coard felt that the proper channel to deal with these issues like this one was through Cde. Strachan as had already been agreed to with Cde. Wilks so.

(11) WFA's Union -   )
(12) MILITARY ALERT -   ) These items wer not discussed
(13) PARTY HEADQUARTERS -)
(14) NACDA'S BOARD -   )

ERIC SEALEY - has expressed desire to organise a goodwill tour to Grenada by a team of boxers. They will need their tickets and accomodation for 8 persons to be paid for by Grenada. This was agreed to and the last week of January and the first week of February were suggested for the visit.

ANGOLAN SOLIDARITY DAY - November 11th, A outdoor meeting to be held in the Sauteurs courtyard. The West Coast and St. Patrick's will be the main areas of mobilisation.

72 - 2

AGRO-INDUSTRIES' RESTAURANT - will be opened during the first week in December. Cde. Radix's suggestion for its name: "The Crucial Factor."

MARRYSHOW DAY - Saturday 11th. Chruch service and graveside ceremony being planned. The NWAFG will organise the indoor meeting/rally to take place at Hindsey School. Cde. Coard will attend it.

TU CONFERENCE : Cde. Strachan&

o everything is going alright

3RD FESTIVAL: Cde. Strachan -

o invitations will go off this month

Hazel-Ann
RECORDING SECRETARY

MINUTES OF THE POLITICAL BUREAU MEETING
WEDNESDAY, 11TH NOVEMBER
1981

Comrades present

Maurice Bishop
Bernard Coard
Selwyn Strachan
Kenrick Radix
Hudson Austin

Comrades absent

George Louison
Unison Whiteman

AGENDA

1. Caribbean and Central American Action meeting
2. Party Schols and visits to S.U.
3. Report on the CDCC Conference
4. Richard Jacobs
5. P.S. for the Ministry of Communications
6. Religious Conference
7. Solidarity with Cuba
8. PA Systems for the 3rd Festival
9. Angola Day Rally
10. PWU Struggle
11. Caribbean Trade Union Conference
12. Activities for November
13. Party Headquarters
14. National Mobilisation's Building
15. Housing
16. Sea World Centre
17. WPJ Congress
18. New Applicants

1. CARIBBEAN AND CENTRAL AMERICAN ACTION MEETING - It was decided that Grenada should "press" to be invited to this meeting which takes place at the end of November. The eprson to go, if we are invited, will be either Cde. Whiteman, Louison or Radix. However, the decision will be taken when the invitation has been received.

2. PARTY SCHOOLS AND VISITS TO S.U. - Twelve short term Party scholarships are being offered to us by the Soviet Union. The Secretariat is to get detailed information from Cde. McPhail in Havana. The S.U. has also restated they are ready to receivedanother 2 CC comrades for rest and recreation there. The OC is to take the decision on who will go.

3. REPORT ON THE CDCC CONFERENCE - Cde. Radix reported that the CDCC meeting held here never reached its ministerial level. The decided to adjourn and reconvene before year's end in New York. The work of the officials was accepted and Grenada retains the chairmanship.

The Jamaican Deputy Foreign Minister, (Galimore) arrived with an armed guard and attempted to use forged currency while here.

4. RICHARD JACOBS - he rang re. going to Mexico and Nicaragua at the same time that he is supposed to be joining Cde. Austin etc. on the GDR, Czechoslovakia and S.U. trip. It was decided that Cde. Jacobs should still go to Mexico and Nicaragua, joing the comrades in S.U. after.

/...5 P.S FOR THE

5. **P.S. FOR THE MINISTRY OF COMMUNICATIONS** - Cde. Byron Campbell will be the P Permanent Secretary in that Ministry when Ron Iton leaves. However, Cdes. Austin, Iton and Campbell will be away at the same time. Cde. Michael Prime will therefore be in charge of the Ministry for that period.

6. **RELIGIOUS CONFERENCE** - A Conference on "RELATION BETWEEN CHRISTIANITY AND REVOLUTION" will be held in Madrid from 5th - 10th December. Grenada is to send 2 delegates. Judy Williams/Ricky Charles and Fr. Martin/Ian St. Bernard were suggested. Cde. Strachan is to follow up on this.

7. **SOLIDARITY WITH CUBA** - Cde. Strachan said that Cde. Gaston wanted the mass organisation, etc. to send solidarity messages to Cuba on the present situation there. If possible, they also want a rally held. The latter also brought copies of Cde. Castro's speeches made in Cuba on the issue. It was agreed that one of the upcoming council meetings should focus on this as a y of expressing solidarity.

8. **PA SYSTEMS FOR THE 3RD FESTIVAL** - Cde. Strachan received a proposal that we purchase our own PA system for the 3rd FEstival. It wcan be bought from Hungary, with parts from Japan and Austria. The Cubans have agreed to train the persons to use it. However, the decision was that we should use the Cubans' own (although still ordering ours), as it will not arrive in time for the Festival.

9. **ANGOLA DAY RALLY** - The rally in solidarity with Angola is to be held tonight at the Sauteurs Courtyard. The programme will include the Angola representative, the SWAPO representative and one comrade from the Party.

10. **PWU STRUGGLE** - The Special G.M. as requested by the Party's PWU Sub-Ctee is scheduled for Thursday, 12th. However, the PWU Executive has publicised a circular saying that they have agreed to hold the meeting, but have scheduled it for Tuesday, 24th and not Thursday, 12th. They stated a few irregularities in the method of approach to hold the Special G.M. However, it was noted that the meeting will go ahead as a mobilisation meeting, but that it will not be a "legal" one according to the PWU Constitution.

11. **CARIBBEAN TRADE UNION CONFERENCE** - The decision was taken to invite the Guyana Agricultural and General Workers Union, after the TUC reeceived a letter from them requesting they be invited.

12. **ACTIVITIES FOR NOVEMBER** - A list of activities (zonal councils, workers parish councils, etc.) totalling 62 was submitted to the Bureau. It was noted that CC comrades will have to start attending these meetings to take some of the work off the backs of the PB members.

13. **PARTY HEADQUARTERS** - The drawings were approved and teh quantities are now to be done, The Party however, is to make a formal request ffor the land to be used and the OC is to discuss a programme of fund-raising to help with the cost of labour for building the headquarters.

14. **NATIONAL MOBILISATION'S MINISTRY BUILDING** - Cde. Strachan suggested that Bereck Knight's house near to Chruch Street be used as the Ministry of National Mobilisation. This was agreed.

15. **HOUSING** - The houses, both at Telescope and Grand Anse are to be allocated. This will be done at Friday's (November, 13th) Bureau meeting.

16. **SEA WORKD CENTRE** - Cde. Radix suggested that this centre be set up in a building near to the Fishing School in True Blue in time for the 3rd Festival.

...3

17. WPJ CONGRESS - To be eheld in December. Our delegates will be decided on
    at next PB meeting - Wednesday, 18th.

18. NEW APPLICANTS - Cde. Strachan suggested that whenever new applicants
    are being brought into the Party that a small ceremony or so be organised
    to mark the occassion. The suggestion was not discussed in detail by the
    Bureau.

Hazel- Ann
RECORDING SECRETARY

MINUTES OF THE POLITICAL BUREAU MEETING OF
WEDNESDAY, 18TH NOVEMBER
1981

Comrades present   Comrades absent-

Maurice Bishop   George Louison
Selwyn Strachan   Unison Whiteman
Bernard Coard
Kenrick Radix
Hudson Austin

74

AGENDA

1. TU Conference Report
2. Bloody Sunday -22nd November
3. International Solidarity Conference
4. NPJ Congress
5. Ministerial designations
6. SELA Meeting -- Panama
7. Relocation of Medical School
8. International Airport
9. Call from Cde. Louison
10. Bankactivities in Grenville
11. Venezuela's Ambassador's visit

(1) **TU CONFERENCE REPORT** - Cde. Strachan reported that there are already 32 delegates here already to attend the conference. He reported that there were a few logistical problems, but that the mobilisation of the workers to attend the opening ceremony was going "okay". The programme chairman for the opening is Cde. Vincent Noel and Both Septhymus Forsyth and the comrade leader are due to speak. It was felt however, that somebody on behalf of the delegates should address the opening.

(2) **BLOODY SUNDAY** - The organisational aspect was looked at by the OC already - the programme is now to be decided upon. The decision - Chairman - Cde. Radix, solidarity messages from all the mass organisations (youth, women, pioneers, farmers, workers, armed forces, etc.) and one solidarity message each from the TU and Int'l solidarity conferences. Each messages to be not more than 5 minutes. Mobilisation is reported to be good and transportation is organised.

(3) **INTERNATIONAL SOLIDARITY CONFERENCE** - Cde. Strachan said - 33 delegates confirmed to attend, could have about 60-70 delegates.

(4) **NPJ CONGRESS** this is from the 17 - 20th December. Cde. Strachan is to attend the congress on behalf of the Party.

(5) **MINISTERIAL DESIGNATIONS** - Cde. Coard's Ministry is that of "Planning, Finance and Trade". Cde. Radix's - "Industry and Fisheries, Attorney General and Justice minister".

(6) **SELA MEETING - PANAMA** - Mathew Williams will be the official at this meeting on Grenada's behalf.

(7) **RELOCATION OF MEDICAL SCHOOL** - The medical school authorities have suggested that the school be re-located in the area opposite "Hog Island". It was agreed to, unless it is opposed to by the armed forces.

...2

(8) INTERNATIONAL AIRPORT - was not discussed.

(9) CALL FROM CDE. LOUISON - A few matters were settled between different comrades bilaterally on issues that were raised by Cde. Louison.

(10) BANK ACTIVITIES IN GRENVILLE - Rumours are reported to be circulating in that town over the recent purchase of the P.B.C. by the N.C.B. Some people are reported to have been pounding down the BBC's doors to withdraw their money from that bank. Cde. Coard reported that he held a 2-hour long meeting he held with Sharon Lycorish of NCB and the workers were supposed to publish a pamphlet "FACTS YOU SHOULD KNOW" on the situation.

(11) VENEZUELA'S AMBASSADOR'S VISIT - Cde. Radix reported on this. They want to send in a military delegation to discuss regional security and they will be donating some equipment to the hospital. The first was agreed to by the Bureau. ie for the military delegation to come to Grenada.

Hazel-Ann
RECORDING SECRETARY

74 - 2

Comrades present:-

Maurice Bishop
Bernard Coard
Selwyn Strachan
Kenrick Radix
George Louison
Unison Whiteman

Comrade absent:-

Hudson Austin - awy

75

Agenda:-

1. Vincent Noel
2. Ricky Singh
3. NYO Congress and rally
4. Grenada/US Friendship Society
5. SWAPO
6. Detainees
7. Richard Hart
8. Correspondence
9. Ministers of Labour Conference
10. Workmen's Compensation Act
11. Christmas tree lightings
12. WPJ Congress
13. Dennis Henry
14. New Applicants to the Party

(1) VINCENT NOEL - This item was disccused in detail.

(2) RICKY SINGH - Cde. Bishop told Cdes. Whiteman and Radix of
a telephone conversation he had with Ricky Singh regarding
the allegation of human rights violations here and the
document Grenada presented at the recent SELA meeting.

(3) NYO CONGRESS AND RALLY - Cde. Coard is to give the feature
address at the opening of the Congress on Saturday and Cde.
Bishop will do likewise at the Rally on Sunday.

(4) GRENADA/US FRIENDSHIP SOCIETY AGREEMENT - This agreemtn is
to be signed by Carlatta Scott and Swinton Lambert

(5) SWAPO - Cde. Coard is to arrange to get the $50,000 promised
to SWAPO sent to their representative at the United Nations.

(6) DETAINEES - Some are to be released

(7) RICHARD HART - He is to replace Miles Fitzpatrick as of August
1982

(8) CORRESPONDENCE -

(9) MINISTERS OF LABOUR CONFERENCE -

(10) WORKMEN'S COMPENSATION ACT -

2/...(11) CHRISTMASS TREE LIGHTINGS

2

(11) CHRISTMAS TREE LIGHTINGS - The only list received was that
    of St. David's.

(12) WFJ CONGRESS - Cdes. Strachan and Sandiford are to attend.

(13) DENNIS HENRY -

(14) NEW APPLICANTS TO THE PARTY -

Hazel-Ann
RECORDING SECRETARY

75 - 2

MINUTES OF POLITICAL BUREAU MEETING
ON MONDAY 28TH DECEMBER, 1981

Present:-

Maurice Bishop   Unison Whiteman   Absent:-
Selwyn Strachan   Hudson Austin   Bernard Coard
George Louison
Kenrick Radix   76

AGENDA:

1. EPICA
2. Nicaragua
3. Agricultural Plan
4. 1982 Work Plan
5. CC Agenda
6. New Year Speech
7. Detainees

8. RC Pastoral letter/Neehall
9. WPJ 2nd Congress Report
10. Visit to Cuba
11. March 13th Anniversary
12. George Lamming

1. <u>EPICA</u> - Regarding the book they are printing on the Grenada
Revolution, 5000 copies will be sent to us at a price of $1.50
(US) each. We are to reserve another 5000 copiesiif possible.
This task is Cde. Strachan's responsibility. It was also agreed
that a Carifta cottage be given to them.

2. <u>NICARAGUA</u> - Cde. Bishop reported that he had a meeting with
Valerie Cornwall and Didicus Jules re. the literary programme
in Nicaragua. They came up with a list of 40 names to be sent
there as tutors/trainers to help in the programme.. However, it
was not celar exactly now many persons were actually needed. The
group also needs a leadert and a top party comrade to assist with
ideological and organisational training. Cdes. Cornwall and Jules
also asked for assistance from the Bureau on informing the comrades who will be going to Nicaragua on the present situation
there. This task is Cde. Louison's own.

The sending of the volunteers to Nicargua is to be co-ordinated
with the Nicargauan Ambassador in Cuba.

Cde. Bishop wanted to get the Bureau's approval on the suggestion
that a few top party comrades be spared to help in this area. It
was agreed/approved.

3. <u>AGRICULTURAL PLAN</u> - Cde. Louison reported that Tamayo's visit
is a follow-up to that of Risquet's. The former has suggestéd a
new system of organisation for the Ministry of Agriculture. He
suggests that there be three sections: organisational, political
and production; that there be two vice ministers, abandon the
Fermanent Secretary and Secretary for Agriculture.

.../2

2

Cde. Louison also disclosed however, that Cde. Rizo has suggested that we will have to do the same for the other ministries once it is done for that of Agriculture.

The general feeling of the Bureau was that we are not quite ready for the system as yet.

4. **1982 WORK PLAN** - Cde. Louison stated that the OC has already looked at the work plans for 1982 of the women, youth and AGWU; the PCB's and IFU are to be looked at - also the Urban Workers Committee. He explained that some OC comrades expressed the view that Cde. Ian St. Bernard be out in charge of the work in St. George's - however, no decision was taken on this.

Cde. Radix expressed the view that in 1982, some Party comrades will have to be put in the area of the economy and production and that meetings with the unemployeds should take place.

5. **CC AGENDA** - The next CC meeting is on Wednesday, 30th and the Bureau decided that the item on the agenda should be "A Political Review of 1981", including the areas of weakensses as identified by the OC and comments on them.

It was suggested that there be special CC meetings to decide on the programme for 1982 and one be held for the purpose of discussing the 1982 One Year Plan and the budget.

6. **NEW YEAR SPEECH** - Cde. Bishop stated that he wanted to get comrades' ideas on what the contents of his new year speexh should be. The following were suggested:- review of the major achievments in 1981, the role of the masses and the growth of democracy, groth of the mass organisations, emphasis on the productivity point, a renewed call for the involvement of the businessmen in the economy, 2% growth in the economy in 1981, 14% more nutmeg sales in 81 than in 80, the soom commencement of the National Bus Service, the development of Carriacou.

The Bureau decided that 1982 be The Year of Economic Construction.

7. **DETAINEES** - A list of 25 suggested names of detainees was presented to the Bureau for consideration to be released. Four additional names were added and the Bureau decided on 22 of the 25 suggested names to be released.

The following items were not discussed:-
8. RC Pastoral letter/Neehall
9. WPJ 2Nd Congress Report
10. Visit to Cuba
11. March 13th Anniversary
12. George Lamming

Hazel-Ann
RECORDING SECRETARY

Comrades present :-   Comrades Absent :-

    Maurice Bishop   Unison Whiteman
    Bernard Coard   Kenrick Radix
    Selwyn Strachan
    George Louison   77
    Hudson Austin

Agenda :-

1. Ron Dellums
2. CDC/Grenlec
3. Dome
4. Airport Meeting Report
5. Outstanding Bills - March 13
6. Journalist Conference
7. Pleassey
8. DPRK - Korea
9. Mass Activities :-

   Lenin's Birthday, Jeremiah Ricardson's Day, May Day,
   Playa de Giron
10. Correspondence
11. Surinamese
12. Fund-raising Committee Report
13. Falkland Islands

1. Ron Dellums is arriving in Grenada on Friday, 9th April and
   leaves on Thursday, 15th. His programme starts on Monday 12th,
   as he will be resting from his arrival until then. Comrade
   Louison was given the task to meet him at the airport. It was
   suggested that arrangements be made for him to see Carriacou.

3. A seminar will be held oin the Dome on Thursday 8th April.
   This will involve all Ministries and is aimed at begining
   paration for the 3-year plan (1983, 1984 and 1985). Comrad
   Coard explained that discussinn will be mainly on the capital
   side of the budget and that as many PB members as possible
   should be there.

4. Comrade Strachan reported on the first part of a meeting
   he and Comrade Austin held with the workers at the site of
   the International Airport. He stated the following :-

   - the meeting lasted 4 hours
   - - it is cleart that the workers and management are to get
       the blame
   - Rullow "got plenty blows"; he is under tremendous pressure
   - there is a friction/gap between the Grenadian and Cuban
     workers
   - the Grenadian workers claim they are not getting recognition
   ,- both sides are cursing each other
   - women workers experiencing problems - inadequate transport etc.
   - claim that management is not giving time to do voluntary
     work and are not giving support for the Militia

Comrade Strachan told them the following as means of solving the problems:-

- the union has to be a vibrant force and complaints must be brought to them
- the union must be involved in decision making re. the workers
- Political Commissar to be appointed ("Piano", Gordon or MacLean)
- Disciplinary committee must be set up
- regular staff meetings must be held

Comrade Austin reported that the usual airport problems were discussed, they included:-

- the access road to the airport to be decided on
- tank
- airport terminal building
- the need for a jeep, trup and car
- need for food loan

He also stated that the Sandino Plant will need 10 Grenadian workers from May

5. The total of the outstanding bills for the March 13 Festival totalled $398,000. Comrade Strachan explained the three "heaviest areas" as i) protocol, ii) mass mobilisation and iii) protocol transport. The breakdown:-

protocol	260,000
mass mobilisation	37,000
protocol transport	101,000
TOTAL	398,000

6. The Journalists Conference will be held here from April 16th to April 19th.

7. Pleassey. Comrade Coard explained that there are three parts to this:-

   i) to ensure that all the parts/equipment would be in the plan (BOU)
   ii) legal element (Miles)
   iii) prices for each item

8. Comrade Strachan will be our representative to the birth anniversary of the North Korean leader, instead of the Comrade Leader.

9. A. Lenin's Birthday - April 22nd. A programme will be organise to observe the day, involving the M's, CM's and A's of the Party.
   B. Jeremiah Richardson - This will be commemorated on April 18th, starting at 3.00 p.m.
   C. May Day - the aim is to bring out 10,000 workers. The Unions are to draw up schedule of visits to work places as a method of mobilising the workers

. Flay de Giron - rallies to observe this will be held in St. Andrew's, St. Georges and St. Patrick's and they are being organised by the Armed Forces.

10. Comrade George Louison has been invited to the Party and Government Conference on Agriculture to be held in the GDR May 12 - 13. They will be sending three tickets - two other comrades are therefore to be identified to accompany him.

12. The Fundraising Committee submitted a report on their activities thus far which stated a balance of $7,607. Comrade Strachan reported that he had held a meeting with them. His suggestion to them was that six simultaneous parties be organised for the six parishes at the end of May.

Another suggestion was that the friendship organisations be asked to donate 10,000 jerseys. They will be printed with "Year of Economic Construction"; "Work Harder, Produce More, Build Grenada". They will then be sold in an attempt to raise some funds - that is to be implemented at around the Carnival season.

Hazel-Ann
RECORDING SECRETARY

THE NEW JEWEL MOVEMENT

GRENADA, CARIBBEAN.

NOT JUST
ANOTHER SOCIETY
BUT A JUST SOCIETY

NEW JEWEL FOR
A UNITED PEOPLE

TO ALL POLITICAL BUREAU MEMBERS

Please acknowledge receipt of the PB minutes dated 7th April, 1982.

NAME	SIGNATURE	DATE	NUMBER
1. Maurice Bishop	*M. Bishop*	16.4.82	A1
2. Bernard Coard	*B. Coard*	16/4/82	A2
3. Selwyn Strachan	*Strachan*	24/4/82	A3
4. George Louison	*George Louison*	16/4/82	A4
5. Hudson Austin	*Austin*	28/4/82	A6
6. Unison Whiteman	*Unison Whiteman*	16/4/82	A5
7. Kenrick Radix			

77 - 4

"Let those who labour hold the reins"

MINUTES OF THE POLITICAL BUREAU
MEETING - 14th APRIL, 1982

Comrades present:-   7?   Comrades absent:-

Maurice Bishop   Selwyn Strachan)
Bernard Coard   Unison Whiteman)   out of
Hudson Austin   Kenrick Radix)   the
George Louison   country

1. <u>Journalists Conference</u> - It was deciddd that the Comrade
   Leader should declare the Conference open; that Comrade
   Whiteman should close it and that Comrade Bernard Coard
   should host the Press Conference which should be sometime
   after the Airport Rally on Sunday 18th. The Conference
   runs from 17 - 19 April, at the Dome.

2. To commemorate 'Playa Giron', the Armed Forces has planned
   four indoor rallies to take place in Carriacou, St. Patrick's,
   St. Andrew's and St. George's. The PB members to attend them
   are Comrades, Hudson Austin, Louison, Coard/Radix/Whiteman
   and Bishop respectively.

3. An invitation was received from Bulgaria to attend the
   100th anniversary of the birth of Dimitrov. This will take
   the form of a International Conference on the Lifework of
   Dimitrov and our Time. It will take place in Bulgaria from
   15th - 17th June, 1982.

   The Bureau felt that Comrade Whiteman would be the person best suited to attend the conference.

4. The Laos 3rd Party Congress is schelduled for 27 - 30th
   April.

5. Comrade Louison will visit the GDR during 12th - 14th May.
   He is to be accompanied by two other comrades.

6. The WMR will hold its conference in Havana, Cuba from
   26th April. A representative from our Party is expected
   to attend.

7. The 27th Party Congress of the Austrailan Communist Party
   will be held from 11th - 14th June. They want the NJM to
   forward its greetings.

The Bureau decided to forward items nos. 3 - 7 to the Organising Committee for discussion and decisions.

Hazel-Ann
RECORDING SECRETARY

YOUTH EMPLOYMENT PROGRAMME A/C

STATEMENT TO 30th JUNE 1982

REVENUE

 Grants - M.N.I.B. $215,000

 Refunds 3,099

               218,099

EXPENDITURE:

 Unemployment Census 14,174

 Unemployment Conferences 15,049

 Renovations to Y.E.P. Office:

  Materials ....15,408)

) 27,713

  Labour .... 12,305)

 Renovations to La Sagesse:

  Materials .... 32,899)

) 60,011

  Labour   .... 27,112)

 Stationery 1,248

 Office Expenses 89

 Vehicle " 7,421

 La Sagesse Training Programme:

  Equipment .... 9,767)

) 30,996

  Other .... 21,229)

 Office Furniture & Equipment 4,448

 Miscellaneous 824

 Travelling & Subsistence 1,727 163,700

  Surplus for Period 54,399

Ramón [signature]
for Y.E.P.

TO: Political Bureau, New Jewel Movement
FROM: Chairperson, Women's Committee, NJM
RE: Problems affecting women Party members
DATE: 11th May, 1982

79

Dear Comrades,

At a recent Women's Committee meeting, it was discovered that many women Party members are feeling under considerable strain. An anlysis of the situation was done and it was felt that we ought to let the Bureau know of the situation and ask the Bureau to consider the matter, and take any decisions which it may think appropriate. Some of the matters discussed are referred to briefly in the minutes of the Women's Committee meeting of 15th April, 1982.

The main problems identified are as follows:-

(1) The special problems of women with children are rarely, if ever considered when fixing hours of study classes and committee or P.C.B. meetings.

When some women members raise the problems of having no one to leave their babies with at 5.00 a.m. or no one to get the children breakfast or ready for school, the attitude of many heads of PCB's, Committees and study groups has frequently been that "you just have to solve that problem". As a result, some women members have been deemed 'in disciplined' as a result of missing meetings, others have taken serious risks with their children, like leaving babies in the care of young children of 10 or 12 years, some have faced the criticisms of the masses for "neglecting" their children. Recently, an incident occured when a sister from St. Andrew's was kept at a meeting in town till 6.30 p.m. On returning to St. Andrew's she found the Day Nursery shut and spent 2 hours searching frantically to find out where the nurses lived to recover her child.

The special problems of workers and of Army comrades <u>are</u> considered when fixing hours of meetings. We feel that the C.C. and serious Party comrades should be aware that women's problems in terms of the care of their children should be considered and women members should not be unfairly condemned, when they are not to be blamed. Likewise, it should be recognised that last minute calls to attend meetings at weekends and on evenings does sometime result in women members being unable to attend because arrangements cannot easily be made at an hour's notice to get babysitting.

Likewise, it should be considered that there are some areas where it is unsafe for women to walk alone late at night or very early in the morning.

We recognise that such consideration entails a risk of some members making children an excuse to avoid doing work; however, we feel that each case must be looked at realistically; moreover in our experience the women with children are among the hardest working and most disciplined members of the Party.

(2) When allocating political tasks it should be considered that most women in our Party have to wash, cook, clean and sometimes also have to care for children and elderly parents, <u>in addition to taking on just as much political work as the men who in most</u>

cases accept little responsibility in the housekeeping area.

At the present time we find that a large number of women, especially those with young children are extremely tired. Also, they are extremely concerned about their neglect of their children in some cases are doing poorly in school. The Party needs to check on overall work-load when allocating political tasks to women members. We have also found in the Women's Committee that the efficiency of our senior women comrades has been greatly increased by giving them even limited staff to assist them (e.g. Tessa now has a Personal Assistant from among the part time workers; Edlyn now assists Claudette in the International area; Faye and Rita work jointly on training, using part time workers to deal with some of the logistical back up).

(3) The Maternity Leave Law must be respected by the Party. The experience of the past 2 years shows us that even some senior Party comrades assume that women members will continue political work almost until she gives birth and will take on work again shortly afterwards. This is damaging to our women's health. The rule should be that women on maternity leave should be free of all political work, except in rare cases where the woman volunteers to undertake a few tasks. Furthermore, women with babies or young children should always be consulted before being directed to go abroad for the Party, to ensure that arrangements can be made to look after her children.

(4) One or two single women with children are finding difficulty in paying full dues, where faters are not paying adequate maintenance. We advised them to write to the O.C. on this.

(5) The Party should seek actively to change the attitude of Party men to the questions of baby-sitting, child care, housework and should ensure that all fathers support thiir children equally both financially and psychologically.

Right now, there are many male Party members who undertake very little or no responsibility in these areas; the Party should make them understand that:-

(a) it is their duty to spend equal time looking after their children whether or not they live in the same house as the mather. Otherwise we will see more and more young women seriously held back in terms of political development because of being burdened full time with children. Right now many young Party men are pressing /sisters to have babies for them, yet afterwards they take little or no responsibility for them.   /the

(b) Where Party men and women live together they must undertake equal responsibility for housework.

(c) It should be clearly understood that Party tasks cannot be used as an excuse for not undertaking (a) and (b). Right now the attitude of Party men is "Sorry I can't do much - any baby care or house work - Party work must come first. But the women Party member could say the same thing! The Party must make it clear that all Party members - men and women - must share housework and baby care equally, in order that both should have an equal opportunity to develop as Party cadres. Otherwise women Party cadres will always be held back in their development both relative to what they are capable of.

(6) Party members must be made aware of what is a proletarian man and woman and what is a proletarian or socialist relationship. We have the example to set for the broad masses of our people. Therefore our relationships whether with other Party members or with non-Party members should be honest, not using or abusing the other person. We believe for example, that it is time married Party men stop running around with several other women; it is time they stopped having "outside children"; it is time unmarried Party men shortly to be married stopped the practice of pressuring women to have children for them, sometimes even using the possibility of marriage as a bribe - or as blackmail; it is also time that women Party members learn to stop gossiping abouth other peoples personal relationships.

We realise that Party members will not all change overnight. However, we feel it is time the Party starts to formulate rules of personal behaviour on the man-woman questions and more than this, seek to raise the ideological level of all Party members on this matter. Too many Party members do not see that the struggle for socialism includes the struggle to create socialist forms of relationships in our society, and especially Applicants need to be carefully educated in this area.

We want to suggest that the Bureau directs the Education Committee to include at least one study session on the woman question on the programme for _all_ M's, CM's and A's at some point during the next six months. The Women's Committee has M-L materials which can be used.

The Bureau may also wish to consider circulating this document to M's and CM's.

Finally, we wish to recognise the real effort and progress made by our senior Party members in overcoming male chauvinist attitude and the practical results this had had (for instance in the development of women in the Militia) despite the problems which still remain. Undoutedly, the NJM is outstanding among other Caribbean Parties in the high degree of equality which it offers to women, both within and outside of the Party.

P. Coard
10th May, 1982.

MINUTES OF THE POLITICAL BUREAU MEETING
ON WEDNESDAY, 15th
SEPT. 1982
_____

80

Comrades present^-.

Comrades absent

Maurice Bishop
George Louison
Unison Whiteman
Hudson Austin

Bernard Coard   - unwell
Kenrick Radix   - away
Selwyn Strachan - away

Agenda

1. Discussion with the Minister of Fisheries - Cuba
2. Soviet Union Party Agreement with NJM
3. Human Rights Conference - New York
4. Chris Stroude
5. New CPO for Keith Joseph/TFG Manager
'6. Party propaganda
7. Letter from Maureen St. Bernard
8. Caricom Action Plan
9. USA Front GRoup
10. Grenada Workers for the GDR
11. Bills in Havana
12. CPE PHASE TWO

1. DISCUSSION WITH THE MINISTER OF FISHERIES   CUBA - Comrade Bishop reprrted on a
meeting that was held with himself, Comrade Radix and the Minister of Fisheries from
Cuba.

Of the ten boats that were donated to us by Cuba only two that are working - eight
are not functioning. The two presently working can collapse any time. It was also
reported that the National Fishing Company has lost about sixty percent of its revenue.

The meeting held, took the following decisions :-

1.1 Do something about the sunken boats - remove them etc. (what is possible)
1.2 Move those that there is no plan to use.
1.3 Try to save two or three
1.4 Send some or the balance to Cuba or Carriacou to be used otherwise if possible.

It was noted that instead of returing the boats that cannot be used back to Cuba, we
should think of creative ways to use them otherwise.

The slipway offered by Cliveland Dolland was also looked at as part of the discussion on this agenda item.

2. <u>SOVIET UNION PARTY AGREEMENT</u> -   Comrades Louison and Cheneve of the CPSU held discussion on the draft agreement and work programme between the two parties as brought by us and agreed,

    a. The Soviets to items for Party Headquarters.
    b. A number of schlarships for Party School - 15 NJM comrades can come from October. NJM to decide on the period of study - three, six or twelve months
    c. The CPSU offered to host 5 NJM comrades for rest and receeation; 5 for a fami- lirisation visit. The NJM offered to host CPSU comrades in Grenada, but their response is that they preferr if comrades assisted with Party building when they come.

In a messafe from Comrade Bourne at our Embassy in Moscow, he indicated that other points raised by the Comrade Leader in discussions held will be considered and we will be notified accordingly,

On the Party Secretariat, Cuban experts are to come to prepare/evaluate quantities and drawings.

On the question of the leadership:s plane, Comrade Bourne indicated that in his meeting with Gosplan on 23rd August, they indicated that they are likely to supply the plane, but needed to know two things:-

i)   If an agreement on co-operation between Grenada and Cuba is possible for the purpose of operation, maintenance and training of Grenadian technicians to use the plane.
ii) If we have a Pilot lined up to fly the plane.

The following will also be given to us by the CPSU:-

a. 2 autobuses (25-seater)
b. 2 Niva cars
c. 3 P.A. amplifiers
d. 12 loudspeakers
e. 6 16 mmprojectors

f. 12 tape recorders
g. 150 cassettes
h. 1 photocopying machine
i. 7 duplicating machines
j. 6 English typewriters

k. 4 Guillotines
m. 2000 folding chairs

3. <u>HUMAN RIGHTS CONFERENCE   NEW YORK</u> - A letter invited the PRG to participate in a Conference on Human Rights to be held in New York was discuss. The conference is to take place on October 1 - 3 and its theme is "Human Rights and the Struggle for Social, Economic and Political Justice". The invitation came from the Conference on Human Rights in the Americas Co-ordinating Committee.

The Bureau decided that either Comrades Creft or Jules should attend, but that further consideration be given to the matter by the Bureau.

Comrade Louison was given the task to speak with Comrade Creft on the matter, in an attempt to convince her to attend the conference.

4. <u>CHRIS STROUDE</u> - He is no longer Political Commissar for the Army and needs to be placed in an area of work. Comrade Bishop reported that himself and Comrade Strachan had discussed the matter and thougℓthat he should be made Political Chief .   His tasks will be to take the political classes, note the problems raised during the classes and pass them on to the Political Organiser to be

solved. However, no name was yet found for the person to fill that post.

The Bureau noted that the comrade has serious organisational weaknesses, although he has many other outstanding strengths.

5. NEW CPO FOR KEITH JOSEPH/TFG MANAGER - This was not discussed. Instead, the Bureau noted that there were many areas like this that needed to be filled with comrades. As part of the reorganisation presently going on in the Party, this matter will have to be dealt with.

It was observed that comrades were needed for:-

TFG
RFG
FWI
Political Organiser/Politiaal Commissar
Propaganda Chief
NACDA
YEP Chief
CPE

6. PARTY PROPAGANDA - To be discussed at the next PB meeting.

7. LETTER FROM AMUREEN ST. BERNARD - The letter from Maurren was discussed by the Bureau and a reply will be sent. She enclosed different letters attacking her.

8. CARICOM ACTION PLAN - Comrades Taylor and Emmanuel to leave for some of the regional island in this reagard.

9. USA FRONT GROUP

The document from WPJ, MONALI and DLM with information on human rights in their respective countries was not yet received except the one from MONALI. WPJ and DLM to be checked in this regard.

10. GRENADA WORKERS FOR GDR)
11. BILLS IN HAVANA) these items
12. CPE PHASE 2) were not discussed

MINUTES OF THE POLITICAL BUREAU MEETING
ON WEDNESDAY, 22nd
September, 1982

Comrades Present:-

    Maurice Bishop
    Bernard Coard
    GeorgeLLouison
    Kenrick Radix
    Selwn Strachan   - late
    Hudson Austin

Comrades absent:-

    Unison Whiteman

81

Agenda:-

1. Wilson Center
2. Papal Nuncio's Visit
3. Venezuela Center
4. Intellectuals Conference/Marryshow Day
5. Mark Nurvine/Dawne Flecther
6. CPE Phase 2
7. Bill Rivere/Lybia Conncection
8. Comrades for key positions
9. Legal Affairs
10. Analysis of Regional Situation

2. **PAPAL NUNCIO'S VISIT** - Comrade Bishop reported on a meeting he held with the Papal Nuncio who was in Grenada on a visit. He s id the meeting was very warm. He said a number of things in relation to the activities of the church and of the behaviour of some priest, including the following:-

1. sermons on the pulpit; their political activists' role; attitude to class bias, school repair, etc.
2. disrespect for laws/regulations - visit to detainees
3. agressive, arrogant, destabilisaing atti ude

The Comrade Leader also made the point to him that the Bishop's attitude is generally one of being another Prime Minister

The Papal NUnico's proposal in response is that a meeting should be called with all the priests and Bishop Charles in which the laws are all laid down.

Comrade Bishop made the following proposals:-

i)   Accreditation of somebody to the Vatican.
ii) All requests for work permits of preests must be sent before they arrive in the country, with their proper CV's.
iii) Removal of the worse elements.

2/...

The Papal Nuncio expressed the opinion that there are some priests/nuns that the PRG can check sometimes, e.g. Sister FRancis Zavier, and the three new brothers in PTC.

The PB has to look at the appointment of an ambassador to the Vatican and structures for dealing .with house keeping matters relevant to the   church.

The Papal Nuncio said that what the Church wants is the right to spiritual freedom. If they are to co-operate with the State in any other areas, it will be that of education .

3. VENEZUELA CENTER   - The Venezuelans want to open a cultural center here. It will operate on guidelines fof a co-ordinating committee, made up of representatives trom the Ministry of Culture here and the Director of the Center. It was noted that the Director of the Centre will be a very key/important person.

The location for the center was already sited - in the Grand Anse area.

4. INTELLECTUALS CONFERENCE - The Intellectuals Conference will take place from 18 - 20 November; Bloody Sunday will be commemorated on November 21 and the Education is Production Too conference will start on November 22nd. November 7 is to be named National Cultural Day and the local committee of intellectuals will be named on that day too, including Don Rojas, Jacob Ross, Merle Hodge, etc.

5. MARK NURVINE/DAWNE FELCHER.   - They want to organise a ''Private Meeting with the Prime Minister'' on 6 - 13 February, 1983. The theme will be ''Another Development in Grenada''. The topics will include that of 1) Habitat, and Food, 2) Peoples Particiaption, 3) Economic Development, 4) International Affairs.

    It is suggested that the persons taking part in the meeting arrive in Grenada four or five days before the start of the meeting and go to Carriacou (Camp Carriacou) where it will be.held .

The NWO delegation came to the PB meeting that morning to discuss the Problems of women party members as put forward in their document to the PB . The delegation comprised Sisters Phyllis Coard, Claudette Pitt and Rita Joseph. They described their concerns as :-

1. Tremendous overwork and tiredness of women Party members
2. Financial problems of women party members
3. Attitude of Party men - non-comprehension by Party men of problems facing women..

The PB, in response, made the following points, apart from others:-

- the three points are very broad and important add the PB shares the concerns
- financial problems are also experienced by men
- the deducation committee will give consideration to the suggestion that the wom n question be studied by the Party.

81 - 2

- CC Sub-Committee looking at the internal state of the Party which will include this
- OC looking at the personal problems of Party comrades regularly on their pre-schelduled agenda
- there should be somebody at the Secretariat level, that comrades can check on their personal problems (suggestion by the women's committee)
- we must see the woman question as one of the contradictions within the society and must see the problems of women globaly
- study must also look at family education (both men and woemn)

In conclusion, the PB made the following three important general points:-

1. a) Need to see this as part of the objective state of development of both the Party and the society.
   b) Historic attitudes - lack of material resources (day care centres, preprimary schools, etc.)
   c) The Party has bnot fully addressed the woman question, although it has been an issue of concern.

2. For all of us(men) we have shon a lack of concern and support for the women we have a relationship with. (This is not to excuse women for wat they do to earn disrespect).

3. The level of human committment. There is an attitude among women members to laziness, mask for excuses, ill discipline.

&&&&&&&&&&&&&&&&&&&&&&&&&&&&&&&&&&&&&&&&&&&

<u>MINUTES OF THE POLITICAL BUREAU MEETING</u>

<u>WEDNESDAY 29TH SEPTEMBER, 1982</u>

<u>Comrades present:-</u>

Maurice Bishop
Selwyn Strachan   82
Kenrick Radix
George Louison
Hudson Austin

<u>Comrades absent:-</u>

Bernard Coard
Unison Whiteman

<u>AGENDA:-</u>

1. Letters to:-   Manley, Hammer, Lamb, Bellafonte
2. Ambassador to the Vatican/Structures re Church
3. Analysis of regional situation
4. Comrades for key positions
5. Militia preparation
6. Robert Vesco
7. Leadership's plane
8. Human Rights Conference Speech
9. Intellectuals Conference
10. Stamp Duty
11. Black Caucus
12. WFDY Conference
13. Land for new Cuban Embassy
14. Soviet Housing

1. Letter to Manley   – re NJM's membership in the   Socialist Internationl. The draft
   was read out, few changes made and Comrade Bishop delegated the task to finalise it.
   The letters to Hammer, Lamb and Bellafonte was not dealt with.

4. Comrades for key positions   Among the comrades needed for key positions are:-
   TFG, RFG, FWI, CPE Chief, NACDA, YEP Chief, National Fisheries Company, Political
   Organiser – Armed Forces.   However, these were not decided on.

5. Militia preparation – the proposal is to change the day for Militia training.
   The proposed change is from every Wednesday to the 1st Wednesday in every month,
   with regular weekend/periodic training; and once a year trining for 7 days of
   15 days .
   The proposed change will require that a law be passed in order for members of
   militia who are employed to get the necessary time off to attend the trainings.
   Each worker is to be allowed a maximum of 15 days.

7. The draft of the speech to be delivered at the Human Rights Conference in New
   York by Sister Creft was considered too historical by the Comrade Leader. The task
   was given to Comrade Kamau McBarnette to do another draft.

11. The Black Caucus in the US have said that they do not get invited to any Caribbean
    activities; as such, they suggested that they be invited to be observers at the up-
  • coming Caricom Heads of Meeting. However, this was decided against.

MINUTES OF THE POLITICAL BUREAU MEETING
WEDNESDAY 27th October, 1982

Comrades present:-   Comrades Absent:-

    Maurice Bishop   83   Bernard Coard
    Selwyn Strachan   Chalkie Ventour - unwell
    George Louison
    Hudson Austin
    Unison Whiteman
    Liam James
    Ewart Layne

The Comrade Leader and Chairman of the Political Bureau, before the start of the meeting, extended a warm welcome to the new members of the Political Bureau - Liam James, Ewart Layne and Chalkie Ventour. He noted that it was the first meeting of the Politbureau since these comrades were made members. He said that the PB looks forward to the contributions of these comrades.

Agenda: A pre set agenda for the PB/EB meetings up until 22nd December(for the next 9 meetings) was drafted/presented to the Bureau by the Comrade Leader. Each member was given a copy. The agenda will follow this format:-

1. Minutes   -   5 minutes
2. Correspondence   -   15 "
3. Items for decisions   -   85 "
4. PB/EB consultation on
   Item 5   -   15 "
5. Discussion on one of
   the "Areas of Work"   -   120 "
                                          ‾‾‾‾‾‾‾‾‾
                                          240 "

Item 1 - Minutes - There were no minutes

Item 2 - Correspondence

2.1 Letter from Wayne Sandiford - To be dealt with at Wednesday, 3rd November meeting.
2.2 Telex from the Korean Embassy in Guyana - They sent a telex to Foreign Affairs re an incident over dinner with their Ambassador about payment of a tick for Comrade Strachan to travel return to Korea.
Response: Reply telex to indicate:-
                             - no demand or attack was
                               made as claimed
                             - the matter was raised by
                               the Chief of Protocol,
                               not by the Minister, but
                               in his preseence.

2.3 Letter from Brazil - Comrade Bishop to follow up on this through his Permanent Secretary - Benny Langaine.

                                       .../2

2.4 Letterffrom <u>Arthur Neckles</u> - Has confirmed willingness to accept the job as General Manager of the National Insurance Scheme. PB agrees to him having the job in principle ρ once okay with Comrade Coard.

2.5 Letter from <u>Lybian People's Bureau</u> - They are requesting our assistance in contacting seven of the regional Parties to come here for follow up discussions held in Lybia with these parties earlier in this year. These parties are:-

    i. Progressive Labour Party - St. Lucia
    ii. Antigua Liberation Movement - Antigua
    iii. Dominica Liberation Movement - Dominica
    iv. People's National Party - Jamaica
    v. Progressive People's Movement - Trinidad
    vi. United People's Movement - St. Vincent
    vii. Movement for National Liberation - Barbados

This was agreed to by the PB.

2.6 Letter from <u>Islamic Foundation</u> - They are requesting that the main route to the International Airportbe called "Palestine Drive." Reply to be sent - a committee will look at the entire naming of the area. Comrade Strachan to follow up on this.

2.7 Letter from <u>American Friends Service Committee</u> - Comrade Strachan received a letter from Athie Martin re an idea of a Summer Camp exchange idea with Grenada. PB's response - Comrade Strachan to study theproposal, then report to PB on it before a decision is taken. No deadline set.

2.8 Letter from <u>Overseas Press Club of Puerto Rico</u> - They have invited Comrade Bishop to bethe main speaker at their lunch and meeting on January 13, 1983. PB's response - Benny Langainge to respond to letter stating the Comrade Leader's inability to acceptthe offer.

2.9 Letter from <u>Brian Murphy</u> - He hasssent a package of newspaper clippings from March 14 1979 to June 29, 1982 on the Grenada Revolution from the leading newspapers in circulation in the United States. Response/Action - Comrade Strachan to reply to the letter and also to get copies of the clippings to all PB members; to the Media Centre, Foreign Affairs. Gail Rizo should/ would be askedto do a n analysis of the document.

2.0 Letter from <u>NJAC</u> - Somebody is being requested to attend the NJAC/ Caribbean Information Centre sponsored two-day conference on Information, Colonialism, Underdevelopment and Development in the Caribbean Region." PB's reponse - OC to decide on representative.

2.10 Communication from <u>Richard Jacobs</u> - Request re provision of jobs for a few displaced PLOpersons. PB's response - should accept between 5 - 10; Comrade Louison to follow up on this.

Item 3 - Items for Decisions -

2.1 <u>November Activities</u> - Many activitieswill be held this month: zonalcouncil meetings, women parish council meetings, special village meetings leading up to Bloody Sunday Rally, conferences, etc. PB's reponse - the Secretariat to assign speakers to the many activities using the CC, plus NWO leadership, NYO leadership,

WC leadership, Comrades Norris Bain and Sydney Ambrose.

2.2 <u>March 13, 1983</u> - Comrade Strachan wanted to know at what level will the celebrationsbe held next year. The guest of honor to be Sam Nujoma and a El Salvador representative to be invited, but a back-up for the guest ofhonor to be also decided on. It was decided that a lot of people will have to be brought out but that ways and means will have to be found to cut down on expenditure. PB's tentative decision - The budget should be within a $500,000 range.

2.3 <u>15 Comradesfor Soviet Union</u> - 15 Party comrades will leave for the Soviet Union on a one year political training; Sister Rita Joseph will lead the group. They leave on Sautrday 6 November,

2.4 <u>Regional Youth Seminar</u>

2.5 <u>Party Headquarters</u>

2.6 <u>Intellectuals Conference</u>

2.7 <u>Education Is Production Too Conference</u>

2.8 <u>Ben Roberts' Land</u>

2.9 <u>Lybian Anniversary</u>

2.0 <u>Meeting with Bob Pastor</u> - The Comrade Leader met with Bob Pastor, a close associate of the US Administration - they discussed US-Grenada relations; the outcome is that both sides (Grenada and the US) will cease all denounciations of each other for a period until he has been able to speak to the Administration. Their response to come to us through Ambassador Williams in Washington.)

until mtg November '82 (10 days after return)

<u>Item 5 - Discussion on the Regional International Situation</u> - The paper presented on this topic and written by Comrade Winston Davis was discussed and briefly commented on. Comrades added these points (among others not recorded):-

- we must see the region as part of the international scenario
- imperialism is on the offensive
- imperialism has recently got some "blows" - forced to cool down
- Europe is seeing the resurgence of the Social Democratic movement
- we must consider what assistance we can give the liberation movements in the region experienceng major internal problems (these pointsabove were made by Comrade Whiteman in his short introduction to the document)
- thedocument is good, but lacks any information on the attitude of the masses in the region to the Grenada Revolution

Some time was spent on discussion on the situation in Guyana:-

- three wings in the PNC (i. left opportunists; ii. nationalists/racists; iii. corrupt/facists/rightists
- the mainoobstacle is the subjective factor - not fully developed

- OECS is more important to Grenada objectivelythan CARICOM

PB's response/action:-
1. A Secretariat to be set up in Butler House for the upcoming CARICOM and OECS meetings. Secretariat to comprise: Dave Bodoo, Claremont Kirton, Dennis Dewar, Lyden Ramdhany, Paul Coulen, Wayne Sandiford, Ashley Taylor, Winston Davis

.../4

Jimmy Emmauel, Veronic Regis and typists/secretaries. Also Nelson Louison. They are to be supervised by Comrade George Louison and to be based in Butler House for the week or two.

2. A document " Human Rightsiin Grenada" is also to be prepared with the assistance of Ron Green who is to be called in to Grenada, with help from Chris Searle who will be here.

3. During the activities of November 7 (specifically Marryshow Day)the Comrade Leader will make a main presentation/speech on the question of regional integration/regional unity, etc.

Agreed to acquire Ben Roberts Land.

* 2.10 of Correspondence (Communication from Richard Jacob) Invitation for Grenada to attend the 60th anniversary of the USSR . Comrade Strachan to attend ~~in principle~~.

TASKS ARRISING:-

1. Cde. Strachan to reply to the Islamic Foundation on their proposal to name the main route to the International Aiport - Palestine Drive. Response:- committee being set up to look at names for that general area; idea a good one.

2. Response to invitation by Overseas Perss Club of Puerto Rico for Comrade Leader on January 13, 1983. Letter to be sent to Benny Langaing to respond stating inability to acceptiinvitation. (Hazel Jove Benny)

3. Comrade Strachan to study proposal from Athie Martin of EFSC for the Summer Camp with Grenada idea, then report to PB on it OK. before responding to Athie Martin.

4. ComradeSStrachan to get copies of the newspaper clippings from Brian Murphy for all PB members; one to go to the Media Centre; another to Foreign Affairs. Gail Rizo to do possible analysis.

5. Reply to ttelex from the Korean Embassy in Guyana re incident over dinner about payment of ticket for Cde. Strachan to travel return to Korea. Response:-

   -) no demand or attack was made as claimed
   - the matter was raised by the Chief of Protocol, not by the Minister, butin his presence.

6. Cde. Louison to respond to information from our Embassy in the Soviet Union re providing jobs for a few PLO displaced persons.

7. The QC to decide on representative to attend the NJAC-CIC sponsored two-day conference on "Information, Colonialism,

Under-Development and Development in the Caribbean Region."

8. ✓ Cde. Leader to follow up on letter from ~~Belize~~ Brazil through his Permanent Secretary. (I gave Benny instructions)

9. ✓ Party Secretariat to assign Party leadership and other decided Party leaders to November Activities.

✓10. SECRETARIAT FOR CARICOM/OECS.

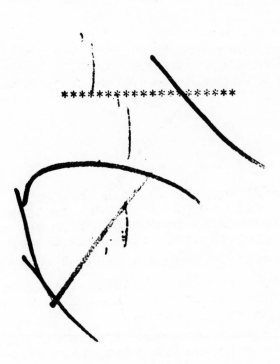

****

Comrades present:-   Comrades absent:-

Maurice Bishop   Ewart Layne   Liam James
Selwyn Strachan   Chalkie Ventour   Unison Whiteman
George Louison
Hudson Austin

84

Agenda:-

1. Minutes
2. Correspondence
3. Items for decisions
4. PB Consultation on Item 5
5. Discussion on one of the
   "Areas of Work" - Workers

1. MINUTES

1.1 Corrections

i)   Ben Roberts land - discussed; PB approved to put it to Cabinet.
       Issue - the seizure of his land. (See page 3).

ii)   Pg. 3 "briefly commented" re discussion on the regional/international
       situation should be "analysed in detail".

iii)   Decision re Cde. Strachan to attend 60th anniversary of the
       USSR in December was not "in principle" but was definte. (see
       page 4).

iv)   Pastor instead of "pastor". (See page 3). "Period" to be "10 days
       after his return to the US, ending approximately mid-November.

v)   Decision to establish Secretariat of OECS/Caricom document preparation
       to have been listed as a task. This to be supervised by Cde. Louison.
       Task accomplished.

1.2 TASKS ARISING

i) Reply to Islamic Foundation: verbal reply given by Cde. Strachan, but
   committee not set up as yet.
ii) Letter to be sent to Benny Langainge - accomplished.
iii) Cde. Strachan to study proposal re Summer Camp (Athie Martin). Done.
     Report: This has been held in other countries already - Mexico, Cuba;
     will involve ten person from the US and Grenada each and five each from
     the Caribbean and Latin America. The objective - "Building Bridges"; to
     learn about Grenada and what is happening here. Idea agreed to in prin-
     ciple.

2/...

iv) Not totally completed; has to be distributed - i.e. distribution of newsclippings to PB members.

v) Reply to telex from the Korean Embassy in Guyana - not known whether it was done. Foreign Affairs to be checked on this.

vi) Cde. Louison to reply to our Embassy in Moscow re providing jobs for a few displaced PLO persons. This not done - deadline next Wednesday.

vii) CC to decide on representative for the NJAC-CIC sponsored conference on Information....etc. Not done - now irrelevant as date already passed.

viii) Response to letter from Brazil re attending anparliamentary conference. Given to Benny for action. (See (d))

ix) Party Secretariat to assign leadership to speak at the mass activities - Done. Few changes were made and may be necessary from time to time.

x) Cde. Louison to set up and supervise the Secretariat for preparation for the OECS and Caricom meetings.

2. CORRESPONDENCE

2.1 Letter from the NSC: Given to Cde. Strachan will respond and follow up.

2.2 Letter from Wayne Sandiford: Asking to be relieved of having to repay monies given to him by default (while in Canada study, he received a stipend, while his salary was being paid in Grenada). Response: money

2.3 must be payd at a rate of $50 monthly from the end of November.

2.3 Memorandum from the DPRK: requesting our co-operation in giving support to them on the issue of South Korea and the way it is being used by the US imperialism. Response: decide to give "wide publicity". Cde. Strachan to follow up on this.

2.4 Letter from NWO re the formation of Health Bridgades. Response: copies to be circulated to all PB members for discussion on Wednesday 10th.

2.5 Letter from Conference of Churches of Grenada: re a visiting delegation from the World Conference of Churches - they will hold a public meeting at Hindsey School on Saturday night (6th) and will be available to meet with Government Ministers of Monday 8th November. Response - Cdes. Whiteman and St.Bernard to meet with the delegation.

3. ITEMS FOR DECISIONS

3.1 Matters Arising from 2-day CC Meeting: A Special Party GM to be held on Saturday 13th November, 4.00 p.m. for Members and Candidate Members; then on Saturday 20th for Applicants. This is for the prupose of reporting to the membership on an Extra-ordinary Central Committee Meeting held recently. (P.B. to hand in view to me)

3.2 Soviet Proposals - Not discussed.

3.3 Upcoming Regional Meetings - OECS and CARICOM: Comrades were breifed on the preparations being made for the upcoming meetings and the issues to be raised at them both bilaterally and unilaterally relating to areas of economic assistance/cooperation, ports, Culture, etc. The delegations to these meetings will be both high powered, including Comrades Bishop, Coard, Louison and Whiteman. The OAS and OLADE meetings are also being held around the same time.

3.4 Prisons/Detainees: Some are to be released - Cde. St.Bernard to check with the Party comrades in the respective areas on the suggested names, then to report on it. (B hope less)

3.5 Line of March Decision: Candidate Members and Members to study Line of March (as presented by Comrade Leader on September 13th) on 11th and 12th December, from 9.00 a.m. - 5.00 p.m. each day (if two days are needed). Applicants' own will be done separately. Cde. Louison to identify additional reading material for use in studying the Line of March (Study on Tuesday 4th 3/.?)

84 - 2

3.6 The Dome - Not discussed
3.7 PB Pre-Set Agenda Change - Not discussed. (~Was discussed~)
3.8 Regional Youth Seminar: This Youth Seminar is to be held at Pope Paul's
Centre, 21 - 28 November, with 35 participants from 14 countries. It is
being financed by two church groups of North America and the topics
down for discussion include:-

- Can Christian Principles Affect Development Issues?
- Chrisitianity: Principles of Dogma
- How an Economic Approaches Affect Development?
- What Political Approaches are necessary for Development?
- Is There A Need For A New International Information Order?
- The Grenada Revolution - Its Effect on Development In The
Region.

The Seminar will end on 28th November, but will also hear reports from the
countries represented, including Haiti. The choice was given to Comrade
Bishop to whatever way possible for him - either have an informal "rap"
with the participants or to formally close the Seminar. The latter was
chosen.

3.9 Party Headquarters - Not discussed.
3.0 Puerto Rico Fisherment Not discussed.

PB CONSULTATION ON ITEM 5: Not relevant - document distributed to comrades.

DISCUSSION ON ONE OF THE "AREAS OF WORK" - WORKERS WORK: This was ~not~ discussed, *Briefly*
because of the limitations of time. However, it is to be discussed along with
the Present Political Situation on Wednesday 10th November.

On the question of the Present Political Situation, Cde. Layne is to prepare
an introduction to the discussion on this topic.

NB: It should be noted that under No. ix of Tasks Arising, it was announced
by Cde. Strahhan that 108 work centres will participate in on the spot
work centre meetings. 108 meetings will not be held, because some will be
held in clusters.

ITEMS FOR DECISIONS THAT WERE NOT DISCUSSED:-
a. The Dome ✓ / YFR ~ PARTY SCHOOL ✓
b. Party Headquarters ✓
✗ c. PB Pre-Set Agenda Change
d. Puerto Rico Fishermen ✓ (VIEQUES)

- NWO ✓
- SOVIET proposals ✓
✓ SECURITY for November
✓ PROPAGANDA "
NAT... SPORTS Council (Blondell's proposal)
I.S.D. Budget
✓ PHIL Agee
RED CROSS proposals
F.E.S. Conference   - CARIBEAN Confer. (WPJ/Kote) ✓

{ TAM
{ Econ..
{ DEmoc
{ InfoNet..
{ Edn..

1. Minutes of the PB to be structured along the lines of the CC minutes. (Done well)
2. Agreement in principle to the idea of the proposal of the work camp as put by Athie Martin.
3. Comrade Leader to address the closing of the Youth Seminar at Pope Paul's Centre on November 28th.
4. Comrade Strachan to respond to NSC letter sent to the Comrade Leader.
5. Money outstanding by Wayne Sandiford to be repaid at $50 monthly.
6. A sub-Committee of Comrades Louison, Bishop and Strachan to look at Decision 16 of the Draft CC Resolution in Time for C. C. Meeting on pry.. RE-ORG..
7. Special Party GM's to be held on Saturday 13 and (20 November) respectively (for CM's and M's, then Applicants) to report on an Extra-Ordinary Meeting of the Central Committee that was held recently.
8. The Comrade Leader will do the presentation at these GM's.
9. All PB comrades are to make notes on the issue to be discussed at the GM; these notes are to be presented to the Comrade Leader by Monday 8th November, in order for him to start making notes on the presentation.
10. Party members to discuss the Line of March as presented by the CC in September, during the weekend of December 11th and 12th (using one or two days as is necessary). (Each Contact on study?)
11. Tightening of the Line of March to be done by November 11th.
12. Comrade Layne to prepare opening presentation on the present political situation for discussion on Wednesday 10th November.
13. NWO's proposal re Health Brigade to be distributed to all PB comrades and discussed on Wednesday 10th November.
14. All relevant comrades to be informed re their relevant area of work to be discussed by the PB on the relevant date. The report they are to prepare to be submitted to PB members one week in advance of the scheduled date for discussion.
15. Comrades St. Bernard and Whiteman to meet with the delegation from the World Council of Churches during their visit to Grenada, on Monday 8th November.
16. Comrade Louison to identify additional reading for comrades to use relevant to the Line of March in order to assist them in the study of the document.
Popr.
17. Our response to request for action re South/north Korea issue - from the Central Committee of the DPRK - and the agression of the US to be to give wide publicity to this action.

MATTERS ARISING:-

1. Hazel to check Benny re reply to two letters sent to the Comrade Leader (i. from Puerto Rico Press Club and ii. re a Parliamentary Conference in Brazil)

2. Copies of newsclippings still to be distributed to PB comrades, Foreign Affairs, etc. (Task outstanding from meeting of 27/10/82.)

3. Reply to Korean Embassy in Guyana - telex to be sent. (Task outstanding from meeting of 27/10/82.)

4. Cde. Strahan to follow up on decision re giving wide publicity to the South/North Korea issue and the aggression of the US.

5. Hazel to?-
   5.1 Distribute copies of NWO Health Bridgade proposal to PB comrades for disucssion on Wednesday, 10th.
   5.2 Inform relevant comrades of their report to be sent to PB one week in advance of the schelduled date for discussion on the PB agenda.
   ~~xxxxxxxxxxxxxxxxxxxxxxPBxxxxxxxxxxxxxxxxofxxxxxxxxxxlippingxxxxxxGrenada~~ as
   ~~xxxxxxxxxxxxxxxxxxxxxxxxxxx~~

6. The OC to follow up on decisions to:-
   i) Hold Special GM### re the Extra Ordinary Central Committee Meeting.
   ii) Weekend Membe ship study on the Line of March.

MINUTES OF THE POLITICAL BUREAU MEETING,
17th November, 1982

① 85

Comrades present:-

Selwyn Strachan
Ewart Layne
~~Hudson Austin~~
Chalkie Ventour
Liam James .
Hudson Austin

Comrades absent:-

Maurice Bishop   } all out
George Lousion   } of the
Unison Whiteman   } country
~~Hudson Austin~~ }

Agenda:-

1. Minutes
2. Correspondence
3. Items for Decisions:-

   i) Welcome Ceremony for the Comrade Leader
   ii) Bloody Sunday Programme
   iii) PRA's Constitutional Ammendement
   iv) MMC Health Bridgage Proposal

   v) Red Cros Visit.Proposals
   vi) Delegate for FES Conference
   vii) Report from Cde. Austin on visit to Cuba
   viii) Present Political Situation

4. PB Consultation on Youth Report
5. Discussion on Youth Work

1. MINUTES

1.1 Corrections

i)   Cde. Ventour reported present, was in fact absent
ii) Decision to open a cinema that will show Soviet films and a bookstore that will sell Soviet books, not "Soveit Cinema" and "Soviet Bookstore".
iii) Issue re procedural steps to be taken before serious disciplinary measures including expulsion are taken against Party comrades - Cde. Layne to have done aresearch and report to the PB.
iv) Issue re Armed forces - on full alert, not "semi alert".
v)   Reported discussion/decision re Brehnev's funeral wrongly reported. To be fully deleted. Discussion/decision took place at PB meeting on Friday, 12th.
vi) Re WCC report "they raised the .....", instead of "they rose the..."
vii) Decision was not taken to reply to Gemma's letter.

1.2 Tasks

i)   Cde. Strachan re ~~Gemma's issue:~~ Disciplinary Committee has not met as yet; meeting scheduled for Friday 19th.
ii) Ongoing: Dome and YFR
iii) Not done. Cde. Strachan himself has been trying to sit on top the propaganda himself.
iv) Done. Suriname said they do not think this is the best time for Ages

to visit there. He will go to West Germany and contact them from there. According to Sister Creft, he raised with her, him taking up permanent residence in Grenada.

v) Done

vi) Not completed. Will be done for 24/11/82

vii) Not done yet.

viii)No report: Cde. Whiteman absent from meeting.

ix) Has been taking place - ongoing.

1.3 Decisions

i) CC should have been directed to follow up on decision that fundraising/propaganda work on the building of the Party's Headquarters needs to be improved/increased.

2. CORRESPONDENCE

2.1 Letter from the NSC: they requested PB representation at all their parish rallies to commemorate/celebrate International Students' Day. The following allocation was decided upon:-

St. Andrew's	: Cde. Hudson Austin
St. Patrick's	: Cde. Liam James
St. David's	: Cde. Chalkie Ventour
St. George's	: Cde. Selwyn Strachan
St. John's) St. Mark's)	: Cde. Ewart Layne

2.2 Letter from Jacqueline Creft: She has sent in her letter of immediate resignation from the Party and has requested that a Minister of Education be identified by December to replace her. Decision: She is to be persuaded to stay on for a while, until a replacement is identified.

3. ITEMS FOR DECISIONS:

3.1 Welcome for the Comrade Leader: It is extremely important to have a big welcome home for the Comrade Leader, on his return from the Caricom Heads of Government Meeting. To this end, the masses from St.Patrick's and St. Andrew's are been organised primarily to go to the ceremony. The CC/Party/PRG/Cabinet members to be mobilised to go the airport for this purpose also. Inclued: 21-Gun Salute, Guard of Honour.

3.2 TAWU's Constitutional Amendment: The proposals for the amendments are to be studied by Cdes. Ventour, Strachan and Bishop.

3.3 Bloody Sunday Programme: The programme is to basically include the following:-

o Culture (Armed Forces Band, etc.)   : from 1.00 p.m.
o Solidarity messages (mass organisations
  etc.)   : " 1.30 p.m.
o Speeches by Foreign Guests: : " 2.00 p.m.
  (Michael Manley, Bellafonte, Lamming)

o Chairing to be done by Fitzie (first
  half of the programme, then by Cde.
  Strachan

o Cde. Leaders speech to begin at 3.30 - 4.00

3.4 **W.H.O Health Bridrare**: This was not discussed
3.5 **FAO CONFERENCE DELEGATE**: This was not discussed.
3.6 **Report from Cde. Austin on visit to Cuba**:

- visit to Cuba was to discuss:-
    i) Airport
    ii) Statellite Dish
    iii) Party Headquarters

on the Airport:-

- main thing is the terminal building, an additional 5,000 square meters was agreed to for this purpose;
- the VIP area will also have a Conference room and a dining room which Cuba will furnish
- terminal building will "air tight" by August 1983.
- in principle, Cuba has already agreed to furnish the Airport
- the generating station to be completed by March 1983; HEB station will also be completed by that time
- we will have to supply the fittings for the Fuel Depot (the list of necessary supplies will be here soon)
- the Fuel Depot must be completed by 1983
- the hill behind the terminal building wheih was causing some concern, will be able to move easily without affecting the Terminal
- the runway will be finished by 1983
- Cuba has agreed to send 100 men to help finish most aspects of the Airport in 1983 and they will then help with other construction projects

on the Statelitte Dish:-

- Cuba will send an expert next month to look at whether the Statellite Dish will be able to carry out the role/function of Cable and Wireless or whether we will need to keep them
- the Soviets will be giving us the Dish with experts from Cuba giving us assistance

Other matters:-

- spoke with the Minister of Transport re the AN26 plane for the leadership
- the parts will come from the Soviet Union and Cuban experts will assemble it in Cuba
- Cuba say that we should get the S.U. to train our pilots; Cuba only upgrade pilots
- Cuba will give us the technicians for the plane
- the possibility of using the plane on a commercial basis between here and Cuba was also discussed

Cde. Austin stated that he will prepare a more detailed report on the discussions held for the PB. He also stated that Comrade Cornwall raised the point that he was not receiving information from Foreign Affairs.
Cde. Clarkson is also complaining of having no work to do. Cde. McPhail has also complained that many times comrades come to Cuba, stay at the house and do not assist financially; that instead of using their advance to pay

/...

4

for accomodation in a hotel, they stay with these comrades and use the money to purchase other things.

Items 4 and 5 were not dealt with because of the limitations in time. The meeting ended at about 10.00 a.m. in order for comrades to go to address the different ISD rallies throughout the country.

DECISIONS:

1. PB comrades' addresses to the different ISD rallies to address the issues of the Caricom Heads of Government meeting, the theme as decided by the NSC ("Students' Action for Peace, Friendship and Solidarity), Brehnev's role in struggling for World peace. to be addressed in this context. There should be one minute's silence observed for the matyrs and the death of Leonid Brehnev.
2. All CC/Party/Cabinet/PRG members to be at Pearl's Aiport on Friday afternoon to welcome the Comrade Leader back from the Caricom Heads of Government meeting.
3. Efforts should be made to identify an appropriate Minister of Education to replace Sister Creft. In the meantime, she is to be persuaded to stay on still.
4. Proposals for ammendments to BAWU's Constitution to be studeied by Cdes. Ventour Strachan and Bishop.
5. PB needs to decide on a separate meeting for the purpose of "catching up" with the pre-schelduled agenda items under "Areas of Work". They are:-

2. i) Work Among the Working Class
1. ii) Present Political Situation
4. iii) Youth Work — (8·12.82)
3. iv) FARMERS

1/12/82 → WOMEN

TASKS:

1. Cde. Strachan to speak with Sister Creft re her remaining as Minister of Education for a while until someone else can be identified.
2. Cdes. Bishop, Strachan and Ventour to study proposed ammendments to BAWU's Constitution.
3. Organising Committee to follow up on decision re fundraising/propaganda for Party Headquarters building. (Meeting this Week) Clean
4. Cde. Layne to report on research re procedural steps to be taken for disciplinary measures.
5. Cde. Ventour to complete additional material on the report of the workers work. Ex (Outstanding from 3/11/82)
6. Cde. Whiteman to respond to CCG re the radio release over Radio Antilles re meeting with the WCC delegation.
7. Cde. Strachan to issue press press release re South/North Korea issue . (Outstanding from 3/11/82.)

ITEMS STILL TO BE DISCUSSED:

1. NWO HEALTH BRIGADE PROPOSAL
2. RED CROSS/VISIT
3. DELEGATE FOR FES CONFERENCE ON ECONOMIC RELATIONS BETWEEN EEC AND THE CARIBBEAN

MINUTES OF THE POLITICAL BUREAU MEETING
WEDNESDAY, 22nd DECEMBER, 1982

86

Comrades present:-

Maurice Bishop	: 8.10	(with excuse)
George Louison	: 7.50	*
Unison Whiteman	: 7.55	
Hudson Austin	: 8.01	*
Ewart Layne	: 8.03	

(*) Left 8.40 to attend meeting with Gosplan)

Comrades absent:-

Liam James)
Selwyn Strachan) away
Chalkie Ventour)

Agenda:

1. Minutes
2. Correspondence
   2.1 Report from Cde. Cornwall re Line of March
   2.2 Letter from Bernard Bourne re Richard Jacobs
   2.3 Report from Clarkson
   2.4 Letter from Bogo re Teacher/Typist
   2.5 "   "   " re Division of Labour of Embassy Staff
   2.6 "   "   " re Consular Affairs
   2.7 Suriname Report
   2.8 Report on meetings held in London recently by Cde. Whiteman
3. Items for decisions:
   3.1 Nicaragua SI Meeting
   3.2 Vatican Ambassador
   3.3 Cari-com/OECS Report
   3.4 IICA Situation
   3.5 Opening/Naming of Florida School
   3.6 UWI Work Plan
   3.7 Wesley College Plan
   3.8 George Lamming and Intellectual Workers Secretariat
   3.9 Christmas/New Year Speeches *(Refer to D.C.)*
   3.0 Approval for Expenditure of roads (January - March 1983)
   3.10 Visits in 1983
   3.11 Don Rojas Visit to Angola
   3.12 Special Party GM in January
   3.13 New Buses
   3.14 Directive to Workers Committee re new Contracts
   3.15 Elaboration of Wages Policy
   3.16 Agricultural re-organisation
   3.17 Security Measures - Christmas/New Years
   3.18 Timing of request for diplomatic Assistance
4. PB Consultation on Item 5
5. "Areas of Work" :-
   5.1 Youth Work
   5.2 Workers Work
      i. Report from PWU Sub-Committee
      ii. Dock Workers *(Consultation)*
      iii. Central Directive to all Party Work Committees re Workers Work
      iv. Assigning PB Comrades to the five areas of workers work as decided

(handwritten notes):

ITEMS: 1. RED CROSS ✓
2. NAM in Cuba ✓ (SPS time)
3. LESSON/ROCK ✓
4. E.B. AGENDA ✓

Co-ord.. of visits of
Rpts from African
delegations.

? ✓ iv. 3.14
✓ vi. 3.15

1. MINUTES

1.1 Corrections

i. Total detainees re release - 53; 21 from Hope Vale and 32 from Richmond Hill

ii. Pg. 2 should read " Cde. Whiteman to withdraw intitation extended by Cde. Taylor to visit Grenada to the Inter-American Commission of Human Rights, using as basis, Grenada's desire for legal submission to be fully considered first.

1.2 Tasks:

i. Done. Letter of response and thanks to be sent.

ii. Done.

iii. Decision recorded.

iv. Dessima to deliver note to relevant person.

v. Merle Hodge and Carrol Davis to be Lecturers/Professors at the University: Hilda Roberts, Margaret Francis, Keith Jeremiah, Ruggles Ferguson to attend the University for the Journalism Course.

vi. Done. Lyden asked to contact Menez, etc.

vii. Kurleigh King out at the time; Person at the Caricom Secretariat redd out the text of the resolution; promised to mail the documents to us.

viii. Done; Cdes. Strachan and Antour to raise matter in SU with Richard and Bourne.

ix. Done; Meeting held, pamphlet to go out by today.

x. Being implemented.

xi. Cde. Whiteman met with IICA representative who came from Barbados.

xii. Not done.

xiii. Lyden and Unis met with Keith Roberts; telex sent to St. Lucia; Jane Belfon going as emmissary tommorrow (23rd December)

xiv. Cde. Layne to follow up on these (measures to be implemented as a result of the Egmont Harbour incident).

2. CORRESPONDENCE

2.1 Report from Cde. Cornwall re Line of March: Suggestions and comments on the Line of March were received from members and candidate members in Cuba. This is to be reproduced and distributed for consideration to CC and Education Committee members. Response to be sent to the comrades, acknowledging receipt of the document and the Party's appreciation for the obvious hard work and thought put into the document.

2.2 Letter from Bernard Bourne re Richard Jacobs:

2.3 Report from Clarkson: Cde. Bishop reported that he had received a 9-page from James Clarkson on the situation in Central America.

2.4 Letter from Bogo re Teacher/Typist (to replace Val): Cde. Cornwall has proposed that a teacher/typist be sent to Cuba from Grenada to do Val's teaching and assiting with the typing. It was decided that Christine Clarkson should be made to assist with the typing presently done by Val. Cde. Whiteman to send reply to Cde. Cornwall.

2.5 Letter from Bogo re division of labour of Embassy Staff: Proposals received from Bogo re division of labour of Embassy staff:

Deputy Head of Mission; in charge of
Consular Affairs: Cde. James Clarkson
2nd Secretary; in charge of Trade,
Accomodation: Cde. Don McPhail
Student's work; personal problems, etc.:Cde. Val Cornwall

86 - 2

3/...

It was also stated that all comrades of the Embassy staff are responsible each for monitoring/events/developments in different areas of the World and that daily morning meetings are held to co-ordinate and share information gathered.

Cde. Whiteman is to respond to Cde. Cornwall re proposed structuring of division of labour, stating PB's approval in principle and Cde. Layne to send letter of authorisation to the military in Cuba stating Cde. Cornwall's powers to deal with military matters on Grenada's behalf.

2.6 <u>Letter from Bogo re Consular Affairs:</u> Cde. James Clarkson is now in charge of Consular Affairs including all immigration/passport/visa arrangements in place pf Cde. Don McPhail, Cde. Whiteman to inform Immigration Department accordingly.

2.7 <u>Suriname Report:</u> Cde. Layne gave the Bureau a very brief report on the situation in Suriname based on a word of mouth report he himself had received from Cde. Rupert Roopnarine. The situation there was described as "dread" with clear evidence of the involvement of the Dutch, British Canadian and American; inability to work with the masses was also noted.

Cde. Roopnarine was due to attend PB at 1.30 p.m. for the prupose of a more detailed report.

2.8 <u>Report on meetings held recently in London with Cde. Whiteman:</u> He tabled his brief report on meetings held while in London during the period of 29th November to 1st December, 1982.

3. ITEMS FOR DECISIONS:

3.1 <u>Nicaragua SI Meeting:</u> A meeting of progressive parties within SI (Cuba, Nicaragua, Jamaica - PNP, Grenada and Hector O'Queli) to be held in Nicaragua from January 5th, 1983 to discuss joint strategy for the SI Congress to he held in Austraila in 1983. Cde. Chris DeRiggs to attend on Grenada's behalf.

3.2 <u>Vatican Ambassador:</u> Cde. Bishop noted that it must be ensured that an Ambassador to the Vatican is appointed/acredited in the person of Jimmy Emmanuel.

3.3 <u>Caricom/OECS Reports</u> : These are still outstanding.

3.4 <u>IICA Situation:</u> Cde. Noel (BGWU) met with the IICA representative from Barbados who came to discuss the IICA issue. The former told him of the Union's position, that:-
      i. Franka should not return to Grenada
      ii. The two sisters that were fired should be rehired.
The IICA represenative stated agreement with No. i, but says it means that it will tkae some time to get cheques signed as a result of this. He stated non-agreement with No. ii.

PB decided that the BGWU (Cde. Noel) to write directly to the Director-General of IICA stating the present situation, giving the background and asking for his personal intefvention in the matter. In the meantime, the normal industrial procedures are to continue - Ministry of Labour, etc.

According to Cde. Whiteman IICA says they will be willing to recognise the union and rehire the two workers.

4/...

3.5 Opening/Naming of Florida School: New primary school to be opened in
Florida - to be named the D"Demo "rant School".

3.6 UWI Work Plan: A few chnages and inclusions were made to the draft UWI
Work Plan as prepared by Carrol Davis and submitted to the PB, but it
was agreed to in principle by the Bureau. Cde. Bishop is to laise
with Carrol Davis in this regard.

3.7 Wesley College Plan: A draft plan for dealing with the Wesley cCollege
issue was also submitted, PB decided on the following to deal with the
issue:-

    i)   Ammend the Education Act to enable the Minister of
        Education to re-locate schools.

    ii)   Use the new powers to relocate the Wesley College to
        the Park.

    iii)   Start meeting with the PTA Executive.

    iv)   Start repairs and logistic arrangement for relocation of
        the school.

3.8

    v)   Make the school Government-owned.

5. YOUTH WORK *~~AMBASSA~~ HATHEW Wilkotongs CALL in to dikoy Security off... re Campbell.*

A 11-page report on the present state of the youth work was presented to
the PB by the Youth Committee. Much of the time during the meeting was
spent reading and clarifing the document, with Cde. Tan Bartholomew pre-
send during that time.

Cde. Bartholomew awas criticised for not carrying out his role as Secretary
of Sports by visiting and been present at sporting activities and or discussing with the different sporting associations in the country.

At the end, the Politbureau requested that Cde. Barhholomew return to the
PB meeting on January 5th, 1983 between 11.00 a.m. and 12.00 noon to discuss the report in more detail. He is to prepare a list of all the sporting associations and a plan to take them over and to also prepare a work
plan for culture which should be dicussed with Cde. Jackie Creft.

Tan to bring check-list of playing-fields.

DECISIONS/TASKS:

1. Suggestions/comments from Members and Candidate Members in Cuba re Line of
March to be reporduced and circulated to CC and Education Committee members.

2. Cde. Whiteman to do the following:-

2.1 Reply to Bogo re:Christime Clarkson to assist with typing *(TO Go on ST. 1st)*
        PB approves in principle proposed division of labour

2.2 Inform Immigration Department re Cde. Clarkson in charge of Consular
Affairs - passports, visas, etc. *(To be early informed. letter)*

3. Ambassador to the Vatican to be acredited.

4. Cde. Noel to send letter to Director-General of IICA re issue here.

5. New Florida School to be called "Demo Grant School".

6. Cde. Bishop to laise with Carrol Davis re UWI Work Plan.

7. Decision on Wesley College (See above, 3.7; Nos. i - v).

8. Reply to be sent to comrades in Cuba re suggestions on Line of March.

9. Cde. Layne to send letter to Cuba re Cde. Cornwall's authorisation to
deal with military matters on Grenad's behalf *(NOT yet.)*

10. Cde. Layne to follow up on decisions taken as a result of the Egmont Harbour
incident, i.e. obtaining list of prohibited ports, puting up OUT OF BOUNDS
sign; training new officers more carefully; careful instructions to the comrades

5/...

11. Cde. DeRiggs to attend SI meeting in Nicaragua from January 5th.
12. Plan for Wesley College issue as decided.(See measures on page 4;
    No. 3.7)
13. Cde. Tan Bartholomew to return for more discussion on the Youth work,
    January 5th with a list of all sporting associations, plan to take
    them over and a work plan for culture discussed with Sister Creft.

Outstanding Agenda Items:

Items for decisions: Nos 3.8 to 3.18 (See page 1)
Areas of Work: Workers Work:
                        i.   Report from PWU Sub-Committee
                        ii.   Dock Workers
                        iii.   Central Directive to all Party Work Committees
                                Re Workers Work
                        iv.   Assigning PB comrades to the five areas of
                                Workers Work as decided.
                        v.   Directive re New Contracts
                        vi.   Wages policy

MINUTES OF THE POLITICAL BUREAU MEETING
WEDNESDAY, 29th DECEMBER, 1982

Comrades present:-

Maurice Bishop
George Louison   : 7.56
Selwyn Strachan   : 7.50
Unison Whiteman   : 7.59
Hudson Austin
Ewart Layne   : 7.45

Comrades absent:-

Liam James   )
Challie Ventour) away

Agenda:-
1. Minutes
2. Correspondence:-
   2.1 Communist Party of Cuba on Demo
   2.2 Ralph Gonsalves
   2.3 Denmark-Grenada Friendship Society
   2.4 Message from M-19, Columbia
   2.5 Suriname
   2.6 Compton's Cable - Caricom/Canada
   2.7 Meetings of 24th and 30th December
   2.8 Outstanding Plans/Budgets/TMS
   2.9 House of Commons Report on Grenada
   2.10 60th Anniversary Report: Cde. Strachan
   2.11 Letter from Fennis Augustine
   2.12 Report from Alva James
3. Items for decisions:-
   3.1 Red Cross Proposal
   3.2 Proposed Non-Aligned Meeting in Grenada
   3.3 Rev. Lettson/Rev. Rock
   3.4 Friday's Economic Bureau Meeting
   3.5 George Lamming and Intellectual Workers Secretariat
   3.6 Christmas/New Year Speeches
   3.7 Approval for Expenditure on roads (January - March 1983)
   3.8 Visits in 1983
   3.9 Don Rojas' Trip to Angola
   3.0 Special Party GM in January
   3.10 New buses
   3.11 Agricultural re-organisation
   3.12 Security Measures - Christmas/New Years
   3.13 Timing of requests for diplomatic assistance
4. PB Consultation on Item 5
5. "Areas of Work":-
   5.1 Workers Work:-
      i.   Report from PWU Sub-Committee
      ii.   Dock Workers
      iii. Central Directive to all Work Committees re workers work.
      iv.   Assigning PB Comrades to the five areas of workers work as decided
      v.   Directive to Workers Committee re new contracts
      vi.   Elaboration of Wages Policy

2/...

1. **MINUTES**
   1.1 <u>Corrections</u>:
       i.   pg. 3; 3.1 should read "progressive parties within SI within the region"; and should include Chile - Ansleme Sule and state El Salvador after the name Hector O'Queli.
       ii. re IICA issue, should read " rehire one of the two workers".
       iii. pg. 2; 2.2 Bourne/Richard, should state letter dealt with outstanding issue and Cdes. Strachan and Ventour to deal with issue while in the S.U.
       iv. re discussion on the Youth work, Cde. Bartholomew to also prepare a check list of all playing fields and other projects to be undertaken by the NYO in 1983 when he returns for discussion on January 5th.

   1.2 <u>Tasks</u>:
       i.   Not done.
       ii. Done; letter to be sent on Friday 31st; Immigration orally informed; letter to follow.
       iii. No reply received on this as yet.
       iv. Cde. Noel notified of decision; not sure if implmented. Decision also included Cde. Noel to pursue normal industrial procedure - Ministry of Labour, etc.
       v.   Ongoing.
       vi. Report to be made on Wednesday 15th January.
       vii. Original deadline impossible; actual relocation unlikely to take place before end of January.
       viii. Not done.
       ix. Not done.
       x.   Cde. Layne spoke to Keith Roberts; important to note/mention the question of co-ordination of channels on the radio.
       xi. Informed of decision; Cde. DeRiggs to meet with Cde. Whiteman re briefing.
       xii. Repition of task no. vii.
       xiii. Task to include No. iv of 1.1 above.

   1.3 <u>Tasks not mentioned</u>:
       i.   Cde. Whiteman to have called in Cde. Mathew Williams re security reports on Cde. Campbell of the Grenada Venezuela Mission. Message was sent to Cde. Williams to come to Grenada.

   1.4 <u>Other</u>:
       1.   The PB decided that given the importance of Cde. Fargurson in getting the Party's paper off the ground away, he should not attend the Journalism Course in San Francisco as decided at last PB meeting.

2. **CORRESPONDENCE:**
   2.1 <u>Communist Party of Cuba on Demo</u>: A condolence message from the Central Committee of the Communist Party of Cuba on the death of "Cacademo" Grant; message to be aired on RFG.
   2.2 <u>Ralph Gonsalves</u>: He wrote on behalf of the Movement for National Unity (the newly formed Party in St. Vincent) expressing the desire to establish fraternal links with NJM and to come to Grenada for that purpose and to discuss the events in St. Vincent. Attached was a copy of the MNU's programme, and press releases re his "break" with the UPM.

       Cde. Strachan is to contact Cde. Gonsalves asking him to come in as he requested.

   2.3 <u>Denmark-Grenada Friendship Society</u>: They have requested that Government change the sentence of death against the four terrorists to that of life imprisonment. The letter was originally sent to Cde. Bishop and copied to Cde. Lambert. Cde. Bishop to reply stating that their concerns have been noted; the Court passed sentence; GIS was reporting the news; the Government has not taken a position on the issue; that ordinary criminals who were sentenced to death before and after the Revolution for ordinary crimes have had their sentences changed to life imprisonment.

3/...

2.4 <u>Message from M-19, Columbia</u>: The 8th National Conference of the M-19 of Columbia sent greetings to the NJM and stated their desire to develop best possible links with our Party. No reply to be sent; letter to be filed.

2.5 <u>Suriname</u>: A report from Cde. Nelson Louison oh his visit to Suriname was received and noted by the Bureau.

2.6 <u>Compton's Cable - Caricom/~~Canada~~Canada</u>: Tx Trudeau's proposed Caricom/ Canada/Commonwealth meeting is planned for 20 - 21 February, 1983, in St. Lucia. Grenada to respond saying the dates are alright, but delegation to attend has not been decided upon as yet.

2.7 <u>Meetings of 24th and 30th December</u>: Meeting of 24th December to have drawn up guidelines for a system to daily monitor the performances of the state and Para statal enterprises - Cde. Louison to have chaired the meeting. The meeting did come off, but Cde. Louison was absent because of the Gosplan session.
Meeting of 30th December of state enterprises comrades from the relevant Ministries - that of Planning and Finance to meet together with Cde. Coard. Cde. Layne to be in attendance.

2.8 <u>Outstanding Plans/Budgets/TMS</u>: List of Ministries and departments who have not submitted either their plan, budget, or TMS or all of these. The relevant responsible PB comrades were asked to ensure those outstanding documents are submitted to the relevant Ministry.

2.9 <u>House of Commons Report on Grenada</u>: Cde. Whiteman tabled the House of Commons Report on Grenada.

2.10 <u>Soviet State 60th Anniversary Celebration Report</u>: Cde. Strachan reported on his recent visit to the Soviet Union to participate in the celebration marking the 60th anniversary of the Soviet State:-
o occassion was tremendously successful and highly organised
o main activity was the joint sitting of the CPSU, Supreme Soviet, Russian Federation; session lasted two days
o 140 foreign delegations; 51 sat on the Presidium (including NJM)
o the entire socialist community was present at t e level of leadership
o Andropov's presentation of one hour was superb/very firm and very well received - tremendous applause by the foreign section
o short addresses were made by the Secretary-Generals of the 15 different republics - all their speeches shown a deep love for the Russian people
o a moving speech was made by a 82-year old Communist who was present at the first Congress called to discuss the formation/establishment of the Soviet State (1922)
o many of the delegations that did not speak at the joint session, spoke at factories; Grenada's presentation was well received

o meetings held with our Party studnets there - they are in a good mood; not clear whether Rita, etc. will return in June or later
o meeting held with Cdes. Einstein Louison and Cecil Prime - they have settled down; suggested that other comrades coming for the five-months course be of a high political level
o meeting held with Cde. Cheneve - looked at the implementation of the Party-to-Party agreement; Cde. Louison to follow up of delivering the leadership's plane - check written agreement; material assistance to be delivered by March 1983; large PA system to arrive before March (in time for the 4th anniversary celebration; introduced the idea of the Party bookstore and independent cinema - was agreed to and enthused by the idea; inter-Party exchanges were discussed -delegation of CPSU comrades led by a CC comrade to come in February; in May or June a Party delgation from NJM to go up; letters from Comrade Leader to Cdes. Tikonov and Andropov were formally delivered at the meeting

4/...

Grenada to prepare article for June WDK issue; statelite Edish delegation arriving in March; East Port delegation arriving 14th January

o   Richard Bourne issue - meeting held jointly with the two parties; tension still exists; each comrade was asked to make presentation on the problem(s) and suggestions for corrective measures; Bourne listed 30 lies/distortions against himself made by Richard; were told by Cde. Strachan that their actions have been damaging to the image of the Party and Revolution, that they were not acting as Party comrades, their behaviour is petty bourgeois in nature; told them each of their strengths and weaknesses; at end of the meeting the following nine points were agreed upon, "To acheive functional co-operation and unity":-

i.   Cde. Jacobs accepts there was no accusation of corruption against himself;
ii.   Both comrades to struggle hard to end written and unspoken polemic;
iii.   Both comrades accept complete honesty and respect;
iv.   Principle of criticism and self-criticism to be adhered to;
v.   Party's committment to wide participation to be instituted;
vi.   Collective leadership; overall leader to be recognised;
vii.   Financial controls;
viii. Embassy to operate on the basis of work Plan
ix.   Monthly reports on the implementation of the above to be sent to the O.C. and copied to the Chairman of the CC.

2.11 Letter from Fennis Augustine: Letter from the NJC re assistance; agreed to. Letter of reply to be sent to Cde. Augustine.

2.12 Report from Alva James: Cde. James made this points to Cde. Whiteman recently:-

o   1983 will be rougher(economically speaking)year than 1982
o   wide feeling in St. David's that "Morain" is involved in stealing
o   re the Grand Boolet issue - the feeling is that the Government should take control of it, but that the debt owed to NCB be paid off;
o   problem of pradeial larceny
o   feeling that Chase has gotten close to Renwick - Nutmeg Association Board of Directors
c   should review profit sharing issue

2.13 Request from Cubana: Cde. Austin reported on a letter he received from Cde. Cornwall which stated that in the latter's conversation with The Director of Cubana in Cuba re lower air fares for students returning home on vacation, he (the Director) expressed a request for special refueling concessions to be granted to them upon the completion of the International Airport - they will bring their fuel and have it stored here.

Our official response to them is that the request is to be studied. Also Cde. Cornwall is to tactfully find out the real source of the request.

Cde. Austin to reply to Cde. Cornwall's letter.

5/...

3. **ITEMS FOR DECISION:-**

3.1 Red Cross Proposal: The Regional Red Cross representative was recently on a visit here and according to Cde. Whiteman, the former has explained a service made available by the association. That is, they can be asked to visit our prisons (must see all the prisoners in their normal environment - cell), and then the option is for them to publish a report or they can informally let people know that the prisoners are alright.

It was decided against accepting the offer at this time.

3.2 Proposed Non-Aligned Meeting in Grenada: At the last Non-Aligned Meeting, it was decided to set up a group/committee of experts to look at small island states; the Cubans want to know whether they can host the meeting - they will be financing it. This was agreed to by the PB, but it was noted that this should be co-ordinated with the Ministry of Planning as there is an upcoming conference to be held also on the same issue - small island states.

3.3 Rev. Lettson/Rev. Rock: The methodist priest, Rev. Lettson was served a deportation order on Thursday 23rd December re his refusal to perform service for both Cdes. Cacademo Grant and T.A. Marryshow. As a result, Ricky Singh called the Comrade Leader on behalf of the new General Secretary of the CCC. Letter to be sent to Rev. Taylor (Methodist Superintendent for the region), copied to Rev. Rock (Sub Superintendent) and Kirton, (the new General Secretary - CCC outlining the background to Rev. Lettson's deportation order and stating that the action/events were regarded as consistent hostility and contempt for the State.

3.4 Friday's Economic Bureau Meeting: Agenda to include:-

   i.   Agriculture Reorganisation
   ii. MNIB
   iii. New taxes
   iv. 1983 Budget/Plan
   v.   Tourism Proposal
   vi. Housing Report

5. **AREAS OF WORK:-**

5.1 Workers Work:-
   i.   PWU Sub-Committee Report: This dealt with the plan by the committee for the upcoming elections next year; the report to complete report/analysis
   ii. Dock Workers: Copies of their Constitution received, but no analysis; Cde. Sawney to be contacted re analysis of present SWWU executive and proposals for work in the Union.
   iii. Central Directive - It was the general feeling that all work committees already knew of the priority being placed on the workers work as stated in the Line of March and that most draft work plans of committees were already submitted to the Organising Committee.
   iv. Assignment of PB comrades...:_ Not discussed.

6/...

Being standardised by Min. of Pl. So that P.B.
can Amart Findings. 1982
                                                            Wages

vi. **Elaboration of Wages Policy** _____ : The Comrade Leader
    pointed out that in 1982 the economy is expected to grow by 2%
    and stated that the question of how much should be salary in-
    creases for workers in the same period should/needs to be addressed.
    However, this was not discussed in detail.   1%
                                                                     AVGE
    Item to be on P.B. Agenda for   *os vs.*
    28.1.83.   *6.29*
                                                                    Inflation.

DECISIONS/TASKS:

1. Suggestions/Comments from Party comrades in Cuba re the Line of March to be
   reproduced and distributed to CC and Education Committee members. (Task outstanding from 22/12/82.)
2. Ambassador to the Vatican to be appointed/accredited. (Outstanding from 22/12/82)
3. Comrade Bishop to alise with Carrol Davis re UWI and report to PB - Wednesday
   5th January. (Outstanding from 22/12/82).
4. Reply to be sent to Cde. Cornwall re suggestions on Line of March. (Outstanding
   from 22/12/82).
5. Letter to military in Cuba re Cde. Cornwall's authorisation to deal with
   military matters. (Outstanding from 22/12/82). (4 H.)
6. Message from Communist Party of Cuba re Cacademo Grant's death to be sent to RFG.
7. Cde. Strachan to contact Cde. Ralph Gonsalves to come to Grenada on the latter's
   request.
8. Cde. Bishop to reply to letter from Denmark Grenada Friendship Society re
   death sentence against the four terrorists sentenced to death.
9. Cde. Liam James to go to Suriname shortly after his report return to Grenada
   from the United Kingdom.
10. Re Caricom/Canada/ Commonwealth Meeting Grenada to respond - dates alright, but
    delegation not decided on as yet.
11. All PB comrades to nesure that the different Ministries and Departments under
    them submitt their Plan/Budget/TMS as relevant.
12. Re request from Cubana Director, Cde. Austin to reply to Cde. Cornwall stating
    that the latter's reply to Cubana is that the request is being conslered and in
    the meantime Cde. Cornwall to find out the real source of the request.
13. Agree in principle to Non?Aligned Committee meeting in Grenada; this to be
    co-ordinated with the Ministry of Planning.
14. Outstanding report re SWWU from Cde. Sawney to be collected and dis-
    tributed to PB comrades.
15. Friday's EB meeting agenda to include:-
    i.   Agriculture Reorganisation
    ii.   MNIB
    iii.   New Taxes
    iv.   1983 Budget/Plan
    v.   Tourism Proposal
    vi.   Housing . Report
16. Cde. Louison to follow up on delivering of leadership's plane from the S.U.
17. Cde. Layne to attend December 30th meeting with State enetrpises, Ministry of
    Planning, Finance, etc.

18 *Response to De Cuti to*
Finis Augustine ... '''''''''''
ITUC Request.

<u>MINUTES OF THE POLITICAL BUREAU MEETING</u>
WEDNESDAY 5TH JANUARY, 1983

<u>Comrades present:-</u>

Maurice Bishop
Selwyn Strachan
Unison Whiteman
Liam James
Hudson Austin
Ewart Layne
George Louison

<u>Comrades absent:-</u>

Chalkie Ventour : away

<u>Agenda:-</u>
1. Minutes
2. Correspondence:
   2.1 GDR re banabas
   2.2 NJM - Washington
   2.3 SI invitation
   2.4 Cde. Ventour
   2.5 Denis Renwick
3. Items for decisions:
   3.1 Venezuela Houses
   3.2 March 13 Proposal
   3.3 House in Carriacou - Military Compound
   3.4 PB Work Plan
   3.5 Archdeacon Huggins
   3.6 Cyrus/Venezuela
   3.7 Devil Desouza
   3.8 Stanley Roberts
   3.9 PB/CC Assignment - Armed Forces Week Activities
   3.10 PB/EB Pre-Scheduled Agenda: January - March, 1983
   3.11 Review of Past Pre-Scheduled Agenda
   3.12 PB Report to CC (*CHRISTMAS*)
   3.13 George Lamming and Intellectual Workers Secretariat
   3.14 Visits in 1983
   3.15 Don Rojas' Trip to Angola
   3.16 Special Party GM in January
   3.17 New Buses
   3.18 Timing of requests for Diplomatic Assistance
4. PB Consultation on Item 5
5. "Areas of Work":-
   5.1 Workers Work:
     i. Socialism Classes
     ii. PB Meeting with WC and CPE every six weeks
     iii. Building for WC.
   5.2 Youth Work

1. <u>MINUTES</u>
   1.1 <u>Corrections:</u>
     i.   ro "Cde. Jacobs accepts...", it should read "no specific
        accusation of corruption against Cde. Jacobs by Cde. Bourne."
     ii. (a)pg. 6 _"the economy is expected"; should read " 2percent
        growth in the economy in 1982".
       (b) re elaboration of wages policy; should read"wages
       increase running at 17 percent as against 6.2 percent
       inflation".
       (c) should also read "wages policy how being studied by
       Ministry of Planning so that the PB can await   results

88

of their technical findings"; matter to come back to
PB on Wednesday 26th January, 1983.

iii. pg. 4 re Grand Bcolet issue, it should include "feeling is
that NCB should take control of Grand Bacolet".

iv. pg. 5, re Red Cross; not for them to publish, but Grenada's
option to publish the report in full.

v. (a) re Non-Aligned meeting in Grenada, "Grenada to host meeting",
the Cubans will help with the financing.

(b) re Ministry of Planning upcoming conference, should read
"as there may be an upcoming conference..."

vi. re Rev. Lettson, not "deportation order" but r vocation
of work permit order to take effect within two weeks".

1.2 Tasks:

i. Done

ii. No reply yet - re accreditation of Ambassador to the
Vatican

iii. Done; written report to be sent by Carrol Davis; appointment of emissaries - a problem

iv. Done.

v. Cde. Layne to write formal note.

vi. Done.

vii. Done; will come to Grenada on ar about 27th January.

viii. Task given to Nelson Louison.

ix. Cde. James leaving today - Suriname.

x. Done

xi. Ongoing.

xii. Done; no reply as yet

xiii. Co-ordination has started.

xiv. Done.

xv. Done.

xvi. Agreement not yet signed.

xvii. Done.

xviii. Done.

2. CORRESPONDENCE:

2.1 GDR re Bananas:- Geest has written to Windban stating that
they have received a request from the GDR to transport the
bananas they have ordered from Grenada.

Cde. Louison is to ~~point out to Geest that the banana industry~~
~~in the Windward Islands is only viable with Grenada's input.~~ contact BEACHE of S.T.V.

2.2 NJM - Washington: A sympathy card on Cacademo's death was received from Party and Party Support Group members in Washington,
D.C. Message to be sent to RFG.

2.3 SI Invitation: SI Congress being held 7 - 10 April in Sydney,
Australia; Congress theme O "World in Crisis: Socialist Res-
ponse. NJM delegates: Chris DeRiggs, Lindwalr Purcell, Caldwell
Taylor (possibly) and for tactically reasons, Cde. Maurice
Bishop's name to be included on the registration form enclosed.

2.4 Cde. Ventour: Telex received stateing that a new health problem
has been identified in Cde. Ventour and so he will not be going

the Black Sea as planned, but instead will have to go
into Hospital.

2.5 **Denis Renwick:** This comrade has reported fell and broke his neck,
he is said to be paralused, WC is requesting that PB/leading
Party comrades visit him in hospital. Agreed.

3. **ITEMS FOR DECISIONS:**

3.1 **Venzuela Houses:** House near Personal Security Unit reportedly
bought by the Venezuela Embassy, sold by Paul Scoon. Cde.
Bishop to speak to the latter, expressing Government's intention to buy the said building. Arrangement to be made for the
purchase of the house.

3.2 **March 13 Proposal:** Proposal to have a much "scaled down" 4th
anniversary celebrations. The last of the three options in
the written 2-page proposal submitted by Cde. Strachan was
agreed to by the PB. Cde. Strachan to hold a Press Conference
in this regard. 14 instead of 20 rallies (mini) to be held.

3.3 **House in Carriacou - Military Compound:** Efforts to be made to
have this house be bought by the Military; house situated in
strategic position to the camp there.

3.4 **PB Work Plan:** Not discussed.

3.5 **Archeadcon Huggins:** Archdeacon Huggins is reported to have made
recent anti-PRG and anti-Revolution sermon in the Chruch at
the Christmas and New Year's church services. It was suggested
that somebody close to the Anglican Church be called in and
spoken to about the matter, who will in turn speak to the
Archdeacon. Cde. Whiteman to follow up on this.   (*)

3.6 **Cyrus/Venezuela:** Cde. Whiteman to call in the Venezuelan Ambassador.

3.7 **"Devil" Desouza:** — Not done

3.8 **Stanley Roberts:** " " " "

3.9 **PB/CC Assignment:** " " " "

3.10 **PB/EB Pre Scheduled Agenda:** Not discussed.

3.11 **Review of Past Pre-Scheduled Agenda:** This was not discussed.

3.12 **PB Report to CC:**

3.13 **George Lamming and Intellectual Workers Secretariat:** This Secretariat
is to be in Grenada - meeting in this regard to have been held this
month. It was noted that offices are needed for the following also:

o Grenada Peace Council
o Grenada-Caribbean IOJ Office
o Grenada Committee for Friendship with the Peoples
o Grenada Human Rihgts Council
o National Science and Technology Center

(*) Cyrus
travelling
on a Vene-
zuelan pass-
port.

It was suggested that when the students from Wesley College on
Lucas Street are relocated, that the building be used for housing
CPE and the present CPE office be used for housing the above-men-
tioned bffices.

However, Cde. Strachan stated that if any building for office
space is to be identified, that it be used for the Workers Committee to use as their Union offices.

It was decided that Regina Taylor make attempts to identify
money to purchase "Albany Inn" which can be used for either
one of these purposes. The PB is also to keep looking for
this purpose.   4/...

The 2nd Conference on National Soverenity, to be held in Grenada on 16 - 20 June; theme - "Food, Science, Technology"; 40 participants; hpping to get Alister McIntyre and William Denas; Regional Planning Committe to meet 29 - 30 January.

3.14 <u>Visits in 1983</u>: The following countries were looked at for possible visits during this year both by the Comrade Leader (in some instances) and the Foriegn Minister alone (in other cases):-

i.	Iran, Iraq, Algeria	: Funds, oil
ii.	Yugloslavia, Korea	: Tourism possibilities
iii.	Romania	
iv.	Angola, Tanzania, Zambia	: Funds, oil products
v.	Kuwait, Suadi Arabia,	:
vi.	Hungary, Czeckoslovakia	
vii.	Sweden	
viii.	Argentina, Brazil, Columbia	
ix.	Austria, Switzerland	

It was also noted that these meetings
will be held this year:

o Caricom - Heads of Government	:	Trinidad
o Non-Aligned	:	India
o Commonwealth	:	

Cde. Whiteman stated that the Government of Kampuchea has inivted Comrades Bishop and Whiteman to visit their country between 1 - 3 March (just before the Non-Aligned Meeting) in place of their Foriegn Minister visiting Grenada in January as was previously planned. It was noted that if agreed to, Vietnam and Laos can be visited around the same time. The visit to Kampuchea was agreed to by the PB.

3.15 <u>Don Rojas' Trip to Angola</u>: This comrade is going to Angola as the Caribbean IOJ Representative; he is to carry with him alletter to Santos from the Comrade Leader inviting him to come to Grenada. Cde. Whiteman to co-ordinate this.

3.16 <u>Special Party GM in January</u>: This GM will be held to disciss the economy - budget/plan etc and for "pushing the Party on the economy". Date; 31st January, 5.00 p.m.

3.17 <u>New Buses</u>: Theft is reported to be taking place on the NTS buses by the conductors. Twelve new buses are being ordered to add to the present amount. It was recommended that a new system of payment be used to ensure the minimum of theft of funds - installing a slot for payment of fares. Cde. Louison is to contact the firm to make the necessary chnages on six of the 12 buses.

3.18 <u>Timing of requests for diplomatic assistance</u>: Not discussed.

3.19 <u>Cacademo Grant</u>: Cde. Louison explained that there is a problem existing over the land owhership on which Cacademo's house was built. Cde. Louison to contact Fred Grant re Government's intention to use the area.

4. AREAS OF WORK:-

5/...

5.1 <u>Workers Work</u>:
    i.   Socialism Classes: Cde. Valdon Boldeau to assign PB/CC
        comrades to visit the Socialism Classes for the period up
        to the end of March. This to be done in time for the PB/
        Socialism Tutors meeting on Thursday, 6th January.

        It was the feeling/concensus that the new year address
        by the Comrade Leader be used first as the material for
        the classes and then to return to the notes on the
        economy.

        Also to be discussed at the Thursday meeting - package of
        measures re emulation at the workplaces.
   ii. PB Meeting with WC......: Decision to hold meetings every
        six weeks with the Workers Committee and the CPE (separately)
        to review the progress being made in this two areas of
        work given the priority for this year; and as one way to
        ensure the leadership supervises this priority.

        The first meting is on February 9th: PB and WC from
        10.00 - 12.00 noon and PB and CPE (plus Didicus and Jackie)
        from 1.00 - 3.00 p.m. and continuing every six weeks there-
        after.
  iii. Building for WC: This was more or less discussed under
        item 3.13. The Workers Committee (especially comrades
        in BGWU and CIWU) have expressed the deep need for a build-
        ing to house their offices , as the present one is too
        small.

5.2 <u>Youth Work</u>: Cde. Tan Bartholomew, Lorriane Felix and Chris
    Brown came to discuss the youth work - a 6-page report on this
    was previously prepared and distributed to PB comrades. The
    document was discussed by the PB and the following was decided:-

    i.   NYO to arrange priorities of matters raised in the
        document.
   ii. Arrange time scheldule for objectives in the document.
  iii. Identify, within 48 hours, a Director of Sports to re-
        place Blondell.
   iv. Cde. Louison to investigate the possibility of getting
        a transcavator from the S.U. to assist with the building
        of NYO hard courts.
    The NYO comrades were told of two houses in the St. Paul's
    area that can be used as a Pioneer Camp as requested/suggested
    by them.

    Cde. Tan Bartholomew to obtain draft laws/statues on the NSO
    and work out a strategy for working with the middle ground in
    the area of sports. Regular meetings should also be held with
    the sporting teams and the Sports Department. A careful study
    of the constitutions of the sporting associations and strategy
    and tactics for capturing them. It was suggested that the em-
    phasis be on cheap sports so as to encourage mass participation
    in sporting activities - e.g. Volleyball, etc.

                                 6/...

DECISIONS/TASKS:

1. Cde. Layne to write a formal note to the Military in Cuba re Cde. Cornwall's authorisation to deal with military matter on Grenada's behalf. (Task/matter outstanding).

2. Cde. Louison to follow up on banana issue.

3. NJM ? Washington message re Cacademo to be sent to RFG.

4. Cdes. Chris DeRiggs, Lindwalr Purcell, Caldwell Taylor (possibly) to attend SI Congress - Sydney; Cde. Leader's name to be included on the registration form.

5. PB/leading Party comrades to Denis Renwick who is in hospital.

6. Cde. Strachan to hold press conference - re decision to have a different March 13 this year.

7. The military to purchse house in Carriacou near to the military compound.

8. Cde. Whiteman to follow up on Archdeacon Huggins issue.

9. Cde. Whiteman to call in the Venezuelan Ambassador re Cyrus.

10. PB to keep looking for a building to house the offices of the Intellectual Workers, etc. and one for the workers.

11. Cde. Regina Taylor to attempt to identify funds for the possible purchase of "Albany Inn".

12. Letter to be sent off to Santos in Angola with Jon Rojas - Cde. Whiteman - letter to come from Cde. Bishop.

13. Special Party GM on the economy - 31st January.

14. Cde. Louison to speak to Fred Grant re Cacademo's house and land spot.

15. The Comrade Leader's new year address to be used in the Socialism classes before the notes on the economy.

16. Six of the twelve new NTS buses to have necessary changes to reduce on possibility of theft by the conductors - Cde. Louison to follow up.

17. Visit to Kampuchea to be made 1 - 3 March, by Cde. Whiteman.

18. Separate meetings to be held every six weeks with the WC and CPE by the PB to supervvise the Number 1 priority for 1983. First meeting is Februrary 9th. Cde. Strachan to list dates of following meetings.

19. Decisions from discussion on Youth work recorded on page 5 (see 5.2).

()()()()()()()()()

MINUTES OF THE POLITICAL BUREAU MEETING
WEDNESDAY 12th JANUARY, 1983

Comrades present:-

    Maurice Bishop
    Selwyn Strachan
    George Louison
    Ewart Layne
    Hudson Austin

Comrades absent:-
    Lian Janes
    Unison Whiteman   } away
    Chalkie Ventour

Agenda:-

1. Minutes
2. Correspondence/Reports:-
    2.1 Cde. Ventour
    2.2 Letter from Kai Schnonhals
    2.3   "   "   Cansave
    2.4 Letters/reports from Cde. Cornwall
    2.5 Security Report
3. Items for Decisions:-
    3.1 UK Festival Committee Request
    3.2 Car for GES Manager
    3.3 Caricom/Canada Meeting
    3.4 Resolution on Agriculture
    3.5 PB/EB Agenda
    3.6 Fort Juedy (Medical School)
    3.7 Devil Desouza
    3.8 Stanley Roberts
    3.9 PB Report to CC
    3.10 Theme for March 13th
    3.11 Director of Sports
4. Areas of Work:-
    4.1 Education Report
    4.2 Workers:-
        a. Socialism Classes
        b. SWWU Report
        c. Workers Committee Report

1. MINUTES
    1.1 Corrections:-
        i.   Pg. 2 re Geest Bananas - Cde. Louison to point out to the Minister
             of Agriculture in St. Vincent, Grenada's intention to continue with
             Geest.
        ii. Pg. 3 re office space needed, include:-
             o Caribbean Education - Production Conference Secretariat
             o Grenada Committee of Intellectuals
        iii. Pg. 4 re visit to Kampuchea - to be made by Cde. Whiteman.
    1.2 Tasks:-
        i.   Tasks not completed - letter to be redone.
        ii. Done; to be followed up by a letter.
        iii. Done.
        iv. Ongoing; Form sent.

    v. Done; visited by Cdes. Austin and Strachan.

    vi. Done.

    vii. Ongoing; message sent to George Prime — follow up.

    viii. Cde. Whiteman left the country; Cde. Louison then asked to follow-up; not done.

    ix. Not done.

    x. Ongoing.

    xi. Cde. Louison spoke to Squires; said that the building is being worked on to start Guest House.

    xii. Ongoing.

    xiii. Now rearranged — same date, but from 1.00 - 10.00 p.m.

    xiv. To be done.

    xv. Being done - ongoing.

    xvi. Done.

    xvii. Ongoing.

    xviii. Ongoing; dates:-

                    February, 9th
                    March, 30th
                    May, 11th
                    June, 22nd

    xix. rearrangement of priorities :
        time scheldue for objectives

        sports director   have returned original two names Keith Joseph, "Ham Folkes"; none other can be found

        transcavator   : will use tractor and added part to perform work of a transcavator

        pionner house   : Deallie house preferred of the two: negotiations for purchase to start by Cde. Bartholomew; then Cde. Wilson and Dolland; matter to be brought to Cabinet.

        NSO strategy   : not started as yet.

2. **CORRESPONDENCE/REPORTS:-**

    2.1 **Cde. Ventour:** Cde. Bishop reported that Cde. Ventour's mother rang him concerned about Cde. Ventour's health. Cde. Layne to contact Keith Roberts re telex that should have been sent off in this regard and to follow up.

    2.2 **Letter from Kai Schopnhels:** Letter sent to the Comrade Leader stating that despite many requests to get involved in some work in Grenada, he has not being invited to even speak at public occasions - only two exceptions to this; has been promised to help in some work - but never materialised; was told by a US citizen that the PRG does not trust him. Decisions:-

        i. Don Rojas to be checked re his background

        ii. Cde. Miguel to be asked to check the Kenyan University

        iii. CPUSA/ Phil Phorna - check

        iv. Cde. Strachan to meet with him, discuss the progress being made on his book and assign him to speak at some zonal council meetings

        v. Cde. Layne to co-ordinate follow up on this and item to return to PB agenda in two weeks.

    2.3 **Letter/Report from Cde. Cornwall:** Cde. Strachan received this letter/ balance report from Cde. Cornwall for the period September to December.

Cde. Cornwall stated the objectives of the missions and the outstanding problems being experienced as:-
i. tendancy to spontaneity
ii. failure to publish an Embassy news.. ter
iii. not being assertive enough in dealins with Cuban comrades
iv. financial difficulties;
v. slow response from Grenada on urgent matters
vi. poor internal distribution system for mails

Solutions to these problems were decided upon by the Embassy and stated
in the letter. A list of 200 activities conducted by the Mission was
attached.

2.3 Letter from Cde. Cornwall to Cde. Strachan:-

document on how Honduras is used by the US against Nicaragua:
copies to be done for the PB

copies of Selected Speeches - Maurice Bishop: 20 copies to be
sent on Saturday;

20 copies of Rupert Bishop's pictures

request for steelebdr to be sent to Cuba in March: to be raised
with Cde. Creft;

The PB noted that the Embassy has improved tremendously since
Cde. Cornwall's appointment to the post in latter 1982.
A letter commending his for his reports, etc. to be sent to him.

2.4 <u>Letter from Cansa</u>: Letter states that they are chaning their
name to Grensave; changing their structures; have requested the
support of Government for their work. Decision - Cde. Creft to
meet with Joan Purcell -who the letter was signed by.

2.5 <u>Security Report</u>: up-to-date report was received.

3. <u>ITEMS FOR DECISIONS</u>: Items Nos. 3.1 to 3.4 were not discussed.
 3.5 Fort Juedy PB/EB Agenda: Cde. Bishop stated a few chnages in the format for the
 PB/EB Pre-Scheduled agenda; the agenda for January - March to be
 prepared for next week's meeting.
 3.6 <u>Fort Juedy (Medical School)</u>: Not discussed.
 3.7 <u>Devil DeSouza</u>: have left the country last Saturday; check to
 be made with Tom at the airport to re-confirm.
 3.8 <u>Stanley Roberts</u>: Cde. Strachan reported that the WC expressed shock
 over his release from detention; they have reported the following:-
  o Stanley states he will organise bolder now
  o is checking workers constantly (SWWU), especially those won over
   by SWWWU Sub-Committee
  o he is about to start plotical education classes (his own)
  o the right wing has been much bolder now - they were also surprised
   of his release
  o Eric Pierre has just returned from a 7-week tour of Israel;
   London, USA
  Decision - The Sub Committee to be asked for a written report.

4/...

3.9 <u>PB Report to CC:</u> Sub-committee of Cdes. Bishop, Louison and Strachan to meet on Thursday, 13th.

3.10 <u>March 13th theme:</u> Not discussed.

3.11 <u>PB/CC Table:</u> Not discussed.

3.12 <u>Director of Sports:</u> Task from discussion on the Youth work; reported difficulty in identifying appropriate person. It was the general feeling that Cde. Tan will have to perform that function indefinitely - until a comrade can be identified.

3.13 <u>Doctor for PB/CC:</u> Not discussed.

3.14 <u>Review of past PB/EB Pre-Scheduled Agenda:</u> To be discussed on 17th January.

3.15 <u>Timing of Request for Diplomatic Assistance:</u> To be discussed on 19th January.

4. **Areas of Work:**

4.1 <u>Education Report:</u> Cdes. Creft and Jules were in attendance for discussion of their written report sent to the PB. The following were to be discussed, but only the first two were completed:-

i. CPE;   ii. Community Centres;   iii. Primary education;   iv. Culture

1. CPE:

   o Committee of Cdes. Louison, Creft, Merle Clarke set up and meeting weekly.
   o Media committee set up and meeting forthnighly.
   o Meeting of CPE and PCB reps held; looked at mobilisation forthnight - 17th - 30th January; 22 - 25 January - days of intensive mobilisation.
   o National Advisory Committee has been restructured: now comprises TU reps, PCB's, Service Clubs.
   o Parish Committees restructured - all TU's, mass organisations now represented.
   o 48 new centres to be opened in February (some churches included); Cde. Creft to follow up with the church leaders
   o CPE leadership needs supervision; daily political guidance of the office staff is weak
   o there is a surplus of CPE teachers
   o transport needed
   o new propaganda work plan drawn up - to be discussed
   o need a full time person to handle CPE propaganda

ii. Community Centres   (Decisions taken after discussion):-

   1. Cde. Strachan contact ET re John Campbell -outstanding designs for the community centres and proposal to send additional person being sent.
   2. Cde. Creft to speak with "Solid" Archibald re possiblity of full time employment with the PRG - specifically for community centres.
   3. Community centres to be built in Marquis, Manacaine, Duquesne and La Poterie.

There was a report that the OC supervises the building of community centres.

This proposal was not decided upon definitely.

iii. This was not discussed.

4.2 Workers Work:

  i. Socialism Classes: The schedule for visits to the classes
by PB/CC was done, but did not take into account PB/ME meetings
on Wednesday and Friday mornings and CC study on Thursdays.
Thus, it is to be re-done.

  ii. SWWU Report: Outstanding to be received from Cde. Sawney - Sub-
Committee plan/strategy for capturing the union.

  iii. Workers Committee Report
Cde. Strachan stated that the PWU Sub-Committee's present approach now is to strike an alliance with Basil Harford. They are
concerned about putting Cde. Ferron Lowe to work in the Ministry
of National Mobilisation, which they realise as the Party's
Ministry (the PWU) because he may lose the respect he has won
in the Management Council.

DECISIONS/TASKS:
1. Cde. Louison to follow up to Geest issue with letter to St. Vincent's Minister of Agriculture.
2. Efforts to be made to purchase house in Carriacou near to Military compound - Cde. Layne.
3. Cde. Louison to speak with Fred Grant re Cacademo's house and land spot. (Task outstanding from 5th January).
4. Letter to be sent to the Military in Cuba re Cde. Cornwall's authority to deal with military matters for Grenada. (task outstanding).
5. Cde. Louison to follow up on Archdeacon Huggins issue - task originally Cde. Whiteman's. (Task outstading from 5th January).
6. Cde. Whiteman to call in Venezuela Ambassador re Cyrus.
7. Sports Director to be identified. (Tan)
8. Negotitiations for purchase of Deallie's House in St. Paul's to start - matter to be brought to Cabinet. (Tan + Donald)
9. Transcavator/tractor with appropriate adjustments to be made available to the youth for work on the play fields.
10. Cde. Layne to follow up on enquiries of Chalkie's health by his mother.
11. Cde. Layne to follow up on K Schnophals issue - See page 1 for decisions.
12. Letter commending Cde. Cornwall re his reporting and performance of the Havana Embassy to be sent off. (Hazel)
13. Document on Honduras to be circulated to PB comrades. (Hazel)
14. Cde. Creft to be checked on: i. request for steelband to go to Cuba in March ii. April scientific conference in GDR.
15. Cde. Creft to be informed that he should meet with Cansave.

All matters outstanding from PB discussion of the Youth work - January 5th.

6/...

16. PB/EB Pre-Schelduled agenda for January - March period to be presented on Wednesday 17th.

17. Check to be made with Tom - ascertain if "Owen" Desouza left the country.

18. SWWU Sub-Committee to be asked for written report re Stanley Roberts.

19. Cdes. Bishop, Louison and Strachan to meet re PB report to CC.

20. Review of Past PB/EB Pre-set agenda for discussion - Wednesday 17th.

21. Timing of requests for diplomatic assistance for discussion on January 19th.

22. Cde. Creft to follow up with Church Leaders re use of the churches as part of the new 48 CPE centres.

23. Decisions re Community Centres:-   (See page 4)

    i. Cde. Strachan to contact ELT.

    ii. Cde. Creft to contact "Solid" Archibald.

    iii. New community centres to be built.

24. Schelduel of PB/CC visits to Socialism Classes to be redone.

25. Outstanding report from Cde. Sawney re SWWU Sub-Committee strategy to be sent to PB. (Hazel)

26. CC Quarterly review meeting 28th March - 1st April.

27. Main areas of work to be taken on PB/EB agendas before Items for decisions.

    Items for Decisions to be discussed: 3.1, 3.2, 3.3, 3.4, 3.10, 3.11, 3.13, 3.14, 3.15.

MINUTES OF THE POLITICAL BUREAU MEETING
ON WEDNESDAY 23rd FEBRUARY, 1983

90

Comrades present:-

Selwyn Strachan
Liam James
Ewart Layne
Hudson Austin
George Louison

Comrades absent:-

Unison Whiteman) away
Chalkie Ventour)
Maurice Bishop - excused

Agenda:-

1. Minutes
2. Correspondence/Reports:-
   2.1 New York Report
   2.2 Cde. Austin's Report
   2.3 Cde. Layne's Report
   2.4 Michael Manley
   2.5 Letter from Caldwell
   2.6 Message from Cde. Bourne
   2.7 National Conference of Delegates of Mass Organisations on the Economy
3. Main Areas of Work:-
   3.1 State Propaganda
   3.2 Farmers Work
   3.3 State of the Party
4. Items for Decisions:-
   4.1 Kenneth Noel
   4.2 Kenrick Radix
   4.3 Jose Henry
   4.4 Venice Hutton
   4.5 Caldwell/Dessima

---

1. MINUTES
1.1 Corrections:-
   i) Pg. 2 re AAJ Conference minutes to include" Co-ordinating committee for the Conference to be headed by Dick Hart and include Allan Alexander, Langston Sibbles, Ashley Taylor. The Comrade Leader to follow up on this.
   ii) Pg. 2, No. 2.7 re Denzil Wilks, minutes to include "Cde. Strachan to meet with him to discuss his work."
   iii) Pg. 2, No. 2.13 re Chappel, minutes to be corrected"... house to be built under the Venezuela Project".

1.2 Tasks:-
   i) Not done
   ii) Done; Leroy McMillan expelled from the party consequently.
   iii) Ongoing; PB decided that the plane should be "packed up" until sale; in the meantime to be serviced and maintained; it is not to be used by any member of the leadership.
   iv) Done; messages sent, but no reply as yet.
   v) Done; issue to be dealt with at the upcoming National

2

Conference of Delegates of Mass Organisations on the Economy.

vi) *Done; date chnaged to 17th March since then.*
vii) *Ongoing*
viii) *Ongoing*
ix) *Decision recorded.*
x)

  10.1 *Task to return to PB next week*
  10.2 *Not started yet*
  10.3 *Decision; not implemented yet*
  10.4 *Done*
  10.5 *(Now included); PB to get a report on the possibility of having more than two terms per year - next week.*

xi)

  11.1 *Not done.*
  11.2 *Started; ongoing*
  11.3 *Ongoing;*
  11.4 *Ongoing*
  11.5 *Done*

2. CORRESPONDENCE REPORTS:

2.1 <u>New York Report</u>:- *Cde. James reported on his visit to Washington, D.C. and New York:-*

o *the political situation and mood of the grenadians is good - the best since the Revolution; mood is high despite the fact that no political work is been done amongst the Grenadians; reasons for the good mood:-*

  - *visit of the National Performing Company in November*
  - *the large number of Grenadians who visited home and are still on a "high" from the visit*
  - *the world bank report on the economy*
  - *recent good news reports in newspapers and magazines*

there are presently no rumours circulating; the "counters" are operating on a very low profile, but doing plenty travelling; (analysis is that they are planning to make a move)

o *met with GRL and discussed their transformation into a mass organisation; they have agreed to this in principle and a work plan is been drawn up in this regard; they have stated improvement - have been studying consistently since July last year and have a work plan and work schedule; there is a serious problem between GRL and Cladwell; they (GRL) have lost respect for him, is called "timid" and "brambling"; he has continued to deteriorate ideologically (his preference for feature address at their March 13 celebrations is Edward Lamb over Harry Bellafonte; GRL has raisee possible purchase of a building in New York to assist them; a house has already been identified;*

o *held meeting with Tourist Office; they have reported a renewal of interest in Grenada; reasons been good news articles recently; average of 250 letters per month received by them on how to get to Grenada; there is also a big interest in*

...3

Carriacou and Camp Carriacou; this interest has to be
exploited now; the tourist office needs to be strengthened
to deal with this work;

o re Grenadians abroad, the Party must look?develop a pers-
pecteve on Grenadians abroad; seek to organise them where-
ever they go, develop, maintain links with them, not to
be hostile to them (even those who left after the Revo)

o thinks the possibility of establishing a radio station
in N.Y. should be looked at; spoke to the CP - they have
agreed that it could be done; Miguel is to follow on discussion with them in this regard

Issues out of the report for PB decisions:-

i) House purchase proposal: agreed, Cde. Coard to
follow up to find the money required;

ii) Possibility of establishing radio station: PB agrees
in principle, Cde. James to follow up through Miguel;

iii) Party to decide/dicuss perspective for Grenadians
abroad; agreed.

2.2 Cde. Austin's Report:- Cde. Austin reported on his
monthly meeting held with the Airport Management and   /site
the Ministry (himself and Cde. Prime):-

i) issue of the "orker Education Classes raised by
Bob Evans and Della Rosa, saying that 30% more
work is expected this year and the classes will
affect this negatively as the classes statt and
end late, thus affecting production: Cdes. HA,
Vincent Noe, Strachan, Layne and Airport Management, Party support Group included if possible,
to meet to solve this problem;

ii) a mecahnism needed for dealing with Plessy now
they are in Grenada: Cde. Prime to chair the
meetings held with them and Airport Management,
with a representative from the Ministry of Planning;

iii) hanger for executive plane to be sand blasted,
also the water tanks; (however the only sand blas-
ter is in prison); he is to be put on payroll in
order to get the work done;

2.3 Cde. Layne's Report:- Re restricted ports and areas;
area of Hog Island to be clarified; Cdes. Layne and
Roberts to visit the area for clarification.

2.4 Michael Manley:- Comrades were reminded of Manley's
arrivale in Grenada today (reason for Comrade Leader's
absence at meeting) and of his book launching tonight.

2.5 Letter from Cladwell: Not discussed.

2.6 Message from Cde. Bourne: Re a 2-man delegation from the
CPSU arriving on 7 March for 10 days; draft progfamme
being drawn up for them to meet with all committees of
the Party, visit and observe Socialism Classes (to be
chosen carefully); they are to be accomodated in Groome's

House"; Cde. James to check Bernadette in this regard.
2.7 <u>National Conference of.......</u>:- Comrades were reminded of this upcoming conference on Thursday 24 February and to be punctual.

3. <u>MAIN AREAS OF WORK:</u>
3.1 <u>State Propaganda</u>:- A 16-page report was submitted to the Bureau on the state propaganda and Cde. McBarnette who apologised for the absence of Cdes. David and Smikle was present for the discussion on the report. The PB criticised the report and pointed out the following to Cde. McBarnette:-

                      raised
    o report   no strategic, policy issues; lacks a clear overal conception of the work and how it is to develop - in order to take policy decisions and give guidance to the work; it does not mention anything about propagandising the Line of March for the year - political education and academic education.

thus, the PB was not satisfied with the report.
It was also noted that report dealt with too many reports on personalities.

Cde. McBarnette stated that he was given some guidelines by the Comrade Leader which included:-

    o present situation in the media houses, difficulties, manpower, space, equipment;
Cde. McBarnette were given these further guidelines for including in the document to be done over:-
    o rationalisation (of space, equipment etc.) possibilities; how to bring the working people into the media; conception on the regional media (which media house will do that); analysis/evaluation of present position re listenership and readership.

Bearing the above in mind, the PB did not discuss this area of work and the document is to be done over, conscious of the new guidelines by Cde. McBarnetteetc.

3.2 <u>Farmers Work</u>:- A 5-page report with a document on the Education Programme for PFU as an appendix was presented to the PB with Cdes. Ehteldred Gittens, Chester Louison and Lucius Hastick were in attendance at the meeting.

The PB expressed total dissatisfaction with the content of the report, that the organisational questions as contained in the document, are for the consideration of the Organising ommittee of the Party and not the PB; the PB is concerned with policy matters, key strategic questions and concerns; analysis of CPE etc.

The discussion on this area of work was postponed until further report - the comrades to do a draft for submission to Cde. Louison (the PB comrades for Farmers Work) by Saturday, 26 February; re-done report to be ciruclated to

the PB members by Monday 28th February for discussion on
Wednesday, 2nd March.

3.3 _State of the Party_:- Cde. Strachan apologised for the
not preparing and the non-submission of a report; the
item is to be discussed one week after the return of
comrades' from the Non-Aligned Movement Conference in
March.

4. _ITEMS FOR DECISIONS_:-

4.1 _Kenneth Noel_:- Has returned from Study abroad; choice of
employment is Foreign Affairs for GFC; he is to be placed
in GFC and Cde. Whiteman to be informed of decision.

4.2 _Kenrick Radix_:- Item put for discussion when the Comrade
Leader is in attendance at meeting.

4.3 _Rose Henry_:- Has been unemployed for the last six months
(since August of 1982) areas been sought for possible employment: She is to be placed in either Tourism, Information or
in the YEP.

4.4 _Vince Hutton_:- Has raised with Cde. Strachan her problems
re maintenance of her son because money cannot be received
from his father, who is Cuban. She wants to know whether the
Party will assist her in enabling the father to return to
Grenada for a while to work: Cde. Strachan is to raise the
issue with Cde. Gaston discreetly.

4.5 _Caldwell/Dessima_:- Cde. James raised that for these comrades'
three months home assignment that a tight programme should
be drawn up in this regard: Cde. James tasked to prepare and
present a draft programme.

DECISIONS/TASKS:-

1. Grenada to re-establish relations with the VSO - cabinet to follow
up with formalised agreement. (Task outstanding from meeting of
16/2/83).

2. Re PB/CPE discussion:- (Outstanding from 16/2/83)

   2.1 Cde. Jules to co-ordinate with Cde. LaCorbinere
       re CPE incentives.

   2.2 CPE to assist the PRA with commencement of secondary
       education in the armed forces.

   2.3 PB to get report on possiblity of having more than
       two terms per year

3. Cde. Coard to identify money for the purchase of the building in
New York for GRL.

4. Cde. James to follow up with Miguel re possibility of establishing a radio station in N.Y.

5. PB agrees in principle to discuss/decide on a perspective for
Grenadians abroad.

6. Cdes. Strachan, Austin, Layne, Noel and Airport Site Party Support
Group to meet to solve all problems related to the holding of the
Worker Education classes.

7. Cdes. Layne and Roberts to visit Hog Island area re decision for
part that is restricted.

8. Cde. James to check Bernadette re accomodating 2-man CPSU delegation
for 10 day period.

9. Report on State propaganda to the PB to be re done taking into consideration the guidelines and criticisms stating in the meeting/

10. Report on Farmers work to be redone, with the guidelines/criticisms and to be circulated to the PB by Monday 28th February after been checked by Cde. Louison on Saturday, 26th February.

11. State of the Party to be discussed one week after the return of comrades' from the Non-Aligned Movement Conference.

12. Kenneth Noel to be placed to work in GFC and Cde. Whiteman to be informed of this decision.

13. Item for decision - Cde. K. Radix to be discussed at meeting with Cde. Bishop's presence.

14. Cde. Strachan to raise with Gaston discreetly, matter related to Vintce Hutton.

15. Cde. James to prepare/present draft programme for visit/home assignment of Cdes. Taylor and Williams.

MINUTES OF THE POLITICAL BUREAU DATED
20TH APRIL, 1983

91

COMRADES PRESENT

Maurice Bishop   Ewart Layne
Unison Whiteman   John Ventour
Selwyn Strachan   Hudson Austin

COMRADES ABSENT

Liam James   -   OUT OF THE COUNTRY
George Louison -   EXCUSE

AGENDA

1. Minutes
2. Correspondence/Reports
3. W.C Work
4. Manouvere
5. Operative situation
6. Items for decision

(a) Protocol building
(b) U.K Festival
(c) Wesley College
(d) Acting Secretary for Information
(e) Ramon Codona
(f) Cde. Bizo
(g) W.P.J Matters
(h) Lenin's Birthday
(i) Cde. Leon Cornwall Letter
(j) 5Th Festival preparations
(k) C.C Plenery
(l) Cde. John Ventour

2. CORRESPONDENCE

- Governor General   - C.P.E Report
- Suriname   - G.M Report
- D.P.K.R Report   - Cde. Unison's Report

2/......................

1. MINUTES

CORRECTIONS

- Re C.C Plenery it should have been Guidelines for reports should be prepared, instead of what was seen on page four under C.C. Plenery line 2.

- It should be decided on the different quarters of the year to hold C.C. Plenery. (Line 5 on page 4)

- Dates and deadlines should be set for preparation of such documents (line 7 on page 4)

- Instead of Airport Site on page 5 sub-heading no. 1 it should have been AIRPORT ACCESS ROAD

- Sub-heading number 2 should have been OTHER AIRPORT MATTERS (page 5)

- Sub-heading number 3 should have been OTHER MATTERS (page 5)

- Someone in the Ministry of Construction should be identified to work with Cuban Comrades.

- Cde. Selwyn Strachan to established contact with Cde. Julien Rizo between Thursday and Friday re Finance and to meet with Plecy.

- A new design should be done re the Protocol Building. It was noted that the Protocol Building was too big. (Last paragraph on page 5)

TASKS - Omitted

- Cde. Selwyn Strachan to speak to Cde. Bernard Coard re the airport question

REPORT ON TASKS

- It was reported that Plecy and Metex and Grenadian Officials held meeting on Monday trying to coodinated and integrate their work anograms.

- Cdes Evans and Smith will report on the results with Cdes Hudson Austin and Bernard Coard after the Cdes meet with both of them.

- Cuban architects to meet on Monday 25th April with Cdes Charlie Campbell Marva moor, with a view of doing new Designs for the Community Centres (Belle Vue, Wester Hall and Concord).

3/..............

2. CORRESPONDENCE

∴ LETTER SUBMITTED BY SISTER JACKIE CHEFT RE GOVERNOR GENERAL PAUL SCOON

- The letter reflected a number of areas not notifying the appropriate bodies before doing such and the number of statements made in different activites which the Minister of Education was present.

- Some of the points highlighted by the Political Bureau are as follows:

- He cannot contradict Government's line

- That there is a church imput :

- Whenever he is visiting school the Ministry of Education should be contacted before entering the schools

- Periodic sessions should be held with him so that he would be in line.

- MEET G.G. this week.

3. WORKERS COMMITTEE

- It was noted by Cde. John Ventour that the Cdes on Workers Committee cannot do the work.

- Plenty of time usually been spent on confusion.

- On Monday 18th when report at W.C meeting most of the tasks were not accomplished.

- The discipline problem is still there, no improvement.

- Cdes on the Committee are demoralised.

B.G.W.U

- Nothing is happening in that Union.

C.I.W.I

- Cde. Winston Ledlow is ill

- Cde. Elliot Bishop is doing his best in that union.

P.W.U

- Plans are on the way for their up coming elections and it appears that the Union stands a good chance.

- Cde. Ventour suggested a number of new names to work on W.C. the following are the names:-

Tessa Stroude	Faye Thompson	Patrick Superville
Sam Brathwaite	Moses Jeffrey	Nelson Louison
Hugh Romain	Rudolph Ogilvie	Nam Folkes
Ramon Lashley	Mc Lean Williams	Claudette Pitt

91 - 3

MINUTES OF THE POLITICAL BUREAU
27th APRIL, 1983

COMRADES PRESENT

Maurice Bishop   Hudson Austin
Selwyn Strachan   Liam James
George Louison   John Ventour
Unison Whiteman   Ewart Layne

AGENDA

1. Minutes
2. Correspondence/Report

ITEMS FOR DECISION

1. Cde. John Ventour
2. C.C Plenary
3. 5th Anniversary
4. Wesley College
5. Acting Secretary for Information
6. Shane Julien
7. U.K Festival
8. May Day Laws
9. Emulation Documents
10. New York Trip
11. Caricom Plan of Action
12. Work Among Grenadian Overseas
13. C,P.E
14. Protocol Building
15. Church

CORRESPONDENCE

1. I.L.O

REPORTS

1. Suriname
2. Cde. Unison Whiteman
3. Cde. Caldwell Taylor
4. Cde. Bernard Bourne
5. Cde. Bernard Coard

1. **CORRESPONDENCE/Reports**

   Letter submitted by Cde. Leon Cornwall re the Afghanistan Revolution re an aritcle to be published in the F.W.I and Party Paper.

   DECISION   Cde. Ferron Lowe to do a draft and pass onto Cde. Selwyn Strachan.

2. Cathy Slone seeking employment in Grenada re the media. A Formal Letter should be done acknowledging receipt of her letter.

2. Letter sent to the Party from the Soviet Union re two auto buses and two ladacars. It should be noted that invoices for the vehicles have already delivered.

4. Bulgarian scholarship - names should reach Bulgaria by the 15th July, 1983.

REPORT FROM CDE. LEON CORNWALL

A report was submitted to the Political Bureau by Cde. Leon Cornwall re him being Grenada Ambassador in Cuba. Cde. Cornwall highlighted the following:-

1. That the party forgets that there is an Embassy in Cuba.

2. F.W.I and Party Paper is scarce re not receiving it on a regular basis.

3. Whenever a delegation is coming to Cuba from Grenada never inform the embassy before. It is only when Cdes land he usually knows.

4. The following was disclosed by the Political Bureau:-

   - The party attitude is quite sickening towards correspondence.

   - It is a historical fact that we have a poor attitude of keeping our Embassies intouch with the latest development in our country.

   - Lack of follow up work on key issues are falling.

   - It was stated that our Party has to work in regards to develop such an area.

   - That Cde. Leon Cornwall always send a constant flow of reports to our Party.

   - Cde. Leon Cornwall should know of all our Party activities viewing that he is a Central Committee member, he should know of the constant development of our Party.

- That a policy decision should be taken when we are sending Cdes to Cuba, noting Cde. Leon Cornwall position.

- Cdes ought to be specifically clear that Cde. Cornwall is a C.C member.

Cde. Maurice Bishop noted:

- All letters should be replied to when sent to the Party and Ministries.

- That Cde. Unison Whiteman do a document for his staff on the Importance of Communication re our Embassies abroad.

- Ensuring that when Cdes write to the Ministry of Foreign Affairs/Party Headquarters a response is sent.

- A system should be put in place in the Party Headquarters to handle the constant flow of correspondence to Cde. Cornwall and other cdes outside the country.

SURINAME

- It was reported by Cde. Lial James re the trip made by the Surinamese to Grenada to observe the Grenada National Manouver was quite successful. He noted that the Cdes left with high spirit.

- Appreciate the trip and found it was quite interesting.

- That a delegation should be sent to Suriname in the future to observe its development.

BERNARD BOURNE

- That a delegation from the Soviet Union will be visiting our country on the 14th - 15th February 1984.

- The delegation would involve Young workers, Farmers, intellecuals etc.

- It was noted that the National Youth Organisation should do the necessary preparation for the group visit.

- A programme should be worked out for the visit.

- A specific plan should be worked out.

4/.........

CDE. CALDWELL TAYLOR

Submitted a report re his work in the U.N. (No analysis was done re the report by the Political Bureau).

CDE. UNISON WHITEMAN TRIP - U.S.A

- the trip went well.

  Things to be done he outline areas follows:-

- Someone full time coordinating Friendship work, and Solidarity Committees.

- Not getting Public Party Paper and other literature re the revolution.

- Cde. Whiteman pointed out that the Investment Promotion trip should be attended by Cde. Lyden Ramdhanny and someone from the Ministry of Trade.

- CDE. BERNARD COARD

- Requesting holiday leave for himself and Family

- Three weeks holiday leave in S.U and one week in Cuba.

- Cde. Selwyn Strachan to tie up trip.

WORKERS COMMITTEE

- MAY DAY

  Cdes did not have their full schedule organised.

  B.G.W.U, C.I.W.U,T.A.W.U - done some work

  P.W.U - focussing on their election.

  Cde. Maurice noted that days of the week have been worked out to meet with the Sub Committee of the Unions.

  Cde. Liam James to sit on top of S.G.W.U work

SOCIALISM CLASSES

It was reported by Cde. Selwyn Strachan that Cde. Brian Meeks has been placed in the Secretariat to assist in coordinating Socialism Classes. He noted that since Cde. Bizo has been place in the Secretariat and visiting the different classes, reports submitted stated that the classes are going well.

Cde. Selwyn Strach an also noted that the analysis of the classes would be handled by Cde. Martin Marryshow.

- 115 classes on paper

- 82 functioning

- 15 not going well

PROBLEMS

- Not enough centralisation.
- Cdes are not following the structures that have been done.

- OTHER MATTERS
- Specialist suggested for taking socialism classes are as follows:-

    (a) Rita Joseph   (b) Wayne Sadiford
    (b) Brian Meeks   (d) Ferron Lowe

It was noted that the Cdes mentioned above will be full time in that particular area. (There are still more names to be added to the list).

PROTOCOL BUILDING

-/ The expansion of the Protocol building will cost the Grenadian Government $150,000.

- That an analysis should be done re the Protocol Building as to where the money could be got.

- Cdes Bob Evans and Bernard Coard to be spoken to by Cdes Hudson Austin and Unison Whiteman re the Protocol Building.

U.K FESTIVAL

- Re the U.K Festival is was noted that sis. Jackie Creft should attend.

- It is reported that sister Jackie was hesitant of going, while discussing the matter with Sister Jackie at the Political Bureau meeting on 27th April, 1983 she still insisted that she is not physically fit to attend. The sister got vexed and then walked out of the meeting. (IT should be noted that Sis. Creft came to the Political Bureau meeting to report on the C.I.E work.)

6/............

C.C PLENARY/POLITICAL AND ECONOMIC BUREAU PRE SCHEDULE AGENDA

- New dates suggested for the C.C Plenary are the 13th - 18th of July, 1983.

- Also the Political Bureau and Economic Bureau pre-schedule agenda was looked at.

C.P.E

- The Chairman of the Political Bureau reported to the Comrades from the C.P.E Centre that maximum input cannot be put into the report due to the lateness of the report reaching most of the Members of the Political Bureau, so the preparation re the Members of the Political Bureau is not what it should have been.

- Another meeting with the C.P.E Comrades is four week from now.

- Submit the full list of Cdes who are C.P.E student Nationally.

- List of Cdes who are active and not active.

- The seminar held was quite successful

- Some of the problems raised never suffaced before but coming from the seminar.

                                            most of
- New Parish coordinators for/the parishes ought to be found.

- St. Andrew's   - new person

- St. Patrick's/St. David's - very weak.

- Children are posing most of the problems for the Cdes at the classes.

- When doing house to house Cdes could creatively link it with C.P.E to solve most of the problems.

- C.P.E Propaganda Committee should be meeting weekly.

- Get very good adverts for the C.P.E propaganda.

- Get Cdes to write the promos and change them from time to time.

- Ask Paul Keen Douglas to assist with a Programme on C.P.E also Sister Merle Collins.

- A C.P.E programme should be played before the news as to the boosting of the propaganda aspect.

- Need someone from the Centre to call the Radio station everyday re the propaganda aspect.

92 - 6

EMULATION

- That emulation be held on a monthly basis.

- The following are proposals made by the Political Bureau

  o That montly report should be submitted to the Political Bureau

  o Analysis of the workshops

  o Monthly Parish Emulation

  8 Propaganda

  o Cdes Jackie Creft, Merle Clarke and Aden Slinger to meet with Cde. Peter David to work out the document that they had done in the past re the Propaganda aspect of C.P.E and that a copy should be sent to the Political Bureau.

  o Ring up the Radio Station re the promos whenever cannot be heard.

  o C.P.E Village Committee should be set up.

  o Fund Raising - in all centres

  o Parish workshops should be held to solve most of the problems - the 6 weeks parish workshop should be used, to help solve some of the problems.

TASKS

1.. Cdes Hudson Austin and Unison Whiteman to meet with Cdes Bernard Coard and Bob Evans re the Protocol Building and its financing.

2. Cde. Hudson Austin to meet with the Cuban at the International Airport.

3. Cde. Ferron Lowe to be informed re draft article to be done re the Afghanistan Revolution.

4. Sister Jackie Creft to get in contact with Cde. Paul Keens Douglas re a programme for C.P.E.

5. Cde. Selwyn Strachan to ensure that a system which has been put in place in the Ministry of National Mobilisation re sending documents to the Embassies and replying to letters are functioning within the Ministry.

MINUTES OF THE POLITICAL BUREAU

4TH MAY, 1983

93

COMRADES   PRESENT

Selwyn Strachan   John Ventour
Unison Whiteman   Liam James
Ewart Layne   Hudson Austin
George Louison

COMRADES   ABSENT

Maurice Bishop - On leave

AGENDA

1. Minutes
2. Correspondence

(a) Letter from Cde. Justin Campbell,
     recording Secretary, requesting to be
     excused from the meeting due to illness.

(b) Letter from Cde. Hazel Ann Williams
     requesting all P.B members to settle their
     account with the Party Secretariat re
     May 2nd Fund raising activity.

(c) Letter from Aiden Slinger C.P.E National
     Coordinator.

(d) Telex from New York Embassy re visit t
     of U.S Congressmen to Grenada May 19th-
     23, 1983.

(e) Telex from Richard Jacobs re World Peace
     Assembly, Prague, September, 1983.

(f) Message from Cde. Seshnev Soviet
     Ambassador re Propaganda assistance.

2. ITEMS FOR DECISION

(a) Cde. John Ventour
(b) Cde. Bishop's New York Visit
(c) Cde. George Louison Re House in St. And.
(d) Wesley College
(e) The Church
(f) Acting Secretary for Information
(g) Work among Frenadians overseas
(h) Shane Julien
(i) Caricom Plan of Action

(j) Patrick Noel - Eastern Main Road
(k) Emulation Document (See Workers Work)

4. Workers Work

5. C.P.E

1. **MINUTES OF P.B MEETING 29th APRIL**

All members felt that the minutes did not adequately express the deliberations of the meeting. Some discussion was held around Cde. Campbell performance as P.B/C/C recording Secretary. It was noted that his performance at the O.C was much greater than at present. Most Comrades expressed the view that Cde. Campbell's psychologically incapable of performing at the P.B. Alternations to Cde. Campbell were examined. It was felt that Cde. HazelAnn Williams would be unable to perform adequately due to her frustration. The O.C recording Secretary Valdon Poldeau was agreeed on in principle as a possible alternative. However, the O.C was directed to settle this due to Cde. Boldeau's organisational tasks.

REPORT ON TASKS

1. Completed. New design for Protocol Building to be presented to the P.B in first two weeks of May.

2. Completed. Designs for Sandino Housing not yet done.

3. No information.

4. No information

5. Completed

6. Not done

2. **CORRESPONDENCE/REPORTS**

(a) Letter from Cde. Campbell was noted.

(b) Letter from Cde. Hazel Ann Williams was noted

(c) Letter from Adien Slinger apologizing for not being able to complete documents requested by the P.B. Promise to have them completed by Friday May 6th.

(d) Telex from New York Embassy informing that the team of U.S congressmen to visit Grenada may 19-23 are requesting free hotel accomodation.

DECISION: 1. Not possible. However, P.R.G will provide ground transportation for sight seeing tour, etc.

2. Cde. Unison Whiteman to arrange negotiations with Hotel Association for concession rates for the Congressmen.

93 - 2

3/............

3. Cde. Whiteman to telephone Cde. Caldwell Taylor to inform
him of the P.B decision and to obtain further information
re congressmen visit.

4. Cde. Liam James pointed out that the visit of the
Congressmen is very important for us because three of
themare from Brooklyn and represent the Caribbean
Community.

Telex from Ambassador to USSR, Richard Jacobs requesting
that he be included in the delegation to the Peace meeting
in Prague, September 1983.

Decision: Agreed to.

Cde. Ventour reported that he held brief meeting with
the soviet Ambassador Cde. Sashnev who expressed great
concern over the absence of our propaganda organs
(newspaper) for three weeks. He also requested to receive
copies of all the Party's propaganda organs where they are
published. Also that he can request propaganda assistance
for us.

DECISION: Cde. Selwyn Strachan to follow up with Cde.
Sashnev.

3. ITEMS FOR DECISION

Cde. John Ventour reported to the meeting on the state of his
health. He pointed out that although he was adhering to
the four hour per day schedule, there was not any marked
improvement in his health. He therefore requested that the
four hour be reduced or he be on total leave for two months.
He also pointed out that the Cuban Dr. Martinez had informed
him that based on the positive results of his blood analysis
it was possible that he begin to work 8 hours per day. This
Cde. Ventour pointed out, however, was not possible due to
the tiredness he felt everyday.

In reply to a question from Cde. Liam James Cde. Ventour
pointed out psychological pressure was possibly one factor
contributing to his present state due to his mothers daily
statements that he was ill, loosing weight, etc. and
expressed the view that he should leave his parents home
soon. In this regard the meeting was informed of his
decision to be married on August 20th, 1983.

DECISION: Cde. Ventour's schedule be reduced to one hour
per day except on days for meetings of the P.B
E.B. and study. At the end of 2 weeks it will
be reviewed.

(b) P.M's visit to the U.S.A at the invitation of
TRANSAFRISA CORP. Cde. Liam James informed the meeting
that this powerful Black Organisation issued an invitation

4/............

93 - 3

- 4 -

sixth

to Cde. Bishop to address their/Annual Dinner on June 4th, 1983.

Invitation has been accepted and will include visits to four U.S cities - New York, Washington, Detroit and Chicago from 3rd -13th June 1983. Three broad strategic objectives for the visit were outlined:-

(i) Conveying to the U.S press and people the image of our P.M as a sober and responsible statemen who is committed to normalising relations with the U.S.A.

(ii) To develop firm unshakeable links and bonds of identity with the black community in the U.S.A

(iii) To promote Tourism primarily among the Black Community.

Cde. James further pointed out that logistical preparation for the visit were already started and that 2 Secretariats one in Grenada and the other in New York - were already establishe established. The delegation was also agreed on. Apart from Cde. Bishop it will include:-

Cde. Unison Whiteman	-	Minister of Foreign Affairs
" Lyden Ramdhanny	-	Minister of Tourisn
" Denis Noel	-	Washington Embassy
" Dessima Williams	-	Ambassador to O.A.S
" Ian Jacobs		
" Merle Collins	-	Foreign Affairs
" Shahiba Strong	-	Protocol
" Liam James	-	Coordinator for entire visit.
" Jenny Francis	-	Secretary
" Kurt Strachan	-	Documentation
" Theresa	-	Cook

One driver/P.S Cde. also security.

Advanced team of Ian Jacobs, Merle Collins and Dessima Williams to leave on Thursday May 5th, 1983.

Cost of Trip - E.C 130,000

Documents already being prepared. Total 15

Books on Grenada Revolution to be sold approximately 1500.

DECISION:- Owusu to check with Cde. Bernard Coard re financial arrangements for obtaining Books from GRENCRAFT.

(ii) Cde. Whiteman to call in the Political Attache of the U.S Embassy in Barbados, FLOWER, at the end of this week informing him that the P.M requests a meeting with President Regan during his VISA to the U.S.A.

(iii)

(iii)   Cde. Selwyn Strachan to meet with the media (Peter
        David, Keith Joseph, Cecil Belfon etc) requesting
        that they tone down the attacks on the U.S during this
        period. Reason. If not can jeapordize the visit.

        Cde. George Louison re Home in St. Andrew's. He informed
        the meeting that a house was located in Felon, Ladigue
        (where cuban doctors used to stay). However, it will
        need repairs costing approx. $25,000.00. Cdes agreed
        to the location of the house. Concerns were expressed
        by Cde. Ventour re security arrangements because the house
        was partly wooden and in one of the worst political areas
        in the country.

        DECISION: 1. Cde. Louison to obtain materials to repair
                       the house from House Repair Scheme and
                       money for labour cost approximately
                       $6,000 from Ministry of Agriculture.

                   2. Cde. Liam James to organise Security
                       arrangements for the house.

(iv)   <u>WORKERS WORK</u>   meeting with Workers Committee
        W.C members present

        James Wardally, Jennifer Donald, Vincent Noel, John
        Jones, Derek Allard, Timothy Toussaint, Val Sawney,
        Winston Ledlow, Michael Prime and Trevor Noel.

        Comrade Strachan informed the members present that due
        to (1) the poor quality of the documents prepared
        by the Committee and (ii) the fact that many members of
        the P.B did not receive copies of the new three months
        workplan in advance in order to properly study them,
        the P.B had decided on the following approach to the
        discussion:-

                   1. Analysis of the strengths and weaknesses of the
                       work

                   2. Problems
                       (a) BGWU
                       (b) Areas of political work among the Working
                            Class
                   3. (a) As a result of (1) and 2 to determine t
                           whether the three months workplan is ree
                           realistic.

        Cde. Ventour began the discussion by pointing out that in
        his opinion the main area of weakness of the Committee, the
        main problem is poor personal discipline on the part of many
        Comrades.

        6/........

Jim Wardally - Main problem is comrades low level of
organisational skills.

Mikey Prime - agreed with Cde. Ventours position but also added
that Cde. Wardally's contribution is also very
relevant

Cde. Selwyn Strachan - supported Cde. Ventours position and
gave several examples:

(i) failure by BGWU to settle the International Airport
Workers contract

(ii) no weekly mobilisation for ideological crash course,
comrades being absent from the course,,improper
organisation re bus tickets to enable workers
to attend the classes.

(iii) failure to keep the party support group functioning.

He further pointed out that the meetings need to decide
whether apart from illdiscipline, there is great need for
assistance in organisational skills to the Comrades.

Cde. Val Sawney: main problem - illdiscipline comrade.
However, other problems are low organisational
skills and low morale which he personally has
experienced. This was due to the specific
problems of the Dock Workers where he has to
physically do most of the work on most
occasion.

Cde. James wardally then volunteered to state reasons for the
low morale of committee members.

(a) the workers Committee was being criticised unfairly

(b) more attention has been given to other Committees
of the Party

(c) Women's Committee

Cde. Vincent Noel then gave one example for the low morale
of Comrades. He recalled that the C.P.E list from the C.P.E
Centre was not received by BGWU until last week after several
efforts and the list when submitted was incorrectly prepared.
This allegation was   by Cde. George Louison who stated
that the lists were submitted to Cde. Derek Allard in February
1983. This was later confirmed by Cde. Allard.

Cde. Strachan then replied to the reasons put forward by Cde.
Wardally re low morale. He pointed out that historically the
Workers Committee was not given priority treatment by the party
re allocation of material resources. Other party committees
received much more assistance than the W.C. However, there was
no lack of manpower resources as suggested by Cde. Vincent Noel.
It was the failure of the Committee to make proper use of and
develop the cadres on the workplaces which has led to this

93 - 6

7/...........

apparent "manpower shortage". He further went onto point out
that it was the illdiscipline - the petty bourgeois conduct of
W.C members who are always exposing themselves before the
Party's rank and file at various forums which has led to the
descrediting of the Committee and criticism from rank and file
Party members. He noted the reason advanced by Cde. Wardally.
Cde. Strachan then ifnormed the Committee members on the need
for clarity on the main problem because this will determine
whether the three months workplan is scientific or ambitious.

Most of the Workers Committee members who spoke disagreed
with Cde. Ventour's position that there was no improvement
in the personal discipline of members during the past month.
Cde. Michael Prime expressed the view that the work will
improve over the next three months.

A criticism was made of Cde. Ventour by Cde. Liam James re
his manner in criticizing Workers Committee members. Cde.
James felt that it could be interpreted as arrogance by the
W.C members and could have also led to the low morale of the
Comrades.

Cde. Ventour apologised for an emotional outburst in criticizing
the Comrades during the meeting but did not accept the criticizm
made by Cde. Liam James.

At this point Cde. Ventour was excused from the meeting.

TASKS

1. Cde. Unison to arrange negotations with Hotel Association
   for concession rates for the Congressmen.

2. Cde. Whiteman to telephone Cde. Caldwell Taylor to
   inform him of the P.B decision and to obtain further
   information re congressmen.

3. Cde. Selwyn Strachan to follow up with Cde. Sashnew
   re meeting.

4. Cde. Liam James to check with Cde. Bernard Coard re
   financial arrangements for obtaining books from GRENCRAFT.

5. Cde. Whiteman to call in the Political Attache of the
   U.S Embassy in Barbados at the end of this week informing
   him that the P.M request a meeting with President Regan
   during his visit to the U.S.A.

6. Cde. Selwyn Strachan to meet with the media re the
   attacks on the U.S during this period.

7. Cde. Lousion to obtain materials to repair house at
   Felon (Ladigue)

8. Cde. Liam James to organise security arrangements for X
   Cde. Louison Home.

9. O.C. re VALDEN as Rec. Secy .. ✓

10. CPE Documents from AIDEN ✓

✓ 11. Rickard to be part of DELEG. TO PRAGUE
                                    Ass. on PEACE

✓ 12. Afghanistan

✓ 13. J.C. re P.K.D. on CPE Promo

✓ 14. OC on Sier. Trip (SPUTNIK Tourist DELEG...)

CENTRAL COMMITTEE

MINUTES OF CENTRAL COMMITTEE SPECIAL ONE-DAY
MEETING ON 26TH APRIL, 1981

Comrades Present:-

Maurice,Bishop	Vincnet Noel	Unison Whiteman
Bernard Coard	Hudson Austin	Ewart Layne
Selwyn Strachan	George Louison	Ian St. Bernard
Chalkie Ventour	Tan Bartholomew	Chris DeRiggs
Leon Cornwall	Phyllis Coard	Kamau McBarnette
Fiztroy Bain	Liam James	

Out of the country:
    Kenrick Radix
    Caldwell Taylor

Agenda:-

1. Farmers - PFU Report
2. Youth - NYD Report

(1) The two documents on teh state of the PFU work, which was sub-
    mitted to the Central Committee on Wednesday 15th , was looked
    at inmmore detail. Comrade Louison gave a summary of the two
    documents which noted among other things that:-

    - the union now has a membership of 406 farmers
    - village meetings have started
    - the work of the big farmers against the union is holding
      back the PFU's work in St. Andrew's and St. Patrick's
    - St. George's needs somebody to do the work
    - St. David's picking up
    - the membership will rise if the material benefits start
      reaching the farmers; seeds, fertilisers, supplies and
      road repairs.
    - right wing farmers still remain a major threat.
    - the farmers have been raising the issue of the merger of
      three boards (cocoa, nutmeg, banana) and to hold elections
      in June
    - PFU to set up office in Grenville
    - there is a need to develop more leadership skills in the
       executive members

    Other Comrades made different points including:-

    - the merger of the three boards has to be carefully timed.
    - tactics hould not be based only on that the progressive
      farmers are saying.
    - May Day celebrations to be used as a test for mobilising
      the farmers.
    - depots should be set up and the number increased based on
      the agricultural production
    - the need for a tight team work approach with the relevant
      ministries and departments to bring the enefits to the
      farmers
    - the political education among the farmers must take a more
      concrete form, exposing the class contradictions
    - agricultural exhibition and emulation programmes must be
      organised

    Comrade Louison was highly rcommended on the comprehensiveness
    of the documents and the following decisions were taken :-

    1. The formation of a three-man committee, Comrades Louison,
       Bain and Bel to (a)produce a pamphlet on the stage of
       negotiations with the big farmers (b) draft guidelines
       on a general policy for time off for workers to attend
       seminars etc., (c)the use of Grenada Farms Corporation's
       vehicles and trasnport generally, (d) draft education
       programme, plan seminars. This is to be submitted to
       the Political Bureau and then sent to Cabinet for ap-
       proval.

2. ComradesLousion, other members of the PFU executive and Mc Lean Williams of the Ministry of Communications, to go to the areas in St. Andrew's, select the roads badly damaged by the recent rains and have them repaired. Comrade Louison and the PFU memebrs must be clearly identified with the repairs.

3. Comrade Louison to go to all Parish Councils, NWO's, NYO's and Militias, with a view to identifying the farmers in these groups and gettingthem to join the PFU. He is also to get from the PCB heads a list of all the farmers in the parish and their political outlook.

4. A committee of representatives from the Party, PFU and State to be responsible for bringing the benefits to the farmers and to determine the grant that should be given to PFU for the purchase of seeds, fertilisers and supplies.

5. On elections, this should be put off, for another year or until the PFU is fully prepared. In .he meantime, a lot of work has to be done.

6. The Political Bureau to work on tactics for stalling the elections for another year.

7. Production co-operatives among the small farmers hshould be organised.

8. The report was accepted and approved.

9. Comrade Louison to present a written report to the Economic Bureau meeting of May 15th on the level of implementation of the above decisions.

****

(2) Comrade Conrwall presented two documents dealing with the youth work. The first, a Report on Youth Work, gave reasons for the bad state of the work, the signs of its poor state and ways of improving the work.

The second document is a two-part Draft Programme For Youth and Student Work. This deals with 1. roots, nature andwork of the March 13th Revolution and 2. the strengthening and building the Revolution among youth and students and deeping their participation.

In his analysis, Comrade Leon Cornwall concluded that the approach to recruiting youths last year was wrong and recommended that only two weeks should be put aside for recruitment at any one time. He stated that the unemployment question was acting as a fetter on the youth work and it needed a solution urgently. The land question is also crucial. Comrade Cornwall presentation was long and detailed, sumaarising the two documents.

Comrade Coard's criticism of the programme was that it did not relate to the present state of the economy.

The following things should be done to push the youth work forward:-

1. Solve the problem of unavailability of land - Comrade Radix is responsible for drafting a law in this regard.

2. Draw up a detailed, comprehensive plan for the development of Sports - a SPRTS PLAN. (To be brought to the meeting with the Cuban officials negotiating the second collaboration agreement, on Tuesday 28th)

3. Same for culture - a CULTURE PLAN - including a budget, for Thursday 30th.

4. A CADET PLAN - for forming cadet cores in every primary and secondary school.

5. The cadres doing the youth work should be of the highest quality - locate the youths in the work places and use them.

6. The speakers at the courses organised by the NYO, should be PB and OC comrades.

/... 7. Draft a

7. Draft a YOUTH EMPLOYMENT PLAN to deal with solving the unemployment problem, lokking at Forestry, Agro-industry, small live-stock, Tourism, Construction, Co-operatives, expanding employment on the State Farms. A committee with representative from the State, Party and Mass organisation (NYO) to do this.

8. Have a youth budget out of the comprehensive YOUTH PROGRAMME.

9. Bogo and Bourne should spend one week each in the G.D.R., Bulgaria and the U.S.SR. to learn from their past and present experiences, tactics, forms and methods. They should meet with the highest level of the youth and students there. They are to negotiate wi h them, assistance for the programme. The YOUTH PLAN should be sent to them in advance, givingthem time to study it.

10. The NYO should merge with the Ministry of Youth, as the NWO has done.

11. Work outaa way to deal with/the rastas and ganja question

It was noted that the Church was trying to replace the CYC with one that is more under their control. They are presently planning to send some 11-year olds to Ireland and Scttland - this to be stopped. Owusu's task.

The C.C. also decided that the Secretariat is to inform all members, candidate members and applicants that they are to march behind either AGWU, CIWU, BGWU banners on May Day and to be in the pavillion.

The Central Committee Weekend meeting schelduled for May 16th-17th will now be on May 30th and 31st.

Hazel-Ann
RECORDING SECRETARY

MINUTES OF CENTRAL COMMITTEE MEETING ON
WEDNESDAY, 27TH MAY 1981

Comrades present:-   Comrades absent:-

Maurice Bishop - Chairman   Bernard Coard   - away
Selwyn Strachan   Phyllis Coard   -   "
Vincent Noel   Hudson Austin   -   "
George Louison   Leon Cornwall   - sick
Kenrick Radix   Tan Bartholomew   "
Unison Whiteman   (on one
Chalkie Ventour   week's
Ewart Layne   rest)
Kamau McBarnette
Liam James
Ian St. Bernard
Oris DeRiggs, Fitzie Bain

AGENDA _ Urban Workers Committee Programme

Before the start of the meeting, Cde. Strachan said that
he had seen Tan the previous day and that the latter
was sick and requested a week's rest, which he agreed
to.

Cde. Noel, Chairman of the Urban Workers Committee
presented the programme of that committee, outlining
the historical development of the present working
class, the political orientation of the trade unions,
the trade union, state and political needs of the
working class, what the Party wants of them and the
tasks from the needs of both the Party and the working
class. The programme included a scheldule for the Cde.
Leader to speak to twenty work places in the next
few weeks.

Comrades felt that the programme was good but lacked
the following:-

    i. the number of people involved in the work
   ii. the possibility of imperialism working
       through the trade unions and the way the
       cttee will deal with that
  iii. the objective problems faced by the workers
       committee over the years and the ways they
       will be solved
   iv. no detailed analysis of the working class over
       the years
    v. scholarships for workers and their children
       as one means of bringing them closer to the
       Revolution
   vi. workers participation
  vii. raising the levels of production and disci-
       pline in creative ways, e.g. emulation,
       quizzes, etc.
 viii. attempt to generally bring the trade union
       movement closer to the Revolution
   ix. address itself in a structured way to get-
       ting workers involved in the programmes of
       the Revolution (e.g. Militia)
   xi. the recruitment of workers into the Party
       (using the sale of party papers and the
       Parish Council meetings)

xii. a breakdown of the amount of workers in
trade unions, how does the workers comit-
tee plan to reach the ununionised ones
xiii. a link between the urban and rurual workers
xiv. material conditions of the working class
xv. the role of the workers in bringing
about the Revolution, their present and
future roles in transforming the society.

Comrades suggested the following as concrete ways
of improving the workers' work and should be included in the detailed programme:-

i. distribution of literature
ii. using the workers to mobilise for rallies
etc.
iii. letting the most outstanding worker sit
with the leadership during rallies, at
the platform
iv. regulating the food and transport costs
v. inter-union windball and cricket compe-
titions
vi. workers committee/cell in places where
there is no union representation
vii. yearly checkups for workers (medical)

Cde. Noel said that a lot of the suggestions were
new, while the Workers Committee had thought of the
others, included them in the programme but had not
elaborated on them. He also said that comrades'
work needs to rationalised and used Cde. Burke to
illustrate his point - the latter is under tremendous pressure. He has much state work, workers
committee's work and other political work, e.g.
the Socialism classes. Cde. Noel said that most
comrades on the workers committee are "falling
down", e.g. Chalkie, Nelson and DeJourge.

Cde. Layne informed the CC that the A Study Group
had suggested to the O.C. that the latter be a su-
pervisory body for the work of the W.C. and that
its work must come up more regularly on the O.C.'s
Agenda for review.

Cde. Bishop concluded that from the programme, the
W.C. had submitted, nothing really needs to be implemented, that it was all "up in the air" still. He
questioned when was the work scheldule going to be
done.

DECISION :-

- The W.C. is to do a more detailed programme/work-
plan/work scheldule in two weeks time. This programme is to elaborate on all the ideas in the
first programme, taking into account all the
above criticisms an suggestions. They are also
to do a comprehensive breakdown of our population.

As a general observation, it was noted that almost all
Party Comrades are reluctant to join a trade union.
It was therefore <u>DECIDED</u> that all Party Comrades -
applicants, candidate members, members - are to join
the appropriate union. In particular, all those who
are public workers must join the T.W.U.

oo-oo

Comrade Whiteman inofrmed the CC of the total collapse of the Publication Committee because of the
departure of some comrades and the placement of
other comrades in different areas of work.

<u>DECISION</u>:- The following comrades are to form the
new Publication/Editorial Committee; Jaqueline
Creft, Kamau McharNette, Ken Lewis, Ruggles Fergur-
son, Carrol Davis, Ian Jacobs and Sandra Ventour.
Cde. Whiteman heads the committee.
It was suggested
that the Party's applicants be given the tasks of
writing an article as one means of deciding the
ones most appropriate to write for the paper. The
paper is now being published on Wednesdays, at the
FWI. Cde. Bishop said that the Party paper should
strive to be trul a mid-week national newspaper.

Cde. DeRiggs raised the question of the present situation with CDC/GES/ESSO. Cde. Bishop briefly informed the Central Committee that Barclays Bank has
granted GES the loan and that ESSO has agreed to
continue supplying oil. He also disclosed that two
new members are now on the GES Board of Directors,
that requests are being made to countries for alternative fuel/power, that Cuban experts are arriving here to check the GES machines and that we can
now spend the allocated $1M on them because the IMF
has approved our loan.

Hazel-Ann
RECORDING SECRETARY

oooooooooOoooooooo

RESOLUTION 1

96

Whereas the Central Committee has noted a number of criticisms levelled in respect to the organisation of meetings of the Central Committee, the need for the better functioning of the h gher organs of the Party and the need for greater administration and implementation generally within the Party;

The Central Committee resolves the following on this day, 5th April, 1981:

1. The Organising Committee appoints three recording secretaries of the highest security clearance for recording all ,meetings of the Political Bureau, Central Committee and organising committee.

   A further three recording secretaries of lower security clearance be appointed by the O.C. for recording meetings of workers, youth, women and other committees of the Party.

2. Copies of all decisions and resolutions taken at these various levels be immediately typed and circulated to the appropriate levels of the Party.

   These bodies should function on the principle of pre-set, agendas and as far as humanly possible and in particular, meetings of O.C. and C.C., presentations by members of these bodies must be in the form of writing, preferably distributed twenty-four hours in advance of these meetings through the recording secretaries.

3. A special sub-committee of the O.C. will be responsible for supervision of the implementation of all decisions made at all levels of the Party utilising resourses of the Party's Secfetariat to physically check implementation on the ground.

4. The Party applies the principle of the utilisation of one, two and three-man sub committees of the P.B., C.C. and O.C. with authority delegated of these decisions on behalf of these bodies within specific areas so as to greatly speed uo decision-taking and implementation.

5. Tight and firm chairmanship be applied in all committees of the Party.

6. The study group and committees of the Party should be utilised as a two-way cobduit between Party members and the higher organs of the Party so that members of the Party can influence higher organs, but also decisions taken at a higher level would be quickly known through the study groups and Party committees for their study, discussion and implementation.

7. All committees of the Party immediately draw up a programme for the specific class or section for which it has responsibility for the period now until 13th March, 1982.

That programme should deal, both with the mobilisation of State and Party resources for the bringing of concrete material benefits to the particular class or strata.

Also, the programme should contain the concrete political objective that the Party committee has for the relevant class, strata and section.

These programmes and the Work Plan deroved from them should be submitted to the C.C. and O.C. within twenty-one days of today, properly typewritten.

8. The rigorous application of the highest standards of discipline, conduct and organisation by all members of all committees, including within that framework, the application of the principle of criticism and self-criticism in all committees and at all levels of the Party.

****

RESOLUTION 2

The Central Committee hereby resolves on this day, April 5th, 1981.

That for the period April 5th to May 17th, the C.C. will continue to meet on Wednesday fortnightly as usual and additionally, will hold a Special Evaluation Session on the weekend 16th to 17th May, 1981.

The agenda for the C.C. for this period will be as follows;

RESOLUTION 2 CONT'D

1. Minutes of decisions
2. Recent developments:-
   a. analysis and implications
   b. shifts in the political situation
   c. tasks arising
   d. resolutions

3. Committee reports - party building
   a. farmers (15th April)
   b. urban workers (29th April)
   c. youth/student/militia (13th May)
   d. party education   )
   e. A.G.W.U./teachers   ) (16-17th May)
   f. All parishes - P.C.B.'S)

4. Affairs of State
   a. agriculture/forestry/N.A.C.D.A. (15th April)
   b. agro-inductries and fisheries (29th April)
   c. national security (13th May)
   d. tourism   )
   e. health and housing   ) (16 - 17th May)
   f. external affairs   )

5. (a) Criticism and self-criticism
   h. Evaluation of period
   c. Determination of next period
   d. Agenda for next period

6. Other business

RESOLUTION 3

Whereas the work .f the Party is being severely held back
by the absence of an adequate and functioning Secretariat.

Be it resolved that at this meeting of the 5th April of the
Central Committee:

> That a massive fund-raising be launched with a
> view to raising the necessary funds to build
> or purchase a Party Headquarters and Secretariat.
>
> Bearing in mind the enormity of the cost involved,
> all organs of the Party, including auzillaries,
> parish councils and party support groups accept
> this task as one of their priorities in the
> coming period and must aim to hold their first
> major fund-raising effort no later than 17th

MORE..........

May, 1981.

For the time being, the primary responsibility for
for the organisation of the fund-raising activities
for this purpose be undertaken by the P.C.B.'S, each
of which must make a written report to the O.C. of
the planning of this proposed programme of activities in regard, no later than 27th April, 1981.

****

Comrades present:-

Unison Whiteman - chairman
Kenrick Radix
George Louison
Vincent Noel
Kamau McBarnette
Fitzie Bain
Phyllis Coard
Ewart Layne

Comrades absent:-

Maurice Bishop - sick
Bernard Coard - with excuse
Owusu James - " "
Bogo Cornwall
Ian St. Bernard - " "
Selwyn Strachan - away
Hudson Austin - "
Chris Deriggs - "
Ian Bartholomew - "
Chalkie Ventour - "

Agenda:-

The Present political situation
Decisions on activities

THE PRESENT POLITICAL SITUATION - Cde. Whiteman, who chaired the meeting, led off the discussion on this topic. He told the CC that there is evidence that the rastas are planning to go on an offensive in the Northern part of the country within days and that we must consider preventative measures.

Cde. Coard (i) said that she thinks its time for a selective pickup eg. Tillman Thomas, Stephen John and Leslie Pierre. She also felt that the key rasta leaders should be picked up, that the Political Bureau should visit the Army camps. A security officer should also speak at the NWO PCT meetings, was her suggestion. Sister Coard estimated that we should prepare to pick up about 50 rastas. She felt:-- we have to handle the situation with "manners"; should look at not only the reation of the rastas, but also at the rest of the masses; the rasta movement has weaken our support base; should not play up the line that this is a move against the rasta movement generally; we don't have the capacity to hold all the rastas in the country; the quality of the guards used to guard the rastas has to be the best - they must be politically educated.

Bain - Cde. Bain reported that some people have been saying that we prohibit people living in the hills; there are some rasta agricultural workers; must find places to house the rastas that are picked up and a programme to keep them occupied - put them on a estate to produce and also give them a library; over the last 3 weeks, people have been coming to him, saying, "Take care of yourself" (they are probably sensing something).

Radix - Cde. Radix felt that we will have to prepare for the reaction from the army and militia; need to have an effective film censorship board (especially after the film, "Reggae Sunsplash") which helped in the recent upsurge of the rastas.

Noel - Cde. Noel said that there is a difference between the rastas who are planning the offensive and the rank and file; the Nya Bingis must be a preparation for a movement; Cde.McBarnette should prepare a propaganda team for the dissemination of the news regionally; must consider the possibility of a national address by the Comrade

Leader; the army should prepare a programme for the rastas who will be picked up - wake up time, eat time, books, films, pacifying music etc. - a rigid programme.

Louison - Cde. Louison said that some rastas look as if they are definitely armed and have received training, from their movements at the Nya Bingis.

Whiteman - He felt that one of our greatest weaknesses is the lack of precise information.

DECISIONS:- The following decisions were taken:-

a. every comrade to gather precise information - list of dangerous, 'counter' rastas and other hostile persons that are probably involved. This to be done by Thursday 25th. midday
b. Comrades to write down lines to deal with action to be taken, slogans, etc.
c. the army to draw up a programme for the P.B. to visit the army camps

Hazel-Ann
RECORDING SECRETARY

97 - 2

<u>RESOLUTION TO CENTRAL COMMITTEE</u>

The Party Comrades of the Study Group Guided by Cde. Selwyn Strachan wish to express our disquiet at the irresponsible attitude and behaviour of some Party Comrades during mass gatherings and other mass forums.

We have noticed that at rallies public meetings, parish councils and other forums at which our Party Leadership has been present, Party Comrades have been guilty of the following:-

1. Comrades lack a sense of commitment to punctually with respect to these events. In fact comrades have been turning up to rallie and meetings extremely late as much as one (1) hour after the scheduled commencement of some of these events even when they have no other commitment before the said event. It should be noted also that some Party Comrades do not turn up at all.

2. Some Comrades have shown a failure or inability to lead the masses in giving attention to and endorsing the main points made by Party Leaders.

3. In fact, instead of inciting and conducting agitational work among the masses, Comrades organise and/or partake in "pocket" discussions even when the Party Leaders including when the Comrade Leader is speaking.

   This attitude towards and pattern of behaviour on the part of Party Comrades lends little to the deepening of the Party's influence among the masses and to the building of the stature of our Party Leaders.

   As members of the vanguard in our Revolutionary Process as a part of the Party which guides and leads our masses we suggest that Comrades will have to adopt a more responsible attitude to these events.

   WE WOULD LIKE TO RECOMMEND THAT:-

1. Party Comrades treat these functions with maximum improtance and as such make a every effort to attend and be on time.

2. Comrades take the lead in applauding and popularising all important points and slogans put forward by Party Leaders.

3. Comrades should demonstrate the maximum amount of attentiveness and enthusiasm. Comrades should cease to to partake in these "pocket" discussions and fully encourage no-Party members to be attentive to address by Party Leaders.

S - G 1 TO CC

THE URGENCY OF SETTING UP STRUCTURES
TO DEAL EFFECTIVELY WITH SOCIAL
PROBLEMS

The Comrades in discussing this problem pointed to the
many personal, social and community problems faced by the masses
and the increasing sense of hopelessness among the masses
concerning the ability of the Party to assist them in solving these.

Some examples given were:-

- farmers going to plant propagation stations and not getting
  (sometimes being refused) plants.

- Bellevue workers not getting profit - sharing for so many
  months - open counter-revolutionary comments of work in the
  Vendomme area.

- the many legal exploitation problems suffered by the masses
  especially in the area of rents, sharecropping and workers
  victimization.

- the many problems being experienced by the guard company which
  are not being solved.

- many broken down machines in Carriacou
- many social problems in areas concerning the Beaurocracy's
- inefficiency,
- frustration of people with Grenville Police.

It was pointed out that

(a) village contacts system is not coping effectively with these.

(b) party offices used to be used by the masses to report problems
     but because of the quality of persons manning Party Offices and
     they not being <u>trained</u> to deal with such problems, we failed
     to assist the masses and so they rarely come now.

It was felt that

Proper structures for dealing with the social problems of the masses need to be set up URGENTLY.

(1) a person in every group-party support, mass org., or Trade Union responsible specifically for this area of work, liasing with.

(2) A full time person at parish level in the PCB and in each mass org., responsible only for social problems, and having as co-ordinators.

(3) National level person/in the party and/in each mass org., or Trade Union entirely dealing with this area of work.

------------------ oOo ------------------------

CENTRAL COMMITTEE MINUTES
HELD ON 22ND JULY, 1981

COMRADES PRESENT

Maurice Bishop
Bernard Coard
Selwyn Strachan
Ian St. Bernard
Kamau Mc Barnette
George Louison
Vincent Noel
Tan Bartholomew

Fitzroy Bain
Kenrick Radix
John Ventour
Ewart Layne
Hudson Austin   - late with excuse
Phyllis Coard
Leon Cornwall   - late with excuse
Liam James   - late with excuse

COMRADES ABSENT

CHRISTOPHER DE RIGGS
UNISON WHITEMAN

AGENDA

1. Minutes

2. Land Reform Document

3. W.C series of reports

4. O.C report on Cde. Vince.

The meeting began at ten minutes past two with 16 Comrades present and two absent. The minutes were read and a number of questions were raised.

LAND REFORM DOCUMENT

A document was submitted to the Central Committee of the party by the Land Reform Committee headed by Cde. George Louison. The document was studied by the Central Committee and the Committee was commended for such great work in putting such detailed information of good quality covering all aspects re Land Reform. Cde. B. Coard said the main question that have to be considered is the overall managerial structure and cost of the programme, and that a key person have to deal with such a programme if it have to be a success. He said that one have to bear in mind, that the youths are the main factor of the Land Reform Programme. He

2/...... stressed that

stressed that it must be of number one priority to bring unemployed youths together from the different parishes to make such a project fruitful. He outlined seven variables to get the whole programme off the ground:-

(1) Machinery

(2) Equipment from Socialist Countries

(3) Pesticide from Socialist Countries

(4) (a) Living barracks from Cuba

    (b) Cash-financial reform ECCA.

(5) Labour - young unemployed

(6) Management - best existing managers

(7) Markets - (a) agro industries

           (b) NIB

           (c) GDR and other Socialist Countries.

He also emphasised the programme needs two thousand five hundred youths and the multiciplity of devicises in getting this figure must be borne in mind on the following:-

(1) Tremendous work of sleepless nights and technical work.

(2) Who will comprise the labour force to get the method working.

He said the P.C.B's should do some proposals and suggestions among the mass Organisations in relation to the programme. He pointed out that a number of youths could use a number of models of national service and devices, including one model that of voluntary action campaigns with the present Land Reform campaign. He concluded by saying that the youths are the existing reserve army of labour.

2. O.C REPORT ON CDE. VINCENT NOEL

On July 22nd, 1981, the Organising Committee of the Party raise the issue re the performance of the Workers Cttee. The O.C had received written information on the performance of the Workers Committee re their work among the Urban Workers, and the failure of the Committee in giving sufficient leadership to the Committee.

3/....... The Central Cttee.

The Central Committee was totally dissatisfied with the work of the Workers Committee, and which developed to a major scandal to the party. The reports which was studied by the Central Committee of the Party from the different Comrades on the W.C arrived at :-

(a) That a shock wave should go through the W.C to move a bit faster on tasks etc.

(b) That Cde. Vincent Noel had failed to push the work forward during the past two (2) years.

(c) That the Workers Committee wasn't working with a work plan and that the sub committees of the WₗC are not functioning.

(d) Cde. Noel accepted that he himself is guilty of been illdiscipline failing to carry out the directives from the party and failing to attend his study group with applicants on the West Coast area.

Cde. Maurice said, if we have to move forward by taking the revolutionary struggles in a serious way, creative measures have to be taken in implementing certain structures, of the party. He said the issue of the Workers Committee came up time and time before, but no surious thought was given to it in a frim and disciplined way and that the Central Committee and the Political Bureau should shoulder some of the blame in this respect.

It was also stated by Cde. B, Coard that the Central Committee and the Political Bureau have to be constructively criticised, of their timidity, unprincipled and softness in dealing with such a situation. After all these charges were laid against Cde. V. Noel the C.C took the following decisions :-

(1) That Cde. Vincent Noel be removed from the Chairmanship of the W.C.

(2) That Cde. Chalkie Ventour should be warned by the C.C to be much more organised re the work of the Workers Committee.

(3) Cde. Selwyn Strachan to replaced Cde. Vincent Noel as chairman of the Workers Committee.

(4) That the Organising Committee do an overall shake up of the Workers Committee and that the best elements remain.

4/....... 5 That the

5. That the principle of our Party of the Political Bureau and Central Committee is dependent on Comrades leading major areas of Party Work, and seeing that Cde. Vincent Noel would no longer be leading such a major area of work they Cde. Noel should be removed from the membership of the Political Bureau and Central Committee of the Party.

The meeting ended at 6.30 p.m.

JUSTIN CAMPBELL
RECORDING SECRETARY for
HAZELANN WILLIAMS.

MINUTES OF CENTRAL COMMITTEE MEETING HELD ON WEDNESDAY, 19TH AUGUST, 1981

100

Comrades present :-

1. Maurice Bishop
2. Selwyn Strachan
3. George Louison
4. Bernard Coard
5. Hudson Austin
6. Chalkie Ventour
7. Ian St. Bernard

8. Bogo Conrwall
9. Liam James
10. Kenrick Radix
11. Ewart Layne
12. Phyllis Coard
13. Fitzie Bain
14. Kamau McBernette

15. Unison Whiteman)
16. Ian Bartholomew) absent
17. Chris DeRiggs

Agenda:-   1a. The Present Political Situation
  b. CC resolutions to Guide the Party's work

Cde. Strachan led off the discussion on the present political situation in the country. He observed that there has been a rapid step up of US imperialism against the Revolution, mainly on the military front. He saw the manouvres in Puerto Rico as an act of preparation for invading our country and said that the US has been operating on many fronts.

His analysis was that we are in one of the most dangerous periods and also noted that in the past couple weeks, some regional islands have become openly hostile. He view the attacks by the Dominica Freedom Party and Eugenie Charles as the most striking..

Cde. Strachan's view was that the social base of the Revolution was widen and that the Carnival (which was organised solely by the working people) could be used to help in the analysis. He described the mood of the NYO Youth Campers as "electric". Cde. Strachan felt that overall, the situation is rough externally and on the internal side - our masses are holding firm. The bourgeoisie, he said had a "wait and see" attitude.

He concluded that the main essence is the stepping up of efforts to turn back the Revolution; both economic and propaganda wise.

The other comrades agreed that the main feature of the present period is the threat to the Revolution being posed by imperialism - US imperialism in particular. Comrades mentioned other things as:-

o The hotel section of the bourgeoisie still warm towards the Revolution.
o The Land Reform Act will cause some general concern.
o The working people are still in full support of the Revolution.
o The Socialism classes has had great impact - the workers are enthusiastic.
o Within the Party, comrades are becoming serious.
o Some people really don't believe that an invasion will come.
o AGWU membership showing more respect and support for the Revolution, their mood is high - they are asking for Government to take over the badly-run estates.
o We must consider Venezuela's attitude towards us and Campines' meeting with Stanley Cyrus.
o The bourgeoisie is "licking their wounds".
o All the recent programmes have had the effect they were intended to have - the farmers programme, youth camp, socialism classes, school uniform and books programme.
o The tighter centralisation in the Party has helped.
o One weakness is that too few people know what to do in a situation of invasion.

2/...o The Youth campers

o The youth campers will be trying to form 47 new NYO groups by
   the end of the camp.
o The camp has had a positive effect in St. Andrew's, but has not
   accomplished its original objective.
o Workers' morale is improving.- there is greater confidence in
   the Party and Government.
o Torchlight issue is significant - the workers there feel that
   state power is on their side.
o US imperialism's aggressiveness is growing - they shot down 2
   Lybian aircrafts.
o The mobilisation for the Militia is important.
o Grenada's isolation is at hand.
o The mood of the masses will not improve is it is not complimented - material benefits must be stepped up.
o Imperialism realised that they cannot rely on local counter-
   revolutionaries to turn back the Revolution.
o The US has lauched a propaganda campaign against us, which has
   had its effects and has alienated our nationals.
o The consciousness and discipline of our people growing.
o The final details for the invasion are being planned - a date may
   have already been fixed.
o The spy flights are probably to gather last bits of information.
o We must have a plan for the CC and the entire Party in a situation of invasion.
o The social base of the Revolution has been broaden, but not
   strengthen. Our best response, has been from former Gairyites.
o Some of the hardest areas for Party work are some areas of our
   traditional supporters.
o The Revolution has gained more supporters than what it has lost.
o 40 - 50% of agricultural workers are willing to attend rallies.
o David Maresh is back with a new TV show on Grenada.

The Comrade Leader shared most of the views already expressed. He commented on the visits to Grenada by many nationals and non- nationals and
felt creative ways need to be found to bring groups here in an organised way. He sighted the Youth and Pioneer Camps as very important
and spoke of the recent militia Route March, resumption of work at
the Airport site and the Torchlight issue.

However, Cde. Bishop also mentioned the negative areas, as follows:-

   1) Grenada's weakness on the international front.
   2) We have lost the propaganda fight on the regional front,
      (we failed to respond to attacks in the media).
   3) Our response to Stanley Cyrus and Michael Sylvester was
      very weak.
   4) The USA has been very successful in bringing about our
      isolation by the CARICOM countries.
   5) The low level and non-involvement of Party cadres in the
      Militia.

Comrade Bishop's views were that this is a total all out assault on
Grenada and that we are facing an impending invasion, which could
come any day now. This he felt, we will have a problem convincing
people of. He also sighted a number of "coincidences" in the evidence
that an invasion was being planned for Grenada.

Cde. Coard, in his presentation also noted that the previous comrades were too "loose" in their analysis, referring to the recent
plans to invade Grenada as imperialism stepping up its aggressiveness.

3/...He questioned where

He questioned where is the peasantry at and where will they be when the Land Reform Act is passed. He also gelt we should get more details on US-Guyana relations, which he felt are not so good.

Cde. (F) Coard suggested that in our foreign affairs thrust, the following countries, individuals, organisations and methods be involved:-

1. France
2. Sweden
3. Non-Aligned countries
4. Socialist countries
5. Caribbean countries
6. Fraternals (NYO and NWO to write fraternal organisations asking for support)
7. Middle ground individuals and groups
8. US Senators, Congressmen, etc.
9. Letter campaign (letter to all Grenadians living abroad)
10. Letter to Grenadians from the missions abroad

<u>DECISIONS REQUIRING FOLLOW-UP ACTION</u>:- See Decisions 1 - 5 above

Hazel-Ann
RECORDING SECRETARY

MINUTES OF CENTRAL COMMITTEE MEETING HELD
WEDNESDAY, 30TH DECEMBER, 1981

101

Comrades present:-

1. Maurice Bishop
2. Selwyn Strachan
3. George Louison
4. Hudson Austin
5. Kenrick Radix
6. Unison Whiteman
7. Liam James
8. Ian St. Bernard
9. Kamau McBarnette
10. Ewart Layne
11. Fitzroy Bain
13. Leon Cornwall
13. Chalkie Ventour

Comrades absent:-

14. Bernard Coard)
15. Phyllis Coard)
16. Chris DeRiggs)   out of
17. Tan Bartholomew)   the country
18. Cladwell Taylor)

<u>Agenda</u>:-   Review of 5th April, 1981 Resolutions

The Central Committee reviewed the three resolutions passed by the said committee on April 5th, 1981.

<u>RESOLUTION 1.1</u>: This resolved that the Organising Clmmittee appoints three high security clearance and three low security clearance Recording Secretaries for recording decisions taken at committee meetings. The C.C. concluded that the three low security clearamce R.S.'s were found, but only two of the three high security clearance ones were found. Presently, only two high security clearance R.S.'s are functioning.

The C.C. therefore decided that the workers, youth and women committees appoint somebody on their committee to perform the duties of the R.S. (i.e. take the minutes of the meetings). The Secretariat will have it typed and circulated thereafter.

<u>RESOLUTION 1.2</u>: This resolved that all decisions,et.c taken at committee meetings be typed and circulated to the appropriate levels in the Party.

The CC analysed that this was been but not in a totally satisfactorily way.

The same resolution resolved to have the Party committees function on preset agendas and have presentations to these committees in the form of writing circulated twenty-four hours before the meeting.

The CC realised that most committees have not been functioning on preset agendas and not in all cases, presentations are written. In instances where they are witten, quite often, it is presented/distributed at the begining of the meeting and not before as resolved.

<u>RESOLUTION 1.3</u>: This resolved that a Special Sub-Committee of the

2/... O.C. be responsible

• O.C. be responsible for the supervision of the implementation of decisions taken.

That Committee is Cdes. Coard and Strachan. The CC concluded that Cde. Coard has been supervising the work of the women and youth. Cde. Strachan has been doing that of the rural and urban workers. Also, Cde. Louison has been supervising the farmers work.

RESOLUTION 1.4: Resolved that the principle of one, two, and three man sub-committees of the P.B., C.C. and O.C. be utilised to speed up implementation of decisions taken as is necessary.

This has been happening.

RESOLUTION 1.5: That tight and firm chairmanship be applied in all committees. This has not been the case in all committees.

RESOLUTION 1.6: That the study groups be used as a two-way conduit between Party members and the higher organs of the Party.

The CC concluded that this was been done effectively prior to the move to all day study twice monthly. It was suggested that the parish GM's could perform this function or that a committee be appointed to deal with this.

RESOLUTION 1.7: That all committees submit work plans and programmes for the period then until March 13th 1982.

The CC found that the farmers and youth committees did theirs on time; the urban workers own was late and was sent back to be re-done; women's own has been done on a month-to-month basis and the rural wokrers (AGWU) did a programme, not a work plan.

RESOLUTION 1.8: That the highest application of standards of disci-pline, conduct and organisation by members of all committees and the application of criticism and self-criticism at those levels.

The CC concluded the highest levels of discipline, etc, were not been adhered to, but that the CC had adhered to the application of criticism and self-criticism.

RESOLUTION 2: That the CC continues to meet fortnightly between April 5th to 17th and also hold a Special Weekend Evaluation session.

The CC did continue to meet fortnighly during that period and the special session was held on June 6th and 7th.

RESOLUTION 3: That a massive fund-raising drive be launched to raise funds for the building or purchase of a Party Headquarters and that the F.C.B.'s submit a written report on this to the O.C. by April 27th, 1981.

This was not done. St. George's F.C.B. submitted a plan - they had one small vevent. St. Patrick's F.C.B. asked to be excused and was agreed. The others failed to do anything.

The Central Committee therefore issued a directive to the Organising Committee that the latter appoints a fundraising committee within two weeks, primarily for the purpose of raising funds for the building of

3/...a Party Headquarters

a Party Headquarters. Along with this, should go a propaganda buildup.

The C.C. is to received a report on the formation of the fundraising committee at the next CC meeting: January 13th, 1982.

The O.C. is also to "get back to" the F.C.B.'s regarding the fundraising events for the Party Headquarters.

In summarising the work of the Central Committee during 1982, Chairman of the C.C., Cde. Bishop, pointed out the following:-

A. STRENGTHS

1. Compared to 1980, there has been progress in the work of the C.C.
2. Attempts at conducting the CC's work more scientifically were made.

B. WEAKNESSES

1. There has not been sufficiently serious followup on decisions taken: lack of implementation.
2. Have not conducted the CC's work along lines that the committee agreed to.
3. Has failed to give guidance to the Party.
4. Circularisation of decisions taken have not been sent down to the lower organs effectively.

Other comrades pointed out the following, in analysing the CC's work during the year:-

1. The C.C. has been self-critical.
2. The committee's ideological unity has developed.
3. The "Gang of 26" was handled firmly.
4. Before the 5th April resolutions, the C.C. did not function properly, after then, the C.C. "started to kick".
5. Too much time wasted in getting meetings started.
6. The C.C. has been guilty of gross ill-discipline regarding study.

The C.C. decided that effective from the next CC meeting, all comrades do the following - when comming to meeting:-

a. Carry a hard back notebook for CC notes only (TOP SECURITY).
b. Carry a file of all their CC minutes.

The Central Committee analysed that a Secretary exclusively to the PB and CC was needed, whose job it would be, among other things, to ensure the implementation of preset agendas, getting minutes to comrades and act as a reminder to comrades of their tasks, meetings, etc. It was therefore decided that the present Recording Secretary to the PB/EB, CC and WC be removed from the Workers Committee (as RS) in order to perform those tasks effectively.

The following is a list of the Party committees that need to have

4/...Recording Secretaries attached

Recording Secretaries attached to them:-

1. Central Committee   )
2. Political/Economic Bureau   ) R.S. - Hazel-Ann
3. Organising Committee   " - R.S. - Justin
4. Urban Workers   "   *
5. Youth   "   *
6. Women   "   *
7. Farmers   "   *
8. Rural Workers (AGWU) Committee *
9. Socialism Tutors   "   - R.S. - Justin
10. National Militia   "   *
11. Propaganda   "   *
13. Teachers   "   *
14. Fundraising   *

   (*) These are to find temporary R.S.'s.

The following are other committees/organs that need Recording Secretaries:-

15. Workers Parish Councils (six)
16. Zonal Councils
17. Women's Councils
18. Youth General Meetings
19. National Party General Meetings
20. Party study (GM level)
21. Parish Co-ordinating Bodies
22. Parish Party General Meetings
23. Farmers Parish Zonal Councils

For security reasons and to have a register of the recipients of the
minutes, the following is to be done:-

a. number the minutes with the code numbering.
b. put two lines through each page of the minutes.
c. have recipients sign for their minutes.
d. purchase a safe to put undelivered minutes/sensitive documents.

The Central Committee looked back at its meetings of June 6th and 7th
and its resolution of June 28th. The resolution resolved to develop a
series of well thought and well planned tactics to crush counter-revolution, braden and deepen all sections of the masses in the Revolution.

It was also resolved to (a) make more active use of the study groups
and GM's and (b) to implement zonal councils, get socialism classes
started, involving the largest section of the masses, hold house
meetings with the middle class, start work with the four main strata:
workers, youth, women, small/middle peasantry.

The tactics for the crushing of counter-revolution were done. More
active use of the study groups was done up to before the new system

5

of studying, the zonal councils were implemented, the socialism classes get started (although presently with some problems: 24 at the village level and 37 at the workplaces), the meetings with the middle class were never started and the work with the four main strata was started.

On the question of the Party's work for 1982, the Central Committee heard that the O.C. was presently looking at the different committee work plans for that year. AGWU, farmers, women and youth and some of the I.C.B's were looked at. On Monday 4th, January, the O.C. will look at the work plans of the workers, national militia, propaganda, education and teachers committees.

Comrades expressed the view that the O.C. should have a work scheldule of all the zonal councils, WIC's for the first half or quarter of the year.

Some comrades also expressed the view that the Central Committee needs to have a 1982 Work Plan and Programme!

It was felt that things were happening in a roundabout style. That is, that the C.C. should have told the different committees what it wants to see included in their work plan, instead of waiting for the plans to be prepared and presented, then to criticise it and if necessary send it back to be redone.

Cde. Radix pointed out that in stating that the Party should play an increasing role in the economy, "we have not come down to specifics".

Cde. Bishop stated that he preferes to see the C.C. go back to study as a Central Committee (together) instead of with the rest of members. He also suggested that the members and candidate members study session be from 8.00 a.m. to 1.00 p.m. instead of 9.00 a.m. to 5.00 p.m. as present.

He also said that more thought must be given to the importance/necessity of rest and suggested that regular excercise be made mandatory for Party comrades.

Out of the CC meeting, these are the decisions taken:-

1. More security for the minutes:-

    a. code numbering of the minutes
    b. signing for the documents
    c. two lines through the pages
    d. purchse of a safe for undelivered documents
2. Central Committee comrades to (a) carry a hard back notebook for

6/...CC notes (top

...6

CC notes (top security) and (b) carry a file of all their CC minutes w
with them to CC meetings.
3. Present CC Recording Secretary to be removed as CC Recording Secretary and to function as Secretary to the PB/EB and CC to ensure
   better functioning of these committees.
4. Workers, youth, women to find temporary RS's for their committees.
5. Education Committee to meet, Tuesday 5th, 10.00 a.m.
6. Propaganda Committee to meet.
7. Teachers Committee to meet and decide on work plan.
8. The O.C. to appoint a fundraising committee. Cde. Strachan to give
   . a report at next CC meeting.
9. The O.C. to "get back to" the I.C.B.'s re. the fundraising for the
   Party Headquarters.
10. The O.C. to look at the week's scheldule re. adding the zonal
    councils, socialism classes, etc.

The C.C. also   briefly discussed the draft New Year speech of
the Comrade Leader. 1982 is to be "Year of Economic Construction."
The speech will speak of the successes of this year: Year of Agriculture and Agro-Industries and call for a step up in the land reform
programme.

The Central Committee decided to meet on Wednesday, January 13th,
8.00 a.m. to 4.00 p.m. The agenda set is :-

1. Review of 1981 for the Party and Revolution.
   (Strenghts, weaknesseses, etc.)
2. Review of work plans and programmes of the committees.
3. Criticism and self-criticism.
4. Line of march. (Preset agenda for the first quarter of 1982.)

Hazel-Ann
RECORDING SECRETARY

101 - 6   *************

Held on the 21st April 1982

'The Meeting began at 9 a.m. with the following cdes present:-

102

Maurice Bishop	Leon ("Bogo") Cornwall
George Louison	Ian St. Bernard'
Unison Louison	Tan Bartholomew
Liam ("Owusu") James	Fitzroy Bain
Ewert ("headache") Layne	

The following cdes were late:-

Bernard Coard

Phyllis Coard

Selwyn Strachan - who was out of the country - Arrived 1200

Absent were:-

Kenrick Radix - out of Country - Cuba

John "Chalkie" Ventour - out of country - GDR

Chris "Kojo" De Riggs - " " " - USA

Hudson Austin - sick

Kamau Mc Barnette - no excuse given

It was noted that according to the present agenda the following should be looked at :-

1 - Agro-Industries

2 - Fisheries

3 - New developments in the political scene

Owing to the absent of Cde. Six it was stated that items #1 and 2 could not be discussed in details as they were his responsibilities. The agenda finally decided upon however, was:

1- Agro Industries/Fisheries

2- The present state of the Party

3- Recent developments with particular emphasis on the political, economical and security situation regionally and hemispherieually as it affects Grenada.

2:....

ITEM #1

In respect to this item it was impossible to deal with a full scale report as stated before. However, both Cdes George Louison and Bernard Coard were in a position to give a report on Fisheries and Agro Industries respectively.

Cde George Louison had held a meeting with a Cuban Commission on Fisheries which had recently visited Grenada. He stated that the analysis of the Commission is basically that while there are objective problems in fisheries they believe the main one is subjective, particularly organisational. An example given was that 60% spare parts negoitiated for has arrived here from Cuba and up to now some boxes have not been opened while others cannot be found! Apart from this a number of other problems were raised.

The Commissions made a number of recommendations.

1. Some boats don't have gears. We need to consider buying some of the gears.

2. Winches could be placed on the boats to assist in pulling ice long line which was proving difficult.

3. Small boats with out board engines were needed to assist in identifying fishes.

4. Changing some of the boat engines so as to make them faster.

5. We need to develop an integrated plan based on our manegerial resources.

6. They are willing to assist in pushing fisheries forward based on the preliminary researches done previously by the Koreans and the Soviets .....

The following were also noted:-

- After one year the boats haven't been dry-docked when this should be done twice a year.

- Halifax harbour previously identified for this was found to be inadequate as it is not deep enough - much work will have to be done to prepare it.

102 - 2

3..... Secondly......

Secondly, labour force is absent there. Grenville was thought to be better. However, further discussion produced an idea of extending a jetty out into the sea thus solving the immediate problem.

On the question of inland fishing the following emerged from the discussions:-

- Grand Etang Lake and Lake Antoine were not potentially suitable for such fishing as plant life is absent there.

- Palmiste and Mardi Gras have potential.

- In all there are about 42 acres available for developing inland fishing.

- The Cubans are prepared to give material assistance in developing this area.

- They are also willing to give manpower assistance in developing management.

Also present at the meeting with Cde George was Roberts of fisheries.

The following were discussions on the report.

- Cde Phill raised the question as to whether the new Fisheries Board was yet functioning to which the reply was no.

- The Cabinet Secretary has been failing in this aspect.

- A number of key new chairman of boards have be having objective problems.

(Then as a by-product of the agenda the boards of other industries such as Agro, Coops and Fisheries were discussed.)

It was also noted that the Grenada/Cuba agreement has been going exceedingly well in comparison to previous years. It was registered, though the level of cheas in Agro Industries and Fisheries were really frightening and further noted that what was really required in Agro Industries and Fisheries is systems which the relevant Minister needs to impliment but has so far failed to do so even though he has been criticised time and time again.

- In comparison the Ministry of Construction has been seriously organising itself with Cde Prime in charge.

- The above Ministry has drawn up a complete document of all projects in the country and the entire manpower requirement, etc needed so as to move ahead rapidly.

- Cde Phill then suggested that either Cde Radix comply with CC decisions or he'll have to be moved to another area of work though he has improved from a year ago! It was noted that the cde has inepressive, creative energy which needs to be harvested.

Recommendations made were:-

1! In respect to Agro Industries and Fisheries the new boards and management have to be set up rapidly and must be made to function.

2! The CC expressed its concern and recommended that all Ministers and in particular the Minister of Agro Industries and Fisheries should act on policy matters, rather than as Managers and Chairmans of Boards, in carrying out their ministerial functions.

3. Weekly reports should be submitted to the Economic Bureau on production and productivity, expenditure, etc.

4, Cde Layne to be used for 2 months as Chairman of the Board of G.F.C. and Agro Industries after which he will be accused.
    - Leroy Neckles as Chairman of the Board of Fisheries.

5. To generally impliment a policy of political Commission particularly in big enterprises so as to deal with personell problems.

The CC noted how unfortunate it was that the Minister responsible for Agro Industries and Fisheries was absent in the face of the foregone discussions.

ITEM #2. STATE OF THE PARTY

Cde Layne was asked to lead off on this item as he had proposed it. The following points were outlined by him:-

(a) Discipline within the Party

(B) Study within the Party

(c) The level of present standards of the Party.

(d) Work performance of Party cdes

(e) The grieving trend of arrogance of Party cdes

(f) Planning in the Party-Work plan/Work schedule

(g) Guidance given to Party applicants. How and who does so.

(h) Specifically the work performance of leading cdes including CC and PB.

(i) The flow of information from the top to the bottom of the Party.

Cde Layne then went on to further explain the above points. He stated that the quality and quantity of work to be done has a bearing on the points stated above. On the question of planning and organising work he stated that some cdes find this difficult to do as many times new tasks are given with prior notice. He also said that there seem to be a total breakdown in planning by committees and organisations which affects Party cdes generally.

In respect to standards, he said many cdes are only carrying a tag - they are really not doing anything. At the same time cdes performance in their area of work is not being assessed, relating to the Pro-Applicants of the Party, he said that some comrades in the Pro-Applicant classes have stated that they don't mind doing the courses but they don't want to be members of the Party.

In terms of arrogance he pointed out that there has been a development of such in the Youth Committee. It is very difficult to advice or speak to them, he stated.

Study - members of the Party have not been involved in study for the year. He further questioned whether C.M. study of 6 hours on Saturday was scientific.

The folllwing were responses to Cde. Layne's contribution 1

CDE. FITZROY

He endorsed the points raised by Cde. Layne and indicated his belief that the level of party organisation has a bearing on the present attitude of Cdes. He cited the socialism tutors meeting as a serious disaster which the party must harnest quickly.

COMRADE TAN

Endorsed the previous speakers and stressed tha his greatest concern was planning within the party. He himself, finds it very difficult to implement his workplan. Looking at the arrogrance displayed by Party Comra des, he said the masses was complaining. He also cited the serious lateness at which meetings and rallies are started. This is annoying the masses Cde. Tan pointed out people are not turning up to meetings our level of organisation is poor. We are in a crisis and we need to do something about it.

CDE. BOGO

Agreed with the previous speakers. Further he said, the present state of the party has to do firstly with the organisation of work. Secondly the quality of our ideological work. Thirdly the rapid growth of the party has unintentionally lowered the quality of party work. He also stated that sufficient time is not given towards organisational guidance.

- We are not developing deep convictions in Comrades so that they can face the day to day struggle of building the society.

- We are creating problems for app by the way in which we carry out our ideological and organisational work.

- Cde. Bogo also accepted a criticism made of him by Cde. Layne in his opening presentation.

7/........

CDE. OWUSU

Belevies that all of us are aware of the lowering of standards
in the party and raised a question as to the basis for recruitment of Proposed applicants into the party, in some cases people
recently hostile to the party.

- This he says this makes the party a laughing stock.
- He cited ~~annoyance~~ arrogance at the highest level of the party and pointed
  out the failure of the party to create structures to shape
  character of Comrades.

- Large numbers of Comrades do not function within a party
  Committee thus making discipline difficult.

COMRADE PHYLLIS

Agreed with most points raised but not all. She made two main
criticisms.

1. The petty bourgeois attitude still existing in a number of
   Comrades, including the leadership.

2. The under-develop structure of the party such as the Secretariat
   etc.

- In respect to the above she cited the following:
- our inability to refuse unrealistic tasks.
- last minute organisation
- our attitude to self criticism
- that our sense of timing is bad
- Cde. Phyl doesn't agree that we have casted our nets to wide
  as was indicated by Cde. Owusu. She agrees that we have made
  some mistakes, but there is good quality among the Pro. A's.
- we need to marry their ideological work with organisational
  work.
- A comparison has shown that the morale of Pro. A's is much
  higher than A's said Cde. Phyl.
- Lastly the O.C needs to decide on what specifically is its
  task-what kind of work it will do and she stressed that a
  disciplinery committee is needed as this takes up too much
  of the O.C's time.

8/.....

COMRADE BERNARD

1. Cde. Layne must be commended for the quality of points he made and the amount of thoughts he put into them.

2. He agrees that there is a crisis in party orgnisation and highlighted that we are discussing these matters of the party in a time when the internal political situation of the country is good.

3. Our main problem is that we are trying to do too much.

- He pointed out that we have listed 25 national events for the year not including 4 Playa Giron rallies in one night.

- our human and other resources do not permit us to do what we are setting ourselves.

- complains have been coming even from technocrats and bureaucrats that excessive demands are being made on them by the Ministers, etc.

- He further endorsed the critical nature of building the character of party comrades. On the question of the prestige of the party and the willingness to join the same he says,

- people have been identifying the quality of their work and wondering how come they did not make it into the Frm A's classes.

- this tells us that the party's prestige is growing despite the weakness we have displayed organisationally.

- The masses are much more clearer now as to who are party members and who are not.

- when the masses stop coming forward with criticisms that is the time we have to worry.

- In this respect he doesn't agree with other Comrades who believes the prestige of the party is falling.

9/......

,CDE. MAURICE

- Also complimented Cde. Layne for the comments he made and the C.C and the party owes the Comrade a depth of gratitude for the thoughts he has given to the matter.

- he further agrees that we are doing too much and we are overworked.

- added to this there are weaknesses in our method of work.

- in respect to party life and norm, one weakness that younger Comrades face is lack of rules and written guidelines.

- rules and guidelines must tell what is expected of an applicant, Pro. A's, C.M and M, their rights and obligations.

- He also stress the need for more serious organised social activities for the party but under clearly defined security principles.

- Following this the decision was taken to draw up a list of Party rules and regulations. A sub Committee of the Party made up of Comrades Phyll and Tan was decided on to draft the above and submit it by Wednesday 28/4/82.

ITEM # 3

RECENT DEVELOPMENTS

This item was discussed in great details and at length. A number of decisions were taken which are attached to this report.

MINUTES OF THE CENTRAL COMMITTEE MEETING
ON SATURDAY, 26th JUNE, 1982

103

Comrades present:-

1. Maurice Bishop
2. Bernard Coard
3. Selwyn Strachan
4. George Louison
5. Unison Whiteman
6. Hudson Austin
7. Kenrick Radix

8. Chalkie Ventour
9. Ian St. Bernard
10. Phyllis Coard
11. Fitzroy Bain
12. Kamau McBarnette
13. Leon Cornwall

Comrades absent:-

14. Liam James — out of country
15. Ewart Layne — sick
16. Chris Dediggs — out of country
17. Tan Bartholomew — sick.

AGENDA:-

1. O.C. analysis of Party
2. Political/Economic Review
3. Criticism/Self-Criticism

- Party's internal state and links with the masses at its worse since the Revolution

(a) Internal Party Organisation
    i.   implementation
    ii.   supervision, control guidance mechanism
    iii.   internal study
    iv.   bureaucratic apparatus - Party Secretariat *

       (*) Part of i and ii but listed separately.

(b) Party's work among the masses

- 6 national rallies held in the last 14 weeks
- the activities this year have been aimless, purposeless, with no direct objectives, etc.

(1) **WORKERS WORK**

   - work about to collapse; need to take stock
   - dissatisfied with quality of work
   - even solving of grievance is not being done
   - rightism in handling of women's grievances

how do the trade un deal with the state apparatus

1. Standards of bourgeois trade unionism not being met.
2. Tendency towards rightism in handling of grievances of workers.

(2) **PEASANTRY**

   - very little work done in the past 6 months
   - the level of political organisational work cannot be felt
   - failure to do propaganda work on the 30 miles of Feeder Roads and its impact on the farmers
   - need of farmers worse than 6 months ago;

Propaganda

- more open to the lines of the big planters and upper petitie bourgeoisie

(3) YOUTH AND STUDENTS

- worse area of mass work in the Party
- quality of political work quite unsatisfactory
- problem of consolidation of large membership
- Pioneers work much better than the above two, best organised of the
three
- the bourgeois forces re-organising their youth arm - religious,
scouts, cubs, etc.

Mass organisation

(4) WOMEN'S ORGANISATION

- also failed to consolidate the large membership
- has a significant number of groups not functioning or semi functioning
- not enough members of their groups active

- political/ideological work among the masses has not got off the
ground
- socialism classes: poor
- Party Paper: a disaster area
- Parish/Zonal Councils not being treated seriously; not enough mo-
bilisational work being done

STATE MEDIA

FWI - not contributed much to the political/ideological work
TFG - palteaued for some time but have slipped backwards due to technical
problems
RFG - very little local news

MOOD OF THE MASSES

- the mood of the masses not as high as recently as May Day
- at the time of Machel's visit, the mood was already slipping
- the mood of the masses was highest on March 13, for the three years
of the Revolution - the broadest section of the masses were involved
in the rally
- the mood now is not as low as last year around this period

REASONS FOR LOW MOOD

Economic: layoffs and rotation in Construction, Health in urban areas;
rural areas - slide in world prices; terms of trade against
Grenada; it's affecting farmers more than anyone else;
However in areas where little benefits have come to the
masses of particular villages, the political work there has
helped to keep the mood good; the Party is not involved in
house-to-house work

3/...

...3

INTERNALLY

Party Lenniniet standards have become worse; no Party study - CM's M's; PCB's very badly off

<u>O.C.</u> functioning in a very b reacratic and routine way giving no assistance to Party committees except in crisis periods. It has not played a role in assisting in the discipline of Party comrades (approach to the work, co-operation in committees, character building, etc.)

<u>PARTY SECRETARIAT</u>: Failure of this to expand has affected the Party's professional nature of its work.

<u>PARTY LEADERSHIP</u>: The CC and PB devoted very little time to Party work and more to state work (economy, defence, etc.); no time for internal Party building, expanding Party structures, building Party's links among the masses, etc.

<u>MILITIA</u>: Difficulties in Regions 1,2,and 3.

<u>CARRIACOU</u>: Mood about 4 (on 1 to 5 scale); however the political work has

Party members' mood is lower than that of the masses. <u>The Armed Forces is on a low also.</u>

TASKS:

1. Rationalisation of Party comrades' work.
2. Training of Party cadres (ideological work and organisational training)
3. Expansion of the Party Secretariat.
4. Introducing systems for control of work, monitoring, guiding work.

CRITICISM/SELF-CRITICISM:

O.C. recommendation re Cde. Leon 'Bogo' Cornwall. Decision - removal from youth work and placed as Ambassador to Cuba.

The <u>Economic Review</u> involved discussion of the Ministry of Finance and Ministry of Planning. The former was a financial report from January to May, 1982. The latter - a report on the Investment Proposals for 1983 - 1985.

Next CC meeting - Friday, July 23rd, 1982. The PB to prepare a pre-set agenda for that meeting.

Comrades Strachan, St. Bernard and Ventour to prepare summary of OC's analysis of the Party to send to Party comrades.

NB - The minutes were prepared from notes taken at the meeting by Comrade Ventour.

Hazel-Ann
RECORDING SECRETARY

MINUTES OF THE CENTRAL COMMITTEE MEETING
HELD ON FRIDAY 27th AUGUST, 1982

104

Comrades present:-

1. Maurice Bishop
2. Selwyn Strachan
3. George Louison
4. Chalkie Ventour
5. Fitzroy Bain

Comrades late:-

6. Hudson Austin
7. Ian Bartholomew
8. Kamau McBarnette
9. Liam James
10. Phyllis Coard) gave excuses re
11. Bernard Coard) their late arrival

Comrades absent:-

12. Unison Whiteman)
13. Kenrick Radix   ) all out of
14. Chris DeRiggs   ) the country
15. Ewart ~~Layne~~)
16. Ian St. Bernard)
17. Leon Cornwall — preparing to leave

Agenda:-

1. Minutes
2. Tasks arising from the Minutes
3. Report from Weekend Members Study: Committee/Workshop Reports
4. Line of March/Way Forward

The meeting started at 8.10 a.m. with 5 of the 11 CC members in the country present. The first almost 2 hours was used for reading the Report from the Weekend Members Study.

At 10.05 a.m., discussion on the agenda items started.

1. MINUTES
1.1 Corrections

(a) The minutes did not reflect the CC's doubts/questioning of a fraternal comrade to help build the Party, as suggested by some comrades.

(b) The task of the four-man committee (Strachan, Coard, Ventour and James) was not clearly defined. It should be stated that the four-man committee was set up for the purpose of conducting a thorough study of the internal state of the Party with a view to making recommendations to the Central Committee. A deadline of the end of October was set for the accomplishment of this task. In this regard, a one day meeting was scheduled.

1.2 Criticism of the minutes

Comrade Phyllis Coard made a gneral criticism of the minutes, stating that it does not reflect decisions taken at CC meetings and that it focuses more on comments made by the different comrades. Other comrades added the following points:-

- there is deficient recording/writing of the minutes
- lacks enough tightness in formulating decisions taken, etc.
- at intervals in the meeting, there should be a pause to give the Recording

Secretary formulations as may be necessary
- for each agenda item there should be a conclusion/consensus
- those ideas with no concensus/conclusions should also be stated
- at the end of each meeting two comrades should sit back with the Recording
  Secretary to compare notes
- after writing up the minutes, they should be shown to Cde. Strachan before
  typing, for the purpose of corrections, etc.

Towards the end of the general discussion on this topic, Cde. Coard made the proposal that the minutes should be written under these five headings:-

1. Main points - made and developed
2. All conclusions
3. Recommendations/Referrals
4. Decisions/Resolutions
5. Tasks Assigned

The above proposal was agreed to by the Central Committee.

3. REPORT FROM WEEKEND MEMBERS STUDY

Two hours of the CC's time was given for the reading of this 52-page document, put
together/comprised of the committees presentations and workshop reports given to
the weekend study of the full members, 20 - 23 August.

However, this item was not discussed in any great detail. It was stated that it
should act as a preliminary help to the formulation of a line of march / way forward in the present/coming period for the Party. Concretely, this means that the
document will go to the Candidate Members, for them to study and make criticisms/
proposals. (It has already reached the full members as they were involved in its
drawing up.)

LINE OF MARCH/WAY FORWARD

The Comrade Leader first stated the reasons for the postponement of the Special
Party General Meeting originally fixed for Thursday 26th August. The reasons he
explained as:-

(a) lack of full CC/PB input in the discussion, as the item re way forward was
    not discussed by the CC/PB up to the morning of the meeting day;

(b) "confusion on the ground";

(c) security - the entire Party was going to be at one location; two separate
    GM's will now be held - one for applicants and another for full members and
    candidate members.

The main points which would have had to be included in the main presentation/
guidelines at the Special G.M. were the following (which were not even yet
discussed centrally by the leading/higher Party organs):-

The character of the Revolution, bearing in mind the character of the society and
of the Party wand what was inherited.
Our economic path must be explained.
Explain what is the dictatorship of the working people.

The tasks were outlined as the following:-

1. Building the Party through:-
   (a) Sinking ML ideas among the working class and working people - Socialism
       Classes
   (b) Organisation of the masses through zonal councils and other organs of popular
       democracy, mass organisations, culture, sports, etc.
2. Building the economy:-
   (a) Raising production.
   (b) Strengthening our ties with the Socialist countries.
3. Strengthening our defense capacity.

The following important points were made:

1. The need to agree with analysis made.
2. Decide on tasks from the analysis and order of prioritisation.
3. The need to creatively apply the guidelines.
4. Organisational/tactical considerations to bear in mind; How does the Party develop its work among the masses?

ese observations were also made:-

Many comrades have lost a sense of perspective over the past few years.
We should have a new Party programme to replace the 1973 Manifesto.
Written explanation(s) re why we are on this path of development has not been done.
We are now more organised than one year ago (quantity has chnaged to quality).
In the last 3 1/2 years our main areas of focus have been on:- bringing benefits to
the masses; mass organisations; popular organs of democracy; construction and
defense

should decentralize sports and cultural activities?
we have had insufficient discussion on the character of the Revolution; we are
now entering a new stage

e following was given as some guidelines to deciding What is the Character of the
volution (political):-

the Revolution is anti-imperialist and is at the national democratic stage
our Party is more and more on the trend of the working class - it has that orientation;
has a working class leadership/has a working class outlook
it is not the Party that holds power by itself; we need and have an alliance with
sections of the national bourgeoisie
the class essence of the Revolution since March 13, 1979 has always been that of the
dictatorship of the working people in alliance with the national bourgeoisie; however,
the latter does not enjoy the same rights as the former
generally, there has been no fear in locking up members of the bourgeoisie - they do
not have control over the State; are not involved in the zonal councils, militia, etc.
we have pursued very good strategy and tactics and have dealt with the things that
really matter
there are different forms/methods/structures for strengthening the alliance with

the national bourgeoisie
the question may be asked why do we need that alliance? To help run the economy
the peasantry and the working class also have an alliance; the material for this is
the exchange of the commodities produced by each other
the working class does not have monopoly over power; it has hegemony over power

t was pointed out that the <u>Non-Capitalist Path or the Path of Socialist Orientation</u>
as not fully understood by all comrades. Under this, these points were made:-

this can be led by different classes and strata - petty bourgeoisie or the working
class must be the dominant class
only the working class can build Socialism because only them that own no property
- we must build the State sector into becoming the dominant sector
- we have set up a rivalry for the banking system through the establishment of the NCB
- have been getting the private sector into areas of investment we want them to get
into
- we cannot have control on foreign trade unless we have control on the financial institutions - the aim is to have total control over these
- MNIB presently has $35M worth of stock; between January - March 1982, 294,000 lbs
of farmers produce was sold by MNIB; one in every ten farmers sell their produce to
the MNIB
- internal distribution; public utilities (electricity, water and telephone) are very
important
- manufacturing sector also important
- must decide on what we want to use tourism for - the total cost of investment in this
area will be $350M (International Airport, hotels, etc.)
$17M will be earned in the 9th year of the International Airport
must concentrate/put effort into tourism/agriculture/industry and the industrialisation
of agriculture
the danger of the path we are taking is that the bourgeoisie will try to take power

n the question of Culture:-

- all local prostitutes should be picked up
- the foreign prostitutes should be deported
- the Ministry of Culture should have control over the cultural groups; they should all
have Political Commissars attached to them

- ideological work is important, even while continuing on the economic development
- the path is very dangerous because it hasn't been tried before.

These key questions/points were raised:-

- How do we effect the alliance with the bourgeoisie?
- At what point do we merge the urban and rural workers committees
- we must try to see how we can tie in the organisational tactics with the broad
overall objectives, bearing in mind the priorities
- we have not been giving the working class enough attention - as much as it needs;
we have treated all committees as equals, but the workers committee should take priority; how do we put this into reality

104 - 4

2. ALL CONCLUSIONS

2.1 The writing of CC minutes needs to be improved.
2.2 Many committee heads/study guides do not pass down the thinking of the CC to

their relevant bodies.

2.3 The security aspect of the Secretariat to be looked at with a view to being improved.

2.4 The weekend members study report to be used as a preliminary help re the discussion/formulation of a line of march/way forward.

2.5 The guidelines for the formulation of a line of march/way forward should be discussed at all levels of the Party.

2.6 There is need for a new Party Programme to replace the 1973 Manifesto.

2.7 The character of the Revolution can be described as anti-imperialist and at the national democratic stage.

2.8 The Party is being guided more and more by the outlook of the working class.

2.9 Must place importance/lay emphasis on our economic development and make strides towards the path of socialist orientation.

2.10 Must recognise the importance of our alliance with sections of the national bourgeoisie at present.

3. DECISIONS/RESOLUTIONS

3.1 The CC minutes to follow the 5-Heading proposal made by Cde. Coard.

3.2 The Education Committee to examine closely and make concrete recommendations re the proposal that YFR building be used to start a Party School. Education Committee meeting dfixed for 14th September.

3.3 The O.C. to follow up on the proposal that a fraternal comrade come to assist us in Party Building.

3.4 The Weekend Members study Report to be used as a guide to the Candidate Members'. and Members' discussion (re the members report contents).

3.5 The guidelines for developing a line of march for the upcoming period to be drafted into resolution or directive form by Comrades Strachan and Ventour. This to be sent to Study Guides and Committee Chairmen.

A presentation on the line of march/way forward to be made by the Comrade Leader at the two upcoming General Meetings.

MINUTES OF EXTRA-ORDINARY MEETING OF THE CENTRAL COMMITTEE OF NJM FROM TUESDAY 12th - FRIDAY 15th OCTOBER, 1982

105

Present:-

Maurice Bishop	Ewart Layne	Chris DeRiggs
George Louison	Phyllis Coard	
Selwyn Strachan	Leon Cornwall	
Unison Whiteman	Kamau McBarnette	
Kenrick Radix	Caldwell Taylor	
Hudson Austin	Fitzroy Bain	
Lian James ✓	Ian St. Bernard	
Chalkie Ventour	Tan Bartholomew ✓	

On Tuesday 12th October, 1982, the Central Committee of NJM was convened by CC Chairman Cde. Maurice Bishop in/an extra-ordinary plenary to discuss a letter of resignation from Cde. Bernard Coard, Deputy Party Leader and to examine the issues raised in the latter related to the state of the Party and the crisis in the work of the higher organs.

Within the period of the meeting, the CC held four sessions totalling 32 hours. The crisis in the work of the higher organs was analysed, the performance of each member of the CC was assessed and a number of decisions on the way forward were taken

Subsequent to two hours of initial deliberations, the CC settled on an approach to the meeting. Cde. Strachan was asked to summarise his discussions with Cde. Coard in relation to the matter of his resignation. Cde. Strachan made the following points:-

i) Cde. Coard had indicated that his decision to resign from PB and CC was taken 6 months previously;

ii) His decision to resign from OC was primarily on account of strain but this was hastened by certain developments - linked to this was the undermining of his authority as Chairman of the OC.

iii) He had made reference to the slackness of the CC and its unwillingness to speak up on issues, the lack of preparation for meetings by CC comrades, and the unwillingness of the CC to study.

iv) In order to take corrective action it would result in personality clashes with the Chairman of the CC.

v) His presence was a fetter to the development of the CC if viewed dialectically.

vi) His resignation is not negotiable.

vii) In the final analysis stringent Leninist measures are required.

The meeting also listened to what was explained to be the main theoretical options presented by Cde. Coard to the Central Committee:-

i) His own resignation

ii) He remains and tolerates slackness of CC and PB

iii) The introduction of Leninist measures, namely:-

a) Change Chairmanship of CC

b) Chop dead weight from CC

c) Put all members of CC into work committees

d) Expand the Political Bureau

The meeting agreed to address itself to the issues raised by Cde. Coard in his conversation with several CC members. Cde. Layne was asked to comment on resolutions and decisions taken by the Central Committee since April, 1981 relating to the introduction of Leninist measures in the Party. Cde. Layne pointed to the following:-

<u>April, 1981:</u> The resolution of the CC addressed itself to:-

      a. Tight chairmanship
      b.   application of high standards of discipline and self-critical approach by all committees
      c. The setting up of a Secretariat and appointment of Recording Secretaries.

<u>September, 1981:</u> Analysis was done on:-

      a. state of comrades' health
      b. lack of personal work plans

      Decisions:-
      a. CC would meet once per month
      b. CC would draft schedule of rest for comrades
      c. CC members would do personal work plans

<u>December, 1981:</u> In this period some 30 hours of review was done - a look was taken at earlier resolutions on strengths and weaknesses. The following was concluded:-

      a. There was a lack of follow up work and a failure to implement major decisions.
      b. Information on decisions taken was not sent down to all levels of the Party.

<u>April, 1982:</u> The CC considered problems related to:-
      a. discipline   e. arrogance throughout the Party
      b. study   f. work performance of members of the
      c. standards   higher organs
      d. planning   g.   of information

<u>June, 1982:</u> The CC analysis of the Party had indicated that:
      i) There was a collapse of nearly all areas of Party work, namely:-

         a. workers   c. women
         b. youth   d. state

In this period the mood of the masses had been described as lower than May Day. The work of the CC had been described as bureaucratic and giving no guidance to work committees.

<u>July, 1982:</u>   In discussing the present state of the Party, the following weaknesses were pointed out:-

      a. control mechanisms were not working
      b. there was looseness in Party organisation
      c. activities were controlling the work of the CC
      d. a Party School was required for Party members to master the science of Marxism-Leninism.

The CC agreed that there were certain recurring, glaring weaknesses:-
      i) the improper functioning of Central Committee and Political Bureau
      ii) the lack of control at the level of Chairmanship
      iii) the low level of discipline by members of the leading organs

Comrades also sited additional evidence of the crisis:-

i) lack of collectivity in building the Party – few PB and CC comrades were giving serious thought to the work and this resulted in low levels of participation in the work;

ii) PB and CC had been "ducking" the real issues;

iii) there was dead weight at CC and PB level and this urgently had to be addressed;

iv) the CC was not studying while seeking to tackle the most explosive issues of the Church and the land.

The CC also addressed itself to the Basis for the crisis:

1. Material Basis: The material basis for the crisis could be found in the backward and underdeveloped nature of our society and the consequent existence of a large petty bourgeois influence in our society. This predominant petty bourgeois composition of the society as a whole reflected in the practical work of the CC.

2. The Political and Ideological Basis: As seen in the failure of the CC to study for close to one year which has weakened the extent to which the ideology of Marxism-Leninism acts as a guide to the actions of the members of the higher organs. This failure to study is definitely linked to the non-Leninist manner of functioning, slackness, timidity and "ducking" from making principled criticisms.

3. The Organisational Basis: Seen in the poor functioning of many Party structures, the non-Leninist practices of comrades of higher organs, the inadequate functioning of other Party members in work committees, the lack of reporting, and the objecively based ____ inability of the O.C. to deal with all matters of discipline further feeds and allows petty bourgeois tendencies to dominate the life of the higher organs of the Party.

CROSSROADS

The CC concluded that the Party stood at the crossroads:-

i. The first route would be the petty bourgeois route which would seek to make B's resignation the issue. This would only lead to temporary relief, but would surely lead to the deterioration of the Party into a social-democratic Party and hence the degeneration of the Revolution. This road would be an easy one to follow given the objectively based backwardness and petty bourgeois nature of the society.

ii. The second route is the Communist route – the road of Leninist standards and functioning, the road of democratic centralism, of selectivity, of criticism and self-criticism and of collective leadership. The Central Committee reaffirmed the position taken by the General Meeting of September 12th and 13th, 1982 – the Party must be placed on a firm Leninist footing.

INDIVIDUAL ASSESSING

The CC agreed on the following format for assessing the performance of each individual CC member:-

1. Discipline – consistent political work.

2. Ideological level – including attitude to study.

3. Work performance – including professional approach, ability to supervide and guide, technical and professional job skills.

4. Relations with the masses – including the question of being an outstanding example.

5. Character/Integrity – including respect for the working class, co-operativeness, modesty, self-criticism, honesty, arrogance and timidity.

6. Analysing ability – including ability to cope with difficult situations,

judgement, appreciation of strategy and tactics, overall leadership
qualities.
7. Dues, attitude to Party and State property.
8. Functionability - general performance as a CC Member.

The scores on the following table summarises the collective assessment of the performance
of each CC member. It should however be pointed out that the CC was particularly disatisfied with the performance of the following comrades:-

        i.   Cde. Kenrick Radix
       ii.   Cde. Caldwell Taylor
     iii.   Cde. Kamau McBarnette
      iv.   Cde. Fitzroy Bain
       v.   Cde. Unison Whiteman

In the case of Cde. Kenrick Radix, the Central Committee had taken note of his lack of
political work, his extremely bad attitude to study and deep seated individualism and
petty bourgeois opportunist attitude to criticism. The consensus was that his performance
was exceedingly below that befitting of a CC member.

In the case of Cde. Caldwell Taylor it was also the view that his performance did not
measure up, particularly his low level of ideological development and sign of deviation
into mysticism.

A S S E S S M E N T

	DISCIPLINE	IDEOLOGICAL LEVEL	WORK PER-FORMANCE	RELATIONS WITH THE MASSES	CHARACTER	ANALYSING ABILITY	DUES	FUNCTIONABILITY
Okusu	3	4	2.5 to 3	4.5 to 5	2.5	3	5	2.5
Kojo	3	3	4	2	2	3.5	1	2.5
Headache	3.5 to 4	4	3.5 to 4	3	2	2	2	3 to 3.5
H.A.	2	2	2	2	2	2	5	2
Chalkie	4	3	3	4	3.5	4	5	3.5
Fitzie	2	1	2	4.5	3	1	2	2
Bogo	2.5	3	2	2 to 2.5	2.5 to 3	2	0	2.5 to 3
Caldwell	0	2	4	3	2.5	2.5	0	2
Dix	0	1	1	2.5	0	1	5	1.5
Unie	2	2.5	3	4	2.5	3.5	5	3
Phyllis	3.5	4	4	1.5	2.5	4	2	3.5 to 4
George	4.5	4 to 4.5	4	4	4	4	2	4.5
Sallo	4.5	4	4.5	4	3.5 to 4	4.5	5	4.5
Maurice	2.5	3	4.5	5	4.5	4	5	3.5
Ian	2.5	2.5	2 to 2.5	3	2.5	2.5	4.5	2
Tan	4.5	2.5	3.5 +	3.5	3.5	2	3	3
Kawau	2	2	2	1.5	1.5	2	2	1.5

Key: Scale of 1 to 5:

5: highest possible score
0: lowest " "
+: upward trend
-: downward trend

1. DISCIPLINE

i. The CC established a Disciplinary Committee under the authority of the O.C. to handle all matters related to Party discipline.

ii. The Disciplinary Committee comprises   following:-
    a. Cde. Selwyn Strachan
    b. Cde. Dave Bartholomew
    c. Cde. Ian St. Bernard
    d. Cde. Nelson Louison
    e. Cde. Faye Thompson

iii. This Committee will draw up a Code of Conduct and Discipline to be submitted to be submitted the CC by December 10, 1982.

2. PARTY CONSTITUTION

i. A Party Sub-Committee has been established to work on the existing draft of the Party's Constitution.

ii. The Committee comprises the following:-

    a. Cde. Maurice Bishop
    b. Cde. George Louison
    c. Cde. Selwyn Strachan

iii. This committee must complete its work by the end of January, 1983.

3. MEETINGS OF THE C.C. AND P.B.

The following procedures will govern the conduct of meetings of CC, PB.:-

        i.   Leninist Chairmanship
        ii. Discussions will be conducted on the basis of pre-scheduled agendas.
             a. Cdes. Strachan and DeRiggs will prepare a dfaft pre-scheduled agenda for CC meetings by the end of November, 1982.
             b. Cdes. Bishop, Strachan and Louison will prepare a draft pre-scheduled agenda for PB meetings by October 22, 1982.
        iii. Decisions will be made in the form of resolutions or conclusions.
        iv. Meetings will start an time and end on time.
        v.   There will be a specific duration for each discussion.
        vi. Members of the CC and PB will take careful notes in all meetings.
        vii. The Chairman will determine who speaks at any given point in time.

4. SEQUENCE OF CC MEETINGS

i.   The CC will meet quarterly for five days of intensive wholistic assessing.
ii. This quarterly review will start at the end of March, 1983.
iii. The regular monthly CC meetings will be pahsed out.
iv. Between the present period and the end of the year, the CC will meet on three (3) ocassions to look at specific areas. The CC will meet on November 4 - 5, 1982 to look at the Economy (8.00 a.m. to 6.00 p.m. on both days).
     The CC will meet from 8.00 a.m. to 6.00 p.m. on December 10, 1982 to look at the re-organisation of the Party. The CC will use the last of the five (5) day study (Tuesday 19 - Saturday 23, October 1982) to take decisions on Land Reform.

5. WORKPLANS AND WORK SCHEDULES

i.   All members of the CC and PB will prepare yearly workplans. The workplans

2/...

for 1983 will be presented to the Secretariat by mid-January, 1983.

iii. All members of the CC and PB will prepare quarterly (3-monthly) workplans. Those for the period January - March, 1983 will be presented by mid-January, 1983.

iv. The aforementioned schedules and workplans will be assessed on a quaartly basis.

v. Each member of the CC and PB will submit self-assesment on the fullfilment of their workplans/schedules in writing on a quarterly basis at the quaterly CC meetings.

vi. These documents will be submitted to the Party Secretariat.

6. CONTROL CARDS/FILES FOR CC MEMBERS

i. A system of building files on each member of the CC will be commenced.

ii. These files will contain such information as:-
a. The records of CC members based on the quarterly assessing.
b. Comrades' workplans and workschedules.

iii. Cde. Strachan will be in charge of this area and the system of filing must commence before the end of October, 1982.

7. PERSONAL ASSISTANTS

i. Each member of the CC will acquire a personal assistant of Secretary by the end of November, 1982.

ii. A Personal Assistant of high political reliability and efficiency will be found for the Comrade Party Leader by the end of December, 1982. All CC members are to assist in obtaining such person.

8. DOCUMENTATION AND MINUTES

i. Documents to be discussed in CC and PB meetings must be submitted to all CC/PB members one week in advance.

ii. The Party Secretariat will prepare guidelines on the format for reporting by middle of November, 1982.

iii. A CC comrade, namely Cde. Strachan be given the task of sending out important CC resolutions to CC comrades abroad.

iv. The minutes of CC and PB minutes will indicate the arrival times of members. A record of punctuality will also be kept of study.

9. CC MEMBERS AND THEIR INVOLVEMENT IN MASS AND POLITICAL WORK

i. Every member of the CC will supervise an area of mass work or political work. The details of this decision will be worked out by the CC at its meeting of December 10,1982.

ii. The Comrade Leader will be put in charge of supervising the rural workers work. Supervision means:-
a. Meeting with the Rural Workers Committee to prepare a Work Plan.
b. At least one monthly meeting with the committee to provide guidance in strategy and tactics and organisation.

iii. Cde. Fitzroy Bain will present a paper on the political issues involved in this are of work by December, 1982.

10. CENTRAL COMMITTEE STUDY

i. The CC will immediately resume study. The first regular session will be Thursday November 11, 1982.

ii. There shall be an intensive 5 day study for the CC to start on Tuesday October 19 and end on Saturday October 23, 1982.

iii. The study material shall be:

    a. Organisational Principles of a Proleterian Party
    b. Lenin on the Transformation of Agriculture
    c. Political Economy of Capitalism

iv. A more scientific method of assessing Comrades' level or preparedness will be utilised. Cde. Louison will prepare a draft evaluation scheme by Tuesday October 19, 1982 and will present it to the CC study group.

v.   Disciplinary action will be taken against CC members who are late or absent without good excuse. This will be subject to the Code of Conduct and Discipline.

vi. A crash course in Marxism-Leninism will be organised for the following comrades:-

    a. Austin   d. Taylor
    b. Bain   e. Bartholomew
    c. Whiteman

Cde. Bernard Coard will be asked to handle this course which will begin in two weeks time for a duration of 8 weeks.

vii. The material for the crash course will include the following:

    a. Dialectics by J.V. Stalin
    b. Found tioms of Leninism by J.V. Stalin
    c. The three sources and three component parts of Marxism

viii. Comrade Louison will act as CC Study Guide.

11. TIMIDITY AND CONSULTATIONS

i.   It is considered a serious violation of the norms of Party life for any CC member to have knowledge of any problem which affects the Leninist functioning of the Party and fails to raise the said problem at CC meetings.

ii. CC members have the right to consultations and bilaterals but should not display timidity in tabling issues for full CC discussion.

12. DEVELOPING LEADERSHIP OUTSIDE OF THE CC

i.   Conscious efforts will be made to develop leadership outside the CC.

ii. In this respect membership of the Party will be fed with information and will be provided with background to the strategy and tactics of CC resolutions.

iii. The CC will utilise the Parish General Meetings to brief members on CC resolutions.

13. MEMBERSHIP OF CC AND PB

The following decisions were made on the question of membership of the CC and PB.

i.   Cde. Radix has been removed from membership of the PB and CC.

ii. Cde. Taylor has been removed from membership of the CC.

iii. The details of Cde. Taylor's future political and state work will be worked out by the PB. Cde. Taylor will be recalled to Grenada in two weeks time to inform him of the CC's decision.

iv. Cde. McBarnette is put on a probationary period of 6 months. He will

./...

take immediate rest from all political and state work for a period of one
month. During this period he will also receive medical attention.
v.   Cde. Bain is put on a probationary period of 6 months.
vi. Cdes. Bain and M. Barnette will be assessed in March, 1983.
vii. Cde. Whiteman will be severely warned for his weak performance.

14. EXPANSION OF THE POLITICAL BUREAU

i.   Cdes. Ventour, Layne and James have been made members of the PB.
ii. Cde. Phyllis Coard will be assessed in March on the question of membership of the Political Bureau.

15. The CC accepts the resignation of Cde. Bernard Coard from the CC and PB. The details of this will be worked out by the Political Bureau.

16. ORGANISATION OF PB's WORK

i.   The PB is directed to organise its work according to the idea of "clusters of work".
ii. The PB will report to the CC on this by December 10, 1982. A sub-committee of Cdes. Strachan, Louison and Bishop to look at it.

17. PARTY PROGRAMME

i.   A Sub-Committee of the Party will draft a new Party Programme.
ii. The sub-committee comprises:

a. Cde. Louison
b. Cde. Phyllis Coard

iii. The deadline for the completion of the draft programme is March, 198

FOREIGN RELATIONS REPORT

THEORETICAL PERSPECTIVE OF FOREIGN POLICY

Foreign policy is the extension internationally of domestic policy. It is the projection on the international scene of the national policy line pursued on the homefront.

This does not mean that a country's domestic policy can be simply shifted to and imposed on the international scene. What it means is that the foreign policy of a country has to be rooted in its domestic situation; in its politics, its philosophy, its economy, its geography - these factors are the main determinants of a country's foreign policy.

While the major determinants of a country's foreign policy are of a domestic nature, external factors also impact upon the foreign policy line. Therefore, the foreign policy must always be sensitive and alert to the dynamic regional and international situations and must be cognizant at all times of the world's constellation and array of forces. Foreign policy has to be flexible enough to respond to changes in these situations and in the international status quo.

GRENADA'S FOREIGN POLICY

Grenada's Foreign Policy reposes on the scientific ideological foundation irreconcilably opposed to the exploitation and domination of nation by nation. This is consistent with Grenada's domestic policy which is opposed to the exploitation of man to man. Thus, Grenada's foreign policy is inevitably manifested through non-alignment, anti-imperialism and peaceful co-existence.

(See "Grenada's Foreign Policy" Annex   )

/ Needs ......

NEEDS AND GOALS OF GRENADA'S FOREIGN RELATIONS

Arising out of its domestic situation a country's foreign relations is geared to fulfilling certain concrete needs and accomplishing clearly defined goals. For Grenada twelve such needs and goals have been outlined:

(1) grants; (2) soft loans; (3) lines of credit;

(4) machinery and equipment (either through loans or gifts;

(5) technical assistance; (6) markets - guaranteed longterm;

(7) tourism; (8) diplomatic support; (9) moral and political support; (10) military and security consideration; (11) material support; (12) electoral support.

These needs and goals are grounded in Grenada's domestic reality of underdevelopment and economic backwardness. Another significant determinant is Grenada's geographic reality as a small island state lacking vital economic endowments such as: (i) a viable infrastructure; (ii) human resources (especially skilled and trained personnel); (iii) a resilient resource base; (iv) a large market; (v) financial resources; (vi) a diversified economy; (vii) natural resources.

The accent on support in Grenada's foreign relations is determined not only by domestic factors but is significantly influenced by the regional and international situation. The Grenada Revolution, the supreme factor delineating Grenada's reality, is confronted by the hostility and might of U.S. imperialism. As a small country Grenada requires extensive and intensive international support to combat successfully U.S. imperialism. The foreign relations must reflect this need for support. Grenada's foreign relations must be the front line of the defence of the Glorious March 13th Revolution.

ISSUES AND CONCERNS OF GRENADA'S FOREIGN POLICY

Grenada's foreign policy has been consistent. The major themes are constantly reflected in the foreign policy statements,

' in ....

in the speeches by the Foreign Minister and other Ministers both in international forums and before the assemblies of Grenadian people.

Common themes are (1) the call for world peace; (2) the question of detente; (3) disarmament; (4) the resumption of the SALT II talks; (5) peaceful coexistence. Also, on the question of peace Grenada has pioneered and continues to champion the concept of the Caribbean as a zone of peace. On this Grenada was able to have a Resolution adopted by the Organization of American States (OAS) at its Assembly in La Paz, Bolivia in 1979.

Central also to Grenada's foreign policy pronouncements and positions are the hallowed principles of non-alignment - anti-imperialism, anti-racism, anti-zionism, anti-colonialism, anti-neo-colonialism, anti-fascism as well as irreconcilable opposition to the hosting of military bases.

The principles of national sovereignty, respect for the territorial integrity of states, the legal equality of states, the right to develop one's own politics-socio-economic process free from outside interference, non-intervention in the domestic affairs of states and ideological pluralism are consistently stated in and defended by Grenada's foreign policy.

Revolutionary Grenada has steadfastly supported the call for a New International Economic Order (NIEO) and for the democratisation of the international economic system especially the international monetary system. Along with this call Grenada has advocated the widening and strengthening of South-South Cooperation, Economic and Technical Cooperation among Developing Countries (ECDC) (TCDC).

Beginning with the Commonwealth Heads of Government Meeting in Lusaka, Zambia, August 1979, Revolutionary Grenada has led

/ the ....

the call for special consideration and assistance for small island states, a category of states facing particular problems. At the meeting of Foreign Ministers of the Non Aligned Movement, New Delhi, India 9-13 February, 1981 Grenada was able to have the movement recommend that the problems of small island states be particularly considered.

(For more on Grenada's position on small island states see the Prime Minister's speech in Aruba in Annex   )

In sum then Grenada's foreign policy is very active. It addresses itself to the international situation and issues of the day reflects the national interest, and concerns.

CONSTRUCT OF THE WORLD

The world, as the Ministry of External Affairs has it, is divided into seven (7) geopolitical regions. They are (1) the Americas; (2) Eastern Europe; (3) the Middle East; (4) Western Europe; (5) The Caribbean; (6) Africa; (7) the Far East.

Of course these geopolitical regions satisfy Grenada's foreign policy needs and interests to different extents and levels. Therefore, the degree of closeness in the relationship between Grenada and each of the regions is not uniformed. This also holds for Grenada's relations with individual countries.

GRENADA DIPLOMATIC MISSIONS

Grenada currently maintains seven (7) embassies abroad. These are in Cuba, Venezuela, the United Kingdom, Belgium (the EEC), Canada, the OAS/USA Mission and the United Nations Mission in the United States.

Plans are fully in train to establish an Embassy in Iraq. Grenada's Ambassador designate to Iraq is Mr. O. Benjamin.

The possibility of setting up an Embassy in the Union of Soviet Socialist Republic (USSR) is also being actively explored and should be realised before the end of 1981.

/Grenada ....

GRENADA AND THE AMERICAS

As can be perceived from the fact that Grenada maintains five missions in the Americas, this is a region of importance to Grenada. For one, many of Grenada's nationals reside in the U.S.A., Canada, and Venezuela. The missions in these countries have the high responsibility of looking after the interests of these nationals abroad. Secondly, many of these nationals are able and are willing to assist the revolutionary process unfolding in Grenada economically, financially and politically. The missions have the task of mobilising the nationals abroad to that end. In this regard the missions have done good work particularly the OAS and UN Missions.

Since Grenada seeks to develop very close relations with the Latin American countries despite the language difference our relations with this region shows Grenada as involved in many organisations and groupings which bring together the countries of the region. SELA, ECLA, OLADE, the OAS, IICA, are examples of groupings in which Grenada develops relations with the Latin American countries. Grenada has diplomatic relations with 11 of the Latin American Countries (See Annex   ) but has ambassadors accredited to only two countries. This will be improved shortly as Cde. Richard Jacobs, Ambassador to Cuba, is Ambassador designate to Panama, Nicaragua and Mexico while Cde. Matthew William, Ambassador to Venezuela, is Ambassador designate to Colombia and Ecuador. Cde. Vernon Simon is the Ambassador designate to Surinam and should present his letters of credence in June 1981. Five Latin American countries have ambassadors accredited to Grenada; only two are resident.

Grenada's most remarkable foreign policy initiative in Latin America was to pioneer the concept of the Caribbean Sea as a Zone of Peace and to have the OAS Assembly in 1979 adopt a positive Resoultion on this in La Paz, Bolivia. Other countries have recently attempted to pretend to be the pioneers and supreme champions of the concept. Grenada must not allow this farce to be

/ successful ......

successful and must tighten up its definition of Caribbean and the Zone of Peace concept and take it into other forums such as the United Nations, the Non-Aligned Movement and CARICOM.

On the El Salvador question Grenada's position is clear and irrevocable: the Junta in El Salvador is a genocidal regime backed solely by U.S. imperialism and devoid of any internal base and consequently any legitimacy. The rtue and authentic representative of the Salvadorean people in the Frente Democratico Revolucionario (FDR).

Grenada has excellent, relations with the Revolutionary Governments, people and countries of Nicaragua and Cuba. Grenada desires the closest relations with these two countries. Grenada has several agreement with Cuba and receives tremendous and invaluable assistance from Cuba in numerous areas - the New International Airport, Fisheries, Education, Military, Agriculture, Health. Cuba has also consistently supported and defended Grenada in international forums.

Nicaragua has also supported Grenada internationally and Grenada has received technical assistance, in the form of military uniforms, from Nicaragua. Grenada in return has supported and defended Nicaragua internationally being the second country to recognise the Provisional Government of National Reconstruction in 1979 and Grenada sent two teachers to assist the Nicaraguans in their literacy programme in 1980.

Grenada has alos received technical assistance from Panama (training of policemen), Mexico (scholarships in sports), Argentina (1,000 tins of wheat in 1980) and Venezuela. The Venezuelans have given assistance in several areas: Health, Communication (a new beacon for Pearls Airport), Sports, Energy. A technical assistance agreement between Venezuela and Grenada exists and covers areas like raods. Brazil has extended to Grenada a line of credit for the new people's plane chartered by LIAT.

/ In ....

In addition the above Grenada will soon be holding discussions with Brazil and Mexico to explore and arrange areas for technical assistance and cooperation. A delegation from Grenada is due to visit Mexico for this purpose in June. Already a delegation headed by Lyden Ramdhanny, member of the P.R.G. has visited Brazil for similar discussions. Out of these discussions the plane emerged.

Grenada's relations with Latin America has been active at many levels. One thinks though that there is room to intensify and widen these relations. For one, Argentina, like Brazil, Mexico and Venezuela, is among the most developed countries in region. Perhaps the same initiative pursued in regards to intensive discussions with Mexico, Brazil and Venezuela for technical assistance and cooperation agreements can be pursued with Argentina who has indicated strong interest in the Caribbean countries of course the domestic policies of repression, the links with South Africa and Israel, the part she played in the Bolivian Coup, and the rumours of her interest in the South Atlantic Treaty Organisation (SATO), are factors which have to be considered and weighed before moving too close to Argentina. However, the possibility should at least be considered.

EASTERN EUROPE

Grenada now has diplomatic relations with all Eastern European Countries. However, Grenada has no diplomatic representation in Eastern Europe nor does she have any ambassador accredited to any Eastern European Country on a non-resident basis. The U.S.S.R., the G.D.R., Bulgaria, Hungary and Czechoslovakia all have ambassadors accredited to Grenada on a non-resident basis.

Despite the lack of representation Grenada's relations with the Eastern European countries is substantial. Grenada has Trade agreements and Scientific and Technical agreements with the USSR, Hungary, Bulgaria, Czechoslovakia, the GDR and Poland. Under these agreements and the many Protocols attached to some of them

Grenada has received material assistance from Eastern Europe - means of transport, scholarships and assistance in agriculture among other areas.

Grenada's relations with Eastern Europe was significantly developed and began to bear fruit after two visits to that region by Deputy Prime Minister Cde. Bernard Coard in 1979 and 1980. The Cde. Deputy Prime Minister also attended the 26 CPSU Congress in 1981 and further developed Grenada's relations with the USSR.

Grenada perceives the key role the Socialist Community has played in defending the developing countries and is consolidating the hard won independence of these countries. Also, the support National Liberation Movement have had from the Socialist Community has been tremendous and often decisive. Thus, for Grenada the Eastern European Countries can be a real source of political and diplomatic support apart from the vast potential they have for technical and economic assistance. For these two reasons Grenada must continue intensifying its relations with Eastern Europe. Therefore, the possibility of establishing an Embassy in Moscow must be seriously and positively explored.

Another initiative in Eastern Europe which must be considered is a visit to Romania. At the recent meeting of Grenada's Heads of Missions in March 1981, Butler House, Belmont, St. George's, Grenada, High Commissioner to Canada, Cde. Jimmy Emmanuel, reported that the Romanians had approached him expressing interest in having the Cde. Prime Minister visit Romania.

THE MIDDLE EAST

Grenada recognises that the Middle East with its petro wealth offers great scope for:

(i)   technical and economic assistance and cooperation;

(ii) Economic Cooperation among Developing Countries (ECDC) - South-South Cooperation;

(iii) a stronger role for the developing countries in the world economy.

Thus, Grenada's foreign relations with the Middle East has been guided by the recognition as well as by Grenada's principles of anti-zionism and anti-imperialism. Grenada has developed close relations with Algeria, Libya, Syria and Iraq. Today it has technical assistance arrangements with Libya, Algeria, Syria and Iraq and has received substantial assistance from these countries. Algeria is providing all the oil, gas, used by the machines employed in the construction of the New International Airport for 1981.

Grenada's relations with these Middle East countries was strengthened and developed after Prime Minister Maurice Bishop visited them in 1980. The Prime Minister brough back over EC$21m. in grants. The possibility of a visit to other Middle East countries such as the United Arab Emirates (UAE) and Kuwait is currently being explored.

Mr. Ashley Taylor, Legal Adviser to the Minister of External Affairs, visited Algeria and Libya in April 1981 as part of the mobilisation for the recently concluded Co-financing Conference for the international airport held in Brussels, Belgium in mid April 1981. Also, it is likely that the Deputy Prime Minister will pay a visit to Libya, Algeria and Iraq this May 1981.

Thus, Grenada has pursued an active policy in the Middle East designed mainly to harness the immense potential the region has for grants, lines of credit, soft loans, technical assistance and energy. However, Grenada's Middle East policy is also geared to develop close relations with the anit-imperialist, anti-zionist forces in the region and to support the Just Struggle of the Palestinian people. Thus, Grenada has recognised the PLO as the legitimate representative of the Palestinian people and remains unswerving in its conviction that no settlement can take place without the involvement of the PLO. Therefore, Grenada has taken a position irreconcilably opposed to the Camp David Agreement.

On the Iraq-Iran war Grenada supports the initiatives taken by the Non-Aligned Movement to mediate between the two countries and bring a Just solution to the conflict. The war between two anti-imperialist countries, tow members of the Non-Aligned Movement, two members of OPEC, two anti-zionist countries is fundamentally regrettable particularly as it consumes tremendous energy and resources which could have been gainfully utilised in the anti-imperialist, anti-zionist struggle.

It must be pointed out here that despite the invaluable assistance Grenada has received from the Mid East, finance, energy, patrol boats from Libya, Grenada has no diplomatic representation in the region. Grenada has diplomatic relations with seven (7) countries in the Middle East but has not even a non-resident ambassador accredited to any of the countries. It is therefore key that Grenada implements the decision to send Mr. O. Benjamin to Iraq as Ambassador

WESTERN EUROPE

Grenada has two missions in Western Europe:

(i) the High Commission to the United Kingdom;

(ii) the mission to the EEC located in Brussels, Belgium.·

Diplomatic relations have been established with 14 West European countries and ambassador accredited to eight.

As a source of tourism and as a market Western Europe is of importance to Grenada. Also, in the United Kingdom are many of Grenada's nationals; this adds importance to relations with Britain particularly as the British Nationality Bill is so topical. However, the Thatcher led government of Britain has adopted a hostile posture to Grenada and there has been very little bilateral contact between the two countries.

Grenada's more fruitful relations with Western Europe has been through the EEC Commission. The EEC has funded projects in Grenada including the building of community centres and the supply of milk.

The best known foreign relations initiative Grenada has made in Western Europe was the recent staging of the Co-financing Conference to mobilise funds for the International Airport.

Grenada has also sought through the Socialist International to develop strong relations withethe Social Democratic Parties of Western Europe some of which are in power in their countries. This is a policy which has tremendous potential for realising material assistance for Grenada. Also, through the Socialist International Grenada can make its contribution to detente disarmament and peace in Europe.

With France Grenada has a programme for Technical Cooperation. This includes road communication, energy bio gas, agriculture, mineral water and the training of teachers in French. These areas were raised by Grenada during the visit of the French Technical and Cultural Mission headed by one Mr. André in October, 1979. The victory of Francois Mitterand of the Socialist Party, a member of the Socialist International, in the recent presidential elections should permit closer cooperation with France.

---

*The EEC Mission covers many countries. See Annex

THE CARIBBEAN

Most of Grenada's relations with the Caribbean has been through the regional institutions: CARICOM and its Ministerial Committees, WISA (soon to be the Organisation of East Caribbean States (OECS). Grenada has been consistent in its attendance of most of the meetings, seminars and workshops organised by regional bodies.

The more important ones are the CARICOM Council of Ministers Meetings, the WISA Council of Ministers Meetings and the Meetings of the Standing Committee of Ministers Responsible for Foreign Affairs. In these forums, Grenada seeks to cooperate closely with its Caribbean counterparts while not sacrificing national goals and principles.

Grenada has agreed with the other Eastern Caribbean Countries on the transformation of the West Indies Associated States Council (WISA) into the Organisation of East Caribbean States (OECS). The OECS should come into being on 4th July. Grenada has agreed in principle but the proposed treaty must be carefully studied.

Despite the hostility of some Caribbean countries Grenada has displayed its good neighbourliness on several occasions; for one, after the Union Island uprising and the apprehension on on its territory of Bumba Charles, Grenada returned the latter to the Government of St. Vincent; again Grenada has offered, despite its weak economy, scholarships to the other countries in its Fisheries Training School.

In order to strenghten and promote its relations with the Caribbean, Grenada has designated a High Commissioner to CARICOM. Already St. Lucia and the Bahamas have agreed to Grenada's request to the Caribbean. St. Vincent has refused arguing to the effect that the relations should be on a multilateral basis; that is, through the regional institutions.

AFRICA

Grenada's main foreign policy concern in Africa thus far has been the situation in Southern Africa. In all international forums Grenada

has been very consistent in its condemnation of South Africa's
apartheid and racism, its illegal occupation of Namibia, its genocidal
repression of the South African and Namibian people and its military
aggression and acts of destabilisation against the Front Line States.

As a concrete manifestation of its commitment to the liberation
struggle in South Africa Grenada in February 1981 gave EC$50,000 to
the Namibian Liberation Fund set up by the Organisation of African
Unity. (OAU)

Due to the acute state of underdevelopment of the economies of
the African countries Grenada does not view Africa as a source of
financial and economic assistance. However, individual countries
such as Nigeria with its booming oil economy can provide substantial
assistance. As a matter of fact Grenada received a grant of some
EC$117,000 from Nigeria for banana rehabilitation in 1981. The po-
tential for intensifying relations with Nigeria exists and is being
developed.

Africa can be a source of great diplomatic moral and political
support. When the imperialist sponsored bomb went off on June 19,
1980 several African countries came out condemning the vicious attack.
Also, when U.S. imperialism attempted to sabotage the Co-financing
Conference held in Brussels recently the African countries of the ACP
all came out with a strong resolution condemning the manoeuvres of
the U.S.A.

Therefore, Grenada must intensify its diplomatic relations with
the African countries. Presently Grenada has relations only with
less than one half of the African countries and does not have an
ambassador accredited to any. Moves have been made to accredit
Cde. Fennis Augustine to the Front Line States. Grenada has recognised
and has established diplomatic relations with the Saharan Arab
Democratic Republic showing once again its support of just liberation
struggles.

FAR EAST

In Asia Grenada has developed close relations with very few countries. Diplomatic relations exists with nine countries and four have ambassadors accredited to Grenada while Grensda has one accredited.

Grenada has been critical of the South Korean fascists and has developed healthy relations with the Democratic People's Republic of Korea (DPRK)(North Korea). Cde. Selwyn Strachan's visit to the DPRK significantly firmed up relations while Korean trade and cultural delegations have visited Grenada. Also, the non-resident Ambassador Mr. Li Jung Ok has made several trips to Grenada. A technical and economic cooperation agreement between Grenada and the DPRK has been discussed and negotiated. One of the areas is an irrigation scheme on the Paradise Estate.

With India Grenada has discussed the possibility of technical assistance. This involves a cotton ginnery for Carriacou. Nothing definite has yet emerged from the discussions.

A Grenada delegation is scheduled to visit Mongolia and Vietnam very shortly. This visit should really widen and deepen Grenada's relations with those two countries of the Far East.

MEMBERSHIP IN INTERNATIONAL ORGANISATIONS

Grenada enjoys membership in several international organisations[*]. This reflects Grenada's active foreign policy geared to promote peace and cooperation among the members of the international community.

THE MOVEMENT OF NON-ALIGNED COUNTRIES

This international organisation is key to Grenada's foreign policy. Grenada joined the Movement in 1979 and was immediately made a member of the Coordinating Bureau. In the Movement Grenada has expressed organised support for the liberation struggles the world over and has

---

[*]
See Annex

reinforced its anti-imperialist, anti-colonialist character.

Reciprocally the Non-Aligned countries as a movement have expressed firm support for the Grenada Revolution. Statements to that effect were adopted by both the Havana Summit, 1979, and the Foreign Ministers' Meeting, New Delhi, February 1981. This moral and political support is indispensable for Grenada confronted as it is by U.S. imperialism; the point is that Grenada's membership in the Non-Aligned Movement is a weapon in the struggle against alien domination.

Grenada's membership in the Movement has earned it the respect and material support of many countries. It was through attendance of the Havana Summit that Prime Minister Maurice Bishop made the vital contact with the Middle East countries and was able to visit Algeria, Iraq, Libya and Syria subsequently and obtained tremendous financial and other assistance.

So far Grenada has not yet been very actively involved in the Coordinating Groups of the Movement; that is the groups of countries responsible for particular areas such as tourism, fisheries, women, housing, etc. Cde. Kendrick Radix recently attended the Fisheries Meeting in Cuba and it is expected that Sis. Phyllis Coard will attend the Women's meeting Cuba this May 1981. Attendance of the Meeting on Tourism in Cyprus, June 1981 should be actively explored. These Coordinating Groups can enhance Grenada's prestige and also bring concrete gains for Grenada.

THE UNITED NATIONS

Grenada has used the United Nations to maintain contact with the many countries in which it has no representation. This adds importance to Grenada's membership in the United Nations.

In that Organisation too Grenada has been able to show support for liberation movements, support initiatives for peace and disarmament and has been able to explain the Grenada Revolution. Grenada has not so far initiated any action in the U.N.

16/...

Membership in the United Nations has allowed Grenada to benefit from U.N. Agencies such as UNESCO, The United Nations Development Programme (UNDP) and The Economic Commission for Latin America (ECLA).

In 1979 Cde. Maurice Bishop addressed the 34th General Assembly of the United Nations while Cde. Selwyn Strachan addressed the 35th General Assembly in 1980.

SOCIALIST INTERNATIONAL

In the Socialist International Grenada has been able to show organised support for peace, peaceful co-existence, disarmament, detenté, cooperation between nations and for the national liberation struggles. Grenada's relations with the SI, developed through the attendance of its meetings by Cde. Unison Whiteman, has earned for Grenada statements of solidarity with the Grenada Revolution. These statements are of vital diplomatic and political importance.

Membership in the SI has also permitted Grenada to develop relations with progressive parties and sectors of Western Europe. Cde. Maurice Bishop's recent attendance of the SI Meeting in Holland served to make good contact with the leading personalities and parties of the SI.

THE COMMONWEALTH

Grenada's main interaction with this grouping was the attendance of the Heads of Governments Meeting in Lusaka, Zambia in 1979. In that meeting Grenada's main initiative in the Commonwealth was made; that is, the advocation of the need for special consideration and assistance for small island states. The Cde. Prime Minister lucidly presented a paper on small island states outlining clearly the severe constraints which these countries must surmount.

FOREIGN POLICY SUCCESSES AND ACHIEVEMENTS

Grenada has scored some successes in its foreign relations. Among these can be cited

    (i) promotion of the special situation of small island states - through its determined efforts Grenada has been able to

17/...

have a wide cross-section of the international
community recognise the particular problems confronting
small island states;

(ii) pioneering and championing of the concept of the
Caribbean Sea as a Zone of Peace - the OAS has recognised
it as such when in 1979, La Paz, Bolivia, Grenada tabled
a resolution which was subsequently passed;

(iii) being the second state to recognise the Provisional
Government of National Reconstruction in Nicaragua, June 1979.
This move consolidated the revolutionary process in
Nicaragua and accelerated Somoza's fall;

(iv) being the first state in the Western Hemisphere to
recognise the Saharan Arab Democratic Republic;

(v) giving material support, EC$50,000 to SWAPO;

(vi) the tremendous invaluable economic, financial and technical
assistance received from external sources.

BALANCE OF FORCES IN THE WORLD

Grenada's foreign policy, as can be perceived from the above
information, is highly active. It is rooted in Grenada's domestic
situation and is guided by Grenada's principles of non-alignment and
anti-imperialism. However, any successful foreign policy must be
aware of and respond to the international conjuncture.

One of the main characteristics of the present international conjuncture is the changing balance of forces. Previously imperialism
led by the U.S.A. held unchallenged sway over mankind. Now the
socialist community is strong and growing still. The U.S.S.R. is the
equal, at least, of the U.S.A. Other poles of power have developed
through the ability of the OPEC countries to exact from the rapacious
West adequate compensation for their natural resource: petroleum.

Thus, today when the U.S. imperialism launches economic aggression
against Revolutionary Nicaragua and Mozambique, refusing to sell them

wheat, the U.S.S.R. can supply the two countries with the necessary wheat. When the U.S.A. refuses to loan money to Nicaragua, Libya provides the money. When the CIA destabilises Angola and sends in mercenaries against the popular MPLA, Cuba moves to assist Angola militarily and successfully. When the U.S.A. tries to stop Grenada building an international airport other countries assist Grenada in the construction of the airport.

The point is that U.S. imperialism no longer holds sway over mankind. Though it remains powerful U.S. imperialism is on the decline. Today as oil rich Saudi Arabia increases its contribution to the International Monetary Fund and its voting power increases the basis for the U.S.A. veto control of the international monetary system is being eroded. Doubtless other oil-rich countries will follow the example of Saudi Arabia.

Thus, Grenada's foreign policy must be cognizant of and reflect this change in the balance of forces. A foreign policy which is not mindful of the international conjuncture is doomed to failure. As a country embarked on the construction of a revolution, the change in the world's balance of forces is for Grenada a positive factor.

106 - 18

LIST OF COUNTRIES WITH WHICH GRENADA
DOES NOT WISH TO DEVELOP CLOSE RELATIONS

(i)   BOLIVIA

(ii)   COMORO ISLANDS

(iii)   CHILE

(iv)   CHINA

(v)   EGYPT

(vi)   EL SALVADOR

(vii)   HAITI

(viii)   HONDURAS

(ix)   ISRAEL

(x)   GUATEMALA

(xi)   PARAGUAY

(xii)   SOUTH KOREA

(xiii)   TAIWAN

(xiv)   SOUTH AFRICA

(xv)   URUGUAY

(xvi)   ZAIRE

GRENADA'S MEMBERSHIP IN INTERNATIONAL AND REGIONAL ORGANISATIONS

CARICOM	-	Caribbean Community
CFTC	-	Commonwealth Technical Assistance Fund
CLAD	-	Latin American Centre for Development Administration
ACP/EEC Lomé Convention		
ECLA	-	Economic Commission for Latin America
FAO	-	Food and Agricultural Organization (UN Agency)
IBRD	-	International Bank for Reconstruction and Development (World Bank)
IMF	-	International Monetary Fund
IFAD	-	International Fund for Agricultural Development
IFC	-	International Finance Corporation
IICA	-	Inter-American Institute for Agricultural Cooperation
	-	Member of Commonwealth of Nations
	-	Non-Aligned Movement
OLADE	-	Latin American Energy Organization
OAS	-	Organization of American States
PAHO	-	Pan-American Health Organization
SI	-	Socialist International
UNO	-	United Nations Organization
UNESCO	-	United Nations Education, Scientific and Cultural Organization
UNCTAD	-	United Nations Conference on Trade and Development
WHO	-	World Health Organization (UN Agency)
WISA	-	West Indies Associated States

OUR COUNTRY IS IN DANGER

DRAFT RESOLUTION FROM THE CENTRAL COMMITTEE OF THE NEW JEWEL
MOVEMENT TO PARTY MEMBERS, SUPPORTERS AND THE BROAD MASSES OF THE
PEOPLE OF GRENADA, ON THE PRESENT NATIONAL SECURITY SITUATION
FACING OUR COUNTRY AND REVOLUTION

The Central Committee of the New Jewel Movement, having met and
analysed the current threat to our Peoples' Revolution, issues the
following call to our people:-

AN IMMEDIATE THREAT TO OUR REVOLUTION NOW EXISTS

(1)   The New Jewel Movement wants all party members as well as the
      entire people of Grenada to be fully conscious that there is
      now a real and serious danger of an immediate military attack
      in one form or another, against our country and revolution.
      Such an attack could come within a matter of days, or even
      hours. This is the most serious threat our country has faced
      since March 13th 1979.

(2)   The proof of this lies in the following:- On Budget Day, last
      Thursday, 17th March, the Comrade Leader of our party and
      Revolution, Prime Minister Maurice Bishop made a speech in
      which he warned of the danger of stepped-up military
      aggression in our region. This was followed, not even
      forty-eight (48) hours later, by the large-scale military
      invasion against Nicaragua which took place in the early
      hours of last Saturday morning, 19th March.

(3)   Our party's analysis of the threat to the region and to
      Grenada in particular, comes not only from the verbal attacks
      of senior officials of the U.S. administration not only from
      the major attacks by President Reagan against both Grenada and
      Nicaragua om March 10th; not only from the large scale
      military manoeuvres right now being conducted in our region.
      Our understanding of the serious threat to our revolution also
      comes from a wide range of concrete intelligence information
      available over several months, and especially in recent weeks,
      demonstrating clearly the detailed planning and organisation
      of an attack on Grenada by counter-revolutionary forces
      abroad working in close collaboration with US imperialism,
      and in particular with the CIA and the US Defence Department.
      We even have the names of the CIA case officers who have
      been working together with Grenadian counter-revolutionaries
      overseas.   2/.....

(4) The only unknown factor, therefore, is the date of the launching of the attack, and the precise form the attack will take. However, based on intelligence reports we do have some definite ideas as to the possible forms of an attack. We repeat that the fact that such an attack is <u>concretely planned for within a matter of days or hours</u> is not in doubt.

(5) <u>SEIZURE OF OUR COUNTRY MEANS THE END OF ALL GAINS</u>

Our people must understand clearly that the military seizure of our country by imperialism would mean the destruction of many lives, would mean widespread repression and brutality, would mean the end of all the benefits our masses have received from the revolution. It would mean that Grenada would be thrown back many years and that the glorious process of construction which has taken place since the revolution would be totally destroyed.

(6) <u>THE NJM HAS LED THE PEOPLE THROUGH PAST THREATS AND ATTACKS</u>

The NJM over many years has led the people through Gairy's brutality and murder. The party mobilized the masses to the Peoples' Convention on Independence, on May 6, 1973, and the Peoples' Congress on November 4th, 1973. The party mobilized the people to seize power and led the people in seizing power on March 13th, 1979. The party has led the people and mobilized the people in the defence of our revolution through the October and November plots of 1979, the bomb attack of June 19th, 1980, the terrorist attack in St. Patrick's on November 18th, 1980, and the 'Amber and the Amberines' threat from US imperialism which was met by our 'Heros of the Homeland' manoeuvre in August 1981.

At this critical time the NJM once more calls on all our people to <u>mobilize actively</u> in defence of the revolution, in defence of our homeland!!!

<u>TASKS FACING THE PARTY, GOVERNMENT AND PEOPLE IN THE LIGHT OF THE THREAT OF MILITARY INVASION</u>

(7) All steps required for the all-out defence of our country must be taken - <u>and they must be taken immediately.</u>

3......

(8) <u>The first and most important task is the immediate and total</u>
<u>mobilisation of all patriots into the militia.</u> All
Grenadians who love their country must join the militia now.
All militia members, no matter how well trained, must show
up for every call-up of the militia at this time, to receive
further intensive training for defence in times of invasion.

Those who believe that Nicaragua has been attacked but we
shall escape, either because we are an island or because we
are small and not important to the United States, or just
because "we are always lucky", are like Ostriches burying
their heads in the sand and putting the lives of their
children and the future of our revolution at risk, Cuba,
the Seychelles and the Comoros are also islands - and all
have been invaded. Our people in every village must ensure
that all patriots sign up to join the militia, and report
for duty immediately.

There will also be an immediate recruitment into certain
sections of the P.R.A., to strengthen our army.

(9) <u>OUR OLDER CITIZENS HAVE A VITAL ROLE TO PLAY</u>

Our Armed Forces will need assistance in many areas
including the guarding of beaches and vital targets in the
country, the digging of trenches throughout the country,
donation of large bags (crocus bag size) and old sheets,
donation of food and water to militia comrades who must go
into immediate training, assistance in giving or lending
vehicles, assistance in first aid for civillians as well as
militia, in looking after children so that young mothers
can go to the battlefront in time of invasion, and cooking
for both the armed forces and the children.

(10) Central Committee members of the party will be in every
parish of the country starting tomorrow. They will be
holding meetings with various groups of citizens and will
be organising medical and service (cooking) support groups
in each parish.

(11) Comrades who want to join the army or militia, who can do
guard duty, drive vehicles, or dig trenches should contact
their local militia or phone 2990 or 2265 (St. George's)
7-623 (St. Andrew's); 9-428 (St. Patrick's); 2009 (St.
David's), St. John's Police Station or St. Mark's Base, 8230.

(12) Comrades who can render first aid assistance, cooking assistance, who can donate food, large bags etc.; or who can look after children during militia call-ups and at time of attack should contact your local party office or phone 3434 or 2383 (St. George's) 7242 (St. Andrew's), 6412 (St. David's) 9340 (St. Patrick's) 8230 (West Coast).

* FORWARD TO DEFEND OUR HOMELAND!!!.
* UNITED, CONSCIOUS AND ORGANISED, WE WILL WIN!!!
* LONG LIVE THE REVOLUTION!!!

March 21st, 1983.

CENTRAL COMMITTEE REPORT ON FIRST PLENARY SESSION
13 - 19 JULY, 1983

Historically, the Central Committee has met on many ocassions to analyse all areas of the Party, State and Mass work. This however, is the first full scale wholistic plenary of the C.C.

Between Wednesdy 13th July, 1983 and Tuesday 19th July, 1983, the C.C. of N.J.M. spent six and a half (6½) days in plenary - a total of 54 hours assessing all areas of Party, Mass and State work. The strengths and weaknesses of the Party's performance were highlighted and a number of conclusions were made.

SECTION I

(i) Main Feature

In its anslysus of the present political and economic situation, the main feature was identified as follows:-

> The continued failure of the Party to transform itself ideologically and organisationally and to excercise firm leadership along a L ninist path in the face of the acute rise in the complexities and difficulties facing the Revolution on all fronts - economic, political, social, military and international.

The evidence to support this conslusion is as follows:-

THE PARTY

Over the period under review our Party has demonstrated many weaknesses - ideologically, politically, and organisationally. Most strikingly, there has been the emergence of deep petty bourgeois manifestations and influence in the party which has led to two ideological trends. This feature came to the fore when the Party had to step up its work amongst the masses, after recognising, as we saw in March, how dangerously close the Party came to losing links with the masses. The petty bourgeois response and attitudes have continued as can be seen by the low rate of attendance at house to house and community work and the lack of consistenty by large sections of the Party in carrying out compulsory areas of Party work.

2/... In the face

In the face of all this, there was a slowing down of the important task of Party building. The Party has also failed to recruit into its ranks members of the working class, the most strategic class.

THE POLITICAL AND ORGANISATIONAL WORK AMONG THE MASSES

In the period, the work of the mass organisations has stagnated and the lack of their presence and influence has opened a definite gap in the political work among the masses. In addition, the political work in the regions has been weak and ineffective, as a result of poor leadership by the P.C.B.'s. In the particular case of St. Andrew's the situation has reached crisis proportions.

Coupled with this, we have witnessed the intensification of the ideological struggle and at the same time the spread of anti-communism within the country, as seen through the Worker Education Classes. The response of the Church has been to step up its activities organisationally and ideologically to spur on this trend and strengthen idealism. At the same time, our propaganda machinery has been incredibly weak leading to the near collapse of our propaganda work among the masses. This has resulted in the overall mood of the masses being low.

THE ECONOMY

While our economy has continued to grow we are experiencing extreme difficulties in mobilising external finance and receiving already promised amounts. This has led to a serious cash flow problem which has slowed down and is even threatening to halt key capital investment projects, caused limited lay-offs and shaken the confidence of broad sections of the masses.

The alliance with the local bourgeoisie aimed at developing a national economy, has become much more complex. Recent IMF negotiations and imperialism's growing attempts to provide ideological guidance and possible finance through CBI to the local bourgeoisie has made the need for a much clearer appreciation

3/...by the entire

by the entire Party of the strategy and tactics on how to maintain that
economic alliance, and use it in the interest of the working peole,
even   more urgent. We need to bear in mind therefore, that the coming
two years will be particularly difficult and complex on the economic
front.

SOCIAL BENEFITS

Notwithstanding an increased milk distribution programme, a more efficient
housing repair programme, a deepening of free health and medical care, expanded education opportunities, economism and consumerism have remained
deep in the society.

MILITARY

In this period, we have seen the development of the Regional Defence
Force, increased agressive U.S. manoeuvres in the region and stepped
up covert activity against our Revolution.

On the other hand, our village militia units have decreased in quantity
and size in most geographic regions, and the workplace militia units
which are now developing ^{are} still at an embryonic stage and thus need
to be strengthened.

REGIONAL

In the Caribbean region there has been signs of increasing co-ordination
between the more developed countries (particularly Jamaica and Barbados)
and U.S. imperialism. They have also begun to increase their pressure on
the OECS countries in their attempts to isolate the Grenada Revolution.
At the same time there have been strong indidations of a gradual shift
in the balance of forces in CARICOM in our favour based on our economic
performance, international work, prestige and growing mass base in their
territories.

INTERNATIONAL

The Reagan administration and U.S. imperialism are growing more and more
aggressive and are at present rushing ahead with plans to deploy nuclear
weapons in Western Europe later this year. This has led to the heightening of East/West tension, posing a grave danger to peace. At the same

4/...time, the World

tine, the World peace movement is growing and the World Socialist
'system is continuing to be consolidated.

(ii) OTHER FEATURES OF THE PERIOD

The C.C. also took note of the following features:-

LOCAL

(a) The positive impact of our regional and international work on
the masses.
- our propaganda victories against Reagan on the Airport
question;
- victories in Ocho Rios and Trinidad CARICOM Summits;
- victories at OECS meetings
- impact of the P.M.'s successful visit to the USA

(b) Greater co-ordination between regional progressive Parties.

(c) Our continued efforts at building links with the Socialist
World.

(d) The growing role of the state sector in the economy.

REGIONAL

(a) The continued victories of FMLN in El Salvador.

(b) The growth of left and progressive organisations in the Caribbean, together with the growing positive sentiments towards
Grenada in the OECS countries and the growth of our mass base
in the Caricom countries.

(c) The improving relations with World Socialism and some Caricom
countries.

(d) The growing contradictions among and within Caricom countries.

(e) Our improving relations with some key Latin American countries
eg. Columbia and Argentina.

(f) Growth in formal and informal relations between Grenada and
other Caricom countries making it objectively more difficult
for U.S. imperialism to achieve their strategic objective of
isolating Grenada.

(g) Our developing relations with Trinidad.

(h) The recent passage of the CBI.

5/... INTERNATIONAL (i) The

INTERNATIONAL

(i)   The consolidation and advancement of the National Liberation strug-
        gles - Namibia, El Salvador, South Africa.

(ii)   The survival of the Front Line states in the face of tremendous
        pressure.

(iii)   The survival and expansion of the Non-Aligned Movement.

(iv)   The aggressive role of U.S. imperialism in Africa, the Middle East,
        Central America and the Caribbean using reactionary regimes - South
        Africa, Israel, El Salvador and Honduras.

(v)   The victories of Margaret Thatcher of Britain and Kohl in West
        Germany.

(vi)   Great strains and problems in the P.L.O.

(vii)   The ongoing senseless Iran-Iraq war.

REVIEW OF THE LINE OF MARCH

During the Plenary, the CC reviewed the Line of March of
the Party which was laid down in September '82. The CC
analysed that events of the period demanded higher ideological conviction, greater sacrifices, stronger leadership of the masses by all Party comrades.

Additionally, the CC calls on all Party comrades to better
prepare the masses for the sacrifices that they will have
to make in the coming period by giving them clearer and
more detailed explanations of what will be required of all
sections of the people /in order that we continue to build and advance
the Revolution.

The CC also agreed that the main feature of the present
political situation demonstrates very clearly that if the
Party was to fail to pursue our Line of March, then our
process will be most definitely turned back. Furthermore in
reviewing the six specific tasks of our Line of March, we
can see that in the few areas where we have made any progress, it was as a direct result of our pursuit of the
Line of March.

Proof of the above can be seen in the following:-

(1) The positive response by the working class to the Reagan attack, and its emergence as the most active and leading class force in the Revolution today is a direct result of the ongoing Socialism classes. In this respect, the failure of the CEE to function has weakened our implementation of priority number one.

(2) Our failure to build the mass organisations, sports and culture, and the organs of popular power has adversely affected the mood and political disposition of the masses.

(3) The Party has failed to make any progress in strengthening its Leninist character.

(4) We have failed to build the sectors which can ensure the sustained growth of our economy, making it possible to expand the programmes of the Revolution from non-tax revenue. However, at the same time, we have witnessed the expansion and development of the state sector and improvement in the structural adjustment of the economy.

(5) The Party has also failed to live up to its responsibility of building the Militia quantitatively and qualitatively. Our only area of progress here has been the workplace Militia.

(6) Despite the fair amount of progress in our international work, we still need to resolutely pursue the follow up work or the potential will never be realised.

"History has therefore proven the correctness of the Line of March, and it must therefore remain the guiding principle for the coming period.

SECTION III

MAIN FOCUS IN THE NEXT QUARTER

Following this review of the Line of March, the C.C. concluded that the main focus of this present period must be:-

...\

(1) Internal Party development, with special emphasis on ideological development and character building.

(2) Stepped up ideological work amongst the working class, students and the working people.

(3) The reorganisation and massive stepping up of the work in CPE.

(4) The adoption of concrete measures to expand and deepen the work in the geographic regions.

1. Internal Party Development:

Here the CC concluded that the following are required:-

a. The systematic development of the internal political and ideological work of the Party. Continuation oof the "weekend" training courses is vital. However, we will have to find more creative methods of implementation since the courses will be held once every six weeks. The main focus of these courses will have to be:-

   i. Further development of the character qualities of Party cadres within an ideological framework.

   ii. Further development of the organisational skills and talents of Party comrades.

b. A methodology of systematic guidance, supervision and control of Party comrades at all levels and in all areas of Party and state work - political, ideological, economic, military and overseas must be developed.

c. A methodology for the professionalisation of the Party's work in all areas. This means that the question of specialisation is of paramount importance.

d. A systematic approach to our work. This has assumed enormous importance since we do not have a "structures" problem. The key is to ensure that our structures function permanently.

e. Gradual weeding out of the worst elements from within the ranks of the Party.

f. A system to/a more careful selection of cadres entering the Party.
   guarantee

g. Permanent structures for the development of the Party overseas.

h. A time perspective for our new Party Constitution.

i. A time perspective for the development of a new Party programme.

j. The creation of a Party School.

k. Time perspective for the construction of a new Party Headquarters.

2. Ideological work:

a. Worker Education classes will commence in the private sector. The appropriate steps governing the implementation of this decision will be worked out by the Workers Committee and the Ministry of National Mobilisation. A special programme for these classes will be developed by the Socialism Tutors Committee. __ _

b. The ideological work among the farmers must be stepped up.

c. The NYO has been directed to make more creative use of their radio programme on RFG.

d. Political Education for all primary and secondary school students.

e. Political eudcation for all teachers.

3. Reorganisation of CPE

The CC analysed the work of the CPE as being weak and identified the main problems as follows:-

a. Subjective weaknesses of the leadership at the national and parish levels.

b. Low involvement and inconsistent attendance of workers in the classes.

c. Inadequate and inefficient mobilisation by the mass organisations.

The CC then concluded that:-

i. Cde. Tan Bartholomew will now lead the CPE.

ii. Material incentives are to be linked to each phase of the programme, with a small incentive to students who successfully complete each level.

iii. The curriculum be expanded to include History and Social Studies, Science and the equivalent of secondary school eucation.

iv. Fundraising activities be stepped up.

v. A more adequate administrative office be found for CPE

vi. The leadership of CPE at the parish level be strengthened through the appointment of new parish co-ordinators.

vii. The C.C. ensures that the mass organisations make CPE a main focus of their work.

110 - 8

9/... 4. Work in the

4. Work in the geographic regions:

The C.C. examined the state of its work in the geographic regions. The work in St. George's was analysed as being the most positive while that of St. Andrew's was cause for great concern. The CC was of the view that consideration should be given to the role of the regional G.M.'s and regional Party committees. This arises from the need for greater Party guidance of the work regionally and the dynamic development of regional structures including the P.C.B.'s.

The parish of St. Andrew's was also identified as a major source of counter-revolution characterised by the following factors:-

a. many social benefits, but little political results;
b. a proliferation of petty rumours in the parish;
c. the continued inflow of marijuana and the increased planting in some areas;
d. evidence of hoarding of money by some elements of the rural bourgeoisie.

The CC therefore concluded the following:-

i. The redeployment of some Party comrades to live and work in the outparishes.

ii. Cde. Ian St. Bernard to visit Carriacou forthnightly.

iii. A task force of two comrades to be identified and sent to Carriacou to live and work there.

iv. Cde. Kamau McBarnette to become the resident Political Chief of St. David's.

v. Special emphasis on house to house, community work, formation of Village Co-ordinating Bodies (VCB's) with Party members as the chiefs and the stepping up of our propaganda work.

vi. That St. Andrew's is a particular problem parish and therefore special attention must be given by all committees to all aspects of their work that affect St. Andrew's.

10/...vii. A task force

vii. A task force of four Party comrades to be located [?]
      Andrew's (to live and work there), one of whom will lead the
      political work there, under the weekly guidance of the Chair-
      man of the O.C.

viii. Counter - intelligence, the P...A. and the Police to find good
      chiefs to be placed in St. Andrew's, immediately.

ix.   St. Andrew's to be given priority in our industrialisation
      programme.

SECTION III

REVIEW OF PARTY COMMITTEES & PILLARS OF THE REVOLUTION

The Central Committee further analysed all other areas of Party work:-

1. **ECONOMY**

   The Central Committee analysed the economic sectors of the country
   and noted the following:-

Problems and Difficulties

i.   Continued serious negative effects of cash flow on
      capital programmes has:-

      a. brought some projects to a halt and threatened
         to halt even key investment projects, such as,
         Airport, GFC, Eastern Main Road, Agro-Industries,
         Farm Roads, etc.

      b. shaken the confidence of small sections of the
         masses and provided the basis for some vicious
         rumours.

ii.   Continued weak performance of the productive sectors -
      Agriculture, Agro-Industries, Fisheries, Tourism.

iii. The failure of one of our most strategic sectors to get
      moving: export (marketing).

iv.   1983/1984 will be difficult years and requires maximum
      efforts of the Party on the economic front. Hence the
      ideological work has to be stepped up to combat conse-
      quent difficulties that these two years will pose for us.

11/... v. Extreme difficulties in

v. Extreme difficulties in mobilising external finance and receiving already promised amounts.

On the positive side:-

i. Continued progress in the structural adjustment of the economy:-

   a. increased domestic savings;

   b. continued positive reduction in the food import bill, from 27.5% in one year to 25.5%. On March 13, 1979, it was 40%;

   c. sizable sections of our overall imports continue to be capital goodssforinvestment and not for consumption;

   d. decrease in the rate of inflation;

   e. drop in unemployment - increase in jobs.

ii. The rise in the production and export of traditional crops.

iii. Continued good performance in export on non-traditional crops.

iv. Further growth in the state ownership of the banking sector.

v. State control of approximately 5000 new acres of land.

vi. Improved performance of GFC and GRC.

vii. Continued good performance of MNIB on the commercial side.

viii. Continued growth in the capital programme despite all the difficulties.

ix. The commencent of long term trade with the socialist community.

x. Continued progress in state planning.

xi. Acquisition of Holiday Inn -(Grenada Beach Hotel). ·

xii. Grenada's improved credit rating.

xiii. We have been able to mobilise massive external assistance over the first four and a half years of the Revolution.

After much deliberations, the Central Committee concluded the following:-

i. The creation of a Ministry of State Enterprised, with Cde. George Louison as the Minister. The new Ministry will be run by two Boards of Directors, one Board comprising the productive sphere headed by Cde. Louison and the other comprising the non-productive sphere to be headed

12/...by Minister Lyden

by Minister Lyden Ramdhany.

ii. Some of the major projects to be considered for collaboration in the upcoming two years are, first of all, a new twenty (20) mega watts power station to be requested from the Soviet Union. Secondly, in the area of Tourism development, we need to build seven (7) more hotels, each one hundred and fifty (150) rooms, through state, private and/or joint venture investments.

Other projects here include water expansion with Soviet assistance, the development of our road network (forty (40) miles of main roads, and many more miles of farm and feeder roads with assistance from Cuba and the Caribbean Development Bank (CDB)). Also to be listed here is the industrialisation of the geographic regions, particularly St. Andrew's. This can be achieved in part through collaboration with countries such as Bulgaria, DPRK, etc. with a focus on Agro-Indusrialisation.

iii. The continuation of our land policy and the study of the possibility of the State securing more land for agriculture.

iv. The private sector must be encouraged to explore investment opportunities offered by the CBI. However, this area must be closely monitored by the Party in keeping with our strategic objectives.

v. We must pursue tactics that will ensure that our CARICOM partners continue to give us solidarity in the trade and investment possibilities of the CBI.

2. INTERNATIONAL WORK

Foreign Affairs

The C.C. analysed the International Relations work of the Party and State and concluded that there was significant improvement in the quality of this work, at the level of the State.

The C.C. noted that the main feature of the International situation was the increased aggression of U.S. imperialism under the leadership of the Reagan administration which is planning to deploy nuclear weapons in Western Europe leading/to heightening of East-West tension and a grave

13/... danger to peace

danger to peace and World civilisation.

The C.C. noted that regionally, there is the begining of a shift in the balance of forces in Caricom towards Grenada, as a result of:-

    a. the continued economic problems of Caricom countries;

    b. the fact that some Caricom countries are contesting seats in regional and international organisations;

    c. the increasing respect for Grenada's economic achievments.

However, it is too early to determine how long this will last. The C.C. concluded that in seeking to improve this work there is need to:-

1. Step up the work in the USA, Western Europe and the Caribbean, especially Trinidad.

2. Reorganise the Ministry of Foreign Affairs to ensure rational and strategic deployment of the staff.

3. Ensure greater co-ordination between Ministry of Foreign Affairs and the International Relations Department of the Party.

4. Follow up on all/contacts made during the Comrade Leader's U.S. visit. This responsibility to be shared between the International Relations Department and the Foreign Affairs Ministry.

5. The International Relations Department to intensify its work with fraternal and Friendship Societies Worldwide, bearing in mind the need for material assistance and the development of political tourism.

6. Ensure that the MDC's, particularly Jamaica and Barbados which are co-ordinating closely with US imperialism, do not succeed in isolating Grenada nor in developing a strategic imperialist control of the region. To achieve this the following measures must be implemented:-

    i.   Move rapidly to firm up relations with Caricom.

    ii.   Be discreet and cautious in our relations with

left opposition parties in OECS states.

iv. Establish a Consulate in Trinidad.

7. Ensure that we move rapidly to firm up relations with the Socialist World.

3. NATIONAL DEFENCE

The CC spent some time analysing the problems and difficulties being encountered in developing this area of work. The CC acknowledged the failure of the Party to live up to its responsibility of building the Militia quantitatively and qualitatively. Our only area of progress here is the workplace militia, and even that needs to be strengthened.

The CC concluded that:-

i. A serious Political Department of the Armed Forces should be organised and that the Chief of such department be vigorously supervised by the O.C.

ii. That dormant and defunct Party cells in the Armed Forces should be revived and a weekly report sent to the O.C. and C.I.C.

iii. That Party comrades should play a leading role in the Militia, so as to inspire and lead the Militia. In addition, the regional Militia Chiefs must submit weekly reports on all party comrades who fail to turn up for militia training.

4. WORKERS WORK

In analysing the work among the working class, the C.C. took particular note of the following:-

i. The Party has failed in its strategic objective to recruit workers into its ranks.

ii. The Workers Education Classes has done relatively well primarily due to the work of the Socialism Tutors Committee.

iii. C.P.E. among the workers was one of the weakest areas of the worker's work, but this was in itself linked to the weakness of the C.P.E. administration centre itself.

iv. The Party Support Groups at the workplaces were begining to show signs of improvement during the last two months but there was need for them to take responsibility for organising production and emulation activities.

The CC then concluded the following:-

i. Party Support Groups: In order to fbetter equip the Party Support Groups with the necessary skills for carrying out their day to nay political task at the work place, the CC decided:-

a. A 24-week ideological training programme for members of Party Support Groups would be organised. (Participonts to be selected immeidately).

b. One day sessions for dealing with right-wing propaganda lines would be organised every two months.

ii. Wages: In order to advise the C.C. on a policy for the rationalisation of wages, an existing committee from the Ministry of Planning was strengthened and tasked to:-

a. submit proposals for standardisation of wages;

b. prepare a draft policy on profit-sharing;

c. submit information on the classification of workers;

d. submit statistics on the size of the Grenadian working class.

iii. Emulation: In order to get this vital area of work among the workers going, it was decided:-

a. To accept the format of the document prepared by Cde. George Louison on this question.

b. To appoint Cde. Kamau McBarnette to be overall Political Head of this area.

c. To appoint an organiser who will be guided by Cde. McBarnette.

iv. Membership on Workers Committee: The CC took note of the need to strengthen the membership of the Workers Commitee. In this respect the C.C. decided to appoint:-

a. Cdes. Fitzroy Bain and Bertie Lessey as members of the Workers Committee representing AGWU Sub-Committee.

b. Identify new heads to lead the work in some of the sub-committees.

16/... v. Regional and international

v. <u>Regional and international Work:</u> In the face of an intensified thrust by imperialism to control the regional trade union movement as seen in the ($2M) offered to these unions through the C.E.I., the C.C. recognised the need to step up our work in this area. To this end, the C.C. decided to:-

a. Direct the Workers Committee to study the possibility of Grenada winning the post of General Secretary and other key positions in the Caribbean Congress of Labour.

b. Direct the W.C. to build and strengthen the International Department of T.U.C. in order to facilitate expanded regional and international work.

c. Direct W.C. to deepen its contact with W.F.T.U. while seeking to maximise the value of its contacts within the I.C.F.T.U.

5. FARMERS

The Central Committee summarised the work of the Farmers Committee as having shown signs of improvement, but expressed concern over the failure to solve persistent problems particularly the total absence of propaganda, the delay in the enactment of the praedial larceny law and the problem of marketing.

The CC concluded that:-

i. The Farmers Committee needs to be strengthened given the strategic role of the farmers in the development of agriculture.

ii. The Committee through the P.F.U. organises a massive recruitment programme linked to the provision of material benefits for the farmers.

iii. All activities of the P.F.U. be consistently highlighted in the media.

iv. The Ministry of Agriculture and the P.F.U. seek to obtain markets locally, regionally and internationally for the farmers produce.

v. The Farmers Committee to be given closer supervision by the Politbureau, C.C. and O.C.

vi. The ideological work among the farmers to be stepped up im-

17/...mediately. vii. The P.F.U.

mediately.

vii.   The F.F.U. seek to start service co-operatives and to work
        out an incentive scheme for the farmers in the co-ops in
        order to convince other farmers of the value of co-ops.

6. TEACHERS

The C.C. summarised the work of the Teachers Committee as fair. It
however, noted that although progressive forces control the G.U.T.,
the majority of teachers remain backward politically.

The C.C. concluded that in order to ensure that the progressive
forces retain effective control of the G.U.T. and deepen the work
among the teachers, the teachers committee must:-

i.   carry out political education among all teachers;
ii.   commence political education of all primary school students;
iii.   assist the Ministry of Education in purging areactionary head
        teachers from schools;
iv.   Co-ordinate with the Ministry of Education to ensure the im-
        plementation of all new strategic programmes in Education.
v.   Ensure that there is continued development of cultural and
        academic level of all teachers (NISTEP and beyound).

7. YOUTH & STUDENTS

In analysing the work of the Youth Committee, the C.C. concluded
that the work among the youth and students was poor. The C.C. noted
particularly that there was a general absence of resoluteness in
pursuing the fundamental task of the construction of hard courts.

The CC concluded:-

i.   That the Youth Committee should focus in the coming period on
        Sport and Culture in order to win the youth masses. The commit-
        tee should creatively lay the basis for taking over the Sports
        Department and thereafter the Sports Associations.
ii.   Streamline the Youth Secretariat bureacracy which is to be re-
        duced from thirteen (13) to four (4), and redeploy the extra
        workers into other areas.
iii.   More creative use be made of the radio programme on RFG.
iv.   The C.C. place special emphasis on proper planning, the train-

ing of cadres, propaganda and international work.

v. There must be greater co-ordination between the students committee and the teachers committee to implement political work among the students, including Pioneers.

vi. The International Department of the NYO must be strengthened.

vii. There must be greater co-ordination between the Youth Committee and the Workers Committee in order to ensure that young workers are recruited into the NYO.

viii. There must be closer supervision by the National Executive of the work at the parish, zonal and group levels.

8. WOMEN'S WORK

1. The C.C. summarised the work of the Women's Committee as being weak and stagnant and concluded this was a result of the failure of the National Leadership to provide effective leadership for the period due to both objective problems and their insensitivity to deep petty bourgeois trends in some of the members of the Women's Committee. This weak national leadership and absence of supervision and control at the parish and zonal levels have exposed the petty bourgeois side of many elements who have not been accustomed to working on their own. This petty bourgeois side has to be seen in the context of the deep petty bourgeois character of our Party.

2. The C.C. discussed an allegation made by the Women's Committee that the Party as a whole has failed to appreciate and pay due regard to the special problems faced by Party women with young children. The CC concluded that this allegation is without sustance. In the view of the CC, there is no doubt that there has been steady and discernible improvement in the arrangements which have been made by the Party to facilitate Party comrades with young children in carrying out their Party duties. The attitude of the Women's Committee on this therefore, reflects a disguised petty bourgeois attitude and reaction.

3. Furthermore, the CC noted that the Political Bureau and Organising Committee have held discussions in the past with the Women's Committee on these questions. At these meetings the point was repeatedly made that the inequality of the woman was one of the contradictions inherent in the capitalist system and had to be resolved by the

Party in a systematic way in accordance with the material development of the society. At these meetings, it was further pointed out that concrete attempts were being made to solve the <u>objective problems</u> faced by the women (through provision of day care centres, kindergardens and pre-primary facilities, jobs, skills-training and educational opportunities) and that the resolution of the <u>subjective difficulties</u> (old culture, old views, old prejudices, old habits and old values) was a matter for the Party as a whole - men and women - to resolve in a principled and systematic way through collective study on the Woman Question and through recognition in practice on the part of both the Party women and men that a conscious attempt at change in attitude and practice was required.

4. The C.C. therefore concluded that in seeking to resolve this problem, the Party cannot encourage weakness, breed cynicism or encourage wrong subjective attitudes, put the Party in the position of a privileged clique, or encourage disunity between men and women in the Party's rank and file, bearing in mind the paramount importance of the need to ensure that both the men and woman unite in the struggle to defeat our principal enemies of capitalism and imperialism and achieve our strategic objective of building Socialism.

5. The CC also agreed to the proposals of the Women's Committee for the revitalising of the women's work.

9. PROPAGANDA

The CC analysed that the Party and State propaganda work is in a state of deep crisis. This state of crisis is the consequence of a number of factors including:-

i. the lack of an ideological perspective of the comrades involved in propaganda work;

ii. the weakness in the number and quality of these comrades;

iii. poor system of management.

Objective factors impacting negatively on the work were also noted.

The Propaganda Committee was criticised for its failure to adequately

20/... project the working

project the working calss and working people as required · the
Party's Line of March in order to guarantee the ideological and
organisational development dof the working class as the leading
social force.

The failure to effectively utilise community work place structures
as a constant source of news about the working class and working
people was also recorded.

The CC concluded:

.i.   Free West Indian and Government Printery to be merged into one
      company with Keith Joseph as Manager, Herby James as Technical
      Head, Ruggles Ferguson as Editor of FWI and JEWEL.

ii.   Peter David to become new Deputy Secretary of Information.

iii. Technical training for personnel from FWI at Cole's Printery
      in Barbados should be pursued.

iv.   Amalgamated approach to be developed in respect to media
      in the form of a Broadcasting Institute.

v.   Merger of GIS and FWI reporters so as to increase the effi-
      ciency of both operations.

vi.   GIS to be approached for 2 technicians to service FWI press,
      while training locals.

vii. FWI and JEWEL to be published weekly on Wednesday and Saturday.

viii. Systematic phasing out of religious programs on GBC start-
      ing with overseas programmes.

10. O.C./SECRETARIAT

i.   The CC concluded that the O.C. has continued to do fair work but
      weaknesses continue to be manifested in overall consistent guid-
      ance, supervision and control of all areas of work simultaneously.
      Consequently, the CC directs that further work be done in the
      area of building systems to control and guide the work of the
      work of the Party.

ii.   The O.C. also expressed concern about the present functioning
      of the Secretariat and directs that further systems be put in
      place to control the quality of work. In this connection, the
      CC has directed the O.C. to identify a Proletarian administrator
      to give day to day leadership to the Secretariat.

27/... (11) SOCIAL

(11) SOCIAL SECTOR

Health:

1. The C.C. noted that some progress had been made in the field of Health care particularly at the level of the expansion of the Primary Health Care Teams throughout the country.

2. The CC noted the existing level of organised mass participation in the delivery of health service and the lack of involvement of the mass organisations and organs of popular democracy in the are of health education.

3. The C.C. directs that consultation begin between the Ministry of Health, mass organisations and the Ministry of National Mobilisation to secure concrete levels of co-ordination in areas such as:-

    i.   The establishment of village health brigades.

    ii. Discussions around the health sector plan.

    iii. The organisation of Health Education Programmes.

Housing:

1. In addressing the work of the Ministry of Housing, the CC considered a proposal for expanding and deepening the Housing Repair Programme. In this respect the CC directs the OC to secure from Housing Ministry a concrete proposal to deepen the provision of cement, sand and gravel.

2. CC also directs that an attempt be made to secure concessional credit for housing components from Columbia and Czechoslovakia.

3. CC further directs the OC to find additional comrades for the Rent Tribunal to ensure greater sharing of the workload, and that a written evaluation by the Chairpersons of the Tribunal, on whether it is correct to extent the rent ceiling above $300 be done.

Education/Sport/Culture:

In this area, the CC noted:-

i.   Both the CPE and NISTEP programmes urgently require stepped up work and attention.

22/... ii. The present un-

ii.   The present 'unsatisfactory disposition of the students to the Revolution, especially secondary school students.

iii.   The continuing poor physical conditions of the school buildings.

iv.   The lack of a standardised curriculum for primary and secondary schools.

v.   The growing influence of the Church and religion among students.

vi.   The drop in discipline among students and teachers and the growing truancy problem.

The CC further noted in the area of Sport, that the organisation and administration are not under firm political control and direction, and have not taken on a mass character.

The CC noted also that the area of culture had seen no significant improvement which can make a meaningful contribution to the political development of the working people.

Consequently:-

i.   CC directs the Ministry of Education and the Teachers Committee to implement the proposal for political education of the primary, secondary and NISTEP teachers.

ii.   NISTEP Programme for secondary schools should commence in September, '83.

iii.   CC directs the Teachers Committee and the Ministry of Education to implement recommendations to remove unsuitable head teachers.

iv.   CC directs the Youth Committee, the Teachers Committee and Ministry of Education to implement political education for students.

v.   School Boards to be reminded that under the Education Act, religious classes are optional in state schools.

vi.   The teachers committee and Ministry of Education to find creative ways for example, through rearranging daily time tables, to ensure the reduction of religious education in schools.

vii.   The Methodist Church will be notified that Wesley College is now state owned.

viii.   The formation of Community School Councils where the balance of forces allows for such to be done, and the political consolidation of existing community school councils.

23/... ix. The estab-

ix.   The establishment of new principals councils to meet monthly.

x.   Appropriate amendment be made to the Education Act to en-
      sure that firmer political and administrative control be ex-
      ercised over private schools.

xi.   Officials in the Ministry of Education to begin the programme
      of bringing young students for one day in each 3 week period.
      ... ... will be started and money will be given
      ... ... with its contribution to the programme

xii. In order to combat the rise in the showing of porporgraphic
      and other types of prohibited movies and the circulation
      of such literature, meetings will be held with individual
      cinema owners, video dealers and other film operators to
      give them formal warning. Their failure to comply will re-
      sult in the suspension or revocation of their licences.

xiii. Officials and C.C. to follow up on the Soviet offer to es-
      ... ...

xiv. ... ... production manager for the
      ... ...

xv.   Officials of Youth Committee to appropriately redeploy unsuit-
      able ... recruits and assume full control of Sport and
      Culture.

(3) ... ...

The ... ... of the C.C. and P.B. had in-
... ... review.

It ... ... C.C. ... all must take the formal responsibility ... ... of Party development along Leninist lines
and ... will ... ... of opposite influence and manifestations to
individual ... ...

In ... ... the C.C. will play a correct Leninist role in
building ... all parts of the Party, along strict Leninist lines,
the C.C. ... all ... of its members to pay particular attention to
improving ... ... improving their personal all rounded development
through ... individual study, daily systematic reflection on all
aspects ... ... and class work and proletarian management   of
time.

MINUTES OF EMERGENCY MEETING OF N.J.M CENTRAL
COMMITTEE DATED 26TH AUGUST, 1983

COMRADES   PRESENT

Maurice Bishop   Selwyn Strachan
Hudson Austin   Unison Whiteman
Liam James   Tan Bartholomew
Ian St. Bernard   Kamau McBarnette
Fitzroy Bain   Leon Cornwall
Chris Deriggs

COMRADE ABSENT

Phyllis Coard   -   Excuse - ill

AGENDA

1. Concern of Party Membership

Central Committee Chairman and Party Leader Comrade Maurice
Bishop called the meeting to order at 8.00 a.m. He asked
Comrade Cornwall to summarise the concern expressed by a
member of senior party member.

Comrade Leon Cornwall reported that he had held discussions
with some senior party Comrades in order to get their views on
a number of issues. This, he said was based on his own feelings
that we do not have an effective way of assessing the feelings
of party membership on key matters.

Comrade Cornwall summarised the feedback as follows:

(i)   Some conclusions of the C.C are not correct.

(ii) Some C.C Comrades are not functioning properly, are
      in a state of rut or performing in a weak manner.

(iii) He had been told by a Comrade from the G.D.R that the
      state of work is bad.

(iv) Similar allegations were made by Cuban Comrades Carlos
      Diaz and Pinero.

(v)   Comrades in the Armed Forces complained that they were
      not happy with the level of party guidance even after
      C.C deliberations and the recent general meeting.

(vi) There was a feeling among some party Comrades that the
      C.C did not criticise itself in a serious way before
      the G.M.

(vii) Cde. Cornwall concluded by recommending that C.C look
      into these concerns.

Other Comrades reported on the feedback that they had received.

CDE. IAN ST.BERNARD: He reported that he had picked up
similar responses: (i)   That the C.C performance in guiding
                             the work has been weak.

                      (ii)   There is a general feeling by
                             Comrades who have been abroad that
                             the work has fallen.

                      (iii) There is concern over the C.C's
                             failure to assign a C.C member to
                             St. Andrew's even after analysing
                             this parish which is the weakest
                             link, also disatisfaction over the
                             nature of the task force so far
                             selected.

                      (iv)   Party Comrades have noted the lack
                             of a serious approach to the Militia

                      (v)   Comrades say that they feel intimi-
                             dated over raising these concerns
                             at the level of G.M's.

                      (vi)   A number of C.C Comrades have been
                             identified as failing to adequately
                             lead and guide the work.

Comrade Tan Bartholomew reported on what had reached him:

                      (1)   Fraternal Comrades had raised certai
                             concerns with him: conversation
                             between Carlos Diaz Kamau and himsel
                             special concern over Army/Militia,
                             Youth.

                      -      Concern by U.J.C about the quality
                             of regional and International work c
                             NYO.

                      -      Concern over the presence of G.D.R
                             Technical delegation down here for
                             a month and having nothing to do,
                             while having to live in unsatisfact-
                             ory housing at the risk of their

111 - 2

personal security - noting that this can tarnish our image in the eyes of fraternals.

    (ii) Comrades in St. Patrick's had expressed concern over:

- Personal problems

- Lack of supervision (implied lack of satisfaction with C.C leadership of work)

- Disciplinery measures taken by O.C against a particular Comrade (Comrade Tan personally agrees with O.C on this)

- Attitude of the Party to the Youth.

- State of work in the Militia

- Party's neglect of work in the Militia. "It does not seem that Imperialism exists anymore".

- A lot of pettyness among soldiers and likely exodus from the Armed Forces next year when 5 (five) years contracts ends.

- Lack of supervision of the work among police, control by RightWing elements, lack of respect for party among police, demoralisation among newly recruited police making it difficult for transformation of this section of the Armed Forces to take place.

Comrade Liam James commented:

(i) We should try to identify the basis for the

(ii) It is clear that little progress has been made in implementing C.C resolutions of five weeks ago.

(iii) We need to convene once more a new wholestic assessing by the Central Committee.

(iv), We need to lock at this situation in a special way - We are <u>seeing the beginning of the disintegration of the party.</u> This period calls for a full meeting of all members of the C.C - last assessment was not deep enough.

3

4/..............

<u>Comrade Strachan:</u>

(i) Sections of the party have begun to rebel against the higher organs of the party. This is serious and dangerous development.

(ii) This silent rebellion will turn into open rebellion and if we do not address it now it will be resolved in a petty bourgeois way.

(iii) At the heart of the matter is the C.C. The situation calls for a more critical review of the C.C - C.C's last assessment of itself was opportunist - C.C did not really criticise itself.

(iv) There is need for a meeting of the full C.C.

(v) Whereas October deliberations Held back the party from a social democratic path, the situation now is qualitatively worse. Membership is now attacking Central Committee.

(vi) Comrades are saying that the C.C is being dishonest with them for example the Dix issue.

Comrade Hudson Austin reported on a meeting he had held with the motorised unit:-

- Comrades are in a serious state of demoralisation.

- Good Comrades are asking to leave

- Comrades are saying that at the end of five (5) years they are not materially better off.

Comrade Austin recommended that the C.C must set aside a day to sit down and look at the Armed Forces. He also recommended that he should be in the work of the Armed Forces full time.

Comrade Unison Whiteman:

(i) The reports have series implications.

(ii) Things are pointing in the direction of a breakdown of confidence in the C.C.

(iii) There is need for a round of G,M's to be assess how wide is the discontent.

(iv) These G.M's can prepare for an overall assessment in six (6) weeks.

4

Cde. Tan Bartholomew:

    (i)   We cannot wait. We need to urgently address the question.

    (ii)   G.M's can follow the C.C's deliberations where Cdes can be given frank explanations.

Cde Fitzroy Bain:

    (1)   We need clarification as regards the depth of the criticism of the C.C.

    (ii)   There is division between party and masses- Concern over the image of the party before the masses.

    (iii) Some responses are genuine while others are petty-bourgeois.

Comrade Kojo commented as follows:

    (i)   It is clear the C.C is facing a confidence crisis.

    (ii)   The reports tell us that these is grave danger of open rebellion and disintegration of our party.

    (iii) The heart of the crisis is the Central Committee.
        - at the level of its composition.

        - at the level of the assignment of duties both in the party and state.

    (iv)   We need to do an assessment based on identified priorit; areas of concern rather than a wholistic.

    (v)   T here is need for full membership of C.C to address these issues.

Comrade Leon Cornwall:

    (i)   We need to begin to think more strategically than tactically - C.C tends to think more tactically.

    (ii)   We need to decide on measures for arresting the situation now and for looking down the road.

Cde. Kamau Mc Barnette commented on the lack of critical responses to the C.C's conclusions at the G.M. He said we need to ask ourselves to what extent do we provide rank and file party members with the opportunity to speak out and do as frankly?

5

Other Comrades commented on the need for C.C Comrades to
lead discussions at Workshops level in future.

COMRADE OWUSU maintained that the basis for timidity in membership is the attitude of some C.C Comrades to criticism and the
fear of membership if being labelled revisionist.

DECISION: (i)   The full C.C of NJM will meet on the 13th, 14th
                 and 15th of September to examine the issues raised
                 in this meeting and to come up with appropriate
                 steps.

           (ii) Cde. Val on Boldeau will be the recording Secretary
                 for this meeting.

SUMMARY REMARKS BY CDE. MAURICE BISHOP

           (i)   The meeting inspite of its short duration has
                 been useful.

           (ii) In agreement with Owusu that we are faced with
                 the threat of disintegration.

           (iii) Agrees also with analysis that Comrades of the
                 party are afraid to raise criticisms.

           (iv) Agrees with the postponement because of the need
                 for C.C members to adequately prepare themselves.

           (v)   By way of preparation C.C members should do the
                 following:

                 (a) rap with party members, particularly senior
                      party members on all the critical issues.

                 (b) rap with key section of the masses with
                      the following in mind:-

                      - the increasing disrespect for the party
                         among certain sections of the masses.

                 (c) rap with leading mass orgs. activists,
                      leading militia types, consistent partici-
                      pants in zonal councils, leaders of party
                      support groups.

           (vi) July C.C resolution should be discussed in work
                 committees and study groups.

           (vii) C.C members should research on the history of the
                 party during the last five or six years. Minutes
                 and conclusions will be useful to look at.

6

(viii) There is reasonable basis to share the concern that many key decisions of the party, if not the majority have been made informally outside of higher organs.

(ix) We should study the history of the C.P.S.U.

(x) We should re-read Standards of Party Life by Pronin.

(xi) We should reflect on the individual strengths and weaknesses of all C.C members.. We should also think about the specific responsibilities of C.C Comrades both at the party and state levels - This should be in writing.

The meeting ended around 10.00 a.m.

Minutes taken by

Cde. Chris DeRiggs.

_____

EXTRAORDINARY MEETING OF THE CENTRAL COMMITTEE NJM

14 - 16 SEPTEMBER, 1983

MEETING STARTED 1.00 P.M

COMRADES PRESENT

Maurice Bishop	Phyllis Coard
Selwyn Strachan	Leon Cornwall
George Louison	Kamau Mc Barnette
Unison Whiteman	Tan Bartholomew
Liam James	Fitzroy Bain
Chalkie Ventour	Chris Deriggs
Ewart Layne	

COMRADES ABSENT

Hudson Austin   -   (out of country)
Ian St. Bernard   -   (sick)

The proposed agenda by Cde. Maurice Bishop was circulated to Cdes for comments.

PROPOSED AGENDA

14TH SEPTEMBER

1. Minutes   (7.00 - 1.10 p.m)
2. Levels of preparation   (I.I0 - 1.20 p.m)
3. Feed back from members work
   Committees and masses   (1.20 - 2.30 p.m)
4. Evaluation of Feed back   (2.30 - 2.45 p.m)
5. Evaluation of C.C (i) Collective
   role/collective work   (2.45 - 6.00 p.m)

   Break at   (4.00 - 4.15 p.m)

2/..............

SEPTEMBER 15TH:

5. Evaluation of C.C
    (ii) Individual assessment   (8.00a.m - 6.00 p.m
           Break   (10.30a.m -10.45 a.m
           Lunch   (1.00p.m - 2.00 p.m

           Break   (4.00p.m - 4.15 p m

Procedures - main   5 minutes
Assessment by 13 other Cdes $13 \times 2 = 26$ minutes
15 Cdes at 31 minutes per person   465 minutes

6. Key areas of implimentation of C.C conclusions

    (i) Regional work/new P.C.B chiefs   (5.15 - 6.00 p.m)

SEPTEMBER 16TH

6. Key areas of implimentation of C.C Conclusions

    (i) Regional Work/PCB Chiefs   (8.00 - 8.30 a.m)

    (ii) C.P.E   (8.30 - 9.30 a.m)

        Militia   (9.30 -10.30 a.m)

        Break   (10.30 -10.45 a.m)

7. (a) Proposed new responsibilities of C.C Cdes
   (b) Proposed responsibilities of C.C Secretariat
   (c) New decisions of C.C
   (d) Proposed meetings/dates and agenda of C.C
   (e) Report to the Party on this meeting
   : - a,b,c,d,e (10.45a.m - 1.00 p.m)

REPORTS AVAILABLE

1. Minutes of Last Emergency C.C
2. Reports from St. George's P.C.B   (1)
3. Report from West Coast P.C.B   (1)
4. Report from St. Andrew's P.C.B   (1)
5. Report from St.David's P.C.B   (2)
6. Report from St. Patrick's P.C.B   (2)
7. Report from Carriacou P.C.B   (1)
8. Report from West Coast G.M   (1)
9. Recommendations from Fedon's and Marryshow seminars
10. Document on internal party development
11. Recommendations from Chris DeBriggs C.M Class
12. Present Political Situation Document.

112-2

13. Worker Education class August '83 report

14. Workers Committee balance of forces document 9th September 1983.

15. Report from Workers Committee on Socialism Classes July - August 4th 1983.

16. Workers Committee analysis of the Working Class for the Month of August.

COMMENTS ON THE AGENDA

Cde. Liam James said the proposed agenda is lacking in focus. It is not consistent with what was agreed in the emergency meeting of the C.C.

Cde. Ventour said that the agenda should be:(

(1) Analysis of the present state of the party and revolution

(2) Analysis of the C.C main problems.

(3) The way forward.

Cde. Layne said the main purpose of this meeting is to discuss the state of the party and revolution and the work of the Central Committee.

Cde. Strachan said that item number six (6) can be taken in the overall assessment of the work.

Cde. James said that he would like the meeting to assess the degree of the state of the rut in the party and to look at the C.C and the way forward in that context.

Cde. Strachan said that item one, assessment of the party and revolution (2)/the C.C line formulation will make the analysis look to mechanistic.

Cde. Bishop said he had no problem with changing the agenda, his main concern is the time limit of the analysis.

Cde. Layne however, felt that the C.C should take all the time necessary to do the analysis given the state of the work. When we have exhausted the discussion on the item we can move on Sister Coard agreed.

The C.C agreed to follow the approach suggested by Cde. Chalkie Ventour.

(1) Analysis of the party and revolution
(2) Analysis of the C.C (main Problem)
(3) The way forward.

(1) ANALYSIS OF THE PRESENT STATE OF THE PARTY AND REVOLU***

Cde. Ewart Layne lead off in the discussion. He said that
had received/minutes of the last C.C plenary, all documents
and report from the P.B and C.C. Therefore his assessment
is based on these reports and feed back from the ground he
had picked up during his short time home.

The situation is that the revolution now faces the greatest
danger since 1979. There is great dispiritiveness and
disatisfaction among the people. Though not in an open way
it can be recognised. The state of the party at present is
the lowest it had ever been. The ineternational prestige o*
the party and revolution is compromised e.g the C.C delegat*
visit to the S.U.

We are faced with the tasks of Managing the state sector in
great economic difficulties, to build the economy in the face
of tremendous pressure from imperialism. Politically, to
raise the consciousness of the working class and working
people in the face of resistance from imperialism and to
build the party into a Marxist Leninist vanguard in a coun**
that is dorminatly pettit bourgeoise and to carry the
proposed constitution to the people in two years time.

Militarily, to organise the defence of the revolution in t**
face of a qualitatively stepped up agression from imperial**
who for years has attempted to carry out its policy of be*c*
more and more into a "gun Boat" policy. The small Caribbee*
islands are being drawn into an alliance against Grenada ar*
all the left organisations in the region.

We have to develop an army with more complicated means.
Tighten our relations with the World Socialist Movement
especailly Cuba, S.U, G.D.R, of which rela*ons are becoming
more and more complex. To steer off isola*ion but not at
the extent of departing from the correct path, and to carry
out all tasks of social development.

In the face of all these tasks the party is crumbling, all
mass organisations are to the ground, organs of people's
democracy is about to collapse. T he internal state of the
party is very dread. There is wide protest against the
higher organs, * prestige has fallen in the eyes of the
party members and the masses. T he C.C has proven its inab*
lity to give leadership to the process e.g this time the C.*
cannot determine the stage the revolution is at. The style
of the C.C is becoming more and more formalistic. The *rov**
and carrying * of working class elements into the party
is low. The style of leadership is carried out by directi***
(members says that democracy is dead in the party). Decis**
making is characterised by spontainety.

The C.C is on a path of right opportunism and is very dish*
to its members e.g in the conclusions of *ne July plenary
was reported that C.C has advanced, every single committee
mass orgs were criticise except the C.C and P.B. The failu*
to match up with incentives to the participants in C.P.E
was not criticised. When Cdes have failed to accomplish

tasks and accuses others for this it very serious. For soon
ideological justifications will be found for these mistakes.

The C.C criticised the NYO for their short comings, at the
same time Cde. Tan Bartholomew has been given additional
responsibility of C.P.E and St. Patrick's P.C.B. He said that
the tasks given to the NYO in this period are giant tasks which
is impossible to accomplish in the end it will only lead to the
fustration of the Cdes in this area.

In his view the main problem is the C.C. The C.C has diverted
from the correct path. This will lead to the total disintegration of the party and the collapse of the revolution; at the
same time when the work on the economic, military and international
fronts becomes much more difficult.

The C.C needs to take a serious view, frankly criticise itself
inorder to move out of this serious dangers in the interest of
the masses and the revolution.

Cde. Ventour supported the points made by Cde. Layne. He said
that the party is facing disintegration. Cdes are complaining
of the amount of tasks, some are showing signs of resignation,
Cdes are afraid to speak up, they show timidity and fear to
express their positions. He said that this can make the C.C
lose a lot of prestige. Cdes do not agree with the C.C
conclusions of July. They also raised that the months have
passed and there is no implimentation of the conclusions. There
is a serious drift away from the party by the key supporters
of the revolution, the vocal Cdes are now passive, they are
not prepared to fight the reactionary lines on the ground.
Community work is not going as was expected, he graded it as
poor to fair. The militia is non existent. In some respects
the masses have gone backwards ideologically using the
present positions on the Korean plane incident and comparing
it with the position of the masses on the Afghistan in the
early days of the revolution. He said that people are getting
their lines from VOA.

Cde. Leon Cornwall also agreed with the analysis made by Cde.
Layne. He said that the honey moon period of the revolution
is over. In the past 4½ years progress was seen in many areas
and the masses were on a high, now the work is becoming much
more difficult and complex. The C.C has failed to develop a
perspective on how the revolution must develop. The C.C has
given too much unrealistic tasks and in pushing Cdes to accomplish it they become fustrated. A striking feature in this
period is the absence of the masses in the activities of the
revolution because of the deep fustrations which exists. He
said that there is confusion among the party masses, we do not
know how we are going to come out of this situation because the
party has not develop a prospective. We tend to push things down
Cdes throat and fustrate them.

All areas of mass organisation work has fallen, which is related
to our lack of prospective on how to impliment solutions. The
serious economic difficulties we face is also affecting the
people.

- 6 -

He said that Cuba had similar problems in their development but they were able to develop a militant mass base because of the strength of the party in developing a perspective and its work

There is a lot of confusion structuraly in the party. There is no clear system of subordination. Structures are created without having a perspective in them. Too much shifting around of Cdes. We have failed to develop Cdes, we also make too much mistakes in who we send to train abroad e.g the Cdes of the Youth Organisations are bitter because training abroad is seen as a passport to transfer them into other areas of work. In some cases we send Cdes to train only to fill the places offered to us.

As a party we are not playing a leading role in the process. Inner party democracy is being down played this is a result of our style of leadership and work, also how we seek to deal with the young Cdes is damagaing the dignity of the party and its membership.

He also agreed that the C.C is on a right opportunist path referring to the conclusions of the July plenary. He continued to say that if the C.C is to gain any respect we must move away from this path. He said that this problem is as a result of the low ideological level of the C.C and the party in general. Cdes see the conclusions of July as a set of administrative measures. There is no system to ensure that Cdes understand the lines of the party. No perspective on the development of the G,M's. He thinks that the solution is an ideologicallyclear and steeled C.C and party which can explain the lines of the party and can impliment it in all areas.

Cde. Fitzroy Bain agreed with the position of the Cdes. He said that the strongest supporters of the regolution are demoralised the party has set too much high standards for the people, we had expected social benefits to do the work for us. Cdes who leave the army are spreading unfavourable lines which is difficult to fight back, it is affecting the credibility of the army in the eyes of the people. There is presently a very low surface mood among the masses which will soon affect their basic mood.

Party Cdes bramble the masses, a small amount of our firmest supporters are leaving the country. The mood of the party is also lower than the masses at this time, there exist a level of mistrust, resentment and fustration among party Cdes. They are not convinced on the lines given by the C.C on Cde. Coard and Cde. Radix. Cdes see double standards in the party e.g when Cdes of the C.C do not do any house to house. Cdes do not have any respect for the D.C, they also show a willingness to resign. Cdes of the Workers Committee are saying that their is at stake, they attend too many meetings, they have no time to visit workplaces and given very little time to address the trade union work. Cdes refer to the case of Sydney Francis and Valentino Sawney who were disciplined recently in saying that Cde. Austin committed a similar offence and he was not disciplined Party Cdes are just going through motions, they lack the spirit to fight on the ground. They criticise the supervision of the C.C, they say that communication from the C.C is weak. They refer to the July Conclusion saying that meetings were held with M's and C.M's no meetings were held with A's but at the

112 - 6

same time A's are expected to carry out the decisions and task
from the July Plenary.

Cde. Bartholomew agreed with all the points made so far saying
that the C.C has not been giving leadership to the process. The
party has been dishonest with its members on a number of issues
which has shaken the confidence of the party masses. The C.C
does not report frankly, the flow or information is a major
problem, internal party democracy has been destroyed and
decisions are handed down without involving the full members

Timidity is a major problem in the party, Cdes are afraid to
speak out frankly because when they do they are termed in
different ways. Members and C.M do not understand basic norms
of party life. Cdes were not consulted when the three Cdes
of the C.C was brought onto the P.B. Cdes do not know the members
of the Central Committee. The D.C has not played the role it
had been assigned to do, it has developed a very arrogant
attitude towards Cdes, it has not developed ways of assisting
Cdes that come before the D.C. The masses have lost confidence
in the party, irregularities takes too much time before it is
solved, e.g water and electricity problems police and soldiers
who left the army are going to Trinidad. They complain about
the condition in the army. The economic problems are not
explained to the people and the Church has grabed a number
of people in this situation. He also reported an incident of
Militia Cdes guarding a Church in this period. He said that
the party has not yet developed a ploicy for dealing with the
Church. The revolution has lost itsability to manners counter
who are very active. He refered to the 300 turn out in the
indoor rally in Sauteurs as a very weak turnout in the context
of the amount of mobilisation done. Mobilisers were actually
chased in some areas.

Cdes complain of the lack of stability in the leadership of the
NYO. He accused the party of bleeding the youth movement.
The best Cadres are pulled out at a time when the youth
movement is in problems. Leading Party Cdes have contributed
to the discrediting of the youth Cdes terrorise the youth
calling NYO "Not yet organise". We are not yet clear on the
relation of the party and the mass organisation. He referred
to occasion where the party is guilty of the above as the O.C
ordered to run all youth from the Tivoli court, Cdes of the
NYO do not get enough support from the party, Cdes complain that
the O.C is not giving them adequate guidance. When members
of the party are tied up for NYO activities they do not turn
up and failed to give any excuse. He continued to say that the
international prestige of the NYO is very poor there is the
possibility of loosing seat on the Bureau of W.F.DY. He raised
the problems experienced by the G.D.R Cdes now in Grenada.
His view is that Cde. Goddard is given too much work as a
result he cannot focus on the youth work in St. George's.

He said that the main problem is in the C.C. The C.C need to
make frank decisions and communicate to its members frankly.

8/...............

Cde. Chris De Riggs registering his agreement with the points
made referred to the 19 characteristics of pettit bourgeois part
that party identified in the weekend of the fedons group seminar
highlighting the points on (i) inconsistency (2) insufficient
planning (3) vascillation (4) agreement in principle windbagism
in practice (5) inadequate vision of the future (6) crisis
management (7) poor attitude towards criticism (8) lack of a
perspective of the future. He said that all these points
characterise the New Jewel Movement at this time. He pointed
to the fact that the C.C has failed to accept the failure for
the work which in his view is very dishonest. This attitude h
discouraged Cdes from criticising the higher organs, the reason
being that Cdes were not encouraged to think critically of the
higher organs. He also refered to the line of march document.
pointing out that no criticism were made of the higher organs
He said that there has always been a tendency for the party to
pay very little attention to the economy which has relevance to
the question of social benefits and the overall development of
the revolution. The C.C needs to prepare lines of educating th
people on the present situation with I.M.F and the present salt
negotiations. The C.C lack a perspective for the development
of the armed forces, the social problem still remains. There i
a serious lack of C.P.E and ideological work in the Armed Forc

The work in the geographic regions is handled unsatisfactoril
using the St. Andrew's issue as evidence. He also raised his
concern over the C.P.E programme. He said that in a context w
the party faces disintegration the C.C has failed miserably. H
concluded that if we continue in this way the party will soon
loose state power.

He went on to say that he has tremendous faith in the C.C. Th
C.C is comprised of the best Cdes the party can produce at this
time, but we have failed to march up collectively to a growing
complex situation.

Cde. Mc Barnette said that so far this meetings gives a clear
indication of how far the C.C is from the rest of the membershi
of the party. He felt that the issues raised have been bubbli
for quite a long time but the C.C had failed to rest it s fing
on the pulse. The structures are there but the C.C has failed
to provide the correct atmosphere for Cdes to perform. The lac
of a prospective shows itself in may ways e.g community work,
failure to deal with the spontaneous work of the masses. Though
the conclusion is that C.P.E is the priority there had been no
structures in the party for C.P.E up to a few weeks ago.

The revolution is suffering from a serious fall of its active
supporters. The party must seek to consolidate. The church
has capitalise on our weaknesses using the tactics and strategie
of the party. Cdes at this time shows deep fear to criticise t
party. The basis must be laid for frank and open criticism in
the party.

Sister Phyllis Coard said that we have recognise that the
situation is very serious. The mood of the party members can b
graded as one (1) or lower. The mood of the masses can be
graded as 1.5. The work of the P.C.B can be described as un-
successful though there have been slight improvements in
St. George's, St. David's and West Coast, it is till very bad i
St. Andrew's and Carriacou. All programmes of the Revolution

are in a very weak condition, while propaganda work is still very bad. The mass organisations are showing less participation in the political work. During the months May to August strenous efforts were made to revive the work but only a mordest 5% improvement was recorded. She analyse the situation as the failure of leadership of the Committees and failure of the C.C to exercise leadership.

As a result, of the C.C failure to deal with the problems in NWO there arise a detoriation and pettit bourgeois behaviour resulting in the removal of key sisters in the work. The guidance of the Wormen's Committee work is now in the hands of a non-party member; Sister Claudette Pitt is now considering resigning, (she also know of 8 Cdes who express a willingness to resign from the party at this time). There is no alternative leader to Claudette because Cdes identied expressed their unwillingness to join the party. The C.C has displayed idealism on the question of women in the party, they cannot cope with the demands of the party at this time. She said that she also notice that the older Cdes are getting tired and sick.

There is a need for the party to assist the NYO in long and short term strategy, their role in the state etc.

The militia/non existent, the army/demoralise the Cdes have genuining complains, growth in militarisation and deep economic problems.

No long and short term goals are set for the propaganda Committee and the masses are moving backward politically.

The Poor quality and low moral of the party is communicated to the masses because party Cdes live and work among the masses, they also display a harsh attitude to the masses. The masses are demoralise because of the party's failure to manners the situation. Party members cannot beat back the reactionary lines on the ground. There are also varing trends among party members, at the level of committees there is dog fight going on. The pettit bourgeois elements are using the situation to excuse themselves from criticism. However, some members have bceome more proletarian in their approach. Members are demoralise by having to carry out unrealistic tasks and decisions. The C.C has failed to analyse the problems correctly and come up with a long term plan development. Cdes sees the July conclusions as being very dishonest.

The question of the ideological development of the C.C is an issue that we need to make a decision on. If this is allowed to continue the party will disintegrate in a matter of 5-6 months with Cdes resigning, applicants cannot make, workers do not want to join the party as a result the few remaining members will bceome over burdened,& fustrated the party will collapse and the revolution cannot continue without the party. The revolution can be turned back within one year. The international support of the working class is lessening. The party need to put the interest of the working people first and foremost.

Cde. Bishop said that in some ways Cdes contributions
have began to address tomorrows agenda.

He said that he is struck by the levels of thought and
preparation of Cdes as evident in their various contributions
Though some conclusions are a bit pre mature, they are
however, correct he agreed that the main problems lies in
the C.C, in his view it have to do with two main factors.

(1) Low ideological levels, insufficient knowledge and
awareness

(3) The lack of perspective as evident in a number of
C.C meetings e.g 16th July. However, points are
coming out more sharply today.

The lack of proper application or strategy and tactics
has led to our party paying no significant attention to the
views of the party and the masses; there is clearly no
channels for communications which has lead to a breakdown
of collective leadership. He said that it was premature
to move from monthly meetings, wholistic pleanry. The C.C
has been able to receive oral and written reports from
the party. Decision were taken outside of the C.C, we
have not set up systems for implimentation and verification.
The C.C is very adhoc in its approach to the work. The
consistant over ruling of decision leeds to a lack of
clarity regarding the role of the higher organs, and
inability for the C.C to provide guidance monitoring and
supervision of the work. This is as a result of the
increasing complexity of the work.

The C.C has not been able to rise to the challenge of
the increasing complexity this has led im to take a
number of unrealistic decisions.

The C.C has made a number of mistakes over the past 18
months because of the weak links with th masses we became
bureauractic and too formalistic in our approach. Visits
to work places have disappeared, increasing non attendance
at zonal councils and parish meetings, visit to communities
to meet people at an informal level, decrease in the
number of discussion and meetings with people in all areas
of work, failure to participate in public activities,
village meetings have disappeared. We have not paid
sufficient regards to the material base in the country.
Changes in the economy, changes in social wages and the
predominant P.B Character of the masses and society as
a whole our propaganda positions have consistently fed
economism. We have failed to point out to the masses that
this period requires a number of sacrafices and if we
are not prepared to build the economy through hard work
we will not make it. We have to take the blame for the
over economic expectations of the people. We need to
develop proper lines on these questions for the people.

He said the mood among the farmers is very low they criticise
and attack workers for not producing.

The mood of the agricultural workers is also very low pointing
to his last visit to one of the state farms.

His understanding of the criticism and complain from the party
has to do with the lack of channels of communications for the
membership to raise their complains and grievances which we need
to address. He agreed that a lot of criticisms have developed
in leading Cdes in the party. He shares the overall concerns
that Cdes have arrived at.

Cde. James agreed that there is a serious crisis in the party.
There are signs of the beginning of disentegration, in the
party, drop in confidence and prestige of the C.C. If the
situation is not rescued there will be no hope for the future
of the party and its ability to hold state power.

The work of the party among the masses has been badly affected
by the mood of the party masses. At present the mood of the
masses is low. We also have to conclude that counter revolution
will seek to exploit the situation that we face. It is also
clear that our ability to hold state power has also decreased.
The problem however, lies in the Central Committee which is the
main link in solving the situation. The C.C will have to take
an honest cold blooded and scientific approach to save the party
and revolution.

Cde. Louison said that he was shocked on his arrival in the
country to see the state of the roads which is in the worst state
it has ever been since the revolution. This he said is because
of the continued decline of the work of the party. He also
pointed out to a split in the P.F.U Executive as evidence of the
present situation. He said that having listen to a number of
Cdes he agree that there is a lot of problems in the leadership
He also pointed to the low ideological level of the C.C and the
continued slow rate of development of a number of Comrades on the
C.C. There is also a clear lack of contact with the masses among
some of the C.C Comrades. He feels however, that sufficeint
weight has not been given to the objective situations and the
problems in the economy which we have failed to explain to the
masses. He also pointed to the fact that while we are loosing
links with the masses the middle class types have been coming
to the revolution for jobs. He said that this is due to the lack
of propaganda work to reach the masses. He said that he is still
to be convince that the ideological levels of the masses have gone
backwards. Some Cdes gives a panicky impression in the way they
make their points.

He feels that/C.C is still capable of leading what is missing/the
ideological level and collective leadership. The main feature of
the July plenary is still correct. The revolution is deficient in
facing the problems squarely and putting things in place.

Cde. Whiteman said that he is shocked at the mood in the country.
He pointed to the failure of the two indoor rallies in St. George's
as an indication of the present situation. He said that there
is not enough two way communications in the party, too much
directives is given regardless of Cdes work plans and schedules
and unrealistic targets are set especially in C.P.E. The
propaganda work has been too idealistic especially on the economy.
He has never seen the road in such a bad condition before. We

have not been able to detect how the enemy operates he feels that there must be some counter revolutionary network in the country. Too much time is spent on small issues instead of fundamental issues e.g the church. He said that we do not fully grasp how the church is working at this time and what tactics and strategy must be employed to counter them. We do not fully know how the masses think and the house to house is not effective in achieving this. His view is that the leadership must spend more time in house to house in order to know what the people are thinking, we also need to think of how to build and substain the mass organisations in the face of economic difficulties.

He described the directive to remove all party Cdes children to public schools as a wrong approach, he said that the decision battle has not come yet, we have to focus on the major contradictions instead of these minor points. He suggested a second leadership structure that can read and summarise reports, he feels that the Leadership spends too much time reading reports.

Cde. Strachan said that he party is now 10 years and 6 months old, though the period we have met on several occasions to look at the work, the problem is that there has been a constant struggle to get the work done, he do not know how long this thing would continue for. The situation the party faces is even at the level of applicants. It is clear that a rebellion has started, it can burst out if it is not solved in a serious way, This is because the C.C have not lived up to expectations.

There is a lot of confusion and unclarity, Cdes are complaining that a large percentage of the party is not working, Cdes are complaining of being over burdened. The party do not give any attention to the economic and social problem of the party members, Cdes have not internalised the channels for communications and use them and even when some of their problems are solved the party do not double check to ensure. There is no system to assess the performance of the C.C members. The C.C is very far from the general membership and the D.C is not playing the role, it helps to demoralise Cdes. A hard look must be taken as to how the D.C must function.

The weekend seminars have shown that there is potential for building a serious M.L party. The sessions brought out both the positive and negative sides of cdes. However, the negative sides was given too much weight. The last rounds of seminar showed a qualitative difference in Cdes discipline. There was an incredible level of thought and participation, these things are happening at the same time when complains are coming up.

The level of attention to internal party development is not given as needed. We accept this in principle but in practice we have been different. The problem we face is in the style and method of our work. He said that a very high level of complacency exist at the level of the C.C. He pointed to the October crisis when the C.C met and took a number of decisions to take the party out of the rut. Cdes began to attend studies on time, prepared and attended meetings on time. However, the fundamental issues were placed aside.

13/......

CC Cdes have not been taking a global look at the work,
instead they only emphasise on their narrow area of work.
He said that we are maintaining the revolution and not leadi
it. Our style of work shows a tendecny to platformism as
op osed to doing the hard slobbing work. He also refered t
the points made in the Fedon group seminar to caharacterise
the party. Busy busy action, temporization and vasillation
in taking hard decisions is eveident in the C.C and more to
Political Bureau e.g the St. Andrew's task force situation.
He said that whenever we postpone a decision we are the one
loose because imperialism is not waiting on us.

He said that in his view a great majority of Cdes love the
party and express a willingness to work in the party but are
not aware of what they should do, using example of Gloria
Hastick who expressed her willingness to remain in the party
but she has been having many problems. He said that the
C.C has not tried to appreciate the problems that Cdes
experienced from time to time. He said that Cdes have used
the rules as a form of resistance refering to the no of
holiday leaves, excuse from community work etc.

He sa d that if we agree that the role of the party is/build
the revolution and if we believe that an ML party can build
what we want then we have to put the party on a M.L footing.
He questioned whether we want to build socialism or just
chanting sologans? Do we have a vision of the future. He is
concern over the fact that the process is without a Leninis
Vanguard. He pointed that in October it was agreed to revie
sister Phyl in regards to her membership on the Bureau but
it was never raised in the July plenary. The C.C must now
find out what are the essential qualities of a M.L party.

BRAOD CONCLUSIONS PROPOSED BY CDE, MAURICE BISHOP

1. There is a state of deep crisis in the party and revoluti

2. The main resson for these weaknesses is the functionin
   of the C.C.

3. The crisis has also become a major contributing factor
   to the Crisis in the country and revolution and the low
   mood of the masses.

4. The crisis have also been compounded by the weakness in
   the material base, electricial block outs, bad roads,
   retrenchments and jobs as an issue.

   To correct this situation the following must be done:

1. Find methods of improving the work an individual and
   collective leadership of the C.C

2. The need to develop a prospective based on M.L criterior
   to guide the work in the coming period.

3. Urgently find creative ways of deepening the links with
   and out work among the masses.

14/......

4. To establish meaningful channels of communications between the leadership and the membership and to formally re-rational ise the work among party Comrades, bearing in mind the ground sewll of complains of over work and lack of of inner party democracy.

5. The C.C need to develop structures for accountability bearing in mind that Cdes are now demanding accounts from the party.

COLLECTIVE AND INDIVIDUAL ANALYSIS OF THE C.C

Cde. Liam James leading off said that this si the last chance for the C.C to pull the party out of this crisis and on a firm M.L path. This crisis is not only among the masses but in the party membership as well. Over the past few months one could have seen that the party and the C.C was not moving forward. The way forward is to take an honest, cold blooded, objective and scientific approach to the situation.

Within the C.C there are many problems all Cdes must be criticise for the lvds of disorganisation, low ideologfcal level and failure to put the party on a firm M.L footing. These weaknesses are so evident that party Cdes are saying that certain Cdes must be chopped from the C.C. It is clear that party Cdes have lost their level of respect for the C.C The removeal of Cdes from the C.C will no way solved the problem in his view all the Cdes of the C.C are by far the best Cdes in the party, what is needed is firm Leninism. He pointed cut that the most fundamental problem is the quality of leadership of the Central Committee and the party provided by Cde. Maurice Bishop. In his view the Cdes has great strength, his ability to inspire and develop Cdes, his ability to raise the regional and international respect for the party and revolution; he has the chrisma to build the confidence of the people both in and out of the country, and to put forward clearly the postions of the party. Today these strengths alone cannot put the party any further in this period. The qualities he lacks is what is needed to push the revolution forward at this time:

(1) A Leninist level of organisation and discipline.

(2) Great depth in ideological clarity.

(3) Brilliance in strategy and tactics.
These qualities which are essential for M.L leadership has prove to be lacking in the Cde. at this time.

Cde. Layne said that based on all analysis, discussions and c conclusions it is quite clear that the C.C has not been able to give ideological leadership to the process. If we are to be honest and frank througho ut the crisis we go through more and more Cdes coming to realise that we face a real possibility of the revolution being turned back.

It is clear that Cde. Bishop lacks theses qualities put forward
by Cde. James. Despite his strengths, the strengths that he
lacks is vitally needed to steer the revolution off the
dangers and to come out of the crisis. The salvation of the
revolution calls for us to take a mature proletarian decision
to save and carry the revolution forward.

Cde. Ventour agreed with the two cdes that the type of
leadership that is neeessary to pull us out of the crisis is
lacking in the Cde. Leader. These criticisms were made to him
on more than one occasion which he accepted. He shows that he
do not have the quality to put the party on a firm M.L footing.

He also criticise the C.C for not criticising the Cde. for areas
of work e.g Armed Forces and Propaganda. However, he thinks
that the main fetter is that the Cde. do not have these qualities.

Cde. Cornwall agreeing with all the Cdes who spoke so far. He
said that we have studied O.P.P. Seven points were made one of
which was a Leninist C.C as a principle for the building of a
M.L. party. He agreed that the root cause is the C.C. For
quite some time we have been seeing the problem. The chairmanship and leadership of the C.C appears very weak. He said that
there are great strength in the Cde. Leader that have carried
the process, but as the complexities grows these qualities
alone is proving inadequate. He also added that the Cde. Leader
ability to supervise and stay ontop of the work is also lacking.
These weaknesses creates a fetter on how we organise to carry the
work forward. Instead we move from one crisis to another and
the frequency of crisis becoming more and more frequent. If
we fail to transform the party we will loose state power, lives
will be lost, history has placed a great responsibility on our
shoulders which we must seek to deal with in the correct and
scientific way.

Cde. De Riggs said that he has been giving the work some deep
thought over the past months. He agreed that the situation
is favourable for counter revolution in this time, state power
can be easily over thrown. The low mood of the party and the
masses is also very clear to him. He said that the C.C has
failed to match up ideologically to the situation. The removal
of any Cde. on the C.C will not help this situation.

The main problem is the question of leadership. There is immi-
diate need for the reorganisation of the C.C in order to re
build the confidence of the membership and masses in the party.
In solving this problem. The interest of the party and
revolution must be taken first, he pointed that he agreed with
all the points made by Cde. James.

Cde. Bartholomew agreed with what he called very frank and open
analysis by the Cdes. He said that he had never reaised any
criticism of the C.C and Leadership though he was disatisfied
with the quality of the leadership. He agreed with all thepoints
points made on the strengths of the Cde. Leader. He continued
to say that his weaknesses were known all the while, but Cdes
were hesitant to raise them. Though he had accepted earlier
criticisms of this, he had never fulfil them in practice. The
quality of the C.C has deteoriated very badly, there is too much

vascillation by the Cde. Leader. The M.E quality is becoming even more critical as the revolution develops.

Cde. Kamau said that since the last C.C meeting he has been giving deep thought to the work of the C.C. Overall the C.C is very weak, disorganised and haphazzard in its approach to the work. His personal work is still disorganise and weak, which is true to say of most C.C Cdes, there is also a serious absence of deep thought and study. He said that the Cde. Leader has shown great strengths and remained in the positive qualities mentioned by Cde. James. However, the main problem remains the role of Cde. Bishop as the leader of the C.C, He said that the C.C continue to be loose and disorganise and unfocus, he said that the Cde. Leader lacks the quality to leade the C.C as spelled out by Cde. James. He agreed that removal of Cdes from the C.C cannot solve the problem until we deal with the question of leadership of the C.C

Sister Phyllis Coard commented that when she read the minutes of the C.C in July she was very shocked. From the beginning of the year she had began to prepare herself more for study though she had not been doing broad reading. However, she feels that the Central Committee cannot move forward unless it involve in more indepth studies. As things began to get more complex the C.C have not met seriously to deal with the fundamental problems and in the absence of the C.C the P.B have not done any better.

She said that she had identified a number of questions for the C.C to deal with in order to move forward, being that we now have to decide what perspective to use and how to develop political education, strategic long term and short term goals for propaganda. The best way to coordinate media propaganda with the propaganda work of the party, how do we develop our lines quickly to the party members, how to structure the C.P.E programme to encourage more participation, the level of party participation in C.P.E, what amount of programmes can the party substain and maintain, qualities to look for in the selection of new party Cdes, how do we improve communications from the higher organs to the lower organs, how to structure the Secretariat, should the NYO become a semi vanguard, how to direct political education, how to organise community work successfully, how to overcome militarisation in the army, how to organise militia to ensure maximum participation, what is the long term future of the zonal councils and how do we sacrafice quantity for quality.

She said that neither the P.B nor the C.C have analyse these fundamental questions that is why these problems exist today, / when and even/it is done it is limited and vasillation follows. She agreed that the leaders of the party has failed to provide the necessary leadership to the party. She commented that the main problem of the C.C is idealism, volunteerism, failure to face up to hard decisions, illness as a result of phycological pressures in this context the Cde. leader has not taken the responsibility, not given the necessary guidance, even in areas where he is directly in charge of the guidance is not adequate He is disorganised very often, avoid responsibilities for dealing with with critical areas of work e.g study class. She criticised

the C.C for not criticising him in the past, some time ago
he pointed out that he was not capable but the C.C ignored
him. Some Cdes are scared to criticise him because he had
been hostile to criticism.

The P.B and C.C leaned on the O.C to take decisions that they
should have taken. Cde. Strachan has taken the full
responsibility to hold the party together when the C.C and
P.B had failed to provide the necessary political guidance
under this pressure he had taken bound away decisions, shown
hostility to criticisms, though she had seen some improvement
of this in the past two weeks. The Cde must be complimented
for the proletarian qualities which he display. A number
of C.C Cdes are demoralise because their work has fallen.
We also need to consider whether the C.C will be stronger
or weaker if Cdes are chopped, in her view it will be weaker.
She agreed to changes in the composition of the C.C. She
concluded that the C.C will have to take the hard decisions
that will improve the quality and levels of the C.C in terms
of ideological and organisational directions.

Cde. Bain said that the analysis is difficult for him in the
given circumstances, problems in work, health and a number
of Cdes being out of the country. The ideological levels of
the C.C is definitely a great concern e.g we are not sharp
in detering the main feature of the period of July plenary,
which he was worried about particularly when the revolution
is 4½ years old. He said that another feature is that we come
up with hasty decision as a result of pre mature thinking.
Cdes are able to identify that the C.C collectively is weak,
he agreed with the points made by Cde. James and added that
it is greater demanding   the leader to give more guide-
ance to the process at this time. ....

5 MIN.

Cdes are looking to the C.C for this quality, it is dangerous
if leading Cdes cannot show these qualities. He said that
he would have preferred is the Cdes had named the C.C Cdes
that the membership was doubtful of. He said that if this
concensus is wide spread and the party do not take action on it
it can lead to more problems, how will these members respond
and what will be the C.C 's answer to it. He feels that
whatever decision must be taken should be given the greatest
thought, not only for now but throughout the future.

Cde. Lousion said that the no. one problem is the quality of
leadership given the process by Cde. Bishop. He loses focus
and spend too much time on details. The points made by Cde.
James and Cornwall have really cristalised the problem which
we have to find ways and means of solving. He said though that
the C.C have not been able to assist the Cds, in developing
these strengths.

He said that the names of C.C Cdes mentioned by the membership as doubtful were "H.A., Uni. Fitzy, Kamau and St. B.
Though in his view reduction or expansion of the C.C cannot
solve the problem. He suggested a cross system for developing
the work, how to find a methodology for helping and forcing
C.C Cdes to develop ideologically. This problem is a fundamental problem we have been extremely weak, the criticisms

are correct we have to come up with a solution quick and
ensure that it is communicated to the party within hours. He
added that we need to spend much more time doing preparation
for study and rigourously execute the tasks. We also have to
get rid of trivial issues.

Cde. Strachan said that one of the most striking thing is that
he .. never heard any member of the C.C ask for a report from
the Political Bureau on its week to week functioning. The P.B
is a committee of the C.C and at no point in time was a report
summoned. The CC Cdes do no get any minutes or report from the
P.B. This is very serious, because the P.B is left to do their
own thing.

He pointed that he is in total agreement with the points made
by Cde. James he again referred to the Fedon study seminar
making the point that Cdes always wait for someone else
to take the lead, which/one of the reason for this rut. We now
have to take the responsibility of demanding higher qualities
from the Cde. Leader. The Cde. should have dealt with him every
time he slipped in the past. He recognise the brillance of the
Cde. but agreed that this is not enough to carry the process
forward and to build a serious M.L party. He used the example
of Cde. Fidel who is always reflecting and thinking saying that
these are the qualities that a M.L leader must have. He said
this is the time when we have to deal with the main problems
of the C.C.

Cde. Unison Whiteman said that the weaknesses mention of the
Cde. Leader are correct. Since October there have been some
improvements in scheduling and study but these improvements are
not fundamental enough. He said that the Cde. Leader had not set
enough time to the fundamental but we have to be careful that we
don't shift too much blame from the the C.C collectively. We
need to have a commitment on the C.C to new norms, prioritisation
greater reflection, better style of work, we have to build up
Comrades,e.g Cde. Leader, we have to assist on higher standards
from him which he is capable of.

Cde. Leader thanked the Cdes for their frankness in their
criticisms. He said that Cdes in the past have given serious
thought to the question of leadership and failed to raise it
for diplomatic reasons which was not good. He is disatisfied
over the fact that C.C Cdes have not raised these points before
with him frankly, though a couple non C.C Cdes have done it.
He picked up an overwhelming sentiment that the qualities
required are not possessed in him. He agreed that the points
are correct especially correct application of strategy and tactics
which cannot be achieved except the other qualities are fulfil.
He had found difficulties of finding a relevant material to
study the question of the functioning of the P.B and C.C which
reflects a weakness, he don't think that he had given adequate
leadership to bodies. He had several problems over the years
especially the style that entails consensus, and unity at all
costs which can result in blunting class struggle. He had tried
to keep a certain kind of relationship with Cdes even though
it is not what it used to be before. He also questioned his
approach as regards to collective leadership, he said that

there is not enough participation and discussions. Too much
decisions are taken by smaller and smaller organs which affects
collective leadership.

On the question of crisis and problems it is correct as the
maximum leader to take the full responsibilities. He needs
time to think of his own role and to give a more precise response
to the problem addressed which he thinks is a correct approach.

After lunch Cde. Ventour took the opportunity to explain to the
C.C that his illness was to a large extent more phycological
than physical. Since he came back the situation had affected him
which reflects a P.B character of lack of staunchness. He said
that he would try his best to pull himself out of this situation
and to serve the party and revolution in the best way he could.

Cde. Bartholomew also pointed to the health Problem he experienced
and the question of his low ideological level of which he is not
satisfied with. He said that he is not capable of taking the
ideological C.M class. Both himself and sister Phyllis Coard
had requested to be personally assessed because of the fact
that they were not in the July plenary, the Cdes were told that
they were not present at the meeting therefore they could not
have been assessed, especially Cde. Tan who was ill and as a
result could not have function. Cdes agreed that it was incorrect
to do it now because of the focus.

THE ROLE OF THE C.C.

Cde. Bishop said that on many occasion we have tried to look at
the role of the C.C. He referred to the documents of June '81
and subsequent minutes of the C.C that dealt with its role.

He proposed that the C.C move to meetings once per month and to
have three wholistic plenary, each year.

He said that the montly meetings must be seen as a medium of
analysis, exchanging information of various sections, and pre-
schedules should cover special areas of party and state work.
He sees that at the end of October the main topic being C.P.E,
in November the study commission/will also have to determine
the role of the C.C//is key in operationalising the sub committee
in terms of reports from various bodies etc. Also getting
to the party guidelines on major issues ensuring conclusion and
resolutions are drawn up after our deliberation and be circulated to the membership.

To develop and maintain links with the masses the leadership
must personally get on the ground among the people, step up
participation in zonal and parish councils, visits schools,
monitor and push production. The role of the C.C must be worked
out in this regard. Develop mechanism for accountability, and
to review constant feedback from the membership and to ensure
channels of communications with them.

made
The C.C must do a constant evaluation of the progress /by members,
receive reports from O.C on the re rationalisation of the work,
prioritise the work of Cdes on the C.C and set targets to be
achieved on a weekly monthly and yearly basis.

Cde. Kamau Mc Barnette said that the C.C needs to explain the
criterior for membership on the C.C and by what mechanism are
Cdes work on the C.C are judge. Ensure the right atmosphere
are convened for free and frank discussions. The party must
be honest and frank with its members and for the last time
explain the truth about Cde. Radix.

Cde. Leon Cornwall said that the C.C must have a propsective
on its role. We need to work out the framework for the kind
of party we would like to build so when Cdes are recruited
we will know what structure we must put them in. The
commission that is travrlling to Cuba and S.U should know
what should be done on their return., They should know how we
are going to build the party, drawing the experience of other
countries. We also need to start working on a party constitution in a concrete way. We must develop commission for
different areas of work. These are concepts that we need to
start.The work on how we are going to build people's power.
A conference should be set up to look at the submission from
the commissions/take decisions and develop the line of march.

Cde. Layne said that he share the views of Cde. Cornwall. He
said that the crisis cannot be solved immediately. There
are a number of fundamental question that the party need to
look at over a period of time. The Party has a very un-
scientific approach to the work, we rush to do things without
deep analysis which further push us into problems. The NJM
does not face a problem of commitment. We need to find the
root of the contradiction or we will continue to face problems.

When Cdes are working hard without any rest it leads to
fustration and demoralisation. We have taken an incorrect
position in terms of what is necessary to build the party.
He pointed to the fact that Cde. Strachan commission visit
to Cuba was not dealt with seriusly. He pointed that there
are committees but no structures, there is no clear role for
the function and future of the V.C.B.& we do not have a C.C
Secretariat. We have to make the question of supervision
a profession. The O.C has been successful in carrying us
to power, the tasks it faces now is enormous. Cdes quality
on the O.C has gone down, Cdes cannot supervise the work
effectively, good ideas are accepted in principle. However,
he complimented the new approach by the O.C, he said that the
O.C has been good but we are asking the Cdes to take too much
heavy ideological and political decisions in the absence of
the functioning of the C.C and P.B.

He made reference to the Etophian Party and the method they
took to develop their party, he said that even though their
method cannot be applied immediately so that it can be develop in the future, we need to have a policy for the development
of Cdes in the party, we have to develop the professional
levels of Cdes in the party, Cdes will make mistakes but they
will be helped and pulled forward.

He said that the struggle for socialism is won, lost or
divided in the army. The party must now be organise in the
work places. Cdes with state post must be prepared to carry
out the lines of the party in the work places. We have
experience in mobilising the masses but we do not know how
to build the party. We have to lay the basis for taking a
strategic approach for the building of a M.L party learning
from the experience of other parties.

Cde. James agreed with the postions of Cde. Cornwall and
Cde. Layne, he made the following proposals:-

1. The C.C must become fully accountable to the members,
   so that Cdes can evaluate the work of the C.C on a whole
   and the C.C members.

2. All C C Cdes must be based in the country at this time
   until the situation is resolved.

3. The C.C and party must study Brutens.

4. Recall the conclusions of the July Plenary.

5. Proposed a modle of joint leadership, marrying the
   strengths of Cdes Bishop and Coard. He went to define
   the responsibilities of the two Cdes.

CDE. MAURICE BISHOP

(i) Direct work among the masses, focus on production
    and propaganda.

(ii) Particular attention to the organs of popular
     democracy, working class, youth masses, visits to
     urban and rural work places.

(iii) Militia mobilisation

(iv) Regional and International work

CDE. BERNARD COARD

(i) Party organisation work
    Chairman of the O.C

(ii) Party organisational development and formation of
     Cdes.

(iii) Strategy and tactics.

The C.C must discuss and ratify all proposals and decisions
sought by the Cdes.

22/..........

P.B weekly chaired by Cde. Bernard Coard. The bothe Cdes will write quarterly reports to the C.C for review. The membership must be told of this decision.

Cde. Deriggs commented on the brillance of the contributions of Cdes Layne, James and Cornwall and supported their positi

He proposed that:

(1) Cde. George Louison be placed to head the St. Andrew's work while maintaining the teachers, farmers and the Ministry of Agriculture work

(2) Cde. Strachan to head C.F.E and propaganda work.

(3) Cde. Bartholomew responsible for Youth and St. Patrick's

(4) Cde. Austin - Construction.

(5) Cde. Layne chief of the Armed Forces with Cde. Cornwall chief of political and academic work.

(6) Cde. Whiteman, Foreign Affairs and Chief of I.R.D of the Party.

(7) Fitzroy Bain - Rural workers work

(8) Cde. Chalkie Ventour Urban Working Class

(9) Sis. Phyllis Coard. St. George's PCB and NWO.

(10) Cde. St. Bernard, West Coast and Carriacou

(11) Cde. Mc Barnette, St. David's P.C.B.

(12) Cde. DeRiggs - Health

(13) Cde. Liam James Ministry of Interior.

Cde. Ventour agreed with Cde. Chris especially with the position on Cde. George Louison. He proposed that Cde. Strachan remain as Deputy chairman of the O.C. He do not agree with the position on H.A. Because he feels that there is great admiration and respect for the Cde. in the Armed Forces. However, he should also retain his position in Construction.

Cde. Mc Barnette agreed with the positions of the Cdes, he complimented Cdes Cornwall, Layne and James for the depth of their contribution. He took the opportunity to put out his interest in propaganda work.

Cde. Layne agreed with the position of Cde. James on the question of Cde. Coard's return to the C.C and P.B. He said that Cde. Bishop qualities are still necessary, but as Cde. James said these qualities cannot push the process forward. The only Cde. who have these qualities is Cde. Bernard Coard

and if one look at the situation in practice he has been
giving ideological and organisational leadership, and
elaborating strategy and tactics even outside of the C.C
e.g the land question. The reason why these qualities are
lacking on the C.C and P.B is because Cde. Coard has been
out of the partys leadership. He sees Cde. James modle as the
best hope of pulling the party out of the crisis. He also f
feels that Cde. Austin should remain in the army because of
his qualities and prestige there.

Cde. Louison said that the scope of the issues raised is
very thorough because it put the work into prospective.
He disagree with the joint leadership proposal, he feels
that this modle cannot solve the problem of Cde. Maurice
Bishop. He welcomes a postion of Cde. Coard being back on
the C.C and P.B and Chairman of the O.C. He is also not
sure that the theoretical postion put forward for joint
leadership is correct. He said the qualities missing have
two dimensions. The level of effort of personel discipline
and struggle that he is able to put in towrds making the
change, and the level of collective mannersing from the C.C
to ensure that he build these qualities, if he fails then
it may be necessary to remove the Cde. in the future. He
did not agree with the basing of all C.C Comrades in the
country. He said that there is need to have a C.C Comrade
as Ambassador to Cuba, and Cde. Layne have only five weeks
to complete his course of which he should be allowed to, if
he complete the training it will bear more fruits in future
He agreed to the monthly meetings of the C.C. He commented
that his personel choice is to work in St. Andrew's, but
he feels his role in the production sector is key and if he
is to be given any additional tasks it should be in this
area, He felt that Cdes are underplaying the role of the
material base. He also agreed that Cde. Austin should
remain in the Armed Forces.

Cde. James said that his proposals is first of all to deal
with the problem that we face. His view is that the fulles
proletarian type support of the C.C can help the Cde.
Leader in developing these qualities, Cde. Bernard is the
only Cde. that have the necessary qualities to merge with
Cde. leader's strength for   r leading the process at this
time.

On Cde. Layne and Cornwall, we all agree that the Army is
in a state of rut and demoralisation along with a serious
ideological drift the army needs at this time Leninist
Leadership in that of Cde. Layne and the political and
Academic work in that of Cde. Cornwall. He agreed with
Cde. DeRiggs proposals, in his view there is no other
choice, especially with the position on St. Andrew's work,
the state eneterprise work is too much for Cde. Lousion.

Cde. Bartholomew said that he is very frightened of the
level of ideological drift in the army, Cdes are saying
that we are talking of imperialism too much, when there
so much problems in the camps. Ministers are buying new c
when soldier cannot get food to eat. They are also sayin
that the army is a bourgeois army making references of

24/........

mable standards.

The masses have lost confidence in the Army's capability to defend the revolution. The political work in the Armed Forces have not been very good. He felt that Cde. Layne and Cde. Cornwall are critical in the army at this time, and that we cannot afford to have a C.C Comrade as Ambassador to Cuba, despite the importance of the relations.

He also agreed that Cde. Louison should be sent to do political work in St. Andrew's because of the problems in the parish and the importance of having a P.B Cde. there. He should remain in N.Y.O and St. Patrick's. He said that he is not capable of handling C.P.E. He agreed that Cde. Coard should be back on the C.C and P.B in a process of joint leadership.

He expressed his concern on the Ministry of Interior. He said that this area is very critical in this period, Cde. James as leader should not be allowed to travel because of the need to sit on top of the work. This excessive travelling does not allow him to effectively supervise the work. P.B minutes should be circulated to the C.C because the C.C is overall responsible for the work.

Cde. Cornwall said that we have two outstanding Cdes in our party being Cdes Bishop and Coard, we have suffered because of the the absence of Cde Coard in the leadership, what is proposed is joint leadership with specific responsibilities and tasks. He has no problem with the points raised by Cde. George but not as reasons to solve the fundamental problem in the party, therefore he strongly supports the points made by Cde. James.

On the Armed forces he said that no one can deny that Cuba is the most important country to the Grenadian process, but he felts that his time is seriously wasted as Ambassador to Cuba because the work is carried out inspite of him. A good party Cde. can carry out the work while he is used more effectively at home. He suggested that Cde. Mc Phail remain to brief Cde. James Parke who will be going up there soon. Cde. Mitchell has improved tremendiously and can do quite a lot of work. Therefore it is quite easy for both himself and Cde. Layne to sit on top of the Army to ensure that it develops.

Cde. Bain felt that the proposals made by Cde. James is a compromise though it is joining strengths of the two Cdes. together. He is confused on how this will work. He would like it to be spelled out clearly, he has problems to conception- -lise it especially when one Cde. will chair the C.C and the other chair the P.B. He will need to give this more thought. He isin agreement that the C.C and P.B have suffered with the absence of Cde. Coard. He also don't know how Cde. Coard is going to accept the formula, he said that some structure should be put in place to allow Cde. Layne to complete his course. However, Cde. Cornwall should remain in the Armed Forces. The C.C has shown too much vasillation on the St. Andrew's issue, Cde. George in his view is the best person for this area. Cde. Austin should not be removed from the armed forces. Cde. Chalkie Ventour is the best person to work

....he Urban Working Class but given his present health
conditions he should be given a personal assistant. He also
agreed with Cde. Bartholomew's point on Cde. James in the
Ministry of Interior. He concluded by saying that there is
need for the C.C to be more on the ground.

Cde. Layne was shocked by the points raised by Cde. Bartholomew
on the Armed Forces in this context, he agreed that himself and
Cde. Cornwall should remain to begin work in the Army. The
explanation to the Cdes in Cuba and S.U can be handled tactically

Cde. Louison felt that Cde. Cornwall is taking an emotional
approach to the question, his purpose in Cuba should be seen in
the context of the overall international work for the Revolution.
The Cde. approach shows a degree of panic in his view.

Cde. Strachan supported the proposals made by Cde. James in
joint leadership. It has been able to recognise the strengths
of the two Cdes due to years of experience of working with them.
The Cde. Leader can unite all classes and strata which is
vitally needed. Cde. Coard has the qualities that he is lacking
therefore a creative way must be used to fuse these qualities
to move the process forward. It is clear that Cde. Coard's
absence is felt over the years. In order to build a Leninist
party we must have a Leninist C.C, therefore he supports the
proposals of Cde. James and DeRiggs. He do not feel that Cde.
Austin should be removed from the Army, he firmly supports the
view that both Cdes Layne and Cornwall should be placed to work
in the Armed Forces immediately, a strong position can be put
to the Cdes of S.U and Cuba so they will understand the situation
He suggested that Merle Collins or Joe Charter can function as
Ambassador to Cuba. The contributions made by Cdes Cornwall,
James and Layne impressed him, all spoken openly and frankly
with great clarity, genuin' proposals were made for the
transformation of the party which will also help to transform
the Cde. Leader into a Marxist Leninist and to Leninise the
C.C. We also have to see out ideological development as key
to the development of the party.

Cde. Whiteman agreed with the position on Cde. Cornwall and
Layne. Cde. Coard should return to the P.B and C.C he do not
agree with joint leadership, he feels that Cde. Coard should
be given specific functions as deputy leader. Agreed that Cde.
Louison should function in St. Andrew's temporarily but should
return to the economy. Considering the fact that Cde. Austin
will remain in the Army Cde. Layne should be allowed to complete
his course. Cde. Cornwall should not be removed from Cuba
because it is not correct to remove the three top officials
from any country at the same time. The proposal to put Cde.
Strachan in C.P.E is correct.

He is not sure whether he should be made head of the I.R.D of
the party because both areas requires a great deal of travelling
and to do work among the left in the region from a party standpoint can lead to problems at state to state levels. He
proposed that his travelling be cut by half.

Sis. Phyllis Coard expressed her agreement with Cde. DeRiggs
except on the point of Cde. Austin, Cde. Strachan as Deputy
chief of the O.C and responsible for C.P.E - She is happy
to hear that Cde. Kojo has considered health as an area of
political work because health is a social programme around
which the masses can be mobilised. She predicted that when
the international Airport is opened there will be serious
demoralisation and counter revolution in St. Andrew's as a result
she supported the idea of Cde. Louison being placed to work
in the parish. She also pointed to the split in the P.F.U
Executive in order to emphasise this need and the fact that
the revolution is built on the alliance of workers and peasants
She said that there is no Cdes in the party who can do what
Cde. Louison is capable of in St. Andrew's.

She also agreed that both Cdes Layne and Cornwall should begin
to function immediately in the Army. It is clear that the
soldiers are disatisfied. The party should be blamed for what
has happened to Cde. Bogo in Cuba.

She suggested that measures should be taken to limit C.C Cdes
travelling, Cdes who can adequately represent the party should
be identified for the purpose. She hunderstood   the situation
for Cde. Unison to guide the party's International work and
not to impliment it. She agrees that the whole party should
study Brutens and that the C.C must study the work of the P.B
and E.B, she also proposed that this minutes should be studied
by the membership because the stage we are at the membership
will not believe what they hear from the C.C. She agreed
with dual leadership not only for a short time but on a long
term basis.

Cde. Louison said that the decision re Cdes Layne and Cornwall
will be hard to sell to the Cdes, they will not be convinced
and it will give a note of instability, on Cuba he feels it is
a mistake that will further strain the relation between the two
countries.

He reminded Cdes of his personal choice to do the St. Andrew's
work, but in his view the two component parts that develop the
revolution is the political work and the rise of the material
base of the revolution . On the material base we have made
little or no progress over the years. It we do not work to
put these things in place the revolution will suffer over
the years to come. To him the work in the Ministry of State
enterprise is more important that the St. Andrew's work.

Cde. Strachan reminded/that the long term plan for St. Andrew's
is industralisation.

Cde. George responded by saying that St.Andrew's requires
maximum attention for at least one year to revive the work.
The social and economic problems are very deep , he don't think
that the Agricultural development work can suffer without
him and his work in the Ministry of State Enterprise can have
a great impact on the work in St. Andrew's than he being there.

He don't see joint leadership as a solution to the fundamental proble. He cannot see the theoretical basis for it, he is not convinced sufficiently that it can work and will not help to develop the strengths in the Cde. Leader. If we/convinced that. he is not developing despite all attempts to help him then we will have to remove him after his best efforts and his best intentions.

Cde. Whiteman addressing the army problems said that we have to find a moderate increase of slary for the soldiers and a food aid package at the end of every month for the soldiers. He belives that no amount of political work can move them without the material aids.

Cde DeRiggs reflecting on the points made by Cde. Louison said that St. Andrews represent a mutiplicity of problems all programmes there are the weakest in the country, it is possible that the people of St. Andrew's can be a constant resistant to the revolution, the extent of the rut is deep pointing to the problems of youth and marijuana smoking in the parish. He is not arguing that the state enterprises work is more important than St. Andrew's but at this pointing time it is critical and urgent for the party to resume control of the situation.

The proposals of joint leadership is to solve the problem that exist the collective mannersing and the Cde. Leader's personal efforts will solve his problem collective leadership is important and critical.

Cde. Ventour said that since the July Plenary he had the impression that Cde. Louison was the best person to head the St. Andrew's work. The work in the parish requires P.B guidance if we do not report this in the G.M Cdes will reise concern. In his view, Cde. Louison cannot do the state Enterprise work at this time along with Teachers and P.F.U.

Cde. Liam James for the purpose of Cde. Hudson Austin who attended the meeting on the 16th because of flight problems, went on to explain all his reasons for his proposals on joint leadership basically making all the points he had made earlier in the meeting saying that if we fail to take these measures we will be guilty of right opportunism. ---. He do not see why C.C members should run away from reality he also gave examples of countries where there are more than one leader of the process e.g Nicaragua.

Cde. Louison questioned whether Cdes are saying that he cannot do the Ministry of State Enterprise work or whether St. Andrew's work is more important or a long term strategy or is it tactical for him to be in St. Andrew's for a period then move into the State Enterprise.

Cde. Cornwall in response said that he do not see the party work in St. Andrew's as a question of tactics, he thinks that this is of strategic importance to the revolution. He is firm that Cde. Louison should go to St. Andrew's because he thinks the Cde have the necessary tools and confidence to do the work.

On the question of joint leadership he also remain very
firm because of the   situation that we face. He referred
to Nicaragua saying that a situation of joint leadership
came about because of the objective situation they faced.
Our situation requires tactical objective strategy.

He also addressed the Cuban Ambassador problems saying that
because of the problem we face. He said that we must
explain our problems to our fraternal parties because they
already know the problems that we experience now,if not they
will see us as jokers. The problem of they accusing us of
instability will be solved if we explain things to these
Comrades.

On the question of he going back to Cuba, he said that there
is a relation between the internal work and the international
work. The key responsibility for him is to build and
strengthen our process.

He supported the view Cde. Whiteman should lead the IRD
of the party.

Sister Phyllis view is that we have to decide whether
George Louison will be in the economy or in politics.
She felt that the Cde. cannot do the state enterprise
along, agriculture, P.F.U and teachers. The present
split in P.FU is because of the lack of political work
among the farmers, she also pointed to his recent failure
in O.C tasks as a sign of over work. The St. Andrew's
work is both tactically and strategically important, it
will also facilitate his teachers and P.F.U work. She
recommended that some one should assist him in the technical
work in the Ministry and Cde. George should focus on
political work for next few years.

Cde. Layne highlighted Sister Phyllis point on the problems
that will develop in St. Andrew's after the International
Airport is completed. The work in this parish is a strategic
question from all points of view. He went on to say that
all the problems in the country cannot be solved immediately.
The strength of our country is in the economy our international prestige is because of our economic performance. Therefore St. Andrew's work is both strategic and immediate
because according to Sis. Phyl we can face a problem of
counter revolution anytime.

On the question of joint leadership, he said that the
starting point is the concrete situation that we face.
We do not have a M.L party or a Leninist C.C. The
situation existed when Cde. Coard lead in ideology,
organisation and strategy and tactics for years. All
parties must be able to work out their political lines.
This is absent in our party because of the absence of
Cde. Coard. We have to be able to organise the party
and masses in order to develop a political line. Cde.
Bishop is the best person to inspire the masses on the
line of the party. In this situation the C.C is called
upon to accept what is the reality.

Cde. Bishop complimented Cdes Layne and Cornwall for their contributions which reflected ideological growth.

He said his honest view is that all strengths and talents the party must utilise of Cdes in the party. The greater the strength of Cdes is the greater responsibility, will be given to them. Leadership, power, authority and prestige that goes with leadership goes with rights. He has never had any problem with sharing power, or even a bad attitude to criticisms. He had worked very well with Cde. Bernard over the years from school days, they share a lot of policy decisions, they both wrote the manifesto, the peoples Congress enditement of Gairy. He referred to 1977 when Cde. Bernard was accused for aggressiveness and wanting to grab power, he had defended him. His position is that he or anybody has the right to be leader for life, he favours cooperation over competition. He feels that Bernard can come back to the P.B because of his skills and intelligence. Cde. James breakdown of responsibility is very useful, however, his concerns is the operationalisation of strategy and tactics. His own idea of his role falls into what Cde. James had outlined. He feels that school visits should have been included under his responsibilities.

He would like to know what is Cde. Bernard's view of the situation and response, if he do not agree what will be the views of the C.C. He need to get some answers on the operationalisation. We have to decide how we will articulate this to the party and masses of which a clear position must be drawn up. His personal concerns are; image of leadership, power struggle, imminent collapse of the revolution.

The formulation of Cdes criticisms have indicated a clear note of no confidence. He said that there are a two way flow he cannot inspire the masses when he have to look over his back or feel that he does not have the full confidence of the Comrades.

He agreed that Cde. Louison should go to St. Andrew's then to experiment in the State Enterprise Ministry, Cde. Austin must remain in the Army. He agreed with Cde. Whiteman's position on the linking of state and party IRD work. He felt that Cde. Coard should be called in to discuss the postion before the final decision is taken.

Cdes felt however, that the C.C should conclude on the decision before Cde. Bernard is spoken to.

Cde. Louison continued to raise his concern in that how will the joint leadership develop the four points in Cde. Bishop.

Cde. James said this proposal will pull us out of the period of crisis and push the party forward along with the full support of the C.C and the best efforts of the Cde. Leader will develop these qualities.

Cde. Louison was not satisfied with the answer.

Cde. James "in the close working together of Cde. Bishop and Coard, the Leader will learn from a working experience. Cde. James brought to the attention of the C.C that Cde. Louison is seeking to disturb the proceedings of the meeting for opportunist reasons.

Cde. George also expressed a willingness to leave the meeting.

Cde. James went on to address the point saying that Cde. Bishop will be Prime Minister and Commander in Chief, he will sign all documents of the C.C. We also have to take a look at how we announce this matter, his view is that this matter must be put forward in a firm and principle way, we also have to decide how we are going to formulate it. The key factor however, is how these two Cdes relate.

On the point of strategy and tactics, is that over the years Cde. Bernard Coard has been able to give guidance to the C.C, this does not mean that he will decide strategy and tactics all by himself. However, he will chair all commissions to determine strategy and tactics. The C.C will discuss and ratify all proposals brought forward. Also in real life the Cde. has developed strategy and tactics for the party.

CDE. Layne addressing the point on vote of no confidence made by Cde. Bishop said he do not agree with this positon he felt that the criticisms were made by all Comrades in the spirit of love for the party, ideological clarity and wanting to build a genuining M.L party, and to build the working class. He sees this as the best way to build the party. Cdes were very frank, the criticised themselves for not being brave enough to do so before. This frankness is critical for the development of an M.L party. It will be sad if the meeting concluded that this was a vote of no confidence. This was done in the insterst of the party and revolution what we are solving here is a problem that we experienced for years.

He used the example of the joining of two parties in G.D.R and their difficulties to say that it is only joining the strengths of two Cdes in the same party. It is our historical duty to solve all problems in our party. He also suggestes that the minutes of this discussions should be studied by members of the party.

Cde. Louison exposed the fact that he was puttin his position for narrow opportunist reasons, he is genuining seeking clarity on the issue.

Cde. James said that he had spoken of Cde. Louison behaviour and he maintain that position.

Sister Phyllis Coard said the most striking thing about this meeting is that Cdes have spoken in an open and frank way if there was any thought of removing the leader Cdes would have said so frankly. The Cde. Leader will have to accept the spirit of the criticisms. She would not like to feel that it was taken by him as a vote of no confidence, this will just discourage Cdes and made them hold back their frankness.

Cde. DeRiggs "the meeting was one of unprecidented frankness and boldness by all Cdes, it was done through the spirit of great love for the revolution and Cde. Leader.

Cornwall. "He had spoken frankly and put forward his position bluntly. If this is the impression, it will hold back Cdes from speaking frankly. They have spotted the weaknesses and strengths and sought to identify a creative solution. The C.C is disposed to asist, the Cde. Leader in all areas, if we fail to do so it will hinder the development of the process.

Cde. Strachan said that while he respect the Cde. Leader's position he feels that the points made were frank, open n and genuine. All Cdes spoke with deep sincerity and profound feelings, Cdes have given a lot of thought to the situation and genuiningly wants to come out of the crisis. These points cannot be seen as a vote of no confidence in the leader-ship. He also complimented the C.C for their frankness. It is extremely important to address the concern raised by the Cde. Leader. He agreed that Cde. Bishop must remain Prime Minister and sign all party and state documents. We also have to ensure that the masses and the counters understand that the party is a united party and there must be no signs of inner fighting. He agreed that we should conclude on. /and the issuet/ speak to Cde. Bernard Coard.

Cde. Mc Barnette said that the exercise has brought to the floor two questions (i) How we are willing to accept our weaknesses and deal with them. (ii) how much we are willing to move forward.

He agreed that the minutes must be brought to full membership. He pointed that the criticisms have not shattered his confi-dence in the Cde. Leader. He said that we need to ensure that this type of criticisms is applied to every one of the C.C if the idea of no confidence is c   it will degenerate the C.C.

Ian Bartholomew said that it took him a lot of guts to made. his points. He think that the C.C have very great respect for Cde. Bishop, there is no doubt that the Cde. will remain Prime Minister in the country. He agreed that the minutes should be studied by the membership. We cannot convince the impression that there is a leadership problem, the most important thing is how the Cdes get along.

32/........

... ventcd agreed with the positions of Layne and James ...
view is joint leadership can work and will work. It is
important to give the minutes to the membership because th
have accused the C.C of being dishonest. Agreed with points
made by Cdes on the vote of no confidence, both the Cde's
strength and weakness were pointed out, and pointed to a crea
way forward. He pointed that Tan and Kamau spoke openly
for the first time an attitude like this can make them become
timid once again.

Sister Phyllis suggested two separate meetings to announce
to the membership one for M's and C.M's and one for applicant

Cde. Louison said that the more the discussions is stretched
out at theoretical and tactical levels he becomes more worrie
He said that Cdes of the party were analysed into three secti
those who can be moulded into communist, those who have to
further develop and those who are weak or this basis he
cannot see the minutes into the hands of all cross section
of the party. He proposed that a summary of the main points
should be brought before the membership.

On the question of joint leadership he said that he would
like to know what is the intention of the C.C, if they will
like to build the qualities or make a leader through joint
leadership and at what stage will the prop be taken off.
As an aspiring M.L he cannot accept joint leadership, he
don't know of any situation of such. He cannot see the
dialectics unfold, he is not sure of the evolution of this
thing, he cannot see joint leadership helping us. He
sees a clear leadership in once embodyment Se had never
understood the science to mean anything different, he is
not convinced that the joint leadership will remain for
any length of time without causing any problem.

Cde. Cornwall felt that the Cde. is confuse because he is
posing in his mind the wrong question. We are saying that
fundamentally the revolution is at stake and that there
is a modle that will help to strengthen the process, or will
it hamper the Revolution. He pointed to a situation where
a Cde. use to be Minister and deputy Minister. This was
tactically correct because of the objective situation. He
feels that Cde. Louison is posing the wrong question, as a
result will come up with wrong conclusion

Cde. Lousion said that the joint leadership would not strength
the Revolution. How will it evolve? What would it eveolve
to? Is it a temporary feature or permanent feature.

Cde. De Riggs disagreed with the context and spirit in
which Cde. Louison made his contribution. He feels the
scientific and theoretical basis as put forward by Cde.
James has been established. We are seeking to find creative
ways to solve the question of leadership of the C.C and the
building of a M.L party for building Socialism. The C.C
in its present form cannot take the country to socialism
which is the long term strategy. We have to safeguard

the Revolution - build socialism. The question of leadership can also be dealt with sometime in the future. He also expressed his disappointment in Cde. Louison.

Cde. Layne said this is a question of fundamental importance. We are called to take decisions to correct the situation the time of manouvering is over. The form of leadership is scientifically decided, based on the situation we face. He used the e.g of the USSR Army where the concept of the Political Commissar and Militarty Leadership had developed and worked. They also defeated the counter revolution and 14 other imperialist powers. The concrete situation we face; the unfolding of the dialectics in the combining the two qualities to strengthen the leadership in a Leninist way for the building of Socialism in Grenada. The attempt to draw the C.C in a personality discussion is a P.B childish attitude.

Cde. George objected. "He has the right to put forward his postion no nne can accuse him of opportunism in his struggle over the years in the party. He raise his points seeking clarity in a genuing way. He regarded Cde. Laynes comments as "shit".

Sister Phyllis Coard said that it is unfair of Cde. Louison to think that there have been demogagry in the meeting. She feels that Cdes have been frank. There has been less demogagry than ever before.

Cde. Layne said that he had been frank and fair. The Cde. is trying to provoke the C.C into a discussion that no Cde. has raised. Cde. George object to the point that this has never been his pintention.

Cde. Bishop pointed to the struggles and difficulties of the RSDLP to point to the fact that Cdes are overbending too quickly to brand lables to each other in the discussion, which we have to be very careful about, because he cannot see how the meeting can proceed. He raised his concerns, that if the minutes of the C.C is given to the membership to study it will be the best way to create disunity and turn back the Revolution. He said that the response to his no confidence point, he is not interested in the Cdes comment. The point is that he alone can solve the problem. He expressed his difficulty in chairing the meeting because of the flying of brands etc.

Cde. Liam James said that he can hold the meeting if he speak up and reign in more on Comrades contributions, and to list all the concerns raise and ask Comrades to comment.

Sister Phyllis Coard said that the other three concerns raised can be taken one by one in order to move forward.

Cde. Layne said that if we take each concern Cdes speak on them if they have opposing positions of anything to add may do so.

The following postions were voted on:

1. On Cde. James proposals

    For   - 9

    Obstain - 2

    Against - 2

2. Formalisation of Joint Leadership:

    For   - 9

    Opposed - 1

    Abstain - 3

Cde. Austin abstained because he was not present for the full discussion for the greater part of the meeting.

3. How to inform the Membership:

    (A) Tell members only through minutes

    For   - 10

    Against - 1

    Abstain - 2

    (B) Tell all three categories in one meeting:

    Against - 11

    Abstain - 2

    (C) Tell all categories in two meetings M's and C.M's the A.'s

    For   - 9

    Against - 2

    Abstain - 2

    (d) Informing the masses:

    Against - 9

    Abstain - 3

    Cde. George Louisen - non participate.

Cde. Kamau moved a motion that these notes should be taken as a decision. It was agreed to put it to a vote.

(4) On Cde. Kamau's Proposals

    For   -   9
    Against   -   0
    Absta in   -   3
    Non participate 1

Cde. Layne proposed a formal vote on the conclusion of the July Plenary. Cde.

Cde. Louison said that there are aspects of the conclusion that can applied to the way forward. We can criticise certain aspects e.g the section on C.C and P.B was incorrect The conclusion failed on these particular issues.

Cde. Layne said that he has further problems with the overall decision of the July Plenary is not inkeeping with the reality therefore he agree with Cde. James to revoke the document and include the correct conclusion in the new document.

Sister Coard agreed with the revoking of the document. She said for the purpose for the history of the party, we have to disassociate ourselves from the document. She suggested a committee to extract the correct conclusions from the document.

Cde. Lousion said that a complete job must be brought before the members. Revoke the document and at the same time put correct position forward we cannot take a propaganda approach.

Cde. James supported Sister Phyllis, he had difficulty in understanding Cde. Louison position.

Cde. Louison said that if we withdraw the document and promis fail to give the Cdes the postions later it will/give the membership clarity.

Cde. Strachan said that if we are not able to extract the correct conclusions for the G.M, it is correct to tell the G.M that the conclusion will come to them in the future.

Cde. James fully supported Cde. Strachan's position, he o don't see how the membership will not accept the postion. They will be happy to hear that the document is revoked.

Cde. Louison said the July conclusions had a multitude of administrative decision, if we say that we revoke the conclusions without putting forward a clear positions at the same time, it can lead to further redecule from the membership. He felt that we should point to the good and bad aspect of the document and put forward a new document, including the conclusions of July that is relevant to the building of the Revolution.

He felts that we should go to the membership with a full
document - giving the Committee a tasks to extract the
relevant conclusion within a certain time in order to
present the new document.

The sub committee agreed on were Cdes Cornwall, James and
Layne. The time is to be taken at the end of the meeting.

Cde. Mc Barnette proposed that we use a break to ask Cde,
Coard to come to the meeting for decision to be put to him.

This was seconded by Cdes Cornwall and Layne. Cde. Maurice
opposed it because of the fact that he has to make a persona...
reflection on the issue. He proposed that the C.C. meet
with Cde. Coard in his absence. He felt that modle would be
counter productive. He suggested that the C.C meet Cde. Ber...
tomorrow while he will be leaving for St. Kitts. He think
that this will be in the ineterst of the C.C.

Cde. James had difficulties with the position, he felt that
Cde. Bishop should stand up and face the situation because
he is part of the Central Committee, he thinks that it can
and will affect Cde. Bernard's position on the issue.

Cde. Bishop said that it is difficult for him to understand
the question of joint leadership and his own role and
function in this modle.

Cde. Layne pointed out that he also had difficulties with
Cde. Bishop position on the ground that it will be difficult
to put this to Cde. Bernard when Cde. Bishop is not present;
because the conclusion will be quite natural as to reasons
why he not present. A pre condition for this thing to work
is a correct attitude on both sides.

Cde. Bishop said that it will be purly artificial based on
his personal postion to sit down for productive discussion,
it will have no usefulness, it will be counter productive
and mechanistic.

Cde. Strachan asked if after the reflection, he will attend
the meeting with Bernard. He said that he has no problem
with that. He said that he do not think that the meeting
will be useful with Bernard when he is present. He said
that two things that is critical for him is time for him
to reflect and Bernard's position at this time. This will
even help him in his own reflection.

Cde. Layne said that he agree that the Cde. Leader would
need time to reflect. However, if he is absent, conseptually
the Cde. will think that he opposed. He felt that it is the
right of the C.C to demand of Cde. Bishop that he be present
for the sake of the future of the revolution.

Cde..Bishop said on the question of the minutes to the membership, that the membership are not at the level. It is ideal...
and devorced from reality to give C.C minutes to members.
Cde Layne disagree.

Cde. Bishop said that the minutes of the C.C cannot be
disturbed to the membership because he has not seen that
in any party. He feels that the party is not at the stage
to provide all points and argument in the meeting.

Cde. Layne said we have much more to loos if we hold back
the minutes of the C.C including the basis for arriving to
the conclusions. The lack of frankness have brought the
party to a near collapse.
....
Cde. James said that this is one of the factors that cause
the party to reach to this stage.   The failure
to give the members clear indication of the meeting will
lead to further lack of confidence of the membership in the
C.C. The Cdes are not nieve   we think they are.

Cde. Cornwall said that the absence of frankness and dealing
with things squarely can lead to more tabarism in the party.

Cde. Bishop proposed adjustment of the meeting which was
supported by Cde. Whiteman

Cde. Layne then points to the incident when himself and
Cde. Cornwall were suspended for serious acts of illdisciplin
in the army. He felt that the response had strengthen the
prestige and standard of the party along with both himself
and Cde.   .

Sister Phyllis Coard then questioned what will the C.C say
to Cde. Bernard in the absence of Cde. Bishop. This however,
was not addressed.

Cde. James suggested that the C.C meet the following day in
the absence of Cde. Maurice to put the decision to Cde Coard
then work out the packages of measures.

Cde. Strachan opposed on the grounds that it is will be too
exploratory.

It was finally agreed to meet at 1.00 p.m. on Saturday 17th with
Cde. Coard.

38/.........

SATURDAY 17TH SEPTEMBER. 1983

Cdes Present

Selwyn Strachan   Phyllis Coard
Hudson Austin   Kamau Mc Barnette
Liam James   Chris De Riggs
Ewart Layne   Leon Cornwall
Chalkie Ventour

Cdes Absent

Maurice Bishop   - out of country
George Lousion   - out of country
Unison Whiteman   - out of country
Jan Bartholomew   - Sick
Fitzroy Bain   - Sick
Ian St. Bernard   - Sick

The meeting started 1.30 p.m. Cde. Bernard Coard attended.

Cde. Strachan addressing Cde. Coard said that the C.C have
been meeting to look at the state of the party and revolution
and to look at the way the process have been developing over
the past four years. It is quite clear that there are great
concerns from the G.M of the party.

Following the emergency C.C all C.C members were called in to
discuss ways and means of pulling ourselves out of this rut.

The revolution is in deep crisis, it faces the dangers of
being turned back, while the C.C is operating in a non Leninist
way. In identifying the root of the problem, it was found
that the C.C is not leading the process and has to take the
full blame. The reason is the weak leadership exercise by
Cde. Maurice Bishop. In trying to find concrete ways of
reviving the situation and to put the party of a firm M.L
base, it was pointed that while these fundamental weaknesses
exists the Cde. Has tremendous strength that will be needed n
ever. But the qualities that are missing are decisive qualitie
to put us on a correct path. Pointing to the four points
referred to by Cdes James and Cornwall and agreeing that
these qualities exist in Cde. Bernard Coard the C.C felt that
Cde. Coard was the only Cde. who had demonstrated practice
these qualities over the years.

As a result a proposal for merging these two strengths throug
joint leadership between Cdes Bishop and Coard was put forwar
by Cde. James and supported by the majority of Cdes. The are
of responsibility was outlined for the two Cdes, all C.C
meetings will be chaired by Cde. Bishop and P.B will be chair
by Cde. Coard. C.C meetings will resume monthly. Cdes felt
that this module can help Cde. Bishop in building the qualitie
missing. This proposal was voted with a majority in favour.

The Cdes will write quarterly reports to the C.C.and on all
fundamental questions The C.C will be involved. Other
proposals were made but they could not be tackeled because
of the need to settle the fundamental issue.

Cdes also outlined the operationalisation of the modle of
joint leadership.

Cde. Cornwall said that they also look at the experienced
of other countries and how the question of leadership is based
on the objective situation that exist.

Cde. Kamau pointed to the fact that everyone spoke with frankness and openess.

Cdes also agreed that the conclusion of the last plenary must
be revoked, because it lack content and dishonest, However,
applicable sections will be attached as an appenxix to the
conclusions of the meeting.

Cde. Ventour pointed that the party was on a right opportunist
path.

Cde. Strachan said that it is the first time he has seen
M.L position being put forward by the Cdes consistantly and
supported by the majority.

Cde. Bernard Coard raised four points being:

1. He would like to see the minutes of the meeting .

2. /The Position of t ose opposed or abstain and what are the
    reasons.

3. Were other options examine, what were these options and
    why were they rejected.

4. Why was not this meeting schedule so that Cde. Bishop
    could be present.

Cde. Austin said, it was only right that he abstain because
he arrived late in the meeting. When he arrived he askedf
for the agenda.

Cde. Louison told him that it is:

(1) analysis of the state of the party and revolution

(2) feedback from the membership and

(3) the way forward. He pointed out that Cde. Bishop said
that he had no problem to joint leadership. Therefore he c uld
n t understand why members who were here for the whole meeting
and could not have taken a postion on this or why it is that
members should vote against. He would like to know what were
their argument for this.

Cde. De Riggs said that Cde. Louison had problems with the either theoretical and operational with joint leadership. He felt these weaknesses cannot be solved by a model of joint leadership. The operationalisation of the proposals will cause difficulties, he do not agree that the minutes should be studied by the membership, he is not clear on how the dialectic will unfold. He said that he has not seen it any where in the science. He supported the idea of tapping the strength of Cdes Bernard Coard, but felt that the joint leadership cannot strengthen Cde. Maurice Bishop's weaknesses, this is not done in any M.L Party. He continued to say that Cde. Whiteman said that we must not seek to shift the blame from oneselve collectively and that the objective situation must be considered. Cde. Bain was not clear on how the joint leadership will work he wanted clarity on the operationalisation.

Cde. Layne said that Cde. Louison said that in some party's that one person heads the state and the other heads the party. but the head of state is subordinate to the head of the party.

Cde. Strachan said that Cde. Louison said that if we agree that the quality missing in the Cde. Leader is possessed in another Cde. why not take the M.L line and change the Cde.

Cde. James recalled his proposals saying that we need to find the scientific solution to get us out of the crisis to put us on the way forward. The scientific solution is based on the objective situation that exist.
                              of Nicaragua
The nine man directorate/was also mentioned because of the heated debate.

Cde. Bishop abstained on voting , though in his presentation he agreed to joint leadership. He placed his concern that he needs clarity on before he vote. He also needed a feed back from Cde. Bernard and some time to reflect on the issue.

Cde. Bernard Coard asked whether Cde. Bishop had agreed in principle.

Cde. Austin said that he gathered from Cde. Maurice that he was conscious of the crisis and that he did not have the necessary qualities, he also pointed that NJM had joint coordination and made reference to thehistoric working relation with himself and Cde. Bernard. He said he cannot understand how two senior Cdes in the party opposed and abstain from this decision.

Cde. De Riggs said that Cde. Maurice in his presentation said that the point made amounts to a vote of no confidence in him, he sees this as a moral crisis on which he need to reflect. Cdes pointed that the points was made from a standpoint of love and deep respect for the Cde. Leader.

Cde. Layne said that this is the first time that Cdes spoke so frankly, which must be encouraged if Cde. Bishop was to see it as a vote of no confidence it will intimidate Cdes and harm the Leninist advancement of the Comrades in the party.

Cde. Cornwall said that conceptually Cde. Bishop had no problem with the concept of the joint leadership, he even agreed with the proposed responsibilities, however, when t he came to the point of no confidence he placed it out of the hands of the C.C by saying that he alone can solved this problem.

Cde. Austing said how he heard Cde. Bishop spoke he felt that some of the criticism was incorrect.

Cde. DeRiggs said that Cde. Bishop said he is not sure that he is the main fetter on the C.C.

Cde. James said that in his criticism he said we are now in a serious crisis, is the last chance for the party. In pulling the party out of the rut we have to be scientific cold blooded and objective.

All C.C Comrades must be criticised. Some Cdes have failed consistantly to the extent that membrs are calling for the removal of some Cdes, but he felt that this is not and will not strengthen the party. The main fetter is that of the leadership provided by the leader of the C.C. He pointed out to the great strength of the Cde. Leader, but said that these strengths cannot carry the struggle forward. He pointed to the quality lacking in the leader which is critical for carrying the process forward, ne said that the Cde with this quality is Cde. Bernard Coard. On this basis he proposed the marriage of the strengths of the two Cdes to push the struggle forward out of this period of crisis.

Sister Coard said that as a result of the weakness of the leader there have been indeciciveness in solving crisis and we loos confidence in the measure we use to get us out of the crisisis and the frequence of the crisis is getting very frequent.

Cde. Deriggs said that Cde. Maurice response were to thank Cdes for the criticism. That the sense of overwhelming centiment / what is required for a M.L leader is found in Cde. difficulties in finding reading materials on how the C.C and P.B should function. He had depended too much on unity and and consensus and collective leadership. That he had not prepared himself for that kind of approach because this was not his intention of how the meeting should go.

OTHER RESPONSE WERE: he gave a history of working relation between himself and Cde. Coard.
- he did not agree that he is the main fetter on the C.C.
- his did not agree that he has bad attitude to criticism
- he said his style of leadership may have cutted necessary debate and that he is not clear of strategy and ta ctics as assigned to Cde. Coard

42/.......

- he would like to know Cde. Coard's position on the issue
- how it will operationalise and seek clarity on the concerns raised.

Four options for leadership were identified in the earlier proceedings:-

(1) Remove Cde. Bishop
(2) Joint Leadership
(3) Have the deputy to play the role that is required.

(4) Remove Cdes from the C.C

On option three (3) Cde. De Riggs said that his own reading is that Cde. George put forward in a general way is that he does not oppose the return of Cde. Coard to the P.B and C.C. Though it was not discussed. It was put forward weakly by Cde. Whiteman as part of the response, it was not done as a concrete proposal. He made it as a response to the fundamental proposal.

Cde. James said that these qualities take years to develop in a Cde. therefore, the Cde. Leader will not be able to lead in this area. Cde. Coard have been leading in this area over the years. We are now recognising it formally and that failure to accept will be right opportunism.

We will not be M.L/ if we have joint leadership in practice and pretend that we have something else.

On point four (4) Cde. Strachan said that the view was expressed that we should take decision on the proposals and call in Comrade Coard. Cde. Bishop said that given that he needs time to reflect and that he need a position from Cde. Coard he will not be able to participate. He is prepared to do so later. He felt that the meeting should go ahead in his absence. Cdes did not agree with the position, they felt that both Cdes should be present in the meeting. The October '82 crisis was also discussed in this light.

Cde. Austin said one of Cde. Austin said one of Cde. Bishop concern is that he would like to know what is Cde. Bernard's disposition on the issue and whether anyone had spoken to Cde. Bernard on the issue before.

Cde. Strachan said that this meeting should give an indication of Cde. Bernard's postion which willbe key for his reflection.

Cde. Layne said that another key issue is that the minutes Cde. Bishop opposed going to the membership.

The Cde. Leaders had strongly opposed to it though he abstained in the voting on the issue. He said he did not understand how Cdes cannot see that this is the surest way of breaking unity in the country undermining his authority, pointing to the level of taybayism in the country.

Cde. Coard said   at every single level in the party there
are lots of bi-laterals beating the party for dishonesty even
to the extent of the study classes.

Cde. Austin said that he was confuse because the C.C was
dicussing what members were discussing; he want to know how it is
possible to report to G,M without submitting the minutes to the
meeting.

Cde. Coard said that his feelings of the present situation are
that within six months the party will disintegrate totally unless a fundamental package of measures bredone. He had thought
it would take 12 months . given the :   of disgust, the
disintegration of the party masses that the lost of state
powere is only a few months away. While all of this is happen
ing imperialism has step up its range of attacks laying the
basis for direct intervention in Central America. They have
set up their troops and using the Korean incident as a basis.
American troops are meters away from Nicaragua.

This is happening at a time when the militia is dis-integrate.
the Army is demoralise, we don't have the capacity of defendi.
the revolution.

The party have never had. such weak links and low . ... with
the masses. The image of the party has detriated in the eyes
of the masses. :

the mood of the party Comrades is at th lowest, it has ever
been. He used the example of the number of Cdes sick.

He is opposed to solving the problem by replacing members of th.
C.C. All the C.C Comrades have important qualities and strenths
to add to the C.C. Cdes know their weaknesses which he has
been always frank with them about. He pointed to the need for
verification using examples of Kamau, Unison, H.A and Kojo. He
also pointed out that it is incorrect to think that Cdes in
State work is not doing political   work   Cdes should not
see their state work as non political work. He said that Cde.
Strachan in an effort to hold the situation together diverted
irationalisation   arnachy etc. accused him of idealism.

He raised the issue of his resignation from the O.C and C.C
and reminded Cdes of his reasons for resigning last year which
he had told Cdes. The C.C had agreed with him for not attending
the C.C meeting because he wanted the issue to discuss. He said
that he was tired and sick of being the only hatchetman and c
critique. The failure of C.C Comrades was to speak up
freely, as a result he concluded that he was the main fetter to
the development of the C.C because everyone was depending on
him for everything especially in the area of the economy.

In July he left the O.C off for many months before he was reflecting
on the party, the problem was the total absence of making deci..
decisiins e.g torchlight and the gang of 26, e.g Cde. Layne
and Einstein on the Army, on when the postion was taken to
put Layne - over Einstein.

44/..........

- 44 -

He said that he had detect a feeling of wanting him to undermine the Comrade Leader's position.

He would not like to return to the C.C and P.B, any tasks given to him he will do it.

He even used the struggle of the formation of the O.C, Cdes Louison, Strachan and himself was accused for organising another seat of power in the party. He felt that when this h reached critical persons on the P.B it was very bad.

He said finally in July last year the C.C unanimously directed the O.C to hold meetings with leaders of committees for rationalisation of Cdes work, as a result _ extended O.C meeting was held, while this meeting was happening other decisions were taken contrary to the C.C decisions so that the O.C could not have the mandate given.

He was seriously affected by the accusation of wanting to undermine the leadership so he resigned from the O.C. He said the Cde Leader found himself vasillating between the M.L trend/on the party. This worsened as the C.C was not aware what was going on and the situation was slipping, and because Comrades were not thinking, therefore the severe of drift and disintegration was not seen, He said that the party and revolution will disintegrate within 24 months. It had reached to a stage where he realise that his ability to influence the process was no longer possible.

The bureau took a thousand easy decision that the O.C had to impliment and failed to take hard decisions. For some periods of time the P.B was not functioning, no agenda, no recording of decisions, he found that he could not take these long meetings for no reason at all.

He had a system for the Bureau to meet three hours for once a week and O.C three hours per week, so that Cdes can spend more time in the field. But Cdes have to be more prepared. Before he was asked to form the idea elaborate these ideas and impliment them, at the same time he had a number of talks behind his back. He would like to operate as he is presently for ever. He said that it will be an emotional strain for him to be back on the C.C under any modle.

The aspect that he had over the years was that he was an ordinary member he would have manners the Cde. Leader years ago, because of his position as deputy Leader and the extent that Cdes will think that he is fighting for leadership, if he comes back and Cde. Bishop falter he would be afraid to criticise him and will resign again. For it to be left for him to manners the leader, he is not prepared to deal with this. He admit that this is a P.B conduct.

However, he had tried to give the party his best support in strategy and tactics he would prefer to operate as in the past year. He also is prepared to take all responsibilities that the C.C offers him but off the C.C. He cannot take emotional

112 - 44

- 3 -

conflict situation that saps his energies. He wants this to
be clearly put to the party.

Unless the C.C is prepared to manners all pettit bourgeois
response he will re-draw.

The issue is to start collective leadership of the C.C.
The lack of frank and bluntness has seriously affected the
party.

The C.C has never been accountable to any one the Bureau had
things 'from the C.C and the C.C hid things from the membership

He said that he have problems with any modle of coming back
the C.C and P.B unless he is forced to.

There are two trends on the C.C Pettit bourgeois Revolutionary
Democratic trend and M.L trend. As the struggle gets tougher
and the taking of decisions becomes harder the level of
vasillation and indecisiveness grows, and the crisis becomes
deeper. The contradiction will become greater, his emotional
strain will also become greater. He has noted a Pettit
Bourgeois Revolutionary trend has becoming greater in Cde.
Louison over the last year. He has planned to raised it with
him. Whatever the decision the C.C take he will have to
ordered because there will be much more taybay behind his
back. He also think that the situation will worsened.

There is no signs in the last 10½ years where the C.C has
consistantly crushed pettit bourgeois characteristics and tred
as soon as it rise.

Cde. Cornwall said that in this meeting he had seen very firm
sought out positions taken, it gives the idea of what the
C.C is capable of doing, he thinks that this is important to
recognise. However, we have not been consistent in this
area. He said that with-out the consistency the party will
rut again.

Cde. Bernard proposed thatfor the next six months the Bureau
should meet as a bureau with all members of the C.C as
alternate Bureau members so that the monthly meetings will
be to take stock.The Bureau meeting will meet to take decisions
on the daily organisation of the work. The Bureau should meet
three hours once a week.

Cde. Strachan felt that these meetings should take place in
the opera ions room of Fort Rupert.

Cde. Coard further proposed that there should be absolutely
no interuption in the meeting.

Cdes also proposed no smoking in meetings.

Comrade Coard continued to question whether the points taken
on operationalisation will satisfy Cde. Leader concern.
Whether he sees the criticisms as a vote of no confidence of
the joint leadership lead to a vote of confidence.   If on this
basis he refused to accept the decision of the C.C on these
models what will be the decision of the C.C.

Cde. Deriggs said that when this situation was dealt with the
decision was taken based on strategy.. The basic concern is t'
character of the C.C.

He said that the only way forward is Cde. Bernard's membership
on the C.C. We must take no action to sacrafice the revolution
and building the revolution and to build the situation. If
joint leadership is decided and one Cde. Comrade don't want
to comply the leadership will be decided.   Cdes have to
be firm and resolute.

Cde. Bernard Coard also questioned the time frame and
propsepective in terms of informing the membership and to start
the work internally and hitting the ground scientifically and
organisationally.

Cde. Starach said that the hold up is based on Cde. Bishop
time for reflection.

Cde. Cornwall felt that this cannot be dragged on indefinitely.
Cdes felt too that the report should not held out any longer
than next Monday and the C.C should continue to meet with Cde.
Coard to work out the package for the way forward. A date was
fixed to meet with Cde. Bishop on Friday. In the meantime
the G.M will be informed of the meetings.

The C.C agreed that three mmeetings would be held to discuss
the minutes with M's,C.M's and A's, it was agreed to cancell
the Fedon's week-end seminar and the members will meet on
Sunday 25th in Bolunge from 9.00 a.m - 10.00 p.m. Breakfast
will be served from 8-9a.m. The C.M's will meet on Monday
27th in Butler House from 5.00 p.m. - 11.00 p.m. and the
following Monday 3rd October from 5.00 p.m. - 8.00 p.m in
Butler house for A.'s.   Transportation and a light snack would
be provided. On September 30th and October 1st the weekend
of Butler seminar the Fedon and Butler group will study the
package of measures and the Marryshow group will use their
schedule seminar to discuss the package.

Cde. Leyne then suggested that the C.C break to use Sunday
to sought out positions, then meet from Monday to Friday from
6.00 a.m - 12.00 noon to work out the package of measures.

Cde. Phyllis Coard suggested that Cde. Bishop be informed of th
meetings that he can join but he should come on Friday to put
forward his positon. She also suggested a system of Comrades
sharing their notes with other Cdes who were absent in the
meeting and Cdes should assist Cde. Boldeau in preparing the
minutes.

Cde. Mc Barnette was asked to assist Cde. Bain

Cde. Cornwall will assist Cde. St. Bernard.

Cde. Layne will brief Cde. Austin.

Cde. Strachan will brief Cde. Bishop

Cde. Cornwall will supervise the writing of the minutes.

———————

EXTRA-ORDINARY GENERAL MEETING

OF

FULL MEMBERS

SUNDAY 25TH SEPTEMBER

1983

EXTRAORDINARY GENERAL MEETING OF FULL MEMBERS

DATE: SUNDAY 25TH SEPTEMBER, 1983

The meeting began at 9.00 a.m chaired by Cde. Liam
James, member of Political Bureau of NJM Central Committee.

AGENDA

1. Distribution of document
2. Chairman's remarks
3. Central Committee report to G.M
4. Discussion
5. Workshops for individual study and discussion
6. Plenary discussion

The documents distributed to the members were:

(a) Minutes of Extra-ordinary meeting of the Central
    Committee of NJM - Tuesday 12th - Friday 15th October 1982.

(b) Extra-ordinary meeting of the Central Committee NJM
    14th - 16th September, 1982.

(c) Central Committee report to membership.

Cde. Liam James as chairman made brief remarks pointing out
that this General Meeting is a very serious one and every
member must approach the deliberations of the meeting in a
spirit of frankness since it has been called resulting from
the comments picked up from the party's membership regarding
the problems faced by the party and revolution and their
disagreement with the conclusions of the regular plenary
session of the Central Committee held from July 18 - 23, 1983.

He further emphasised and stressed that all comrades must show
a high level of security consciousness with the documents and
their contents, emphasising that this is an internal party
matter and must not be discussed outside of party bounds.

113 - 2

2/...........

CENTRAL COMMITTEE REPORT

The Central Committee report to the membership was
presented by Cde. Ewart Layne, member of the Political
Bureau of NJM Central Committee. The report was characterised
with a spirit of frankness, straight-forwardness, criticism
and self-criticism. It pointed out that the present crisis
faced by the party and revolution is the worse ever in 4½
years since we are faced with the reality of the degeneration
of the party, its possible disintegration in six months and
the resulting overthrow of the revolution that can come in one
year's time if we don't take effective measures to remedy the
situation. The report gave concrete evidence which testified
to the fact that this process is already in train.

It is a spirit of criticism and self criticism ascertained
the reasons for the crisis facing the party and revolution
pointing squarely at the Central Committee as the source of
the problem. In so doing the views held which stated that the
Organising Committee (O.C) and Disciplinary Committee (D.C)
were dispelled since as the report pointed out the problems
of these committees are symptomatic to the real problem, that
of the Central Committee.

The report analysed that the Central Committee's main
problem is that of the weak quality of leadership provided
by Cde. Maurice Bishop, Chairman of the Central Committee and
leader of the party. It frankly pointed out that Cde. Maurice
Bishop has tremendous strengths that are necessary for the
process but these by themselves cannot carry the party out of
its present crisis. The qualities are also needed, those of:

1. A Leninist level of organisation and discipline
2. Great depth in ideological clarity.
3. Brillance in strategy and tactics
4. The capacity to exercise Leninist supervision, control
   and guidance of all areas of party work are today not
   present in the Comrade.

3/..........

113 - 3

Thus the Central Committee has been making errors for
the last 12 months, vacillating and taking a right opportunist
path.

The report also pointed out that the weak functioning of the
Central Committee, its vacillatory positions, the unwillingness
of its members to study, thinks, take hard decisions and
struggle for their implementation have led Cde. Bernard Coard
to resign from the Central Committee September 1982.

Continuing in the same spirit of open self criticism the
Central Committee report criticised the C.C for not giving
policy guidelines on the different areas of party work.

It is based on the above that the Central Committee reported
to the G.M its decision to establish a model of joint leadership
of the party by marrying together the strengths of Cdes Maurice
Bishop and Bernard Coard with the areas of work spelt out for
each C e. As we stated this model of joint leadership is an
acknowledgement of reality existing in our party for the last
ten years and authority is now being given commensurate with
responsibility so as to improve and make more efficient the
party's work.

The Central Committee also made six other conclusions and
decisions and demenaded of every party member that they always
uphold and struggle at all times for nine principles which
toget er with the model of joint leadership and decisive for
overcoming this gr ve cri is and putting the p rty on a
Marxist Leninist path. These nine principles enunciated are:

1. Iron Discipline
2. Firmly uphold and apply the principle of democratic
    Centralism emphasising criticism and self criticism and
    collective le dership.

3. Leninist level of organisation.
4. Open warmth and selflessness in dealing with the masses
5. Sink but don't drown amongst the masses.
6. Kill all arrogance
7. Greater scientific thought and reflection on the problems
    and difficulties of the party and revolution

8. An end to all vacillation
9. Bold, firm and a creative style of thought and action.

The Central Committee in its report warned the members
against the illusion that the crisis that we are now in can
be quickly and easily solved. It instead called on them to
wage a long and persistent struggle as the only guarantee
to a solution to these ever recurring problems.

After the Central Committee's report Cde. Liam James
called on the members to be frank, open, cold-blooded and
objective in their deliberations and overcome the tendency to
be timid. He then pointed out to the members the reason for
Cde. Maurice Bishop's absence stating that since the C.C
meeting on Friday 17th September. Cde. Bishop said he needed
time to think and reflect on the Central Committee's conclusion
and would be able to meet on Friday 24th September in the
C.C plenary to put forward his position. However, Cde. Bishop
did not turn up on the appointed date and gave the same reason
for his absence. Today, he stated, the same is true for his
absence at the General Meeting.

Cde. James then read a note from Cde. Bernard Coard which
stated that he understood that Cde. Bishop would be absent
from the G.M and as such he felt it was not fitting for him to
be present since this may inhibit free and frank discussions.
However, Cde. Coard pointed out if the G.M requests his presence
he would be willing to comply.

Cde. Murie Francois in response called for both Cdes Bishop
and Coard to be present at the G.M. Cde. Maureen St. Bernard
proposed that both Cdes be sent for. Cde. Lester Redhead
pointed to the nature of the crisis we are facing and requiring
that both Cdes must be present. Cde. Tessa Stroude joined the
other Comrades in stating that both Cdes must be here at the
G.M. This also was the position of Cde. Wayne Sandiford.

5/...........

Cde. Liam James then asked - do you think that both Cdes should be sent for? In reply Cde. Chester Louison said that Cde. Maurice Bishop should be given more time to reflect. In response to Cde. Chester Louison six Comrades reiterated the position that both Cdes must be here. Cde. Nelson Louison said that both Cdes should be here while Cde. Anslem De Bourg pointed out that if both Comrades accept that we are faced with a serious crisis then they must be here. Cde. Valdon Boldeau agreed with Cde. DeBourg and further stated that this G.M would assist Cde. Bishop's reflection. Cde. Keith Ventour stated that he is shocked/that both Cdes are not here and that they must hear the position of the G.M. Cde. Chester Humphrey reasoned that it is not possible to resolve the questions put forward by the C.C if both Cdes are not present, in so doing he rejected the position taken by Cde. C. Louison. Cde. Lex Mc Bain called for their presence and further stated that it was unprincipled for Cde. Bishop to absent himself from the C.C meeting. Cde. Gordon Raeburn endorsed the views of the above Cdes that both must be present. Cde. Claudette Pitt also endorsed that position, stated that the C.C had not been hearing from the membership and she further questioned the absence of other C.C members.

Cde. Liam James explained that Cde. Chris DeRiggs and Cde. George Louison were at present out of the country.

Continuing in the same manner Cde. Chris Stroude said it was important that both Cdes be present. Cde. Rudolph Ogilvie stated that if Cde. Bishop is given more time to reflect in isolation he would sink. Cde. Keith Roberts stated his firm agreement with Cde. R. Ogilvie and called for the presence of both Cdes. Cde. Reginald Fleming stated that the call for both Cdes to come to the G.M is to uphold democratic centralism (applause). Cde. Peter David stated that Cde. Bishop already had a week to reflect and that the views of the members are critical for him to move forward. Cde. Einstein Louison stated

that the   6/.........

that the highest level in the party is here, there is at this
time no higher level and if the situation is so terrible he is
wondering why both comrades are not here. He called for both
to be sent for. Cde. Ronnie Spooner stated his agreement with
everyone except Cde. Chester Louison, He further stated that
if the C.C and membership accept that the crisis is so bad then
both Cdes must be present so that collectively we can analyse
the crisis. He called for the G.M to use whatever necessary
means to get the Cdes here (applause).

Cde. Faye Thompson asked whether Cde. Bishop would come,
she suggested that a letter demanding his presence should be
sent signed by all members. Cde. Peter David suggested that
a delegation to get Cde. Bishop to come to the G.M. Cde.
Chester Humphrey asked for the C.C's view on the matter.
Cde. Rudolph Ogilvie stated that Cde. Coard is willing to come
therefore we must ensure that Cde. Bishop is coming before
requesting Cde. Coard's presence. Cde. Rita Joseph stated her
disagreement with Cde. R. Ogilvie and stated that if Cde. Bishop
does not come Cde. Coard should still be present. Cde. Keith
Ventour stated his agreement with Cde. R. Joseph.

Cde. Ewart Layne said that Cde. Bishop's attitude to the
criticism by the C.C and its decision was petit bourgeois in
character. He pointed out that the C.C warned Cde. Bishop that
if he responds in this way to criticism this could only
discourage Cdes from openly criticising him and would only
guarantee that we don't come out of the crisis and thus the
disintegration of the party and the eventual loss of state power.

Cde. Layne informed the G.M that Cde. Bishop asked for time
to reflect which was given to him up until Friday 23rd. He also
said he needs to know Cde. Coard's views. This he knew by
Monday 19th based on the records of the meeting held by the C.C
with Cde. Coard. In addition Cde. Coard held a direct personal
talk with Cde. Bishop and reiterated his position on the matter,

namely, that emotionally his preference is to remain outside
of the C.C but given the dangers of the revolution at this time
he is willing to return to the C.C and P.B at whatever level
determined by the C.C.

Cde. Layne went on to state that however, the C.C has no
communication from Cde. Bishop on his position although he
continues to do his state work normally, operating from his
residence while failing to attend the C.C meeting on Friday
23rd. This, Cde. Layne, pointed out could only be seen as contempt for the C.C, contempt for democratic centralism on the
part of Cde. Bishop. On this score Cde. Layne stated that the
issue we face today is what path would the party take. Will we
build a Marxist Leninist party as voted for by the General
Membership in 1982 when the line of March was presented? Will
we institute democratic centralism for all? Will the Minority
submit to the Majority? Will there be one discipline binding
on all or will it be for everyone except the leader? Will we
practice criticism and self criticism frankly and openly as
demanded by Cde. Lenin or will the C.C be intimidated by one man?
Are we going to build a petit bourgeois social democratic party
with one man above everyone, where people fufil decisions they
like and do not fulfil those they do not like, where there is
one discipline for some and a next set for others, where some
can be criticised and others are above criticism?

This is the first and most fundamental issue the party
membership faces today, which ever decision is taken will determine the future of the party and revolution, Cde. Layne stated.
He went on to point out that it is either the building of a
Marxist Leninist party and the struggle to build socialism or a
petit bourgeois social democratic party and ultimately the
degeneration of the party and revolution like in Egypt and
Somalia. What faces us is the road of opportunism or Leninist
principles.

8 /........

If the road of opportunism is chosen he said he cannot
see any aspiring communist, any aspiring Marxist Leninist,
any Comrade who stands for principle remaining a member of
the C.C. He informed the G.M that he had spoken to all C.C
members who voted for the Majority position, including
Cde. Hudson Austin who although late for the C.C plenary but
who is a principled Comrade and that all these C.C members
have agreed that if the road of opportunism is chosen they would
have no alternative but to resign for the C.C on the ground
of principle. The membership is then free to choose a new
Central Committee but none of the Cdes would be standing for
re-election. However, they are willing to continue functioning
as ordinary party members and in order to remove any suspicion
or grounds for rumour that they are working to undermine the n
new C.C, they are all prepared to serve and defend the revolution overseas. Thus the membership must choose which road
whether it is opportunism or Marxism Leninism. Cde. Layne
then quoted a passage from the material.

⌣ Cde. Unison Whiteman on a point of order informed the
G.M that Cde. Bishop turned up on Saturday 24th for a C.C
meeting at 1.30 p.m but the meeting did not take place.

Cde. Liam James explained to the G.M that the meeting was
specifically to discuss and agree on the Central Committee
report to the G.M but the document was not yet rolled off.
Thus it was not possible for the meeting to be held.

Cde. Tessa Stroude asked whether Cde. Bishop sent an
excuse for his non attendance to the Friday 23rd C.C meeting

Cde. Selwyn Strachan said that Cde. Bishop informed him
that he had not finished reflecting and he had nothing new to
say, thus he wanted more time to reflect. He also said that
he went to bed late on Thursday night. Cde. Strachan stated
his firm endorsement of the points made by Cde. Layne. He

stated that the issue is one of democratic centralism. We
have analysed the problems, got to the root of the problems
and came up with a solution. And this is the first time that
the C.C has been so frank and principled. The C.C has to be
blamed for covering up and for its right opportunist positions.
We have contributed to the crisis. This right opportunism
of the C.C is seen in the covering up of Cde. Coard's resignation and Cde. Kenrick Radix removal from the C.C. And he
was part of the covering up and brambling on these issues.
But now a clear majority in the C.C has taken decisions and
they must be upheld on the principle of democratic centralism.

Cde. Leon Cornwall said that the behaviour and attitude
of Cde. Maurice Bishop to the frank, open and comradely
criticisms and the C.C decision based on the criticism was
petit bourgeois in nature. Cde. Bishop during the C.C extra-
ordinary plenary accepted, and this is recorded, that the
party and revolution face their most dangerous crisis and if
things continue we can lose state power. Cde. Bishop also
agreed to the fact that the source of the crisis is with the
Central Committee, Cde. Cornwall informed the G.M. In fact
no C.C member disagreed with this. When Cde. Bishop was
criticised everyone including himself spoke in agreement with
the criticism. However, on the question of action, what is to
be done vacillations begun. Despite this Cde. Bishop said
he had no problem with joint leadership and that his conception
of his role in the revolution accorded with those spelt out
in the proposal. Comrades but Cde. Bishop had not shown that
consistency in action as his verbal expressions may indicate.
Instead he has been in practice resisting the criticism of
the majority position. Cde. Cornwall pointed out that this
action violates the fundamental principle of a Marxist Leninist
party, that of democratic centralism which is the soul of a
Marxist Leninist Party and those aspiring to build such a
party. That failure to uphold democratic centralism in this

care would lead to serious problems in the future and the
inability of the C.C to apply this to other party Comrades
and committees in the future. Cde. Cornwall stated that on
Tuesday 20th Cdes Strachan, James, Layne, Austin and himself
spoke with Cde. Bishop, at the end Cde. Bishop said "I will
definitely come to the C.C meeting on Friday but not before".
He also said in the same positive manner words to this effect
to Cde. Layne of Thursday at 10.30 p.m. However, he failed
to turn up to the C.C meeting and thus joined with Cde. Layne
in saying that Cde. Bishop showed contempt to the C.C decision
and democratic centralism. He also reminded the G.M that many
party Comrades members, candidates and appliacnts even Comrades
who are not even potential applicants have been seriously
criticised by the party, however they continued to work and
struggle for the interest of the revolution. He went on to
say that we must decide on what type of party we are building.
If it is a Marxist Leninist Party then all, not some of the
Leninist principles must be applied. But if it is a social
democratic party then we must leave the 'people's books' alone.
He finally endorsed the postion that no aspiring Leninist can
remain on the C.C if the party fails to apply this C.C decision
on the way forward and therefore is prepared to resign.

Cde. Basil Gahagan call on the G.M to take a decision to
call for Cde. Bishop. A vote was taken 46 Cdes for , 1
against and one abstained. A delegation headed by Cde. Ian
St. Bernard, member of the NJM Central Committee and consisting
of Cdes Basil Gahagan, Murie Francois, Keith Ventour, Chester
Humphrey and Wayne Sandiford left to convey to Cde Bishop the
will of the G.M.

At 11.10 a.m Cde. Bernard Coard arrived at 12.42 Cde.
Ian St. Bernard reported to the G.M on behalf of the delegation
Cde. St. Bernard pointed out that the delegation met Cde.
Bishop and explained the position of the G.M after they had
heard the C.C report. Cde. Bishop said he prefered for the

11/..........

delegation to carry to the G.M his position. He said he
read the C.C report and had not yet formulated his position
on it. He outlined his position on joing leadership saying
he has always accepted this and refered to the joint coordinating secretaries established in March 1973 when NJM was
formed. He stated that as leader of the party and revolution
he accepts the blame for the weakness of the C.C. When asked
to come to the G.M to explain his position he was not favourable
to this, however, after some insisting by the delegation he
said he would reach at 12.30 p.m. Cde. St. Bernard said that
in his opinion Cde. Bishop would come.

Cde. Keith Ventour added that the atmosphere in the meeting
with Cde. Bishop was emotional. He pointed out that Cde. Bishop
said that he got the C.C report late and didn't agree with certain
aspects in it. Cde. Chester Humphrey added that Cde. Bishop said
that there were many things he was trying to think out and as
such contribute to the meeting. Cde. Wayne Sandiford added
that Cde. Bishop said that there were some concerns he had and
wants to raise but does not think it is wise to raise them in
the G.M. Cde. Layne interpreted all these as manifestations
of violation of democratic centralism by Cde. Bishop.

At. 12.52 p.m Cde. Bishop arrived.

Cde. Fitzroy Bain said that one member of the delegation said
Cde. Bishop said that there were things in the C.C report he was
not in agreement with what were they?

Cde. Murie Francois asked Cde. Unison Whiteman for an
explanation about his abstention in the voting. Cde. Whiteman
said that Cde. Bishop had some concerns some of which have
not been addressed, thus demanding that he comes here is not
correct. Cde. Spooner asked - "What were those concerns?"
Cde. Whiteman responded that one concern is that he needs to
adjust psychologically and secondly there were certain important
points not reflected in the minutes. Cde. Peter David said that

12/........

the G.M was concern about Cde. Bishop's absence and thus he
should explain.

Cde. Bishop in response said that he assumed that the C.C
would explain his position to the G.M. He added that the
discussions in the C.C Plenary has raised concerns to him.
When stripped bare and until he has completed his reflections
then he can face the G.M with a clean conscience. He is now
relatively confused and emotional. There are several things
that concern him and thus require a lot of mature reflection.
He said that he shared the basic C.C conclusion on the crisis
in the country, and party and that the source of the drisis
lies in the C.C. He added that he firmly believes that the
more authority and power one has then the greater the responsibility for failures belongs to that person. He pointed out that
the concept of joint leadership does not bother him because
of his history of struggle especially from the 1973 merger which
gave rise to NJM. He said that many Comrades had criticised
him in relation to his acceptance of joint leadership in the
past in the form of joint coordinating secretaries. However,
the masses have their own conception and perception that may
not be necessarily like ours who study the science. Our history
shows that the masses build up a personality cult around a single
individual. He admitted that his style of leadership has led to
vacillation, indecisiveness in many cases. He confessed that
maybe his conception of leadership is idealistic because of the
historical abuse of power and one may leadership. He and his
contempories have distaste for one man leadership and he has a
strong position on this. He further pointed out that his style
of leadership is an error since it calls for consensus, unity
at all cost and this cause vacillation. And he is not sure
that he has overcome this.

Secondly he said that he feels strongly that the party must
have a clear position on areas of demorcation of responsibility
ans systems of accountability. He is of the view that some
Comrades held strong reservations and they should have raised
them in an open and principled way. He said that if they
held them for long and then sudden spring then then there
must be need for reflection.

then in an open and principle way. He said that if they
held them for long and then suddenly spring them then there
must be need for reflection.

He informed the G.M that in the JULY C.C. plenary there was
assessment held and that many points that are now being made
about him that were not made then. He stated that he is always
open to criticism but he should have been approached first
before the meeting so he would be able to work out a clear and
cogent response. He went on to say that there is a fine line
separating a petit bourgeois and a scientific response. He
felt that if he had those conclusions on a member he would have
concerned them before although this may not be a scientific
position.

He also said that he is concern about the minutes being
given to the G.M. If minutes are given which show what each
member of the C.C has said it can develop ideas of groupings
and fractions and vacillations in the C.C. He is afraid that
it would eventually reach the masses and reaction and would
thus undermine the revolution and give rise to suspicions that
there is a power struggle in the C.C. He said that if we are
to rebuild links with the masses then by solving the problem
by being frank it would undermine the confidence of the leadership. He sees this clearly and does not understand why other
C.C members cannot see this. He pointed out that in the past
the C.C has decided on not communicating sensitive matters of
defence. He said that at the emergency C.C meeting a large
part of the meeting was spent discussing whether Cde. Valdom
Boldeau, the C.C recording secretary should be present at the
extra-ordinary C.C plenary. At the emergency C.C meeting some
Cdes had apprehension but now 2 weeks later they have no
apprehension in giving the minutes to the G.M.

He then said that he is concerned about what is the
real meaning of the C.C's position. He is having horrors.
If it is what he is thinking of then he does not see himself
as being on the C.C or on the C.C as a leader. He said that
the C.C pointed out that his strengths were the ability to
agitate the masses, to articulate the position of the party and
government to the masses and to hold high the banner of the
revolution in the region and internationally and his weaknesses
were lack of Leninist level of organisation and discipline,
brillance in strategy and tactivs and all that have been said.
But the C.C said that precisely those qualities he lacks are
those required to carry the revolution forward because those
he has can't take it further. Thus the strengths of two Cdes
are to be married together. He is suspicious that Comrades have
concluded that the party must be transformed into a Marxist
Leninist party and thus he is the wrong person for the leader.
He can't accept this compromise, it is unprincipled. He
explained that for him to put out his strengths it must be as
a result of a deep conviction, love for the poor and working
people and out of a feeling of confidence from the C.C. He
is not satisfied because the totality of points made is pointing
him in a direction he is trying to run from. It is not joint
leadership but a compromise in the interim. "What is the
genuine substantial preference of the Comrades he asked?

Cde. Bishop went on to say that only he can solve the
problem he is now facing because any assistance and talk
about this not being a case of no confidence will be seen by
him as tactical. He further said that he is considering the
option of withdrawing from the P.B and C.C but has not yet
resolved this. Therefore the C.C as the vanguard of the
vanguard has a duty to meet in his absence and come up with
clear conclusions on how to come out of the crisis. He at ted
that the C.C should not wait for him because supposing after
his reflection he decides to withdraw, then many vital weeks
would have been lost. His only concern he stated is about
certain areas in the report that concerns him about his role

in the future but the C.C should go ahead and meet and whatever line is taken can be communicated to him.

Cde. James stated that in his view Cde. Bishop must remain in the G.M and hear from the members. He went on to say that we must distinguish between emotional and psychological reactions from decisions of the C.C. The C.C is the highest body and its decisions are binding on all - this is a fundamental Leninist principle. It must not be for some but for all. He stated that what is at stake given the depth of the crisis is the future of the revolution. The number one priority for every one must be the interest of the party and revolution. Our whole approach to this question must always be totally cold blooded, honest and objective. We must ask ourselves what is the correct solution, what is the way forward.

On the question of raising it with him before Cde. James said that theire is no Leninist rule that demands this, that no party rule requires this. If a comrade choses to do this it is out of that comrade's own liking. Cde. James informed the G.M that the C.C has removed Comrades from the P.B and C.C before and no such approach as Cde. Bishop desired in his case was used.

On the question of the minutes going to the G.M Cde. James said that the heart, the essence of the minutes is the position taken on joint leadership and the critifisns of Cde. Bishop. The C.C can't lie anymore unless we decide we are not building a Marxist Leninist party. It is therefore critical that the G.M see the positions taken by everyone since it would help in their assessing C.C members.

Cde. Francis Gill stated that it is necessary for Cde. Bishop to be here and stay at the G.M. He needs to hear the discussions of all the members. Cde. Gill said that the emotionalism that

not surprise him because of the petit bourgeois nature of the
party. He further stated that the criticisms he has read in
the minutes have been frank and he does not see any petit
bourgeois manifestations in them. The main issue is that of
settling the leadership question. He agrees that Cde. Bishop
does not have the ideological clarity. At first many members
thought that the problem rested with the Organising Committee
but now he has realised that the Organising Committee cannot
have problems if the C.C does not have. Cde. Gill stated that
all of us have the weakness of not frankly raising criticisms
and Cde. Bishop should appreciate that now comrades are willing
to do so. This is a sign of the growing maturity of the C.C and
G.M.

Cde. Gill said that he appreciated Cde. Bishop's concern on
the minutes going to the G.M but failure to give information
holds back the party. For too long the majority of the party
has been operating in ignorance. Cde. Gill said that he has
always seen lways seen leadership in the party as being joint.
He had serious concerns when Cde. Coard resigned. He further
stated that it is necessary for Cde. Bishop to have bilateral and
collective discussions with the membership. He said that in
his view there is no other way forward except a qualitative
change taking place in the C.C. Cde. Gill then read out a
quotation from Karl Marx "We have chosen a path in which we
can accomplish the most for mankind, then nobody can bow us
because they are only sacrafice for everyone. Then we enjoy
no poor limited egoistic joy for our happiness belongs to
thousands. Our deeds will live on working eternally."

Cde. Anslem Debourg said that there is a crisis in the party.
The C.C is the highest organ, once it is split then no party
and no revolution. He said that the question of collective
leadership is a fundamental principle of Marxism Leninism.
That collective leadership could only advance and push the
revolution forward. He referred to Cde. Bishop's statement
on page 10 in the minutes where Cde. Bishop said, "he is struck

17/............

by the levels of thought and preparation of Cdes as evident in their various contributions". Cde. Debourg said that this is a hint to there being a conspiracy in the C.C. Cde. Debourg said that he does not think that Cde. Coard's resignation was correct and criticised him for this.

Cde. Lorianne Lewis said that in the past the C.C has not been frankly criticising each other now out of the blues it has been done with Cde. Bishop and if we are to put the party on a Marxist Leninist footing we must not suddenly jump to cricirise. She also aked how would we bring the question of joint leadership to the masses since there are many people who would not like to see Cde. Coard as leader?"

Cde. Liam Janes answered that joint leadership is an internal party matter and is not to be brought to the masses. Cde. Bishop would remain a Prime Minister and Commander in Chief of the Armed Forces. He said that the key to defeating rumour mongering is the proletarian acceptance, attitude and disposition of the two Comrades. In the past imperialism and reaction spread rumours about power struggle in the party but this made no headway because the closeness of the two comrades.

Cde. Ewart Layne said that if we strip things of personal feelings and ground them on the organisational principles of a proletarian party and the concrete situation in our country then the C.C conclusions are correct. He said that no Marxist Leninist principle says that you must first privately raise criticism. Cde. Layne refered to the resolution of the C.C plenary of April 1981 when there was a unanimous call for tight chairmanship. He also said that came up in December 1981, October 1982 and July 1983 all being critical of Cde. Bishop's leadership. He also said that the C.C resolution of October 1982 said that there was nothing wrong with Cdes holding bilate als and consultations on party matters however, these matters must then be eventually brought before the party C.C.

On the minutes Cde. Layne said that we are not fooling anyone.
The members know what is going on. We must be frank and
honest. He then quoted a passage from the material, 'Democracy
and centralism' which all members studied a few weeks ago
"Lenin considered the development of criticism and self
criticism in every way among the indispensable conditions for
strengthening the party and for improving its work. The
party of communists criticised itself, and by criticising
inevitably strengthens itself. Principled, open criticism was
considered by Lenin to be the duty of a revolutionary. He
pointed out that it had a place in the arsenal of every party
organisation. Lenin warned that the party must critically
examined the results of its activity, and should not hide from
the party members and the people the shortcomings in its work.

"The party cannot fulfil its role of leader of the working
class and all working people if it fails to notice its own
shortcomings; if it is unable to expose the negative aspects
in its work, if it is afraid to openly and honestly acknowledge
mistakes and cannot correct them in time."

"Lenin wrote in this connection: 'A political party's attitude
towards its own mistakes is one of the most important and
surest ways of judging how earnest the party is and how it fulfil
in practice its obligations towards its class and the working
people. Frankly acknowledging a mistake, ascertaining the
reasons for it, analysing the conditions that have led up to it,
and thrashing out the means of its rectification - that is the
hallmark of a serious party; that is how it should perform its
duties; and how it should educate and train its class and then
the masses!'

"Open criticism of its own defects is not a sign of the
weakness but of the great strength of a Marxist party, and a
means of strengthening it further. Lenin insisted that a
party could learn to win and succeed only when it could face
the truth, even the worst, squarely".

19/...........

Cde. Layne further stated that Cde. Bishop is of the opinion that there is a plot and conspiracy to remove him but at this time for tactical reasons we are going half way. This Cde. Layne considers to be gross contempt for the intelligence of the C.C. For him to feel that under every chair, in every window there is a conspiracy going on is nothing but contempt.

Cde. Lex Mc Bain said that since April 1981 the resolutions of the C.C has been pointing to weak leadership given the C.C but nothing was being done. Therefore if we met and taken another such resolution and do nothing then soon the party would disintegrate and the revolution overthrown.

Cde. Ronnie Spooner said that since April '81 with all the resolutions it can be said that the C.C has been a talk shop. Information was not being sent down. The C.C was not taking firm measures. He said that a weekend seminar the party membership identified 19 features of a social Democratic Party and it's clear that they all are applicable to our own party. The failure of the C.C to pass on information to the membership shows that the C.C was operating as a clique and did not trust the membership. He stated that Cde. Bishop as the leader of the party should be the first person to abide by and uphold democratic centralism. His failure to do so is nothing but a petit bourgeois manifestation. He further pointed out that Marxism Leninism is not a dogma but a guide to creative action and in this regard sited the nine man joint leadership in Nicaragua. He firmly stated that he supports joint leadership in the party, and further went on to say that it is because of the C.C and party's vacillation we are in this situation. As the old people say 'what happens in the dark must come out to light'. He however, confidently said that today shows that the party is prepared to come forward'. Referring to Cde. Bishop he said that one never knows his strengths if he does not know his weaknesses.

113 - 20

20/...........

Cde. Nelson Louison endorsed Cdes Layne and Gill's position.
He said that this is the first time that the C.C is telling
the membership the truth. He noted that many Comrades have
been seeing the problems and not saying anything. We must
decide whether we are building a Marxist Leninist party or a
social democratic one. He noted that many National Liberation
Movements have failed because of this failure to build a Marxist
Leninist party. He pointed out his disagreement with Cde.
Bishop's position when he earlier said that the opinions of
the members cannot help him and that he alone can help himself.
This Cde. N. Louison said is a petit bourgeois position. He
then quoted from the document 'Supreme Principle of Party
Leadership' which was recently studied by the whole party,
"Lenin severly condemned any attempt to ignore the opinions of
ordinary party members, to look upon them as merely the executors
of the will of leading personalities. For him, a party member
was an active, conscientious, political fighter, a master of
his party, prepared to bear complete responsibility for its work."

Cde. Wayne Sandiford said that he criticises Cde. Bernard
Coard for resigning from the C.C and that he is worried how
Cde. Bishop is seeing the criticisms of the C.C and G.M as
some kind of conspiracy. He said that he does not want to be
part of any conspiracy. He then pointed out that many
Comrades have been moved from their orignal areas of work and
placed in others. He gave himself as an example of this saying
that one morning he was told that he is moved from the Ministry
of Trade and is now a full time Worker Education Tutor. This
change although abrupt he tired to take in a proletarian way
and has been making his best efforts. He further stated that
in Cde. Bishop's speech he sited four concerns, namely a wrong
approach, the minutes going to the membership, he needs to
reflect and that this maybe a conspiracy. Cde. Sandiford said that
these four concerns are not concerns of principle they instead
reflect Cde. Bishop's petit bourgeois side.

21/...........

113 - 21

Cde. Liam James then suggested that the workshops should begin. Cde. Mikey Prime thensaid that the G.M must decide whether Cde. Bishop leaves the G.M or not.

A vote was taken on the matter 51 Cdes were for Cde. Bishop staying and one (1) abstained (Chester Louison)

Then the Workshop begun.

At. 4.00 p.m the plenary session of the G.M begun with workshops reports. Please see the appendix for the composition and reports of work shops.

After the workshops reports Cde. Liam James said that the workshops in their reports sited three (3) areas which need clarification. They are. Cde. George Louison's attitude at the C.C plenary; what is Cde. Austin's role in the Armed Forces and what problems. Cde. Leon Cornwall experienced as ambassador to Cuba.

Cde. Liam James informed the G.M that Cde. George Louison's behaviour and position at the C.C plenary was right opportunism. He was vulgar and refered to the position taken by one Comrade as 'a load of shit'. He also tried to disrupt the meeting when the majority of the Central Committee was not supportive of his position by taking up his bag and threatening to walk out of the meeting. Cde. James however, said that Cde. Louison should further explain his behaviour to the G.M when he returns from abroad. He then called Cde. L. Cornwall to explain the problems he experienced.

Cde. Cornwall said that when the issue of all C.C members being based in Grenada came up at the C.C plenary there were some Cdes who did not favour this especially on the question of Cde. Layne and himself remaining. Thus he informed the C.C that there were some problems he experienced in Cuba mainly caused by the way in which the party was operating that made it

113 - 22   · · · ·

unecessary for a C.C member to be based in Cuba as ambassador
since a lot of information was being channelled from Grenada
to Cuba by our party and government without his knowledge.

He said tht this was drawn to the C.C's attention several
times both in terms of personal talks he had with C.C members,
reports to Grenada and a long letter he wrote to the C.C on
these matters. And failure to take corrective action was in
fact amounting to a waste of his time as a C.C member and a
lowering of the image of the party's Central Committee since
basic information that any ambassador should know was not
being provided to him. He sited the continous failure for the
newspapers to be sent to the embassy and the fact that other
embassies were providing him with their newspapers and always
asking him for copies of Grenada's. This became a source of
personal embarrasment. Also he was not informed except one
hour before the plane landed in Cuba when Cde. Bishop was coming
to Cuba in March on his way to New Delhi and this information
was given to him not by Grenada but by the Cuban Comrades. This
he said is unheard of. Also on several occasion when other
leaders of the revolution travel to Cuba the same occured. He
said that on other matters instead of he as ambassador to Cuba
and a C.C member informing the Cuban comrades they instead were
informing him. This he said can only be interpreted as if
he was not a confidentail person of the Grenada Revolution and
NJM and could only serve to lower the prestige of the C. C as
well as waste his time since things were going ahead inspite
of is presence in Cuba. He also sited an example of when he
was asked by Grenada to pass on some information to Cuba and was
experiencing difficulties to get that meeting but instead a Cuban
Comrade - not a member of the C.C of the Cuban Communist Party
was able to fly in to Grenada and immediately get a meeting with
four members of our Political Bureau including Cde. Bishop and
deal with the same matter that he was supposed to deal with.
Thus he reasoned because of how we were operating it was not
useful for a C.C member to be wasting his time.

Cde. Hudson Austin pointed out that for more than a year
he had been concentrating all of his efforts as Minister of
Construction on the many construction projects that have been
taking place as such very little of his time has been given
to the Armed Forces. He explained that in the Ministry of
Construction he works closely with Cde. Mikey Prime the Permanent
Secretary who is the only Permanent Secretary that is a party
Member . He said that there is a clear division of labour
between himself and Cde. Mikey Prime and that his Ministry
has a good relation with the Union which unionises the workers.
However, he said all this has been to the expense of the Armed
Forces and he is very concern/about this. He said that he
proposed in the July plenary of the C.C 17 points for building
and strengthening the Armed Forces and latter he wrote a letter
to Cde. Bishop outlining how the Armed Forces can be strengthened.
He said that is concern is great because the lessons of Poland
showed that when the revolution was in danger and there was
chaos in the party and society it was only the Armed Forces
that ~~was able to rescue~~ the situation.

Cde. Unison Whiteman explained to the G.M that he had a
number of reservations on the question of joint leadership for
theoretical and practical reasons. He said he never read about
such a situation. He had heard of a leader and a deputy leader
with the latter having specific responsibilities. He said that
whenever a leader is missing qualities collective leadership
and not joint leadership solves the problem. On the question
of the minutes going to the membership he felt that instead of
this a comprehensive report highlighting all the arguments
should have been given.

Cde. Chester Louison said he abstained from the voting
this morning because he was concerned about Cde. Bishop's
emotional state.

Cde. Fitzroy Bain said that there is a split in views
in the C.C on the proposals and that whatever the results
it must be for the party's survival. He said that he had strong,

feelings and he had problems with the report read by
Cde. Layne. He said that we have to be careful that we don't
move from right opportunism to left opportunism. He asked how
can the resignation of the Comrades help the C.C.? He said
that this is to intimidate the meeting and that he strongly
criticises this. He went onto say that Cde. George Louison
is absent from this meeting and that Cde. G. Louison has strong
feelings on the matters being discussed however, we have gone
ahead and held the G.M in Cde. G. Louison absence instead of
waiting until he is back. He said that this is not just a
case of majority and minority since in the past the minority
has held views and the C.C has not gone ahead with the position
that was held by majority. He said he is unhappy about labelling
comrades and that more ideologically developed comrades put
forward positions and others like himself who are of a lower
ideological level feel timid in the face of these. He said that
Cde. Coard's resignation last year exposed the weaknesses of the
party and when Cde. Coard resigned he had openly called such
a resignation a counter revolutionary. He said that there has
been some caucusing in the C.C., that Comrades are always
talking to each other and that he has no problems with joint
leadership but this can mash up the party since there was
caucusing. He went on to say that he does not know if this is
a plot, he is not sure on the caucusing and what comrades said
to each other but if there is a plot we have to crush it. He
admitted that the criticisms of Cde. Bishop are correct and just
and that Cde. Bishop's style of handling the situation and
criticisms was petit bourgeois. He said that he knows that
his ideological level is low and the other Comrades have a
higher ideological level but he does not like these things.
He ended by saying he knows that the Comrades had well thought
out positions and were frank but he must say what is on his
mind.

Cde. Peter David replying to Cde. F. Bain said that
the latter is coming up in a subtle way with some conspiracy
theory. He said that we must struggle to be always frank and

must struggle to be always frank and call a spade a spade. He
said that Cde. F. Bain cannot seek to blame other Comrades who
have been struggling to raise their ideological level, that
he must not feel intimidated by should make all efforts to raise
his. He went on to say that we have always been good at making
quick decisions on small issues but vacillate on taking decisions
on fundamental issues. He reminded Cde. F. Bain that he himself
said that the C.C Comrades who voted for joint leadership had
well though out positions yet he is hinting that there is a
conspiracy and this decision can mash up the revolution. Cde.
David said that if there were a conspiracy it was a conspiracy
to build the party and revolution.

Cde. L. Cornwall said that he was happy to see the level of
discussion of the members and it is being carried out at a high
ideological level grounded in the theory of Marxism Leninism. He
said that this shows that the party is maturing. In relation to
the position taken by Cde. F. Bain he said that Cde. Bain pointed
out that he had problems with the report given by Cde. Layne
however, when the C.C met to consider the report before it was
presented the G.M, Cde. Bain voted in favour of the report being
presented as is to the G.M. However, if Cde. Bain is referring to
the points made by Cde. Layne in relation to the decision that the
majority of C.C members would resign from the C.C if the party
membership fails to demand that the Leninist principle of
democratic centralism be upheld and adhered to Cde. Cornwall
said that the decision of the majority is one of principle.
He said that for too long our C.C has been vacillating and failing
to take decisions when one or two C.C members oppose such. This
he said has made the party work weak and ineffective and is
responsible for the deep crisis we now face. He pointed out that
failure to take this decision and uphold democratic centralism has
grave consequences for the party and revolution. That if we fail
to apply democratic centralism, which is the heart and soul of a
Marxist Leninist party or any party aspiring to be transformed
into such, on this issue that we now face then on other matters
ordinary party members would reject C.C decisions that they do not

like. This he claims would march up the party. He went on to
say that we have always spoken about the importance of democratic centralism in the party; that on the morning of March
13th 1979 if democratic centralism was not upheld when the
Political Bureau took the decision for the attack on True Blue
barracks, if at that critical moment the party members said
that they needed time to reflect then there would have been no
revolution and the party leadership would have been wipe out
since Gairy left orders to exterminate the entire leadership.
This is why if we fail to stand by principles but bend them
for one man it would be unprincipled for C.C members who have any
respect for principles to remain on the C.C.

He went on to say that he finds it very strange that Cde.
Bain never raised the issue of postponing the G.M before because
Cde. George Louison is out of the country. He stated that
the C.C took this decision to hold the G.M since Saturday 17th
but between that time and today Cde. Bain never even raised the
matter of postponing the G.M, in fact he did not raise it this
morning and now it is almost 10.00 p.m. Why is he now raising this?
He also said that no one must feel intimidated because of the
differences in ideological level, instead it is the duty of
every C.C member, every party member to struggle hard and study
hard so that the ideological level of the entire C.C and party
can be raised in order to work out the correct solutions to
problems we face now and the even more complex ones we would face
in the future.

He went on to say that when the C.C criticised Cde. Bishop
it was not done from a position of self righteousness. We all
have weaknesses but it was the opinion of every single one of the
C.C that the weaknesses of Cde. Bishop as leader of the C.C and
party were persisting for a long time and causing vacillations
in the C,C thus seriously affecting the party work. He then
stated that on Cde. B. Coard's resignation the C.C pointed
out in October that given the problems in the C.C that it
was correct to do so. He informed the G.M that a great dependency

syndrome h d developed in the C.C because everybody was
expecting Cde. Coard to do all the thinking and preparations
for C. C meetings and to ensure that whatever decisions were
implemented. This he said only held back the development of the
C.C nd jeopardised collective leadership. Since Cde. Coard's
resign tion many C.C members have realised that they must take
on their responsibility as a C.C member to think and prepare
for meetings. It is this long struggle to take on their
responsibilities since Cde. Coard's resignation that has made
it possible for the ordinary party members themselves to be
now boldly speaking up. In the past this never happened but now
everyone has sensed that they must now shoulder their responsibility. This is the positive effect of Cde. Coard's resignation

Cde. F. Bain then spoke repeating his position on the statement made by the majority of C.C members to resign if the C.C
decision is not carried through. He further said that he got
the C.C report late and that the did not see any conspiracy by
the C,C.

Cde. F. Gill said he does not see any conspiracy but instead
we are breaking new grounds. He said that we all have petit
bourgeois weaknesses which can be seen in our style of work.
He called for the party to embark on serious ideological training
and said that Cde. F. Bain's position reflects a low ideological
level and understanding. He said that this issue is one of
principle — will we stand by principles we speak of or would be
cast them aside for Cde. Bishop's sake? He further said that what
was in the minutes were already known by most party members and
that the bringing of the minutes to the membership was forced on
the C.C because the members would not have accepted anything
without seeing the minutes.

Cde. Einstein Louison said that some Comrades are trying
to justify a serious kind of complacency that frightens him.
This matter is one of life or death of the revolution. It was
the members who forced this on to the C.C. On Cde. Bishop's
concerns he said that what is clear is that Cde. Bishop lost

touch with the reality around him. He also said that this is true
for Cde. F. Bain. He pointed out that Cde. Bishop had been
failing to supervise the work and thus he criticises him for
this slackness. He said that we are at a point when we must
struggle hard to build a Marxist Leninist party which is the
only guarantee that we will build socialism. He said that the
matters raised concerning Cde. George Louison's position is not
a personal attack on him, his position at the C.C meeting was
definitely right opportunist. He went on to say that the C.C
comrades who did not vote for the decision but instead previously
agreed to all the analyses of the crisis and problems reminds him
of what Karl Marx said about some philosophers. He quoted, "The
philosophers have only interpreted the world, in various ways;
the point, however, is to change it."

Cde. U. Whiteman said that his position is clear that Cde. B.
Coard should be on the C.C and P.B but he has never heard or
read about joint leadership. He said that may be he is not being
creative but his is his position. He said that someone told him
that the General Hospital is having problems because there is no
clearly defined head of the hospital.

Cde. Keith Roberts said he is surprised to hear of the positions
of certain C.C members especially those of Cde. Bishop and Bain
who hint that this is a conspiracy. He said that Cde. Bishop must
truly accept the criticism in a principled way. He quoted from
another document studied by the entire party 'communist - a title
of honour' which said, "Lenin considered the conscientious
carrying out of collectively taken decisions to be the highest
manifestation of unity. He wrote: 'Dsicussing the problem,
expressing and hearing different opinions ascertaining the views
of the majority of the organised Marxist, expressing these views
in the form of decisions adopted by delegates and carrying out
conscientiously-this is what reasonable people all over the world
call unity.

29/...............

"After a decision has been taken by the relevant bodies
Lenin pointed out, all party members must act as one man. A
communist's devotion to the party is tested by his ability to
uphold the common cause and the way he implements party decisions.
To be a communist means, above all, to merge one's own desires
and actions with the desires and actions of the party."

Cde. K. Roberts went on to say that Cde. Bishop has by his
words and action shown great mistrust in the Comrades around
him. a high and unbelievable level of individualism. Cde. Roberts
stated that we all get wisdom from the collective wisdom of the
party and we must all struggle to raise our ideological level in
the interest of the revolution.

Cde. Valdon Boldeau said that he is happy with the C.C
discussions and conclusions. For sometime now he has been unhappy
with how the party was operating. He is now happy to see the
C.C openly and frankly discussing its problems and is prepared
to solve them. He further stated that the critifism of Cde.
Bishop at the C.C plenary was honest and made from the standpoint
of genuine respect and to pull the party out of the crisis.
He said that he supports the model of joint leadership. He
reminded Cde. Bishop that C.C decisions are binding on every
party member and as leader he must be more willing to stand firm
with the C.C decision. Cde. Boldeau stated that if Cde. Bishop
does not fulfil the decision this would lead to disrespect for
the C.C and for himself.

Cde. Chris Stroude said that since the formation of NJM the
party's policy was one of taking state power and to build socialism
and communism even if we ourselves would not be around to see
communism. Therefore we can't afford to reach part of the way and
mark time. He pointed out that we have to deeply study Marxism
Leninism and Lenin's teachings on democratic centralism. He said
he was shocked to hear about and to personally hear Cde. Bishop
position. He reminded Cde. Bishop that at the first weekend
seminar of the party a few weeks ago he himself addressed the
and explained the Leninist principles of party building and called

30 ....

on all to always uphold them. Cde. Stroude pointed out
that he agrees with joint leadership and that this is a
reality in the party that must be recognised. He said
that if the revolution is turned back it would have regional
and international implications. He said that he is surprised
that Cde. Bishop is trying to hide the truth from the members
by witholding the minutes. He said that there is nothing
wrong in calling the position taken by someone as being
opportunist. When someone is taking a counter revolutionary
position we say it is a counter revolutionary position.
He said that if opportunism is not struggled against it would
stifle the party.

Cde. Basil Gahagan said that we must be critic of positions
that are opportunist. He said that he is shocked with Cde.
Bishop's position. It reveals a low ideological level and
understanding. He further went on to say that the party has
lost contact with the masses and the C.C has lost contact with
the party membership. It is this lost of contact that is
now causing this paranoa of power struggle and conspiracy.

. Cde. Lester Redhead commended the C.C for its frankness
and stated that he is disatisfied with Cde. Bishop's position
He said that the Comrade lacks these leadership qualities
which Cde. Coard has therefore he supports joint leadership.
He said that over the last year many committees bound away
because of lack of C.C guidance. He said that the party
members were not felled. He further stated that Cde. Bishop
has not taken the criticism in a frank, wholehearted manner
nad if we are to build a Marxist Leninist party it must be
based on all the Leninist principles of party building. He
further stated that many party members are developing because
they have a positive and proletarian attitude to the criticisms
that the C.C always give them. Thus Cde. Bishop must see
these criticisms for his own good and the party.

Cde. Chester Humphrey said that what is taking place reminds
him of what Cde. Coard said when the party celebrated Lenin's
birthday. What Cde. Coard said referred to how different
comrades respond to criticism i.e either in a proletarian or
a petit bourgeois way. He said that Cde. Coard said on that

3/..........

that day that:

(a) there are those who accept criticism and attempt to correct their way.

(b) there are those who refuse criticism and make no attempt to change.

(c) there are those who accept or say they accept but don't do anything to change.

The latter category he said was by far the most dangerous. He said that Cde. Bishop pointed out both to the C.C and G.M that these two bodies can't do anything to help him and only he himself can help himself. This Cde. Humphrey criticised as petit bourgeois individualism and attempts to find solution for his problem outside of the party. Cde. Humphrey asked what is the main issue? He answered we are trying to rescue a dangerous situation. He asked what is necessary to rescue the situation.? He answered that one necessary ingredient is that of strengthening the C.C and party leadership and this is why he firmly supports joint leadership of the party between Cde. Bishop and Cde. Coard, the two most outstanding comrades of t e party with different necessary strengths. He further stated that no textbook on Marxism would give you this. We must be creative and always take into account our reality.

Cde. Keith Ventour stated that he firmly agrees with joint leadership. He said that both Cdes Bishop and Coard must act in a proletarian way always in the interest of the party. He said however, in his view the problem is with Cde. Bishop and his petit bourgeois attitude to the revolution. He said that the only way to solve this is for Cde. Bishop to genuinely accept the criticism. He further stated that no one is president for life. He then quoted at length from the document studied by the whole party 'Supreme Principle of Party Leadership' which said, "The Leninist way of presenting the question of the relation between the masses and their leaders, between the leaders and the led deserves attention. Lenin stressed that if is the masses themselves who throw up worthy leaders from their ranks. The masses follow thier leaders, but at the

same time they guide the latter, and correct them whenever
necessary. Genuine leaders of the people not only teach
the masses but learn from them, too.

   'And for that very reason,' Lenin wrote, 'the whole party
must constantly, steadily and systematically train suitable
persons for the Central bodies, must see clearly, as in the
palm of its hand, all the activities of every candidate for
these high posts, must come to know even their personal
characteristics, their strong and weak points, their victories
and defeats. In this way, and in this way alone, shall we
enable the whole body of influential party workers (and not
the chance assortment of persons in a circle or grouplets)
to know their leaders and to put each of them in his proper
category.'

   "Drawing in large circles of people in the elaboration and
implementation of decisions, assessing the opinion of the
majority and expressing its will these are the Leninist
principles of party life. They guarantee the all-sidedness
and correctness of party decisions. Forgetting or violating
these principles inevitably brings with it the isolation of
the leaders from the masses, and the adoption of thoughless,
erroneous decisions.

   "A genuinely scientific, Marxist Leninist approach to the
problem of collective leadership presupposes a correct solution
of the question of the authority of the leaders of the revolutionary working class movement.

   "Marxism Leninism does not deny the important role of the
leaders of the working class. While acknowledging the decisive
role of the people in the development of society, Marx,
Engels and Lenin considered that a leading personality, although
he cannot change the course of history to his liking, does
nevertheless play an important role in it. A leader can, by
his activity accelerate the pace of events, indicate a less
difficult path towards a goal, or, on the contrary, slow down
 the movement forward and make it more difficult. Leading
personalities are those who have understood, earlier, more
clearly and more deeply than others, a new situation and the
needs of social development, and have headed a mass movement."

33/.........

Cde. Keith Ventour went on to say that the C.C must
manners all forms of opportunism. He then stated that
Cde. Bishop now seems more relaxed than this morning (applause).
He said that this morning Cde. Bishop seemed to be confused,
contemptous and mistrustful of the party membership. Now he
has a more relaxed look and he hopes that it is a good sign
which shows his willingness to genuinely accept the C.C and
G.M criticisms and the decision of the C.C (applause).

Cde. Moses Jeffrey stated his firm agreement with the C.C
analysis and resolution. He said that this is the most serious
day in the life of the party because of the frankness and
honesty with which the vast majority of comrades are carrying
on the discussion. As a result his confidence in the party
is growing and the C.C is showing maturity. He said that
Cde. Bishop's position is based on deep jolted emotions,
lack of confidence in the ability of th party to assist him,
non acceptance of the practical application of democratic
centralism. He said that there has been for too long a certain
link between the C.C and the members. That the continous
failure of the C.C to give the members accurate information
has not prepared them to struggle with deep conviction. He
said that many members were not convinced of the many lines
the C.C gave as to the problems of the party work thus he
asked - how can we convince the masses when we ourselves are
not convinced? If the C.C has not confidence in the party
members how can we effectively work among the masses. He
said that the only conspiracy that exists in the party is the
conspiracy of the C.C against democratic centralism and against
the party rank and file members. He noted that now the cadres
are maturing and understanding in a better way Marxism Leninism
and that the foetus of a Marxist Leninist party is developing.
He said that he hopes that Cde. Bsihop has learnt the lesson
that there are no untouchables in the party.

Cde. Ruggles Ferguson said he endorses the views of other
Comrades. He said that we must not lose sight of imperialism
as our main enemy. That imperialism is becoming more dangerous
ous in several parts of the world-peace is at stake in the
world because of imperialism. Therefore we must build a
Marxist Leninist Party. He said he is surprised with Cde.
Bishop's position. That frankness and openess must remain
a main feature in party life. He therefore appeals to the

reason and proletarian instincts of Cde. Bishop.

Cde. Gellineau James stated that this ia a historic meeting and it shows th t the party is developing and maturing along a Marxist Leninist path. He said that he is disturbed by Cde. Bishop, Bain and G.Louison's positions. He then refered to the day when he was removed from the party's Central Committee he said that he had to wage a stout struggle with himself to accept the C.C decision in a proletarian manner. He promised to send a letter to the C.C which he wrote on the day to show what was his attitude to the C.C decision. He also referred t the early days of the revolution when he was removed as commander of the militia unit but again made all efforts to accept this in the best spirit. He therefore said that Cde. Bishop has no other alternative than to show he is capable of accepting criticism and moving forward.

Cde. Bertrand Lessey said that he supported the C.C resolution. The frankness here in the G.M and at the C.C meeting shows that the party wants to make a decisive break with the past. Thus all efforts must be made to ensure that we move forward united only on the principles of Marxism Leninism.

Cde. Mikey Prime said he strongly endorses the C.C resolution-it is one of frankness, firmness and decisiveness. He said that he spoke to some C.C members, those who are closer to the membership, just before the extra-ordinary C.C plenary and he told them that if the C.C does not move away from this 'dilly-dallying' there won't be any positive change in the conditions of the country. He said that we must learn the lesson ot today that decisiveness is always keep in building a Marxist Leninist party.

Cde. Edlyn Lambert said that if the women of the party did not speak the meeting would not have ended. She said that she is shocked and disappointed with Cde. Bishop's attitude at the dedisions of the C.C and to democratic centralism and free frank and honest criticism. She said that if Cde. Bishop sees the party and C.C as of no help to him then he does not have a party political problem. She said that the matters in the C.C minutes are of no threat to the revolution since t

35/............

majority of the party members know of the problems an[...]
of the C.C. The threat to the revolution she said is [...]
continuous failure of the C.C to tell the members the tr[...]
and to act to overcome weaknesses and shortcomings. Sh[...]
Cde. Bishop that in May he called on every party member t[...]
the extra mile. She then asked how can we walk the extr[...]
mile if you do not set the pace for us? She asked him t[...]
of the many lives that would be lost if the party does n[...]
out of this crisis so the revolution can move forward. [...]
then said that it is fitting for Cde. Bishop to now tell [...]
what he intends to do.

Cde. Claudette Pitt said that she is proud to be a member
of the NJM. She said that she is happy to see that the [...]
members of the C.C are standing up for firm Leninist Princi[...]
She reminded Cde. Bishop that in a weekend seminar of th[...]
he said that democratic centralism is a norm of party l[...]
She said she is shocked to hear his position today and [...]
unwillingness in practice to accept the C.C decision [...]
leadership. She reminded him that in the years before [...]
revolution he always singled out the excellent hard w[...]
Coard and that he said in those days had it not been [...]
tremendous hard work energy and foresight of Cde. Coar[...]
of them including himslef would have given up the strugg[...]
She said that she strongly supports the C.C decisions.

Cde. Lorianne Lewis stated that on many occasions w[...]
hot then cold. She sited the March threat as an exam[...]
She said that many Comrades have called for firmness i[...]
but don't do so in practice. She asked how far have w[...]
in drafting the new party programme and the constituti[...]

Cde. Peter David said that he was wondering that when
Cde. Bernard Coard is back on the C.C and P.B whether C[...]
then go back in a rut. However, he said that he can se[...]
development ofquite a number of C.C Comrades and as a resul[...]
feels confident that this won't be so. He said that [...]
by the C.C to the membership must be constant, He the[...]
that is quite sure that the reflection that Cde. Bisho[...]
doing in isolation would have led to nothing. He then [...]
on Cde. Bishop to make sure that all his reflections fr[...]
to be reflections on how we will be marching along th[...]
to build socialism with the full knowledge that only [...]
Leninist party can lead guide and direct the people [...]
fully undertake this task.

Cde. Faye Thompson said that Cde. Bishop's behaviour was unexpected and rude. From now on he must reflect on how the revolution will be moving forward.

Cde. Rudolph Ogilvie said he firmly supported th C.C report. He said that the session is a firm step to strengthen the party. He is now more confident in the party because this shows the willingness of the party to solve its problems and to build socialism according to the time tested principles of scientific socialism. He rejects Cde. Bishop's position that this is a conspiracy and criticises him for taking such a stand which is the stand of the petit bourgeois.

Cde. Maureen St. Bernard said that Cde. Bishop must mingle more with the party membership he is too isolated from the party's rank and file this is why he can't understand the changes taking place in the party.

Cde. Murie Francois said that Cde. Bishop should accept the criticism. She said she is not surprise at Cde. Bish position because this is the same petit bourgeois position he has been taking for a long time on the Rural Workers Committee of the Party.

At this point Cde. Peter David read a resolution which was unanimously voted for by everyone at the G.M.

The members then called on Cdes Coard and Bishop to speak.

Cde. Bernard Coard said that today is indeed a historical day in the life of the party (applause). He said the C.C meetings he attended from Monday 19th September amazed him because unlike the past every C.C member was putting forward well thought out, clear and reasoned positions on the way forward for building the party and transforming it into a genuine Marxist Leninist party. He said that in the past most C.C members would be silent in C.C meetings because they did not to have ideas on how the party and revolution is to be built. However, now he witness a qualitative difference. He also said that the G.M showed quality and though. He said in his conversations with Cde. Jorge Risket, member of the Politicul Bureau of the PCC Central Committee. Cde. Risket always said that some people come to socialism by their head, others by their heart and still others by ....

37/...........